W9-DCA-404

Jake
Swiacki

Walker
Weldon
2011

SADLIER-OXFORD

Progress in Mathematics

$\dfrac{1}{5}$

· Authors ·

Catherine D. LeTourneau

Alfred S. Posamentier

with

Elinor R. Ford

· · · · · · · · · · · · Program Consultants · · · · · · · · · · · ·

Madelaine Gallin
Former Math Coordinator
Community School District #6
New York, NY

Frank Lucido
Associate Professor in
Bilingual/Multicultural Education
Texas A&M University
Corpus Christi, TX

Lucy Lugones
Math Coordinator
St. Luke's School
Whitestone, NY

Tim Mason
Title 1 Specialist
Palm Beach County School District
West Palm Beach, FL

R. James Milgram
Professor of Mathematics
Stanford University
Palo Alto, CA

Rosalie Pedalino Porter
Consultant Bilingual/ESL Programs
Amherst, MA

Sadlier-Oxford
A Division of William H. Sadlier, Inc.
www.sadlier-oxford.com

The publisher gratefully acknowledges Rose Anita McDonnell (1905–2003) and her colleagues for the important role they played in the development of *Progress in Mathematics* for more than sixty years.

Reviewers

The publisher wishes to thank the following teachers and administrators, who read portions of the series prior to publication, for their valuable contributions.

Grades 3-6 Reviewers

Madonna Atwood
Teacher
St. Louis, MO

John Palladino
Professor at Eastern Michigan University
Ypsilanti, MI

Debra Wright
Principal
Winter Haven, FL

Grade-Level Reviewers

Marie Bicsak
Math Coordinator
Mt. Clemens, MI

Sara Kobylarz
Grade 3 Teacher
Bronx, NY

Br. Ralph Darmento, F.S.C.
Deputy Superintendent of Schools
Newark, NJ

Suzanne Ryan
Grade 4 Teacher
Orono, MN

Candace Govin
Grades 4–8 Math Teacher/Coordinator
Plantation, FL

Sr. Adriana Cernoch
Grade 6 Teacher
Dallas, TX

Brandy Roth
Grade 3 Teacher
Kissimmee, FL

Elizabeth M. Johnson
Grade 5 Teacher
Bettendorf, IA

Linda Hamby
Grade 5 Teacher
DesPeres, MO

Barbara Murphy
Grade 4 Teacher
Chesterfield, MO

Sr. Martha Carmody, O.P.
Grade 4 Teacher
Springfield, IL

Jacqueline A. Byrd
Grade 5 Teacher
Chesterfield, MO

Sr. Maristella Dunlavy, O.P.
Principal
Springfield, IL

Jeannine Frey
Grade 3 Teacher
Chesterfield, MO

Mary E. Stokes
Grade 5 Teacher
Oak Forest, IL

Printed in the United States of America
ISBN: 0-8215-8205-4
123456789/10 09 08 07 06 05

Dear Family

Progress in Mathematics, now in its sixth decade of user-proven success, is a complete basal mathematics program. Written by experienced teacher-authors, it integrates a traditional course of study and today's academic Standards with the most up-to-date methods of teaching.

Progress in Mathematics is designed to meet the individual needs of all learners. Teachers who use *Progress* come to understand that students may progress as quickly as they can or as slowly as they must.

In Grade 5, the concepts of fractions and decimals will be further developed, and your fifth grader will use all four operations with these number types. There will also be an increased emphasis on algebraic thinking. Other topics that are studied include: statistics, geometry, measurement, probability, percents, and proportions. Special attention is given to critical thinking, problem solving, mental math, and journalizing.

But overall success in achieving the goals of this program depends on ongoing teacher-family-student interaction. It is important for you to encourage your fifth grader to achieve success in mathematics and enjoy it as well. You can help your student see math as useful and practical by relating it to everyday situations. It is also helpful to provide a quiet space and time for homework, and to reinforce the idea that by practicing math concepts and skills in your home environment, your student can have fun while learning mathematics.

Throughout the school year, you and your student can access *Math Alive At Home* pages at www.sadlier-oxford.com. These pages include the math vocabulary of each chapter plus fun-filled activities that will help you relate the math your student is learning in school to the real world.

We know that by using **Progress in Mathematics** your fifth grader will not only learn to value math, but become a confident problem solver and learn to reason and communicate mathematically as well.

The Authors

Contents

Introduction to Problem Solving

✶ Develops concept or skill with manipulatives.   *Algebra* Lesson promotes algebraic reasoning.

★Develops concept or skill with manipulatives.   Algebra Lesson promotes algebraic reasoning.

★Develops concept or skill with manipulatives.   *Algebra* Lesson promotes algebraic reasoning.

Fractions: Addition and Subtraction

Fractions: Multiplication and Division

* Develops concept or skill with manipulatives.   _Algebra_ Lesson promotes algebraic reasoning.

*Develops concept or skill with manipulatives.   *Algebra* Lesson promotes algebraic reasoning.

*Develops concept or skill with manipulatives.   Algebra Lesson promotes algebraic reasoning.

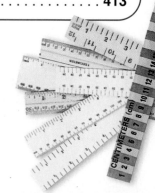

*Develops concept or skill with manipulatives.   Algebra Lesson promotes algebraic reasoning.

★ Develops concept or skill with manipulatives.   **Algebra** Lesson promotes algebraic reasoning.

Skills Update

A Review of Mathematical Skills from Grade 4

Progress in Mathematics includes a "handbook" of essential skills, Skills Update, at the beginning of the text. These one-page lessons review skills you learned in previous years. It is important for you to know this content so that you can succeed in math this year.

If you need to review a concept in Skills Update, your teacher can work with you, using manipulatives, which will help you understand the concept better.

The Skills Update handbook can be used throughout the year to review skills you may already know. Since many lessons in your textbook refer to pages in the Skills Update, you can use a particular lesson at the beginning of class as a warm-up activity. Or your class may choose to do the Skills Update lessons at the beginning of the year so that you and your teacher can assess your understanding of these previously learned skills.

You may even want to practice specific skills at home. If you need more practice than what is provided on the Skills Update page, you can use the practice pages available online at www.sadlier-oxford.com. These practice pages have an abundance of exercises for each one-page lesson.

Place Value to Thousands

▶ You can show 158,706 in a place-value chart. The value of each digit in a number depends on its place in the number.

In 158,706 the value of:

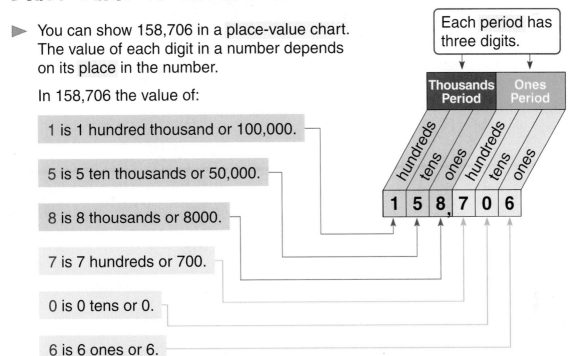

Each period has three digits.

1 is 1 hundred thousand or 100,000.

5 is 5 ten thousands or 50,000.

8 is 8 thousands or 8000.

7 is 7 hundreds or 700.

0 is 0 tens or 0.

6 is 6 ones or 6.

▶ Standard Form: 158,706

Remember:
Four-digit numbers may be written with or without a comma. In numbers *larger* than 9999, use a comma to separate the periods.

Word Name:

one hundred fifty-eight thousand,

seven hundred six

Write the place of the underlined digit. Then write its value.

1. 22<u>4</u>2　　　**2.** 6<u>3</u>,666　　　**3.** <u>1</u>99,999　　　**4.** 88<u>0</u>,888

Place a comma where needed in each. Then write the period name for the underlined digit.

5. 3 4 2 5 <u>9</u>　　　**6.** <u>1</u> 6 4 3 2　　　**7.** 2 0 <u>0</u> 0 6 0　　　**8.** <u>8</u> 0 5 0 2 7

Write the number in standard form.

9. forty-five thousand, seven hundred sixty-two　　　**10.** five thousand, six

11. nine hundred thousand, seven　　　**12.** ten thousand, nineteen

Write the word name for each number.

13. 7046　　　**14.** 37,008　　　**15.** 231,075　　　**16.** 923,780

Compare and Order Whole Numbers

Compare 363,420 and 381,787.

			Remember:
			< means "is less than."

▶ **To compare whole numbers:**
 • Align the digits by place value.

363,420
381,787

> Remember:
> < means "is less than."
> > means "is greater than."
> = means "is equal to."

 • Start at the left and find the first
   place where the digits are different.

363,420   3 = 3
381,787

 • Compare the value of these digits
   to find which number is greater.

363,420   8 > 6
381,787

So 381,787 > 363,420.   You could also say 363,420 < 381,787.

Order from greatest to least: 69,520; 19,478; 160,434; 63,215

▶ **To order whole numbers:**
 • Align the digits by place value.

 • Compare the digits in each place, starting with the greatest place.

69,520	69,520	69,520
19,478	19,478	19,478
160,434	160,434	160,434
63,215	63,215	63,215

There are no hundred thousands in the other numbers. 160,434 is the greatest.	6 = 6 and 1 < 6 19,478 is the least.	3 < 9 63,215 < 69,520

In order from greatest to least the numbers are:
160,434; 69,520; 63,215; 19,478

The order from least to greatest: 19,478; 63,215; 69,520; 160,434

Compare. Write <, =, or >.

1. 1563 __?__ 1519

2. 67,234 __?__ 67,234

3. 479,059 __?__ 479,065

Write in order from least to greatest.

4. 9458; 9124; 948; 972

5. 3951; 3068; 369; 3547

6. 99,407; 91,568; 90,999; 93,697

7. 216,418; 215,783; 213,614; 221,986

Round Whole Numbers

To round a number to a given place:

- Find the place you are rounding to.

- Look at the digit to its right.
  If the digit *is less than 5*, round down.
  If the digit is *5 or more*, round up.

▶ Round 13,528 to the nearest *ten*.

13,5<u>2</u>8
↓
13,530

| 8 > 5 |
| Round **up** |
| to 13,530. |

▶ Round 13,528 to the nearest *hundred*.

13,<u>5</u>28
↓
13,500

| 2 < 5 |
| Round **down** |
| to 13,500. |

▶ Round 13,528 to the nearest *thousand*.

1<u>3</u>,528
↓
14,000

| 5 = 5 |
| Round **up** |
| to 14,000. |

Round to the nearest ten.

| **1.** 27 | **2.** 25 | **3.** 51 | **4.** 86 | **5.** 174 | **6.** 397 |
| **7.** 469 | **8.** 875 | **9.** 2587 | **10.** 4351 | **11.** 9289 | **12.** 3542 |

Round to the nearest hundred.

13. 158	**14.** 426	**15.** 375	**16.** 896	**17.** 719	**18.** 950
19. 1047	**20.** 3888	**21.** 5942	**22.** 6891	**23.** 3098	**24.** 8762
25. 37,405	**26.** 62,345	**27.** 88,088	**28.** 65,097	**29.** 58,706	**30.** 66,636

Round to the nearest thousand.

31. 9155	**32.** 7983	**33.** 4550	**34.** 6237	**35.** 8396
36. 33,888	**37.** 15,942	**38.** 93,192	**39.** 87,983	**40.** 46,237
41. 326,150	**42.** 145,706	**43.** 357,029	**44.** 563,498	**45.** 807,476
46. 821,593	**47.** 450,513	**48.** 435,127	**49.** 205,120	**50.** 761,604

Add and Subtract Whole Numbers

To add or subtract whole numbers:

- Estimate.

- Align the numbers. Add or subtract, starting with the ones. Regroup when necessary.

▶ Add: 3458 + 2596 = __?__ .

Round to estimate: 3000 + 3000 = 6000.

Add the ones. Regroup.	Add the tens. Regroup.	Add the hundreds. Regroup.	Add the thousands.
$\begin{array}{r} 1 \\ 3\ 4\ 5\ 8 \\ +2\ 5\ 9\ 6 \\ \hline 4 \end{array}$	$\begin{array}{r} 1\ 1 \\ 3\ 4\ 5\ 8 \\ +2\ 5\ 9\ 6 \\ \hline 5\ 4 \end{array}$	$\begin{array}{r} 1\ 1\ 1 \\ 3\ 4\ 5\ 8 \\ +2\ 5\ 9\ 6 \\ \hline 0\ 5\ 4 \end{array}$	$\begin{array}{r} 1\ 1\ 1 \\ 3\ 4\ 5\ 8 \\ +2\ 5\ 9\ 6 \\ \hline 6\ 0\ 5\ 4 \end{array}$
14 ones = 1 ten 4 ones	15 tens = 1 hundred 5 tens	10 hundreds = 1 thousand 0 hundreds	**Think** 6054 is close to the estimate of 6000.

▶ Subtract: 2842 − 1645 = __?__ .

Round to estimate: 3000 − 2000 = 1000.

More ones needed. Regroup. Subtract.	More tens needed. Regroup. Subtract.	Subtract.
$\begin{array}{r} 3\ 12 \\ 2\ 8\ \cancel{4}\ \cancel{2} \\ -1\ 6\ 4\ 5 \\ \hline 7 \end{array}$	$\begin{array}{r} 13 \\ 7\ \cancel{8}\ 12 \\ 2\ \cancel{8}\ \cancel{4}\ \cancel{2} \\ -1\ 6\ 4\ 5 \\ \hline 9\ 7 \end{array}$	$\begin{array}{r} 13 \\ 7\ \cancel{8}\ 12 \\ 2\ \cancel{8}\ \cancel{4}\ \cancel{2} \\ -1\ 6\ 4\ 5 \\ \hline 1\ 1\ 9\ 7 \end{array}$
4 tens 2 ones = 3 tens 12 ones	8 hundreds 3 tens = 7 hundreds 13 tens	**Think** 1197 is close to the estimate of 1000.

Estimate by rounding. Then add or subtract. (Watch for + or −.)

1. 215 + 687

2. 4306 + 3849

3. 6287 + 318

4. 659 − 286

5. 7583 − 2948

6. 3717 − 839

Whole Number Operations I

Multiply One Digit

Multiply: $7 \times 816 = \underline{\ ?\ }$.

First, estimate by rounding: 7×816.

$7 \times 800 = 5600$

Then multiply.

Multiply the ones. Regroup.	Multiply the tens. Add the regrouped tens. Regroup again.	Multiply the hundreds. Add the regrouped hundreds.

$$\begin{array}{r} \overset{4}{8\ 1\ 6} \\ \times \quad 7 \\ \hline 2 \end{array}$$

7×6 ones $= 42$ ones
42 ones $=$
4 tens 2 ones

$$\begin{array}{r} \overset{1\ 4}{8\ 1\ 6} \\ \times \quad 7 \\ \hline 1\ 2 \end{array}$$

7×1 ten $= 7$ tens
7 tens $+$ 4 tens $=$
11 tens $=$
1 hundred 1 ten

$$\begin{array}{r} \overset{1\ 4}{8\ 1\ 6} \\ \times \quad 7 \\ \hline 5\ 7\ 1\ 2 \end{array}$$

7×8 hundreds $= 56$ hundreds
56 hundreds $+$ 1 hundred $=$
57 hundreds $=$
5 thousands 7 hundreds

Think
5712 is close to
the estimate of 5600.

Estimate by rounding. Then multiply.

1. $\begin{array}{r} 25 \\ \times\ 3 \\ \hline \end{array}$
2. $\begin{array}{r} 62 \\ \times\ 4 \\ \hline \end{array}$
3. $\begin{array}{r} 58 \\ \times\ 5 \\ \hline \end{array}$
4. $\begin{array}{r} 42 \\ \times\ 6 \\ \hline \end{array}$
5. $\begin{array}{r} 19 \\ \times\ 7 \\ \hline \end{array}$

6. $\begin{array}{r} 956 \\ \times\ 5 \\ \hline \end{array}$
7. $\begin{array}{r} 619 \\ \times\ 8 \\ \hline \end{array}$
8. $\begin{array}{r} 534 \\ \times\ 4 \\ \hline \end{array}$
9. $\begin{array}{r} 519 \\ \times\ 5 \\ \hline \end{array}$
10. $\begin{array}{r} 348 \\ \times\ 9 \\ \hline \end{array}$

Find the product.

11. $\begin{array}{r} 87 \\ \times\ 6 \\ \hline \end{array}$
12. $\begin{array}{r} 93 \\ \times\ 7 \\ \hline \end{array}$
13. $\begin{array}{r} 79 \\ \times\ 8 \\ \hline \end{array}$
14. $\begin{array}{r} 41 \\ \times\ 5 \\ \hline \end{array}$
15. $\begin{array}{r} 32 \\ \times\ 4 \\ \hline \end{array}$

16. $\begin{array}{r} 759 \\ \times\ 3 \\ \hline \end{array}$
17. $\begin{array}{r} 825 \\ \times\ 4 \\ \hline \end{array}$
18. $\begin{array}{r} 329 \\ \times\ 6 \\ \hline \end{array}$
19. $\begin{array}{r} 478 \\ \times\ 8 \\ \hline \end{array}$
20. $\begin{array}{r} 976 \\ \times\ 9 \\ \hline \end{array}$

21. 9×49
22. 8×93
23. 7×358
24. 5×953

One-Digit Quotients

Divide: $73 \div 9 = \underline{\ ?\ }$.

Decide where to begin the quotient.

Divisor $\rightarrow 9\overline{)73} \leftarrow$ Dividend

$9\overline{)73}$

Think
$9 > 7$ **Not enough tens**
$9 < 73$ **Enough ones**

The quotient begins in the ones place.

Estimate: About how many 9s are in 73?

$8 \times 9 = 72$
$9 \times 9 = 81$ $\leftarrow$ | 73 is between 72 and 81. Try 8. |

| Divide the ones. | | Multiply. | | Subtract and compare. | | Write the remainder. |

$\dfrac{8}{9\overline{)7\ 3}}$

$\begin{array}{r} \times\ 8 \\ 9\overline{)7\ 3} \\ 7\ 2 \end{array}$

$\begin{array}{r} 8 \\ 9\overline{)7\ 3} \\ -7\ 2 \\ \hline 1 \end{array}$
$1 < 9$

$\begin{array}{r} 8\ R1 \\ 9\overline{)7\ 3} \\ -7\ 2 \\ \hline 1 \leftarrow \end{array}$ Remainder

| Check by multiplying and adding. |

$\begin{array}{r} 8 \leftarrow \textbf{Quotient} \\ \times\ \ 9 \leftarrow \textbf{Divisor} \\ \hline 7\ 2 \\ +\ \ 1 \leftarrow \text{Remainder} \\ \hline 7\ 3 \leftarrow \text{Dividend} \end{array}$

| The remainder must be less than the divisor. |

Divide and check.

1. $5\overline{)47}$ 2. $4\overline{)39}$ 3. $3\overline{)25}$ 4. $7\overline{)59}$ 5. $8\overline{)76}$

6. $6\overline{)51}$ 7. $9\overline{)87}$ 8. $6\overline{)49}$ 9. $7\overline{)60}$ 10. $4\overline{)23}$

11. $4\overline{)31}$ 12. $6\overline{)38}$ 13. $5\overline{)33}$ 14. $8\overline{)79}$ 15. $7\overline{)68}$

Find the quotient and the remainder.

16. $58 \div 6$ 17. $65 \div 8$ 18. $29 \div 4$ 19. $62 \div 7$

20. $32 \div 7$ 21. $49 \div 5$ 22. $75 \div 8$ 23. $89 \div 9$

24. $26 \div 3$ 25. $51 \div 9$ 26. $47 \div 6$ 27. $53 \div 8$

Whole Number Operations III

REVIEW OF GRADE 4 SKILLS

Two-Digit Quotients

Divide: 82 ÷ 3 = _?_ .

Decide where to begin the quotient.	3)82	Think............................. 3 < 8 **Enough tens**

The quotient begins in the tens place.

Estimate: About how many 3s are in 8?

$2 \times 3 = 6$ ← Try 2.
$3 \times 3 = 9$

Divide the tens.	Multiply.	Subtract and compare.	Bring down the ones.
$\begin{array}{r} 2 \\ 3\overline{)8\ 2} \end{array}$	$\begin{array}{r} \times 2 \\ 3\overline{)8\ 2} \\ \rightarrow 6 \end{array}$	$\begin{array}{r} 2 \\ 3\overline{)8\ 2} \\ -6 \\ \hline 2 \end{array}$ ← 2 < 3	$\begin{array}{r} 2 \\ 3\overline{)8\ 2} \\ -6 \downarrow \\ \hline 2\ 2 \end{array}$

Repeat the steps to divide the ones.

Divide the ones.	Multiply.	Subtract and compare.	Check.
$\begin{array}{r} 2\ 7 \\ 3\overline{)8\ 2} \\ -6 \downarrow \\ \hline 2\ 2 \end{array}$	$\begin{array}{r} \times \\ 2\ 7 \\ 3\overline{)8\ 2} \\ -6 \downarrow \\ \hline 2\ 2 \\ \rightarrow 2\ 1 \end{array}$	$\begin{array}{r} 2\ 7\ R1 \\ 3\overline{)8\ 2} \\ -6 \downarrow \\ \hline 2\ 2 \\ -2\ 1 \\ \hline 1 \end{array}$ ← 1 < 3	$\begin{array}{r} 27 \\ \times\ 3 \\ \hline 81 \\ +\ 1 \\ \hline 82 \end{array}$

Divide and check.

1. 2)58   **2.** 4)84   **3.** 6)96   **4.** 3)79   **5.** 7)89

6. 7)85   **7.** 5)73   **8.** 4)69   **9.** 6)93   **10.** 8)97

Find the quotient and the remainder.

11. 47 ÷ 3   **12.** 85 ÷ 2   **13.** 77 ÷ 5   **14.** 59 ÷ 4

15. 83 ÷ 6   **16.** 91 ÷ 8   **17.** 81 ÷ 7   **18.** 74 ÷ 6

Fractions

A fraction is a number that names one or more *equal parts* of a whole or region, or of a set.

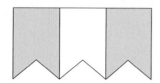

2 of the 3 equal parts of the banner are green. $\frac{2}{3}$ of the banner is shaded.

2 of the 3 cars in this parking lot face right. $\frac{2}{3}$ of the cars face right.

3 equal segments are between 0 and 1.

Point P is $\frac{2}{3}$ of the way between 0 and 1.

$\frac{2}{3}$

The numerator tells the number of equal parts being considered.

The denominator tells the number of equal parts in the whole or set.

Standard Form: $\frac{2}{3}$

Word Name: two thirds

Write the fraction for the shaded part or point on the number line.

1.

2.

3.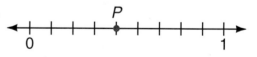

Draw a model to show each fraction.

4. $\frac{5}{7}$ as part of a whole

5. $\frac{7}{8}$ as part of a set

6. $\frac{3}{10}$ as a point on a number line

Write the fraction in standard form.

7. six elevenths

8. four twentieths

9. The numerator is 6, the denominator is 13.

Write the word name for each fraction.

10. $\frac{1}{2}$

11. $\frac{2}{7}$

12. $\frac{5}{9}$

13. $\frac{6}{11}$

14. $\frac{7}{8}$

15. $\frac{8}{13}$

Fractions I

Algebra
Equivalent Fractions

Equivalent fractions name the *same part* of a whole,
a region, or a set.

One half ($\frac{1}{2}$) of the whole
is shaded blue.

Two fourths ($\frac{2}{4}$) of the whole
is shaded blue.

Four eighths ($\frac{4}{8}$) of the
whole is shaded blue.

$$\frac{1}{2} = \frac{2}{4} = \frac{4}{8}$$

$\frac{1}{2}$, $\frac{2}{4}$, and $\frac{4}{8}$ are
equivalent fractions since
they name the same part
of the whole.

Equivalent Fractions Chart

1				1 whole
$\frac{1}{2}$		$\frac{1}{2}$		2 halves
$\frac{1}{3}$	$\frac{1}{3}$	$\frac{1}{3}$		3 thirds
$\frac{1}{4}$	$\frac{1}{4}$	$\frac{1}{4}$	$\frac{1}{4}$	4 fourths
$\frac{1}{5}$	$\frac{1}{5}$ $\frac{1}{5}$ $\frac{1}{5}$ $\frac{1}{5}$			5 fifths
$\frac{1}{6}$ $\frac{1}{6}$ $\frac{1}{6}$ $\frac{1}{6}$ $\frac{1}{6}$ $\frac{1}{6}$				6 sixths
$\frac{1}{8}$ $\frac{1}{8}$ $\frac{1}{8}$ $\frac{1}{8}$ $\frac{1}{8}$ $\frac{1}{8}$ $\frac{1}{8}$ $\frac{1}{8}$				8 eighths
$\frac{1}{9}$ $\frac{1}{9}$ $\frac{1}{9}$ $\frac{1}{9}$ $\frac{1}{9}$ $\frac{1}{9}$ $\frac{1}{9}$ $\frac{1}{9}$ $\frac{1}{9}$				9 ninths
$\frac{1}{10}$ $\frac{1}{10}$ $\frac{1}{10}$ $\frac{1}{10}$ $\frac{1}{10}$ $\frac{1}{10}$ $\frac{1}{10}$ $\frac{1}{10}$ $\frac{1}{10}$ $\frac{1}{10}$				10 tenths
$\frac{1}{12}$ $\frac{1}{12}$ $\frac{1}{12}$ $\frac{1}{12}$ $\frac{1}{12}$ $\frac{1}{12}$ $\frac{1}{12}$ $\frac{1}{12}$ $\frac{1}{12}$ $\frac{1}{12}$ $\frac{1}{12}$ $\frac{1}{12}$				12 twelfths

$$1 = \frac{2}{2} = \frac{3}{3} = \frac{4}{4} = \frac{5}{5} = \frac{6}{6} = \frac{8}{8} = \frac{9}{9} = \frac{10}{10} = \frac{12}{12}$$

Use the chart above to find equivalent fractions.

1. $\frac{1}{2} = \frac{?}{6}$ **2.** $\frac{1}{3} = \frac{?}{6}$ **3.** $\frac{1}{4} = \frac{?}{8}$ **4.** $\frac{1}{5} = \frac{?}{10}$

5. $\frac{1}{3} = \frac{?}{9}$ **6.** $\frac{1}{4} = \frac{?}{12}$ **7.** $\frac{8}{10} = \frac{?}{5}$ **8.** $\frac{6}{9} = \frac{?}{12}$

Use the chart above to compare. Write <, =, or >.

9. $\frac{3}{4}$? $\frac{6}{8}$ **10.** $\frac{1}{3}$? $\frac{4}{9}$ **11.** $\frac{7}{10}$? $\frac{4}{6}$ **12.** $\frac{6}{12}$? $\frac{5}{10}$

13. $\frac{2}{8}$? $\frac{1}{5}$ **14.** $\frac{3}{5}$? $\frac{1}{2}$ **15.** $\frac{4}{6}$? $\frac{8}{12}$ **16.** $\frac{3}{5}$? $\frac{8}{10}$

Write the missing number to complete the equivalent fraction.

17. $\frac{2}{5} = \frac{?}{10}$ **18.** $\frac{3}{4} = \frac{6}{?}$ **19.** $\frac{2}{10} = \frac{?}{5}$ **20.** $\frac{3}{5} = \frac{?}{10}$ **21.** $\frac{2}{6} = \frac{?}{12}$

22. $\frac{3}{6} = \frac{6}{?}$ **23.** $\frac{3}{4} = \frac{?}{12}$ **24.** $\frac{4}{8} = \frac{?}{12}$ **25.** $\frac{2}{3} = \frac{6}{?}$ **26.** $\frac{6}{9} = \frac{8}{?}$

Fractions II

Add and Subtract Fractions: Like Denominators

Add: $\frac{2}{4} + \frac{1}{4} = \underline{\ ?\ }$.

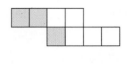 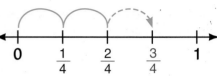

▶ To **add fractions** with *like* denominators:

- Add the numerators.

- Write the sum over the common denominator.

$$\frac{2}{4} + \frac{1}{4} = \frac{3}{\ }$$

$$\frac{2}{4} + \frac{1}{4} = \frac{3}{4}$$

Think........
$2 + 1 = 3$

Subtract: $\frac{3}{5} - \frac{1}{5} = \underline{\ ?\ }$.

▶ To **subtract fractions** with *like* denominators:

- Subtract the numerators.

- Write the difference over the common denominator.

$$\frac{3}{5} - \frac{1}{5} = \frac{2}{\ }$$

$$\frac{3}{5} - \frac{1}{5} = \frac{2}{5}$$

Think........
$3 - 1 = 2$

Study these examples.

$$\begin{array}{r} \frac{5}{9} \\ + \frac{2}{9} \\ \hline \frac{7}{9} \end{array}$$

Think..
$$\frac{5 + 2}{9}$$

$$\begin{array}{r} \frac{8}{9} \\ - \frac{2}{9} \\ \hline \frac{6}{9} \end{array}$$

Think..
$$\frac{8 - 2}{9}$$

Use fraction strips or number lines to model each sum or difference. Then write an addition or a subtraction sentence.

1. $\frac{3}{6} + \frac{2}{6}$
2. $\frac{4}{6} - \frac{3}{6}$
3. $\frac{2}{5} + \frac{2}{5}$
4. $\frac{5}{7} - \frac{2}{7}$

Add or subtract.

5. $\frac{5}{9} + \frac{3}{9}$
6. $\frac{5}{8} + \frac{2}{8}$
7. $\frac{8}{10} - \frac{5}{10}$
8. $\frac{4}{5} - \frac{2}{5}$

9. $\begin{array}{r} \frac{7}{10} \\ + \frac{2}{10} \\ \hline \end{array}$
10. $\begin{array}{r} \frac{1}{5} \\ + \frac{3}{5} \\ \hline \end{array}$
11. $\begin{array}{r} \frac{4}{9} \\ + \frac{4}{9} \\ \hline \end{array}$
12. $\begin{array}{r} \frac{7}{8} \\ - \frac{3}{8} \\ \hline \end{array}$
13. $\begin{array}{r} \frac{10}{12} \\ - \frac{8}{12} \\ \hline \end{array}$

Fractions III

Tenths and Hundredths

A number less than one can be written
either as a fraction or as a decimal.

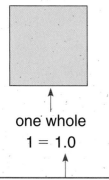

one whole
$1 = 1.0$

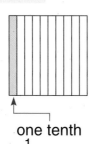

one tenth
$\frac{1}{10} = 0.1$

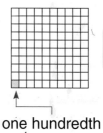

1 tenth =
10 hundredths

one hundredth
$\frac{1}{100} = 0.01$

A decimal point
separates the whole number
part from the decimal part.

0 shows no ones.

0 shows no tenths.

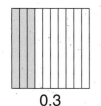

0.3

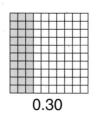

0.30

$0.3 = 0.30$

Equivalent decimals show
the same amount.

Write a fraction and a decimal for each.

1.

2.

3.

4.

Write as a decimal.

5. $\frac{2}{10}$ **6.** $\frac{5}{10}$ **7.** $\frac{9}{100}$ **8.** $\frac{6}{100}$ **9.** $\frac{17}{100}$ **10.** $\frac{23}{100}$

Compare. Write <, =, or >.

11. 0.5 _?_ 0.50   **12.** 0.06 _?_ 0.6   **13.** 0.9 _?_ $\frac{9}{10}$ **14.** 0.8 _?_ $\frac{8}{100}$

Write an equivalent decimal.

15. 0.4   **16.** 0.7   **17.** 0.20   **18.** 0.10   **19.** 0.3   **20.** 0.9

Geometric Concepts

Description	Figure	Symbol	Read As
A point is an exact location in space, usually represented by a dot.	•P	P	point P
A line is a set of points in a plane that forms a straight path and extends indefinitely in opposite directions.	A — B	$\overleftrightarrow{AB}$ or $\overleftrightarrow{BA}$	line AB
A line segment is part of a line with two endpoints.	C — D	$\overline{CD}$ or $\overline{DC}$	line segment CD or DC
A ray is part of a line that starts at an endpoint and extends indefinitely in one direction.	E — F	$\overrightarrow{EF}$	ray EF
A plane is a flat surface that extends indefinitely in all directions.	•R •K •J	RJK	Plane RJK
Intersecting lines are lines that meet at a common point.	A D C P B	$\overleftrightarrow{AB}$ and $\overleftrightarrow{CD}$ intersect at P.	Line AB and line CD intersect at point P.
Parallel lines are lines in the same plane that never intersect.	E F G H	$\overleftrightarrow{EF} \parallel \overleftrightarrow{GH}$	Line EF is parallel to line GH.

Identify each figure. Then name it using symbols.

1.  O P

2. Y X

3. R S

4. 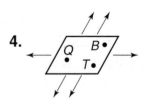 Q B• T•

Draw and label each figure. You may use dot paper.

5. $\overline{DM}$ 6. $\overleftrightarrow{XY}$ 7. $\overrightarrow{FE}$ 8. point Z 9. plane SQR

10. lines EM and DR intersecting at X 11. parallel lines XR and YT

Identify Polygons

▶ A polygon is a closed plane figure formed by line segments. The line segments are called sides. Pairs of sides meet at a point called a vertex (plural: vertices).

vertices
side
angle

7 sides
7 angles

▶ Polygons are classified by the number of sides or vertices (or angles).

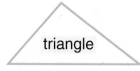 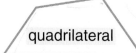 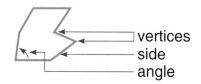

triangle

3 sides
3 vertices

quadrilateral

4 sides
4 vertices

pentagon

5 sides
5 vertices

hexagon

6 sides
6 vertices

Decide if each figure is a polygon. Write *Yes* or *No*.

1.

2.

3.

4.

Name each polygon.

5.

6.

7.

8.

Complete the table.

	Figure	Name	Number of Sides	Number of Vertices
9.		?	?	?
10.	?	?	?	5
11.	?	?	6	?
12.		?	?	?

Customary Units of Length

The inch (in.), foot (ft), yard (yd), and mile (mi) are customary units of length.

| 12 inches (in.) = 1 foot (ft) |
| 36 inches = 1 yard (yd) |
| 3 feet = 1 yard |
| 5280 feet = 1 mile (mi) |
| 1760 yards = 1 mile |

about 1 in. long

about 1 ft tall

about 1 yd wide

The distance a person can walk in 20 minutes is about 1 mile.

▶ Before you can compare measurements in different units, you need to rename units.

Compare: 4 ft __?__ 52 in.

You can make a table.

ft	1	2	3	4	5
in.	12	24	36	48	60

4 ft = 48 in.   48 < 52   So 4 ft < 52 in.

Which unit would you use to measure? Write *in., ft, yd,* or *mi.*

1. length of an eraser

2. width of a board

3. distance between 2 cities

4. height of a desk

5. length of a soccer field

6. width of a quarter

Write the letter of the best estimate.

7. length of a pencil   **a.** 4 yd   **b.** 4 in.   **c.** 4 ft

8. height of a basketball player   **a.** 6 ft   **b.** 6 in.   **c.** 6 yd

Compare. Use <, =, or >.

9. 8 ft __?__ 96 in.   **10.** 6 yd __?__ 2 ft   **11.** 1 mi __?__ 3000 yd

Measurement I

Customary Units of Capacity and Weight

▶ The cup (c), pint (pt), quart (qt), and gallon (gal) are customary units of liquid capacity.

2 cups = 1 pint (pt)
2 pints = 1 quart (qt)
2 quarts = 1 half gallon
4 quarts = 1 gallon (gal)

1 c

1 pt

1 qt

1 half gal

1 gal

▶ The ounce (oz) and pound (lb) are customary units of weight.

16 ounces (oz) = 1 pound (lb)

about 1 oz

about 1 lb

Which unit would you use to measure? Write *c, pt, qt,* or *gal.*

1. juice in a pitcher
2. ice cream in a carton
3. paint in a can
4. water in a swimming pool
5. milk in a recipe
6. water in a bucket

Which unit would you use to measure the weight of each? Write *oz* or *lb.*

7. a toaster
8. a television
9. a dog
10. an envelope
11. a feather
12. a bag of oranges

Complete each table.

13.

pt	1	2	?	4	5	6
c	2	?	6	?	?	?

14.

oz	16	32	?	64	?	96	?	?
lb	1	2	3	?	5	?	7	8

Metric Units of Length

The centimeter (cm), decimeter (dm), meter (m), and kilometer (km) are metric units of length.

1 m	= 100 cm
1 m	= 10 dm
1 km	= 1000 m

about 1 cm wide

about 1 dm long

about 1 m long

The Brooklyn Bridge in New York is about 1 km long.

Which metric unit of length is best to measure each?
Write *cm, m,* or *km.*

1. length of a car

2. depth of the ocean

3. height of a person

4. width of a tape

5. thickness of a sandwich

Write the letter of the best estimate.

6. length of an umbrella   **a.** 1 m   **b.** 1 dm   **c.** 1 km

7. width of a postage stamp   **a.** 0.22 cm   **b.** 2.2 cm   **c.** 22 cm

Complete each table.

8.

dm	1	2	3	?	5	6
cm	10	?	?	40	?	?

9.

km	1	2	?	4	5
m	1000	?	3000	?	?

Compare. Write <, =, or >.

10. 5 m __?__ 48 dm

11. 100 cm __?__ 2 m

12. 1000 m __?__ 1 km

Measurement III

Metric Units of Capacity and Mass

▶ The milliliter (mL) and liter (L) are metric units of liquid capacity.

1000 milliliters (mL) = 1 liter (L)

20 drops of water is about 1 mL.

about 1 L

▶ The gram (g) and kilogram (kg) are metric units of mass.

1000 grams (g) = 1 kilogram (kg)

A paper clip has a mass of about 1 g.

A hardcover dictionary has a mass of about 1 kg.

Which metric unit is best to measure the capacity of each? Write *mL* or *L*.

1. a bucket
2. a perfume bottle
3. a test tube
4. a bathtub
5. a can of juice
6. an eyedropper

Which metric unit is best to measure the mass of each? Write *g* or *kg*.

7. a computer
8. a peanut
9. an electric iron
10. a sugar cube
11. a comb
12. a bowling ball

Complete each table.

13.

L	1	2	?	?	?	?	?	8
mL	1000	?	?	4000	?	?	?	?

14.

kg	1	?	3	?	?	?	?	8
g	1000	?	?	4000	?	?	?	?

Make Pictographs

Make a pictograph to organize the data at the right.

▶ To make a pictograph:

- List each kind of book.

- If necessary, round the data to nearby numbers.

  $298 \longrightarrow 300 \qquad 54 \longrightarrow 50$

- Choose a symbol or picture to represent the number of books for each kind to make the *key*.
  Let 🔲 = 100 books.

- Draw symbols to represent the data for each kind of book.

- Label the pictograph. Write the *title* and the *key*.

Books in the Jackson Public Library	
Kind	**Number of Books**
Science	298
Medicine	54
Biography	195
Art	147
Fiction	554
History	256

> This is about 150 art books.

Books in the Jackson Public Library	
Science	🔲 🔲 🔲
Medicine	🔲
Biography	🔲 🔲
Art	🔲 🔲
Fiction	🔲 🔲 🔲 🔲 🔲 🔲
History	🔲 🔲 🔲
Key: Each 🔲 stands for 100 books.	
Each 🔲 stands for 50 books.	

Make a pictograph for each set of data.

1.

Students Taking Part in After-School Activities	
Activities	**Number of Students**
Clubs	50
Sports	63
Chorus	38
School Paper	14
Student Council	7

2.

Compact Disc Sales	
Music	**Compact Discs Sold**
Classical	105
Country	886
Jazz	212
Rap	384
Rock	790
R & B/Soul	450

Statistics I

Make Bar Graphs

Organize the data at the right in a horizontal bar graph.

▶ To make a horizontal bar graph:

  • Use the data from the table to choose an appropriate scale.

  • Draw and label the scale on the horizontal axis. Start at 0.

  • Draw and label the vertical axis. List the name of each item.

  • Draw horizontal bars to represent the data.

  • Write the title of the bar graph.

▶ You can make a vertical bar graph by placing the scale along the vertical axis and the items along the horizontal axis.

Heights of Some U.S. Waterfalls	
Name	Height in Feet
Akaka	442
Bridalveil	620
Lower Yellowstone	310
Niagara	182
Silver Strand	1170

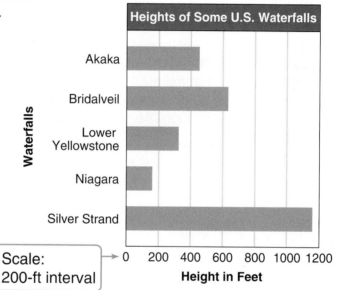

Scale: 200-ft interval

Make a horizontal bar graph for the data listed below.

1.

Results of Canned Food Drive	
Class	Number of Cans
3A	125
3B	102
4A	96
4B	85
5A	141
5B	115

Make a vertical bar graph for the data listed below.

2.

Favorite Sports Activity	
Sport	Number of Students
Baseball/Softball	25
Basketball	18
Gymnastics	14
Soccer	28
Tennis	12

Equally/Not Equally Likely Outcomes

For each of the spinners *A* and *B* there are three different possible results or outcomes: red, blue, green.

▶ Spinner *A* is divided into 3 equal sections, and each section is a different color. Since there is 1 equal section of each color, each color has the same chance of occurring. The outcomes are equally likely.

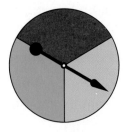

Since there is 1 red section out of a total of 3 sections, the probability of landing on red is 1 out of 3.

Spinner A

▶ Spinner *B* is divided into 6 equal sections. Since there is *not* an equal number of sections for each color, each color does not have the same chance of occurring. The outcomes are not equally likely.

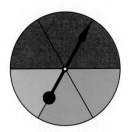

Since there are 3 red sections, the spinner is more likely to land on red than on green or blue.

Spinner B

Since there are 3 red sections out of a total of 6 sections, the probability of landing on red is 3 out of 6.

List the different outcomes. Then write whether the outcomes are *equally likely* or *not equally likely*.

1.
2.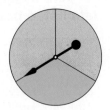
3.
4.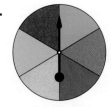

Use the spinner on the right to find the probability of landing on:

5. red   6. blue

7. green   8. yellow

Probability I

List Outcomes

▶ You can make an organized list to show all possible outcomes of an experiment.

In an experiment, Tamara spins the two given spinners. Find all possible outcomes. How many possible outcomes are there?

- Look at the spinners to find the possible outcomes.

  Spinner 1: Blue (B) or Red (R)

  Spinner 2: 1, 2, or 3

Spinner 1

- Make an organized list of the possible pairs of outcomes. Then count the number of outcomes.

B, 1	R, 1
B, 2	R, 2
B, 3	R, 3

So there are 6 possible outcomes.

Spinner 2

**Make a list of all possible outcomes for each experiment.
Then write the total number of outcomes.**

1. toss a coin and toss a green/red counter

2. toss a coin and spin the spinner

3. pick a card without looking and roll a number cube

4. spin the spinner and pick a cube without looking

Dear Student,

Problem solvers are super sleuths. We invite you to become a super sleuth by using these *four* steps when solving problems.

1) Read **2)** Plan **3)** Solve **4)** Check

Sleuths use clues to find a solution to a problem. When working together to solve a problem, you may choose to use one or more of these *strategies* as clues:

Strategy File

Use These Strategies
Combine Strategies
Find a Pattern
Use a Model/Diagram
Guess and Test
More Than One Solution
Use Simpler Numbers

Strategy File

Use These Strategies
Work Backward
Use More Than One Step
Logical Reasoning
Write an Equation

Strategy File

Use These Strategies
Make a Table
Interpret the Remainder
Write a Number Sentence
Make an Organized List
Draw a Picture

Read ▸ **Create a mental picture.**
List the facts and the questions.

As you read a problem, create a picture in your mind.
Make believe you are there in the problem.
This will help you think about:
- what facts you will need;
- what the problem is asking;
- how you will solve the problem.

After reading the problem, it might be helpful to sketch
the picture you imagined so that you can refer to it.

Name or list all the facts given in the problem. Be aware
of *extra* information not needed to solve the problem.
Look for *hidden* information to help solve the problem.
Name the question or questions the problem asks.

Plan ▸ **Choose and outline a plan.**

Plan how to solve the problem by:
- looking at the picture you drew;
- thinking about what you did when you solved similar problems;
- choosing a strategy or strategies for solving the problem.

Solve ▸ **Work the plan.**

Work with the listed facts and the strategy to find the
solution. Sometimes a problem will require you to add,
subtract, multiply, or divide. Multistep problems require
more than one choice of operation or strategy. It is good
to *estimate* the answer before you compute.

Check ▸ **Test that the solution is reasonable.**

Ask yourself:
- "Have I answered the question?"
- "Is the answer reasonable?"

Check the answer by comparing it to the estimate. If the
answer is not reasonable, check your computation.

Strategy: Logical Reasoning

Tom, Roger, and Sue each had a different fruit for lunch today. One had a banana, one had an apple, and one had an orange. Tom and the boy who had a banana are cousins. Sue did *not* have an apple. What did each person have for lunch?

Read ▷ **Visualize yourself in the problem as you reread it. List the facts and question.**

Facts: Each had a different fruit. Tom and the boy who had a banana are cousins. Sue did not have an apple.

Question: What did each person have?

Plan ▷ To solve the problem, make a table and use logical reasoning to eliminate the false conclusions.

When you write **yes** in a box, write **no** in the corresponding boxes in both that row and that column.

	Banana	Apple	Orange
Tom			
Roger			
Sue			

Solve ▷ Since Tom and the boy who had a banana are cousins, write **yes** under "Banana" across from "Roger" and write the **no** in the corresponding boxes. Since Sue did *not* have an apple, write **no** across from Sue under that column.

	Banana	Apple	Orange
Tom	no	yes	no
Roger	yes	no	no
Sue	no	no	yes

So Sue did have an orange.
(Write the **yes** and **no** in the "Orange" column.)

So Tom did have an apple.
(Write **yes** in the remaining box.)

Check ▷ Compare the completed chart to the facts given in the problem.

Strategy: Interpret the Remainder

Ms. Cooper needs 115 decorations for cakes.
Decorations come 9 to a box. How many boxes
should she order? When the cakes are decorated,
how many decorations from the last box will
not be used?

Read Visualize yourself in the problem as you
reread it. List the facts and questions.

Facts: 115 decorations needed
9 decorations per box

Questions: How many boxes should
be ordered? How many
decorations will *not* be used?

Plan To find how many boxes should be ordered,
divide:

$$115 \div 9 = \underline{\ ?\ }$$
decorations   per box   boxes

To find how many decorations will *not* be used,
subtract the remainder from 9.

Solve

```
      1 2  R 7
  9)1 1 5
    - 9 ↓
      2 5
    - 1 8
        7
```

Twelve boxes will not be enough.
So she will need to order 13 boxes of decorations.

$$9 - 7 = 2$$

Two decorations will *not* be used from
the last box.

Check Check division by using multiplication and addition.
$$9 \times 12 + 7 = 115$$

Strategy: Use More Than One Step

Marvin is reading a 341-page book. He has already read 128 pages of the book. If he skipped the 19 pages of maps, how many more pages does he have left to read to finish the book?

| read 128 pages skipped 19 pages | _?_ pages left to read |

Read ▸ **Visualize yourself in the problem as you reread it. List the facts and the question.**

Facts: He has read 128 pages.
He skipped 19 pages.

Question: How many more pages does he have left to read?

Plan ▸ To find the number of pages left, you must use two steps.

Step 1: Add the number of pages Marvin read and skipped.

Step 2: Subtract that sum from the total number of pages.

Solve ▸
```
    1
  1 2 8  pages read
+   1 9  pages skipped
  1 4 7
```

```
        13
    2  3 11
    3̶ 4̶ 1̶  total number of pages
  - 1 4 7
    1 9 4
```

Marvin has 194 pages left to read.

Check ▸ Use the commutative property and addition to check your computation.

```
    1
    1 9
 +1 2 8
  1 4 7
```

```
  1   1
    1 9 4
 +1 4 7
  3 4 1  The answer checks.
```

Strategy: Make a Table

Rory multiplied a two-digit number by a one-digit number greater than 1. The product was between 40 and 45. What were the numbers?

×
product

Read ▸ **Visualize yourself in the problem as you reread it. List the facts and the question.**

Facts: The factors were a two-digit number and a one-digit number greater than 1. The product was between 40 and 45.

Question: What were the numbers?

Plan ▸ Make a table to record the factors and products.

To find the factors, list:
- one-digit numbers greater than 1. (2, 3, 4, . . .)
- two-digit numbers. (10, 11, 12, . . .)

Since the least two-digit number is 10 and 5 × 10 = 50, the one-digit number is less than 5.

Multiply the factors to find the products that equal 41, 42, 43, or 44.

> Remember: Not all problems have just one solution.

Solve ▸

Factors	21 × 2	22 × 2	23 × 2	13 × 3	14 × 3	15 × 3	11 × 4
Product	42 Yes	44 Yes	46 No	39 No	42 Yes	45 No	44 Yes

So there is *more than one solution.*
The factors are 2 × 21, 2 × 22, 3 × 14, and 4 × 11.

Check ▸ Reread the problem. Compare the completed table to the facts given in the problem. Are all the solutions reasonable? Yes.

INTRODUCTION TO PROBLEM SOLVING

27

Applications: Mixed Review

Choose a strategy from the list or use another strategy you know to solve each problem.

1. Cool Cola at the circus comes in personal, average, and family sizes. The personal size is 6 oz and sells for $1.09. The average size is 12 oz and sells for $1.89. The family size is 24 oz and sells for $2.79. Which is the best buy? How do you know?

Strategy File

Use These Strategies
Logical Reasoning
Interpret the Remainder
Use More Than One Step
Make a Table

2. Mr. Posio has 123 circus stickers to pass out to his class. He gives 4 stickers to each student. How many students are there in Mr. Posio's class? How many stickers are left over?

3. The circus attendance in April was less than the attendance in May but greater than the attendance in June. The circus attendance in July was between the attendance in April and in May. Write these months in increasing order of attendance.

4. The circus has tigers named Leo, Clem, and Fred. Gary, Mary, and Barry are the trainers. Mary does *not* train Clem. She watches Gary train Leo before her act. Match the trainers with their tigers.

5. Ms. Gretchen needs 69 fruit bars for her students at the circus. There are 8 fruit bars in a box. How many boxes of fruit bars should Ms. Gretchen order?

6. Adam saved $138 to buy a $270 bicycle. He worked at the Stellar Circus each week and received $30 the first week. For each additional week, Adam received $2 more than the preceding week. How many weeks did he work to have enough money to pay for the bicycle?

Place Value, Addition, and Subtraction

Lincoln Monument: Washington

Let's go see old Abe
Sitting in the marble and the moonlight,
Sitting lonely in the marble and the moonlight,
Quiet for ten thousand centuries, old Abe.
Quiet for a million, million years.

Quiet—

And yet a voice forever
Against the
Timeless walls
Of time—
Old Abe.

Langston Hughes

In this chapter you will:

Explore a billion
Read, write, compare, order, and round numbers
Use addition properties and subtraction rules
Use rounding and front-end estimation
Read and write Roman numerals
Solve by the Guess-and-Test strategy

Critical Thinking/Finding Together

In 1863 Abraham Lincoln began a speech, "Four score and seven years ago…" In 1922 the Lincoln Memorial in Washington, DC, was built. If *score* means 20, use *score* to describe the number of years between the year Lincoln was referring to when he gave the speech and 1922.

What Is a Billion?

Materials: paper, pencil, base ten cube stamp, construction paper, almanac, newspapers, magazines

Find the products in exercise 1.
Record each number sentence and the answer.
Look for a pattern.

1. $10 \times 1 = \underline{?}$
   $10 \times 10 = \underline{?}$
   $10 \times 100 = \underline{?}$
   $10 \times 1000 = \underline{?}$
   $10 \times 10{,}000 = \underline{?}$
   $10 \times 100{,}000 = \underline{?}$
   $10 \times 1{,}000{,}000 = \underline{?}$
   Predict the product of $10 \times 10{,}000{,}000$;
   $ 10 \times 100{,}000{,}000.$

2. Describe the pattern in the products when 10 is multiplied by a multiple of 10.

The number that is $10 \times 100{,}000{,}000$ is one billion, or 1,000,000,000. One billion is the next counting number after 999,999,999.

3. How is 1,000,000,000 like 1,000,000; 10,000,000; and 100,000,000? How is it different?

4. If 1,000,000,000 = 10 hundred millions, then 1,000,000,000 = 100 ten millions.
   How many millions is one billion equal to? how many thousands?

Use the base ten cube as a thousand model. Stamp 10 base ten cubes on a sheet of construction paper.

5. How many sheets of paper each with 10 base ten cubes pictured would be needed for 10 thousand? 100 thousand? 1 million? 10 million? 100 million? 1 billion?

Answer questions 6–8.

If you could travel 1 mile per second,
you could get to places very quickly.
At 1 mile per second:

6. About how many minutes would it take
   you to travel 1000 miles? 1,000,000 miles?
   1,000,000,000 miles?

7. About how many hours would it take you
   to travel 1000 miles? 1,000,000 miles?
   1,000,000,000 miles?

8. About how many days would it take
   you to travel 1,000,000 miles?
   1,000,000,000 miles?

Communicate

9. How did you discover about how
   many minutes it would take you to
   travel 1000 miles; 1,000,000 miles; and
   1,000,000,000 miles at 1 mile per second?

10. How did you discover about how many
    hours it would take you to travel 1000 miles;
    1,000,000 miles; and 1,000,000,000 miles
    at 1 mile per second?

11. How did you discover about how many days it
    would take you to travel 1,000,000 miles; and
    1,000,000,000 miles at 1 mile per second?

Write About It

12. Use the almanac, newspapers, and magazines
    to find numbers in the billions. Write a short
    description of the kinds of activities that involve
    references to billions.

1-2

Place Value to Billions

The average distance of the planet Pluto from the Sun is about 3,674,488,000 miles.

You can show this number in a place-value chart.

In 3,674,488,000,
the billions period has:
   3 with a value of 3 billions
   or 3,000,000,000.
the millions period has:
   6 with a value of 6 hundred
   millions or 600,000,000;
   7 with a value of 7 ten
   millions or 70,000,000;
   4 with a value of 4 millions
   or 4,000,000.

Billions Period			Millions Period			Thousands Period			Ones Period		
hundreds	tens	ones	hundreds	tens	ones	hundreds	tens	ones	hundreds	tens	ones
	3,	6	7	4,	4	8	8,	0	0	0	

Standard Form: 3,674,488,000

Commas separate the periods.

Word Name: three billion,

   six hundred seventy-four million,

   four hundred eighty-eight thousand

Remember:
Four-digit numbers may be written with or without a comma.

Study these examples.

Standard Form: 40,000,000,000
Word Name: forty billion
Short Word Name: 40 billion

Standard Form: 70,000,000
Word Name: seventy million
Short Word Name: 70 million

Practice

Write the place of the underlined digit. Then write its value.

1. 5,476,807,139
2. 3,960,135,741
3. 7,708,304,016
4. 9,428,001,230
5. 16,350,846,760
6. 39,714,062,030
7. 24,398,407,268
8. 90,165,270,000
9. 365,123,145,000
10. 190,477,653,002
11. 401,743,000,295
12. 839,200,430,000

Write the number in standard form.

13. three million, five hundred forty thousand, thirty-seven

14. forty million, one hundred thousand, two hundred five

15. two hundred twenty million, five thousand, eight

16. three billion, six hundred six million, seventy-seven thousand, four hundred three

17. seventy-nine billion, one

18. eighty-one million

19. nine hundred forty billion

20. thirteen million, two

21. 800 million

22. 40 billion

23. 500 billion

Write the word name for each number.

24. 1,042,003,051

25. 4,725,000,000

26. 72,200,000,020

27. 12,025,617,809

28. 500,476,807,139

29. 23,539,417,148

Write the short word name for each number.

30. 6,000,000

31. 100,000,000

32. 20,000,000

33. 30,000,000,000

34. 6,000,000,000

35. 500,000,000,000

Problem Solving

36. The average distance from Earth to the planet Saturn is about 773,119,750 miles. Write the word name of this number.

37. At times, the planet Pluto is about five billion miles from Earth. Write this number in standard form.

CRITICAL THINKING

Rearrange the digits in the given statement to make new true statements.

38. $7234 < 7243$

42 _?_ _?_ $<$ _?_ _?_ 24

_?_ 7 _?_ _?_ $>$ _?_ _?_ 4 _?_

39. $62,249 < 63,975$

69, _?_ _?_ 2 $>$ 69, _?_ 7 _?_

_?_ _?_, _?_ 42 $<$ 9 _?_, _?_ _?_ 3

Expanded Form

The value of each digit of a number can be shown
by writing the number in expanded form.

A place that holds a
zero may be omitted
in expanded form.

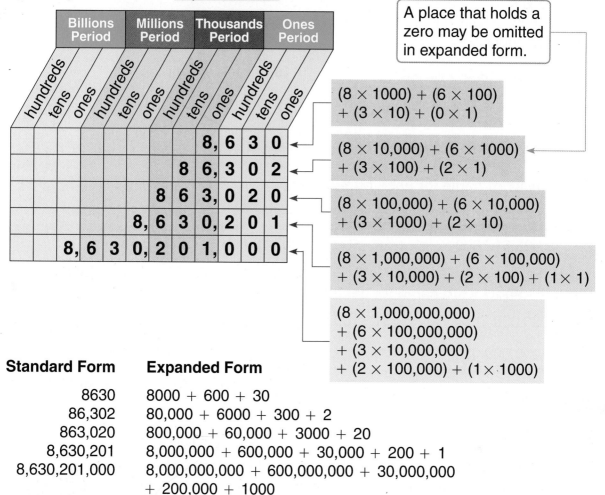

$(8 \times 1000) + (6 \times 100)$
$+ (3 \times 10) + (0 \times 1)$

$(8 \times 10,000) + (6 \times 1000)$
$+ (3 \times 100) + (2 \times 1)$

$(8 \times 100,000) + (6 \times 10,000)$
$+ (3 \times 1000) + (2 \times 10)$

$(8 \times 1,000,000) + (6 \times 100,000)$
$+ (3 \times 10,000) + (2 \times 100) + (1 \times 1)$

$(8 \times 1,000,000,000)$
$+ (6 \times 100,000,000)$
$+ (3 \times 10,000,000)$
$+ (2 \times 100,000) + (1 \times 1000)$

Standard Form	Expanded Form
8630	8000 + 600 + 30
86,302	80,000 + 6000 + 300 + 2
863,020	800,000 + 60,000 + 3000 + 20
8,630,201	8,000,000 + 600,000 + 30,000 + 200 + 1
8,630,201,000	8,000,000,000 + 600,000,000 + 30,000,000 + 200,000 + 1000

Complete the expanded form of each number.

1. $1487 = (\underline{\ ?\ } \times 1000) + (\underline{\ ?\ } \times 100) + (\underline{\ ?\ } \times 10) + (\underline{\ ?\ } \times 1)$

2. $87,020 = (\underline{\ ?\ } \times 10,000) + (\underline{\ ?\ } \times 1000) + (\underline{\ ?\ } \times 10)$

3. $180,764 = (1 \times \underline{\ ?\ }) + (8 \times \underline{\ ?\ }) + (7 \times \underline{\ ?\ }) + (6 \times \underline{\ ?\ }) + (4 \times \underline{\ ?\ })$

4. $32,530,008 = (3 \times \underline{\ ?\ }) + (2 \times \underline{\ ?\ }) + (5 \times \underline{\ ?\ }) + (3 \times \underline{\ ?\ }) + (8 \times \underline{\ ?\ })$

5. $4,700,930,002 = (4 \times \underline{\ ?\ }) + (7 \times \underline{\ ?\ }) + (9 \times \underline{\ ?\ })$
$+ (\underline{\ ?\ } \times 10,000) + (\underline{\ ?\ } \times 1)$

Write each in standard form.

6. 4000 + 500 + 60 + 9

7. 20,000 + 2000 + 900 + 80 + 7

8. 400,000 + 300 + 50

9. 3,000,000 + 9000 + 40 + 8

10. 60,000,000 + 3,000,000 + 400,000 + 5000 + 7

11. 1,000,000,000 + 200,000,000 + 50,000,000 + 300 + 9

Write in expanded form.

12. 8998

13. 6745

14. 15,243

15. 37,418

16. 672,115

17. 350,001

18. 700,946

19. 2,200,002

20. 13,004,205

21. 604,003,020

22. 2,005,940,000

Choose the correct answer.

23. In the number 62,725, the 6 means:
   a. 6 × 1000   **b.** 6 × 100   **c.** 6 × 100,000   **d.** 6 × 10,000

24. In the number 2,784,349, the 2 means:
   a. 2 × 1000   **b.** 2 × 10,000   **c.** 2 × 1,000,000   **d.** 2 × 100,000,000

25. In the number 34,056,971,000, the 3 means:
   a. 3 × 1000   **b.** 3 × 10,000   **c.** 3 × 10,000,000   **d.** 3 × 10,000,000,000

Problem Solving

26. The distance from the center of Earth to the center of the Sun is 92,955,807 miles. Write this number in expanded form.

MENTAL MATH

Use the number 14,567,903,104. What number is:

27. 10,000 greater?

28. 1,000,000 less?

29. 10,000,000,000 greater?

30. 100,000,000 less?

Thousandths

Each one of the ten parts of 0.01 is 0.001.

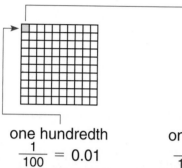

one hundredth
$\frac{1}{100} = 0.01$

one thousandth
$\frac{1}{1000} = 0.001$

Ones	Tenths	Hundredths	Thousandths
0•	0	0	3
0•	0	6	8
0•	3	5	4

0 ones, 0 tenths, 0 hundredths, 3 thousandths

0 ones, 0 tenths, 6 hundredths, 8 thousandths

0 ones, 3 tenths, 5 hundredths, 4 thousandths

1 hundredth = 10 thousandths

Remember:
0.4 = 0.40 = 0.400
Equivalent decimals show the same amount.

Standard Form   **Word Name**

0.003   three thousandths
0.068   sixty-eight thousandths
0.354   three hundred fifty-four thousandths

Practice

Write as a decimal.

1. $\frac{5}{1000}$ 2. $\frac{9}{1000}$ 3. $\frac{4}{100}$ 4. $\frac{3}{10}$ 5. $\frac{4}{1000}$ 6. $\frac{7}{1000}$

Write the value of the underlined digit.

7. 0.3̲62   8. 0.04̲9   9. 0.503̲   10. 0.9̲18   11. 0.005̲

12. 0.5̲18   13. 0.06̲7   14. 0.6̲53   15. 0.52̲4   16. 0.09̲3

Write the decimal in standard form.

17. seven thousandths

18. nine hundred four thousandths

19. fifty-six thousandths

20. sixty-three thousandths

21. one hundred three thousandths

22. three hundred two thousandths

Write the word name for each decimal.

23. 0.461   **24.** 0.159   **25.** 0.009   **26.** 0.112   **27.** 0.258

28. 0.053   **29.** 0.158   **30.** 0.002   **31.** 0.273   **32.** 0.419

Write an equivalent decimal.

33. 0.9   **34.** 0.09   **35.** 0.23   **36.** 0.25   **37.** 0.72

38. 0.80   **39.** 0.50   **40.** 0.650   **41.** 0.300   **42.** 0.010

Write the letter of the correct answer.

43. Three hundred three thousandths is ___?___
    a. 303,000   **b.** 0.303   **c.** 303   **d.** 0.33

44. One hundred thirteen thousandths is ___?___
    a. 0.113   **b.** 0.013   **c.** 113,000   **d.** 113

45. Four hundred fifty-seven thousandths is ___?___
    a. 0.407   **b.** 457   **c.** 0.457   **d.** 457,000

46. Six hundred forty thousandths is ___?___
    a. 640,000   **b.** 600,040   **c.** 0.640   **d.** 0.064

Problem Solving

47. Minerva walked a distance of forty-five thousandths of a kilometer to the museum. Write this distance in standard form.

48. Mike rides 0.8 km on his bicycle. Write this distance as thousandths of a kilometer.

49. A car travels at a speed of 0.917 mile per minute. Write the word name of this speed.

CRITICAL THINKING

Use Mental Math and place value to find how much less _A_ is than _B_.

50. A. 0.751   **51. A.** 0.138   **52. A.** 0.369   **53. A.** 0.7

    B. 0.752   **B.** 0.148   **B.** 0.37   **B.** 0.71

Decimals Greater Than One

You can write a number greater than one as a decimal.

 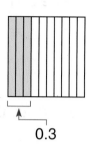 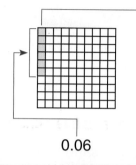 

1   0.3   0.06   0.004

Ones	Tenths	Hundredths	Thousandths
1•	3	6	4

▶ A place-value chart can help you read decimals.
- If there is a whole number, read the whole number first. Then read the decimal point as *and*.
- Read the decimal as a whole number before reading the place value of the last digit.

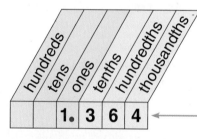

1 one, 3 tenths, 6 hundredths, 4 thousandths

Standard Form
1.364

Word Name
one and three hundred sixty-four thousandths

Read the number. Then write the word name.

1. 0.392   2. 2.307   3. 19.3   4. 1.002   5. 17.017

6. 53.147   7. 103.551   8. 317.03   9. 37.730   10. 932.73

Write the place of the underlined digit. Then write its value.

11. 7.6̲78   12. 75.19̲6   13. 8̲0.103   14. 35.64̲3   15. 13̲8.2

16. 4̲25.13   17. 90̲.121   18. 6.2̲31   19. 9.47̲8   20. 1.41̲1

Write the number in standard form.

21. seven and fourteen hundredths   **22.** one and two thousandths

23. sixty-three and two tenths   **24.** three and five hundredths

25. three and four thousandths   **26.** forty-five and six tenths

27. one hundred forty-five and two thousandths

28. sixty-one and three hundred eighteen thousandths

29. one hundred thirty-eight and five hundred forty-one thousandths

Write the word name for each number.

30. 10.392   **31.** 2.307   **32.** 19.3   **33.** 1.002   **34.** 8.017

35. 3.147   **36.** 12.551   **37.** 37.03   **38.** 5.730   **39.** 319.723

Use the number 958.826. What number is:

40. one tenth greater?   **41.** one hundredth less?   **42.** one thousandth greater?

43. three and one tenth less?   **44.** twenty and two thousandths greater?

Problem Solving

45. Marla's time for the bicycle race was fifty-nine and one hundred twenty-two thousandths seconds. Write this time in standard form.

46. Steve's time for the bicycle race was 48.235 seconds. Write the word name for his time.

CHALLENGE — Algebra

Write the pattern rule. Then complete the pattern.

47. 0.3, 0.4, 0.5, _?_ , _?_

48. 0.6, 0.5, 0.4, _?_ , _?_

49. 1.9, 2, 2.1, _?_ , _?_

50. 0.09, 0.08, 0.07, _?_ , _?_

51. 0.005, 0.006, 0.007, _?_ , _?_

52. 3.26, 3.25, 3.24, _?_ , _?_

Compare and Order Numbers

Compare 8,532,314,516 and 8,539,417,148.
Which is greater?

Remember:
$<$ means "is less than."
$>$ means "is greater than."

▶ You can compare whole numbers by
comparing the digits in each place-value
position. Start at the left and check each
place until the digits are different.

8,532,314,516
8,539,417,148

| $8 = 8$ |
| $5 = 5$ |
| $3 = 3$ |

$\boxed{9 > 2}$

8,539,417,148 $>$ 8,532,314,516   or   8,532,314,516 $<$ 8,539,417,148

Order from least to greatest:
  1,353,678,945; 1,359,712,148; 358,643,208; 1,353,432,816

▶ You can order whole numbers by
comparing them in the same way.

1,353,678,945	1,353,678,945	1,353,678,945
1,359,712,148	1,359,712,148	1,359,712,148
358,643,208	358,643,208	358,643,208
1,353,432,816	1,353,432,816	1,353,432,816

No billions.	$3 = 3$ and $9 > 3$	$6 > 4$
358,643,208	1,359,712,148 is	1,353,678,945 $>$ 1,353,432,816
is least.	greatest.	

The order from least to greatest:
  358,643,208; 1,353,432,816; 1,353,678,945; 1,359,712,148

The order from greatest to least:
  1,359,712,148; 1,353,678,945; 1,353,432,816; 358,643,208

Practice

Compare. Write $<$ or $>$.

1. 479,059 _?_ 479,056   **2.** 2,873,303 _?_ 2,808,323   **3.** 2,124,371 _?_ 256,721

4. 2,356,100,910 _?_ 2,561,009,102   **5.** 7,495,851,787 _?_ 7,489,987,565

6. 3,410,999,246 _?_ 3,410,989,243   **7.** 6,355,601,501 _?_ 999,031,276

Write in order from least to greatest.

8. 4,767,831; 4,984,321; 4,113,121; 4,801,125

9. 9,238,456,348; 9,760,816; 989,507,555; 9,238,940,067

Write in order from greatest to least.

10. 162,550,743; 99,927,483; 159,294,604; 162,475,988

11. 2,458,599,763; 2,196,536,401; 2,423,038,972; 2,314,043,179

Compare and Order Decimals

To compare and order decimals, use the same rules for comparing and ordering whole numbers.

▶ Compare 6.2 and 6.17. Which is greater?

| 6.20 ←─ | 6.2 = 6.20 | | 6.20 | 6 = 6 | | 6.20 | 2 > 1 |
| 6.17 | | | 6.17 | | | 6.17 | |

6.2 > 6.17   or   6.17 < 6.2

▶ Order from least to greatest: 9.631; 9.615; 8.92.

9.631	8 < 9		9.631	6 = 6		9.631	3 > 1
9.615	8.92 is least.		9.615			9.615	9.631 is
8.920							greatest.

The order from least to greatest: 8.92; 9.615; 9.631
The order from greatest to least: 9.631; 9.615; 8.92

Compare. Write <, =, or >.

12. 7.083 ? 7.83   **13.** 10.8 ? 10.80   **14.** 3.9 ? 4.12

15. 9.34 ? 3.94   **16.** 4.453 ? 4.532   **17.** 1 ? 0.99

Write in order from least to greatest and from greatest to least.

18. 6.161; 6.311; 6.62   **19.** 3.814; 3.872; 3.853   **20.** 5.05; 5.051; 5.053

21. 7.413; 7.423; 7.42   **22.** 13.3; 13.321; 13.335   **23.** 6.163; 6.316; 6.631

Rounding Numbers

Suppose you live in California and someone asks you what California's state population is. You could give the exact figure—33,871,648—or you might give a number that has been rounded to a given place.

Round 33,871,648 to the nearest *million*.

▶ To round a number to a given place, you can use a number line:

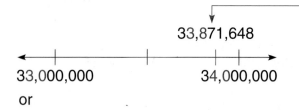

33,871,648

33,000,000   34,000,000

> 33,871,648 is closer to 34,000,000.
> Round **up** to 34,000,000.

or

Use the rules for rounding. Find the place you are rounding to, then look at the digit to its right.

33,871,648
↓
34,000,000

> 8 > 5
> Round **up**
> to 34,000,000.

If the digit is *less than 5*, round down.

If the digit is *5 or more*, round up.

California's state population to the nearest million is 34,000,000.

▶ To round a number to the greatest place:

- Find the digit in the greatest place.

- Look at the digit to its right and round as usual.

6,589,105
↓
7,000,000

> 5 = 5
> Round **up**
> to 7,000,000.

32,152,083
↓
30,000,000

> 2 < 5
> Round **down**
> to 30,000,000.

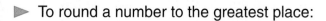

Round each number to the place of the underlined digit.
You may use a number line to help you.

1. 1<u>6</u>3,128   **2.** <u>9</u>25,684   **3.** <u>1</u>,675,213   **4.** 6,5<u>8</u>9,105

5. <u>3</u>6,813,431   **6.** 12,4<u>3</u>5,129   **7.** 2<u>3</u>5,198,051   **8.** 84,19<u>3</u>,103

Practice

Round to the greatest place.

9. 53,678   10. 99,407   11. 783,229   12. 359,048

13. 114,726   14. 5,748,111   15. 1,098,093   16. 7,523,670

17. 20,248,973   18. 37,561,444   19. 86,124,826   20. 15,543,901

Rounding Decimals and Money

To round decimals and money amounts, use the same rules for rounding whole numbers.

▶ Round 36.375 to the nearest:

Whole Number	**Tenth**	**Hundredth**
36.375	36.375	36.375
↓	↓	↓
36	36.4	36.38

Do not write zeros to the right.

▶ Round $473.28 to the nearest:

Ten Cents	**Dollar**	**Ten Dollars**	**Hundred Dollars**
$ 473.28	$473.28	$473.28	$473.28
↓	↓	↓	↓
$ 473.30	$473	$470	$500

Round each to the nearest *whole number*, *tenth*, and *hundredth*.

21. 6.148   22. 1.792   23. 3.732   24. 24.873   25. 39.925

26. 73.159   27. 29.866   28. 548.501   29. 112.549   30. 332.532

Round each to the nearest *ten cents*, *dollar*, *ten dollars*, and *hundred dollars*.

31. $427.89   32. $642.87   33. $792.46   34. $225.98   35. $146.72

36. $119.28   37. $542.76   38. $125.58   39. $918.92   40. $699.45

Problem Solving

41. The world's largest rock crystal ball weighs 106.75 pounds. Round this weight to the nearest tenth.

42. Julie bought two books for $14.98 and $19.45. Find the total cost of the books to the nearest dollar.

Addition Properties/Subtraction Rules

▶ The properties of addition can help you add quickly and correctly.

| addend + addend = sum |

- **Commutative Property of Addition**
  Changing the *order* of the addends does not change the sum.

.Think..
"order"

$6 + 9 = 15$

$9 + 6 = 15$

$$\begin{array}{cc} 6 & 9 \\ +9 & +6 \\ \hline 15 & 15 \end{array}$$

- **Associative Property of Addition**
  Changing the *grouping* of the addends does not change the sum.

.Think..
"grouping"

$(2 + 3) + 6 = 2 + (3 + 6)$

$5 + 6 = 2 + 9$

$11 = 11$

- **Identity Property of Addition**
  The sum of *zero* and a number is the same as that number.

.Think..
"same"

$9 + 0 = 9$

$0 + 9 = 9$

$$\begin{array}{cc} 9 & 0 \\ +0 & +9 \\ \hline 9 & 9 \end{array}$$

▶ Use the properties to find shortcuts when adding more than two numbers.

Change the order.

Add down.   Add up.

$$\begin{array}{cc} 3 & \\ 0 & 3 \\ 4 & 7 \\ 7 & 14 \\ +6 & 20 \\ \hline 20 & \end{array}$$

$$\begin{array}{ccc} 3 & 20 \\ 0 & 17 \\ 4 & 17 \\ 7 & 13 \\ +6 & \\ \hline 20 & \end{array}$$

Change the order and the grouping.

$$\begin{array}{c} 3 \\ 4 \\ 6 \\ +7 \\ \hline 20 \end{array} \quad 10 \quad 10$$

$(3 + 7) + (4 + 6) = 20$

$10 + 10 = 20$

Find the missing number. Name the property of addition that is used.

1. $8 + 7 = \square + 8$

2. $8 = 0 + \square$

3. $(6 + 1) + 9 = 6 + (1 + \square)$

4. $\square + 4 = 4$

5. $5 + \square = 6 + 5$

6. $3 + (5 + 6) = (3 + \square) + 6$

Practice

Add. Use the properties of addition to find shortcuts.

7.	8.	9.	10.	11.	12.
9	4	5	4	1	9
3	2	4	7	2	4
7	6	5	6	6	1
+1	+8	+3	+2	+8	+5

13. $2 + 7 + 0 + 5 + 3$ **14.** $1 + 6 + 5 + 0 + 4$ **15.** $2 + 0 + 4 + 8 + 1$

Subtraction Rules

Subtraction is the *inverse* of addition.
It "undoes" addition.

$$7 + 4 = 11$$
$$11 - 4 = 7$$

$$\begin{array}{r} 7 \\ +4 \\ \hline 11 \end{array} \qquad \begin{array}{r} 11 \\ -\ 4 \\ \hline 7 \end{array}$$

The **rules of subtraction** can help you subtract quickly and correctly.

minuend − subtrahend = difference

- When the minuend is equal to the subtrahend, the difference is always *zero*.

$$9 - 9 = 0 \qquad \begin{array}{r} 9 \\ -9 \\ \hline 0 \end{array}$$

- When zero is the subtrahend, the difference is equal to the *minuend*.

$$9 - 0 = 9 \qquad \begin{array}{r} 9 \\ -0 \\ \hline 9 \end{array}$$

Find the missing addend.

16. $7 + \boxed{4} = 11$

Think....
$$11 - 7 = 4$$
So $7 + 4 = 11$

17. $6 + \square = 15$ **18.** $\square + 9 = 18$

19. $8 + \square = 14$ **20.** $\square + 4 = 12$ **21.** $7 + \square = 7$ **22.** $8 + \square = 13$

23. $\square + 9 = 9$ **24.** $7 + \square = 14$ **25.** $\square + 2 = 11$ **26.** $9 + \square = 15$

Problem Solving

27. There are 16 books on a shelf. Hannah takes 7 books from the shelf. How many books are left on the shelf?

28. Ramon puts 14 books in a box. Eight of the books are textbooks. How many books are *not* textbooks?

29. In a 5-day period, Luis spends 4 h, 3 h, 5 h, 3 h, and 5 h pruning trees. He then adds to find the total number of hours. Does the order in which he adds the numbers affect the sum? Explain.

Estimate Sums and Differences

Mr. Blackwell asked his class to estimate the sum: 4164 + 987 + 3895 + 4213, and the difference: 8365 − 3821.

4000 + ...
8000 − ...

You can use front-end estimation to estimate sums and differences.

▶ To *estimate sums* using **front-end estimation**:
  • Add the front digits. Then write zeros for the other digits.
  • Adjust the estimate with the back digits.

Add the front digits. Write zeros for the other digits.

```
    4164
     987
    3895
 + 4213
about 11,000
```

Adjust the estimate with the back digits.

```
 4164
  987  ⟩ about 1000
 3895
+4213  ⟩ about 1000
```

Think
```
   11,000
    1,000
 +  1,000
   13,000
```

Adjusted estimate:
11,000 + 1000 + 1000 = 13,000

Rough estimate: 11,000

The estimated sum is 13,000.

▶ To *estimate differences* using **front-end estimation**:
  • Subtract the front digits.
  • Write zeros for the other digits.

```
      8365
    − 3821
about  5000
```

The estimated difference is 5000.

Study these examples.

```
  $324.54 ⟶ $324.54
   276.37     276.37  ⟩ about $100
 + 436.93   + 436.93
about $900.00
```

```
      9561            $943.86
    −  742          − 137.13
about  9000    about  $800.00
```

Rough estimate: $900
Adjusted estimate:
  $900 + $100 = $1000

Estimate the sum or difference. Use front-end estimation.

1. 4987 2526 + 2844	**2.** 6325 3691 + 2236	**3.** 232 7625 + 3475	**4.** $115.27 372.62 +236.91	**5.** $947.60 25.89 + 550.09
6. 6626 − 4813	**7.** 7242 − 5759	**8.** 8934 − 812	**9.** $887.56 − 259.60	**10.** $932.55 − 47.28

11. 6325 + 3632 + 8422 + 1362   **12.** 7459 + 1359 + 813 + 5231

Estimation by Rounding

▶ Rounding is another estimation strategy.
To estimate by rounding:

- Round each number to the greatest place of the least number.
- Add or subtract the rounded numbers.

$$
\begin{array}{r}
\overset{1\,1}{6917} \rightarrow 6920 \\
78 \rightarrow 80 \\
+\ 434 \rightarrow +\ 430 \\
\hline
\text{about} \quad 7430
\end{array}
\qquad
\begin{array}{r}
\$5.78 \rightarrow \$5.80 \\
3.26 \rightarrow 3.30 \\
+\ 0.83 \rightarrow +\ 0.80 \\
\hline
\text{about} \quad \$9.90
\end{array}
\qquad
\begin{array}{r}
5931 \rightarrow 5900 \\
-\ 723 \rightarrow -\ 700 \\
\hline
\text{about} \quad 5200
\end{array}
$$

▶ When an estimated
difference is **zero**, round
to the next greatest place.

$$
\begin{array}{r}
\$39.48 \rightarrow \$40.00 \\
-\ 35.62 \rightarrow -\ 40.00 \\
\hline
\text{about} \quad \$ \quad 0
\end{array}
\qquad
\begin{array}{r}
\$39.48 \rightarrow \$39.00 \\
-\ 35.62 \rightarrow -\ 36.00 \\
\hline
\text{about} \quad \$3.00
\end{array}
$$

Estimate the sum or difference. Use rounding.

13. 2732 6146 + 7378	**14.** 3257 612 + 5701	**15.** 4239 624 + 38	**16.** $ 4.67 15.08 + 41.13	**17.** $41.07 92.53 + 3.12
18. 7893 − 5421	**19.** 8934 − 819	**20.** 9434 − 9251	**21.** $83.72 − 8.44	**22.** $932.55 − 47.48

23. 2357 + 4612 + 5318 + 675   **24.** 6531 + 7735 + 943 + 39

TEST PREPARATION

25. Which subtraction has an estimated difference of 3000?

     A 5785 − 1315   **B** 5168 − 3209   **C** 5185 − 2316   **D** 5774 − 3894

Addition: Three or More Addends

How many pairs of sneakers did Allan Sporting Goods store sell during the three-month period?

First, you can round to estimate the sum.

$$100 + 200 + 100 = 400$$

To find how many pairs of sneakers the store sold, add: $119 + 206 + 94 = $ __?__ .

Month	Pairs of Sneakers Sold
April	119
May	206
June	94

Add the ones. Regroup.

```
      1
    119
    206
  +  94
      9
```

19 ones = 1 ten 9 ones

Add the tens. Regroup.

```
     11
    119
    206
  +  94
     19
```

11 tens = 1 hundred 1 ten

Add the hundreds.

```
     11
    119
    206
  +  94
    419
```

Think.....
419 is close to the estimate of 400.

Allan Sporting Goods store sold 419 pairs of sneakers.

Study these examples.

```
  111
  1715
  4673
+ 2586
  8974
```

```
   111
   2358
    793
   4312
 + 6135
  13,598
```

```
   1 1
  $3.59
   1.43
 + 0.85
  $5.87
```

```
   11 2
  $13.59
   24.38
   47.15
 + 32.23
 $117.35
```

Use rounding to estimate. Then add.

1.
```
   54
   32
 + 23
```

2.
```
   43
   25
 + 31
```

3.
```
  183
  214
+ 302
```

4.
```
  516
  242
+ 321
```

5.
```
  624
  143
+ 232
```

6.
```
  501
  243
+  76
```

7.
```
  251
   39
+ 490
```

8.
```
   3429
   5182
 + 2404
```

9.
```
   3297
   4356
 + 1579
```

10.
```
   6783
   3452
 +  594
```

Practice

Use rounding to estimate. Then find the sum.

11.	$26.34	12.	$19.57	13.	$52.09	14.	$23.21	15.	$56.25
	14.72		70.46		43.17		17.64		9.18
	+ 37.18		+ 13.12		+ 17.45		+ 1.92		+ 13.46

16.	$16.83	17.	$29.54	18.	$95.12	19.	$45.73	20.	$ 8.75
	23.19		47.21		3.81		18.92		19.16
	41.62		25.38		19.09		21.45		27.32
	+ 19.18		+ 31.09		+ 21.35		+ 3.28		+ 3.26

Align and add.

21. 2386 + 1396 + 2176 + 7266

22. 5449 + 2176 + 2347 + 3248

23. 3829 + 1760 + 1857 + 704

24. 8176 + 45 + 589 + 1259

25. 1105 + 1075 + 589 + 2863

26. 2749 + 3890 + 917 + 44

Problem Solving

27. Three rivers form a river system and have lengths of 513 miles, 247 miles, and 397 miles. Altogether, how long are these rivers?

28. Linda has 107 stamps from North America, 319 stamps from Africa, 43 stamps from Asia, and 168 stamps from Europe. How many stamps does Linda have in all?

CRITICAL THINKING

Look carefully at the numbers in a problem. The size and type of numbers will help you decide which computation method to use when an exact answer is needed.

Computation Methods
• Mental Math
• Paper and Pencil

Add. Use Mental Math or Paper and Pencil. Explain the method you used.

29. 274 + 289 + 87 + 300

30. 7000 + 100 + 600 + 17

31. 117 + 117 + 147 + 1570

32. 5389 + 126 + 3427 + 8653

33. 6000 + 500 + 40 + 3

34. 5734 + 3268 + 521 + 1614

35. 2100 + 330 + 900 + 70

36. 6398 + 235 + 8709 + 5002

1-11

Subtraction with Zeros

Julia collected 4000 pennies for the charity drive. Raymond collected 3135 pennies. How many more pennies did Julia collect than Raymond?

First, you can use front-end digits to estimate.
4000 − 3000 = 1000

To find how many more, subtract:
4000 − 3135 = _?_ .

▶ To **subtract** when the minuend has zeros:

- Regroup as many times as necessary before starting to subtract.

- Subtract.

More hundreds, tens, and ones are needed. Regroup all.		Subtract.		Check.

$$\begin{array}{r} \overset{9\ \ 9}{3\ \cancel{10}\ \cancel{10}\ 10} \\ \cancel{4}\ \cancel{0}\ \cancel{0}\ \cancel{0} \\ -\ 3\ 1\ 3\ 5 \\ \hline \end{array}$$

$$\begin{array}{r} \overset{9\ \ 9}{3\ \cancel{10}\ \cancel{10}\ 10} \\ \cancel{4}\ \cancel{0}\ \cancel{0}\ \cancel{0} \\ -\ 3\ 1\ 3\ 5 \\ \hline 8\ 6\ 5 \end{array}$$

$$\begin{array}{r} \overset{1\ 1\ 1}{865} \\ +\ 3135 \\ \hline 4000 \end{array}$$

4 thousands =
3 thousands 10 hundreds   0 tens   0 ones =
3 thousands   9 hundreds 10 tens   0 ones =
3 thousands   9 hundreds   9 tens 10 ones

Think
865 is close to the estimate of 1000.

Julia collected 865 more pennies than Raymond.

Study these examples.

$$\begin{array}{r} \overset{9\ \ 9}{6\ \cancel{10}\ \cancel{10}\ 12} \\ \cancel{7}\ \cancel{0}\ \cancel{0}\ 2 \\ -\ 3\ 2\ 5\ 8 \\ \hline 3\ 7\ 4\ 4 \end{array}$$

$$\begin{array}{r} \overset{9\ \ 15}{8\ \cancel{10}\ \cancel{16}\ 13} \\ \cancel{9}\ \cancel{0}\ \cancel{6}\ \cancel{3} \\ -\ 4\ 3\ 7\ 6 \\ \hline 4\ 6\ 8\ 7 \end{array}$$

$$\begin{array}{r} \overset{9\ \ 9}{4\ \cancel{10}\ \cancel{10}\ 10} \\ \cancel{5}\ \cancel{0}\ \cancel{0}\ \cancel{0} \\ -\ \ \ 6\ 9\ 8 \\ \hline 4\ 3\ 0\ 2 \end{array}$$

$$\begin{array}{r} \overset{9\ \ 9}{8\ \cancel{10}\ \cancel{10}\ 10} \\ \$\cancel{9}\ \cancel{0}.\cancel{0}\ \cancel{0} \\ -\ \ 7\ 2.5\ 6 \\ \hline \$1\ 7.4\ 4 \end{array}$$

Estimate using front-end digits. Then find the difference.

| 1. | 800 − 526 | 2. | 700 − 439 | 3. | 300 − 124 | 4. | 902 − 514 | 5. | 600 − 78 |

| 6. | 9000 − 4572 | 7. | 8000 − 2333 | 8. | 6006 − 1737 | 9. | 8060 − 5274 | 10. | 3000 − 543 |

| 11. | $7.00 − 5.21 | 12. | $6.00 − 3.92 | 13. | $8.00 − 2.97 | 14. | $5.09 − 1.35 | 15. | $4.00 − 0.83 |

| 16. | $87.00 − 64.27 | 17. | $93.00 − 78.42 | 18. | $60.03 − 14.59 | 19. | $48.00 − 7.03 | 20. | $30.20 − 4.53 |

Align and subtract.

21. 4000 − 784

22. 9000 − 8762

23. 5003 − 1784

24. 7020 − 4721

25. 7200 − 6548

26. 5081 − 329

27. 8700 − 421

28. 9300 − 7842

29. 4800 − 703

Find the missing minuend.

| 30. | ? − 764 = 136 | 31. | ? − 459 = 241 | 32. | ? − 623 = 278 | 33. | ? − 596 = 257 | 34. | ? − 861 = 263 |

| 35. | ? − 5278 = 2722 | 36. | ? − 4927 = 1073 | 37. | ? − 3452 = 3548 | 38. | ? − 1777 = 1226 | 39. | ? − 2182 = 1848 |

Problem Solving

40. Bobby has 2000 international coins. One hundred twenty-three coins are from Asia. How many coins are *not* from Asia?

41. Carla had $30.00. She bought a book for $7.95. How much money did she have left?

CRITICAL THINKING Algebra

Find the value.

42. $504 - n$ when $n = 113$

43. $n + 309$ when $n = 519$

44. $6097 + n$ when $n = 9362$

45. $9002 - n$ when $n = 2754$

Replace the variable, n, with the given number and then compute.

Larger Sums and Differences

Study these examples. First, you can round to estimate. Then add or subtract as usual.

Add: 115,463 + 97,912 + 122,877 = __?__ .

TODAY'S NEWS
115,463
Watch Game!

Estimate.	Add. Regroup where necessary.
100,000	112 11
100,000	115,463
+ 100,000	97,912
about 300,000	+ 122,877
	336,252

.Think.............
336,252 is close to
the estimate of 300,000.

Subtract: 820,410 − 647,635 = __?__ .

Estimate.	Subtract. Regroup.
	11 9 13 10
	7 12 10 14 11 10
800,000	8 2 0, 4 1 0
− 600,000	− 6 4 7, 6 3 5
about 200,000	1 7 2, 7 7 5

.Think.............
172,775 is close to
the estimate of 200,000.

Practice

Use rounding to estimate. Then add or subtract. (Watch for + or −.)

1. 36,587	**2.** 28,764	**3.** 65,446	**4.** 49,765
87,943	64,537	1,915	18,976
+ 13,156	+ 35,936	+ 47,291	+ 7,359

5. 26,542	**6.** 34,896	**7.** 41,132	**8.** 62,764
− 17,986	− 15,984	− 17,545	− 58,685

9. 115,609	**10.** 356,789	**11.** 471,009	**12.** 365,786
205,399	141,217	180,007	274,982
+ 411,111	+ 222,888	+ 277,777	+ 186,214

13. 672,244	**14.** 681,337	**15.** 524,700	**16.** 938,400
− 456,688	− 278,456	− 316,672	− 619,711

Use rounding to estimate. Then find the sum or difference. (Watch for + or −.)

17.	$247.00 + 166.72	18.	$621.21 − 354.25	19.	$516.83 + 378.35	20.	$700.01 − 549.34
21.	$357.97 + 689.80	22.	$370.05 − 151.29	23.	$721.63 + 494.09	24.	$270.05 − 179.71

Align. Then add or subtract. (Watch for + or −.)

25. 45,162 + 215 + 3614 + 7   **26.** 204,106 + 403 + 7000 + 10,691

27. 746,500 − 28,781   **28.** 978,432 − 739,853

Write each group of numbers in order from greatest to least.
Then add and subtract the two greatest numbers.

29. 38,745; 39,547; 37,845; 39,845   **30.** 77,178; 71,718; 77,781; 71,871

31. 40,060; 40,600; 40,006; 46,000   **32.** 54,980; 54,908; 54,809; 54,890

Problem Solving

Use the table for problems 33–34.

33. What is the combined seating capacity of Yankee Stadium and Wrigley Field?

34. How much more seating capacity does Cleveland Browns Stadium have than Angel Stadium?

Arena	Seating Capacity
Yankee Stadium, NY	57,545
Cleveland Browns Stadium, OH	73,200
Wrigley Field, IL	36,765
Angel Stadium, CA	45,050

35. Every cubic millimeter of blood contains about 7500 white blood cells. A count less than 1500 above this number is still considered healthy. Is a white cell count of 8750 considered healthy? Explain.

36. Earth's total surface area is about 199,560,000 square miles. Approximately 139,692,000 square miles are covered with water. About how much of Earth's surface is covered by land, to the nearest million?

CRITICAL THINKING   Algebra

37. Replace each □ with a digit from 0 to 9 so that the addition is correct. Use each digit only once.

```
    □ □ □
 +  □ □ □
  □ □ □ □
```

Roman Numerals

The ancient Romans used letters to write numbers.
Study this table of Roman numerals and their values.

I	II	III	IV	V	VI	VII	VIII	IX	X
1	2	3	4	5	6	7	8	9	10
V	X	XV	XX	XXV	XXX	XXXV	XL	XLV	L
5	10	15	20	25	30	35	40	45	50
X	XX	XXX	XL	L	LX	LXX	LXXX	XC	C
10	20	30	40	50	60	70	80	90	100
C	CC	CCC	CD	D	DC	DCC	DCCC	CM	M
100	200	300	400	500	600	700	800	900	1000

▶ To find the value of a Roman numeral,

add:
- if the letter is repeated.
  XX = 10 + 10 = 20
  CCC = 100 + 100 + 100 = 300

| A letter is never repeated more than three times. |

- if a letter with a smaller value comes
  after a letter with a larger value.
  XV = 10 + 5 = 15
  DCX = 500 + 100 + 10 = 610

subtract:
- if a letter with a smaller value comes
  before a letter with a larger value.
  XL = 50 − 10 = 40
  CM = 1000 − 100 = 900

CDLXIV

▶ Sometimes you must both add and subtract.

CDLXIV = (500 − 100) + (50 + 10) + (5 − 1)
              400   +   60   +   4   =   464

Complete each to write the Roman numeral in standard form.

1. CCLXIII = 100 + _?_ + 50 + _?_ + _?_ + _?_ + _?_ = _?_

2. CMXCIV = (1000 − _?_) + (_?_ − 10) + (_?_ − _?_) = _?_

Write the Roman numeral in standard form.

3. XXXIV	4. MVII	5. LV	6. DXXI
7. CCLXX	8. DCCXC	9. XCIX	10. MDIII
11. XLVII	12. MCCLVI	13. CXLV	14. MDCCXCI
15. MMCLI	16. MMDCCCIII	17. MDCCLXXXV	18. MDCCCXLV

Write each as a Roman numeral.

19. 18	20. 24	21. 31	22. 52	23. 14	24. 73
25. 180	26. 193	27. 387	28. 504	29. 919	30. 623
31. 731	32. 876	33. 415	34. 327	35. 613	36. 287
37. 1321	38. 1449	39. 2001	40. 3555	41. 2765	42. 3046

Write the date of the admittance of each state into the Union as a standard numeral.

43.
Florida

MDCCCXLV

44.
New Mexico

MCMXII

45.
Ohio

MDCCCIII

46.
Oregon

MDCCCLIX

Problem Solving

47. The Statue of Liberty was dedicated in 1886. Write this date as a Roman numeral.

48. Dr. Evans saw the date MDIX on a building in Rome. Write this number as a standard numeral.

CHALLENGE

49. Use some of the digits 1, 3, 5, 7, 9 only once to write 5 numbers less than 2000 and then express each number as a Roman numeral. Share your work with a classmate.

Problem-Solving Strategy:
Guess and Test

Ed needs to take his cat, bird, and snake to the veterinarian. His car can hold only 2—1 pet and himself. If left alone together, the cat (*C*) will eat the bird (*B*), and the snake (*S*) will eat the bird (*B*). How many trips will Ed (*E*) need to make?

Read

Visualize yourself in the problem above as you reread it. List the facts and the question.

Facts: Ed and 3 pets go to the veterinarian. *C* and *B* or *B* and *S* cannot be left alone together. Only 1 pet and Ed fit into the car.

Question: How many trips does he need to make?

Plan Make a guess. Draw a picture to test each guess.

Solve

		Home		Veterinarian

1st Ed takes the bird because the cat will not eat the snake. $C, S \xrightarrow[\text{1st}]{E, B}$

2nd Ed returns, leaving the bird. $C, S \xleftarrow[\text{2nd}]{E} B$

3rd Ed takes the cat and leaves it at the veterinarian's. $S \xrightarrow[\text{3rd}]{E, C} B$

4th Ed returns with the bird. $S \xleftarrow[\text{4th}]{E, B} C$

5th Ed takes the snake and leaves the bird home. $B \xrightarrow[\text{5th}]{E, S} C$

6th Ed returns after leaving the snake with the cat. $B \xleftarrow[\text{6th}]{E} C, S$

7th Ed takes the bird. Now the 3 pets are at the veterinarian's. $\xrightarrow[\text{7th}]{E, B} C, S$

So Ed needs to make 7 trips.

Check Did more than two go in the car? No.
Was the cat or snake ever left alone with the bird? No.

Use Guess and Test to solve each problem.

1. Pat's dad is 2 ft 1 in. taller than Pat. The sum of their heights is 10 ft 5 in. How tall is Pat?

Read Visualize yourself in the problem above as you reread it. Focus on the facts and question.

List what you know.

Facts: Dad's height is 2 ft 1 in. more than Pat's. Sum of their heights is 10 ft 5 in.

Question: How tall is Pat?

Plan Guess a height for Pat. Add 2 ft 1 in. to find his dad's height. Then test whether the sum of their heights equals 10 ft 5 in. Record each guess in a chart.

Pat	4 ft
Dad	6 ft 1 in.
Sum	10 ft 1 in.

Solve .... **Check**

2. Drew wrote a 4-digit number less than 2000. The sum of its digits is 20. Only the digits in the ones place and hundreds place are even. The digit in the ones place is double the digit in the thousands place. What number did Drew write?

3. Grace has a cat, a bird, and a package of birdseed. She wants to get all three home safely, but her bicycle basket will hold only *one* at a time. The cat will eat the bird if the two are left alone together. The bird will eat the birdseed if they are left alone. How many trips does Grace need to make to get everything home safely?

4. Five coins fell out of Doug's pocket. He lost 27¢. What coins did Doug lose?

5. In the subtraction example at the right, each letter stands for a different digit. Find the value of X, Y, and Z.

$$\begin{array}{r} X\ Y\ X \\ -\ \ \ Z\ X \\ \hline X\ Y \end{array}$$

Write Your Own

6. Write a problem that requires you to use the Guess and Test strategy. Then solve it. Share your work with a classmate.

Problem-Solving Applications: Mixed Review

Read Plan Solve Check

Solve each problem and explain the method you used.

1. A U.S. census is taken every ten years. The first U.S. census was taken in 1790. At that time, the population was recorded as 3,929,000. How many times greater is the 9 in the hundred thousands place than the 9 in the thousands place?

2. By the 1800 census the population had reached 5,308,000. Is this an increase of more or less than 2 million over the 1790 population? Explain.

3. By 1810, the population had increased to 7,240,000. What is the increase over the 1800 census?

4. The center of population in 1980 was 0.25 miles west of De Soto, Missouri. Write 0.25 as a fraction. Write its word name.

5. In 1990, the center of population moved southwest by $\frac{5}{10}$ of a mile more than 39 miles. Write this distance as a decimal.

6. Between 1790 and 1990, the center of population for the United States shifted 818.6 miles. What is 818.6 rounded to the nearest one?

7. Write the year 1790, when the first U.S. census was taken, in Roman numerals.

8. This chart shows the census population of the ten most populated states in 2000. Write the states in order from greatest to least population.

9. Which states have populations of about 20 million?

10. Which states have populations of between 8 million and 12 million?

11. Which state has about double the population of Georgia?

2000 U.S. Census	
State	**Population**
California	33,871,648
Florida	15,982,378
Georgia	8,186,453
Illinois	12,419,293
Michigan	9,938,444
New Jersey	8,414,350
New York	18,976,457
Ohio	11,353,140
Pennsylvania	12,281,054
Texas	20,851,820

Choose a strategy from the list or use another strategy you know to solve each problem.

12. The fourth census took place in a year that can be written as a Roman numeral using these letters: *X, C, D, C, M, X, C.* What is the standard numeral for the year of the fourth census?

13. A rural village's population is between 800 and 1000. The sum of the digits in its population is 21, and the digits in the ones and the hundreds places are the same. What might be the population of the village?

14. In 2000, Alaska's population was less than Virginia's but greater than Wyoming's. Hawaii's population was between Alaska's and Virginia's. Write these states in increasing order of population.

15. Between 1800 and 2000, the U.S. population increased by 276,113,906. The population was almost 280,000,000 in 1990. If the population increases by the same amount in the next 200 years, will the population in 2200 be more than 1 billion? Explain.

> **Strategy File**
>
> **Use These Strategies**
> More Than One Solution
> Guess and Test
> Logical Reasoning
> Use a Graph
> Use More Than One Step

Use the circle graph for problems 16–18.

16. Which age group represented more than half the U.S. population in 2000? Explain.

17. What percent of the U.S. population was under the age of 18 in 2000?

18. Which age group represented between 10% and 25% of the population?

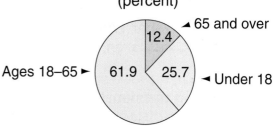

**U.S. Population
Age Distribution 2000
(percent)**

◄ 65 and over
12.4
Ages 18–65 ► 61.9 25.7 ◄ Under 18

Write Your Own

19. Write in your Math Journal which problems you solved using the same strategy and explain why. Then write a problem modeled on these problems and have a classmate solve it.

Check Your Progress
Lessons 1–15

In the number 308,610,547,823, write the digit in the: *(See pp. 30–33.)*

1. ten-billions place   **2.** millions place   **3.** hundred-thousands place

Write the number in standard form. *(See pp. 30–39, 54–55.)*

4. three hundred four billion, six hundred thousand   **5.** CCLXI

6. 1,000,000,000 + 40,000 + 80 + 3   **7.** eight and twelve thousandths

Write the word name for each number.

8. 360,071   **9.** 1,009,124,008   **10.** 6.71   **11.** 0.531   **12.** CMLXI

Compare. Write $<$, $=$, or $>$. *(See pp. 40–41.)*

13. 185,035,013 _?_ 185,503,013   **14.** 10.09 _?_ 10.1   **15.** 9.63 _?_ 9.630

Write in order from least to greatest.

16. 6,135,936; 6,315,396; 6,531,639; 6,153,693   **17.** 3.12; 31.2; 0.312

Round each number to the place of the underlined digit. *(See pp. 42–43.)*

18. 474,19<u>8</u>,575   **19.** <u>3</u>13,983,156   **20.** 145.7<u>2</u>8   **21.** $766.1<u>3</u>

Find the missing addend. *(See pp. 44–45.)*

22. 8 + ☐ = 15   **23.** ☐ + 9 = 17   **24.** 14 = ☐ + 7   **25.** 11 = 6 + ☐

Use rounding to estimate. Then add or subtract. *(See pp. 46–53.)*

26.	**27.**	**28.**	**29.**	**30.**
25,736	503,149	$235.17	600,000	$907.15
12,548	180,590	137.23	− 421,351	− 35.43
+ 36,985	+ 248,762	+ 427.45		

Problem Solving
(See pp. 56–59.)

31. The sum of two numbers is 34.
Their difference is 18.
What are the two numbers?

(See *Still More Practice*, p. 477.)

Logic and Venn Diagrams

▶ In logic, the negation of a statement is formed by denying that statement. When a statement is true, its negation is false. When a statement is false, its negation is true.

> A statement, in logic, is a sentence that is either true or false.

Inserting or removing *not* in a statement forms the negation of that statement.

Statement	**Negation**
A triangle has 3 sides. (True)	A triangle does not have 3 sides. (False)
In standard form, 80 million is not 80,000,000. (False)	In standard form, 80 million is 80,000,000. (True)

▶ Venn diagrams may be used to illustrate *All, Some,* or *No* statements.

> Venn diagrams are drawings, usually circles, that show relationships.

This Venn diagram shows that:

All vowels are letters of the alphabet.

Some letters of the alphabet are vowels.

No whole numbers are letters of the alphabet.

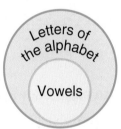

Tell whether the statement is *True* or *False*. Then write the negation of the statement and tell whether it is *True* or *False*.

1. A square has 5 sides.

2. A circle is a plane figure.

3. The word name of 19.3 is nine and three tenths.

4. The sum of a number and zero is not zero.

5. In the number 3,624,749, the 2 means $2 \times 10,000$.

6. One thousandth greater than 59.725 is not 59.726.

Draw a Venn diagram to illustrate each statement.

7. All roses are flowers.

8. No triangles are squares.

9. Some numbers are fractions.

10. All rectangles are quadrilaterals.

11. No spheres are cylinders.

12. Some plants are green.

Chapter 1 Test

In the number 21,825,493,076, write the digit in the:

1. hundred-thousands place
2. billions place
3. ten-millions place

Write each number in standard form.

4. three billion, two million, forty-five thousand, eighty-three
5. nine and twenty-one thousandths
6. 8,000,000 + 4000 + 60 + 2

Write the word name for each number.

7. 1,000,935,009
8. 10.08
9. 9.036

Compare. Write <, =, or >.

10. 800,905,174 __?__ 800,905,147
11. 3.215 __?__ 3.125
12. 9.07 __?__ 9.070

Write in order from greatest to least.

13. 1,745,236; 1,475,236; 1,745,632; 1,475,263
14. 9.47; 9.56; 9.37; 9.68

Find the missing number. Name the property of addition that is used.

15. 9 + 5 = ☐ + 9
16. 7 = 0 + ☐
17. (5 + 2) + 3 = 5 + (2 + ☐)

Write each as a Roman numeral.

18. 999
19. 1750

Problem Solving

Use a strategy you have learned.

20. The area of Oregon is 97,073 square miles and the area of California is 158,706 square miles. What is the total area of the two states?

Tell About It

21. How can you use the properties of addition to help you find the missing numbers in exercises 15–17? Explain.

Performance Assessment

Use front-end estimation and rounding to estimate the answers.
Tell which estimation strategy produces an estimate closer to the actual answer and explain why.

22. 90,043 + 53,621 + 1,285 = __?__
23. $300.06 − $181.09 = __?__

Test Preparation

Choose the best answer.

1. Choose the standard form.

   fifty million, three
   - **a.** 53,000,000
   - **b.** 50,300,000
   - **c.** 50,000,300
   - **d.** 50,000,003

2. Which illustrates the Associative Property of Addition?
   - **a.** $3 + 7 = 7 + 3$
   - **b.** $(3 + 7) + 6 = 3 + (7 + 6)$
   - **c.** $(7 + 0) + 3 = (0 + 7) + 3$
   - **d.** $(3 + 7) + 6 = (3 + 7) + 6$

3. Choose the order from least to greatest.

   520,804; 502,480; 502,840
   - **a.** 502,480; 502,840; 520,804
   - **b.** 502,840; 502,480; 520,804
   - **c.** 520,804; 502,480; 502,840
   - **d.** 502,840; 520,804; 502,480

4. Round to the place of the underlined digit.

   $\underline{6},381,576$
   - **a.** 6,400,000
   - **b.** 6,000,500
   - **c.** 6,380,000
   - **d.** 6,000,000

5. Subtract.

   $\begin{array}{r} 5005 \\ -\ 1636 \\ \hline \end{array}$
   - **a.** 4,379
   - **b.** 4,369
   - **c.** 3,379
   - **d.** 3,369

6. Use front-end estimation to estimate the sum.

   $\begin{array}{r} 5,273 \\ 8,549 \\ +\ 7,992 \\ \hline \end{array}$
   - **a.** 18,000
   - **b.** 19,000
   - **c.** 21,000
   - **d.** 22,000

7. Choose the word name.

   0.009
   - **a.** nine thousandths
   - **b.** nine thousand
   - **c.** nine hundred
   - **d.** nine hundredths

8. Choose the Roman numeral.

   2040
   - **a.** MMLX
   - **b.** MMXL
   - **c.** MMLIV
   - **d.** MMXLV

9. Choose the standard form.

   $2,000,000 + 400,000 + 30 + 4$
   - **a.** 2,434
   - **b.** 2,400,340
   - **c.** 2,004,034
   - **d.** 2,400,034

10. Choose the order from greatest to least.

    5.81; 5.813; 5.081
    - **a.** 5.081; 5.81; 5.813
    - **b.** 5.813; 5.81; 5.081
    - **c.** 5.81; 5.081; 5.813
    - **d.** 5.813; 5.081; 5.81

11. Round to the nearest hundredth.

    7.932
    - **a.** 7.90
    - **b.** 7.93
    - **c.** 7.932
    - **d.** 7.923

12. Add.

    $1105 + 1075 + 479 + 2973$
    - **a.** 6532
    - **b.** 6522
    - **c.** 5632
    - **d.** 5622

13. Find the difference.

    $\begin{array}{r} \$631.31 \\ -\ 364.35 \\ \hline \end{array}$
    - **a.** $276.96
    - **b.** $266.96
    - **c.** $265.96
    - **d.** $256.96

14. Choose the place and the value of the underlined digit.

    $9.4\underline{7}8$
    - **a.** hundreds; 700
    - **b.** tens; 70
    - **c.** hundredths; 0.07
    - **d.** thousandths; 0.007

15. Round 5,281,756 to the nearest million.

a. 5,300,000
b. 5,000,000
c. 5,280,000
d. 6,000,000

21. What is the place value of the digit 9 in 8.239?

a. 9 hundredths
b. 9 tenths
c. 9 ones
d. 9 thousandths

16. Find the difference.

```
  5040
-  276
```

a. 4764
b. 4664
c. 5236
d. 5316

22. Choose the standard form.

MCMLXXXI

a. 1981
b. 2081
c. 1881
d. 2071

17. Find the sum.

```
 $431.88
+ 868.32
```

a. $1300.10
b. $1300.20
c. $1299.10
d. $1299.20

23. Which illustrates the Commutative Property of Addition?

a. $325 + 13 = 300 + 35 + 13$
b. $32 + (40 + 6) = (32 + 40) + 6$
c. $179 + 200 = 200 + 179$
d. $565 + 0 = 565$

18. Find the missing addend.

$\square + 8 = 19$

a. 8
b. 9
c. 11
d. 27

24. Estimate the difference by rounding.

```
  5079
-  853
```

a. 4000
b. 4200
c. 4300
d. 5000

19. Rachel flew 2500 miles on Monday, 1265 miles on Tuesday, and 485 miles on Wednesday. How many miles altogether did she fly in three days?

a. 4250 miles
b. 4150 miles
c. 3250 miles
d. 3150 miles

25. Ben saved $73. He gave $18 less to charity than he saved. How much did he give to charity?

a. $65
b. $55
c. $81
d. $91

20. In May, 13,637 people attended the circus, which was 8,478 people less than the attendance in June. In July, the attendance was 3,342 more than June's. How many people attended the circus in July?

a. 25,357 people
b. 25,457 people
c. 22,115 people
d. 22,015 people

26. Jack made two stops during his 50-mile bike trip. He first stopped after 20 miles. His second stop was 15 miles before the end of the trip. How many miles did he travel between his first and second stops?

a. 30 miles
b. 25 miles
c. 20 miles
d. 15 miles

27. What strategy did you use to solve problem 25?

28. Explain how the Use More Than One Step strategy helps you solve problems 20 and 26.

The Runner

Run, run, runner man,
As fast as you can,
Faster than the speed of light,
Smoother than a bird in flight.
Run, run, runner man,
No one can catch the runner man,
Swifter than an arrow,
Outrunning his own shadow.
Run, run, runner man,
Faster than tomorrow.
Run, run, runner man,
Quicker than a rocket!
Into deep space spinning a comet!
Run, run, runner man,
Lighting the heavens of the night,
Run, run, runner man,
Out of sight,
Run, run, runner man, run!

Faustin Charles

Multiplication

In this chapter you will:
Use properties, special factors, and patterns
Estimate and multiply up to 3-digit numbers and money
Solve problems with hidden information
   by using more than one step

Critical Thinking/Finding Together
You are training for a marathon. Each week you need
to run five miles more than the previous week. If you
need to run a total of 130 miles, how many miles will
you run during each of the next four weeks?

Factors and Products

There are 5 packs. Each pack contains 6 cartons of juice. How many cartons of juice are there in all?

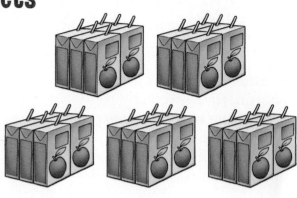

To find how many cartons in all, you can add:

$$6 + 6 + 6 + 6 + 6 = 30$$

```
  6
  6
  6
  6
+ 6
 30
```

or

you can multiply, since there are equal sets.

5 sixes   =   30

$$5 \quad \times \quad 6 \quad = \quad 30$$

number of sets   **number in each set**   **number in all**

.Think.........................
Multiplication is
repeated addition.

```
  6 ←——— in each set
× 5 ←——— sets
 30 ←——— in all
```

There are 30 cartons of juice in all.

Study this example.

$$8 + 8 + 8 + 8 = 32$$
4 eights   = 32
$$4 \times 8 \quad = 32$$

factor   **factor**   **product**

```
  8 ←——— factor
× 4 ←——— factor
 32 ←——— product
```

$4 \times 8 = 32$
is a multiplication sentence.

Write as a multiplication sentence. Name the factors and product.

1. $9 + 9 + 9$ 3×9

2. $4 + 4 + 4 + 4 + 4$

3. $2 + 2 + 2 + 2 + 2 + 2 + 2 + 2$

4. $3 + 3 + 3 + 3 + 3 + 3$

5. $8 + 8 + 8 + 8 + 8 + 8 + 8 + 8 + 8$

6. $5 + 5 + 5 + 5$

7. $6 + 6$

8. $7 + 7 + 7 + 7 + 7 + 7 + 7$

Find the product.

9. 8 ×3	**10.** 7 ×4	**11.** 5 ×5	**12.** 0 ×6	**13.** 1 ×7	**14.** 9 ×9	
15. 2 ×6	**16.** 7 ×7	**17.** 3 ×9	**18.** 6 ×8	**19.** 5 ×3	**20.** 6 ×6	

Practice

Find the missing factor.

21. 8 ×? 48	**22.** 7 ×? 42	**23.** ? ×9 54	**24.** ? ×6 18	**25.** 4 ×? 0

Think
6 × 8 = 48

26. ? ×5 35	**27.** ? ×4 36	**28.** ? ×3 24	**29.** ? ×6 0	**30.** ? ×7 63	**31.** 9 ×? 81

Compare. Write <, =, or >.

32. 6 × 3 __?__ 3 × 7   **33.** 9 × 0 __?__ 8 × 0

34. 5 × (2 × 3) __?__ 5 × (3 × 3)   **35.** 9 × 7 __?__ 8 × 8

36. (3 × 2) × 6 __?__ 3 × (2 × 4)   **37.** (2 × 3) × 6 __?__ 2 × (3 × 2)

Problem Solving

38. Each pack holds 4 videotapes. How many videotapes are in 9 packs?

39. Nine large books will fit on one shelf. How many large books will fit on 8 shelves?

40. When you multiply 7 by itself, what is the product?

41. Two factors are 8 and 9. What is the product?

42. The product is 81. One factor is 9. What is the other factor?

43. The product is 36. One factor is 6. What is the other factor?

MENTAL MATH — Algebra

Compute. Work from left to right.

44. 6 × 6 + 4 − 2   **45.** 9 × 8 + 6 − 10   **46.** 6 × 7 − 8 − 6

47. 2 × 3 × 5 − 8   **48.** 7 × 1 + 6 − 1   **49.** 6 × 5 + 7 + 3

2-2

Properties of Multiplication

The properties of multiplication can help you multiply quickly and correctly.

factor × factor = product

- **Commutative Property of Multiplication**
  Changing the *order* of the factors does not change the product.

  .Think..
  "order"

  $$9 \times 6 = 54$$
  $$6 \times 9 = 54$$

  $$\begin{array}{cc} 6 & 9 \\ \times 9 & \times 6 \\ \hline 54 & 54 \end{array}$$

- **Associative Property of Multiplication**
  Changing the *grouping* of the factors does not change the product.

  .Think.....
  "grouping"

  $$(2 \times 3) \times 3 = 2 \times (3 \times 3)$$
  $$6 \times 3 = 2 \times 9$$
  $$18 = 18$$

- **Identity Property of Multiplication**
  The product of *one* and a number is the same as that number.

  .Think...
  "same"

  $$1 \times 7 = 7$$
  $$7 \times 1 = 7$$

  $$\begin{array}{cc} 7 & 1 \\ \times 1 & \times 7 \\ \hline 7 & 7 \end{array}$$

- **Zero Property of Multiplication**
  The product of *zero* and a number is zero.

  .Think.......
  "0 product"

  $$0 \times 4 = 0$$
  $$4 \times 0 = 0$$

  $$\begin{array}{cc} 4 & 0 \\ \times 0 & \times 4 \\ \hline 0 & 0 \end{array}$$

Practice

Name the property of multiplication used.

1. $5 \times 2 = 2 \times 5$

2. $9 \times 0 = 0$

3. $3 \times (2 \times 4) = (3 \times 2) \times 4$

4. $1 \times 8 = 8$

5. $0 \times 6 = 0$

6. $(2 \times 2) \times 4 = 2 \times (2 \times 4)$

7. $4 \times 1 = 4$

8. $9 \times 8 = 8 \times 9$

9. $0 \times 0 = 0$

10. $1 \times 1 = 1$

Find the missing number. Use the properties of multiplication.

11. $\underline{?} \times 4 = 4 \times 6$

12. $9 \times \underline{?} = 9$

13. $2 \times \underline{?} = 0$

14. $1 \times 7 = \underline{?}$

15. $6 \times 8 = 8 \times \underline{?}$

16. $0 \times 6 = \underline{?}$

17. $3 \times (2 \times 4) = (3 \times \underline{?}) \times 4$

18. $(4 \times 2) \times 4 = \underline{?} \times (2 \times 4)$

Distributive Property

Distributive Property of Multiplication Over Addition
When the same factor is *distributed* across two addends, the product does not change.

.Think............
"same factor across addends"

factor — addends

$2 \times (3 + 4) = (2 \times 3) + (2 \times 4)$
$\times$
$\times$
$2 \times 7 = 6 + 8$
$14 = 14$

Copy and complete.

19. $3 \times (5 + 2) = (3 \times 5) + (\underline{?} \times 2)$

20. $\underline{?} \times (4 + 2) = (6 \times 4) + (6 \times 2)$

21. $2 \times (3 + 6) = (\underline{?} \times 3) + (\underline{?} \times 6)$

22. $5 \times (\underline{?} + \underline{?}) = (5 \times 2) + (5 \times 3)$

23. $4 \times (2 + 3) = (4 \times \underline{?}) + (4 \times \underline{?})$

24. $6 \times (5 + 2) = (\underline{?} \times \underline{?}) + (\underline{?} \times \underline{?})$

25. Seven students gave oral reports for their science project. Of those reports, three were each 8 minutes long and the rest were each 5 minutes long. How long did it take for all the reports to be given?

26. Ray and Sue discovered that they had visited the same museums in New York during the summer. Ray visited 2 museums during each of his 3 days there. If Sue visited 3 museums a day, how many days was her trip?

Write About It

27. In your Math Journal write how:
- the Commutative Property of Multiplication differs from the Associative Property of Multiplication;
- the Associative Property or Distributive Property can be helpful to you in mental math computation.

Mental Math: Special Factors

▶ Study this pattern for multiplying with 10:

$10 \times 1 = 10$	$10 \times 3 = 30$	$10 \times 5 = 50$
$10 \times 2 = 20$	$10 \times 4 = 40$	$10 \times 6 = 60$

▶ Study this pattern for multiplying with a multiple of 10:

$40 \times 2 = 80$	$60 \times 5 = 300$
$40 \times 3 = 120$	$60 \times 6 = 360$
$40 \times 4 = 160$	$60 \times 7 = 420$

.Think..........
Multiples of 10 are
0, 10, 20, 30, 40, 50, ...

▶ To multiply a whole number and a multiple of 10:
  • Multiply the nonzero digits.
  • Count the number of zeros in the factors.
    Then write the same number of zeros in the product.

$30 \times 8 = 240$
one zero

$$\begin{array}{r} 8 \\ \times 30 \\ \hline 240 \end{array}$$ one zero

$6 \times 90 = 540$
one zero

$$\begin{array}{r} 90 \\ \times\ 6 \\ \hline 540 \end{array}$$ one zero

---

Find the products.

1. 10×7
10×8
10×9

2. 10×2
20×2
30×2

3. 20×6
30×6
40×6

4. 30×8
40×8
50×8

5. 4×10
5×10
6×10

6. 6×10
6×20
6×30

7. 7×20
7×30
7×40

8. 9×30
9×40
9×50

Multiply.

9. $\begin{array}{r} 20 \\ \times\ 4 \\ \hline \end{array}$

10. $\begin{array}{r} 50 \\ \times\ 7 \\ \hline \end{array}$

11. $\begin{array}{r} 40 \\ \times\ 8 \\ \hline \end{array}$

12. $\begin{array}{r} 60 \\ \times\ 9 \\ \hline \end{array}$

13. $\begin{array}{r} 70 \\ \times\ 6 \\ \hline \end{array}$

14. 6×50

15. 8×60

16. 9×20

17. 3×40

18. 2×70

19. 7×80

20. 5×30

21. 4×60

Find the product.

22. 2
× 30

23. 7
× 50

24. 8
× 40

25. 9
× 60

26. 8
× 70

27. 6
× 90

28. 8
× 80

29. 5
× 50

30. 4
× 30

31. 9
× 40

32. 8 × 50

33. 7 × 30

34. 8 × 20

35. 6 × 40

36. 70 × 2

37. 30 × 5

38. 80 × 7

39. 5 × 60

40. 60 × 4

41. 90 × 6

42. 70 × 4

43. 40 × 2

44. 3 × 70

45. 7 × 50

46. 9 × 90

47. 8 × 80

Problem Solving

48. A movie theater in a shopping center has 40 rows of seats with 9 seats in each row. How many people in all can the theater seat?

49. The theater sold 6 cartons of popcorn at the Saturday matinee. If there were 30 bags in each carton, how many bags of popcorn in all did it sell?

50. The theater sold 40 orange drinks at each of 2 shows each night for 5 nights. How many orange drinks in all did it sell?

51. The theater sold 30 sandwiches at each of 3 shows each day for 5 days. How many sandwiches in all did it sell?

CRITICAL THINKING

52. Name two factors of 10 whose sum is 7.

53. Name two factors of 30 whose difference is 7.

54. Name two factors of 20 whose sum is 12.

55. Name two factors of 12 whose difference is 4.

Patterns in Multiplication

Study these patterns for multiplying with 100, 1000,
or their multiples:

1 × 7 = 7	2 × 8 = 16	4 × 5 = 20
10 × 7 = 70	20 × 8 = 160	40 × 5 = 200
100 × 7 = 700	200 × 8 = 1600	400 × 5 = 2000
1000 × 7 = 7000	2000 × 8 = 16,000	4000 × 5 = 20,000
10 × 70 = 700	20 × 80 = 1600	40 × 50 = 2000
100 × 70 = 7000	200 × 80 = 16,000	400 × 50 = 20,000
1000 × 70 = 70,000	2000 × 80 = 160,000	4000 × 50 = 200,000

▶ To multiply a whole number and 100, 1000,
or their multiples:
• Multiply the nonzero digits.
• Count the number of zeros in the factors.
  Then write the same number of zeros in the product.

600 × 3 = 1800   2 zeros

$$\begin{array}{r} 3 \\ \times 600 \\ \hline 1800 \end{array}$$ 2 zeros

8000 × 40 = 320,000   4 zeros

$$\begin{array}{r} 40 \\ \times \ 8000 \\ \hline 320,000 \end{array}$$ 4 zeros

Find the products.

1. 10 × 6
100 × 6
1000 × 6

2. 10 × 8
100 × 8
1000 × 8

3. 20 × 3
200 × 3
2000 × 3

4. 60 × 5
600 × 5
6000 × 5

5. 10 × 4
100 × 4
1000 × 4

6. 10 × 9
100 × 9
1000 × 9

7. 30 × 7
300 × 7
3000 × 7

8. 50 × 8
500 × 8
5000 × 8

9. 10 × 40
100 × 40
1000 × 40

10. 30 × 70
300 × 70
3000 × 70

11. 20 × 50
200 × 50
2000 × 50

12. 90 × 40
900 × 40
9000 × 40

Practice

Multiply.

13.   7
    × 400

14.   9
    × 300

15.   8
    × 4000

16.   6
    × 7000

17.   3
    × 8000

18.   10
    × 900

19.   30
    × 600

20.   20
    × 5000

21.   80
    × 3000

22.   90
    × 2000

23. 8 × 600

24. 6 × 400

25. 5 × 3000

26. 9 × 6000

27. 700 × 6

28. 200 × 9

29. 6000 × 8

30. 7000 × 5

31. 4 × 300

32. 6 × 500

33. 8 × 30,000

34. 6 × 60,000

35. 20 × 3000

36. 30 × 2000

37. 10 × 40,000

38. 20 × 20,000

Problem Solving

Use the pictograph for problems 39–45.

How many books of each type were sold?

39. romance

40. biography

41. mystery

42. classics

43. How many books in all were sold?

44. How many more romance books were sold than biography books?

45. How many books were sold that were *not* classics?

46. There are 50 parcels of flyers. Each parcel contains 100 flyers. How many flyers are there in all?

47. There are 60 reams of paper. Each ream contains 500 sheets. How many sheets are there in all?

Books Sold at a Bookstore						
Romance	▯	▯	▯	▯	▯	▯
Biography	▯	▯	▯	▯	▮	
Mystery	▯	▯	▯	▯	▯	▮
Classics	▯	▯	▯			
Key: Each ▯ = 100 books.						

CHALLENGE — Algebra

Find each product.

48. 10 × 20 × 30

49. 20 × 40 × 50

50. 20 × 30 × 40

51. 80 × 10 × 700

52. 60 × 50 × 200

53. 30 × 50 × 100

54. 40 × 50 × 8000

55. 20 × 30 × 6000

56. 20 × 40 × 9000

Estimate Products

About how many pounds will 487 boxes of toys weigh if a box of toys weighs 113 pounds?

To find about how many pounds, estimate: 487 × 113

▶ To estimate the product of two numbers:
  • Round each factor to its greatest place.
  • Multiply.

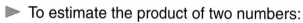

$$113 \longrightarrow 100$$
$$\times 487 \longrightarrow \times 500$$
$$\text{about} \quad 50{,}000$$

487 × 113 = about 50,000
↓   ↓
500 × 100

The boxes of toys will weigh about 50,000 pounds.

Study these examples.

$$657 \longrightarrow 700$$
$$\times 91 \longrightarrow \times 90$$
$$\text{about} \quad 63{,}000$$

$$\$48.36 \longrightarrow \$50.00$$
$$\times 674 \longrightarrow \times 700$$
$$\text{about} \quad \$35{,}000.00$$

Write $ and . in the product.

Round to estimate each product.

1. 72 ×16	**2.** 87 ×11	**3.** 61 ×27	**4.** 56 ×19	**5.** 29 ×38
6. 383 ×162	**7.** 627 ×215	**8.** 783 ×457	**9.** 919 ×189	**10.** 502 ×305
11. 114 × 25	**12.** 162 × 33	**13.** 139 × 21	**14.** 124 × 15	**15.** 219 × 38
16. $8.75 × 7	**17.** $7.61 × 47	**18.** $2.17 × 23	**19.** $29.93 × 174	**20.** $36.45 × 238
21. $7.17 × 23	**22.** $9.61 × 57	**23.** $59.37 × 245	**24.** $78.12 × 343	**25.** $98.23 × 478

Choose the best estimate.

26. 2463×89 **a.** 100,000   **b.** 21,000   **c.** 180,000   **d.** 31,000

27. $78 \times \$24.32$ **a.** \$1600   **b.** \$1400   **c.** \$2400   **d.** \$2100

Practice

Estimation by Clustering

When a number of addends "cluster" around a certain number, an estimate for the sum may be obtained by multiplying that number by the number of addends.

Think
Addends "cluster" around 700.

Estimate: $692 + 703 + 711 + 691 + 708$

$700 + 700 + 700 + 700 + 700$

$5 \times 700 = 3500 \longleftarrow$ **estimated sum**

Estimate: $\$18.92 + \$21.37 + \$23.46 + \$19.31$

$\$20 + \$20 + \$20 + \$20$

$4 \times \$20 = \$80 \longleftarrow$ **estimated sum**

Estimate the sum. Use clustering.

28. $23 + 19 + 24 + 17$ **29.** $102 + 96 + 98 + 103$ **30.** $823 + 790 + 799$

31. $\$10.12 + \$9.99 + \$10.45$ **32.** $\$71.12 + \$69.89 + \$70.99 + \$67.45$

33. $\$32.54 + \$29.43 + \$30.21$ **34.** $\$512.50 + \$501.99 + \$498.65 + \$496.04$

Problem Solving

Choose a computation method. Solve and explain the method you used.

Computation Methods
• Estimate
• Exact Answer

35. One carton of apples weighs 32 pounds. How many pounds will 200 cartons of apples weigh?

36. One box of oranges weighs 48 pounds. Will 550 boxes of oranges weigh less than 25,000 pounds?

37. Ms. Chan bought 18 baskets of fruit at $10.85 a basket. Did she spend more than $200? Explain.

38. A pound of potatoes costs $1.19. About how much will 54 pounds of potatoes cost? Explain.

Update your skills. See page 5.

Zeros in the Multiplicand

Each of three classes uses 2708 mL of distilled water in a science experiment. How much distilled water is used altogether by the three classes?

First, estimate by rounding: 3 × 2708.

$$3 × 3000 = 9000$$

To find how much distilled water is used, multiply: 3 × 2708 = ___?___ .

Multiply the ones. Regroup.

```
        2
    2 7 0 8  ←——— multiplicand
  ×       3  ←——— multiplier
        4    ←——— product
```

3 × 8 ones = 24 ones
            = 2 tens 4 ones

Multiply the tens. Then add the regrouped tens.

```
        2
    2 7 0 8
  ×       3
      2 4
```

3 × 0 tens = 0 tens
0 tens + 2 tens = 2 tens

Multiply the hundreds. Regroup.

```
    2   2
    2 7 0 8
  ×       3
    1 2 4
```

3 × 7 hundreds
  = 21 hundreds
  = 2 thousands 1 hundred

Multiply the thousands. Then add the regrouped thousands.

```
    2   2
    2 7 0 8
  ×       3
    8 1 2 4
```

3 × 2 thousands = 6 thousands
6 thousands + 2 thousands
            = 8 thousands

The three classes use 8124 mL of distilled water.

Think
8124 is close to the estimate of 9000.

Study these examples.

```
      7
    6 0 8 0
  ×       9
  5 4,7 2 0
```

6 × 90,500 = ___?___
6 × 90,500 = 6 × (90,000 + 500)
           = (6 × 90,000) + (6 × 500)
           = 540,000 + 3000 = 543,000

Use the Distributive Property.

Use rounding to estimate. Then multiply.

1. 1109
   × 3

2. 6043
   × 4

3. 5180
   × 7

4. 9205
   × 5

5. 6089
   × 8

6. 4009
   × 5

7. 8400
   × 8

8. 3090
   × 6

9. 7008
   × 9

10. 9060
    × 4

11. 23,016
    × 5

12. 68,509
    × 8

13. 40,243
    × 7

14. 52,050
    × 4

15. 80,403
    × 6

16. 83,600
    × 3

17. 90,053
    × 5

18. 40,070
    × 8

19. 80,003
    × 7

20. 89,000
    × 9

Find the product. You may use the Distributive Property.

21. 6 × 9081

22. 9 × 3014

23. 7 × 4209

24. 5 × 4870

25. 4 × 20,859

26. 8 × 68,806

27. 5 × 70,042

28. 3 × 68,006

29. 8 × 25,070

30. 9 × 90,506

31. 6 × 76,080

32. 7 × 58,004

33. 9 × 91,006

34. 4 × 78,500

35. 5 × 90,003

36. 8 × 79,000

37. 3 × 70,008

38. 7 × 90,098

39. 4 × 170,009

40. 6 × 703,007

Problem Solving

41. A train travels an average of 9075 miles per week. How many miles does it travel in 6 weeks?

42. A factory can make 6500 boxes in an hour. How many boxes can it make in 5 hours?

43. How many days are there in 3600 weeks?

44. How many feet are there in 8003 yards?

TEST PREPARATION

45. Due to Earth's rotation, a point on the equator travels about 1700 km every hour. How far does a point on the equator travel in 9 hours?

    A 16 300 km   **B** 1530 km

    C 15 300 km   **D** 2600 km

46. Mars orbits the Sun at a rate of 15 miles per second. How many miles does Mars travel in its orbit in 30 minutes?

    F 27,000 miles   **G** 2700 miles

    H 4500 miles   **J** 450 miles

Multiply Two Digits

Ms. Sheridan buys 17 bags of apples.
Each bag contains 24 apples.
How many apples in all does
Ms. Sheridan buy?

First, estimate by rounding: 17 × 24.

$$20 \times 20 = 400$$

To find how many apples in all,
multiply: 17 × 24 = __?__ .

▶ To multiply by two digits:

Multiply by the ones.	Multiply by the tens.	Add the partial products.

```
        2                    2                      2
        2 4                  2 4                    2 4
       ×1 7                 ×1 7                   ×1 7
7 × 24 → 1 6 8              1 6 8                  1 6 8  ← partial
              10 × 24 → 2 4 0                    +2 4 0  ← products
                                                   4 0 8
```

You can omit this zero.

Ms. Sheridan buys 408 apples.

.Think.....................................
 408 is close to the estimate of 400.

Study these examples.

```
    1
    7 8              4 0 2          2 2 3
   ×2 0            ×   1 3          1 1 1
   1 5 6 0          1 2 0 6         3 6 5 9
                   +4 0 2         ×      4 2
                    5 2 2 6        7 3 1 8
                                +1 4 6 3 6
                                1 5 3,6 7 8
```

Practice

Complete each multiplication.

```
1.      7 8     2.      4 7     3.      6 0     4.      2 7 6    5.      4 0 5 9
       ×2 6            ×3 4            ×4 8            ×   5 2           ×     6 7
        4 6 8           1 8 8           4 8 0           5 5 2           ? ? ? 1 3
     +1 5 6 ☺         +1 4 1         +? ? 0         +? ? ? ?         +? ? ? ? ?
      ? ? ? ?          ? ? ? ?         ? ? ? ?         ? ? ? ? ?        ? ? ? ? ? ?
```

Use rounding to estimate. Then multiply.

6. 62
    × 18

7. 54
    × 26

8. 46
    × 37

9. 70
    × 52

10. 83
     × 64

11. 413
     × 48

12. 572
     × 63

13. 620
     × 44

14. 206
     × 37

15. 639
     × 58

16. 2741
     ×   35

17. 1052
     ×   29

18. 8506
     ×   74

19. 7009
     ×   86

20. 6927
     ×   67

Find the product.

21. 27 × 429

22. 30 × 625

23. 47 × 804

24. 92 × 520

25. 50 × 3693

26. 74 × 6240

27. 23 × 4127

28. 48 × 3219

29. 90 × 4120

30. 83 × 7059

31. 76 × 9008

32. 39 × 7853

Problem Solving   Use the bar graph.

33. How many cherries are there in 32 cartons?

34. How many plums are there in 48 cartons?

35. How many kiwis are there in 56 cartons?

36. How many strawberries are there in 67 cartons?

37. Which contain more fruit: 40 cartons of strawberries or 50 cartons of cherries?

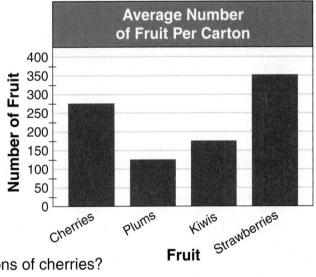

Average Number of Fruit Per Carton

Number of Fruit — Fruit
Cherries   Plums   Kiwis   Strawberries

DO YOU REMEMBER?

Align and add.

38. 1425 + 5700 + 28,500

39. 2428 + 6070 + 121,400

40. 2912 + 8320 + 124,800

41. 2125 + 29,750 + 127,500

42. 2616 + 6540 + 130,800

43. 8532 + 56,880 + 663,600

Multiply Three Digits

Norma's father has a vegetable farm of 126 rows of tomato plants. Each row has 178 plants. How many tomato plants are on the farm?

First, estimate by rounding: 126 × 178.

$$100 \times 200 = 20,000$$

To find how many tomato plants are on the farm, multiply: 126 × 178 = ? .

▶ To multiply by three digits:

Multiply by the ones.	Multiply by the tens.	Multiply by the hundreds. Add the partial products.

```
    1 7 8                 1 7 8                 1 7 8
  × 1 2 6               × 1 2 6               × 1 2 6
  1 0 6 8 ← 6 × 178     1 0 6 8               1 0 6 8
                        3 5 6 ◌ ← 20 × 178    3 5 6 ◌
                                            + 1 7 8 ◌ ◌ ← 100 × 178
                                              2 2,4 2 8
```

................Think................
22,428 is close to
the estimate of 20,000.
....

There are 22,428 tomato plants on the farm.

Study this example.

Find the product of $n \times 6350$ when $n = 528$.

A **variable,** such as n, is a letter or symbol that is used to represent a number.

$n \times 6350 = $? .

$528 \times 6350 = 3,352,800$

Complete each multiplication.

1.
```
      4 2 7
    × 3 2 4
    1 7 0 8
    8 5 4 ◌
  + ? ? ? ? ◌ ◌
    ? ? ? ? ? 8
```

2.
```
      6 0 7
    × 2 1 4
    2 4 2 8
      6 0 7
  + ? ? ? 4
    ? ? ? ? ? ?
```

3.
```
      3 7 0
    × 8 6 3
    1 1 1 0
    2 2 2 0
  + ? ? ? ?
    ? ? ? ? ? ?
```

4.
```
      5 1 9 2
    ×   2 7 4
    2 0 7 6 8
    3 6 3 4 4
  + ? ? ? ? ?
    ? ? ? ? ? ?
```

Practice

Use rounding to estimate. Then multiply.

5. 541
   × 122

6. 345
   × 211

7. 217
   × 115

8. 431
   × 134

9. 501
   × 272

10. 244
    × 152

11. 420
    × 135

12. 305
    × 271

13. 360
    × 417

14. 742
    × 343

Find the product.

15. 354 × 120

16. 417 × 131

17. 252 × 204

18. 475 × 218

19. 624 × 382

20. 728 × 618

21. 683 × 4234

22. 527 × 6049

23. 482 × 2979

24. 236 × 1143

25. 962 × 4085

26. 819 × 2709

27. $n \times 328$ when $n = 274$

28. $n \times 853$ when $n = 418$

29. $275 \times n$ when $n = 362$

30. $415 \times n$ when $n = 672$

31. There are 245 rows of corn plants. Each row has 125 plants. How many corn plants are there in all?

32. There are 135 baskets of potatoes. Each basket holds 115 potatoes. How many potatoes are there in all?

33. Dennis picks an average of 465 bushel baskets of apples during the season. If each basket holds 118 apples, how many apples does Dennis pick during the season?

34. A supermarket receives 625 cases of oranges. Each case holds 135 oranges. How many oranges in all does the supermarket receive?

35. A fruit distributor received 575 cartons of plums during the week. The average number of plums per carton is 125. At the end of the week, 62,950 plums had been sold to supermarkets. Were all the plums received sold at the end of the week? Explain your answer.

36. In your Math Journal, explain why in exercises 1–4 (page 80):

   • there are 3 partial products

   • the zeros are written in the partial products in exercise 3.

2-9 Zeros in the Multiplier

A movie theater sold out all 405 seats for each show. If there were 698 shows, how many seats were sold?

First, estimate by rounding:

405 × 698.

↓ ↓

400 × 700 = 280,000

To find how many seats were sold, multiply: 405 × 698 = *n*.

Long Way

```
      6 9 8
    × 4 0 5
    3 4 9 0  ←——— 5 × 698
    0 0 0 0  ←——— 0 × 698
+ 2 7 9 2 0 0  ←——— 400 × 698
  2 8 2,6 9 0
```

The theater sold 282,690 seats.

Short Way   There are 0 tens in 405, so omit the second partial product.

```
      6 9 8
    × 4 0 5
    3 4 9 0  ←——— 5 × 698
+ 2 7 9 2 0 0  ←——— 400 × 698
  2 8 2,6 9 0
```

.Think...
282,690 is close to the estimate of 280,000.

Study these examples.

```
    3 0 0 2
  ×   7 0 0
2,1 0 1,4 0 0
```
700 has 0 ones and 0 tens, so omit the partial products.

Remember to write this digit directly under the multiplier place.

```
    3 2 5 6
  ×   3 5 0
  1 6 2 8 0 0  ←——— 50 × 3256
+ 9 7 6 8 0 0  ←——— 300 × 3256
1,1 3 9,6 0 0
```
350 has 0 ones, so omit the partial product.

Complete each multiplication. Use the short way.

1.
```
      7 1 4
    × 6 0 0
  ? ? ? ? 0 0
```

2.
```
        4 0 2
      × 3 0 7
      2 8 1 4
+ ? ? ? 6 0 0
  ? ? ? ? ? ?
```

3.
```
        9 5 6
      × 5 8 0
      7 6 4 8 0
+   ? ? 8 0
  ? ? ? ? ? ?
```

4.
```
        3 5 8 0
      ×   7 0 6
      2 1 4 8 0
+ ? ? ? 6 0
  ? ? ? ? ? ?
```

Practice

Use rounding to estimate. Then multiply.

5. 219
   × 304

6. 391
   × 104

7. 604
   × 206

8. 508
   × 709

9. 760
   × 306

10. 360
    × 703

11. 362
    × 202

12. 937
    × 209

13. 846
    × 407

14. 928
    × 607

15. 457
    × 320

16. 936
    × 430

17. 869
    × 650

18. 947
    × 730

19. 898
    × 860

Find the product.

20. 600 × 739

21. 900 × 846

22. 700 × 4004

23. 500 × 8009

24. 720 × 365

25. 740 × 438

26. 860 × 549

27. 930 × 714

28. 507 × 367

29. 604 × 863

30. 708 × 905

31. 403 × 870

32. 230 × 1258

33. 470 × 2479

34. 605 × 4059

35. 209 × 7086

36. 601 × 3583

37. 807 × 7859

38. 920 × 7003

39. 640 × 8705

Problem Solving

40. The art guild had its exhibit for 105 days. It sold 436 tickets for each day. How many tickets did it sell for its exhibit?

41. The average family uses 370 gallons of water a day. How many gallons of water does the average family use in 120 days?

42. A bar of iron weighs 500 pounds. How many pounds will 738 bars of iron weigh?

43. A machine produces 420 chips in one minute. How many chips does it produce in 150 minutes?

CRITICAL THINKING

Write the multiplication sign in the right place to get the given product.

44. 1 2 3 4 5 6 = 56,088

45. 3 3 3 3 3 3 = 109,989

46. 1 3 5 7 9 0 = 122,130

47. 1 0 2 4 6 8 = 81,968

48. 2 2 4 4 6 6 = 98,252

49. 9 8 7 6 5 4 = 533,304

2-10 Multiplication with Money

Marion bought 8 boxes of greeting cards at $6.95 a box. How much did Marion pay for the greeting cards?

First, estimate by rounding: 8 × $6.95.

$$8 \times \$7.00 = \$56.00$$

To find how much Marion paid, multiply: 8 × $6.95 = n.

▶ To multiply an amount of money:

- Multiply as usual.

- Write a decimal point in the product two places from the right.

- Write the dollar sign in the product.

```
  $6.9 5
×     8
$5 5.6 0
```

Write the decimal point 2 places from the right.

Write the dollar sign.

Think

Marion paid $55.60. $55.60 is close to the estimate of $56.00.

Study these examples.

```
  $0.8 9        $2.1 5         $2.0 4
×    4 6      ×     9 7      ×    3 2 0
    5 3 4        1 5 0 5        4 0 8 0
+ 3 5 6 0    + 1 9 3 5 0    + 6 1 2 0 0
 $4 0.9 4     $2 0 8.5 5     $6 5 2.8 0
```

Write the dollar sign and the decimal point.

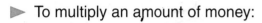

Find the product. Write the dollar sign and decimal point.

1.
```
  $0.8 3
×      9
  ? ? 7
```

2.
```
  $3.5 4
×      9
? ? 8 6
```

3.
```
  $0.6 5
×      4
  ? ? ?
```

4.
```
  $7.3 8
×      6
? ? ? ?
```

5.
```
  $8.6 9
×      8
? ? ? ?
```

6.
```
  $0.7 4
×      8
  ? ? ?
```

7.
```
  $0.3 9
×      7
  ? ? ?
```

8.
```
  $2.6 3
×      9
? ? ? ?
```

9.
```
  $1 0.4 5
×        6
  ? ? ? ?
```

10.
```
  $1 2.3 8
×        9
? ? ? ? ?
```

Practice

Use rounding to estimate. Then find the product.

11. $3.73
    × 9

12. $5.46
    × 7

13. $3.14
    × 8

14. $9.03
    × 5

15. $7.80
    × 6

16. $0.57
    × 38

17. $2.90
    × 70

18. $9.80
    × 55

19. $0.69
    × 43

20. $0.86
    × 30

21. $4.50
    × 605

22. $2.18
    × 340

23. $9.06
    × 214

24. $7.24
    × 416

25. $6.18
    × 524

Multiply.

26. 43 × $3.04

27. 79 × $8.47

28. 86 × $9.32

29. 51 × $7.46

30. 62 × $5.78

31. 93 × $6.85

32. 540 × $4.09

33. 215 × $6.07

34. 432 × $7.80

35. 279 × $84.27

36. 514 × $34.65

37. 483 × $65.19

38. 375 × $28.29

39. 762 × $41.58

40. 627 × $50.59

Problem Solving

41. Pancho earns $6.75 an hour as a laboratory assistant. How much does he earn in 32 hours?

42. Mr. Montes buys 29 copies of books for his class. Each book costs $9.75. How much do all the books cost?

43. A class of 38 students goes on a field trip. Each student pays $8.65 for the trip. How much does the class pay for the trip?

44. Tina bought 15 pounds of cherries at $1.68 per pound. Roy bought 14 pounds of cherries at $1.80 per pound. Who paid more?

CRITICAL THINKING

Write a multiplication example for each.

45. Multiply a 2-digit number by a 2-digit number so that the product is a:

    a. 3-digit number

    b. 4-digit number

46. Multiply a 3-digit number by a 3-digit number so that the product is a:

    a. 5-digit number

    b. 6-digit number

Problem-Solving Strategy:
Use More Than One Step

September						
S	M	T	W	TH	F	S
			1	2	3	4
5	6	7	8	9	10	11

October						
S	M	T	W	TH	F	S
					1	2
3	4	5	6	7	8	9
10	11	12	13	14	15	16
17	18	19	20	21	22	23

Kenny swims 23 laps every day. How many laps did he swim in the months of September and October?

Read

Visualize yourself in the problem above as you reread it. Focus on the facts and the question.

List what you know.

Facts: Swims 23 laps every day
Swims months of September and October

Question: How many laps did he swim in September and October?

Plan

Is all the information you need listed in the problem? No.
Is there hidden information in the problem? Yes.

Hint
There are 30 days in September and 31 days in October.

First add to find the total number of days.

Then estimate and multiply to find the number of laps Kenny swam: $61 \times 23 = n$.

Solve

Total days: $30 + 31 = 61$ days

Estimate. Use rounding. $60 \times 20 = 1200$
about 1200 laps

Then multiply.
$$
\begin{array}{r}
23 \\
\times 61 \\
\hline
23 \\
+138 \\
\hline
1403
\end{array}
$$

Think
The product 1403 is close to the estimate of 1200.

Kenny swam 1403 laps in September and October.

Check

Did you answer the question asked? Yes.

Check your computation by changing the order of the factors.

$$
\begin{array}{r}
61 \\
\times 23 \\
\hline
183 \\
+122 \\
\hline
1403
\end{array}
$$
The answer checks.

Find the hidden information to solve each problem.

1. Jan earns $4.50 an hour babysitting.
   She babysits 3 hours each week.
   How much money will Jan make in a year?

Read ▸ Visualize yourself in the problem above
as you reread it. Focus on the facts
and questions.

List what you know.

Facts: $4.50 an hour babysitting
babysits 3 hours each week

Question: How much will Jan earn in a year?

Plan ▸ Is there information not stated in the problem? Yes.

.Hint
There are 52 weeks in a year.

First multiply to find the amount
Jan earns each week: $4.50 × 3 = n.

To find the amount of money Jan will earn in a year,
multiply: 52 × n = ___?___ .

Solve ┄┄┄┄┄ **Check**

2. Mr. Hudson uses three cups of flour in every loaf of bread. He bakes 67
   loaves of bread a day. How many cups of flour does he use in a week?

3. There are 52 bookshelves of fiction and 21 bookshelves of
   nonfiction in the library. About $1\frac{1}{2}$ dozen books fit on each
   shelf. About how many books can fit on all the shelves?

4. Hector can fit two dozen coins on a page of his coin album.
   If his album has 125 pages, how many coins can he put in it?

5. Frank types 88 words per minute. If it took him $1\frac{1}{4}$ hours
   to type a report, about how many words are in the report?

6. Write and solve a problem that has hidden
   information. Have someone solve it.

Problem-Solving Applications: Mixed Review

Read **Plan** **Solve** **Check**

Solve each problem and explain the method you use.

1. KidCo's first product is beaded bracelets. Each bracelet uses 9 in. of bead wire. Will 1500 in. of wire be enough for 150 bracelets?

2. Each bracelet uses 30 beads. How many beads are needed to make this first batch?

3. The next KidCo product is matching necklaces. Each necklace uses 120 beads. How many beads will be needed to produce 75 necklaces?

4. Each necklace uses 72 in. of wire. Will a 5000-in. roll of wire be enough to make 75 necklaces? If not, how much more wire will be needed?

5. The total cost of materials is $3 for each bracelet. KidCo plans to sell the bracelets for $5 each. How much profit will it make if it sells all 150 bracelets?

6. Each necklace costs $11.25 to make. How much will it cost to make 75 necklaces?

7. KidCo rented a booth at Town Hall Market. It sold 18 pairs of earrings at $4.50 each and 8 belts at $8.05 each. How much money did KidCo collect from the sales?

8. KidCo owners had flyers printed. Each word costs 12 cents to set. About how much did it cost to set this flyer?

9. Bulk mail costs 16¢ a piece. KidCo mailed 750 flyers. How much did the owners pay for this service?

10. On Saturday morning there were 205 people at the Town Hall Market. There were double that number in the afternoon. How many people came to the Town Hall Market on Saturday?

Announcing:

KidCo Products

Town Hall Market

Every Saturday

• Beaded Belts •
Bracelets • Earrings
• Baked Goods •
and More!

Choose a strategy from the list or use another strategy you know to solve each problem.

11. KidCo owners disagreed on how much to charge for necklaces. Some wanted to charge $15, and others wanted to charge $16.50. How much more will they collect on 75 necklaces if they charge the higher price?

Strategy File

Use These Strategies
Guess and Test
Logical Reasoning
More Than One Solution
Use More Than One Step

12. Shawn took in $69.15 for 2 hours work on Saturday, selling belts for $8.05 and earrings for $4.50. How many of each did Shawn sell?

13. KidCo belts are made of braided cords. Each belt uses 96 in. of cord. Will a 120-ft roll of cord be enough to make a dozen belts?

14. Bob and Kay both work part-time at KidCo. Bob works every fourth day and Kay works every third day. Both work on March 1. On what other days in March do they both work?

15. Renting a booth at the market costs $15.75 per Saturday or $53 for four Saturdays. If a booth is rented every Saturday from May 2 to June 25 at the lower rate, what will the savings be?

16. Last year Kelly sold 24 necklaces. This year she sold twice that number. How many necklaces did Kelly sell in the past two years?

Use the table for problems 17–18.

17. How much will be earned if all the teddy bears are sold?

18. All the corn muffins were sold. How much was earned?

New KidCo Products		
Product	**Teddy Bears**	**Corn Muffins**
Cost of Materials	$7	$0.89 per doz
Product Price	$11	$1.80 per doz
Time Required	85 min each	200 min for 25 doz
Number Made	80	25 doz

Write Your Own

19. Write in your Math Journal which problem you solved using two strategies and explain why. Then write a problem modeled on this problem and have a classmate solve it.

Write as a multiplication sentence. *(See pp. 66–67.)*
Name the factors and product.

1. 7 + 7 + 7 + 7 + 7

2. 6 + 6 + 6 + 6 + 6 + 6 + 6

Find the missing factor.

3. 4 × __?__ = 20

4. __?__ × 7 = 42

5. 9 × __?__ = 54

Name the property of multiplication used. *(See pp. 68–69.)*

6. 2 × 6 = 6 × 2

7. 0 × 8 = 0

8. 4 × (3 × 2) = (4 × 3) × 2

9. 1 × 4 = 4

10. 3 × (2 + 4) = (3 × 2) + (3 × 4)

Find the product. *(See pp. 70–73, 76–85.)*

11. 8 × 30

12. 6 × 20

13. 40 × 9

14. 80,500 × 7

15. 15 × 67

16. 3023 × 83

17. 215 × 356

18. 605 × 4582

19. 372 × $1.59

20. 625 × $4.37

21. 394 × $7.85

Use rounding to estimate. Then multiply. *(See pp. 74–85.)*

22. 86 × 24	23. 246 × 26	24. 607 × 47	25. 318 × 64	26. 215 × 31
27. 416 × 258	28. 346 × 517	29. 237 × 608	30. 6289 × 413	31. 7385 × 329
32. $4.29 × 32	33. $7.48 × 62	34. $26.42 × 104	35. $72.48 × 320	36. $6.75 × 342

Problem Solving
(See pp. 84–89.)

37. The drama club sold 364 tickets. The tickets cost $2.75 each. How much money did the club make on the ticket sales?

38. Pencils are packed 12 dozen per box. How many pencils are there in 30 boxes?

(See Still More Practice, p. 478.)

Exponents

When a number is used as a factor several times, it can be written with an **exponent**. The exponent tells how many times the number, called the *base*, is used as a factor.

$$2 \times 2 \times 2 \times 2 \times 2 \times 2 = 2^6 \leftarrow \text{exponent}$$

2 used as a factor 6 times | base

The example shows that 2 is used as a factor six times and the product is 64.

$$2^6 = 2 \times 2 \times 2 \times 2 \times 2 \times 2 = 64 \leftarrow \text{product}$$

Read: "two to the sixth power"

Study these examples.

$$7^1 = 7$$
Read: "seven to the first power"

$$7^2 = 7 \times 7 = 49$$
Read: "seven squared"

$$7^3 = 7 \times 7 \times 7 = 343$$
Read: "seven cubed"

Write each product using an exponent.

1. $9 \times 9 \times 9 \times 9 \times 9$

2. $6 \times 6 \times 6$

3. $10 \times 10 \times 10 \times 10$

4. $7 \times 7 \times 7 \times 7 \times 7 \times 7 \times 7$

5. $5 \times 5 \times 5 \times 5 \times 5 \times 5 \times 5 \times 5 \times 5 \times 5$

Find the product.

6. 2^2　　**7.** 3^4　　**8.** 4^3　　**9.** 5^3　　**10.** 1^{10}　　**11.** 10^4

12. 9^1　　**13.** 6^3　　**14.** 8^3　　**15.** 2^7　　**16.** 4^5　　**17.** 10^9

Find each product to discover a pattern.

18. $2^4 = \underline{\ ?\ }$
$2^3 = \underline{\ ?\ }$
$2^2 = \underline{\ ?\ }$
$2^1 = \underline{\ ?\ }$
$2^0 = \underline{\ ?\ }$

19. $5^4 = \underline{\ ?\ }$
$5^3 = \underline{\ ?\ }$
$5^2 = \underline{\ ?\ }$
$5^1 = \underline{\ ?\ }$
$5^0 = \underline{\ ?\ }$

20. $10^4 = \underline{\ ?\ }$
$10^3 = \underline{\ ?\ }$
$10^2 = \underline{\ ?\ }$
$10^1 = \underline{\ ?\ }$
$10^0 = \underline{\ ?\ }$

21. Any nonzero number that has an exponent of zero has a value of __?__ .

Chapter 2 Test

Find the missing factor.

1. $6 \times \underline{\ ?\ } = 42$ **2.** $64 = 8 \times \underline{\ ?\ }$ **3.** $15 = \underline{\ ?\ } \times 3$

Name the property of multiplication used.

4. $9 \times 1 = 9$ **5.** $3 \times 4 = 4 \times 3$ **6.** $(5 \times 7) \times 2 = 5 \times (7 \times 2)$

7. $12 \times 0 = 0$ **8.** $4 \times (5 + 3) = (4 \times 5) + (4 \times 3)$

Find the product.

9. 4×4
4×40
4×400

10. 9×6
9×60
9×600

11. 3×7
3×70
3×700

12. 8×5
8×50
8×500

13. $\begin{array}{r} 164 \\ \times\ 56 \\ \hline \end{array}$ **14.** $\begin{array}{r} 279 \\ \times\ 34 \\ \hline \end{array}$ **15.** $\begin{array}{r} 312 \\ \times 284 \\ \hline \end{array}$ **16.** $\begin{array}{r} 673 \\ \times 406 \\ \hline \end{array}$ **17.** $\begin{array}{r} 5120 \\ \times\ 700 \\ \hline \end{array}$

Use rounding to estimate. Then multiply.

18. $\begin{array}{r} 4076 \\ \times\ \ \ 4 \\ \hline \end{array}$ **19.** $\begin{array}{r} 428 \\ \times\ 47 \\ \hline \end{array}$ **20.** $\begin{array}{r} 5085 \\ \times\ \ 68 \\ \hline \end{array}$ **21.** $\begin{array}{r} 547 \\ \times 305 \\ \hline \end{array}$ **22.** $\begin{array}{r} 7457 \\ \times\ 263 \\ \hline \end{array}$

23. $\begin{array}{r} \$35.24 \\ \times\ \ \ \ \ 6 \\ \hline \end{array}$ **24.** $\begin{array}{r} \$2.15 \\ \times\ \ \ 52 \\ \hline \end{array}$ **25.** $\begin{array}{r} \$0.25 \\ \times\ \ \ 43 \\ \hline \end{array}$ **26.** $\begin{array}{r} \$11.42 \\ \times\ \ \ 579 \\ \hline \end{array}$ **27.** $\begin{array}{r} \$26.75 \\ \times\ \ \ 489 \\ \hline \end{array}$

Problem Solving

Use a strategy you have learned.

28. Farmer Zeke sold 600 bushels of corn for $2.50 a bushel. He sold 350 bushels of soybeans for $5.00 a bushel. How much did Farmer Zeke make altogether?

Tell About It

29. Explain how to use the Distributive Property to multiply $7 \times 500{,}080$.

Performance Assessment

Choose the computation method.
Use the numbers in the box to write multiplication sentences that you can solve using:

101	33
2853	50

30. mental math   **31.** paper and pencil

Test Preparation

Choose the best answer.

1. Estimate $489 + 502 + 495 + 512$.
   Use clustering.

   a. 20,000
   b. 2000
   c. 20
   d. 2.00

2. Which two numbers have a product of 420?

   a. 70 and 60
   b. 7 and 60
   c. 70 and 600
   d. 7 and 600

3. Choose the order from least to greatest.

   640,705; 604,750; 604,570

   a. 604,570; 604,750; 640,705
   b. 604,750; 604,570; 640,705
   c. 640,705; 604,570; 604,750
   d. 604,750; 640,705; 604,570

4. Round to the place of the underlined digit.

   7,3<u>6</u>9,842

   a. 7,300,000
   b. 7,360,000
   c. 7,370,000
   d. 8,000,000

5. Multiply.

   $\begin{array}{r} 362 \\ \times\ 275 \end{array}$

   a. 99,550
   b. 99,500
   c. 90,550
   d. 90,500

6. Which number has a 7
   in the hundredths place?

   a. 703.52
   b. 175.68
   c. 607.49
   d. 906.07

7. Find the sum.

   $2854 + 563 + 49 + 307$

   a. 3773
   b. 3763
   c. 3873
   d. 3863

8. Which illustrates the Associative Property
   of Multiplication?

   a. $7 \times 10 = 10 \times 7$
   b. $1 \times 9 = 9$
   c. $5 \times 0 = 0$
   d. $3 \times (4 \times 5) = (3 \times 4) \times 5$

9. Estimate the product. Use rounding.

   $\begin{array}{r} \$71.16 \\ \times\ \ 323 \end{array}$

   a. $24,000.00
   b. $2400.00
   c. $21,000.00
   d. $2100.00

10. Choose the standard form.

    $7,000,000 + 30,000 + 300 + 4$

    a. 7,300,034
    b. 7,030,304
    c. 7,300,304
    d. 7,030,034

11. Find the missing factor.

    $9 \times \underline{\ ?\ } = 0$

    a. 1
    b. 9
    c. 0
    d. 10

12. Find the product.

    750×328

    a. 246,000
    b. 24,000
    c. 240,000
    d. 24,600

13. Find the difference.

    $\begin{array}{r} 8040 \\ -\ 3921 \end{array}$

    a. 5921
    b. 5129
    c. 4119
    d. 4029

14. Multiply.

    $40 \times 50,000$

    a. 20,000
    b. 200,000
    c. 2,000,000
    d. 20,000,000

15. Choose the multiplication sentence.

$8 + 8 + 8 + 8 + 8 + 8$

   a. $6 \times 8 = 48$
   b. $8 \times 8 = 64$
   c. $6 \times 6 = 36$
   d. none of these

16. The sum of 41,075 and 22,957 is:

   a. 63,032
   b. 64,032
   c. 64,022
   d. 63,022

17. Find the difference.

   79,000
  − 17,278

   a. 61,278
   b. 62,722
   c. 62,278
   d. 61,722

18. $3 \times (4 + 5) = (3 \times 4) + (3 \times 5)$ illustrates which property?

   a. commutative
   b. distributive
   c. associative
   d. identity

19. A roll of film costs $5.59 and its processing costs $8.50. If Ted pays for both the film and its processing with a $20 bill, how much change would he get?

   a. $13.10
   b. $6.91
   c. $5.91
   d. $14.09

20. What is the place value of the digit 9 in 8.239?

   a. 9 hundredths
   b. 9 tenths
   c. 9 ones
   d. 9 thousandths

21. Men first landed on the moon in 1969. Write this date as a Roman numeral.

   a. MCMLXIX
   b. MCMXLIX
   c. MMCLXIX
   d. MMCXLIX

22. Which statement is true?

   a. $100 \times 324 > 10 \times 3240$
   b. $20 \times 300 = 60 \times 100$
   c. $300 \times 820 < 244 \times 1000$
   d. $400 \times 300 = 60 \times 200$

23. The first dinosaurs appeared on Earth about 230 million years ago. What is this number in standard form?

   a. 230,000
   b. 230,000,000
   c. 230,000,000,000
   d. 23,000,000

24. A museum displays slides of its exhibits on 6-sided racks. Each side has 12 rows of slides. Each row holds about 18 slides. About how many slides are there on each rack?

   a. about 2400 slides
   b. about 1200 slides
   c. about 2000 slides
   d. about 1000 slides

Explain how you solved each problem. Show all your work.

25. An airport checks in an average of 1500 passengers per hour. Each passenger checks in an average of 60 pounds of baggage. How many pounds of baggage are handled by the airport in one day?

26. Ada has 47 red buttons in her collection. She has three times as many blue buttons as she has green buttons. If there are 175 buttons of all three colors in the collection, how many blue buttons does Ada have?

Division

A Microscopic Topic

I am a paramecium
that cannot do a simple sum,
and it's a rather well-known fact
I'm quite unable to subtract.

If I'd an eye, I'd surely cry
about the way I multiply,
for though I've often tried and tried,
I do it backward . . . and divide.

Jack Prelutsky

In this chapter you will:

Use the meanings of division and patterns
Explore divisibility rules and short division
Estimate using compatible numbers
Learn about the order of operations
Make a table and find a pattern to
solve problems

Critical Thinking/Finding Together

The first minute you look at a
slide under a microscope
you see 5 bacteria. The
number of bacteria doubles
every minute. If you look at the
slide every minute, how many
bacteria will you see in the
tenth minute?

Understanding Division

Gil arranges 45 books into stacks. Each stack contains 5 books. How many stacks in all does Gil make?

To find how many stacks in all, you can find a missing factor:

$$n \times 5 = 45$$
$$n = 9$$

or

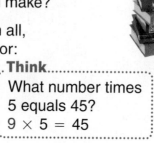

.Think..........
What number times
5 equals 45?
$9 \times 5 = 45$

you can divide since you are separating a set into equal groups.

$$\underset{\uparrow}{45} \quad \div \quad \underset{\uparrow}{5} \quad = \quad \underset{\uparrow}{9}$$

dividend   divisor   quotient

$$9 \leftarrow \textbf{quotient}$$
$$5\overline{)45} \leftarrow \textbf{dividend}$$
$$\uparrow$$
$$\textbf{divisor}$$

Gil makes 9 stacks in all.

$45 \div 5 = 9$ is a division sentence.

▶ Division is the inverse of multiplication. It "undoes" multiplication.

Since $9 \times 5 = 45$, then $45 \div 5 = 9$ ◄
and $45 \div 9 = 5$. ◄

These are related division facts.

Find the value of n.

1. $9 \times 4 = 36$
$36 \div 4 = n$
$36 \div 9 = n$

2. $6 \times 7 = 42$
$42 \div n = 6$
$42 \div n = 7$

3. $8 \times 3 = 24$
$n \div 3 = 8$
$n \div 8 = 3$

Write four related facts using the given numbers.

4. 6, 3, 18

.Think..........
$6 \times 3 = 18$
$3 \times 6 = 18$
$18 \div 3 = 6$
$18 \div 6 = 3$

5. 3, 9, 27

6. 4, 7, 28

7. 7, 8, 56

8. 8, 9, 72

9. 5, 8, 40

10. 6, 8, 48

11. 2, 8, 16

12. 7, 6, 42

13. 5, 4, 20

14. In your Math Journal, write what you notice about the four related facts in exercises 4–13. What does this tell you about multiplication and division?

Rules of Division

Here are some rules of division that can help you divide quickly and correctly.

dividend ÷ divisor = quotient

- When the divisor is *one,* the quotient is the same as the dividend.

$$8 \div 1 = 8 \qquad 1\overline{)8}\;\; {}^{8}$$

- When the divisor and the dividend are the *same* number, the quotient is always one.

$$7 \div 7 = 1 \qquad 7\overline{)7}\;\; {}^{1}$$

- When the dividend is *zero,* the quotient is zero.

$$0 \div 3 = 0 \qquad 3\overline{)0}\;\; {}^{0}$$

- The divisor can *never* be zero.

Divide.

15. $43\overline{)43}$ **16.** $37\overline{)0}$ **17.** $1\overline{)97}$ **18.** $91\overline{)0}$ **19.** $58\overline{)58}$ **20.** $35\overline{)35}$

21. $39\overline{)0}$ **22.** $51\overline{)51}$ **23.** $85\overline{)85}$ **24.** $1\overline{)65}$ **25.** $98\overline{)0}$ **26.** $49\overline{)49}$

27. $561 \div 561$ **28.** $0 \div 483$ **29.** $612 \div 612$ **30.** $0 \div 165$

Write a division sentence for each.

31. The quotient is 1. The divisor is 60. What is the dividend?

32. The dividend is 49. The quotient is 7. What is the divisor?

33. The dividend is 40. The divisor is 8. What is the quotient?

34. The divisor is 16. The quotient is 0. What is the dividend?

Problem Solving

35. Ruth has a CD case that holds 36 CDs. She divides the case into four equal sections for rock, jazz, vocal, and dance music. How many CDs can each section hold?

36. Seth bought a music CD that has a total playing time of 1 hour and 12 minutes. Each song is 6 minutes long. How many songs are on the CD?

Division Patterns

3-2 Algebra

Use division facts and patterns with zero
to divide with multiples of 10, 100, or 1000.

Study these division patterns:

Fact: 8 ÷ 2 = 4

  80 ÷ 2 = 40
  800 ÷ 2 = 400
  8000 ÷ 2 = 4000
  80,000 ÷ 2 = 40,000

Fact: 30 ÷ 6 = 5

  300 ÷ 6 = 50
  3000 ÷ 6 = 500
  30,000 ÷ 6 = 5000
  300,000 ÷ 6 = 50,000

Remember:
Look for a basic
division fact when
dividing with multiples
of 10, 100, or 1000.

Fact: 24 ÷ 8 = 3

  240 ÷ 80 = 3
  2400 ÷ 80 = 30
  24,000 ÷ 80 = 300
  240,000 ÷ 80 = 3000

Fact: 7 ÷ 1 = 7

  70 ÷ 10 = 7
  700 ÷ 100 = 7
  7000 ÷ 1000 = 7
  70,000 ÷ 10,000 = 7

Fact: 18 ÷ 2 = 9

  180 ÷ 2 = 90
  1800 ÷ 20 = 90
  18,000 ÷ 200 = 90
  180,000 ÷ 2000 = 90

Practice

Find the quotients. Look for a pattern.

1.
9 ÷ 3
90 ÷ 3
900 ÷ 3
9000 ÷ 3
90,000 ÷ 3

2.
48 ÷ 6
480 ÷ 6
4800 ÷ 6
48,000 ÷ 6
480,000 ÷ 6

3.
30 ÷ 5
300 ÷ 50
3000 ÷ 50
30,000 ÷ 50
300,000 ÷ 50

4.
12 ÷ 4
120 ÷ 40
1200 ÷ 40
12,000 ÷ 40
120,000 ÷ 40

5.
45 ÷ 9
450 ÷ 90
4500 ÷ 900
45,000 ÷ 9000
450,000 ÷ 90,000

6.
56 ÷ 7
560 ÷ 70
5600 ÷ 700
56,000 ÷ 7000
560,000 ÷ 70,000

Divide. Write the basic fact you use.

7. 7)350

8. 9)720

9. 3)1800

10. 8)6400

11. 80)240

12. 60)420

13. 50)300

14. 30)120

15. 50)2000

16. 40)2800

17. 60)3600

18. 20)18,000

19. 40)16,000

20. 700)49,000

21. 800)480,000

22. 300)270,000

Use basic facts and patterns to find the value of _n_.

23. $720 \div 9 = n$

24. $60 \div 3 = n$

25. $800 \div 2 = n$

26. $2400 \div 6 = n$

27. $1200 \div n = 40$

28. $3500 \div n = 70$

29. $2800 \div n = 40$

30. $6300 \div n = 90$

31. $4200 \div 60 = n$

32. $30,000 \div 50 = n$

33. $64,000 \div 80 = n$

34. $45,000 \div 90 = n$

35. $54,000 \div 60 = n$

36. $630,000 \div n = 900$

37. $560,000 \div n = 8000$

Compare. Write <, =, or >.

38. $3600 \div 6$ __?__ $4000 \div 8$

39. $4200 \div 70$ __?__ $4800 \div 80$

40. $70,000 \div 7$ __?__ $80,000 \div 2$

41. $45,000 \div 90$ __?__ $25,000 \div 5$

 Problem Solving Use the bar graph.

The graph shows the different distances traveled by 4 families in 5 days. If each family traveled the same distance each day, how many miles did each family travel per day?

42. Ayala

43. Tan

44. Ford

45. Smith

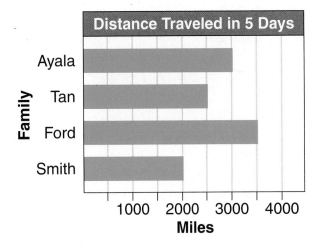

Distance Traveled in 5 Days

Family / Miles

DO YOU REMEMBER?

Write the digit in the tens place.

46. 39   **47.** 247   **48.** 6531   **49.** 78,093   **50.** 189,704

Write the digit in the hundreds place.

51. 563   **52.** 849   **53.** 7442   **54.** 65,104   **55.** 282,312

Write the place of the red digit.

56. 9472   **57.** 8435   **58.** 67,892   **59.** 60,948   **60.** 349,925

61. 17,539   **62.** 417,058   **63.** 502,931   **64.** 896,127   **65.** 642,573

3-3 Three-Digit Quotients

Manuel has 866 baseball cards in all. He divides them equally among his 7 friends. How many cards does each friend get? How many cards are left over?

To find how many cards each friend gets, divide: $866 \div 7 = n$.

▶ Use the division steps.

• Decide where to begin the quotient.

$$7\overline{)866}$$

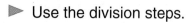

> **Think**
> $7 < 8$
> **Enough hundreds**

Divide the hundreds first.

• Divide the hundreds.
  Estimate: $\underline{\ ?\ } \times 7 = 8$
  $1 \times 7 = 7$
  $2 \times 7 = 14$
  Try 1.

$$\begin{array}{r} 1 \\ 7\overline{)8\ 6\ 6} \\ -7\downarrow \\ \hline 1\ 6 \end{array}$$

Division Steps
• Decide where to begin the quotient.
• Estimate.
• Divide.
• Multiply.
• Subtract and compare.
• Bring down.
• Repeat the steps as necessary.
• Check.

• Divide the tens.
  Estimate: $\underline{\ ?\ } \times 7 = 16$
  $2 \times 7 = 14$
  $3 \times 7 = 21$
  Try 2.

$$\begin{array}{r} 1\ 2 \\ 7\overline{)8\ 6\ 6} \\ -7\downarrow \\ \hline 1\ 6\ \downarrow \\ -1\ 4\ \\ \hline 2\ 6 \end{array}$$

• Divide the ones.
  Estimate: $\underline{\ ?\ } \times 7 = 26$
  $3 \times 7 = 21$
  $4 \times 7 = 28$
  Try 3.

$$\begin{array}{r} 1\ 2\ 3\ \text{R5} \\ 7\overline{)8\ 6\ 6} \\ -7\downarrow \\ \hline 1\ 6\downarrow \\ -1\ 4\downarrow \\ \hline 2\ 6 \\ -2\ 1 \\ \hline 5 \end{array}$$

Remember:
Write the remainder in the quotient.

• Check: $123 \times 7 + 5 = 866$

Each friend gets 123 baseball cards. There are 5 baseball cards left over.

Divide and check.

1. $3\overline{)372}$ 2. $4\overline{)568}$ 3. $2\overline{)295}$ 4. $6\overline{)999}$

5. $4\overline{)872}$ 6. $6\overline{)712}$ 7. $7\overline{)917}$ 8. $8\overline{)904}$

9. $3\overline{)2184}$ 10. $5\overline{)4455}$ 11. $2\overline{)1168}$ 12. $5\overline{)4366}$

13. $7\overline{)2436}$ 14. $6\overline{)4559}$ 15. $8\overline{)7462}$ 16. $9\overline{)1098}$

Find the quotient and the remainder. Then check.

17. $568 \div 3$ 18. $907 \div 8$ 19. $817 \div 7$ 20. $694 \div 4$

21. $857 \div 2$ 22. $762 \div 5$ 23. $805 \div 6$ 24. $877 \div 3$

25. $3739 \div 6$ 26. $1841 \div 5$ 27. $4039 \div 9$ 28. $3964 \div 5$

29. $1379 \div 4$ 30. $2167 \div 8$ 31. $2586 \div 6$ 32. $3048 \div 7$

Problem Solving

33. There are 3150 canceled stamps in 9 boxes. If each box contains the same number of canceled stamps, how many canceled stamps are in each box?

34. The Art Guild has 1438 flyers to give out. If 5 members of the Guild share the job equally, how many flyers will each give out? How many flyers will be left over?

35. Ms. Fox needs to put 1032 books on shelves. If a shelf holds 8 books, what is the least number of shelves Ms. Fox needs?

36. Seven ticket agents sold 4662 tickets. Each agent sold the same number of tickets. How many tickets were sold by each agent?

TEST PREPARATION

37. The art club creates holiday cards for the Ace retirement home. There are 8 members of the club, each of whom creates 6 cards. The 13 residents of the retirement home each take the same number of cards. What is the minimum number of remaining cards?

     A 4   **B** 7   **C** 9   **D** 10

Larger Quotients

▶ To divide large dividends, keep repeating the division
steps until the division is completed.

- Divide: $44{,}776 \div 6 = n$

```
        7 4 6 2  R4
   6)4 4,7 7 6
   − 4 2 ↓
       2 7
     − 2 4 ↓
         3 7
       − 3 6 ↓
           1 6
         − 1 2
             4
```

- Divide: $480{,}897 \div 9 = n$

```
        5 3,4 3 3
   9)4 8 0,8 9 7
   − 4 5 ↓
       3 0
     − 2 7 ↓
         3 8
       − 3 6 ↓
           2 9
         − 2 7 ↓
             2 7
           − 2 7
               0
```

Check:
$6 \times 7462 + 4 = 44{,}776$

Check:
$9 \times 53{,}433 = 480{,}897$

Practice

Complete each division.

1.
```
      7 8 ? ?
   6)4 7,1 3 0
   − 4 2 ↓
       5 1
     − ? ? ↓
         ? 3
       − ? ? ↓
           ? 0
         − ? ?
             ?
```

2.
```
      9 5 ? ?  R ?
   8)7 6,4 3 8
   − 7 2 ↓
       4 4
     − ? ? ↓
         ? 3
       − ? ? ↓
           ? 8
         − ? ?
             ?
```

3.
```
    ? ? ? ? ?  R ?
   9)8 2 7,4 3 8
   − 8 1 ↓
       1 7
     − ? ↓
        ? 4
      − ? ? ↓
          ? ?
        − ? ? ↓
            ? ?
          − ? ?
              ?
```

4. **MATH JOURNAL** Write in your Math Journal the possible
remainders when you divide by 8; by 9.
Explain why.

Divide and check.

5. $5\overline{)34{,}061}$ 6. $6\overline{)38{,}558}$ 7. $7\overline{)43{,}511}$ 8. $8\overline{)50{,}519}$

9. $9\overline{)19{,}014}$ 10. $8\overline{)35{,}356}$ 11. $5\overline{)42{,}736}$ 12. $7\overline{)25{,}361}$

13. $6\overline{)211{,}994}$ 14. $8\overline{)670{,}197}$ 15. $5\overline{)349{,}782}$ 16. $9\overline{)767{,}893}$

17. $7\overline{)596{,}081}$ 18. $9\overline{)850{,}609}$ 19. $3\overline{)295{,}058}$ 20. $4\overline{)230{,}178}$

Find the quotient.

21. $8\overline{)65{,}714}$ 22. $5\overline{)39{,}719}$ 23. $6\overline{)52{,}736}$ 24. $7\overline{)93{,}712}$

25. $7\overline{)43{,}296}$ 26. $9\overline{)48{,}732}$ 27. $6\overline{)73{,}501}$ 28. $8\overline{)36{,}098}$

29. $5\overline{)102{,}315}$ 30. $4\overline{)362{,}003}$ 31. $3\overline{)271{,}514}$ 32. $6\overline{)483{,}015}$

33. $4\overline{)675{,}153}$ 34. $9\overline{)869{,}563}$ 35. $5\overline{)686{,}347}$ 36. $7\overline{)532{,}456}$

Problem Solving

37. There were 12,744 people who attended the 6 performances of a play presented by a theater guild. If an equal number of people attended each of the performances, how many people attended each performance?

38. The British Library's *General Catalogue of Printed Books to 1995* contains about six million records from three files: British Library Catalogue, Humanities and Social Sciences Catalogue, and Science Reference and Information Service Catalogue. A typical reader would need 6 months to scan 198,000 catalog pages. If a typical reader can scan an equal number of catalog pages each month, how many catalog pages can he scan in one month?

Write About It

39. Explain without computing why each quotient is incorrect.
    - 19,003 ÷ 3 = 6334 R11
    - 15,000 ÷ 4 = 375
    - 12,005 ÷ 5 = 1240

40. If a divisor is 4, what can you say about the remainder?

Zeros in the Quotient

A farmer has 826 bags of seed to plant in 8 fields. He uses the same number of bags of seed in each field. How many bags of seed does he use in each field? How many bags of seed are left over?

To find how many bags of seed are used in each field, divide: $826 \div 8 = n$.

Decide where to begin the quotient.	$8\overline{)826}$	**Think** $8 = 8$ **Enough hundreds**

Divide the hundreds first.

Estimate: $\underline{?} \times 8 = 8$
$1 \times 8 = 8$

Try 1.

Divide the hundreds.	Divide the tens.	Divide the ones.	Check.

Divide the hundreds.
$$\begin{array}{r} 1 \\ 8\overline{)8\ 2\ 6} \\ -8 \\ \hline 2 \end{array}$$

Divide the tens.
$$\begin{array}{r} 1\ 0 \\ 8\overline{)8\ 2\ 6} \\ -8 \\ \hline 2 \\ -0 \\ \hline 2\ 6 \end{array}$$

$8 > 2$
Not enough tens
Write zero in the tens place.

Divide the ones.
$$\begin{array}{r} 1\ 0\ 3 \text{ R2} \\ 8\overline{)8\ 2\ 6} \\ -8 \\ \hline 2 \\ -0 \\ \hline 2\ 6 \\ -2\ 4 \\ \hline 2 \end{array}$$

Check.
$$\begin{array}{r} 103 \\ \times\ \ 8 \\ \hline 824 \\ +\ \ 2 \\ \hline 826 \end{array}$$

The farmer uses 103 bags of seed in each field. There are 2 bags left over.

Study these examples.

$$\begin{array}{r} 2\ 1\ 0 \text{ R2} \\ 3\overline{)6\ 3\ 2} \\ -6 \\ \hline 3 \\ -3 \\ \hline 2 \end{array}$$

Not enough ones
Write zero in the quotient.

$$\begin{array}{r} 2\ 0\ 0\ 5 \\ 5\overline{)1\ 0,0\ 2\ 5} \\ -1\ 0 \\ \hline 0\ 2 \\ -0 \\ \hline 2\ 5 \\ -2\ 5 \\ \hline 0 \end{array}$$

Not enough hundreds or tens
Write zeros in the quotient.

$$\begin{array}{r} 1\ 0,2\ 0\ 8 \\ 4\overline{)4\ 0,8\ 3\ 2} \\ -4 \\ \hline 0\ 8 \\ -8 \\ \hline 3\ 2 \\ -3\ 2 \\ \hline 0 \end{array}$$

Divide and check.

1. $4\overline{)830}$ 2. $6\overline{)652}$ 3. $5\overline{)604}$ 4. $3\overline{)722}$

5. $6\overline{)662}$ 6. $5\overline{)537}$ 7. $8\overline{)828}$ 8. $9\overline{)927}$

9. $6\overline{)6120}$ 10. $8\overline{)2565}$ 11. $5\overline{)1545}$ 12. $7\overline{)7063}$

13. $8\overline{)1200}$ 14. $6\overline{)1248}$ 15. $3\overline{)18,162}$ 16. $4\overline{)20,172}$

17. $6\overline{)36,570}$ 18. $5\overline{)25,065}$ 19. $7\overline{)21,030}$ 20. $9\overline{)40,582}$

Problem Solving
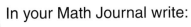

21. A farmer plants 2745 tomato plants in 9 rows. Each row has the same number of tomato plants. How many tomato plants are in each row?

22. Mr. Rivera plants 2800 corn plants in 8 rows. Each row has an equal number of corn plants. How many corn plants are in each row?

23. Julia stores 3535 cans of juice on 7 shelves in a stockroom. Each shelf has the same number of cans of juice stored on it. How many cans of juice are stored on each shelf?

24. Ms. Murphy buys juice for the 308 students in the camp. There are 6 cans of juice in a pack. How many packs of juice should Ms. Murphy order?

25. Mr. O'Brien needs 250 fruit bars for all the children in the camp. There are 8 fruit bars in a box. How many boxes of fruit bars should Mr. O'Brien order?

26. A vendor packs 784 apricots in 6 cases. Each case holds the same number of apricots. How many apricots are in each case? How many apricots are left over?

27. In your Math Journal write:

- When a zero must be placed in the quotient.

- What a zero in the quotient indicates.

CRITICAL THINKING — Algebra

28. Find the missing factor:

- $n \times 0 = 9$

- $n \times 0 = 0$

29. How do the multiplication sentences in exercise 28 show that you can *never* divide by 0?

3-6

Short Division

A travel agent sold an equal number of tickets for each of 7 destinations. If the agent sold a total of 2996 tickets, how many tickets did he sell for each destination?

To find how many tickets were sold for each destination, divide: $2996 \div 7 = n$.

▶ To divide using short division:

- Divide to find the first digit of the quotient.

$$7\overline{)2\ 9\ ^19\ 6} \qquad \begin{array}{l} 4 \times 7 = 28 \\ 29 - 28 = 1 \end{array}$$

- Multiply and subtract mentally.

$$7\overline{)2\ 9\ ^19\ ^56} \qquad \begin{array}{l} 2 \times 7 = 14 \\ 19 - 14 = 5 \end{array}$$

- Write each remainder in front of the next digit in the dividend.

$$7\overline{)2\ 9\ ^19\ ^56} \qquad \begin{array}{l} 8 \times 7 = 56 \\ 56 - 56 = 0 \end{array}$$

- Repeat the steps until the division is completed.

- Check. $\qquad 7 \times 428 = 2996$

The travel agent sold 428 tickets for each destination.

Study these examples.

$$8\overline{)6\ 4,4\ ^44\ ^48} \qquad \begin{array}{l} \textbf{Not enough hundreds} \\ \text{Write zero.} \end{array}$$

quotient: 8 0 5 6

$$7\overline{)7\ 5,^52\ ^37\ ^24\ 3} \qquad \begin{array}{l} \text{Write the} \\ \text{remainder.} \end{array}$$

quotient: 1 0, 7 5 3 R3

Use short division to divide. Then check.

1. $2\overline{)723}$ **2.** $4\overline{)965}$ **3.** $3\overline{)756}$ **4.** $5\overline{)125}$

5. $4\overline{)7364}$ **6.** $5\overline{)8740}$ **7.** $3\overline{)6147}$ **8.** $7\overline{)6566}$

9. $9\overline{)47,376}$ **10.** $8\overline{)56,365}$ **11.** $6\overline{)85,742}$ **12.** $4\overline{)104,232}$

Practice

Use short division to find the quotient.

13. $2\overline{)806}$ 14. $4\overline{)408}$ 15. $2\overline{)614}$ 16. $7\overline{)749}$

17. $4\overline{)8360}$ 18. $3\overline{)3015}$ 19. $6\overline{)6246}$ 20. $7\overline{)7630}$

21. $9\overline{)93,609}$ 22. $8\overline{)80,416}$ 23. $6\overline{)72,186}$ 24. $8\overline{)84,008}$

25. $5\overline{)78,025}$ 26. $4\overline{)28,084}$ 27. $9\overline{)96,228}$ 28. $7\overline{)14,357}$

29. $3\overline{)120,066}$ 30. $5\overline{)303,450}$ 31. $7\overline{)284,914}$ 32. $9\overline{)162,459}$

Problem Solving

33. An airplane travels 3920 miles in 7 hours. How many miles does it travel in one hour?

34. There are 3488 greeting cards in packs. Each pack holds 8 cards. How many packs of cards are there in all?

35. A loaf of bread uses 9 ounces of flour. How many loaves of bread can 3501 ounces of flour make?

36. A machine produces 3360 clips in 8 minutes. How many clips does it produce in one minute?

37. There are 378 people going on a field trip. Nine buses are hired for the trip. If the same number of people ride in each bus, how many people ride in each bus?

38. There were 10,050 tickets sold for a 3-game series. If the same number of tickets was sold for each game, how many tickets were sold for each game?

39. A bicyclist is planning a 1500-mile trip. His average speed is 8 miles per hour. Will the trip take more or less than 200 hours? Explain your answer.

MENTAL MATH

Find the quotient.

40. $9000 \div 30$ 41. $1600 \div 40$ 42. $3600 \div 60$

43. $15,000 \div 500$ 44. $81,000 \div 900$ 45. $63,000 \div 700$

46. $240,000 \div 800$ 47. $180,000 \div 200$ 48. $420,000 \div 600$

49. $480,000 \div 8000$ 50. $540,000 \div 6000$ 51. $630,000 \div 9000$

Explore Divisibility

Materials: paper, pencil

A number is <u>divisible</u> by another number when you divide and the remainder is zero.

Some numbers in the hundred chart below are divisible by 2. List and examine these numbers.

1. What do the ones digits of all the numbers have in common?

2. What rule can you write to show that a number is divisible by 2?

3. Use your rule to write some numbers that are divisible by 2. Check by dividing.

Suppose you want to test the numbers in your list of numbers that are divisible by 2 for divisibility by 4.

4. Divide to find which numbers are divisible by 4.

5. Now divide to find which of these numbers: 316; 520; 8634; 1722; 68,616; and 95,628 are divisible by 4. Then find the two-digit number formed by the tens and ones digits of each of these given numbers. What do you notice about the two-digit numbers?

6. What rule can you write to show that a number is divisible by 4?

7. Use your rule to write some numbers that are divisible by 4. Check by dividing.

Now test the numbers in the hundred chart for divisibility by 3.

8. Divide to find which numbers are divisible by 3. List the numbers.

1	2	3	4	5	6	7	8	9	10
11	12	13	14	15	16	17	18	19	20
21	22	23	24	25	26	27	28	29	30
31	32	33	34	35	36	37	38	39	40
41	42	43	44	45	46	47	48	49	50
51	52	53	54	55	56	57	58	59	60
61	62	63	64	65	66	67	68	69	70
71	72	73	74	75	76	77	78	79	80
81	82	83	84	85	86	87	88	89	90
91	92	93	94	95	96	97	98	99	100

9. Find the sum of the digits of each number divisible by 3. What do you notice about each of these sums?

10. What rule can you write to show that a number is divisible by 3?

11. Use the rule for divisibility by 3 as a model to write a rule for divisibility by 9.

Now test the numbers in the hundred chart for divisibility by 5.

12. Divide to find which numbers are divisible by 5. List and examine these numbers.

13. What are the ones digits of these numbers?

14. What rule can you write to show that a number is divisible by 5?

15. Use the rule for divisibility by 5 as a model to write a rule for divisibility by 10.

Communicate

16. If a number is divisible by 4, is it always divisible by 2? Explain your answer.

17. If a number is divisible by 10, is it always divisible by 5? Explain your answer.

18. If a number is divisible by 9, is it always divisible by 3? Explain your answer.

19. If a number is divisible by 3 and 2, by what number is it also divisible? How do you know?

Write About It

20. Create boxes such as these. Then challenge your classmates to find what number does *not* belong and explain why.

21	72
105	202

75	20
4	45

18	603
906	27

22	72
52	36

Divisibility and Mental Math

Divisibility rules can help you decide if one number is divisible by another number.

The chart below shows the divisibility rules for 2, 5, 10, 4, 3, 9, and 6.

Rule A number is divisible	Example
by 2 if its ones digit is divisible by 2.	20, 42, 84, 936, 1048 are divisible by 2. **Think** All even numbers are divisible by 2.
by 5 if its ones digit is 0 or 5.	60, 135, 4890, 53,965 are divisible by 5.
by 10 if its ones digit is 0.	70, 860, 4050, 96,780 are divisible by 10.
by 4 if its tens and ones digits form a number that is divisible by 4.	$6128 \longrightarrow 28 \div 4 = 7.$ $31,816 \longrightarrow 16 \div 4 = 4.$ 6128 and 31,816 are divisible by 4.
by 3 if the sum of its digits is divisible by 3.	$27 \longrightarrow 2 + 7 = 9$ and $9 \div 3 = 3.$ $3591 \longrightarrow 3 + 5 + 9 + 1 = 18$ and $18 \div 3 = 6.$ 27 and 3591 are divisible by 3.
by 9 if the sum of its digits is divisible by 9.	$216 \longrightarrow 2 + 1 + 6 = 9$ and $9 \div 9 = 1.$ $5058 \longrightarrow 5 + 0 + 5 + 8 = 18$ and $18 \div 9 = 2.$ 216 and 5058 are divisible by 9.
by 6 if it is divisible by both 2 and 3.	516 is divisible by both 2 and 3. 516 is divisible by 6.

Practice

Tell which numbers are divisible by 2.

1. 24 **2.** 47 **3.** 98 **4.** 436 **5.** 569 **6.** 760

7. 6135 **8.** 9842 **9.** 7764 **10.** 57,961 **11.** 79,778 **12.** 490,893

Tell which numbers are divisible by 5. Tell which are divisible by 10.

13. 65 **14.** 90 **15.** 873 **16.** 745 **17.** 4000 **18.** 9154

19. 35,960 **20.** 45,782 **21.** 73,590 **22.** 94,615 **23.** 870,520 **24.** 791,621

Tell which numbers are divisible by 4.

25. 96   **26.** 82   **27.** 324   **28.** 422   **29.** 3820   **30.** 9416

31. 79,131   **32.** 83,536   **33.** 20,904   **34.** 72,072   **35.** 131,616   **36.** 806,300

Tell which numbers are divisible by 3. Tell which numbers are divisible by 9.

37. 69   **38.** 87   **39.** 135   **40.** 159   **41.** 4320   **42.** 3519

43. 71,415   **44.** 83,721   **45.** 95,580   **46.** 81,693   **47.** 100,512   **48.** 560,373

Tell which numbers are divisible by 6.

49. 84   **50.** 93   **51.** 204   **52.** 396   **53.** 1029   **54.** 5415

55. 11,712   **56.** 30,609   **57.** 28,514   **58.** 72,144   **59.** 503,640   **60.** 712,820

Write whether each number is divisible by 2, 3, 4, 5, 6, 9, and/or 10.

61. 1425   **62.** 2360   **63.** 4390   **64.** 6570   **65.** 8735   **66.** 9822

67. 12,360   **68.** 19,585   **69.** 23,130   **70.** 335,412   **71.** 240,120   **72.** 350,262

Problem Solving   Use the chart.

A number of students at Kennedy School are to be divided into equal groups for activities during the school's field day.

Can the number of students be divided into groups of 2? groups of 3? groups of 4? groups of 5? groups of 6? groups of 9? groups of 10?

	Number of Students	Number of Students in Each Group						
		2	3	4	5	6	9	10
73.	48	?	?	?	?	?	?	?
74.	180	?	?	?	?	?	?	?
75.	315	?	?	?	?	?	?	?
76.	1080	?	?	?	?	?	?	?

CRITICAL THINKING

77. How many numbers between 200 and 225 are divisible by 10? by 5? by 2? by 3? by 9? by 4? by 6?

78. How many numbers between 150 and 200 are divisible by both 3 and 5? by both 4 and 10? by both 6 and 9?

Estimation: Compatible Numbers

Seven Siberian tigers at the city zoo eat 2075 pounds of meat each week. If the tigers eat equal amounts, about how many pounds of meat does each tiger eat each week?

To find about how many pounds, estimate: 2075 ÷ 7.

▶ To estimate quotients using compatible numbers:

- Use a basic fact to help you find compatible numbers.

- Divide.

$$2075 \div 7$$

> **Think**
> $2100 \div 7 = 300$

> Compatible numbers are numbers that are easy to compute mentally.

Each tiger eats about 300 pounds of meat each week.

▶ Compatible-number estimation may use different sets of numbers to estimate a quotient.

Estimate: 17,652 ÷ 4

> **Think**
> $17,652 \div 4$ ⟶ $16,000 \div 4 = 4000$
> ⟶ $20,000 \div 4 = 5000$

So 17,652 ÷ 4 is about 4000, or 17,652 ÷ 4 is about 5000.

> Both estimates are correct.

Study these examples.

Estimate: 8325 ÷ 41

> **Think**
> $8000 \div 40 = 200$

So 8325 ÷ 41 is about 200.

Estimate: 63,356 ÷ 56

> **Think**
> $60,000 \div 60 = 1000$

So 63,356 ÷ 56 is about 1000.

Write each division using compatible numbers.

1. 1758 ÷ 4
2. 3951 ÷ 5
3. 7453 ÷ 8
4. 8326 ÷ 9

5. 9875 ÷ 23
6. 4282 ÷ 34
7. 63,792 ÷ 59
8. 84,796 ÷ 78

Estimate the quotient.

9. 1957 ÷ 4
10. 4893 ÷ 5
11. 6397 ÷ 8
12. 3319 ÷ 9

13. 2679 ÷ 83
14. 8529 ÷ 92
15. 4813 ÷ 68
16. 7945 ÷ 94

17. 83,592 ÷ 94
18. 39,125 ÷ 58
19. 61,958 ÷ 75
20. 38,958 ÷ 49

Estimate to compare. Write <, =, or >.

21. 27,903 ÷ 7 _?_ 35,903 ÷ 9
22. 5798 ÷ 3 _?_ 11,938 ÷ 6

23. 2829 ÷ 23 _?_ 4173 ÷ 13
24. 12,636 ÷ 24 _?_ 15,296 ÷ 32

25. 46,879 ÷ 18 _?_ 49,362 ÷ 19
26. 69,135 ÷ 27 _?_ 56,238 ÷ 16

Problem Solving

27. Jane earned $557 for a 5-day job. About how much did she earn each day?

28. Mr. Duffy earns $38,796 a year. About how much does he earn in one month?

29. Bamboo is so low in nutrients that a giant panda eats as much as 80 lb of it in 12 hours. About how many pounds can it eat in one hour?

30. While hunting, a cheetah can cover 1310 ft of ground in as few as 60 strides. About how many feet does it travel in 5 strides?

DO YOU REMEMBER?

Match each definition with a term in the box.

31. the written form of a number that shows the place value of each of its digits

32. one of two or more numbers that are multiplied to form a product

33. an approximate answer; to find an answer that is close to the exact answer

34. to find addends that are nearly alike in order to estimate their sum

standard form

estimate

expanded form

clustering

factor

Teens as Divisors

You may have to change your estimate more than once
when the divisor is a number from 11 through 19.

Divide: $11{,}378 \div 13 = n$.

| Decide where to begin the quotient. | $13\overline{)11{,}378}$ $13\overline{)11{,}378}$ | **Think** $13 > 11$ **Not enough thousands** $13 < 113$ **Enough hundreds** |

The quotient begins in the hundreds place.

Estimate: $13\overline{)11{,}378}$

Try 9.

Think
$$\begin{array}{r} 10 \\ 10\overline{)100} \end{array}$$

A quotient digit *cannot* be greater than 9.

| Divide the hundreds. | | Divide the tens. | Divide the ones. | Check. |

$$
\begin{array}{r}
9 \\
13\overline{)1\,1{,}3\,7\,8} \\
1\,1\,7
\end{array}
$$

Too large.
Try 8.

$$
\begin{array}{r}
8 \\
13\overline{)1\,1{,}3\,7\,8} \\
-1\,0\,4 \\
\hline
9\,7
\end{array}
$$

$$
\begin{array}{r}
8\,7 \\
13\overline{)1\,1{,}3\,7\,8} \\
-1\,0\,4 \\
\hline
9\,7 \\
-9\,1 \\
\hline
6\,8
\end{array}
$$

$$
\begin{array}{r}
8\,7\,5 \text{ R3} \\
13\overline{)1\,1{,}3\,7\,8} \\
-1\,0\,4 \\
\hline
9\,7 \\
-9\,1 \\
\hline
6\,8 \\
-6\,5 \\
\hline
3
\end{array}
$$

$$
\begin{array}{r}
8\,7\,5 \\
\times \quad\quad 1\,3 \\
\hline
2\,6\,2\,5 \\
+ \quad 8\,7\,5 \\
\hline
1\,1\,3\,7\,5 \\
+ \quad\quad\quad 3 \\
\hline
1\,1{,}3\,7\,8
\end{array}
$$

Complete each division.

1.
$$
\begin{array}{r}
9 \\
15\overline{)1\,3\,5} \\
-?\,?\,? \\
\hline
?
\end{array}
$$

2.
$$
\begin{array}{r}
8 \text{ R } \underline{?} \\
17\overline{)1\,4\,9} \\
-?\,?\,? \\
\hline
?
\end{array}
$$

3.
$$
\begin{array}{r}
9 \\
17\overline{)1\,5\,2\,1} \\
1\,5\,3
\end{array}
$$

Try 8.

$$
\begin{array}{r}
8\,? \text{ R } \underline{?} \\
17\overline{)1\,5\,2\,1} \\
-?\,?\,? \\
\hline
?\,?\,? \\
-?\,?\,? \\
\hline
?
\end{array}
$$

Divide and check.

4. $14\overline{)129}$

5. $18\overline{)144}$

6. $13\overline{)403}$

7. $15\overline{)780}$

8. $19\overline{)950}$

9. $15\overline{)498}$

10. $14\overline{)747}$

11. $17\overline{)884}$

Find the quotient and the remainder. Then check.

12. 19)1578   **13.** 17)1462   **14.** 18)1693   **15.** 15)1159

16. 18)3427   **17.** 17)2869   **18.** 14)3609   **19.** 13)3921

20. 12)10,512   **21.** 18)16,038   **22.** 17)13,243   **23.** 19)18,981

24. 14)73,501   **25.** 12)13,732   **26.** 13)13,296   **27.** 15)16,438

28. 11)115,932   **29.** 13)148,732   **30.** 14)193,475   **31.** 16)167,652

Problem Solving

32. A tank containing 336 gallons of fuel can be emptied in 12 minutes. How many gallons of fuel can be emptied in one minute?

33. A plane uses 570 gallons of gasoline in a 15-hour trip. How many gallons of gasoline does it use in one hour?

34. Albert traveled 4000 miles in 16 days. If he traveled the same number of miles each day, how many miles did he travel each day?

35. Melissa puts 420 photos in an album. Each page of the album holds 14 photos. How many pages does she fill?

36. There are 540 children enrolled in Valley School. If there are 18 classrooms in the school, what is the average number of students in each classroom?

CRITICAL THINKING

Find the errors in the division process. Then make the corrections.

37.
```
         9 R3
  12)1 0 8 3
    −1 0 8
          3
```

38.
```
        1 3
  17)1 7 5 1
    −1 7
        5 1
      −5 1
          0
```

39.
```
       1 5  1
  13)1 9,5 1 3
    −1 3
      6 5
     −6 5
          1 3
        −1 3
             0
```

40.
```
         8 6 3
  18)1 5 5,3 4 0
    −1 4 4
      1 1 3
     −1 0 8
          5 4
        −5 4
            0
```

Two-Digit Divisors

Mr. Jansen has 1825 tickets to distribute to his
23 salespersons. If he distributes the tickets equally
among his salespersons, how many tickets does
each one receive? How many tickets are left over?

To find how many tickets each salesperson receives,
divide: $1825 \div 23 = n$.

Decide where to begin the quotient.	$23\overline{)1825}$ $23\overline{)1825}$

Think

$23 > 18$ **Not enough hundreds**

$23 < 182$ **Enough tens**

The quotient begins in the tens place.

Estimate: $23\overline{)1825}$

Try 9.

Think

$\begin{array}{r} 9 \\ 20\overline{)180} \end{array}$

Divide the tens.

$$\begin{array}{r} 9 \\ 23\overline{)1\,8\,2\,5} \\ 2\,0\,7 \end{array}$$

Too large
Try 8.

$$\begin{array}{r} 8 \\ 23\overline{)1\,8\,2\,5} \\ 1\,8\,4 \end{array}$$

Too large
Try 7.

$$\begin{array}{r} 7 \\ 23\overline{)1\,8\,2\,5} \\ -1\,6\,1 \downarrow \\ \hline 2\,1\,5 \end{array}$$

Divide the ones.

$$\begin{array}{r} 7\,9 \text{ R8} \\ 23\overline{)1\,8\,2\,5} \\ -1\,6\,1 \downarrow \\ \hline 2\,1\,5 \\ -2\,0\,7 \\ \hline 8 \end{array}$$

Check.

$$\begin{array}{r} 7\,9 \\ \times\quad 2\,3 \\ \hline 2\,3\,7 \\ 1\,5\,8 \\ \hline 1\,8\,1\,7 \\ +\qquad 8 \\ \hline 1\,8\,2\,5 \end{array}$$

Each salesperson receives 79 tickets.
There are 8 tickets left over.

Study these examples.

$$\begin{array}{r} 1\,0 \text{ R33} \\ 45\overline{)4\,8\,3} \\ -4\,5 \downarrow \\ \hline 3\,3 \end{array}$$

Not enough ones
Write zero in the
quotient.

$$\begin{array}{r} 1\,6\,0 \\ 29\overline{)4\,6\,4\,0} \\ -2\,9 \downarrow \\ \hline 1\,7\,4 \\ -1\,7\,4 \\ \hline 0 \end{array}$$

No ones
Write zero in
the quotient.

Complete each division.

1. 41)8 6 → 2 R ?
   −? ?
   ?

2. 32)6 7 2 → 2 ?
   −? ?
   ? ?
   −? ?
   ?

3. 47)4 2 1 6 → 9
   4 2 3

   Try ?

   47)4 2 1 6 → ? ? R ?
   −? ? ?
   ? ? ?
   −? ? ?
   ? ?

Divide and check.

4. 32)96
5. 22)88
6. 41)205
7. 17)153

8. 61)854
9. 43)688
10. 34)680
11. 27)621

12. 51)358
13. 65)201
14. 82)331
15. 46)283

16. 35)1019
17. 76)3733
18. 44)1456
19. 63)3792

20. 59)1193
21. 36)2884
22. 43)3886
23. 72)4332

24. 45)9542
25. 62)6905
26. 81)9729
27. 76)9884

Problem Solving

28. Roy feeds the birds in the zoo 6500 ounces of birdseed in 52 weeks. How many ounces of birdseed does he feed the birds each week?

29. If 6036 people visit the zoo in 12 days, what is the average number of people who visit the zoo each day?

30. A club collected $5500 in annual membership fees. The annual membership fee is $25. How many club members paid their fees?

CRITICAL THINKING

Find the number.

31. A number between 130 and 140 when divided by 12 has a quotient that contains the same two digits and has no remainder.

32. A number between 2700 and 2800 when divided by 25 has a quotient that contains three odd digits and has no remainder.

Divide Larger Numbers

Buses transported 162,448 fans to games for a season. If 52 fans went on each bus trip, how many trips did the buses make?

To find how many trips, divide: 162,448 ÷ 52 = *n*.

- Decide where to begin the quotient.

  52)162,448

  Divide the thousands first.

  Think
  52 < 162
  Enough thousands

- Divide the thousands.

  Estimate: 52)162,448

  Try 3.

  Think
  $$\frac{3}{50)150}$$

  $$\begin{array}{r} \times\ \ \ 3 \\ 52\overline{)1\ 6\ 2,4\ 4\ 8} \\ \underline{-1\ 5\ 6}\downarrow \\ 6\ 4 \end{array}$$

- Repeat the steps: *estimate, divide, multiply, subtract,* and *compare.*

- Check.

  52 × 3124 = 162,448

  $$\begin{array}{r} 3\ 1\ 2\ 4 \\ 52\overline{)1\ 6\ 2,4\ 4\ 8} \\ \underline{-1\ 5\ 6}\downarrow\ \ \ \ \\ 6\ 4\downarrow\ \ \\ \underline{-5\ 2}\downarrow\ \\ 1\ 2\ 4\ \\ \underline{-1\ 0\ 4}\downarrow \\ 2\ 0\ 8 \\ \underline{-2\ 0\ 8} \\ 0 \end{array}$$

There were 3124 bus trips made.

Study these examples.

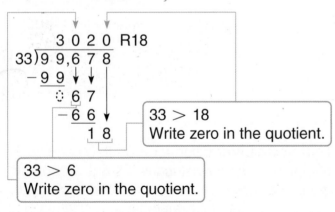

$$\begin{array}{r} 3\ 0\ 2\ 0\ \text{R18} \\ 33\overline{)9\ 9,6\ 7\ 8} \\ \underline{-9\ 9}\downarrow\downarrow\downarrow \\ 6\ 7\ \\ \underline{-6\ 6}\downarrow \\ 1\ 8 \end{array}$$

33 > 18
Write zero in the quotient.

33 > 6
Write zero in the quotient.

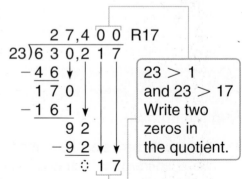

$$\begin{array}{r} 2\ 7,4\ 0\ 0\ \text{R17} \\ 23\overline{)6\ 3\ 0,2\ 1\ 7} \\ \underline{-4\ 6}\downarrow \\ 1\ 7\ 0 \\ \underline{-1\ 6\ 1}\downarrow \\ 9\ 2 \\ \underline{-9\ 2}\downarrow\downarrow \\ 1\ 7 \end{array}$$

23 > 1
and 23 > 17
Write two zeros in the quotient.

Divide and check.

1. 63)31,550
2. 34)32,200
3. 57)22,850
4. 72)56,890
5. 62)29,145
6. 43)42,145
7. 54)37,841
8. 92)82,890
9. 27)553,529
10. 16)521,613
11. 29)884,560
12. 21)430,629

Estimate. Then find the quotient.

13. 42)193,242
14. 32)876,821
15. 27)105,595
16. 26)174,590
17. 58)349,334
18. 64)493,444
19. 91)364,460
20. 82)582,692
21. 77)273,080
22. 47)991,985
23. 39)928,210
24. 53)483,651

Divide. Use mental math or paper and pencil.
Explain the method you used.

25. 90)63,000
26. 39)45,164
27. 80)32,320
28. 41)12,500
29. 56)420,810
30. 45)180,000
31. 27)101,520
32. 17)170,006

Problem Solving

33. There are 43,560 apples to be shipped to stores. If 72 apples are packed in each box, how many boxes of apples are to be shipped?

34. There are 38,912 pears to be boxed. If each box contains 64 pears, how many boxes are needed for the pears?

35. A stadium has 98,400 seats in all. How many rows of seats does the stadium have if each row has 96 seats?

36. If there are 32 nails in a box, how many boxes are needed to pack 65,852 nails?

37. If a bus seats 52 passengers, how many buses will be needed to transport 162,478 fans to games for the entire season?

CRITICAL THINKING

38. What is the greatest number of digits you can have in a quotient if you divide a 6-digit number by a 2-digit number? What is the least number? Explain how you found your answers.

Divide Money

Ms. Taylor paid $133.65 for 27 identical boxes of school supplies. How much did she pay for each box of supplies?

To find the cost of a box of supplies, divide: $133.65 ÷ 27 = *n*.

▶ To divide money:

- Place the dollar sign and the decimal point in the quotient.

$$\begin{array}{r} \$. \\ 27\overline{)\$\ 1\ 3\ 3.6\ 5} \end{array}$$

- Divide as usual.

$$\begin{array}{r} \$4.9\ 5 \\ 27\overline{)\$\ 1\ 3\ 3.6\ 5} \\ -\ 1\ 0\ 8 \\ \hline 2\ 5\ 6 \\ -\ 2\ 4\ 3 \\ \hline 1\ 3\ 5 \\ -\ 1\ 3\ 5 \\ \hline 0 \end{array}$$

- Check: 27 × $4.95 = $133.65

Ms. Taylor paid $4.95 for each box.

Study these examples.

$$\begin{array}{r} \$3.0\ 7 \\ 42\overline{)\$\ 1\ 2\ 8.9\ 4} \\ -\ 1\ 2\ 6 \\ \hline 2\ 9\ 4 \\ -\ 2\ 9\ 4 \\ \hline 0 \end{array}$$

29 < 42
Write zero in the quotient.

$$\begin{array}{r} \$2.3\ 0 \\ 53\overline{)\$\ 1\ 2\ 1.9\ 0} \\ -\ 1\ 0\ 6 \\ \hline 1\ 5\ 9 \\ -\ 1\ 5\ 9 \\ \hline 0 \end{array}$$

There are no pennies. Write zero in the quotient.

Practice

Complete each division.

1.
$$\begin{array}{r} \$2.?\ ? \\ 6\overline{)\$\ 1\ 6.1\ 4} \\ -\ 1\ 2 \\ \hline 4\ 1 \\ -\ ?\ ? \\ \hline ?\ ? \\ -\ ?\ ? \\ \hline ? \end{array}$$

2.
$$\begin{array}{r} \$7.?\ ? \\ 13\overline{)\$\ 9\ 7.7\ 6} \\ -\ ?\ ? \\ \hline ?\ ? \\ -\ ?\ ? \\ \hline ?\ ? \\ -\ ?\ ? \\ \hline ? \end{array}$$

3.
$$\begin{array}{r} \$?.?\ ? \\ 29\overline{)\$\ 2\ 0\ 0.6\ 8} \\ -\ 1\ 7\ 4 \\ \hline ?\ ?\ ? \\ -\ ?\ ?\ ? \\ \hline ?\ ? \\ -\ ?\ ? \\ \hline ? \end{array}$$

Divide and check.

4. 4)$15.12   5. 3)$6.27   6. 8)$159.60   7. 7)$107.10

8. 54)$14.04   9. 47)$39.95   10. 67)$62.31   11. 24)$13.68

12. 19)$114.00   13. 26)$208.00   14. 15)$139.50   15. 42)$153.30

16. 28)$157.92   17. 31)$186.62   18. 53)$365.70   19. 85)$177.65

20. 34)$173.06   21. 47)$325.24   22. 32)$322.56   23. 11)$250.25

24. 17)$402.05   25. 23)$530.15   26. 19)$1179.71   27. 21)$1997.10

Problem Solving

Use the table for problems 28–31.

How much does each box of each kind of card cost?

28. Thank you cards

29. Get well cards

30. Birthday cards

31. Anniversary cards

Quantity	Item	Total Cost
25 boxes	Thank you cards	$ 86.25
32 boxes	Get well cards	$155.20
46 boxes	Birthday cards	$273.70
18 boxes	Anniversary cards	$125.10

Choose a computation method. Use mental math or paper and pencil. Explain the method you used. Write whether you estimated or found an exact answer.

32. Mark earned $536.10 in 6 days. If he earned the same amount of money each day, how much did he earn each day?

33. Fifteen part-time workers earned $424.80. About how much did each worker receive if the money was divided equally?

34. An art supply kit costs $67.75 per student per year. Is $2300 enough to supply an art class of 28?

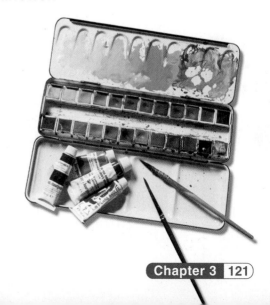

Order of Operations

The order of operations is a set of rules that is used to simplify mathematical expressions with more than one operation.

Compute: $3 + 7 \times 1 - 4 \div 2$

▶ To simplify a mathematical expression using the order of operations:

- *First* multiply or divide. Work from left to right.

- *Then* add or subtract. Work from left to right.

$3 + \underbrace{7 \times 1}_{} - \underbrace{4 \div 2}_{}$

$\underbrace{3 + 7}_{} \quad - \quad 2$

$10 \quad - \quad 2 \ = 8$

Compute: $(8 \times 3) \div (4 + 2)$

▶ When there are parentheses in a mathematical expression, do the operations within the parentheses *first*. Then follow the order of operations.

- Do operations with parentheses.

- Divide.

$\underbrace{(8 \times 3)}_{} \div \underbrace{(4 + 2)}_{}$

$24 \quad \div \quad 6 \ = 4$

Study these examples.

$\underbrace{(56 \div 8)}_{} - 2 + \underbrace{(5 + 6)}_{} \times 3$

$7 \quad - 2 + \underbrace{11 \times 3}_{}$

$\underbrace{7 \quad - 2}_{} + \quad 33$

$5 \quad + \quad 33 = 38$

$19 + \underbrace{21 \div 7}_{} \times 8 - 13$

$19 + \underbrace{3 \quad \times 8}_{} - 13$

$19 + \quad 24 \quad - 13$

$\underbrace{43}_{} \qquad - 13 = 30$

Compute.

1. $8 \times 2 \div 4$

2. $4 \times 6 + 3$

3. $2 \times 7 - 4$

4. $81 \div 9 - 3$

5. $64 \div 8 + 5$

6. $8 + 3 \times 4 - 5$

7. $9 + 45 \div 5 - 3$

8. $9 \times 4 \div 6 + 7$

9. $48 \div 6 \times 3 - 5$

10. $27 - 16 \div 4 + 2$

11. $18 - 3 \times 2 + 9$

12. $81 \div 9 - 2 \times 3$

Practice

Use the order of operations to compute.

13. $4 - 9 \div 3 - 1$

14. $16 \div 4 + 2 \times 6$

15. $(3 \times 7) + (64 \div 8)$

16. $(18 - 9) \div (1 + 2)$

17. $20 + 6 \div 3 - 7$

18. $24 - 8 \div 4 \times 3$

19. $18 \times (11 - 6)$

20. $7 + (19 - 2) \times 3$

21. $3 + 5 \times 10 \div 2 + 8$

22. $17 + 63 \div 3 \times 6 - 9$

23. $59 - 45 \div 5 \times 3 + 41$

24. $134 - 8 \div 4 \times 2$

25. $10 \times 4 + (49 \div 7) \times 2$

26. $(35 \div 5) \times 2 + 3 \times 6$

27. $18 - 3 \div 3 + (63 \div 3) - 6$

28. $19 - 4 \times 2 + (19 - 3) \div 4$

29. $(28 \div 7) + 5 - 3 + (7 \times 2)$

30. $4 + (29 - 2) \div 9 + (16 + 2)$

31. $(4 \times 8) - 5 + (0 \div 6)$

32. $(24 \div 6) - 3 + (2 \times 4)$

33. $2 + (3 \times 6) + n$ when $n = 10$

34. $(12 + 72) \div n$ when $n = 6$

35. $(28 + n) \times 4$ when $n = 32$

36. $(9 \times 8) - (n \times 6)$ when $n = 3$

37. $n \times 2 \div 2 + 24$ when $n = 8$

38. $6 + n - 3 \times 6 \div 9$ when $n = 2$

Rewrite each number sentence using parentheses to make it true.

39. $25 - 5 \times 10 \div 2 = 0$

40. $19 - 4 + 3 \div 7 = 18$

41. $3 + 6 \times 5 + 5 = 50$

42. $9 - 5 \times 2 + 6 = 14$

43. $8 + 24 \div 14 - 8 = 12$

44. $27 - 5 + 4 \div 3 = 24$

45. $9 + 5 \div 2 - 4 = 3$

46. $4 \times 3 + 5 - 2 = 30$

CHALLENGE

Use the order of operations to compute.

47. $y + 48 \div n$ when $n = 6$; $y = 12$

48. $a \times b - 12$ when $a = 13$; $b = 29$

49. $4 \times (a + b) + 2$ when $a = 6$; $b = 3$

50. $(n - y) \div (2 \times y)$ when $n = 200$; $y = 40$

Problem-Solving Strategy:
Make a Table/Find a Pattern

A shop rents bicycles and 3-wheeled buggies. Every day Larry checks the 60 wheels on the 25 vehicles for safety. How many of each type of vehicle does he have?

Read

Visualize yourself in the problem above as you reread it. Focus on the facts and the question.

List what you know.

Facts: Shop rents bicycles and
3-wheeled buggies.
There is a total of 25 vehicles.
There is a total of 60 wheels.

Question: How many of each vehicle does the shop rent?

Plan

Make a table to find the different combinations of bicycles and buggies. Look for a pattern to find the combination that has exactly 25 vehicles and 60 wheels.

Bicycles	10	11	12	13
Buggies	15	14	13	12
Wheels	20 + 45 = 65	22 + 42 = 64	24 + 39 = 63	26 + 36 = 62

Notice the pattern in the table. As the number of buggies decreases by 1, so does the total number of wheels. So to get from 65 wheels to 60 wheels, subtract: $65 - 60 = 5$.

Solve

To find the number of buggies, subtract: $15 - 5 = 10$.
There are 10 buggies $(15 - 5)$
and 15 bicycles $(10 + 5)$.

Check

15 bicycles: $2 \times 15 = 30$ wheels
10 buggies: $3 \times 10 = 30$ wheels
$25 \overset{?}{=} 10 + 15$ Yes. $60 \overset{?}{=} 30 + 30$ Yes.

Make a table and find a pattern to solve each problem.

1. Cassie's grandparents gave her $1 for her first birthday. Each year after, they gave her $1 more than the year before. How much money will they have given her by her 20th birthday?

 Read Visualize yourself in the problem above as you reread it. Focus on the facts and the question.

List what you know.

Facts: 1st birthday—$1
every birthday after—$1 more than the year before

Question: How much money will they have given her by her 20th birthday?

Plan List the addends.
$1 + $2 + $3 + $4 + $5 + $6 + . . . + $18 + $19 + $20

Try solving a similar problem and look for a pattern.
By adding the first and last addends in the sequence the sums are equal.
There are 3 sets of 7.

Think
$3 \times 7 = 21$

$$1 + 2 + 3 + 4 + 5 + 6$$
7
7
7

First add the first and last addends from the problem.
Divide the last number by 2 to find the number of sets.
Then multiply the number of sets by the sum.

Solve   **Check**

2. Nancy bought a bag of red, white, and blue balloons for the party. There were 49 balloons in the bag. If there are 2 times as many red as blue and half as many white as blue, how many of each color balloon are in the bag?

3. The temperature at 10:00 P.M. was 37°F. If it dropped 2°F every hour until 4:00 A.M. and then rose 4°F each hour after that, what was the temperature at noon the next day?

Write Your Own

4. Write a problem using the Make a Table/Find a Pattern strategy. Have someone solve it.

Problem-Solving Applications: Mixed Review

Read ▶ **Plan** ▶ **Solve** ▶ **Check**

Solve each problem. Explain the method you used.

1. The Stampton Post Office sold 3768 stamps yesterday. The office was open for 8 hours, and business was steady all day. About how many stamps were sold each hour?

2. Mae came to the post office and bought a sheet of 40 stamps for $14.80. What is the cost of each stamp?

3. Allen bought a sheet of 50 stamps for $40.00. How much did each stamp cost?

4. In a busy hour, 3 clerks can each serve about the same number of customers. There are 90 customers. About how many customers can each clerk serve in an hour?

5. The office has 444 post office boxes arranged in rows. There are 37 equal rows of boxes. How many boxes are in each row?

6. There are 12 mail carriers in Stampton. Monday, they delivered 24,780 letters. Each carrier delivered the same number of letters. How many letters did each carrier deliver?

7. A new commemorative Earth stamp is produced on sheets of 40 stamps. One clerk has 840 of the stamps at her station. A customer wants to buy 22 sheets of stamps. Does the clerk have enough?

8. Mr. Jared delivered 8456 letters. He delivered the same number of letters each hour during a 7-hour period. About how many letters did he deliver each hour?

9. Mr. Jared's mail truck logged 51 mi, 47 mi, 63 mi, 54 mi, 44 mi, and 65 mi. What is the average number of miles the truck traveled each day in one workweek?

Choose a strategy from the list or use another strategy you know to solve each problem.

10. There are four postal clerks in cubicles along one wall of the post office: Art, Clay, Don, and Mark. Don is to the left of Mark and at one end. Mark is between Art and Don. Clay is at one end. Who are in the middle cubicles?

11. The first 52 customers to arrive at the post office on Monday came in groups of 4 or 5. How many groups of each size were there?

12. A postal clerk can work a 6-hour or an 8-hour shift. If she worked 44 hours one week, how many shifts of each length did she work?

13. It costs $168 to rent a post office box for one year. At that rate how much does it cost to rent a box for five months?

14. Each page of Cathy's stamp album holds 12 stamps. If she has 377 stamps to put in her album, how many more stamps does she need to fill a page?

15. Danielle sorts letters into bins. She sorts 302 letters into the first bin, 413 letters into the second bin, and 524 letters into the third. If the pattern continues, how many letters will she put into the sixth and seventh bins?

Strategy File

Use These Strategies
Make a Table/Find a Pattern
Interpret the Remainder
Use a Graph
More Than One Solution
Guess and Test
Logical Reasoning
Use More Than One Step

Use the bar graph for problems 16 and 17.

16. Letters are delivered 6 days a week. About how many letters were delivered each day during the first week of August? during the fourth week? during the whole month?

17. What is the average number of letters delivered each week in August?

August Postal Data

CRITICAL THINKING

18. Zip codes help postal workers sort mail. How many 5-digit zip codes begin with the digits 100_ _? Write in your Math Journal about the strategies you use to solve this problem.

Check Your Progress
Lessons 1–16

Write four related facts using the given numbers. *(See pp. 96–97.)*

1. 6, 7, 42   **2.** 5, 9, 45   **3.** 8, 9, 72   **4.** 3, 4, 12

Find the quotients. *(See pp. 98–99.)*

5. $63 \div 9$
$630 \div 9$
$6300 \div 9$
$63{,}000 \div 9$

6. $54 \div 6$
$540 \div 60$
$5400 \div 600$
$54{,}000 \div 6000$

7. $35 \div 7$
$350 \div 70$
$3500 \div 70$
$35{,}000 \div 70$

Use basic facts to find the value of *n*.

8. $64{,}000 \div 80 = n$ **9.** $150{,}000 \div n = 3000$ **10.** $n \div 60 = 400$

Divide and check. *(See pp. 100–107, 114–121.)*

11. $9\overline{)3027}$ **12.** $8\overline{)5866}$ **13.** $24\overline{)49}$ **14.** $41\overline{)984}$

15. $31\overline{)1836}$ **16.** $15\overline{)945}$ **17.** $86\overline{)68{,}906}$ **18.** $73\overline{)78{,}146}$

19. $28\overline{)\$56.56}$ **20.** $17\overline{)\$35.02}$ **21.** $26\overline{)\$286.26}$ **22.** $64\overline{)\$204.80}$

Write whether each number is divisible by 2, 3, 4, 5, 6, 9, and/or 10. *(See pp. 108–111.)*

23. 90   **24.** 795   **25.** 4152   **26.** 6252   **27.** 70,320

Estimate the quotient. *(See pp. 112–113.)*

28. $845 \div 9$ **29.** $1015 \div 29$ **30.** $1836 \div 15$

Use the order of operations to compute. *(See pp. 122–123.)*

31. $36 - 3 \times 7 + 10 \div 5$ **32.** $(35 \div 7) + 2 \times 3 - 4$

Problem Solving

(See pp. 114–115, 124–127.)

33. Lois has 36 colored pencils. They are either green or red. For every green pencil, Lois has 3 red pencils. How many red pencils does Lois have?

34. Ralph put 1620 canceled stamps in 18 boxes. If he put the same number of stamps in each box, how many stamps were in one box?

(See *Still More Practice*, p. 479.)

Translate Algebraic Expressions

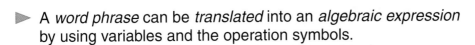

An algebraic expression uses one or more variables and the operation symbols $+$, $-$, $\times$, $\div$.

$$n + 3 \qquad b - 2 \qquad a \times b \text{ or } ab \qquad n \div m \text{ or } \frac{n}{m}$$

▶ A *word phrase* can be *translated* into an *algebraic expression* by using variables and the operation symbols.

Word phrase	Algebraic expression
a more than 7	$7 + a$
b less than 5	$5 - b$
the product of 7*m* and *n*	$7m \times n$ or $7mn$
the sum of *c* and *d*, divided by 9	$(c + d) \div 9$ or $\dfrac{c + d}{9}$

Translate the word phrase into an algebraic expression.

1. *c* increased by 6

2. 5 decreased by *b*

3. twice the product of *m* and *n*

4. *x* divided by *y*

5. 4 less than *a*

6. *m* more than *n*

7. three times *n* increased by 2

8. 10 less than half the sum of *a* and *b*

9. the quotient when 13 added to *m* is divided by 10

10. the difference when twice *c* is subtracted from 25

Represent by an algebraic expression.

11. a distance that is 10 meters shorter than *d* meters

12. a number that is 6 less than a number *n*

13. the cost of *x* suits if each suit costs $150

14. a weight that is 25 lb heavier than *m* lb

15. an amount of money that is twice *y* dollars

16. the width of a rectangle that is half of its length ℓ

17. the total number of days in *w* weeks and *d* days

Chapter 3 Test

Find the value of *n*.

1. $4 \times 7 = n$
   $n \div 7 = 4$

2. $5 \times n = 30$
   $30 \div 5 = n$

3. $n \times 9 = 72$
   $72 \div n = 9$

Divide.

4. $30\overline{)900}$

5. $8\overline{)5600}$

6. $5875 \div 4$

7. $5050 \div 3$

Find the quotient and check.

8. $8\overline{)5982}$

9. $17\overline{)8891}$

10. $51\overline{)1377}$

11. $68\overline{)53,176}$

12. $57\overline{)\$182.40}$

13. $23\overline{)\$276.92}$

Write whether each number is divisible by 2, 3, 4, 5, 6, 9, and/or 10.

14. 360

15. 7155

16. 8472

17. 43,140

Estimate to compare. Write $<$, $=$, or $>$.

18. $298 \div 3 \underline{\ ?\ } 282 \div 4$

19. $1392 \div 7 \underline{\ ?\ } 1821 \div 6$

Problem Solving

Use a strategy you have learned.

20. The scoutmaster ordered 14 buses for 952 people. If he assigned the same number of people to each bus, how many passengers were in each bus?

Tell About It

21. Ray and Mary each estimate a quotient using compatible numbers. Mary uses the same dividend as Ray, but she uses a greater divisor. Whose estimate is higher? Why? Give an example to support your answer.

Performance Assessment

Explain where you can place one set of parentheses in the mathematical expression at the right to result in an answer:

$$30 - 3 \times 10 + 9 \div 3$$

22. greater than 100

23. between 10 and 30

Choose the best answer.

1. In 10,234,567,890 which digit is in the ten-millions place?

   a. 0   **b.** 1
   c. 3   **d.** 9

2. Which is ordered greatest to least?

   a. 8.524; 8.534; 8.53
   b. 8.534; 8.53; 8.524
   c. 8.53; 8.534; 8.524
   d. none of these

3. Estimate.

   $$563,682$$
   $$472,289$$
   $$+\ 186,451$$

   a. 130,000
   b. 930,000
   c. 1,100,000
   d. 1,300,000

4. 3046×6

   a. 18,276
   b. 21,276
   c. 33,412
   d. 18,876

5. Which are divisible by 3?

   a. 18,585; 325,714; 1823
   b. 69,132; 276,204; 2301
   c. 418,608; 45,806; 2002
   d. 115,321; 35,432; 2106

6. $44\overline{)112,928}$

   a. 810
   b. 2160 R1
   c. 2566 R24
   d. 2516 R14

7. Compute.
   Use the order of operations.

   $2 \times 6 + 36 \div 9 - 5$

   a. $\frac{1}{3}$ **b.** 11
   c. 16   **d.** 24

8. Choose the standard form of the number.

   seven billion, three hundred six thousand

   a. 7,000,306,000
   b. 7,000,360,000
   c. 7,306,000,000
   d. 7,360,000,000

9. Which shows 15,695,823 rounded to its greatest place?

   a. 10,000,000
   b. 16,000,000
   c. 200,000,000
   d. 20,000,000

10. Subtract.

    $$726,423$$
    $$-\ 318,619$$

    a. 231,516
    b. 407,804
    c. 914,722
    d. 417,804

11. $217 \times \$25.81$

    a. \$326.98
    b. \$1410.77
    c. \$5600.77
    d. not given

12. Which compatible numbers are used to estimate

    $19\overline{)3817}$?

    a. $20\overline{)4000}$
    b. $9\overline{)3600}$
    c. $40\overline{)2000}$
    d. not given

13. $32\overline{)\$2398.40}$

    a. \$36.81
    b. \$112.14
    c. \$174.95
    d. not given

14. Which number is 1000 more than

    $4\overline{)81,608}$?

    a. 1242
    b. 3402
    c. 20,402
    d. 21,402

15. Which statement illustrates the Associative Property of Multiplication?

a. $3 \times (2 \times 6) = (3 \times 2) \times (3 \times 6)$
b. $3 \times (2 \times 6) = (3 \times 2) \times 6$
c. $3 \times (2 + 6) = (3 \times 2) + (3 \times 6)$
d. $3 \times (2 \times 6) = (2 \times 6) \times 3$

16. Which has an estimated product of 60,000?

a. 329×14
b. 2345×23
c. 289×23
d. 2915×23

17. Choose the standard form.

$600,000 + 400 + 90$

a. 60,490
b. 64,900
c. 600,490
d. 604,900

18. The product is 64. One factor is 8. What is the other factor?

a. 4
b. 6
c. 8
d. 12

19. Marvin bought one shirt for $28.95, a second shirt for $19.99, and a pair of jeans for $27. How much did Martin spend in all?

a. $76.94
b. $75.94
c. $75.95
d. $76.95

20. Jake has 918 cards. He gives an equal number to each of 17 classmates. At most, how many cards does Jake give to each classmate?

a. 27 cards
b. 36 cards
c. 48 cards
d. 54 cards

21. Which statement is true?

a. $100 \times 524 > 10 \times 5240$
b. $30 \times 500 = 15 \times 1000$
c. $300 \times 820 < 244 \times 1000$
d. $60 \times 5000 = 15 \times 200$

22. Estimate the quotient.

$43,362 \div 198$

a. 20
b. 200
c. 2000
d. 20,000

23. Choose the value of the underlined digit.

$0.59\underline{3}$

a. 3 tenths
b. 3 hundredths
c. 3 thousandths
d. not given

24. The divisor is 95. The quotient is 1. What is the dividend?

a. 0
b. 1
c. 90
d. 95

25. Last year Lita read 24 books. This year she read twice that number. How many books did Lita read in the past two years?

a. 72 books
b. 54 books
c. 48 books
d. 36 books

26. At an imaginary bank, each clerk serves the same number of customers. If 3 clerks serve 81 customers in one hour, how many clerks serve 324 customers in one hour?

a. 27 clerks
b. 18 clerks
c. 12 clerks
d. 9 clerks

Explain how you solve the problem. Show all your work.

27. Tom writes a number pattern in which the first number in the pattern is divisible by 2, the second number is divisible by 3, the third number is divisible by 9, and then the pattern repeats itself. Which of these numbers, 240, 250, 260, and 270 could be the 12th number in Tom's pattern?

Number Theory and Fractions

Unfortunately for me, LUNCH is pizza and apple pie. Each pizza is cut into 8 equal slices. Each pie is cut into 6 equal slices. And you know what that means: **fractions**

From *Math Curse* by Jon Scieszka

In this chapter you will:

Explore factors, primes, composites, and multiples

Rename equivalent fractions, improper fractions, and mixed numbers

Find whether a fraction is closer to 0, $\frac{1}{2}$, or 1

Compare and order fractions

Solve problems using organized lists

Critical Thinking/Finding Together

You ate $\frac{1}{4}$ of a pizza and your friend ate $\frac{1}{6}$ of the remainder. What fraction of the pizza was left?

Explore Prime and Composite Numbers

Materials: color tiles, paper, pencil

A rectangular array is an arrangement in which objects are displayed in rows and columns.

Any nonzero whole number can be represented by a rectangular array.

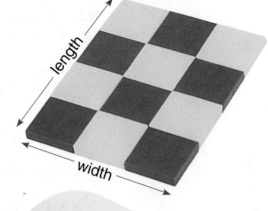

1. Use color tiles to show all the rectangles into which 12 tiles can be arranged. (The figure above shows one rectangle.)

2. How many rectangles can be formed with 12 tiles?

Rectangles can be named by their length times their width. The rectangle above is a 4 × 3 rectangle, with length of 4 tiles and width of 3 tiles.

3. Name all the rectangles formed with 12 tiles.

The length and width of each rectangle are factors of the number. Both 4 and 3 are factors of 12.

4. Name all the factors of 12.

5. How many factors does 12 have?

6. What do you notice about the number of rectangles formed with 12 tiles and the number of factors of 12?

Use color tiles to show all rectangles represented by each number. Write the rectangles and factors for each number.

7. 5	**8.** 9	**9.** 3	**10.** 8	**11.** 10
12. 4	**13.** 15	**14.** 7	**15.** 13	**16.** 6
17. 25	**18.** 20	**19.** 23	**20.** 17	**21.** 19
22. 14	**23.** 18	**24.** 16	**25.** 22	**26.** 21

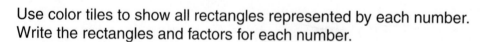

Refer to exercises 7–26.

27. Which numbers have exactly 2 rectangles? more than 2 rectangles?

28. Which numbers have exactly 2 factors? more than 2 factors?

If a whole number is represented by exactly 2 rectangles, then the number is a **prime number**.

29. Which of the numbers in exercises 7–26 are prime numbers?

30. How many factors does a prime number have?

If a whole number is represented by more than 2 rectangles, then the number is a **composite number**.

31. Which of the numbers in exercises 7–26 are composite numbers?

32. How many factors does a composite number have?

33. What do you notice about the number of rectangles and the number of factors of a whole number?

34. Use color tiles to show all rectangles represented by 1. Is 1 a prime number or a composite number? Explain why.

35. Is 2 a prime number or a composite number? Explain your answer.

DO YOU REMEMBER? — *Algebra*

Find the missing factor.

36. $4 \times n = 32$

37. $7 \times n = 56$

38. $5 \times n = 40$

39. $n \times 6 = 48$

40. $n \times 9 = 81$

41. $n \times 10 = 90$

42. $6 \times n = 42$

43. $9 \times n = 45$

44. $3 \times n = 27$

Factors, Primes, and Composites

Factors are numbers that are multiplied to find a product.

$$5 \times 6 = 30 \qquad 5 \times 2 \times 3 = 30$$

factors   factors

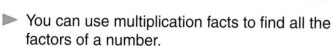

► You can use multiplication facts to find all the factors of a number.

Find all the factors of 30.

$1 \times 30 = 30$ Factors of 30: 1, 2, 3, 5, 6, 10, 15, 30
$2 \times 15 = 30$
$3 \times 10 = 30$
$5 \times 6 = 30$

► A prime number is a number greater than 1 that has *exactly* two factors, itself and 1.

The factors of 2 are 1 and 2.
So 2 is a prime number.

.Think........
 2 × 1 = 2

► A composite number is a number greater than 1 that has *more than* two factors.

The factors of 6 are 1, 2, 3, and 6.
So 6 is a composite number.

> The number 1 is *neither* prime *nor* composite.

List all the factors of each number. Tell if the number is prime or composite.

1. 4
2. 9
3. 13
4. 19
5. 31
6. 49

7. 57
8. 21
9. 37
10. 16
11. 65
12. 69

13. 53
14. 18
15. 32
16. 52
17. 59
18. 63

19. A prime number has exactly _?_ factors.

20. A composite number has _?_ factors.

Practice

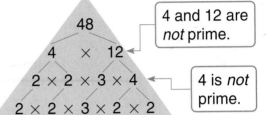

Prime Factorization

A composite number can be shown as the product of prime factors.
This is called prime factorization.

▶ You can use a *factor tree* to find the prime factorization of a number.

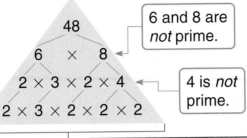

6 and 8 are *not* prime.

4 and 12 are *not* prime.

4 is *not* prime.

4 is *not* prime.

The prime factorization of a number is always the same. The order of the factors does *not* matter.

Prime factorization of 48:
$2 \times 2 \times 2 \times 2 \times 3 = 2^4 \times 3$

The exponent of a number tells how many times the number, called the base, is used as a factor.

Write each number as a product of prime numbers.

21.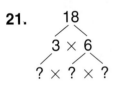
18
3×6
$? \times ? \times ?$

22.
45
$5 \times ?$
$? \times ? \times ?$

23.
72
9×8
$3 \times ? \times 2 \times ?$
$? \times ? \times ? \times ? \times ?$

24.
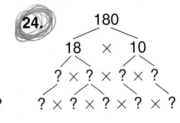
180
18×10
$? \times ? \times ? \times ?$
$? \times ? \times ? \times ? \times ?$

**Use a factor tree to find the prime factorization of each.
Use exponents when appropriate.**

25. 78   26. 90   27. 28   28. 75   29. 50   30. 96

31. 120   32. 128   33. 108   34. 132   35. 138   36. 144

Identify the base and exponent of each number.

37. 4^3 38. 2^4 39. 6^2 40. 2^3 41. 7^2 42. 5^2

CHALLENGE

43. List all the even prime numbers less than 50.

44. List all the odd composite numbers less than 50.

Practice

Greatest Common Factor

The greatest common factor (GCF) of two or more numbers is the largest number that is a factor of these numbers.

▶ To find the greatest common factor (GCF):
- List the factors of each number.
- List the common (same) factors of the numbers.
- Find which common factor is the greatest.

Find the greatest common factor (GCF) of 12 and 27.

$1 \times 12 = 12$　　　$1 \times 27 = 27$
$2 \times 6 = 12$　　　$3 \times 9 = 27$
$3 \times 4 = 12$

Factors of 12:　　Factors of 27:
1, 2, 3, 4, 6, 12　　1, 3, 9, 27

Common factors of 12 and 27: 1, 3
Greatest common factor (GCF) of 12 and 27: 3

Study this example.

Find the greatest common factor (GCF) of 16, 28, and 32.

$1 \times 16 = 16$　　　$1 \times 28 = 28$　　　$1 \times 32 = 32$
$2 \times 8 = 16$　　　$2 \times 14 = 28$　　　$2 \times 16 = 32$
$4 \times 4 = 16$　　　$4 \times 7 = 28$　　　$4 \times 8 = 32$

Factors of 16:　　　Factors of 28:　　　Factors of 32:
1, 2, 4, 8, 16　　　1, 2, 4, 7, 14, 28　　　1, 2, 4, 8, 16, 32

Common factors of 16, 28, and 32: 1, 2, 4
Greatest common factor (GCF) of 16, 28, and 32: 4

Practice

List the factors, common factors, and GCF of each number.

	Number	Factors	Common Factors	GCF
1.	6	? ? ? ?	? ?	?
	10	? ? ? ?		
2.	18	? ? ? ? ? ?	? ? ? ?	?
	24	? ? ? ? ? ? ? ?		

List the factors of each number. Then circle the common factors of each pair of numbers.

3. 6 and 9   **4.** 3 and 15   **5.** 4 and 11   **6.** 18 and 24

7. 16 and 20   **8.** 11 and 26   **9.** 8 and 12   **10.** 10 and 30

List the common factors of each set of numbers. Then circle the GCF.

11. 15 and 21   **12.** 24 and 32   **13.** 12 and 72   **14.** 27 and 36

15. 24 and 36   **16.** 16 and 20   **17.** 14 and 32   **18.** 18 and 36

19. 3, 9, and 15   **20.** 4, 8, and 12   **21.** 24, 36, and 20

Find the GCF of each set of numbers.

22. 45 and 60   **23.** 24 and 40   **24.** 18 and 21   **25.** 16 and 48

26. 30 and 45   **27.** 48 and 56   **28.** 36 and 63   **29.** 36 and 42

30. 12, 15, and 18   **31.** 7, 35, and 49   **32.** 16, 20, and 24

Problem Solving

33. Ms. Durkin wants to package 16 math books and 28 science books equally without mixing the books and with none left over. What is the greatest number of books she can put in each package? How many packages in all will she have?

34. In her coin book, Sylvia wants to arrange 18 French coins and 24 Spanish coins in equal rows on the page. What is the greatest number of Spanish or French coins she can arrange in each row? How many rows will she have?

CRITICAL THINKING

Write True or False for each statement. Explain your answer.

35. One is a common factor of every set of numbers.

36. Zero can be a common factor of a set of numbers.

37. Two numbers can have no common factors.

38. The greatest common factor of two prime numbers is 1.

4-4

Fraction Sense

▶ A fraction can be estimated as closer to 0, $\frac{1}{2}$, or 1.

The number line and the rules below show how a fraction is determined to be *closer to 0, closer to $\frac{1}{2}$,* or *closer to 1.*

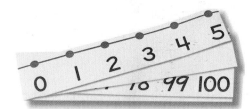

> $\frac{11}{12}$ is *closer to 1.*
> Its numerator is about equal to its denominator.

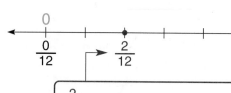

> $\frac{2}{12}$ is *closer to 0.*
> Its numerator is much less than its denominator.

> $\frac{7}{12}$ is *closer to $\frac{1}{2}$.*
> Double the numerator. It is about equal to its denominator.

▶ A fraction can also be estimated by replacing its numerator and/or denominator with compatible numbers.

$\frac{19}{41}$ is about $\frac{20}{40}$ or $\frac{1}{2}$. $\frac{28}{31}$ is about $\frac{30}{30}$ or 1.

$\frac{129}{131}$ is about $\frac{130}{130}$ or 1. $\frac{99}{216}$ is about $\frac{100}{200}$ or $\frac{1}{2}$.

Practice

Write whether each fraction is *closer to 0, closer to $\frac{1}{2}$,* or *closer to 1.*

1. $\frac{5}{8}$ 2. $\frac{1}{9}$ 3. $\frac{6}{7}$ 4. $\frac{8}{11}$ 5. $\frac{7}{15}$ 6. $\frac{19}{20}$

7. $\frac{21}{43}$ 8. $\frac{5}{38}$ 9. $\frac{16}{29}$ 10. $\frac{45}{47}$ 11. $\frac{3}{100}$ 12. $\frac{119}{121}$

Estimate each fraction using compatible numbers.

13. $\frac{31}{59}$ 14. $\frac{16}{25}$ 15. $\frac{87}{91}$ 16. $\frac{201}{400}$ 17. $\frac{105}{201}$ 18. $\frac{498}{501}$

Finding Equivalent Fractions

▶ You can *multiply* or *divide* the numerator and denominator by the *same nonzero number* to find equivalent fractions.

$$\frac{2 \times 2}{6 \times 2} = \frac{4}{12} \qquad \frac{2 \div 2}{6 \div 2} = \frac{1}{3} \qquad \frac{2}{6} = \frac{4}{12} = \frac{1}{3}$$

These are equivalent fractions.

▶ You can also multiply or divide the numerator and denominator by the same nonzero number to find a missing numerator or denominator in equivalent fractions.

$$\frac{5}{8} = \frac{n}{24}$$

Think
$8 \times n = 24$
$8 \times 3 = 24$

$$\frac{5 \times 3}{8 \times 3} = \frac{15}{24}$$

$$\frac{5}{8} = \frac{15}{24} \quad \text{equivalent fractions}$$

$$\frac{18}{27} = \frac{2}{n}$$

Think
$18 \div n = 2$
$18 \div 9 = 2$

$$\frac{18 \div 9}{27 \div 9} = \frac{2}{3}$$

$$\frac{18}{27} = \frac{2}{3} \quad \text{equivalent fractions}$$

Write three equivalent fractions for each.

19. $\frac{1}{9}$ **20.** $\frac{2}{5}$ **21.** $\frac{3}{7}$ **22.** $\frac{7}{9}$ **23.** $\frac{5}{6}$ **24.** $\frac{7}{8}$

Write the missing number to complete the equivalent fraction.

25. $\frac{4}{5} = \frac{n}{25}$ **26.** $\frac{7}{8} = \frac{21}{n}$ **27.** $\frac{21}{49} = \frac{n}{7}$ **28.** $\frac{32}{40} = \frac{4}{n}$

29. $\frac{2}{3} = \frac{4}{a} = \frac{8}{b}$ **30.** $\frac{5}{8} = \frac{10}{a} = \frac{15}{b}$ **31.** $\frac{6}{7} = \frac{12}{a} = \frac{18}{b}$

Problem Solving

32. Four ninths of the class watched the glee club concert. Explain if the class attendance at the concert is less than or more than $\frac{1}{2}$ of the class.

33. The fifth grade's class banner is $\frac{7}{8}$ yd long. The sixth grade's class banner is $\frac{14}{16}$ yd long. Which banner is longer? Explain.

Write About It

34. Use an example to explain in your Math Journal why you can multiply or divide the numerator and denominator of a fraction by the same number without changing its value.

4-5

Fractions in Lowest Terms

Eighteen of the 24 stamps in Ben's collection are foreign. Write a fraction in lowest terms to show what fractional part of the stamps in Ben's collection are foreign.

▶ A fraction is in lowest terms, or in simplest form, when its numerator and denominator have no common factor other than 1.

To **rename a fraction** as an equivalent fraction in lowest terms, or in simplest form:

- Find the greatest common factor (GCF) of the numerator and the denominator.

Factors of 18: 1, 2, 3, 6, 9, 18
Factors of 24: 1, 2, 3, 4, 6, 8, 12, 24
GCF of 18 and 24: 6

- Divide the numerator and the denominator by their greatest common factor (GCF).

$$\frac{18}{24} = \frac{18 \div 6}{24 \div 6} = \frac{3}{4} \longleftarrow \boxed{\text{lowest terms}}$$

In lowest terms, $\frac{3}{4}$ of the stamps in Ben's collection are foreign.

> Remember: When 1 is the GCF of the numerator and denominator, the fraction is in lowest terms.

Is each fraction in lowest terms? Write Yes or No. Explain why.

1. $\frac{3}{5}$ 2. $\frac{2}{6}$ 3. $\frac{2}{9}$ 4. $\frac{2}{4}$ 5. $\frac{6}{8}$ 6. $\frac{4}{7}$

7. $\frac{5}{10}$ 8. $\frac{2}{11}$ 9. $\frac{2}{10}$ 10. $\frac{4}{8}$ 11. $\frac{7}{8}$ 12. $\frac{3}{12}$

13. $\frac{6}{15}$ 14. $\frac{12}{31}$ 15. $\frac{10}{19}$ 16. $\frac{7}{21}$ 17. $\frac{10}{25}$ 18. $\frac{23}{26}$

Choose the equivalent fraction in lowest terms.

19. $\frac{6}{8}$ a. $\frac{2}{3}$ b. $\frac{1}{3}$ c. $\frac{2}{4}$ d. $\frac{3}{4}$

20. $\frac{9}{45}$ a. $\frac{1}{5}$ b. $\frac{2}{10}$ c. $\frac{2}{5}$ d. $\frac{3}{15}$

21. $\frac{18}{27}$ a. $\frac{1}{3}$ b. $\frac{2}{3}$ c. $\frac{6}{9}$ d. $\frac{4}{6}$

Practice

Name the GCF of the numerator and the denominator.

22. $\frac{3}{6}$ 23. $\frac{6}{9}$ 24. $\frac{4}{10}$ 25. $\frac{3}{12}$ 26. $\frac{5}{15}$ 27. $\frac{8}{24}$

28. $\frac{6}{18}$ 29. $\frac{9}{12}$ 30. $\frac{8}{20}$ 31. $\frac{6}{24}$ 32. $\frac{4}{22}$ 33. $\frac{8}{12}$

34. $\frac{5}{25}$ 35. $\frac{4}{20}$ 36. $\frac{7}{21}$ 37. $\frac{4}{18}$ 38. $\frac{6}{15}$ 39. $\frac{9}{63}$

Write each fraction in simplest form.

40. $\frac{30}{40}$ 41. $\frac{20}{80}$ 42. $\frac{16}{24}$ 43. $\frac{24}{48}$ 44. $\frac{20}{28}$ 45. $\frac{24}{36}$

46. $\frac{28}{35}$ 47. $\frac{24}{32}$ 48. $\frac{32}{44}$ 49. $\frac{18}{63}$ 50. $\frac{45}{72}$ 51. $\frac{33}{66}$

52. $\frac{34}{51}$ 53. $\frac{14}{42}$ 54. $\frac{20}{32}$ 55. $\frac{35}{40}$ 56. $\frac{18}{45}$ 57. $\frac{36}{72}$

58. $\frac{33}{36}$ 59. $\frac{15}{75}$ 60. $\frac{38}{57}$ 61. $\frac{52}{65}$ 62. $\frac{45}{60}$ 63. $\frac{63}{147}$

Write each answer in simplest form.

64. There were 8 stamp collections at the Hobby Fair. If there were 24 hobbies in all, what fractional part of the hobbies were stamp collections?

65. Three out of 30 visitors to the Hobby Fair are stamp collectors. What fractional part of the visitors are stamp collectors?

66. Seven out of 28 stamps in Kyle's collection are from Europe. What fractional part of Kyle's collection is *not* from Europe?

67. At a recent spelling bee, 15 out of 24 contestants were girls. What fractional part of the contestants were boys?

68. A scientist worked 36 hours on an experiment last week. She spent 15 hours doing research and 12 hours recording data. The rest of the time she spent writing her report. What fractional part of her time was spent writing her report?

Write About It

69. What is the greatest common factor of the numerator and the denominator of any fraction in lowest terms? Explain how you can identify when a fraction is in simplest form.

Update your skills. See page 9.

Fractions in Greater Terms

A fraction is in greater terms than its equivalent fraction when its numerator and denominator are *greater than* the numerator and denominator of its equivalent fraction.

$$\frac{1}{2} = \frac{3}{6} = \frac{6}{12}$$

$\frac{3}{6}$ and $\frac{6}{12}$ are in greater terms than $\frac{1}{2}$. $\frac{1}{2}$, $\frac{3}{6}$, and $\frac{6}{12}$ are equivalent.

▶ To **rename a fraction** as an equivalent fraction in greater terms, *multiply* the numerator and the denominator by the *same* number.

$$\frac{1}{2} = \frac{1 \times 3}{2 \times 3} = \frac{3}{6} \leftarrow \text{greater-terms fraction}$$

$$\frac{1}{2} = \frac{1 \times 6}{2 \times 6} = \frac{6}{12} \leftarrow \text{greater-terms fraction}$$

▶ To find a missing numerator or denominator in a greater-terms fraction:
- Find what number the given numerator or denominator was multiplied by.

$$\frac{2}{3} = \frac{14}{n}$$

Think
$2 \times n = 14$
$2 \times 7 = 14$

- Multiply the other term of the given fraction by the same number.

$$\frac{2 \times 7}{3 \times 7} = \frac{14}{21} \quad \text{So } \frac{2}{3} = \frac{14}{21}.$$

Study these examples.

$$\frac{6}{8} = \frac{n}{64}$$

Think
$8 \times n = 64$
$8 \times 8 = 64$

$$\frac{6 \times 8}{8 \times 8} = \frac{48}{64} \quad \text{So } \frac{6}{8} = \frac{48}{64}.$$

$$\frac{20}{25} = \frac{40}{n}$$

Think
$20 \times n = 40$
$20 \times 2 = 40$

$$\frac{20 \times 2}{25 \times 2} = \frac{40}{50} \quad \text{So } \frac{20}{25} = \frac{40}{50}.$$

Practice

Choose the equivalent fraction in greater terms.

1. $\frac{1}{5}$ **a.** $\frac{3}{16}$ **b.** $\frac{4}{20}$ **c.** $\frac{3}{10}$ **d.** $\frac{5}{10}$

2. $\frac{3}{4}$ **a.** $\frac{10}{12}$ **b.** $\frac{9}{10}$ **c.** $\frac{5}{8}$ **d.** $\frac{12}{16}$

Find the missing term.

3. $\frac{6}{8} = \frac{n}{16}$ 　　 4. $\frac{2}{3} = \frac{n}{9}$ 　　 5. $\frac{4}{6} = \frac{12}{n}$ 　　 6. $\frac{7}{8} = \frac{21}{n}$ 　　 7. $\frac{5}{9} = \frac{40}{n}$

8. $\frac{4}{5} = \frac{n}{45}$ 　　 9. $\frac{3}{4} = \frac{15}{n}$ 　　 10. $\frac{3}{5} = \frac{15}{n}$ 　　 11. $\frac{7}{10} = \frac{n}{50}$ 　　 12. $\frac{6}{8} = \frac{n}{64}$

13. $\frac{7}{10} = \frac{n}{20}$ 　　 14. $\frac{2}{3} = \frac{24}{n}$ 　　 15. $\frac{4}{9} = \frac{20}{n}$ 　　 16. $\frac{7}{12} = \frac{49}{n}$ 　　 17. $\frac{10}{15} = \frac{20}{n}$

18. $\frac{8}{10} = \frac{n}{60}$ 　　 19. $\frac{2}{5} = \frac{16}{n}$ 　　 20. $\frac{3}{4} = \frac{36}{n}$ 　　 21. $\frac{8}{20} = \frac{n}{80}$ 　　 22. $\frac{6}{11} = \frac{n}{55}$

23. $\frac{5}{8} = \frac{n}{32}$ 　　 24. $\frac{5}{7} = \frac{40}{n}$ 　　 25. $\frac{8}{9} = \frac{72}{n}$ 　　 26. $\frac{3}{11} = \frac{9}{n}$ 　　 27. $\frac{7}{12} = \frac{28}{n}$

Find equivalent fractions.

28. $\frac{1}{3} = \frac{2}{6} = \frac{?}{12} = \frac{8}{?} = \frac{?}{48}$ 　　　 29. $\frac{3}{4} = \frac{?}{8} = \frac{?}{16} = \frac{24}{?} = \frac{48}{?}$

30. $\frac{3}{5} = \frac{6}{?} = \frac{12}{?} = \frac{?}{40} = \frac{?}{80}$ 　　　 31. $\frac{5}{6} = \frac{10}{?} = \frac{20}{?} = \frac{?}{48} = \frac{80}{?}$

32. $\frac{4}{7} = \frac{?}{14} = \frac{?}{28} = \frac{32}{?} = \frac{64}{?}$ 　　　 33. $\frac{8}{9} = \frac{?}{18} = \frac{32}{?} = \frac{64}{?} = \frac{?}{144}$

34. $\frac{1}{2} = \frac{?}{8} = \frac{?}{16} = \frac{?}{64} = \frac{?}{128}$ 　　　 35. $\frac{2}{3} = \frac{?}{6} = \frac{8}{?} = \frac{?}{24} = \frac{?}{48}$

36. $\frac{4}{5} = \frac{?}{10} = \frac{?}{20} = \frac{32}{?} = \frac{64}{?}$ 　　　 37. $\frac{3}{7} = \frac{?}{14} = \frac{12}{?} = \frac{36}{?} = \frac{108}{?}$

Problem Solving

38. Eden has $\frac{1}{3}$ of a pie left. She cuts this into two pieces of equal size. Write and explain what fraction shows the two pieces as part of the whole pie.

39. Seven twelfths of the flowers in the box are red. Write an equivalent fraction to show what part of the flowers in the box are *not* red.

TEST PREPARATION

40. Which fraction is *not* equivalent to the shaded area?

　A $\frac{9}{12}$ 　**B** $\frac{18}{24}$ 　**C** $\frac{16}{20}$ 　**D** $\frac{6}{8}$

41. Which fraction is equivalent to the unshaded area?

　F $\frac{6}{20}$ 　**G** $\frac{9}{12}$ 　**H** $\frac{12}{24}$ 　**J** $\frac{8}{32}$

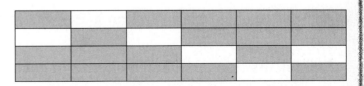

Multiples: LCM and LCD

▶ The multiples of a number are the products of that number and 0, 1, 2, 3, 4, . . .

Multiples of 3							

Multiples of 3

$\begin{array}{r} 3 \\ \times\,0 \\ \hline 0 \end{array}$ $\begin{array}{r} 3 \\ \times\,1 \\ \hline 3 \end{array}$ $\begin{array}{r} 3 \\ \times\,2 \\ \hline 6 \end{array}$ $\begin{array}{r} 3 \\ \times\,3 \\ \hline 9 \end{array}$ $\begin{array}{r} 3 \\ \times\,4 \\ \hline 12 \end{array}$ $\begin{array}{r} 3 \\ \times\,5 \\ \hline 15 \end{array}$ and so on.

Multiples of 4

$\begin{array}{r} 4 \\ \times\,0 \\ \hline 0 \end{array}$ $\begin{array}{r} 4 \\ \times\,1 \\ \hline 4 \end{array}$ $\begin{array}{r} 4 \\ \times\,2 \\ \hline 8 \end{array}$ $\begin{array}{r} 4 \\ \times\,3 \\ \hline 12 \end{array}$ $\begin{array}{r} 4 \\ \times\,4 \\ \hline 16 \end{array}$ $\begin{array}{r} 4 \\ \times\,5 \\ \hline 20 \end{array}$ and so on.

▶ Nonzero multiples that are *the same* for two or more numbers are called common multiples.

Multiples of 3: 3, 6, 9, 12, 15, 18, 21, 24, . . .
Multiples of 4: 4, 8, 12, 16, 20, 24, 28, 32, . . .
Common multiples of 3 and 4: 12, 24, . . .

▶ The least common multiple (LCM) of two or more numbers is the *least number* that is a *multiple* of those numbers.

Least common multiple (LCM) of 3 and 4: 12

Study this example.

Multiples of 2: 2, 4, 6, 8, 10, 12, . . .
Multiples of 3: 3, 6, 9, 12, 15, . . .
Multiples of 6: 6, 12, 18, 24, . . .

Common multiples of 2, 3, and 6: 6, 12, . . .
Least common multiple (LCM) of 2, 3, and 6: 6

Practice

List the first twelve nonzero multiples of each number.

1. 5   **2.** 7   **3.** 8   **4.** 9   **5.** 1   **6.** 10

List the first four common multiples of each set of numbers.

7. 3, 5   **8.** 6, 9   **9.** 4, 8   **10.** 3, 9   **11.** 3, 4, 9

Find the least common multiple (LCM) of each set of numbers.

12. 2, 4   **13.** 6, 8   **14.** 9, 12   **15.** 3, 10   **16.** 10, 15

17. 3, 4, and 9   **18.** 5, 6, and 10   **19.** 2, 7, and 8   **20.** 12, 16, and 18

Least Common Denominator (LCD)

The least common denominator (LCD) of two or more fractions is the least common multiple (LCM) of the denominators.

Find the least common denominator (LCD) of $\frac{3}{4}$, $\frac{2}{5}$, and $\frac{9}{10}$.

- Find the common multiples of the denominators.

  Multiples of **4**: 4, 8, 12, 16, 20, . . .
  Multiples of **5**: 5, 10, 15, 20, . . .
  Multiples of **10**: 10, 20, 30, . . .

- Find the LCM of the denominators. This is the least common denominator (LCD).

  LCM of **4**, **5**, and **10**: 20
  So LCD of $\frac{3}{4}$, $\frac{2}{5}$, and $\frac{9}{10}$: 20

Find the least common denominator (LCD) of each set of fractions.

21. $\frac{1}{2}$, $\frac{3}{4}$ **22.** $\frac{2}{3}$, $\frac{1}{9}$ **23.** $\frac{1}{3}$, $\frac{3}{5}$ **24.** $\frac{3}{4}$, $\frac{1}{6}$ **25.** $\frac{5}{6}$, $\frac{5}{8}$

26. $\frac{1}{3}$, $\frac{7}{10}$ **27.** $\frac{5}{8}$, $\frac{7}{12}$ **28.** $\frac{3}{10}$, $\frac{2}{15}$ **29.** $\frac{2}{3}$, $\frac{3}{11}$ **30.** $\frac{2}{9}$, $\frac{4}{15}$

31. $\frac{3}{4}$, $\frac{2}{5}$, and $\frac{9}{20}$ **32.** $\frac{1}{3}$, $\frac{5}{6}$, and $\frac{7}{12}$ **33.** $\frac{1}{12}$, $\frac{3}{16}$, and $\frac{5}{18}$

Problem Solving

34. Blue paper sells in multiples of 6 sheets, and green paper sells in multiples of 8 sheets. What is the least number of sheets of each color Ted can buy to have the same number of each color?

35. Trisha colors every third square in her art design yellow and every fourth square in her art design red. Of 36 squares in the design, how many will be colored both red and yellow?

CRITICAL THINKING

36. What is the least common multiple of a prime number and any other prime number? Explain.

37. What is the least common multiple of 1 and any other number? Give examples to support your answer.

Mixed Numbers

Rodney feeds his kittens two and three fourths cups of milk each day.

Write: $2\frac{3}{4}$
Read: two and three fourths

$2\frac{3}{4}$ is a mixed number.

$$1 \quad + \quad 1 \quad + \quad \frac{3}{4}$$
$$2 \qquad\qquad + \quad \frac{3}{4}$$

▶ A **mixed number** is made up of a *whole number* and a *fraction*. A mixed number is greater than 1.

$$\boxed{\text{whole number}} \longrightarrow 2\frac{3}{4} \longleftarrow \boxed{\text{fraction}}$$

▶ A mixed number can be shown on a number line.

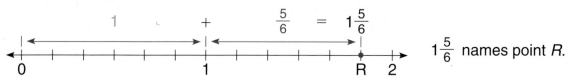

$1\frac{5}{6}$ names point *R*.

Study these examples.

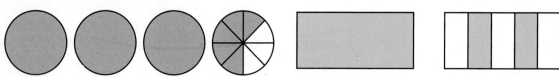

Write: $3\frac{5}{8}$
Read: three and five eighths

Write: $1\frac{2}{5}$
Read: one and two fifths

Practice

Write the mixed number that represents the shaded part.

1.

2.

Write as a mixed number.

3. seven and one sixth

4. four and five eighths

5. eleven and four fifths

6. nine and six sevenths

Write the mixed number for each point.

7.

8.

9.

10.

Draw a picture and a number line that shows each mixed number.

11. $1\frac{4}{7}$ **12.** $3\frac{1}{2}$ **13.** $2\frac{5}{8}$ **14.** $4\frac{3}{5}$ **15.** $2\frac{5}{9}$

Rounding Mixed Numbers

To **round a mixed number** to the nearest whole number, compare the fraction part to $\frac{1}{2}$.

- If the value of the fraction is *less than* $\frac{1}{2}$, round down.

  $5\frac{1}{4}$ rounds to 5.

  $\frac{1}{4} < \frac{1}{2}$
  Round **down**.

- If the value of the fraction is *greater than* or *equal to* $\frac{1}{2}$, round up.

  $8\frac{5}{6}$ rounds to 9.

  $\frac{5}{6} > \frac{1}{2}$
  Round **up**.

  $10\frac{4}{8}$ rounds to 11.

  $\frac{4}{8} = \frac{1}{2}$
  Round **up**.

Round each mixed number to the nearest whole number.

16. $3\frac{1}{3}$ **17.** $9\frac{5}{7}$ **18.** $6\frac{4}{8}$ **19.** $18\frac{1}{5}$ **20.** $19\frac{10}{13}$ **21.** $12\frac{4}{9}$

22. $7\frac{1}{2}$ **23.** $10\frac{3}{8}$ **24.** $5\frac{13}{15}$ **25.** $11\frac{4}{9}$ **26.** $8\frac{5}{8}$ **27.** $13\frac{6}{12}$

Problem Solving

28. A recipe calls for $2\frac{1}{3}$ cups of flour. About how many cups of flour will be needed for the recipe?

29. Sabina studied for $3\frac{3}{8}$ hours. About how many hours did she study?

Fractions Greater Than or Equal to One

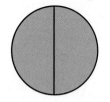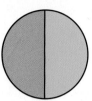

A fraction that *is greater than* or *is equal to* one has its numerator greater than or equal to its denominator. This type of fraction is called an improper fraction.

$\frac{3}{2}$ 3 > 2   So $\frac{3}{2}$ > 1 and $\frac{3}{2}$ is an improper fraction.

$\frac{2}{2}$ 2 = 2   So $\frac{2}{2}$ = 1 and $\frac{2}{2}$ is an improper fraction.

▶ You can express a fraction greater than or equal to one as a whole number or a mixed number. The number line shows that:

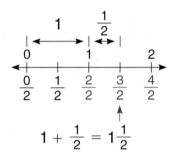

$\frac{2}{2} = 1$ $\frac{3}{2} = 1\frac{1}{2}$ $\frac{4}{2} = 2$

whole number   mixed number   whole number

$1 + \frac{1}{2} = 1\frac{1}{2}$

▶ To **rename a fraction** greater than or equal to one as a whole number or a mixed number in simplest form:

- Divide the numerator by the denominator.
- Write the quotient as the whole number part of the mixed number.
- Write the remainder as the numerator and the divisor as the denominator of the fraction part.
- Express the fraction in simplest form.

$\frac{22}{6} = \underline{\quad?\quad}$

$\frac{22}{6} \longrightarrow 6\overline{)22}^{\ 3\ R4}$

$\frac{22}{6} = 3\frac{4}{6}$

$3\frac{4}{6} = 3\frac{2}{3}$ ⟵ simplest form

Study these examples.

$\frac{18}{9} \longrightarrow 9\overline{)18}^{\ 2} = 2$

$\frac{39}{7} \longrightarrow 7\overline{)39}^{\ 5\ R4} = 5\frac{4}{7}$

Choose the fractions in each set that are greater than or equal to one.

1. a. $\frac{9}{8}$ b. $\frac{7}{7}$ c. $\frac{3}{5}$ d. $\frac{6}{7}$ e. $\frac{10}{7}$ f. $\frac{8}{4}$

2. a. $\frac{5}{11}$ b. $\frac{17}{4}$ c. $\frac{25}{5}$ d. $\frac{5}{8}$ e. $\frac{9}{2}$ f. $\frac{36}{6}$

Practice

Write a numerator to give each fraction a value equal to 1.

3. $\frac{n}{4}$ **4.** $\frac{n}{6}$ **5.** $\frac{n}{3}$ **6.** $\frac{n}{8}$ **7.** $\frac{n}{10}$ **8.** $\frac{n}{7}$

9. $\frac{n}{12}$ **10.** $\frac{n}{9}$ **11.** $\frac{n}{15}$ **12.** $\frac{n}{11}$ **13.** $\frac{n}{13}$ **14.** $\frac{n}{5}$

Write a numerator to give each fraction a value greater than 1.

15. $\frac{n}{4}$ **16.** $\frac{n}{9}$ **17.** $\frac{n}{5}$ **18.** $\frac{n}{7}$ **19.** $\frac{n}{10}$ **20.** $\frac{n}{6}$

21. $\frac{n}{8}$ **22.** $\frac{n}{11}$ **23.** $\frac{n}{19}$ **24.** $\frac{n}{3}$ **25.** $\frac{n}{15}$ **26.** $\frac{n}{12}$

Write each as a whole number or a mixed number in simplest form.

27. $\frac{10}{9}$ **28.** $\frac{44}{7}$ **29.** $\frac{24}{8}$ **30.** $\frac{18}{3}$ **31.** $\frac{6}{4}$ **32.** $\frac{50}{6}$

33. $\frac{42}{10}$ **34.** $\frac{37}{7}$ **35.** $\frac{53}{6}$ **36.** $\frac{41}{3}$ **37.** $\frac{30}{8}$ **38.** $\frac{65}{7}$

39. $\frac{75}{9}$ **40.** $\frac{45}{8}$ **41.** $\frac{26}{2}$ **42.** $\frac{110}{5}$ **43.** $\frac{192}{9}$ **44.** $\frac{210}{8}$

Tell which whole number each fraction is closer to.
You may use a number line.

45. $\frac{9}{2}$ **46.** $\frac{13}{3}$ **47.** $\frac{19}{5}$ **48.** $\frac{40}{7}$ **49.** $\frac{65}{9}$ **50.** $\frac{88}{6}$

Problem Solving

Write the answer as a mixed number.

51. A piece of lumber is 43 inches long. If it is cut into 6 equal pieces, how long is each piece?

52. If 6 identical items weigh a total of 23 pounds, how much does each item weigh?

CRITICAL THINKING

53. Ms. Rill served 4 different pies for the party: apple, blueberry, cherry, and banana. She cut each pie into eighths. After the party, she found that there were 3 slices of apple pie, 2 slices of blueberry pie, 1 slice of cherry pie, and 5 slices of banana pie left. Write a fraction and a mixed number to express the number of pies eaten. Explain the method you used to find your answer.

Compare and Order Fractions

Compare: $\dfrac{5}{8}$? $\dfrac{7}{8}$.

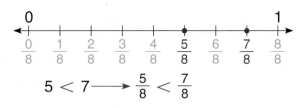

▶ To **compare fractions**
with *like denominators*,
compare the numerators.

$$5 < 7 \longrightarrow \dfrac{5}{8} < \dfrac{7}{8}$$

Compare: $\dfrac{5}{6}$? $\dfrac{1}{2}$.

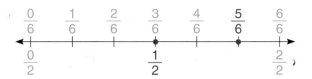

▶ To **compare fractions**
with *unlike denominators*:

- Find the least common denominator
  (LCD) of the fractions.

LCD of $\dfrac{5}{6}$ and $\dfrac{1}{2}$: 6

- Use the LCD to rename the fractions
  as equivalent fractions with the
  same denominator.

$$\dfrac{5}{6} = \dfrac{5}{6}$$

$$\dfrac{1}{2} = \dfrac{1 \times 3}{2 \times 3} = \dfrac{3}{6}$$

- Compare the numerators.

$$5 > 3 \longrightarrow \dfrac{5}{6} > \dfrac{3}{6}$$

So $\dfrac{5}{6} > \dfrac{1}{2}$.

Compare: $1\dfrac{1}{4}$? $1\dfrac{7}{8}$.

▶ To **compare mixed numbers**:

- Compare the whole numbers.

$1 = 1$

- Compare the fractions.

LCD of $\dfrac{1}{4}$ and $\dfrac{7}{8}$: 8

$$\dfrac{1}{4} = \dfrac{1 \times 2}{4 \times 2} = \dfrac{2}{8} \qquad 2 < 7 \longrightarrow \dfrac{2}{8} < \dfrac{7}{8}$$

$$\dfrac{1}{4} < \dfrac{7}{8} \quad \text{So } 1\dfrac{1}{4} < 1\dfrac{7}{8}.$$

Study these examples.

$\dfrac{19}{6}$? $\dfrac{17}{6}$ Think $19 > 17$

$\dfrac{19}{6} > \dfrac{17}{6}$

$3\dfrac{4}{5}$? $5\dfrac{4}{5}$ Think $3 < 5$

$3\dfrac{4}{5} < 5\dfrac{4}{5}$

$\dfrac{21}{4}$? $5\dfrac{3}{4}$ Think $\dfrac{21}{4} = 5\dfrac{1}{4}$

$\dfrac{21}{4} < 5\dfrac{3}{4}$

Compare. Write $<$, $=$, or $>$.

1. $\frac{3}{4}$ ___?___ $\frac{2}{4}$ 2. $\frac{4}{9}$ ___?___ $\frac{7}{9}$ 3. $\frac{5}{6}$ ___?___ $\frac{11}{12}$ 4. $\frac{4}{5}$ ___?___ $\frac{12}{15}$

5. $\frac{5}{5}$ ___?___ $\frac{10}{10}$ 6. $1\frac{5}{9}$ ___?___ $1\frac{2}{3}$ 7. $3\frac{2}{5}$ ___?___ $3\frac{4}{5}$ 8. $\frac{15}{4}$ ___?___ 4

Practice

Ordering Fractions

To **order fractions**:

Order: $\frac{1}{3}$, $\frac{2}{9}$, $\frac{1}{4}$

- Use the LCD to rename the fractions as equivalent fractions with the same denominator.

LCD of $\frac{1}{3}$, $\frac{2}{9}$, and $\frac{1}{4}$: 36

$$\frac{1}{3} = \frac{1 \times 12}{3 \times 12} = \frac{12}{36}$$
$$\frac{2}{9} = \frac{2 \times 4}{9 \times 4} = \frac{8}{36}$$
$$\frac{1}{4} = \frac{1 \times 9}{4 \times 9} = \frac{9}{36}$$

- Compare the fractions.

$$\frac{8}{36} < \frac{9}{36} < \frac{12}{36}$$

.Think........
$8 < 9 < 12$

So $\frac{2}{9} < \frac{1}{4} < \frac{1}{3}$.

- Arrange the fractions in order from *least to greatest* or from *greatest to least*.

From least to greatest: $\frac{2}{9}$, $\frac{1}{4}$, $\frac{1}{3}$

From greatest to least: $\frac{1}{3}$, $\frac{1}{4}$, $\frac{2}{9}$

**Draw a number line to show each set of numbers.
Then order the numbers from least to greatest.**

9. $\frac{2}{7}$, $\frac{4}{7}$, $\frac{3}{7}$ 10. $\frac{5}{13}$, $\frac{12}{13}$, $\frac{8}{13}$ 11. $\frac{1}{2}$, $\frac{1}{3}$, $\frac{1}{6}$ 12. $\frac{4}{5}$, $\frac{1}{4}$, $\frac{7}{8}$

Write in order from greatest to least.

13. $\frac{4}{5}$, $\frac{7}{10}$, $\frac{3}{4}$ 14. $\frac{11}{12}$, $\frac{3}{8}$, $\frac{5}{6}$ 15. $2\frac{7}{9}$, $2\frac{5}{6}$, $2\frac{2}{3}$ 16. $1\frac{4}{5}$, $1\frac{7}{10}$, $1\frac{3}{4}$

Problem Solving

17. Three teams played the same number of tournament games. Of their games, Team A won $\frac{7}{10}$, Team B won $\frac{2}{3}$, and Team C won $\frac{4}{5}$. Which team won the fewest games? Explain why.

18. In a broad-jump contest, Lily jumped $3\frac{1}{2}$ ft in her first jump, $3\frac{2}{5}$ ft in her second jump, and $3\frac{5}{6}$ ft in her third jump. Which was her longest jump? Explain why.

Chapter 4 153

Problem-Solving Strategy:
Make an Organized List

A pet shop keeps a pair of dogs in each cage. If there are 6 dogs: a shepherd, a collie, a poodle, a retriever, a terrier, and a bulldog, how many possible pairs can be formed?

Read

Visualize yourself in the problem above as you reread it. List the facts and the question.

Facts: • a pair of dogs in each cage
• 6 dogs: a shepherd, a collie, a poodle, a retriever, a terrier, and a bulldog

Question: How many possible pairs can be formed?

Plan

Make a list of the possible pairs. Let the first letters of the dogs' names stand for each pair.

> **Hint**
> The **order** of the letters does not matter.

Solve

A shepherd can be housed with any of the 5 other dogs.

    S and C
    S and P
    S and R
    S and T
    S and B

A collie can be housed with any of the 4 other dogs.

    C and P
    C and R
    C and T
    C and B

A poodle can be housed with any of the 3 other dogs.

    P and R
    P and T
    P and B

A retriever can be housed with any of the 2 other dogs.

    R and T
    R and B

A terrier can be housed with the other dog that is left.

    T and B

Count the number of pairs.
$5 + 4 + 3 + 2 + 1 = 15$

So 15 pairs can be formed from the 6 different dogs.

Check

Make a second list that begins with a different choice of dog. Both lists should have the same number of pairs.

Make an organized list to solve each problem.

1. Tamisha has 3 shirts: one yellow, one blue, and one orange; 2 pairs of shorts: one white and one black; and 2 vests: one plaid and one flowered. How many different three-piece outfits can she make?

Read Visualize yourself in the problem above as you reread it. Focus on the facts and the question.

List what you know.

Facts: 3 shirts—1 yellow, 1 blue, 1 orange
2 pairs of shorts—1 white, 1 black
2 vests—1 plaid, 1 flowered

Question: How many three-piece outfits can she make?

Plan To find how many outfits Tamisha can make, make an organized list showing the possible combinations she can use.

Shirts	Shorts	Vests
yellow	white	plaid
yellow	white	flowered
yellow	black	plaid
yellow	black	flowered

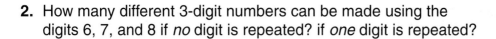

Solve **Check**

2. How many different 3-digit numbers can be made using the digits 6, 7, and 8 if *no* digit is repeated? if *one* digit is repeated?

3. The juice in a machine costs 60¢ a bottle. The machine will accept only exact change, it cannot give change, and it will not accept pennies or half dollars. How many different combinations of coins can you use to buy a bottle of juice?

Write Your Own

4. Write a problem using the Make an Organized List strategy. Have someone solve it.

Problem-Solving Applications: Mixed Review

Solve each problem and explain the method you used.

1. At last week's track meet, Stacy ran $\frac{9}{12}$ of a mile, Jules ran $\frac{4}{5}$ of a mile, and Raul ran $\frac{3}{4}$ of a mile. Which two students ran the same distance?

2. Regina ran $2\frac{8}{20}$ miles. Write this number in lowest terms.

3. There were 63 students at the track meet and 9 of them ran in the 100-meter race. What fractional part of the students ran in the race?

4. Ashlee ran $\frac{1}{4}$ of the race before tagging Adam. Then Adam ran $\frac{8}{32}$ of the race. Who ran farther? Explain.

5. Ruby ran $\frac{12}{3}$ miles. Then she ran 3 more miles. How far did she run?

6. Jake ran $\frac{5}{6}$ of a mile. Frank ran $\frac{15}{20}$ of a mile. Who ran farther?

7. Of the 63 students at the track meet, 34 are girls. What fractional part of the students are boys?

8. There are 36 boys and 45 girls in the track meet. The coach wants an equal number of boys or girls on each team. What is the greatest number of boys or girls the coach can have on a team? How many teams in all will he have?

9. From 4:30 P.M. to 6:30 P.M. the Route 1 bus stops every 12 min at the gym's bus stop. The Route 2 bus stops there every 15 min. If both buses are now at the stop and the schedule is kept, how long will it be before both buses will be at the stop again?

Write *True* or *False*. Explain your answer.

10. Some improper fractions equal whole numbers.

11. A fraction whose denominator is 1 more than its numerator is sometimes in lowest terms.

Choose a strategy from the list or use another strategy you know to solve each problem.

12. The judges at the track meet will award prizes to the top 4 teams. How many different ways can the top 4 teams place?

13. The long-jump winner jumped $8\frac{1}{2}$ ft. Did the winner jump more than 100 in.?

14. There were 12 students at last week's track meet. A little less than half were girls. Write a fraction that might represent the part of the team that was girls.

15. The team from Dellmont won $\frac{1}{5}$ of the medals, the team from Edgarton won $\frac{1}{3}$ of the medals, and the team from Fredonia won 11 of the 30 medals given at the meet. Five girls were on the teams. Which team won the most medals?

Strategy File

Use These Strategies
More Than One Solution
Use a Graph
Use More Than One Step
Logical Reasoning
Make an Organized List

Use the table for problems 16–18.

16. All teams had one member who threw the javelin at least 82 m. What team came closest to 90 m? Explain how you found your answer.

17. The average throw was 84 m. Which team threw the farthest? the least far? Explain how you found your answer.

18. Which team threw between 80 and 85 m?

Javelin Throw	
Team	**Meters**
Spartans	$82\frac{2}{5}$
Lions	$85\frac{1}{2}$
Eagles	$85\frac{8}{10}$
Vikings	$83\frac{1}{4}$

Use the graph for problems 19 and 20.

19. How many students participated in the meet?

20. In which two events did a total of $\frac{1}{4}$ of the students participate?

Track Meet Participants

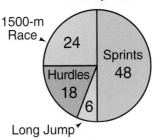

1500-m Race — 24
Sprints — 48
Hurdles — 18
6
Long Jump

Write Your Own

21. Write in your Math Journal which problems you solved using the same strategy, and explain why. Write a problem modeled on one of these problems and have a classmate solve it.

Check Your Progress
Lessons 1–12

Write whether each number is prime or composite. *(See pp. 134–137.)*

1. 43 **2.** 39 **3.** 24 **4.** 57 **5.** 18 **6.** 101

Find the prime factorization of each. Use exponents when appropriate.

7. 16 **8.** 27 **9.** 32 **10.** 44 **11.** 56

Find the greatest common factor (GCF) of each set of numbers. *(See pp. 138–139.)*

12. 6 and 15 **13.** 9 and 21 **14.** 8 and 12 **15.** 2, 6, and 18

Find equivalent fractions in higher terms. *(See pp. 140–145.)*

16. $\frac{1}{4} = \frac{?}{8} = \frac{?}{12}$ **17.** $\frac{3}{7} = \frac{6}{?} = \frac{9}{?}$ **18.** $\frac{5}{9} = \frac{?}{18} = \frac{15}{?}$

Write each fraction in lowest terms. *(See pp. 142–143.)*

19. $\frac{9}{21}$ **20.** $\frac{16}{24}$ **21.** $\frac{24}{30}$ **22.** $\frac{4}{12}$ **23.** $\frac{14}{35}$ **24.** $\frac{21}{42}$

Find the least common denominator (LCD) of each set of fractions. *(See pp. 146–147.)*

25. $\frac{1}{4}, \frac{1}{8}$ **26.** $\frac{1}{3}, \frac{3}{10}$ **27.** $\frac{4}{5}, \frac{1}{2}$ **28.** $\frac{5}{9}, \frac{2}{3}, \frac{7}{27}$

Draw a picture and a number line to show each mixed number. *(See pp. 148–149.)*

29. $2\frac{1}{4}$ **30.** $3\frac{2}{3}$ **31.** $4\frac{3}{5}$ **32.** $6\frac{4}{7}$

Write as a whole number or a mixed number in simplest form. *(See pp. 150–151.)*

33. $\frac{11}{6}$ **34.** $\frac{36}{9}$ **35.** $\frac{22}{3}$ **36.** $\frac{24}{5}$ **37.** $\frac{47}{7}$

Compare. Write <, =, or >. *(See pp. 152–153.)*

38. $\frac{5}{9}$? $\frac{7}{9}$ **39.** $\frac{5}{9}$? $\frac{10}{18}$ **40.** $\frac{2}{3}$? $\frac{1}{2}$ **41.** $2\frac{3}{8}$? $2\frac{5}{16}$

Problem Solving
(See pp. 154–156.)

42. Tom uses three 1–6 number cubes. He is looking for different ways to roll the sum of 12. How many ways will he find?

43. Football practice lasted $2\frac{1}{6}$ hours yesterday. About how many hours was the football practice?

(See *Still More Practice*, p. 480.)

Density of Fractions

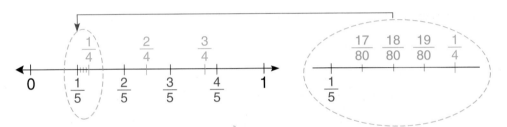

An infinite number of fractions can be found between any two fractions. This is called the **Density Property of Fractions.**

Find 3 fractions between $\frac{1}{5}$ and $\frac{1}{4}$.

▶ To find fractions between two fractions:

   ❶ Rename the fractions as equivalent fractions in higher terms with the same denominator.

   ❷ Look at the numerators and write the whole numbers between them.

   ❸ Write the new fractions. Use the whole numbers as the numerators and the common denominator as the denominators.

   ❹ Repeat the steps until the desired number of fractions is found.

$$\frac{1}{5} = \frac{1 \times 4}{5 \times 4} = \frac{4}{20} \longrightarrow \frac{4 \times 2}{20 \times 2} = \frac{8}{40} \longrightarrow \frac{8 \times 2}{40 \times 2} = \frac{16}{80}$$

$$\frac{1}{4} = \frac{1 \times 5}{4 \times 5} = \frac{5}{20} \longrightarrow \frac{5 \times 2}{20 \times 2} = \frac{10}{40} \longrightarrow \frac{10 \times 2}{40 \times 2} = \frac{20}{80}$$

No whole numbers between 4 and 5: continue renaming.	One whole number between 8 and 10: continue renaming.	Three whole numbers between 16 and 20: 17, 18, 19

Three fractions between $\frac{1}{5}$ and $\frac{1}{4}$: $\frac{17}{80}, \frac{18}{80}, \frac{19}{80}$

Find three fractions between each pair of fractions.

1. $\frac{1}{10}, \frac{1}{6}$ 2. $\frac{1}{3}, \frac{2}{5}$ 3. $\frac{1}{2}, \frac{3}{5}$ 4. $\frac{7}{10}, \frac{3}{4}$ 5. $\frac{4}{5}, \frac{5}{6}$

6. $\frac{1}{2}, \frac{5}{6}$ 7. $\frac{7}{15}, \frac{3}{5}$ 8. $\frac{1}{3}, \frac{3}{8}$ 9. $\frac{1}{4}, \frac{2}{7}$ 10. $\frac{3}{4}, \frac{5}{6}$

Find the prime factorization of each. Use exponents when appropriate.

1. 36   **2.** 24   **3.** 52   **4.** 112   **5.** 148

Find the greatest common factor (GCF) for each set of numbers.

6. 6 and 21   **7.** 9 and 15   **8.** 12, 16, and 24

Write whether each fraction is *closer to 0, closer to* $\frac{1}{2}$, or *closer to 1*.

9. $\frac{13}{27}$ **10.** $\frac{39}{40}$ **11.** $\frac{5}{61}$ **12.** $\frac{17}{28}$ **13.** $\frac{197}{200}$

Find the missing term.

14. $\frac{9}{10} = \frac{n}{100}$ **15.** $\frac{4}{5} = \frac{n}{60}$ **16.** $\frac{2}{9} = \frac{10}{n}$ **17.** $\frac{3}{4} = \frac{24}{n}$

Write each fraction in lowest terms.

18. $\frac{8}{12}$ **19.** $\frac{4}{8}$ **20.** $\frac{12}{15}$ **21.** $\frac{18}{27}$ **22.** $\frac{36}{54}$

Find the least common denominator (LCD) of each set of fractions.

23. $\frac{4}{5}, \frac{1}{2}$ **24.** $\frac{2}{3}, \frac{4}{7}$ **25.** $\frac{3}{8}, \frac{1}{4}$ **26.** $\frac{1}{2}, \frac{5}{6}, \frac{7}{18}$

Write each as a whole number or mixed number in simplest form.

27. $\frac{19}{4}$ **28.** $\frac{37}{8}$ **29.** $\frac{48}{8}$ **30.** $\frac{57}{9}$ **31.** $\frac{84}{12}$

Problem Solving

Use a strategy you have learned.

32. How many different three-digit numbers can be made using 0, 1, and 2 if digits can be repeated?

Tell About It

33. Which is greater, $\frac{9}{5}$ or $\frac{9}{8}$? $\frac{3}{7}$ or $\frac{6}{7}$? Explain your answer.

Performance Assessment

Use a number line.
Tina cut 3 different lengths of ribbon: $1\frac{1}{2}$ yd, $\frac{2}{3}$ yd, and $1\frac{5}{9}$ yd.

34. Show each on a number line.

35. Use $<$ and $>$ to compare the lengths in 2 different ways.

36. Order the lengths from greatest to least.

Test Preparation

Choose the best answer.

1. Which is the GCF of 48 and 84?

   a. 4
   b. 6
   c. 12
   d. 24

7. Which is the LCM of 6, 8, and 12?

   a. 4
   b. 26
   c. 48
   d. 24

2. Which statement is true?

   a. $2\frac{3}{7} > 2\frac{1}{4}$
   b. $1\frac{3}{7} < 1\frac{1}{4}$
   c. $1\frac{3}{7} = 1\frac{1}{4}$
   d. $2\frac{1}{4} > 2\frac{3}{7}$

8. Which fraction is closest to 0?

   a. $\frac{3}{4}$
   b. $\frac{1}{2}$
   c. $\frac{1}{12}$
   d. $\frac{7}{8}$

3. Which numbers are in order from greatest to least?

   a. 5.4; 5.04; 5.340
   b. 5.430; 5.4; 5.04
   c. 5.430; 5.4; 5.433
   d. 5.04; 5.4; 5.430

9. Estimate the quotient.

   $$42{,}252 \div 208$$

   a. 20
   b. 200
   c. 2000
   d. 20,000

4. Which gives an answer of 441?

   a. 525×84
   b. $31{,}752 \div 72$
   c. $3744 + 676$
   d. $8040 - 7506$

10. The difference between 5004 and 2879 is:

   a. 3125
   b. 3135
   c. 2125
   d. 2135

5. Which numbers are divisible by 3?

   A. 1572   **B.** 3071   **C.** 3456

   a. A and B only
   b. A and C only
   c. B and C only
   d. A, B, and C

11. Which decimal has 2 in the thousandths place and 5 in the tenths place?

   a. 2.158
   b. 9.225
   c. 2007.5
   d. 9.542

6. As a mixed number, $\frac{53}{9}$ is equal to:

   a. $5\frac{8}{9}$ **b.** $5\frac{1}{9}$

   c. $6\frac{8}{9}$ **d.** $6\frac{1}{9}$

12. As a fraction in higher terms, $\frac{2}{3}$ is equal to:

   a. $\frac{10}{12}$ **b.** $\frac{14}{21}$

   c. $\frac{12}{16}$ **d.** $\frac{8}{18}$

13. Which fractions are in lowest terms?

A. $\frac{5}{9}$ B. $\frac{3}{31}$ C. $\frac{15}{27}$ D. $\frac{9}{11}$

    a. A, B, D
    b. A, C, D
    c. A, B, C
    d. B, C, D

14. As a fraction, $4\frac{3}{10}$ is equal to:

    a. $\frac{43}{10}$ **b.** $\frac{17}{10}$

    c. $\frac{33}{10}$ **d.** $\frac{7}{10}$

15. Which is the best estimate for $8.95 + $13 + $10.09?

    a. $31
    b. $32
    c. 31
    d. 32

16. A decimal has been rounded to the nearest whole number. The rounded number is 14. Which of these numbers could be the decimal?

    a. 14.724
    b. 14.563
    c. 14.495
    d. 14.912

17. John has 45 feet of rope and Jeanine has 60 feet. What is the longest length they can cut from each rope so that all the pieces are equal in length?

    a. 180 feet
    b. 90 feet
    c. 30 feet
    d. 15 feet

18. Which is ordered from least to greatest?

    a. $\frac{2}{3}, \frac{5}{6}, \frac{3}{4}$ **b.** $\frac{2}{3}, \frac{3}{4}, \frac{5}{6}$

    c. $\frac{5}{6}, \frac{3}{4}, \frac{2}{3}$ **d.** $\frac{3}{4}, \frac{2}{3}, \frac{5}{6}$

19. Which fractions are each equivalent to $\frac{2}{5}$?

    a. $\frac{4}{10}, \frac{6}{15}, \frac{8}{20}$ **b.** $\frac{4}{10}, \frac{6}{12}, \frac{8}{20}$

    c. $\frac{4}{9}, \frac{6}{15}, \frac{8}{20}$ **d.** $\frac{4}{10}, \frac{6}{15}, \frac{9}{21}$

20. Choose the quotient.

    $7\overline{)35,916}$

    a. 51,310
    b. 5130
    c. 513 R6
    d. 5130 R6

21. Jan has three times as many baseball cards as Jeric. Jan has 87 baseball cards. How many baseball cards does Jeric have?

    a. 84 baseball cards
    b. 261 baseball cards
    c. 29 baseball cards
    d. 90 baseball cards

22. A roll of ribbon is 250 inches long. How much longer should the roll be so that Ellen can cut an exact number of 15-inch streamers, with no ribbon left over?

    a. 15 inches
    b. 5 inches
    c. 265 inches
    d. 255 inches

Explain how you solved the problem. Show all your work.

23. How many 3-digit numbers can you make using the digits 1, 2, 3, and 4 if the hundreds digit is prime and repetition of a digit is not permitted?

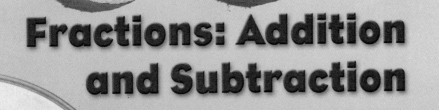

Fractions: Addition and Subtraction

Grandmother's Almond Cookies

No need cookbook, measuring cup.
Stand close. Watch me. No mess up.

One hand sugar, one hand lard
(cut in pieces when still hard),

two hands flour, more or less,
one pinch baking powder. Guess.

One hand almond, finely crushed.
Mix it with both hands. No rush.

Put two eggs. Brown is better.
Keep on mixing. Should be wetter.

Sprinkle water in it. Make
cookies round and flat. Now bake

one big sheet at three-seven-five.
When they done, they come alive.

Janet S. Wong

In this chapter you will:

Learn to add or subtract with renaming
Estimate sums and differences of
   mixed numbers
Use the Work Backward strategy

Critical Thinking/Finding Together

One cup of condensed milk weighs 11 oz.
How many ounces of milk will remain
unused after a grandmother opens three
6-oz cans for a recipe that requires $1\frac{1}{2}$
cups of milk?

Update your skills. See page 10.

Rename Fraction Sums: Like Denominators

In a science experiment, Plant A grew $\frac{6}{8}$ in. one week and $\frac{7}{8}$ in. the next week. How many inches did it grow during the two weeks?

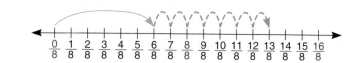

To find how many inches Plant A grew, add: $\frac{6}{8} + \frac{7}{8} = n$.

▶ To **add fractions** with like denominators:

- Add the numerators.

- Write the sum over the common denominator.

- Write the sum in simplest form.

$$\frac{6}{8} + \frac{7}{8} = \frac{6 + 7}{8}$$

$$= \frac{13}{8}$$

Think
$$\begin{array}{r} 1\ R5 \\ 8\overline{)13} \end{array}$$

$$= 1\frac{5}{8}$$ ← simplest form

Plant A grew $1\frac{5}{8}$ in. during the two weeks.

Study these examples.

$$\frac{11}{13} + \frac{2}{13} = \frac{11 + 2}{13}$$

$$= \frac{13}{13} = 1$$

Think
$$\begin{array}{r} 1 \\ 13\overline{)13} \end{array}$$

$$\frac{7}{12} + \frac{11}{12} = \frac{7 + 11}{12}$$

$$= \frac{18}{12}$$

Think
$$\begin{array}{r} 1\ R6 \\ 12\overline{)18} \end{array}$$

$$= 1\frac{6}{12} = 1\frac{1}{2}$$

$$\begin{array}{r} \frac{1}{6} \\ + \frac{1}{6} \\ \hline \frac{2}{6} = \frac{1}{3} \end{array}$$

Think
$$\frac{1 + 1}{6}$$

Write an addition sentence, with the sum in simplest form for each number line.

1.

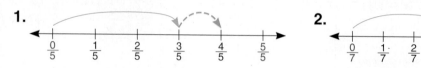

2.

3.

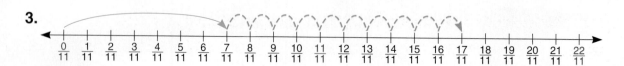

Use number lines to model each sum. Write an addition sentence with the sum in simplest form.

4. $\frac{4}{5} + \frac{3}{5}$
5. $\frac{3}{10} + \frac{9}{10}$
6. $\frac{10}{12} + \frac{2}{12}$
7. $\frac{3}{10} + \frac{3}{10}$

Add.

8. $\frac{5}{12} + \frac{4}{12}$
9. $\frac{5}{7} + \frac{6}{7}$
10. $\frac{11}{12} + \frac{1}{12}$
11. $\frac{7}{24} + \frac{17}{24}$

12. $\frac{7}{14} + \frac{9}{14}$
13. $\frac{9}{15} + \frac{9}{15}$
14. $\frac{7}{16} + \frac{9}{16}$
15. $\frac{15}{11} + \frac{7}{11}$

16. $\frac{1}{9}$
$+ \frac{5}{9}$

17. $\frac{3}{14}$
$+ \frac{2}{14}$

18. $\frac{3}{8}$
$+ \frac{7}{8}$

19. $\frac{7}{12}$
$+ \frac{13}{12}$

20. $\frac{18}{20}$
$+ \frac{4}{20}$

21. $\frac{10}{14}$
$+ \frac{4}{14}$

22. Write in your Math Journal the different types of answers you get when adding fractions with like denominators. Give an example of each.

Write an addition sentence.

23. What is the sum of $\frac{15}{21}$ and $\frac{8}{21}$?

24. How much is $\frac{18}{16}$ increased by $\frac{14}{16}$?

Problem Solving

25. Sherry bought $\frac{5}{8}$ yd of yellow ribbon for a gift box. Then she bought $\frac{3}{8}$ yd of red ribbon for a school project. How much ribbon did Sherry buy in all?

26. The robot traveled $\frac{2}{9}$ of a mile on Monday and $\frac{4}{9}$ of a mile on Tuesday. How far did it travel in the two days?

27. Some fifth graders experimented with the growth of plants in different types of soil. They recorded the results in a table. What was the total amount of plant growth over the two-week period for each type of soil?

Plant Growth			
Period	Soil A	Soil B	Soil C
Week 1	$\frac{6}{12}$ in.	$\frac{4}{12}$ in.	$\frac{3}{12}$ in.
Week 2	$\frac{7}{12}$ in.	$\frac{8}{12}$ in.	$\frac{3}{12}$ in.

DO YOU REMEMBER?

Find the least common multiple (LCM) of each set of numbers.

28. 5, 7
29. 9, 12
30. 8, 10
31. 4, 6, and 12
32. 10, 15

Add Fractions: Unlike Denominators

Dave worked $\frac{3}{4}$ of an hour on his model plane. His dad worked on it for $\frac{2}{3}$ of an hour. How much time did both work on the model plane?

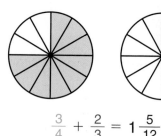

To find the amount of time, add: $\frac{3}{4} + \frac{2}{3} = n$.

$$\frac{3}{4} + \frac{2}{3} = 1\frac{5}{12}$$

▶ To **add fractions** with unlike denominators:

- Find the least common denominator (LCD) of the fractions.

  Multiples of 4: 4, 8, 12, 16, . . .
  Multiples of 3: 3, 6, 9, 12, . . .
  LCD of $\frac{3}{4}$ and $\frac{2}{3}$: 12

- Use the LCD to rename the fractions as equivalent fractions with the same denominator.

$$\frac{3}{4} = \frac{3 \times 3}{4 \times 3} = \frac{9}{12}$$
$$+ \frac{2}{3} = \frac{2 \times 4}{3 \times 4} = \frac{8}{12}$$

- Add. Then write the sum in simplest form.

$$\frac{17}{12} = 1\frac{5}{12}$$

Rename the sum.

Dave and his dad worked $1\frac{5}{12}$ h on the model plane.

▶ The properties of addition for whole numbers also apply to fractions.

Commutative Property

..Think..
"order"

$$\frac{3}{4} + \frac{2}{3} = \frac{2}{3} + \frac{3}{4}$$
$$1\frac{5}{12} = 1\frac{5}{12}$$

You can check addition by applying the *Commutative Property*.

Identity Property

..Think..
"same"

$$\frac{3}{4} + 0 = \frac{3}{4}$$
$$0 + \frac{3}{4} = \frac{3}{4}$$

Study these examples.

$$\frac{3}{16} = \frac{3}{16}$$
$$+ \frac{5}{8} = \frac{5 \times 2}{8 \times 2} = \frac{10}{16}$$
$$\frac{13}{16}$$

$$\frac{5}{6} + \frac{2}{3} = \frac{5}{6} + \frac{2 \times 2}{3 \times 2}$$
$$= \frac{5}{6} + \frac{4}{6}$$
$$= \frac{9}{6} = 1\frac{3}{6} = 1\frac{1}{2} \longleftarrow$$

Simplest form

Add.

1. $\frac{2}{3}$
$+ \frac{1}{6}$

2. $\frac{2}{5}$
$+ \frac{3}{10}$

3. $\frac{1}{6}$
$+ \frac{2}{5}$

4. $\frac{1}{3}$
$+ \frac{5}{9}$

5. $\frac{1}{3}$
$+ \frac{7}{12}$

6. $\frac{2}{3}$
$+ \frac{1}{5}$

Find the sum. Use the Commutative Property to check your answers.

7. $\frac{1}{2} + \frac{1}{7}$

8. $\frac{4}{15} + \frac{2}{3}$

9. $\frac{3}{10} + \frac{1}{4}$

10. $\frac{2}{3} + \frac{1}{8}$

11. $\frac{2}{3} + \frac{4}{9}$

12. $\frac{5}{8} + \frac{1}{2}$

13. $\frac{4}{5} + \frac{9}{10}$

14. $\frac{5}{6} + \frac{5}{9}$

Find the value of *n*. Name the property of addition that is used.

15. $\frac{4}{7} + \frac{3}{14} = n + \frac{4}{7}$

16. $0 + n = \frac{3}{10}$

Problem Solving

17. Lin spent $\frac{1}{10}$ of her allowance for a gift and $\frac{2}{5}$ for a movie ticket. What part of her allowance did she spend in all?

18. Two of nine team members are taller than 5 ft. Seven eighteenths are between 4 ft 9 in. and 5 ft. What fraction of the team is taller than 4 ft 9 in.?

19. June and Paul recorded the distances they swam each day.

a. On which day did they swim a total of half a mile? How do you know?

b. Who swam farther on Wednesday and Thursday? How do you know?

c. On which day did they swim the shortest combined distance? How do you know?

Day	Distance in Miles	
	June	Paul
Monday	$\frac{1}{10}$	$\frac{1}{5}$
Tuesday	$\frac{1}{6}$	$\frac{1}{3}$
Wednesday	$\frac{1}{2}$	$\frac{3}{8}$
Thursday	$\frac{3}{8}$	$\frac{1}{4}$

CHALLENGE — Algebra

Find the value of *n*.

20. $\frac{5}{6} + \frac{n}{6} = 1$

21. $7\frac{5}{12} + 2\frac{6}{n} = 9\frac{11}{12}$

22. $n + 9\frac{3}{16} = 12\frac{3}{16}$

23. $3\frac{3}{7} + n = 5\frac{5}{7}$

24. $5\frac{7}{10} + n = 6$

25. $\frac{3}{4} + n + \frac{4}{5} = 1\frac{4}{5}$

Add Three Fractions

Adrian bought $\frac{1}{2}$ pound of bananas, $\frac{2}{3}$ pound of pears, and $\frac{3}{4}$ pound of strawberries. How many pounds of fruit did he buy in all?

To find the amount of fruit Adrian bought, add: $\frac{1}{2} + \frac{2}{3} + \frac{3}{4} = n$.

▶ To **add three fractions**, use the same rules for adding two fractions.

- Find the least common denominator (LCD) of the fractions if the denominators are *unlike*.

LCD of $\frac{1}{2}$, $\frac{2}{3}$, and $\frac{3}{4}$: 12

- Use the LCD to rename the fractions as equivalent fractions with the same denominator.

$$\frac{1}{2} = \frac{1 \times 6}{2 \times 6} = \frac{6}{12}$$
$$\frac{2}{3} = \frac{2 \times 4}{3 \times 4} = \frac{8}{12}$$

- Add. Then write the sum in simplest form.

$$+\frac{3}{4} = \frac{3 \times 3}{4 \times 3} = \frac{9}{12}$$
$$\frac{23}{12} = 1\frac{11}{12}$$

Adrian bought $1\frac{11}{12}$ pounds of fruit.

Study these examples.

$$
\begin{array}{l}
\frac{3}{7} \\
\frac{1}{7} \\
+\frac{2}{7} \\
\hline
\frac{6}{7}
\end{array}
$$

$$\frac{1}{4} = \frac{1 \times 3}{4 \times 3} = \frac{3}{12}$$
$$\frac{1}{3} = \frac{1 \times 4}{3 \times 4} = \frac{4}{12}$$
$$+\frac{5}{12} = \frac{5}{12}$$
$$\frac{12}{12} = 1$$

$$\frac{5}{12} + \frac{7}{12} + \frac{5}{6} = \frac{5}{12} + \frac{7}{12} + \frac{5 \times 2}{6 \times 2}$$
$$= \frac{5}{12} + \frac{7}{12} + \frac{10}{12}$$
$$= \frac{22}{12} = 1\frac{10}{12} = 1\frac{5}{6} \leftarrow$$

Simplest form

Add.

1.
$$
\begin{array}{r}
\frac{1}{5} \\
\frac{2}{5} \\
+\frac{1}{5} \\
\hline
\end{array}
$$

2.
$$
\begin{array}{r}
\frac{1}{9} \\
\frac{2}{9} \\
+\frac{4}{9} \\
\hline
\end{array}
$$

3.
$$
\begin{array}{r}
\frac{3}{8} \\
\frac{1}{8} \\
+\frac{2}{8} \\
\hline
\end{array}
$$

4.
$$
\begin{array}{r}
\frac{1}{10} \\
\frac{7}{10} \\
+\frac{2}{10} \\
\hline
\end{array}
$$

5.
$$
\begin{array}{r}
\frac{3}{13} \\
\frac{4}{13} \\
+\frac{5}{13} \\
\hline
\end{array}
$$

6.
$$
\begin{array}{r}
\frac{2}{12} \\
\frac{6}{12} \\
+\frac{7}{12} \\
\hline
\end{array}
$$

Practice

Find the sum.

7. $\dfrac{1}{3}$
$\dfrac{2}{3}$
$+\dfrac{5}{9}$

8. $\dfrac{1}{5}$
$\dfrac{1}{10}$
$+\dfrac{3}{5}$

9. $\dfrac{3}{4}$
$\dfrac{3}{8}$
$+\dfrac{1}{8}$

10. $\dfrac{1}{4}$
$\dfrac{1}{12}$
$+\dfrac{1}{3}$

11. $\dfrac{1}{6}$
$\dfrac{2}{9}$
$+\dfrac{1}{18}$

12. $\dfrac{2}{5}$
$\dfrac{1}{4}$
$+\dfrac{9}{20}$

13. $\dfrac{4}{5} + \dfrac{3}{10} + \dfrac{1}{4}$

14. $\dfrac{2}{3} + \dfrac{1}{5} + \dfrac{3}{10}$

15. $\dfrac{5}{6} + \dfrac{7}{8} + \dfrac{1}{4}$

Associative Property of Addition

The *Associative Property of Addition* for whole numbers also applies to fractions.

Think "grouping"

$$\left(\dfrac{2}{11} + \dfrac{1}{11}\right) + \dfrac{5}{11} = \dfrac{2}{11} + \left(\dfrac{1}{11} + \dfrac{5}{11}\right)$$

$$\dfrac{3}{11} + \dfrac{5}{11} = \dfrac{2}{11} + \dfrac{6}{11}$$

$$\dfrac{8}{11} = \dfrac{8}{11}$$

Find the value of *n*. Then check by adding.

16. $\left(\dfrac{2}{9} + \dfrac{1}{9}\right) + \dfrac{4}{9} = \dfrac{2}{9} + \left(\dfrac{1}{9} + n\right)$

17. $\dfrac{3}{10} + \left(\dfrac{2}{10} + \dfrac{1}{10}\right) = \left(\dfrac{3}{10} + n\right) + \dfrac{1}{10}$

18. $\left(\dfrac{3}{4} + n\right) + \dfrac{5}{6} = \dfrac{3}{4} + \left(\dfrac{2}{3} + \dfrac{5}{6}\right)$

19. $n + \left(\dfrac{1}{2} + \dfrac{1}{6}\right) = \left(\dfrac{2}{5} + \dfrac{1}{2}\right) + \dfrac{1}{6}$

Problem Solving

20. Zaffar bought $\dfrac{2}{3}$ qt of fresh orange juice, $\dfrac{3}{4}$ qt of fresh mango juice, and $\dfrac{1}{2}$ qt of fresh grape juice. How many quarts of fruit juice did he buy?

21. Yvonne sifted together $\dfrac{3}{4}$ cup of rye flour, $\dfrac{3}{5}$ cup of wheat flour, and $\dfrac{7}{10}$ cup of white flour. How many cups of flour did she sift?

22. Ms. Russell added $\dfrac{1}{8}$ teaspoon of pepper, $\dfrac{1}{2}$ teaspoon of salt, and $\dfrac{1}{4}$ teaspoon of curry powder to the stew. How many teaspoons of seasoning did she add to the stew?

23. Mr. Clarke bought $\dfrac{3}{8}$ pound of peanuts, $\dfrac{3}{4}$ pound of pecans, and $\dfrac{5}{6}$ pound of walnuts. How many pounds of nuts did he buy?

Add Mixed Numbers

Esther used $2\frac{1}{4}$ yd of gold ribbon and $1\frac{1}{4}$ yd of blue ribbon to make certificates. How many yards of ribbon did she use for the certificates?

$$3\frac{2}{4} = 3\frac{1}{2}$$

To find how many yards of ribbon were used for the certificates, add: $2\frac{1}{4} + 1\frac{1}{4} = n$.

▶ To **add mixed numbers** with fractions with *like* denominators:

- Add the fractions.

- Add the whole numbers.

- Write the sum in simplest form.

$$
\begin{array}{r}
2\frac{1}{4} \\
+\,1\frac{1}{4} \\
\hline
\frac{2}{4}
\end{array}
\qquad
\begin{array}{r}
2\frac{1}{4} \\
+\,1\frac{1}{4} \\
\hline
3\frac{2}{4} = 3\frac{1}{2}
\end{array}
$$

Simplest form

Esther used $3\frac{1}{2}$ yards of ribbon for the certificates.

Add: $7\frac{2}{5} + 5\frac{3}{10} = n$.

▶ To **add mixed numbers** with fractions with *unlike* denominators:

- Find the LCD of the fractions.

- Use the LCD to rename the fractions as equivalent fractions with the same denominator.

- Add the fractions. Then add the whole numbers.

- Write the sum in simplest form.

LCD of $\frac{2}{5}$ and $\frac{3}{10}$: 10

$$
\begin{array}{rcl}
7\frac{2}{5} = 7\frac{2 \times 2}{5 \times 2} & = & 7\frac{4}{10} \\
+\,5\frac{3}{10} & = & 5\frac{3}{10} \\
\hline
& & 12\frac{7}{10}
\end{array}
$$

Study these examples.

$$
\begin{array}{r}
3\frac{1}{9} \\
+\,5 \\
\hline
8\frac{1}{9}
\end{array}
$$

$$
\begin{array}{rcl}
5\frac{5}{12} & = & 5\frac{5}{12} \\
+\ \frac{1}{4} = \frac{1 \times 3}{4 \times 3} & = & \frac{3}{12} \\
\hline
& & 5\frac{8}{12} = 5\frac{2}{3}
\end{array}
$$

$$
\begin{array}{rcl}
6\frac{1}{4} = 6\frac{1 \times 3}{4 \times 3} & = & 6\frac{3}{12} \\
2\frac{1}{6} = 2\frac{1 \times 2}{6 \times 2} & = & 2\frac{2}{12} \\
+\,8\frac{1}{3} = 8\frac{1 \times 4}{3 \times 4} & = & 8\frac{4}{12} \\
\hline
& & 16\frac{9}{12} = 16\frac{3}{4}
\end{array}
$$

Add.

1. $3\frac{4}{11}$
$+\,2\frac{1}{11}$
_____

2. $8\frac{5}{12}$
$+\,9\frac{1}{12}$
_____

3. $9\frac{1}{6}$
$+\,2\frac{3}{4}$
_____

4. $10\frac{3}{5}$
$+\,3$
_____

5. $4\frac{1}{3}$
$+\,7\frac{1}{6}$
_____

6. $\quad\frac{4}{5}$
$+\,8\frac{1}{6}$
_____

7. $6\frac{3}{7}$
$3\frac{1}{7}$
$+\,2\frac{2}{7}$
_____

8. $5\frac{1}{9}$
$3\frac{4}{9}$
$+\,4\frac{1}{9}$
_____

9. $9\frac{1}{3}$
$2\frac{1}{4}$
$+\,3\frac{1}{12}$
_____

10. $2\frac{2}{5}$
$6\frac{1}{3}$
$+\,4\frac{1}{15}$
_____

11. $8\frac{1}{4}$
$2\frac{2}{5}$
$+\,5\frac{3}{20}$
_____

12. $2\frac{1}{3}$
$5\frac{3}{8}$
$+\,\quad\frac{1}{4}$
_____

13. $6\frac{1}{4} + 5\frac{2}{4}$

14. $3\frac{5}{12} + \frac{1}{3}$

15. $8\frac{2}{5} + 5$

16. $7\frac{1}{6} + 3\frac{1}{6} + 5\frac{1}{6}$

17. $8\frac{2}{5} + 7\frac{1}{4} + \frac{1}{10}$

18. $9 + 8\frac{1}{3} + 3\frac{1}{12}$

19. Explain in your Math Journal how the properties of addition can be used to solve $3\frac{1}{3} + 6\frac{1}{4} + 1\frac{2}{3}$ mentally.

Problem Solving

20. Ethel bought $1\frac{5}{12}$ yd of white fabric and $2\frac{1}{2}$ yd of yellow fabric to make curtains. How many yards of fabric did she buy?

21. The chef spent $4\frac{1}{4}$ h cooking dinner and $1\frac{2}{3}$ h cooking breakfast and lunch. How many hours did he spend cooking?

22. In the long-jump competition, Mac's first jump was $22\frac{1}{8}$ ft. His second jump was $21\frac{2}{3}$ ft, and his third jump was $20\frac{3}{4}$ ft. Find the sum of his jumps in feet.

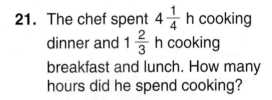

TEST PREPARATION

23. Lauren practiced playing the piano $1\frac{1}{4}$ hours in the morning, 3 hours in the afternoon, and 2 hours and 45 minutes in the evening. For what fraction of the day did she practice?

A $\frac{1}{3}$ **B** $\frac{7}{24}$ **C** $\frac{1}{4}$ **D** $\frac{5}{24}$

5-5 Rename Mixed Number Sums

When a *sum* contains *a fraction greater than or equal to one*, **rename** the fraction as a whole or mixed number. Then add the whole numbers.

▶ Add: $5\frac{3}{4} + 3\frac{5}{6} = n.$

$$5\frac{3}{4} = 5\frac{3 \times 3}{4 \times 3} = 5\frac{9}{12}$$
$$+\ 3\frac{5}{6} = 3\frac{5 \times 2}{6 \times 2} = 3\frac{10}{12}$$

$$8\frac{19}{12} = 8 + 1\frac{7}{12}$$

Rename $\frac{19}{12}$ as $1\frac{7}{12}$.

$$= 9\frac{7}{12}$$

▶ Add: $9\frac{1}{6} + 1\frac{1}{3} + 3\frac{1}{2} = n.$

$$9\frac{1}{6} \qquad\qquad = 9\frac{1}{6}$$
$$1\frac{1}{3} = 1\frac{1 \times 2}{3 \times 2} = 1\frac{2}{6}$$
$$+\ 3\frac{1}{2} = 3\frac{1 \times 3}{2 \times 3} = 3\frac{3}{6}$$

$$13\frac{6}{6}$$

Rename $\frac{6}{6}$ as 1.

$$= 13 + 1$$
$$= 14$$

Study this example.

$$6\ \frac{3}{5} = 6\frac{3 \times 3}{5 \times 3} = 6\frac{9}{15}$$
$$+\ \quad\frac{13}{15} \qquad\qquad = \quad\frac{13}{15}$$

$$6\frac{22}{15} = 6 + 1\frac{7}{15} = 7\frac{7}{15}$$

Rename each as a mixed number in simplest form.

1. $6\frac{11}{9}$ **2.** $10\frac{5}{5}$ **3.** $14\frac{7}{7}$ **4.** $9\frac{10}{8}$ **5.** $8\frac{6}{4}$ **6.** $11\frac{9}{6}$

7. $3\frac{20}{15}$ **8.** $21\frac{14}{12}$ **9.** $32\frac{16}{14}$ **10.** $17\frac{28}{25}$ **11.** $19\frac{24}{18}$ **12.** $25\frac{15}{10}$

13. $36\frac{8}{8}$ **14.** $42\frac{16}{15}$ **15.** $53\frac{27}{24}$ **16.** $83\frac{12}{8}$ **17.** $75\frac{19}{17}$ **18.** $41\frac{13}{11}$

Add.

19. $4\frac{5}{7}$ **20.** $4\frac{1}{8}$ **21.** $6\frac{5}{6}$ **22.** $3\frac{8}{9}$ **23.** $5\frac{3}{8}$ **24.** $5\frac{2}{4}$

    $+\ 2\frac{3}{7}$ $+\ 5\frac{7}{8}$ $+\ 4\frac{4}{6}$ $+\ 6\frac{2}{9}$ $+\ 3\frac{7}{8}$ $+\ 3\frac{4}{4}$

Find the sum.

25. $4\frac{3}{4}$ **26.** $8\frac{5}{6}$ **27.** $7\frac{5}{9}$ **28.** $\frac{3}{5}$ **29.** $6\frac{2}{5}$ **30.** $3\frac{5}{12}$

    $+\,2\frac{7}{20}$ $+\,2\frac{5}{12}$ $+\,4\frac{8}{18}$ $+\,9\frac{8}{20}$ $+\,\frac{2}{3}$ $+\,9\frac{7}{8}$

31. $4\frac{1}{5}$ **32.** $3\frac{4}{9}$ **33.** $3\frac{3}{4}$ **34.** $5\frac{1}{8}$ **35.** $6\frac{1}{2}$ **36.** $2\frac{5}{6}$

    $6\frac{9}{10}$ $6\frac{2}{3}$ $5\frac{3}{8}$ $\frac{3}{4}$ $9\frac{1}{4}$ $9\frac{1}{3}$

    $+\,2\frac{2}{5}$ $+\,4\frac{2}{9}$ $+\,7\frac{5}{8}$ $+\,6\frac{1}{2}$ $+\,3\frac{2}{3}$ $+\,\frac{1}{12}$

37. $6\frac{5}{9} + 4\frac{2}{3}$ **38.** $\frac{3}{4} + 2\frac{4}{5}$ **39.** $3\frac{5}{8} + 7\frac{2}{3}$

40. $8\frac{1}{2} + 5\frac{7}{12} + 3\frac{2}{3}$ **41.** $3\frac{3}{10} + 2\frac{3}{4} + 6\frac{1}{5}$ **42.** $4\frac{1}{3} + \frac{5}{8} + 1\frac{1}{4}$

Write _always_, _sometimes_, or _never_.

43. When you add two mixed numbers, the fractional part of the sum is more than 1. Give examples to support your answer.

Problem Solving

44. A $10\frac{1}{2}$-ft ladder has a $4\frac{3}{4}$-ft extension. What is the height of the ladder when totally extended?

45. Harriet exercised $14\frac{2}{3}$ min in the morning and $23\frac{5}{6}$ min in the afternoon. How long did she exercise in all?

46. The Madrigal family drank $2\frac{2}{3}$ bottles of spring water for breakfast, $2\frac{1}{8}$ bottles for lunch, and $1\frac{3}{4}$ bottles for dinner. How many bottles of spring water did the family drink for their three meals?

MENTAL MATH

Add. Look for sums of 1.

47. $10 + 3\frac{1}{2} + 4\frac{1}{2}$ **48.** $6\frac{1}{4} + 11 + 5\frac{3}{4}$ **49.** $9\frac{4}{5} + 7\frac{1}{5} + 3$

50. $6\frac{1}{2} + 4\frac{1}{2} + 5\frac{3}{4}$ **51.** $3\frac{1}{3} + 6\frac{1}{5} + 10\frac{2}{3}$ **52.** $8\frac{3}{4} + 2\frac{2}{7} + 9\frac{1}{4}$

Rename Differences: Like Denominators

Mary ran $\frac{8}{9}$ mi on Saturday. Ellen ran $\frac{5}{9}$ mi on the same day. How much farther did Mary run than Ellen?

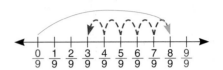

To find how much farther, subtract: $\frac{8}{9} - \frac{5}{9} = n$.

▶ To **subtract fractions** with *like* denominators:

- Subtract the numerators.

- Write the difference over the common denominator.

- Write the difference in simplest form.

$$\frac{8}{9} - \frac{5}{9} = \frac{8-5}{9}$$

Think
GCF of 3 and 9: 3

$$= \frac{3}{9}$$

$$= \frac{3 \div 3}{9 \div 3} = \frac{1}{3} \quad \leftarrow \boxed{\text{simplest form}}$$

Mary ran $\frac{1}{3}$ mi farther than Ellen.

Study these examples.

$$\frac{13}{7} - \frac{6}{7} = \frac{13-6}{7}$$
$$= \frac{7}{7} = 1$$

Think
$$7)\overline{7}^{\,1}$$

$$\frac{17}{8} - \frac{6}{8} = \frac{17-6}{8}$$
$$= \frac{11}{8}$$
$$= 1\frac{3}{8}$$

Think
$$8)\overline{11}^{\,1\ R3}$$

$$\begin{array}{r} \frac{2}{3} \\ -\frac{2}{3} \\ \hline \frac{0}{3} = 0 \end{array}$$

Think
$$\frac{2-2}{3}$$

Write a subtraction sentence, with the difference in simplest form, for each number line.

1.
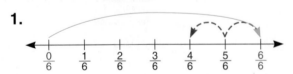

2.
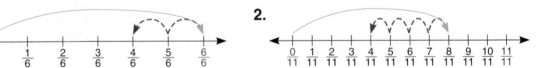

3.
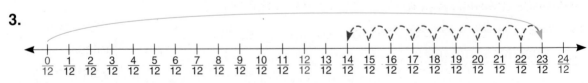

Use number lines to model each difference. Write a subtraction sentence with the difference in simplest form.

4. $\frac{5}{8} - \frac{1}{8}$

5. $\frac{5}{6} - \frac{1}{6}$

6. $\frac{11}{12} - \frac{5}{12}$

7. $\frac{7}{10} - \frac{3}{10}$

Subtract.

8. $\dfrac{19}{12} - \dfrac{7}{12}$

9. $\dfrac{21}{10} - \dfrac{10}{10}$

10. $\dfrac{7}{8} - \dfrac{7}{8}$

11. $\dfrac{25}{9} - \dfrac{7}{9}$

12. $\begin{array}{r} \frac{7}{8} \\ -\ \frac{3}{8} \\ \hline \end{array}$

13. $\begin{array}{r} \frac{10}{12} \\ -\ \frac{8}{12} \\ \hline \end{array}$

14. $\begin{array}{r} \frac{17}{15} \\ -\ \frac{1}{15} \\ \hline \end{array}$

15. $\begin{array}{r} \frac{19}{8} \\ -\ \frac{11}{8} \\ \hline \end{array}$

16. $\begin{array}{r} \frac{18}{20} \\ -\ \frac{4}{20} \\ \hline \end{array}$

17. $\begin{array}{r} \frac{10}{14} \\ -\ \frac{10}{14} \\ \hline \end{array}$

Find the value of *n*.

18. $\dfrac{3}{11} + \dfrac{n}{11} = \dfrac{7}{11}$

> **Think**
> $\dfrac{7}{11} - \dfrac{3}{11} = \dfrac{4}{11}$; so $\dfrac{3}{11} + \dfrac{4}{11} = \dfrac{7}{11}$

19. $\dfrac{3}{9} + \dfrac{n}{9} = \dfrac{5}{9}$

20. $\dfrac{6}{21} + \dfrac{n}{21} = \dfrac{8}{21}$

21. $\dfrac{n}{13} + \dfrac{4}{13} = \dfrac{7}{13}$

22. $\dfrac{9}{23} + \dfrac{n}{23} = \dfrac{18}{23}$

23. $\dfrac{n}{17} + \dfrac{8}{17} = \dfrac{15}{17}$

24. $\dfrac{n}{15} + \dfrac{11}{15} = \dfrac{14}{15}$

25. $\dfrac{8}{25} + \dfrac{n}{25} = \dfrac{18}{25}$

26. Write in your Math Journal the different types of answers you get when subtracting fractions with like denominators. Give an example of each.

Write a subtraction sentence.

27. What is the difference between $\dfrac{15}{21}$ and $\dfrac{8}{21}$?

28. How much less than $\dfrac{18}{13}$ is $\dfrac{5}{13}$?

Problem Solving

29. Lucas needs $\dfrac{4}{9}$ yd of ribbon for a gift box. He has $\dfrac{7}{9}$ yd of ribbon. How much ribbon will he have after wrapping?

30. In one minute, a full freight train travels $\dfrac{2}{6}$ mi and an empty freight train travels $\dfrac{4}{6}$ mi. Which train travels faster? By how much?

DO YOU REMEMBER?

Complete the sentences. Use the words in the box.

31. The symbol $>$ or $<$ is used to show a(n) ? statement.

32. In $16 \div 8 = 2$, 16 is the ? .

33. In 5^3, 3 is called the ? .

34. A ? is a symbol, usually a letter, that is used to represent a number.

> exponent
> divisor
> variable
> inequality
> dividend

Subtract Fractions: Unlike Denominators

A piece of ribbon $\frac{1}{6}$ yd long is cut from a ribbon that is $\frac{2}{3}$ yd long. How much of the ribbon is left?

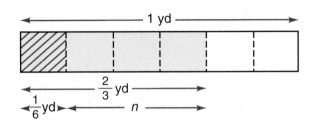

To find how much of the ribbon is left, subtract: $\frac{2}{3} - \frac{1}{6} = n$.

▶ To **subtract fractions** with *unlike* denominators:

- Find the least common denominator (LCD) of the fractions.

  LCD of $\frac{2}{3}$ and $\frac{1}{6}$: 6

- Rename the fractions as equivalent fractions with the LCD as the denominator.

$$\frac{2}{3} = \frac{2 \times 2}{3 \times 2} = \frac{4}{6}$$
$$-\frac{1}{6} \qquad\qquad = \frac{1}{6}$$
$$\overline{\qquad\qquad\qquad \frac{3}{6} = \frac{1}{2}} \leftarrow$$

- Subtract the fractions.

- Write the difference in lowest terms.

lowest terms

The piece of ribbon that is left is $\frac{1}{2}$ yard long.

Complete each subtraction.

1. $\frac{5}{9}\qquad\qquad = \frac{?}{9}$
$-\frac{1}{3} = \frac{1 \times ?}{3 \times ?} = \frac{?}{9}$
$\overline{\qquad\qquad \frac{?}{9}}$

2. $\frac{3}{7} = \frac{3 \times ?}{7 \times ?} = \frac{?}{14}$
$-\frac{2}{14}\qquad\qquad = \frac{?}{14}$
$\overline{\qquad\qquad \frac{?}{14} = \frac{?}{?}}$

3. $\frac{2}{3} = \frac{2 \times ?}{3 \times ?} = \frac{?}{9}$
$-\frac{2}{9}\qquad\qquad = \frac{?}{9}$
$\overline{\qquad\qquad \frac{?}{?}}$

Subtract.

4. $\frac{7}{8}$
$-\frac{1}{2}$

5. $\frac{3}{8}$
$-\frac{5}{16}$

6. $\frac{9}{12}$
$-\frac{1}{3}$

7. $\frac{7}{9}$
$-\frac{2}{3}$

8. $\frac{9}{10}$
$-\frac{4}{5}$

9. $\frac{2}{3}$
$-\frac{8}{15}$

10. $\frac{5}{6}$
$-\frac{1}{2}$

11. $\frac{4}{5}$
$-\frac{3}{10}$

12. $\frac{17}{36}$
$-\frac{1}{3}$

13. $\frac{2}{3}$
$-\frac{3}{18}$

14. $\frac{8}{15}$
$-\frac{1}{3}$

15. $\frac{3}{4}$
$-\frac{5}{12}$

Find the difference.

16. $\frac{2}{3}$ **17.** $\frac{5}{7}$ **18.** $\frac{3}{4}$ **19.** $\frac{5}{8}$ **20.** $\frac{4}{5}$ **21.** $\frac{3}{4}$
$-\frac{7}{24}$ $-\frac{5}{28}$ $-\frac{7}{16}$ $-\frac{7}{24}$ $-\frac{4}{15}$ $-\frac{5}{20}$

22. $\frac{4}{11}$ **23.** $\frac{7}{8}$ **24.** $\frac{8}{9}$ **25.** $\frac{6}{7}$ **26.** $\frac{9}{10}$ **27.** $\frac{5}{6}$
$-\frac{5}{22}$ $-\frac{5}{24}$ $-\frac{5}{36}$ $-\frac{5}{21}$ $-\frac{3}{20}$ $-\frac{7}{30}$

Subtract.

28. $\frac{4}{6} - \frac{2}{12}$ **29.** $\frac{11}{18} - \frac{1}{6}$ **30.** $\frac{23}{36} - \frac{5}{12}$ **31.** $\frac{14}{16} - \frac{1}{4}$

32. $\frac{5}{9} - \frac{5}{18}$ **33.** $\frac{15}{26} - \frac{1}{2}$ **34.** $\frac{17}{27} - \frac{1}{3}$ **35.** $\frac{4}{5} - \frac{3}{20}$

Problem Solving

36. Nelia had $\frac{2}{3}$ cup of fruit. She put $\frac{3}{6}$ cup into the salad she was making. What fractional part of a cup of fruit was left?

37. Marsha needs $\frac{2}{3}$ qt of paint for a project. She has $\frac{7}{12}$ qt of paint. How much more paint does she need for the project?

38. Chris had $\frac{3}{4}$ yd of ribbon. He used $\frac{3}{8}$ yd for a bow. How much of the ribbon was *not* used for the bow?

39. Juan ran $\frac{6}{8}$ of a mile and Charles ran $\frac{1}{4}$ of a mile. How much farther did Juan run than Charles?

40. Denroy walked $\frac{7}{8}$ mile on Monday. He walked $\frac{1}{4}$ mile less on Tuesday. How far did he walk on Tuesday?

41. Naty had $\frac{11}{12}$ of a tank of gas. She used some and had $\frac{1}{3}$ of a tank left. How much gas did she use?

CHALLENGE

Find each sum. Then find how much greater it is than 1.

42. $\frac{2}{3}$ and $\frac{1}{2}$ **43.** $\frac{2}{3}$ and $\frac{4}{9}$ **44.** $\frac{5}{6}$ and $\frac{1}{4}$ **45.** $\frac{4}{5}$ and $\frac{3}{10}$

46. $\frac{43}{64}$ and $\frac{5}{8}$ **47.** $\frac{5}{6}$ and $\frac{13}{48}$ **48.** $\frac{5}{38}$ and $\frac{17}{19}$ **49.** $\frac{16}{17}$ and $\frac{5}{51}$

More Subtraction of Fractions

Flora uses $\frac{2}{3}$ yd of a $\frac{3}{4}$-yd strip of wood to make a name plate. How long is the piece of wood that is left?

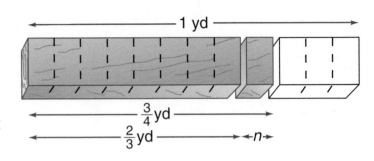

1 yd

$\frac{3}{4}$ yd

$\frac{2}{3}$ yd ← n →

To find the length of the wood that is left, subtract: $\frac{3}{4} - \frac{2}{3} = n$.

- Find the least common denominator (LCD) of the fractions.

LCD of $\frac{3}{4}$ and $\frac{2}{3}$: 12

- Rename the fractions as equivalent fractions with the LCD as the denominator.

$$\frac{3}{4} = \frac{3 \times 3}{4 \times 3} = \frac{9}{12}$$

- Subtract the fractions.

$$-\frac{2}{3} = \frac{2 \times 4}{3 \times 4} = \frac{8}{12}$$

- Write the difference in simplest form.

$$\frac{1}{12}$$ ← Simplest form

The piece of wood that is left is $\frac{1}{12}$ yd long.

Complete each subtraction.

1.
$$\frac{3}{5} = \frac{3 \times ?}{5 \times ?} = \frac{?}{15}$$
$$-\frac{1}{3} = \frac{1 \times ?}{3 \times ?} = \frac{?}{15}$$
$$\frac{?}{15}$$

2.
$$\frac{5}{6} = \frac{5 \times ?}{6 \times ?} = \frac{?}{24}$$
$$-\frac{3}{8} = \frac{3 \times ?}{8 \times ?} = \frac{?}{24}$$
$$\frac{?}{24}$$

3.
$$\frac{1}{2} = \frac{1 \times ?}{2 \times ?} = \frac{?}{18}$$
$$-\frac{2}{9} = \frac{2 \times ?}{9 \times ?} = \frac{?}{18}$$
$$\frac{?}{?}$$

Subtract.

4.
$$\frac{1}{3}$$
$$-\frac{1}{4}$$

5.
$$\frac{4}{5}$$
$$-\frac{3}{4}$$

6.
$$\frac{7}{9}$$
$$-\frac{1}{2}$$

7.
$$\frac{2}{5}$$
$$-\frac{1}{3}$$

8.
$$\frac{4}{5}$$
$$-\frac{1}{2}$$

9.
$$\frac{3}{4}$$
$$-\frac{1}{6}$$

10.
$$\frac{6}{7}$$
$$-\frac{2}{3}$$

11.
$$\frac{3}{5}$$
$$-\frac{1}{8}$$

12.
$$\frac{7}{10}$$
$$-\frac{2}{3}$$

13.
$$\frac{5}{6}$$
$$-\frac{5}{8}$$

14.
$$\frac{3}{7}$$
$$-\frac{1}{3}$$

15.
$$\frac{9}{10}$$
$$-\frac{1}{4}$$

Find the difference.

16. $\dfrac{5}{6}$
$-\dfrac{2}{9}$

17. $\dfrac{4}{5}$
$-\dfrac{1}{3}$

18. $\dfrac{8}{9}$
$-\dfrac{5}{12}$

19. $\dfrac{13}{15}$
$-\dfrac{4}{9}$

20. $\dfrac{6}{7}$
$-\dfrac{3}{4}$

21. $\dfrac{9}{10}$
$-\dfrac{2}{3}$

22. $\dfrac{5}{7}$
$-\dfrac{3}{5}$

23. $\dfrac{7}{9}$
$-\dfrac{2}{3}$

24. $\dfrac{5}{6}$
$-\dfrac{4}{5}$

25. $\dfrac{7}{8}$
$-\dfrac{2}{3}$

26. $\dfrac{4}{5}$
$-\dfrac{3}{7}$

27. $\dfrac{1}{2}$
$-\dfrac{2}{11}$

Subtract.

28. $\dfrac{1}{2} - \dfrac{1}{3}$

29. $\dfrac{3}{4} - \dfrac{2}{5}$

30. $\dfrac{4}{5} - \dfrac{1}{6}$

31. $\dfrac{5}{6} - \dfrac{4}{9}$

32. $\dfrac{2}{3} - \dfrac{1}{4}$

33. $\dfrac{7}{8} - \dfrac{5}{6}$

34. $\dfrac{8}{9} - \dfrac{3}{4}$

35. $\dfrac{14}{15} - \dfrac{2}{9}$

Add or subtract. Then compare. Write <, =, or >.

36. $\dfrac{7}{8} - \dfrac{1}{6}$? $\dfrac{2}{3} + \dfrac{1}{5}$

37. $\dfrac{1}{4} + \dfrac{2}{9}$? $\dfrac{9}{10} - \dfrac{1}{6}$

38. $\dfrac{5}{6} - \dfrac{1}{3}$? $\dfrac{1}{6} + \dfrac{1}{3}$

39. $\dfrac{1}{3} + \dfrac{1}{5}$? $\dfrac{2}{3} - \dfrac{1}{4}$

40. $\dfrac{4}{5} - \dfrac{1}{10}$? $\dfrac{1}{5} + \dfrac{1}{2}$

41. $\dfrac{2}{5} + \dfrac{1}{7}$? $\dfrac{2}{3} - \dfrac{3}{7}$

Write a subtraction sentence for each.

42. How much less than $\dfrac{5}{7}$ is $\dfrac{1}{2}$?

43. How much greater than $\dfrac{5}{6}$ is $\dfrac{6}{7}$?

Problem Solving

44. On Tuesday $\dfrac{3}{4}$ inch of snow fell. On Thursday $\dfrac{1}{5}$ inch of snow fell. How much more snow fell on Tuesday than on Thursday?

45. Tess has $\dfrac{5}{8}$ of an inch of loose-leaf paper in her binder. Cal has $\dfrac{2}{3}$ of an inch in his. Who has less loose-leaf paper? How much less?

46. Pat, Jett, and Vic went to the library during their break. Jett stayed in the library for $\dfrac{1}{10}$ hour less than Pat. Vic stayed in the library for $\dfrac{1}{4}$ hour more than Jett. If Vic stayed in the library for $\dfrac{4}{5}$ hour, how much time did each one stay in the library?

Subtract Mixed Numbers

Sylvia had $7\frac{3}{4}$ yards of fabric. She used some of the fabric to make curtains and had $2\frac{1}{4}$ yards left. How much fabric did she use for the curtains?

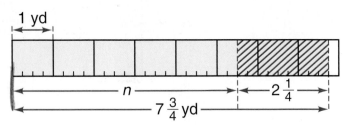

$$n + 2\frac{1}{4} = 7\frac{3}{4}$$

To find how much fabric was used, subtract: $7\frac{3}{4} - 2\frac{1}{4} = n$.

▶ To **subtract mixed numbers** with fractions of *like* denominators:

- Subtract the fractions.
- Subtract the whole numbers.
- Write the difference in simplest form.

$$
\begin{array}{r}
7\frac{3}{4} \\
- 2\frac{1}{4} \\
\hline
\frac{2}{4}
\end{array}
\qquad
\begin{array}{r}
7\frac{3}{4} \\
- 2\frac{1}{4} \\
\hline
5\frac{2}{4} = 5\frac{1}{2}
\end{array}
$$

⟵ Simplest form

Sylvia used $5\frac{1}{2}$ yards of fabric for curtains.

Subtract: $8\frac{3}{4} - 1\frac{2}{3} = n$.

▶ To **subtract mixed numbers** with fractions of *unlike* denominators:

- Find the LCD of the fractions.

LCD of $\frac{3}{4}$ and $\frac{2}{3}$: 12

- Rename the fractions as equivalent fractions with the LCD as the denominator.

- Subtract the fractions. Then subtract the whole numbers.

- Write the difference in simplest form.

$$
\begin{array}{r}
8\frac{3}{4} = 8\frac{3 \times 3}{4 \times 3} = 8\frac{9}{12} \\
- 1\frac{2}{3} = 1\frac{2 \times 4}{3 \times 4} = 1\frac{8}{12} \\
\hline
7\frac{1}{12}
\end{array}
$$

⟵ Simplest form

Study these examples.

$$
\begin{array}{r}
9\frac{3}{10} \\
- 7\frac{3}{10} \\
\hline
2\frac{0}{10} = 2
\end{array}
$$

$$
\begin{array}{r}
5\frac{2}{3} = 5\frac{2 \times 2}{3 \times 2} = 5\frac{4}{6} \\
- 5\frac{1}{6} = \qquad\qquad\; = 5\frac{1}{6} \\
\hline
\frac{3}{6} = \frac{1}{2}
\end{array}
$$

$$
\begin{array}{r}
3\frac{2}{5} = 3\frac{2 \times 2}{5 \times 2} = 3\frac{4}{10} \\
- 3\frac{4}{10} = \qquad\qquad\; = 3\frac{4}{10} \\
\hline
\frac{0}{10} = 0
\end{array}
$$

Subtract.

1. $3\frac{2}{5}$
$-2\frac{1}{5}$

2. $2\frac{4}{7}$
$-1\frac{3}{7}$

3. $4\frac{7}{8}$
$-2\frac{3}{8}$

4. $5\frac{5}{6}$
$-3\frac{3}{6}$

5. $5\frac{11}{16}$
$-5\frac{3}{16}$

6. $6\frac{8}{9}$
$-3\frac{8}{9}$

7. $5\frac{4}{12}$
$-5\frac{1}{3}$

8. $6\frac{5}{9}$
$-4\frac{1}{2}$

9. $6\frac{4}{5}$
$-2\frac{1}{3}$

10. $8\frac{2}{3}$
$-3\frac{1}{5}$

11. $8\frac{3}{4}$
$-7\frac{1}{6}$

12. $8\frac{5}{6}$
$-8\frac{4}{9}$

13. $9\frac{3}{8} - 4\frac{5}{16}$

14. $6\frac{3}{7} - 2\frac{5}{21}$

15. $2\frac{1}{5} - 1\frac{1}{20}$

16. $8\frac{5}{6} - 5\frac{1}{3}$

17. $5\frac{2}{3} - 5\frac{2}{9}$

18. $3\frac{12}{18} - 3\frac{2}{3}$

19. $7\frac{15}{20} - 4\frac{3}{5}$

20. $2\frac{4}{7} - 1\frac{1}{2}$

Problem Solving

21. A motorcyclist rode $9\frac{5}{7}$ miles on flat and hilly roads. If he rode $2\frac{1}{21}$ miles on hilly roads, how many miles did he ride on flat roads?

22. A recipe calls for $2\frac{5}{9}$ cups of flour. Lou has only $1\frac{13}{30}$ cups of flour on hand. How many more cups of flour does she need to make the recipe?

23. From a $5\frac{5}{6}$-ft piece of rope, Val cut off $2\frac{1}{3}$ ft. How much rope was left?

24. Cindy ran the 60-yd hurdles in $11\frac{2}{3}$ s. She ran the same race in $1\frac{1}{2}$ s more than Elsie. What was Elsie's time?

25. In your Math Journal write when the fractional part of the difference of two mixed numbers is equal to zero; when the whole-number part of the difference is equal to zero. Use models to explain your answers.

CHALLENGE — Algebra

Compare. Write <, =, or >.

26. $9\frac{5}{10} - 6\frac{3}{10} \ \underline{?} \ 5\frac{2}{5} - 2\frac{1}{5}$

27. $6\frac{3}{4} - 2\frac{1}{4} \ \underline{?} \ 10\frac{2}{3} - 6\frac{1}{3}$

28. $8\frac{4}{7} - 5\frac{3}{14} \ \underline{?} \ 7\frac{4}{5} - 4\frac{3}{10}$

29. $9\frac{12}{20} - 2\frac{3}{10} \ \underline{?} \ 8\frac{1}{4} - 1\frac{1}{8}$

Subtraction with Renaming

Susan had 3 yards of ribbon.
She used $1\frac{2}{6}$ yards for edging.
How many yards of ribbon
did she have left?

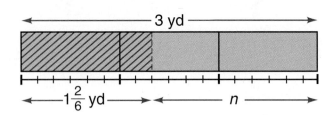

3 yd

$1\frac{2}{6}$ yd n

To find the number of yards left,
subtract: $3 - 1\frac{2}{6} = n$.

▶ To **subtract** a *mixed number* from
   a *whole number:*

- Rename the whole number as
  a mixed number.

- Subtract the mixed numbers.

- Write the difference in simplest form.

$$\begin{array}{r} 3 = 2\frac{6}{6} \\ -1\frac{2}{6} = 1\frac{2}{6} \\ \hline 1\frac{4}{6} = 1\frac{2}{3} \end{array}$$

.Think..........
$3 = 2 + 1$
$ = 2 + \frac{6}{6} = 2\frac{6}{6}$

Simplest form

Susan had $1\frac{2}{3}$ yards of ribbon left.

Study these examples.

$$\begin{array}{r} 7 = 6\frac{4}{4} \\ -6\frac{1}{4} = 6\frac{1}{4} \\ \hline \frac{3}{4} \end{array}$$

.Think.......
$7 = 6 + 1$
$ = 6 + \frac{4}{4}$
$ = 6\frac{4}{4}$

$$9 - \frac{2}{3} = 8\frac{3}{3} - \frac{2}{3}$$
$$= 8\frac{1}{3}$$

.Think.......
$9 = 8 + 1$
$ = 8 + \frac{3}{3}$
$ = 8\frac{3}{3}$

Rename each whole number as a mixed number.

1. $2 = 1\frac{?}{2}$

2. $5 = 4\frac{?}{3}$

3. $7 = 6\frac{?}{8}$

4. $9 = 8\frac{?}{5}$

5. $6 = 5\frac{?}{4}$

6. $3 = 2\frac{?}{3}$

7. $8 = 7\frac{?}{7}$

8. $4 = \underline{\ ?\ }\frac{?}{9}$

9. $8 = \underline{\ ?\ }\frac{?}{4}$

10. $6 = \underline{\ ?\ }\frac{?}{6}$

11. $5 = \underline{\ ?\ }\frac{?}{2}$

12. $4 = \underline{\ ?\ }\frac{?}{3}$

13. $10 = \underline{\ ?\ }\frac{?}{5}$

14. $12 = \underline{\ ?\ }\frac{?}{7}$

15. $14 = \underline{\ ?\ }\frac{?}{11}$

16. $11 = \underline{\ ?\ }\frac{?}{9}$

Subtract.

17. $7 - 3\frac{2}{3}$ 18. $6 - 2\frac{1}{2}$ 19. $4 - 1\frac{3}{8}$ 20. $5 - 1\frac{1}{4}$ 21. $10 - 7\frac{3}{5}$ 22. $7 - 2\frac{2}{7}$

23. $9 - 2\frac{1}{6}$ 24. $6 - 4\frac{1}{5}$ 25. $4 - 1\frac{1}{2}$ 26. $6 - 2\frac{2}{3}$ 27. $7 - 3\frac{4}{9}$ 28. $3 - 1\frac{6}{10}$

29. $3 - 2\frac{2}{5}$ 30. $7 - 6\frac{1}{8}$ 31. $4 - 2\frac{6}{9}$ 32. $8 - 5\frac{2}{4}$ 33. $10 - 5\frac{5}{6}$ 34. $4 - 1\frac{1}{9}$

35. $3 - 2\frac{1}{6}$ 36. $7 - 6\frac{8}{12}$ 37. $8 - 4\frac{7}{12}$ 38. $4 - 1\frac{2}{3}$ 39. $16 - 9\frac{5}{8}$ 40. $3 - 1\frac{9}{10}$

Find the difference.

41. $6 - 2\frac{3}{5}$ 42. $8 - \frac{1}{4}$ 43. $9 - \frac{3}{5}$ 44. $7 - 4\frac{3}{10}$

45. $5 - 3\frac{2}{9}$ 46. $7 - 6\frac{1}{6}$ 47. $4 - \frac{3}{4}$ 48. $2 - \frac{1}{5}$

Problem Solving

49. A piece of tin $2\frac{3}{8}$ ft long was cut from a 4-ft sheet of tin. How much of the sheet was left?

50. Max lives $4\frac{5}{6}$ miles from school. Don lives 6 miles from school. How much farther away from school does Don live than Max?

51. Explain in your Math Journal why renaming is needed when a mixed number is subtracted from a whole number.

CRITICAL THINKING — Algebra

Write the next two numbers to complete the pattern.
Explain the method you used.

52. $6, 5\frac{1}{2}, 5, 4\frac{1}{2}, \underline{\ ?\ }, \underline{\ ?\ }$

53. $8, 6\frac{1}{2}, 5, 3\frac{1}{2}, \underline{\ ?\ }, \underline{\ ?\ }$

54. $7, 5\frac{2}{3}, 4\frac{1}{3}, 3, \underline{\ ?\ }, \underline{\ ?\ }$

55. $9, 7\frac{3}{4}, 6\frac{1}{2}, 5\frac{1}{4}, \underline{\ ?\ }, \underline{\ ?\ }$

More Renaming in Subtraction

Alice is biking to the park, $4\frac{1}{2}$ miles from her home. She has already gone $2\frac{5}{6}$ miles. How much farther does she have to go to reach the park?

To find how much farther Alice has to go, subtract: $4\frac{1}{2} - 2\frac{5}{6} = n$.

- Find the LCD of the fractions.

LCD of $\frac{1}{2}$ and $\frac{5}{6}$: 6

- Express the fractions as equivalent fractions with the LCD as the denominator.

$$4\frac{1}{2} = 4\frac{1 \times 3}{2 \times 3} = 4\frac{3}{6}$$
$$-2\frac{5}{6} \qquad\qquad = 2\frac{5}{6}$$

$$\frac{3}{6} < \frac{5}{6}$$

- Rename the *minuend* if the fraction in the minuend is less than the fraction in the subtrahend.

$$4\frac{1}{2} = 4\frac{3}{6} = 3\frac{9}{6}$$
$$-2\frac{5}{6} = 2\frac{5}{6} = 2\frac{5}{6}$$
$$\rule{2cm}{0.4pt}$$
$$1\frac{4}{6} = 1\frac{2}{3}$$

$$4\frac{3}{6} = 3 + 1 + \frac{3}{6}$$
$$= 3 + \frac{6}{6} + \frac{3}{6}$$
$$= 3 + \frac{9}{6}$$

- Subtract. Write the difference in simplest form.

Simplest form

Alice has to go $1\frac{2}{3}$ miles farther to reach the park.

Study this example.

$$5\frac{1}{3} = 5\frac{1 \times 8}{3 \times 8} = 5\frac{8}{24}$$
$$-4\frac{7}{8} = 4\frac{7 \times 3}{8 \times 3} = 4\frac{21}{24}$$

$$\frac{8}{24} < \frac{21}{24}$$

$$5\frac{8}{24} = 4\frac{32}{24}$$
$$-4\frac{21}{24} = 4\frac{21}{24}$$
$$\rule{2cm}{0.4pt}$$
$$\frac{11}{24}$$

Think

$$5\frac{8}{24} = 4 + 1 + \frac{8}{24}$$
$$= 4 + \frac{24}{24} + \frac{8}{24}$$
$$= 4\frac{32}{24}$$

Practice

Rename each mixed number.

1. $5\frac{1}{5} = 4 + 1 + \frac{1}{5}$
$\qquad = 4 + \frac{5}{5} + \frac{1}{5}$
$\qquad = 4\frac{?}{5}$

2. $8\frac{2}{3} = 7 + 1 + \frac{2}{3}$
$\qquad = 7 + \frac{?}{3} + \frac{2}{3}$
$\qquad = 7\frac{?}{3}$

3. $6\frac{3}{7} = 5 + 1 + \frac{3}{7}$
$\qquad = 5 + \frac{?}{7} + \frac{?}{7}$
$\qquad = 5\frac{?}{7}$

Subtract.

4. $6\frac{1}{2}$
$-3\frac{3}{4}$

5. $10\frac{1}{4}$
$-\ 9\frac{3}{8}$

6. $4\frac{1}{6}$
$-2\frac{2}{3}$

7. $8\frac{1}{5}$
$-2\frac{5}{10}$

8. $8\frac{1}{3}$
$-4\frac{5}{12}$

9. $8\frac{1}{3}$
$-2\frac{4}{15}$

10. $7\frac{3}{4}$
$-2\frac{7}{8}$

11. $6\frac{1}{3}$
$-4\frac{4}{9}$

12. $12\frac{1}{6}$
$-\ 7\frac{7}{12}$

13. $10\frac{3}{10}$
$-\ 4\frac{3}{5}$

14. $8\frac{1}{3}$
$-3\frac{7}{15}$

15. $6\frac{1}{2}$
$-5\frac{9}{10}$

16. $9\frac{1}{4}$
$-2\frac{3}{7}$

17. $12\frac{1}{4}$
$-\ 8\frac{2}{3}$

18. $2\frac{1}{5}$
$-1\frac{2}{3}$

19. $5\frac{1}{4}$
$-2\frac{5}{6}$

20. $6\frac{1}{9}$
$-4\frac{1}{2}$

21. $2\frac{1}{4}$
$-\ \frac{3}{5}$

Find the difference.

22. $8\frac{3}{8} - 5\frac{3}{4}$

23. $7\frac{1}{2} - 4\frac{7}{10}$

24. $9\frac{1}{3} - 8\frac{5}{6}$

25. $6\frac{1}{4} - \frac{3}{8}$

26. $5\frac{1}{4} - 4\frac{2}{3}$

27. $4\frac{3}{4} - 2\frac{5}{6}$

28. $10\frac{1}{5} - \frac{1}{3}$

29. $3\frac{1}{8} - \frac{3}{5}$

30. $11\frac{3}{8} - 8\frac{2}{3}$

31. $5\frac{1}{5} - \frac{7}{9}$

32. $8\frac{2}{3} - 4\frac{4}{5}$

33. $7\frac{4}{7} - \frac{3}{4}$

Write a subtraction sentence for each.

34. What number is $\frac{5}{7}$ less than $3\frac{1}{2}$?

35. Find the difference between $7\frac{3}{8}$ and $5\frac{2}{3}$.

36. Chuck roller-skates $4\frac{1}{3}$ miles from his home to school. After he goes $2\frac{7}{8}$ miles from his home, he passes Arnie's house. How far from school is Arnie's house?

37. Dad caught a trout that weighed $7\frac{3}{8}$ pounds. Tom caught one that weighed $3\frac{3}{4}$ pounds. How many pounds heavier was Dad's trout than Tom's trout?

38. From a $10\frac{1}{3}$-ft piece of rope, a $5\frac{5}{6}$-ft piece was cut off. How much rope was left?

39. Owen needs $6\frac{2}{5}$ yd of wire. He has $4\frac{3}{4}$ yd. How much more wire does he need?

Write About It

40. Explain how to rename $5\frac{1}{6}$ so that you could subtract $3\frac{2}{9}$ from it.

Estimate Sums and Differences of Mixed Numbers

▶ You can use **rounding** to estimate sums and differences of mixed numbers.

When rounding a mixed number to the nearest whole number and *the fraction is*:

- *greater than* or *equal to* $\frac{1}{2}$, round *up*.
- *less than* $\frac{1}{2}$, round *down*.

Estimate: $12\frac{5}{6} + 11\frac{4}{9} + 14\frac{1}{2}$.

- Round each mixed number to the nearest whole number.
- Add the rounded numbers.

$$12\frac{5}{6} + 11\frac{4}{9} + 14\frac{1}{2}$$
$$\downarrow \qquad \downarrow \qquad \downarrow$$
$$13 \ + \ 11 \ + \ 15$$
$$= 39$$

Think
$$\frac{5}{6} > \frac{1}{2}$$
$$\frac{4}{9} < \frac{1}{2}$$
$$\frac{1}{2} = \frac{1}{2}$$

estimated sum

Estimate: $13\frac{1}{9} - 8\frac{2}{3}$.

- Round each mixed number to the nearest whole number.
- Subtract the rounded numbers.

$$13\frac{1}{9} - 8\frac{2}{3}$$
$$\downarrow \qquad \downarrow$$
$$13 \ - \ 9$$
$$= 4$$

Think
$$\frac{1}{9} < \frac{1}{2}$$
$$\frac{2}{3} > \frac{1}{2}$$

estimated difference

▶ You can also use **front-end estimation** to estimate sums and differences of mixed numbers.

Estimate: $9\frac{1}{3} + 4\frac{1}{5} + 5\frac{7}{9}$.

- Add the whole number parts.
- Adjust the estimate with the fraction parts.

$$9\frac{1}{3} + 4\frac{1}{5} + 5\frac{7}{9} \longrightarrow 18$$

Adjusted estimate:
$$18 + 1 = 19$$

Think
$\frac{7}{9}$ is about 1.

$$9\frac{1}{3} + 4\frac{1}{5} + 5\frac{7}{9} \approx 19$$

is approximately equal to

Estimate: $15\frac{5}{9} - 6\frac{1}{4}$.

- Subtract the whole number parts.

$$15\frac{5}{9} - 6\frac{1}{4} \longrightarrow 9$$

$$15\frac{5}{9} - 6\frac{1}{4} \approx 9$$

Estimate the sum or difference by rounding. Then compute and compare.

1. $9\frac{1}{3} + 2\frac{3}{8}$

2. $8\frac{2}{3} + 3\frac{3}{4}$

3. $14\frac{1}{3} + 12\frac{1}{2}$

4. $16\frac{2}{7} + 13\frac{5}{9}$

5. $11\frac{3}{5} + 4\frac{7}{8}$

6. $16\frac{1}{4} + 4\frac{3}{8}$

7. $19\frac{2}{9} + 15\frac{3}{4}$

8. $15\frac{1}{8} + 14\frac{8}{9}$

9. $7\frac{1}{5} + 3\frac{4}{9} + 5\frac{1}{3}$

10. $4\frac{2}{11} + 7\frac{1}{8} + 9\frac{3}{10}$

11. $8\frac{3}{5} + 9\frac{4}{7} + 3\frac{5}{6}$

12. $8\frac{7}{12} - 4\frac{3}{4}$

13. $10\frac{1}{5} - 2\frac{3}{10}$

14. $18\frac{2}{9} - 4\frac{1}{2}$

15. $15\frac{2}{3} - 4\frac{7}{8}$

16. $6\frac{4}{7} - 2\frac{1}{3}$

17. $5\frac{7}{10} - 2\frac{3}{5}$

18. $9\frac{2}{3} - 2\frac{5}{6}$

19. $8\frac{3}{4} - 3\frac{2}{7}$

Estimate the sum or difference. Use front-end estimation.

20. $12\frac{1}{8} + 3\frac{2}{3}$

21. $9\frac{8}{11} + 7\frac{2}{9} + 6\frac{1}{10}$

22. $9\frac{4}{5} + 8\frac{3}{4} + 4\frac{1}{3}$

23. $9\frac{5}{16} - 6\frac{1}{5}$

24. $10\frac{3}{5} - 4\frac{2}{3}$

25. $18\frac{7}{12} - 5\frac{2}{7}$

26. $25\frac{1}{8} - 13\frac{11}{15}$

Use estimation strategies to predict the sum or difference. Choose the correct answer.

27. $11\frac{3}{5} + 4\frac{7}{8}$ **a.** less than 15   **b.** between 15 and 16   **c.** greater than 16

28. $13\frac{4}{7} - 9\frac{1}{4}$ **a.** less than 4   **b.** between 4 and 5   **c.** greater than 5

Problem Solving

29. Ben ran $2\frac{3}{8}$ mi on Saturday and $6\frac{5}{6}$ mi on Sunday. About how many miles did he run that weekend?

30. Which estimation method would give a more reasonable estimate for $10\frac{1}{3} - 9\frac{5}{9}$? Why?

CRITICAL THINKING — Algebra

Find the value of *n* that will give a sum or difference in the given range. Explain the method you used.

31. $6\frac{2}{7} + n$ is between 8 and 9.

32. $8\frac{7}{12} + n$ is between 12 and 13.

33. $9\frac{2}{9} - n$ is between 4 and 5.

34. $10\frac{2}{3} - n$ is between 6 and 7.

Problem-Solving Strategy:
Work Backward

At a bake sale, Ms. Talbot sold $6\frac{1}{3}$ dozen muffins before lunch. After lunch, she made 2 dozen more muffins. Then Ms. Talbot sold another $7\frac{1}{2}$ dozen. She had $1\frac{1}{2}$ dozen muffins left. How many muffins did she have at the start of the sale?

Read

Visualize yourself in the problem above as you reread it. List the facts and the question.

Facts: before lunch—$6\frac{1}{3}$ doz sold

after lunch —2 doz more made

$7\frac{1}{2}$ doz sold

$1\frac{1}{2}$ doz left

Question: How many muffins did she have at the start of the sale?

Plan

First write a number sentence to show what happened.

Total − doz sold + doz made − doz sold = doz left

n − $6\frac{1}{3}$ +   2   − $7\frac{1}{2}$ = $1\frac{1}{2}$

To find the original number, start with the number left and work backward. Use the inverse operation to undo each step.

Solve

$1\frac{1}{2} + 7\frac{1}{2} - 2 + 6\frac{1}{3} = n$

$9\quad\ \ - 2 + 6\frac{1}{3} = n$

$7\quad + 6\frac{1}{3} = 13\frac{1}{3}$

> Think
> Use the order
> of operations.

Ms. Talbot had $13\frac{1}{3}$ dozen muffins at the start of the sale.

Check

Begin with the total and work *forward*.

$13\frac{1}{3} - 6\frac{1}{3} +\quad 2\quad - 7\frac{1}{2} \overset{?}{=} 1\frac{1}{2}$

$7\quad +\quad 2\quad - 7\frac{1}{2} \overset{?}{=} 1\frac{1}{2}$

$9\quad\ - 7\frac{1}{2} \overset{?}{=} 1\frac{1}{2}$

$1\frac{1}{2} = 1\frac{1}{2}$ The answer checks.

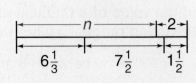

Use the Work Backward strategy to solve each problem.

1. The final cost of Jack's bicycle was $94.00. This included a discount of $10.25 and tax of $5.50. What was the original price of the bicycle without the tax and discount?

 Visualize yourself in the problem above as you reread it. Focus on the facts and the question.

List what you know.

Facts: final cost — $94.00
discount — $10.25
tax — $5.50

Question: What was the original price of the bicycle without the tax and discount?

 First write a number sentence to show what happened. Then work backward.

Cost = price − discount + tax
$94.00 = n − $10.25 + $5.50
$94.00 − $5.50 + $10.25 = n

Solve .... **Check**

3	$3\frac{1}{2}$	1
?	$\frac{5}{2}$	?
4	?	?

2. Find the missing addends in the magic square. (*Hint:* Find the sums first. Remember: All the sums are the *same*.)

3. Nick ordered 2 suits for $249.95 each and a pair of slacks. The total cost was $554.85. What was the cost of the slacks?

4. After Dad cut fencing to put around his garden, he had $\frac{3}{4}$ ft of fencing left over. He had already cut three $3\frac{1}{4}$-ft pieces, one $2\frac{1}{3}$-ft piece, and one $3\frac{1}{2}$-ft piece. How long was the fencing originally?

5. The Dinger Catering Service prepared punch for 3 wedding receptions on one Saturday. If they served $10\frac{1}{3}$ gal of punch at the first, $13\frac{1}{2}$ gal at the second, $13\frac{2}{3}$ gal at the third, and had $2\frac{1}{2}$ gal left over, how much punch did they prepare for the day?

Problem-Solving Applications: Mixed Review

Solve each problem and explain the method you used.

1. At Pet Palace, Meg spent $\frac{1}{5}$ h bathing a terrier and $\frac{3}{5}$ h cutting its hair. How long did Meg spend grooming the terrier?

2. Meg opened a new bottle of dog shampoo in the morning. She used $\frac{1}{4}$ of the bottle before noon and $\frac{2}{5}$ of the bottle after noon. How much of the bottle of shampoo did she use in all?

3. A sheepdog's hair was $4\frac{3}{4}$ in. long. Meg trimmed off $1\frac{3}{8}$ in. How long was the dog's hair after cutting?

4. A bottle of flea spray was $\frac{5}{6}$ full at the beginning of the day. At the end of the day, the bottle was $\frac{1}{3}$ full. How much of the bottle was used that day?

5. The tallest client at Pet Palace, Hercules, is $30\frac{1}{8}$ in. tall. The shortest, Muffin, is $11\frac{3}{16}$ in. tall. How much taller is Hercules than Muffin?

6. Koji worked for $3\frac{1}{4}$ h before lunch and $3\frac{1}{4}$ h after lunch. How long did he work in all?

7. Koji gave a dalmatian $2\frac{1}{2}$ dog biscuits. He gave a poodle $1\frac{1}{2}$ biscuits, a collie $2\frac{3}{4}$ biscuits. How many biscuits did Koji give to the dogs in all?

8. In a 50-lb bag of dog food, $19\frac{1}{4}$ lb are meat protein and $18\frac{7}{8}$ lb are vitamin compound. To fill the bag, how many pounds of the third ingredient, cereal compound, are needed?

Choose a strategy from the list or use another strategy you know to solve each problem.

9. Avi cut $\frac{2}{3}$ in. off a poodle's hair, but it was not short enough, so he cut another $\frac{1}{4}$ in. Then the dog's hair was perfect at $5\frac{1}{2}$ in. How long was the poodle's hair before cutting?

Strategy File

Use These Strategies
Work Backward
Guess and Test
Use More Than One Step
Logical Reasoning
Find a Pattern
Use a Graph

10. Loxy and Foxy are cats. Together they weigh 16 lb. Loxy weighs $\frac{1}{2}$ lb more than Foxy, and each cat weighs more than 7 pounds. How much could each cat weigh?

11. Ace, Champ, and Ruffy are dogs that weigh $23\frac{3}{4}$ lb, $23\frac{5}{6}$ lb, and $23\frac{5}{8}$ lb. Ace and Ruffy together weigh more than double Champ's weight. Ace weighs more than Ruffy. Place the dogs in order from lightest to heaviest.

12. A puppy weighed $1\frac{3}{4}$ lb at birth. Each day it gained $\frac{1}{8}$ lb. What was its weight after one week?

Use the circle graph for problems 13–15.

13. What fractional part of the clients were dogs? How do you know?

14. What fractional part of the clients were cats? How do you know?

15. From which group of pets does Pet Palace obtain most of its clients?
Group A: large and miniature dogs
Group B: miniature and small dogs
How much greater is this group than the other? How do you know?

Pet Palace Clients

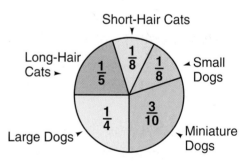

Write Your Own

16. Write in your Math Journal which problem you solved using more than one strategy and explain why. Then write a problem modeled on that problem and have a classmate solve it.

Add. *(See pp. 164–167, 170–173.)*

1. $\frac{9}{8}$
$+\frac{1}{8}$

2. $\frac{5}{6}$
$+\frac{1}{6}$

3. $\frac{7}{17}$
$+\frac{15}{17}$

4. $\frac{2}{5}$
$+\frac{1}{10}$

5. $\frac{1}{4}$
$+\frac{1}{12}$

6. $\frac{7}{10}$
$+\frac{1}{2}$

7. $6\frac{7}{9}$
$+1\frac{4}{9}$

8. $9\frac{7}{16}$
$+2\frac{5}{16}$

9. $7\frac{1}{2}$
$+1\frac{1}{4}$

10. $6\frac{1}{5}$
$+4\frac{3}{10}$

11. $8\frac{5}{12}$
$+2\frac{1}{2}$

12. $5\frac{3}{5}$
$+2\frac{2}{3}$

Subtract. *(See pp. 174–185.)*

13. $\frac{15}{11}$
$-\frac{1}{11}$

14. $\frac{13}{7}$
$-\frac{6}{7}$

15. $\frac{7}{12}$
$-\frac{1}{3}$

16. $\frac{1}{2}$
$-\frac{3}{8}$

17. $\frac{2}{3}$
$-\frac{1}{9}$

18. $\frac{5}{6}$
$-\frac{1}{2}$

19. $9\frac{3}{5}$
$-3\frac{1}{4}$

20. $4\frac{2}{3}$
$-2\frac{1}{2}$

21. $6\frac{1}{8}$
$-3\frac{1}{2}$

22. $4\frac{1}{4}$
$-3\frac{3}{8}$

23. $2\frac{7}{16}$
$-1\frac{3}{4}$

24. $14\frac{1}{3}$
$-9\frac{3}{5}$

Add or subtract. *(See pp. 164–185.)*

25. $\frac{7}{13} + \frac{4}{13}$

26. $\frac{15}{16} - \frac{3}{16}$

27. $\frac{3}{5} + \frac{1}{3} + \frac{4}{15}$

28. $13\frac{1}{24} - 11\frac{1}{2}$

29. $7 - 2\frac{3}{5}$

30. $9\frac{7}{8} + 2\frac{5}{16} + 4\frac{1}{2}$

Estimate. Use front-end estimation. *(See pp. 186–187.)*

31. $10\frac{3}{5} + 14\frac{2}{3}$ 32. $2\frac{5}{6} - 1\frac{7}{12}$ 33. $1\frac{1}{2} + 3\frac{3}{8}$ 34. $3\frac{5}{8} - 1\frac{1}{2}$

Problem Solving
(See pp. 180–185, 188–190.)

35. Vicky came home from the matinee at 5:45 P.M. The travel time to and from the cinema was $\frac{1}{2}$ hour each way. She spent $2\frac{1}{4}$ hours at the cinema. What time did she leave home?

36. Carla bought $3\frac{1}{8}$ lb of peaches and $2\frac{5}{6}$ lb of grapes. How many more pounds of peaches than grapes did she buy?

(See Still More Practice, p. 481.)

Unit Fractions

A unit fraction is a fraction with a numerator of 1.

$\frac{1}{2}, \frac{1}{3}, \frac{1}{4}, \frac{1}{5}, \frac{1}{11}, \frac{1}{20}$ are unit fractions.

▶ To express a non-unit fraction as the sum of two or more different unit fractions:

$$\frac{3}{4} = \frac{1}{?} + \frac{1}{?}$$

- Find the unit fractions that have a least common denominator (LCD) equal to the denominator of the non-unit fraction.

..Think....................
What unit fractions have an LCD of 4?
$\frac{1}{2}$ and $\frac{1}{4}$
....

$$\frac{3}{4} \overset{?}{=} \frac{1}{2} + \frac{1}{4}$$

- Check if the sum of the unit fractions is equal to the given non-unit fraction.

$$\frac{1}{2} = \frac{1 \times 2}{2 \times 2} = \frac{2}{4}$$
$$+ \frac{1}{4} \qquad\qquad = \frac{1}{4}$$
$$\rule{3cm}{0.4pt}$$
$$\frac{3}{4}$$

So $\frac{3}{4} = \frac{1}{2} + \frac{1}{4}$. [unit fractions]

Write each fraction as the sum of different unit fractions.

1. $\frac{5}{6} = \frac{1}{?} + \frac{1}{?}$

2. $\frac{7}{10} = \frac{1}{?} + \frac{1}{?}$

3. $\frac{5}{8} = \frac{1}{?} + \frac{1}{?}$

4. $\frac{4}{9} = \frac{1}{?} + \frac{1}{?}$

5. $\frac{2}{3} = \frac{1}{?} + \frac{1}{?}$

6. $\frac{7}{12} = \frac{1}{?} + \frac{1}{?}$

7. $\frac{8}{15} = \frac{1}{?} + \frac{1}{?}$

8. $\frac{9}{20} = \frac{1}{?} + \frac{1}{?}$

9. $\frac{3}{5} = \frac{1}{?} + \frac{1}{?}$

10. $\frac{9}{14} = \frac{1}{?} + \frac{1}{?}$

11. $\frac{10}{21} = \frac{1}{?} + \frac{1}{?}$

12. $\frac{7}{24} = \frac{1}{?} + \frac{1}{?}$

Problem Solving

13. A design of a school pennant took up 64 out of 100 squares of a sheet of grid paper. Did the design take up $\frac{1}{4}$, $\frac{8}{10}$, $\frac{16}{25}$, or $\frac{16}{20}$ of the squares? Express the fraction as the sum of different unit fractions.

Chapter 5 Test

Add.

1. $\frac{11}{14}$
   $+\frac{3}{14}$

2. $\frac{11}{12}$
   $+\frac{1}{2}$

3. $\frac{5}{6}$
   $+\frac{3}{4}$

4. $2\frac{1}{5}$
   $+1\frac{4}{5}$

5. $6\frac{5}{7}$
   $+3\frac{3}{4}$

6. $4\frac{2}{3}$
   $+1\frac{1}{15}$

Subtract.

7. $\frac{19}{10}$
   $-\frac{7}{10}$

8. $\frac{7}{9}$
   $-\frac{2}{3}$

9. $\frac{4}{5}$
   $-\frac{2}{3}$

10. $8\frac{7}{8}$
    $-2\frac{1}{2}$

11. $9\frac{5}{9}$
    $-3\frac{5}{18}$

12. $10\frac{2}{3}$
    $-7\frac{1}{12}$

Add or subtract.

13. $\frac{5}{7} + \frac{1}{3} + \frac{4}{21}$

14. $5 - 3\frac{2}{7}$

15. $7\frac{3}{20} - 4\frac{3}{5}$

16. $3\frac{1}{4} + 1\frac{3}{5} + 2\frac{1}{10}$

17. $6\frac{7}{18} + 3\frac{2}{3} + 1\frac{1}{6}$

Use rounding to estimate.

18. $5\frac{5}{7} + 2\frac{1}{2}$

19. $9\frac{2}{3} - 4\frac{1}{5}$

20. $10\frac{1}{8} + 12\frac{4}{5} + 3\frac{5}{6}$

Problem Solving

Use a strategy you have learned.

21. Anthony needs $6\frac{7}{8}$ yd of wire. He has $4\frac{1}{3}$ yd. How much more wire does he need?

Tell About It

22. An estimated sum of two mixed numbers is about 8. One of the numbers is $3\frac{5}{8}$. What might be the other number? How do you know?

Performance Assessment

Draw a diagram.
Use these 5 straws to make plane figures. Use 1 straw per side.

23. How many units does it take to make a rectangle?

24. About how many units does it take to make the largest possible triangle?

25. How many units shorter is the distance around the rectangle than the distance around the triangle?

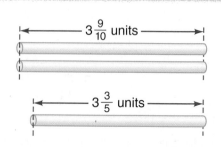

$3\frac{9}{10}$ units

$3\frac{3}{5}$ units

$1\frac{1}{2}$ units

Test Preparation

Choose the best answer.

1. What is the value of 7 in 376,148,206?
   - **a.** 7000
   - **b.** 70,000
   - **c.** 70,000,000
   - **d.** 80,000,000

2. $900 − $46.54
   - **a.** $854.54
   - **b.** $864.56
   - **c.** $946.54
   - **d.** $853.46

3. How many times greater than 30×20 is 30×2000?
   - **a.** 10   **b.** 100   **c.** 200   **d.** 1000

4. Find the missing dividend.

   $n \div 4 = 12$
   - **a.** 3   **b.** 16
   - **c.** 36   **d.** 48

5. Which is a prime number?
   - **a.** 9   **b.** 13
   - **c.** 15   **d.** 25

6. Which shows $\frac{18}{54}$ in lowest terms?
   - **a.** $\frac{1}{4}$ **b.** $\frac{1}{3}$ **c.** $\frac{1}{2}$ **d.** none of these

7. Find the missing number.

   $7 = 6\frac{n}{11}$
   - **a.** 6   **b.** 7
   - **c.** 11   **d.** 33

8. $8\frac{6}{7} − 2\frac{1}{7}$
   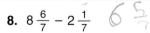
   - **a.** $5\frac{5}{7}$ **b.** $8\frac{3}{7}$
   - **c.** $10\frac{1}{7}$ **d.** not given

9. Round 592,067,208 to its greatest place.
   - **a.** 550,000,000
   - **b.** 592,000,000
   - **c.** 500,000,000
   - **d.** none of these

10. Estimate.

    4632×221
    - **a.** 80,000
    - **b.** 100,000
    - **c.** 1,000,000
    - **d.** 10,000,000

11. $\begin{array}{r} 946 \\ \times\ 608 \\ \hline \end{array}$
    - **a.** 264,109   **b.** 575,168
    - **c.** 755,618   **d.** 576,168

12. $34\overline{)26{,}588}$
    - **a.** 782   **b.** 799 R22
    - **c.** 882   **d.** 881 R29

13. What is the GCF of 12 and 24?
    - **a.** 6   **b.** 8
    - **c.** 12   **d.** 24

14. Name the mixed number.
    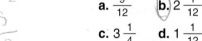
    - **a.** $2\frac{4}{5}$ **b.** $2\frac{5}{6}$ **c.** $2\frac{7}{8}$ **d.** $3\frac{5}{6}$

15. $\frac{1}{2} + \frac{5}{6} + \frac{3}{4}$

    - **a.** $\frac{9}{12}$ **b.** $2\frac{1}{12}$
    - **c.** $3\frac{1}{4}$ **d.** $1\frac{1}{12}$

16. $12\frac{3}{3} − 2\frac{1}{3}$
    - **a.** $9\frac{2}{3}$ **b.** $10\frac{1}{3}$
    - **c.** $14\frac{1}{3}$ **d.** $10\frac{2}{3}$

17. What is the prime factorization of 108?

    a. $3^2 \times 2^3$
    b. $3^3 \times 2^2$
    c. $3^2 \times 2^2$
    d. $3^3 \times 2^3$

18. Which of these numbers is divisible by 2, 3, and 4?

    a. 3916
    b. 3912
    c. 3915
    d. 2053

19. $4\frac{5}{9} - 2\frac{2}{3} = n$

    a. $2\frac{1}{3}$ **b.** $2\frac{8}{9}$

    c. $2\frac{1}{9}$ **d.** $1\frac{8}{9}$

20. Kate is permitted 1000 calories a day on her diet. She consumed 279 calories at lunch and 342 at breakfast. How many calories may she consume at dinner?

    a. 389 calories
    b. 379 calories
    c. 631 calories
    d. 621 calories

21. In a book closet, mathematics books are kept in stacks of 4. If each student carries no more than one stack, what is the least number of students needed to carry books for a class of 23?

    a. 5 students
    b. 6 students
    c. 27 students
    d. 19 students

22. What is the least common multiple of 6 and 15?

    a. 3
    b. 30
    c. 45
    d. 60

23. Find the sum.
$3268 + 156{,}729 + 7034$

    a. 166,031
    b. 167,031
    c. 156,031
    d. 157,031

24. Which fraction is closer to $\frac{1}{2}$?

    a. $\frac{5}{62}$ **b.** $\frac{19}{20}$

    c. $\frac{12}{26}$ **d.** $\frac{20}{23}$

25. I am a number. If you multiply me by 2, the result is 346 more than the result of multiplying me by 0. What number am I?

    a. 0
    b. 1
    c. 173
    d. 346

26. Tony collected $1072.61 from 49 customers at his booth at the antiques fair. About how much did he receive from each person if each person gave him approximately the same amount?

    a. about $15
    b. about $10
    c. about $25
    d. about $20

**Explain how you solved the problem.
Show all your work.**

27. Christina started with a number, added $\frac{2}{5}$ to it, and then subtracted $1\frac{1}{10}$. She ended up with the number $2\frac{3}{10}$. What was Christina's original number?

28. Mr. Diaz needs $8\frac{5}{16}$ feet of molding to finish a closet. He has $7\frac{1}{8}$ feet of molding. How many more feet of molding does Mr. Diaz need?

CHAPTER 6

Fractions: Multiplication and Division

Arithmetic

Multiplication is vexation.
Division is as bad;
The Rule of Three it puzzles me,
And fractions drive me mad.

Anonymous

$\frac{1}{10}$

$\frac{1}{12}$

$\frac{1}{10}$

$\frac{1}{10}$

$\frac{1}{12}$

In this chapter you will:

Multiply fractions and mixed
  numbers using the GCF
Explore division with models
Learn about reciprocals and
  dividing fractions and
  mixed numbers
Estimate mixed-number
  products and quotients
Solve problems using
  simpler numbers

**Critical Thinking/
Finding Together**

By how many sixteenths
is $\frac{1}{3}$ of $\frac{3}{4}$ more than
$\frac{1}{4}$ of $\frac{3}{4}$?

Multiply Fractions

Tracy had a tray of ice cubes that was $\frac{2}{3}$ full.
She used $\frac{1}{4}$ of the ice cubes. What fractional part
of the entire ice-cube tray did she use? To find what
fractional part of the tray she used, find $\frac{1}{4}$ of $\frac{2}{3}$

Materials: paper, ruler, colored pencils or crayons

Step 1 Fold a rectangular sheet of paper
in thirds *horizontally* to represent
the ice-cube tray. Open it up
and then draw a line along each
fold. Shade two of the horizontal
sections to show $\frac{2}{3}$, which is how
much of the tray is full.

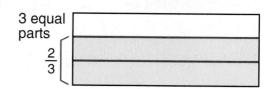

3 equal parts

$\frac{2}{3}$

Step 2 Fold the paper in fourths *vertically*.
Open it up and then draw a line along
each fold. Mark off $\frac{1}{4}$ of the shaded
vertical sections, which is how much
of the entire ice-cube tray Tracy used.

Into how many sections did you finally
divide the rectangle? What fractional part
of the rectangle is marked off?

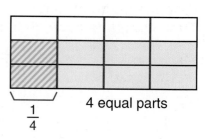

$\frac{1}{4}$ 4 equal parts

Step 3 Write a multiplication sentence that tells what
fractional part of the entire tray Tracy used.

1. Explain what $\frac{1}{4}$ of $\frac{2}{3}$ means.

2. Is the product of $\frac{1}{4} \times \frac{2}{3}$ less than 1?

3. Can the product of two fractions
less than 1 be greater than 1?
Why or why not? Give an example
to support your answer.

4. Can the product of two fractions less
than 1 be greater or less than each
of the original fractions? Why? Give
an example to support your answer.

Practice

Use the pair of diagrams to complete the statement.

5.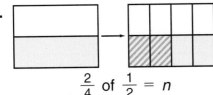

$$\frac{2}{4} \text{ of } \frac{1}{2} = n$$

6.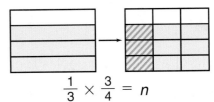

$$\frac{1}{3} \times \frac{3}{4} = n$$

Write a multiplication sentence for each diagram.

7.  **8.**  **9.** 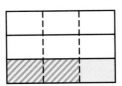 **10.**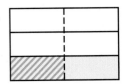

Draw a diagram to show each product. Then write a multiplication sentence.

11. $\frac{4}{5} \times \frac{1}{4}$ **12.** $\frac{2}{9} \times \frac{1}{3}$ **13.** $\frac{1}{5} \times \frac{2}{3}$ **14.** $\frac{1}{4} \times \frac{3}{8}$

15. $\frac{5}{6} \times \frac{1}{3}$ **16.** $\frac{2}{3} \times \frac{4}{5}$ **17.** $\frac{3}{4} \times \frac{1}{2}$ **18.** $\frac{3}{8} \times \frac{1}{3}$

Find the diagram that matches each statement. Then complete each statement.

19. $\frac{1}{3} \text{ of } \frac{1}{3} = n$ **20.** $\frac{3}{4} \text{ of } \frac{1}{3} = n$ **21.** $\frac{1}{2} \text{ of } \frac{1}{4} = n$ **22.** $\frac{2}{3} \text{ of } \frac{1}{5} = n$

a. 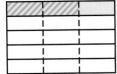 **b.** 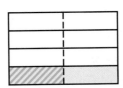 **c.**  **d.**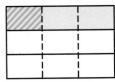

Communicate

23. How does shading and marking off help you find the product of two fractions?

24. Study the relationship between the numerators of the factors and the numerator of the product. What do you observe? Explain your answer. Is the same true for the denominator?

25. Use what you have observed to write a rule in your Math Journal on how you multiply fractions. Compare your rule to those of your classmates.

Multiply Fractions by Fractions

One third of a swimming pool is roped off for nonswimmers. Three fourths of this space is used for swimming lessons. What fractional part of the pool is used for swimming lessons?

To find what fractional part of the pool is used for swimming lessons, multiply: $\frac{3}{4} \times \frac{1}{3} = n$.

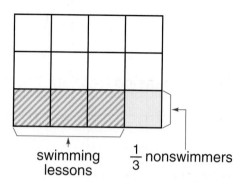

swimming lessons $\frac{1}{3}$ nonswimmers

▶ To **multiply** a *fraction* by a *fraction*:

- Multiply the numerators.
- Multiply the denominators.
- Write the product in simplest form.

$$\frac{3}{4} \times \frac{1}{3} = \frac{3 \times 1}{4 \times 3}$$

$$= \frac{3}{12} = \frac{1}{4}$$

simplest form

One fourth of the pool is used for swimming lessons.

▶ To check multiplication use the *Commutative Property*.

$$\frac{1}{2} \times \frac{3}{4} = \frac{1 \times 3}{2 \times 4}$$ Check: $\frac{3}{4} \times \frac{1}{2} = \frac{3 \times 1}{4 \times 2}$ **Think** "order"

$$= \frac{3}{8}$$ $$= \frac{3}{8}$$

Study these examples.

$$\frac{3}{5} \text{ of } \frac{1}{6} = \frac{3}{5} \times \frac{1}{6}$$

$$= \frac{3 \times 1}{5 \times 6}$$

$$= \frac{3}{30} = \frac{1}{10}$$

Compare: $\frac{1}{2} \times \frac{1}{4} \ ? \ \frac{1}{2} \times \frac{1}{5}$

$$\frac{1 \times 1}{2 \times 4} \ \underset{?}{\quad} \ \frac{1 \times 1}{2 \times 5}$$

$$\frac{1}{8} > \frac{1}{10}$$

Complete each multiplication.

1. $\frac{2}{3} \times \frac{4}{5} = \frac{2 \times ?}{3 \times ?}$

$$= \frac{8}{?}$$

2. $\frac{3}{5} \times \frac{1}{2} = \frac{? \times 1}{? \times 2}$

$$= \frac{?}{10}$$

3. $\frac{5}{7} \times \frac{1}{4} = \frac{? \times ?}{? \times ?}$

$$= \frac{?}{?}$$

Multiply.

4. $\frac{1}{3} \times \frac{1}{8}$

5. $\frac{1}{4} \times \frac{3}{5}$

6. $\frac{4}{5} \times \frac{1}{7}$ $\frac{4}{35}$

7. $\frac{1}{3} \times \frac{2}{9}$ $\frac{2}{27}$

Find the product. Use the Commutative Property to check your answers.

8. $\frac{7}{10} \times \frac{1}{3}$

9. $\frac{3}{4} \times \frac{3}{5}$

10. $\frac{3}{8} \times \frac{5}{7}$

11. $\frac{5}{6} \times \frac{2}{9}$

12. $\frac{3}{4}$ of $\frac{2}{9}$

13. $\frac{4}{5}$ of $\frac{4}{7}$

14. $\frac{3}{10}$ of $\frac{2}{5}$

15. $\frac{5}{8}$ of $\frac{4}{9}$

Find the missing fraction. Then check by multiplying.

16. $\frac{3}{4} \times n = \frac{5}{6} \times \frac{3}{4}$

17. $\frac{6}{7} \times \frac{1}{4} = n \times \frac{6}{7}$

18. $n \times \frac{2}{9} = \frac{2}{9} \times \frac{4}{5}$

Compare. Write $<$, $=$, or $>$.

19. $\frac{2}{5} \times \frac{1}{4}$ ___?___ $\frac{1}{4} \times \frac{2}{3}$

20. $\frac{5}{9} \times \frac{3}{5}$ ___?___ $\frac{5}{6} \times \frac{3}{4}$

21. $\frac{1}{4} \times \frac{3}{8}$ ___?___ $\frac{3}{16} \times \frac{1}{2}$

22. $\frac{3}{5} \times \frac{1}{6}$ ___?___ $\frac{3}{9} \times \frac{1}{2}$

23. $\frac{3}{5} \times \frac{2}{3}$ ___?___ $\frac{7}{8} \times \frac{2}{5}$

24. $\frac{5}{6} \times \frac{9}{10}$ ___?___ $\frac{1}{2} \times \frac{4}{5}$

Problem Solving

25. It took Peter $\frac{3}{4}$ of the morning to do yard work. He spent $\frac{2}{3}$ of this time pulling weeds. What part of the morning did he pull weeds?

26. Five sixths of the books on the shelf are nonfiction. Three fourths of these books are science books. What part of the books on the shelf are science books?

27. Half of Ms. Silver's class participates in after school sports. One third of those students play volleyball. What fraction of Ms. Silver's class does *not* play volleyball in after school sports?

28. Tanika puts two fifths of a month's allowance into her savings account. She spends half of the rest on a CD. What fraction of her month's allowance does she have left?

CRITICAL THINKING — Algebra

Using each of the digits 2, 3, 4, and 5 only once, find two fractions that will have a product *n* such that:

.Think..........
$\frac{?}{?} \times \frac{?}{?} = n$

29. *n* is a product close to 1.

30. *n* is the greatest product possible.

31. *n* is the least product possible.

Multiply Fractions and Whole Numbers

Cara walks $\frac{1}{4}$ mile to the library.
Kareem walks three times this distance.
What part of a mile does Kareem walk?

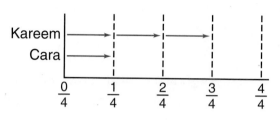

To find what part of a mile Kareem
walks, multiply: $3 \times \frac{1}{4} = n$.

▶ To **multiply** a *fraction* and a *whole number*:

$$3 \times \frac{1}{4} = \frac{1}{4} + \frac{1}{4} + \frac{1}{4}$$

• Rename the whole number as a
fraction with a denominator of 1.

$$3 \times \frac{1}{4} = \frac{3}{1} \times \frac{1}{4}$$

• Multiply the numerators. Then multiply
the denominators.

$$= \frac{3 \times 1}{1 \times 4}$$

• Write the product in simplest form.

$$= \frac{3}{4} \leftarrow$$

Kareem walks $\frac{3}{4}$ mile to the library.

simplest form

▶ The properties of multiplication for whole numbers
also apply to fractions.

Identity Property

$$1 \times \frac{5}{6} = \frac{5}{6}$$

.Think..
"same"

Zero Property

$$0 \times \frac{2}{3} = 0$$

.Think..
"0 product"

Study these examples.

$$5 \times \frac{4}{5} = \frac{5}{1} \times \frac{4}{5}$$
$$= \frac{5 \times 4}{1 \times 5}$$
$$= \frac{20}{5} = 4$$

$$7 \times \frac{5}{21} = \frac{7}{1} \times \frac{5}{21}$$
$$= \frac{7 \times 5}{1 \times 21}$$
$$= \frac{35}{21} = 1\frac{14}{21} = 1\frac{2}{3} \leftarrow$$

simplest form

Multiply.

1. $16 \times \frac{1}{8}$

2. $20 \times \frac{1}{4}$

3. $18 \times \frac{1}{6}$

4. $24 \times \frac{1}{3}$

5. $36 \times \frac{1}{9}$

6. $42 \times \frac{1}{7}$

7. $12 \times \frac{5}{12}$

8. $17 \times \frac{15}{17}$

Practice

Find the product.

9. $22 \times \frac{1}{2}$ **10.** $30 \times \frac{1}{10}$ **11.** $0 \times \frac{1}{5}$ **12.** $15 \times \frac{2}{3}$

13. $2 \times \frac{3}{8}$ **14.** $10 \times \frac{3}{50}$ **15.** $2 \times \frac{3}{7}$ **16.** $2 \times \frac{4}{11}$

17. $40 \times \frac{7}{16}$ **18.** $15 \times \frac{4}{25}$ **19.** $45 \times \frac{5}{27}$ **20.** $24 \times \frac{5}{16}$

Fractional Part of a Whole Number

Kerr received $12 in Sacajawea gold dollars. He put $\frac{3}{4}$ of it in the bank. How much did he put in the bank?

To find how much he put in the bank, find: $\frac{3}{4}$ of $12 = n$.

$\frac{3}{4}$ of $12

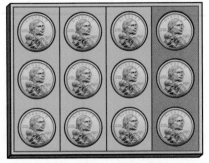

"of" means $\times$

Kerr put $9 in the bank.

3 out of 4 equal groups

$$\frac{3}{4} \times 12 = \frac{3}{4} \times \frac{12}{1} = \frac{3 \times 12}{4 \times 1}$$
$$= \frac{36}{4} = 9$$

Multiply.

21. $\frac{2}{7}$ of $14 **22.** $\frac{3}{8}$ of $24 **23.** $\frac{4}{5}$ of $35 **24.** $\frac{5}{6}$ of $18

25. $\frac{3}{10}$ of 15 **26.** $\frac{2}{3}$ of 20 **27.** $\frac{5}{9}$ of 25 **28.** $\frac{4}{11}$ of 12

Problem Solving

29. Kim lives $\frac{3}{4}$ km from her school. Chet lives 4 times that distance from school. How far from the school does Chet live?

30. One third of the 24 students in class read books on sports. How many students in the class do not read books on sports?

DO YOU REMEMBER?

Find the greatest common factor (GCF) of each set of numbers.

31. 4 and 8 **32.** 6 and 12 **33.** 9 and 18 **34.** 5 and 20

35. 7 and 21 **36.** 8 and 18 **37.** 16 and 20 **38.** 10 and 25

Multiply Fractions Using the GCF

You can sometimes simplify fractions using the GCF before multiplying.

Multiply: $\frac{20}{21} \times \frac{7}{8} = n$.

$$\frac{20}{21} \times \frac{7}{8} = \frac{20 \times 7}{21 \times 8}$$

$$= \frac{\overset{1}{(4 \times 5)} \times \overset{1}{(7 \times 1)}}{\underset{1}{(7 \times 3)} \times \underset{1}{(4 \times 2)}}$$

$$= \frac{5 \times 1}{3 \times 2} = \frac{5}{6}$$

Think
20 = 4 × 5
7 = 7 × 1
21 = 7 × 3
8 = 4 × 2

Think
$\frac{4}{4} = 1$ and $\frac{7}{7} = 1$

> The **greatest common factor (GCF)** of two or more numbers is the greatest number that is a factor of these numbers.
> **GCF:**
> 20 = 1, 2, 4, 5, 10, 20
> 8 = 1, 2, 4, 8
> 7 = 1, 7
> 21 = 1, 3, 7, 21

▶ To **multiply fractions using the GCF:**

- Divide *any* numerator and denominator by their GCF.

- Multiply the numerators. Then multiply the denominators. The product will be in simplest form.

- Rename the product as a whole or mixed number when needed.

$$\frac{20}{21} \times \frac{7}{8} = \frac{\overset{5}{20} \times \overset{1}{7}}{\underset{3}{21} \times \underset{2}{8}}$$

GCF of 20 and 8: 4
GCF of 7 and 21: 7

$$= \frac{5 \times 1}{3 \times 2} = \frac{5}{6}$$

simplest form

Study these examples.

$$\frac{2}{5} \times 25 = \frac{2}{5} \times \frac{25}{1}$$

Think
GCF of 25 and 5: 5

$$= \frac{2 \times \overset{5}{25}}{\underset{1}{5} \times 1} = \frac{2 \times 5}{1 \times 1}$$

$$= \frac{10}{1} = 10$$

whole number

$$49 \times \frac{5}{14} = \frac{49}{1} \times \frac{5}{14}$$

Think
GCF of 49 and 14: 7

$$= \frac{\overset{7}{49} \times 5}{1 \times \underset{2}{14}} = \frac{7 \times 5}{1 \times 2}$$

$$= \frac{35}{2} = 17\frac{1}{2}$$

mixed number

Complete each multiplication.

1. $\dfrac{4}{7} \times \dfrac{35}{36} = \dfrac{\overset{1}{4} \times \overset{?}{35}}{\underset{1}{7} \times \underset{?}{36}}$

$$= \frac{1 \times ?}{1 \times ?} = \frac{?}{?}$$

2. $\dfrac{3}{8} \times 16 = \dfrac{3}{8} \times \dfrac{16}{?} = \dfrac{3 \times \overset{?}{16}}{\underset{?}{8} \times ?}$

$$= \frac{3 \times ?}{? \times ?} = \frac{?}{?} = ?$$

Multiply using the GCF.

3. $\frac{1}{2} \times \frac{2}{3}$

4. $\frac{1}{4} \times \frac{2}{7}$

5. $\frac{2}{9} \times \frac{1}{6}$

6. $\frac{3}{4} \times \frac{1}{9}$

7. $\frac{4}{9} \times \frac{3}{5}$

8. $\frac{4}{7} \times \frac{3}{8}$

9. $\frac{4}{15} \times \frac{5}{9}$

10. $\frac{2}{3} \times \frac{3}{13}$

11. $\frac{6}{7} \times \frac{7}{8}$

12. $\frac{3}{10} \times \frac{7}{9}$

13. $\frac{3}{4} \times 16$

14. $\frac{4}{25} \times 10$

15. $\frac{7}{12} \times 24$

16. $\frac{4}{21} \times 49$

17. $\frac{5}{16} \times 32$

18. $32 \times \frac{5}{6}$

19. $33 \times \frac{4}{11}$

20. $35 \times \frac{5}{42}$

21. $24 \times \frac{3}{8}$

22. $25 \times \frac{2}{15}$

Find the product in simplest form.

23. $\frac{3}{10} \times \frac{25}{27}$

24. $\frac{8}{27} \times \frac{9}{20}$

25. $\frac{9}{14} \times \frac{7}{15}$

26. $\frac{7}{8} \times \frac{6}{21}$

27. $\frac{2}{9} \times \frac{21}{26}$

28. $14 \times \frac{3}{7}$

29. $36 \times \frac{7}{8}$

30. $20 \times \frac{3}{25}$

31. $\frac{5}{12} \times 8$

32. $\frac{3}{19} \times 30$

33. $\frac{5}{8} \times \frac{4}{15}$

34. $\frac{3}{4} \times 18$

35. $\frac{5}{7} \times \frac{8}{15}$

36. $72 \times \frac{5}{12}$

37. $\frac{5}{6} \times 54$

38. Explain in your Math Journal why your answer is already in lowest terms when you multiply fractions using the GCF.

Problem Solving

39. There are 20 members of the basketball team. Three fifths are fifth-grade students. How many members of the basketball team are fifth-grade students?

40. Mary Ellen had $\frac{2}{3}$ of a pie left. She ate $\frac{3}{8}$ of it at lunchtime. How much of the pie did she eat at lunchtime? How much of the pie was left?

CHALLENGE — Algebra

Multiply using the GCF.

41. $\frac{3}{10} \times 5 \times \frac{2}{3}$

42. $8 \times \frac{5}{12} \times \frac{3}{10}$

43. $\frac{3}{7} \times \frac{14}{27} \times \frac{3}{8}$

44. $\frac{4}{9} \times \frac{5}{36} \times \frac{3}{20}$

45. $\frac{5}{7} \times \frac{9}{20} \times 14$

46. $\frac{11}{24} \times \frac{3}{22} \times \frac{8}{33}$

Rename Mixed Numbers as Fractions

Rename $2\frac{3}{8}$ as a fraction greater than one.

$$2\frac{3}{8} = 1 + 1 + \frac{3}{8}$$

$$= \frac{8}{8} + \frac{8}{8} + \frac{3}{8}$$

$$= \frac{19}{8}$$

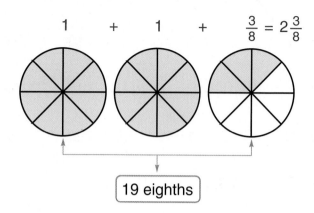

$$1 \quad + \quad 1 \quad + \quad \frac{3}{8} = 2\frac{3}{8}$$

19 eighths

▶ To **rename** a *mixed number* as a *fraction greater than one*:

- Multiply the whole number by the denominator.

- Add the product to the numerator.

- Write the sum as the numerator and the given denominator as the denominator.

Multiply:
$8 \times 2 = 16$

Then add:
$16 + 3 = 19$

$$2\frac{3}{8} = \frac{(8 \times 2) + 3}{8}$$

$$= \frac{16 + 3}{8}$$

$$= \frac{19}{8}$$

Rename each as a fraction greater than one.

1. $2\frac{1}{2} = \frac{(2 \times ?) + ?}{2}$

$$= \frac{?}{2}$$

2. $6\frac{3}{4} = \frac{(4 \times ?) + ?}{4}$

$$= \frac{?}{4}$$

3. $10\frac{3}{5} = \frac{(? \times 10) + ?}{?}$

$$= \frac{?}{?}$$

Rename each mixed number. Write the letter of the correct answer.

4. $11\frac{3}{5}$ **a.** $\frac{55}{3}$ **b.** $\frac{5}{58}$ **c.** $\frac{58}{5}$ **d.** $\frac{3}{55}$

5. $12\frac{4}{7}$ **a.** $\frac{7}{88}$ **b.** $\frac{84}{7}$ **c.** $\frac{7}{84}$ **d.** $\frac{88}{7}$

6. $15\frac{5}{6}$ **a.** $\frac{95}{6}$ **b.** $\frac{85}{6}$ **c.** $\frac{6}{95}$ **d.** $\frac{6}{85}$

Practice

Rename each as a fraction greater than one.

7. $2\frac{1}{8}$ 8. $5\frac{3}{4}$ 9. $3\frac{1}{7}$ 10. $6\frac{7}{10}$ 11. $11\frac{2}{3}$ 12. $4\frac{3}{5}$

13. $6\frac{1}{17}$ 14. $7\frac{5}{21}$ 15. $3\frac{3}{16}$ 16. $10\frac{1}{2}$ 17. $9\frac{5}{6}$ 18. $8\frac{7}{9}$

19. $2\frac{4}{7}$ 20. $3\frac{7}{25}$ 21. $10\frac{2}{5}$ 22. $12\frac{1}{6}$ 23. $5\frac{2}{9}$ 24. $7\frac{4}{11}$

25. $15\frac{1}{4}$ 26. $8\frac{2}{3}$ 27. $14\frac{4}{5}$ 28. $10\frac{5}{8}$ 29. $12\frac{3}{4}$ 30. $5\frac{9}{10}$

31. $4\frac{5}{12}$ 32. $3\frac{5}{7}$ 33. $5\frac{9}{14}$ 34. $3\frac{4}{13}$ 35. $4\frac{2}{17}$ 36. $2\frac{17}{19}$

Rename the mixed number as a fraction greater than one.

37. A sheet of tin is $4\frac{5}{9}$ ft long.

38. A book page is $7\frac{1}{10}$ in. wide.

39. A bag of fertilizer weighs $31\frac{3}{8}$ lb.

40. A gasoline tank contains $20\frac{3}{4}$ gal.

Problem Solving

41. A piece of lumber that is 40 in. long has been cut into 7 equal pieces. How long is each piece? Write the length as a mixed number.

42. The flying time from New York to Los Angeles is $5\frac{2}{3}$ h. Write this time as a fraction greater than one.

43. How many equal pieces of wood that weigh between 15 and 16 ounces can be made from a 110-ounce block if the whole block is used? How much will each piece weigh?

Write About It

44.   Explain in your Math Journal:

- how to use drawings or models to prove that $2\frac{3}{4} = \frac{11}{4}$.

- the relationship among $2\frac{5}{6}$, $1\frac{11}{6}$, and $\frac{17}{6}$.

Multiply Fractions and Mixed Numbers

Arlene bought $4\frac{2}{3}$ yards of material. She used $\frac{6}{7}$ of it for a dress. How much material did she use for the dress?

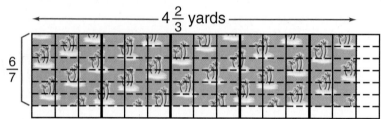

$4\frac{2}{3}$ yards

$\frac{6}{7}$

To find how much material was used for the dress, multiply: $\frac{6}{7} \times 4\frac{2}{3} = n$.

▶ To **multiply** a *fraction* and a *mixed number*:

- Rename the mixed number as a fraction greater than one.

- Simplify using the GCF where possible. Then multiply the numerators and multiply the denominators.

- Rename the product as a whole or mixed number when needed.

$$\frac{6}{7} \times 4\frac{2}{3} = \frac{6}{7} \times \frac{14}{3}$$

$$= \frac{\overset{2}{\cancel{6}} \times \overset{2}{\cancel{14}}}{\underset{1}{\cancel{7}} \times \underset{1}{\cancel{3}}}$$

$$= \frac{2 \times 2}{1 \times 1} = \frac{4}{1}$$

$$= 4 \leftarrow \boxed{\text{whole number}}$$

.Think.......
GCF of 6
and 3: 3
GCF of 14
and 7: 7

Arlene used 4 yards for the dress.

Study these examples.

$$\frac{6}{11} \times 2\frac{2}{9} = \frac{6}{11} \times \frac{20}{9}$$

$$= \frac{\overset{2}{\cancel{6}} \times 20}{11 \times \underset{3}{\cancel{9}}} = \frac{2 \times 20}{11 \times 3}$$

$$= \frac{40}{33} = 1\frac{7}{33} \leftarrow \boxed{\text{mixed number}}$$

$$3\frac{3}{5} \times \frac{5}{6} = \frac{18}{5} \times \frac{5}{6}$$

$$= \frac{\overset{3}{\cancel{18}} \times \overset{1}{\cancel{5}}}{\underset{1}{\cancel{5}} \times \underset{1}{\cancel{6}}} = \frac{3 \times 1}{1 \times 1}$$

$$= \frac{3}{1} = 3 \leftarrow \boxed{\text{whole number}}$$

Practice

Find each product. Rename as necessary.

1. $\frac{4}{7} \times 3\frac{1}{2} = \frac{4}{7} \times \frac{?}{2}$

   $= n$

2. $6\frac{2}{5} \times \frac{3}{8} = \frac{?}{5} \times \frac{?}{8}$

   $= n$

3. $\frac{8}{9} \times 2\frac{3}{4} = \frac{?}{9} \times \frac{?}{?}$

   $= n$

Find the product.

4. $3\frac{1}{2} \times \frac{1}{3}$

5. $2\frac{1}{2} \times \frac{3}{5}$

6. $\frac{5}{14} \times 2\frac{1}{3}$

7. $\frac{1}{9} \times 5\frac{1}{3}$

8. $\frac{2}{3} \times 4\frac{1}{5}$

9. $\frac{3}{7} \times 5\frac{3}{5}$

10. $2\frac{1}{5} \times \frac{4}{11}$

11. $1\frac{5}{7} \times \frac{5}{12}$

12. $6\frac{1}{8} \times \frac{4}{7}$

13. $4\frac{1}{4} \times \frac{2}{3}$

14. $\frac{9}{12} \times 1\frac{1}{3}$

15. $\frac{3}{14} \times 2\frac{1}{3}$

16. $\frac{3}{4} \times 1\frac{2}{6}$

17. $\frac{7}{8} \times 2\frac{2}{7}$

18. $2\frac{1}{2} \times \frac{2}{15}$

19. $2\frac{4}{5} \times \frac{5}{7}$

20. $\frac{6}{7} \times 4\frac{1}{3}$

21. $\frac{6}{7} \times 2\frac{1}{3}$

22. $2\frac{2}{5} \times \frac{5}{6}$

23. $4\frac{1}{5} \times \frac{6}{7}$

Using the Distributive Property

The **Distributive Property** is sometimes used when multiplying a fraction and a mixed number.

$$\frac{2}{3} \times 9\frac{3}{10} = \frac{2}{3} \times \left(9 + \frac{3}{10}\right) = \left(\frac{2}{3} \times 9\right) + \left(\frac{2}{3} \times \frac{3}{10}\right)$$

$$= \left(\frac{2}{3} \times \frac{9}{1}\right) + \left(\frac{2}{3} \times \frac{3}{10}\right)$$

$$= \left(\frac{2 \times \overset{3}{\cancel{9}}}{\cancel{3} \times 1}\right) + \left(\frac{\overset{1}{\cancel{2}} \times \overset{1}{\cancel{3}}}{\cancel{3} \times \cancel{10}_{5}}\right) = \left(\frac{2 \times 3}{1 \times 1}\right) + \left(\frac{1 \times 1}{1 \times 5}\right)$$

$$= \frac{6}{1} + \frac{1}{5} = 6 + \frac{1}{5} = 6\frac{1}{5}$$

Multiply. Use the Distributive Property.

24. $\frac{1}{8} \times 8\frac{8}{11}$

25. $\frac{1}{6} \times 12\frac{3}{5}$

26. $\frac{1}{5} \times 10\frac{5}{9}$

27. $\frac{1}{3} \times 15\frac{3}{8}$

28. $\frac{3}{4} \times 4\frac{1}{3}$

29. $\frac{8}{9} \times 18\frac{1}{4}$

30. $\frac{3}{7} \times 14\frac{1}{9}$

31. $\frac{5}{6} \times 18\frac{9}{10}$

Problem Solving

32. Celia had $4\frac{1}{2}$ yards of ribbon. She used $\frac{5}{6}$ of it for her project. How many yards of ribbon did she use for her project? How many yards were *not* used?

33. Arnold lives $8\frac{3}{4}$ miles from the library. Miriam lives $\frac{4}{5}$ of this distance from the library. How far does Miriam live from the library?

Multiply Mixed Numbers

Stan bought $2\frac{1}{4}$ feet of wood for shelving. Ralph bought $1\frac{2}{3}$ times as much. How many feet of wood did Ralph buy?

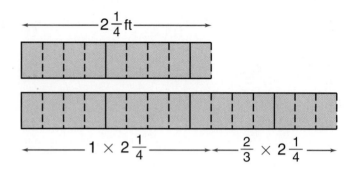

To find how many feet of wood, multiply: $1\frac{2}{3} \times 2\frac{1}{4} = n$.

▶ To **multiply** a *mixed number* by a *mixed* or *whole number*:

- Rename both factors as fractions greater than or equal to one.

- Simplify using the GCF where possible.

- Multiply the numerators. Then multiply the denominators.

- Rename the product as a whole or mixed number when needed.

$$1\frac{2}{3} \times 2\frac{1}{4} = \frac{5}{3} \times \frac{9}{4}$$
$$= \frac{5 \times \overset{3}{\cancel{9}}}{\underset{1}{\cancel{3}} \times 4}$$
$$= \frac{5 \times 3}{1 \times 4} = \frac{15}{4}$$
$$= 3\frac{3}{4} \longleftarrow \boxed{\text{mixed number}}$$

Ralph bought $3\frac{3}{4}$ feet of wood.

Study these examples.

$$8 \times 4\frac{1}{2} = \frac{8}{1} \times \frac{9}{2}$$
$$= \frac{\overset{4}{\cancel{8}} \times 9}{1 \times \underset{1}{\cancel{2}}} = \frac{4 \times 9}{1 \times 1}$$
$$= \frac{36}{1} = 36 \longleftarrow \boxed{\begin{array}{c}\text{whole}\\\text{number}\end{array}}$$

$$4\frac{1}{6} \times 3 = \frac{25}{6} \times \frac{3}{1}$$
$$= \frac{25 \times \overset{1}{\cancel{3}}}{\underset{2}{\cancel{6}} \times 1} = \frac{25 \times 1}{2 \times 1}$$
$$= \frac{25}{2} = 12\frac{1}{2} \longleftarrow \boxed{\begin{array}{c}\text{mixed}\\\text{number}\end{array}}$$

Practice

Find each product. Rename as necessary.

1. $9 \times 1\frac{1}{6} = \frac{?}{1} \times \frac{?}{6}$

$= \frac{? \times ?}{1 \times 6}$

$= n$

2. $1\frac{1}{10} \times 5 = \frac{?}{10} \times \frac{?}{1}$

$= \frac{? \times ?}{10 \times 1}$

$= n$

3. $3\frac{1}{2} \times 3\frac{1}{3} = \frac{?}{2} \times \frac{?}{3}$

$= \frac{? \times ?}{? \times ?}$

$= n$

Multiply.

4. $6 \times 3\frac{1}{6}$

5. $9 \times 1\frac{2}{3}$

6. $4 \times 2\frac{2}{5}$

7. $3 \times 4\frac{4}{9}$

8. $7\frac{1}{2} \times 2\frac{2}{5}$

9. $1\frac{1}{3} \times 5\frac{1}{4}$

10. $3\frac{3}{5} \times 1\frac{2}{3}$

11. $6\frac{1}{4} \times 2\frac{2}{5}$

12. $3\frac{3}{4} \times 3\frac{1}{3}$

13. $6\frac{1}{4} \times 1\frac{1}{5}$

14. $8\frac{2}{3} \times 2\frac{1}{2}$

15. $3\frac{3}{8} \times 3\frac{1}{2}$

16. $4\frac{2}{7} \times 3$

17. $4\frac{1}{6} \times 12$

18. $1\frac{1}{7} \times 7$

19. $5\frac{2}{5} \times 15$

20. $2\frac{1}{3} \times 1\frac{2}{7}$

21. $4\frac{2}{5} \times 2\frac{1}{2}$

22. $6\frac{1}{8} \times 2\frac{2}{7}$

23. $9\frac{2}{3} \times 1\frac{1}{2}$

24. $\frac{7}{8} \times 2\frac{2}{5}$

25. $\frac{3}{10} \times 4\frac{4}{9}$

26. $7\frac{1}{2} \times 2\frac{4}{5}$

27. $1\frac{1}{2} \times 4\frac{2}{3}$

Compare. Write <, =, or >.

28. $1\frac{6}{7} \times 21 \underline{\ ?\ } 6 \times 1\frac{5}{6}$

29. $18 \times 2\frac{2}{9} \underline{\ ?\ } 2\frac{1}{2} \times 16$

30. $2\frac{1}{2} \times 1\frac{2}{3} \underline{\ ?\ } 2\frac{2}{5} \times 1\frac{1}{2}$

31. $3\frac{1}{2} \times 2\frac{1}{4} \underline{\ ?\ } 3\frac{1}{4} \times 2\frac{1}{2}$

Problem Solving

32. Lilia made 2 dresses. Each dress needed $2\frac{3}{16}$ yards of fabric. How many yards of fabric did she use?

33. Vito is $4\frac{2}{3}$ feet tall. His father is $1\frac{1}{4}$ times as tall. How tall is Vito's father?

34. The hour hand of a clock moves 30 degrees every hour. How many degrees does it move in $2\frac{3}{4}$ hours?

35. Cayo uses $9\frac{1}{2}$ ounces of flour to make a loaf of bread. How much flour does he use to make 6 loaves of bread?

Write About It

36. Keep a daily log for a school week. Use mixed numbers and fractions to record, to the nearest quarter of an hour, the time you spend at school, doing homework, and playing. At the end of the school week, find the total time spent for each category.

37. Suppose the total time you found in each category is the same every school week. Explain how you would find how much time you spend on each activity in a month.

Division of Fractions

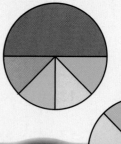
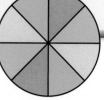

How many eighths are in 3?
To find how many,
divide: $3 \div \frac{1}{8} = n$.

Materials: fraction circles and strips, colored pencils or crayons

Step 1 Find 3 fraction circles that show eighths. Shade all of the eighths.

Step 2 Count the number of eighths shaded. How many eighths are there altogether?

8 equal parts   8 equal parts   8 equal parts

Step 3 Write a division sentence that tells how many eighths are in 3.

1. The diagram at the right shows how to model the number of two thirds in 2.

   Use fraction strips to model $2 \div \frac{2}{3}$ as shown. How many $\frac{2}{3}$s are in 2? What is $2 \div \frac{2}{3}$?

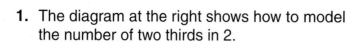

$\frac{2}{3}$ $\frac{2}{3}$ $\frac{2}{3}$

2. The diagram at the right shows how to model the number of tenths in $\frac{4}{5}$.

   Use fraction strips to model $\frac{4}{5} \div \frac{1}{10}$ as shown. How many $\frac{1}{10}$s are in $\frac{4}{5}$? What is $\frac{4}{5} \div \frac{1}{10}$?

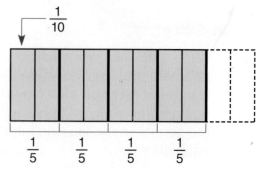

$\frac{1}{10}$

$\frac{1}{5}$ $\frac{1}{5}$ $\frac{1}{5}$ $\frac{1}{5}$

3. How many fourths are in 2?

4. How many halves are in 4?

5. How many $\frac{1}{6}$s are in $\frac{1}{3}$?

6. How many $\frac{1}{10}$s are in $\frac{2}{5}$?

Use fraction circles or strips to model each quotient.
Then write a division sentence. Look for a pattern.

7. $4 \div \dfrac{1}{2}$ **8.** $2 \div \dfrac{1}{8}$ **9.** $3 \div \dfrac{3}{4}$ **10.** $2 \div \dfrac{2}{5}$

11. $\dfrac{3}{4} \div \dfrac{1}{4}$ **12.** $\dfrac{9}{11} \div \dfrac{3}{11}$ **13.** $\dfrac{3}{8} \div \dfrac{2}{8}$ **14.** $\dfrac{7}{9} \div \dfrac{2}{9}$

Write a division sentence for each diagram.

15. 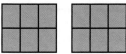 **16.**

17. **18.**  **19.**

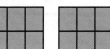

20. When you divide a whole number by a fraction, how does the quotient compare with the whole number? Explain your answer.

21. If you divide fractions with like denominators, when will the quotient be a whole number? Give an example to support your answer.

22. Explain how you divide fractions with like denominators.

CHALLENGE — **Algebra**

Use the diagram to complete each division sentence.

23.

$\dfrac{2}{3} \div \underline{\ ?\ } = 4$

24.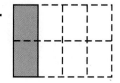

$\underline{\ ?\ } \div \dfrac{1}{8} = 2$

25.

$\dfrac{1}{2} \div \underline{\ ?\ } = \underline{\ ?\ }$

Reciprocals

Two numbers with a product of 1 are called **reciprocals** of each other.

$$\frac{\overset{1}{\cancel{2}}}{\cancel{7}} \times \frac{\overset{1}{\cancel{7}}}{\cancel{2}} = \frac{1}{1} = 1 \quad \text{So } \frac{2}{7} \text{ and } \frac{7}{2} \text{ are reciprocals.}$$

$$\frac{2}{7} \bowtie \frac{7}{2}$$

$$1\frac{1}{4} \times \frac{4}{5} = \frac{\overset{1}{\cancel{5}}}{\cancel{4}} \times \frac{\overset{1}{\cancel{4}}}{\cancel{5}} = \frac{1}{1} = 1 \quad \text{So } 1\frac{1}{4} \text{ and } \frac{4}{5} \text{ are reciprocals.}$$

Find the reciprocal of 2.

▶ To find the **reciprocal of a number:**

- Write the number as a fraction. $2 = \frac{2}{1}$

- Invert the fraction by exchanging the position of the numerator and the denominator. $\frac{2}{1} \bowtie \frac{1}{2}$

- Check if the product of the numbers is 1. $\frac{\overset{1}{\cancel{2}}}{1} \times \frac{1}{\cancel{2}} = \frac{1}{1} = 1$

> 2 and $\frac{1}{2}$ are reciprocals.

Study these examples.

$$\frac{5}{9} \bowtie \frac{9}{5} \quad \frac{\overset{1}{\cancel{5}}}{\cancel{9}} \times \frac{\overset{1}{\cancel{9}}}{\cancel{5}} = \frac{1}{1} = 1$$

$\frac{9}{5}$ is the reciprocal of $\frac{5}{9}$.

$$2\frac{1}{3} = \frac{7}{3} \quad \frac{7}{3} \bowtie \frac{3}{7} \quad \frac{\overset{1}{\cancel{7}}}{\cancel{3}} \times \frac{\overset{1}{\cancel{3}}}{\cancel{7}} = \frac{1}{1} = 1$$

$\frac{3}{7}$ is the reciprocal of $2\frac{1}{3}$.

Practice

Find the value of *n*, the missing reciprocal, in each multiplication sentence.

1. $7 \times n = 1$ **2.** $3 \times n = 1$ **3.** $\frac{1}{6} \times n = 1$ **4.** $\frac{1}{8} \times n = 1$

5. $\frac{7}{11} \times n = 1$ **6.** $\frac{8}{9} \times n = 1$ **7.** $\frac{3}{2} \times n = 1$ **8.** $\frac{7}{3} \times n = 1$

9. $3\frac{1}{2} \times n = 1$ **10.** $4\frac{2}{3} \times n = 1$ **11.** $2\frac{5}{6} \times n = 1$ **12.** $5\frac{2}{7} \times n = 1$

Write the reciprocal of each number.

13. 11   **14.** $\frac{1}{5}$ **15.** $\frac{5}{8}$ **16.** $\frac{9}{2}$ **17.** $\frac{15}{7}$ **18.** $6\frac{3}{5}$

Write _always_, _sometimes_, or _never_ to make each statement true.

19. The reciprocal of a whole number _?_ has a numerator of 1.

20. The reciprocal of a mixed number is _?_ a fraction greater than one.

21. The reciprocal of a fraction is _?_ a whole number.

Use the numbers in the box for problems 22–24.

22. Write the fractions that are less than 1.
Then write their reciprocals.

23. Write the fractions that are greater than 1.
Then write their reciprocals.

$$\boxed{\begin{array}{ccc} \frac{1}{4} & \frac{9}{8} & \frac{3}{10} \\ & \frac{6}{5} & \frac{2}{7} \end{array}}$$

24. What numbers have reciprocals less than 1? greater than 1?

25. When is the reciprocal of a number greater than the
number? less than the number? Give examples.

26. What number is its own reciprocal? Why?

27. Is there any number that does _not_ have a reciprocal?
Explain your answer.

CRITICAL THINKING

**Complete the related multiplication and division sentences
to discover a pattern.**

reciprocals

28. $6 \times 2 = 12$, so $12 \div$ _2_ $= 6$. Also, $12 \times \frac{1}{2} = 6$.

Multiplication and division are inverse operations.

29. $8 \times \frac{1}{4} = \frac{8}{4} = 2$, so $2 \div$ _?_ $= 8$. Also, $2 \times$ _?_ $= 8$.

30. $10 \times \frac{1}{12} = \frac{10}{12} = \frac{5}{6}$, so $\frac{5}{6} \div$ _?_ $= 10$. Also, $\frac{5}{6} \times$ _?_ $= 10$.

31. Dividing by a number is the same as multiplying by
the _?_ of that number.

Divide Whole Numbers by Fractions

A carpenter cut a 4-ft board into $\frac{2}{3}$-ft boards.
How many pieces of board did the carpenter make?

To find the number of $\frac{2}{3}$-ft boards,
divide: $4 \div \frac{2}{3} = n$.

You can use a diagram:

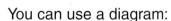

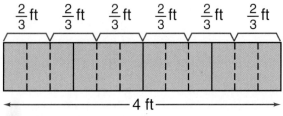

.Think.................
How many $\frac{2}{3}$s are in 4?
....

$$4 \div \frac{2}{3} = 6$$

or

You can multiply by the reciprocal of the divisor since dividing by a
number is the same as multiplying by the reciprocal of that number.

▶ To **divide** a *whole number* by a *fraction*:

- Rename the whole number as a
  fraction with a denominator of 1.

- *Multiply* by the *reciprocal* of the divisor.

- Simplify using the GCF where possible.
  Then multiply the numerators and multiply
  the denominators.

- Rename the product as a whole or
  mixed number when needed.

$$4 \div \frac{2}{3} = \frac{4}{1} \div \frac{2}{3}$$

.Think............
$\frac{2}{3}$ and $\frac{3}{2}$ are
reciprocals.
....

$$= \frac{4}{1} \times \frac{3}{2}$$

$$= \frac{\overset{2}{\cancel{4}} \times 3}{1 \times \underset{1}{\cancel{2}}} = \frac{2 \times 3}{1 \times 1} = \frac{6}{1}$$

$$= 6 \longleftarrow \boxed{\text{whole number}}$$

The carpenter made 6 pieces of $\frac{2}{3}$-ft board.

Study these examples.

$$8 \div \frac{3}{4} = \frac{8}{1} \div \frac{3}{4}$$

.Think............
$\frac{3}{4} \times \frac{?}{?} = 1$
....

$$= \frac{8}{1} \times \frac{4}{3} = \frac{8 \times 4}{1 \times 3} = \frac{32}{3}$$

$$= 10\frac{2}{3} \longleftarrow \boxed{\text{mixed number}}$$

$$10 \div \frac{1}{3} = \frac{10}{1} \div \frac{1}{3}$$

.Think............
$\frac{1}{3} \times \frac{?}{?} = 1$
....

$$= \frac{10}{1} \times \frac{3}{1} = \frac{10 \times 3}{1 \times 1} = \frac{30}{1}$$

$$= 30 \longleftarrow \boxed{\text{whole number}}$$

Copy and complete the table to find the quotient for each division.

	Division Expression	Reciprocal of Divisor	Multiplication Sentence	Quotient
1.	$6 \div \frac{3}{8}$	?	$6 \times \frac{8}{3} = $?	?
2.	$12 \div \frac{4}{5}$	?	$12 \times \frac{5}{4} = $?	?
3.	$5 \div \frac{7}{8}$	$\frac{8}{7}$	?	?
4.	$7 \div \frac{3}{4}$	$\frac{4}{3}$	?	?

Divide.

5. $3 \div \frac{1}{2}$

6. $4 \div \frac{1}{3}$

7. $18 \div \frac{6}{17}$

8. $6 \div \frac{3}{5}$

9. $12 \div \frac{3}{4}$

10. $8 \div \frac{1}{6}$

11. $24 \div \frac{12}{13}$

12. $9 \div \frac{3}{7}$

13. $7 \div \frac{4}{5}$

14. $15 \div \frac{9}{11}$

15. $7 \div \frac{2}{7}$

16. $5 \div \frac{4}{9}$

17. $6 \div \frac{5}{8}$

18. $4 \div \frac{3}{10}$

19. $20 \div \frac{8}{9}$

20. $13 \div \frac{3}{10}$

Problem Solving

21. How many pieces of $\frac{1}{4}$-yd copper tubing can be cut from a 10-yd piece of copper tubing?

22. Edward jogs $\frac{3}{4}$ mile a day. How many days will it take him to jog 8 miles?

23. How many pieces of $\frac{5}{9}$-m board can be cut from a 15-m board?

24. How many $\frac{7}{8}$-qt containers can be filled with 14 qt of strawberries?

25. Which quotient is greater: $5 \div \frac{1}{10}$ or $5 \div \frac{3}{10}$? Explain your answer.

26. Which quotient is less: $10 \div \frac{1}{5}$ or $10 \div \frac{3}{5}$? Explain your answer.

TEST PREPARATION

27. Myra walks at the rate of $\frac{1}{16}$ mile per minute. How long, in hours, would it take her to walk 3 miles?

A $5\frac{1}{3}$ hours **B** $\frac{3}{16}$ hour **C** $\frac{4}{5}$ hour **D** $1\frac{1}{4}$ hours

Divide Fractions by Fractions

Rosa spent $\frac{5}{6}$ hour solving word problems in math. If she averaged $\frac{1}{12}$ hour on each problem, how many word problems did she solve?

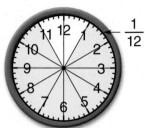

To find the number of word problems, divide: $\frac{5}{6} \div \frac{1}{12} = n$.

.Think..........

How many twelfths are in $\frac{5}{6}$?

▶ To **divide** a *fraction* by a *fraction*:

- Multiply by the reciprocal of the divisor.

$$\frac{5}{6} \div \frac{1}{12} = \frac{5}{6} \times \frac{12}{1}$$

.Think..........

$\frac{1}{12}$ and $\frac{12}{1}$ are reciprocals.

- Simplify using the GCF where possible.

- Multiply the numerators. Then multiply the denominators.

$$= \frac{5 \times \overset{2}{\cancel{12}}}{\underset{1}{\cancel{6}} \times 1} = \frac{5 \times 2}{1 \times 1}$$

- Rename the product as a whole or mixed number when needed.

$$= \frac{10}{1} = 10 \leftarrow \boxed{\text{whole number}}$$

Rosa solved 10 word problems.

Study these examples.

.Think..........

$$\frac{9}{10} \div \frac{3}{5} = \frac{9}{10} \times \frac{5}{3}$$

$\frac{3}{5} \times \frac{?}{?} = 1$

$$= \frac{\overset{3}{\cancel{9}} \times \overset{1}{\cancel{5}}}{\underset{2}{\cancel{10}} \times \underset{1}{\cancel{3}}} = \frac{3 \times 1}{2 \times 1}$$

$$= \frac{3}{2} = 1\frac{1}{2} \leftarrow \boxed{\text{mixed number}}$$

.Think..........

$$\frac{4}{25} \div \frac{3}{7} = \frac{4}{25} \times \frac{7}{3}$$

$\frac{3}{7} \times \frac{?}{?} = 1$

$$= \frac{4 \times 7}{25 \times 3}$$

$$= \frac{28}{75} \leftarrow \boxed{\text{fraction}}$$

Complete each division.

1. $\frac{2}{3} \div \frac{5}{6} = \frac{2}{3} \times \frac{6}{5} = n$

2. $\frac{4}{5} \div \frac{4}{7} = \frac{4}{5} \times \frac{7}{4} = n$

3. $\frac{3}{8} \div \frac{15}{16} = \frac{3}{8} \times \frac{?}{?} = n$

4. $\frac{3}{7} \div \frac{6}{7} = \frac{3}{7} \times \frac{?}{?} = n$

5. $\frac{4}{25} \div \frac{2}{3} = \frac{?}{?} \times \frac{?}{?} = n$

6. $\frac{9}{10} \div \frac{3}{5} = \frac{?}{?} \times \frac{?}{?} = n$

Practice

Divide.

7. $\dfrac{1}{2} \div \dfrac{1}{6}$
8. $\dfrac{1}{4} \div \dfrac{1}{12}$
9. $\dfrac{3}{4} \div \dfrac{1}{6}$
10. $\dfrac{5}{6} \div \dfrac{1}{9}$

11. $\dfrac{3}{8} \div \dfrac{1}{4}$
12. $\dfrac{5}{8} \div \dfrac{1}{2}$
13. $\dfrac{1}{3} \div \dfrac{4}{15}$
14. $\dfrac{3}{14} \div \dfrac{1}{7}$

15. $\dfrac{4}{9} \div \dfrac{1}{6}$
16. $\dfrac{4}{5} \div \dfrac{7}{15}$
17. $\dfrac{5}{12} \div \dfrac{1}{4}$
18. $\dfrac{4}{9} \div \dfrac{1}{12}$

19. $\dfrac{3}{4} \div \dfrac{3}{8}$
20. $\dfrac{3}{5} \div \dfrac{3}{10}$
21. $\dfrac{3}{7} \div \dfrac{3}{7}$
22. $\dfrac{7}{10} \div \dfrac{7}{20}$

23. $\dfrac{2}{3} \div \dfrac{8}{9}$
24. $\dfrac{8}{15} \div \dfrac{2}{5}$
25. $\dfrac{3}{5} \div \dfrac{4}{15}$
26. $\dfrac{4}{7} \div \dfrac{3}{14}$

27. $\dfrac{7}{9} \div \dfrac{5}{6}$
28. $\dfrac{5}{12} \div \dfrac{2}{3}$
29. $\dfrac{2}{3} \div \dfrac{3}{4}$
30. $\dfrac{2}{11} \div \dfrac{10}{13}$

31. $\dfrac{2}{3} \div \dfrac{2}{5}$
32. $\dfrac{4}{5} \div \dfrac{3}{7}$
33. $\dfrac{8}{9} \div \dfrac{4}{5}$
34. $\dfrac{5}{8} \div \dfrac{2}{9}$

Compare. Write $<$, $=$, or $>$.

35. $\dfrac{1}{2} \div \dfrac{1}{3}$ __?__ $\dfrac{1}{4} \div \dfrac{1}{6}$
36. $\dfrac{1}{5} \div \dfrac{1}{7}$ __?__ $\dfrac{1}{8} \div \dfrac{1}{9}$

37. $\dfrac{1}{6} \div \dfrac{5}{12}$ __?__ $\dfrac{1}{5} \div \dfrac{3}{5}$
38. $\dfrac{1}{8} \div \dfrac{3}{4}$ __?__ $\dfrac{1}{9} \div \dfrac{2}{3}$

39. $\dfrac{4}{9} \div \dfrac{2}{3}$ __?__ $\dfrac{16}{25} \div \dfrac{4}{5}$
40. $\dfrac{5}{6} \div \dfrac{2}{9}$ __?__ $\dfrac{4}{7} \div \dfrac{3}{14}$

Problem Solving

41. Gerald cuts a $\dfrac{7}{8}$-yd piece of leather into $\dfrac{1}{16}$-yd strips for key holders. How many strips does he cut?

42. Karen divides $\dfrac{3}{4}$ cup of salad dressing into $\dfrac{1}{8}$-cup portions. How many portions of salad dressing does she have?

43. The reciprocal of a number is the quotient of $\dfrac{1}{3}$ and $\dfrac{5}{6}$. What is the number?

44. The reciprocal of a number is the product of $\dfrac{1}{3}$ and $\dfrac{5}{6}$. What is the number?

MENTAL MATH

Compute.

45. $\dfrac{3}{4} \times \dfrac{5}{6} \div \dfrac{3}{4}$

46. $\left(\dfrac{37}{56} \times \dfrac{11}{14}\right) \div \dfrac{37}{56}$

47. $\left(\dfrac{28}{5} \times \dfrac{3}{41}\right) \div \dfrac{28}{41}$

Divide Fractions by Whole Numbers

Mrs. Kelly divided a half loaf of raisin bread equally among her 6 grandchildren. What fractional part of the loaf of bread did each grandchild receive?

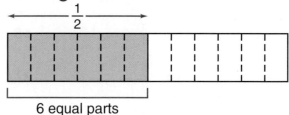

$\frac{1}{2}$

6 equal parts

To find how much bread each received, divide: $\frac{1}{2} \div 6 = n$.

.Think..........
What is $\frac{1}{2}$ divided into 6 equal parts?

▶ To **divide** a *fraction* by a *whole number*:

- Rename the whole number as a fraction with a denominator of 1.

- Multiply by the reciprocal of the whole-number divisor.

- Simplify using the GCF where possible.

- Multiply the numerators. Then multiply the denominators.

- Write the answer in simplest form.

$$\frac{1}{2} \div 6 = \frac{1}{2} \div \frac{6}{1}$$

.Think..........
$$\frac{6}{1} \times \frac{?}{?} = 1$$

$$= \frac{1}{2} \times \frac{1}{6}$$

$$= \frac{1 \times 1}{2 \times 6}$$

$$= \frac{1}{12} \leftarrow$$ Simplest form

Each grandchild received $\frac{1}{12}$ of the loaf of bread.

Study this example.

$$\frac{9}{10} \div 12 = \frac{9}{10} \div \frac{12}{1}$$

.Think..........
$\frac{9}{10}$ divided into 12 equal parts equals what number?

$$= \frac{9}{10} \times \frac{1}{12} = \frac{\overset{3}{\cancel{9}} \times 1}{10 \times \underset{4}{\cancel{12}}}$$

$$= \frac{3 \times 1}{10 \times 4} = \frac{3}{40}$$

Complete each division.

1. $\frac{1}{4} \div 3 = \frac{1}{4} \div \frac{3}{?}$

$$= \frac{1}{4} \times \frac{?}{?}$$

$$= \underline{\ ?\ }.$$

2. $\frac{2}{3} \div 10 = \frac{2}{3} \div \frac{10}{?}$

$$= \frac{2}{3} \times \frac{?}{?}$$

$$= \underline{\ ?\ }$$

3. $\frac{3}{5} \div 9 = \frac{?}{5} \div \frac{9}{?}$

$$= \frac{?}{5} \times \frac{?}{?}$$

$$= \underline{\ ?\ }$$

Divide.

4. $\frac{1}{5} \div 2$ 5. $\frac{1}{7} \div 4$ 6. $\frac{5}{8} \div 10$ 7. $\frac{3}{16} \div 9$

8. $\frac{12}{33} \div 4$ 9. $\frac{9}{10} \div 3$ 10. $\frac{6}{7} \div 4$ 11. $\frac{15}{19} \div 6$

12. $\frac{4}{17} \div 6$ 13. $\frac{6}{7} \div 9$ 14. $\frac{12}{25} \div 6$ 15. $\frac{6}{7} \div 15$

16. $\frac{4}{9} \div 36$ 17. $\frac{5}{8} \div 40$ 18. $\frac{9}{17} \div 27$ 19. $\frac{9}{10} \div 81$

20. $\frac{7}{8} \div 49$ 21. $\frac{6}{7} \div 42$ 22. $\frac{4}{11} \div 8$ 23. $\frac{3}{4} \div 9$

24. $\frac{3}{20} \div 21$ 25. $\frac{2}{3} \div 50$ 26. $\frac{5}{6} \div 20$ 27. $\frac{7}{8} \div 14$

28. $\frac{5}{12} \div 25$ 29. $\frac{11}{12} \div 22$ 30. $\frac{9}{10} \div 27$ 31. $\frac{3}{11} \div 12$

32. $\frac{6}{7} \div 8$ 33. $\frac{4}{25} \div 12$ 34. $\frac{12}{13} \div 16$ 35. $\frac{10}{11} \div 15$

Compare. Write $<$, $=$, or $>$.

36. $\frac{1}{2} \div 10$ __?__ $\frac{1}{4} \div 5$ 37. $\frac{1}{5} \div 8$ __?__ $\frac{2}{5} \div 8$ 38. $\frac{1}{5} \div 6$ __?__ $\frac{1}{6} \div 5$

39. $\frac{3}{4} \div 6$ __?__ $\frac{3}{4} \div 9$ 40. $\frac{1}{3} \div 4$ __?__ $\frac{2}{6} \div 4$ 41. $\frac{5}{6} \div 25$ __?__ $\frac{4}{7} \div 28$

Problem Solving

42. One third of the class is divided into 3 equal groups. What part of the class is each group?

43. Three fourths of a squad is divided into 2 teams. What part of the squad is each team?

44. Jenny has $\frac{7}{8}$ yard of ribbon to use for 3 dresses. If the same amount of ribbon is used for each dress, how many yards of ribbon are used for one dress?

45. Camilo has $\frac{3}{5}$ hour to solve 12 math problems. If he spends the same amount of time on each problem, what part of an hour does he spend on each problem?

Divide Mixed Numbers by Fractions

Carol has $2\frac{1}{2}$ pounds of nuts. How many $\frac{1}{4}$-pound bags can she fill?

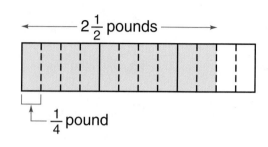

To find the number of $\frac{1}{4}$-pound bags, divide: $2\frac{1}{2} \div \frac{1}{4} = n$.

Think
How many fourths are in $2\frac{1}{2}$?

▶ To **divide** a *mixed number* by a *fraction*:

- Rename the mixed number as a fraction greater than one.

- Multiply by the reciprocal of the divisor.

- Simplify using the GCF where possible.

- Multiply the numerators. Then multiply the denominators.

- Rename the product as a whole or mixed number when needed.

$$2\frac{1}{2} \div \frac{1}{4} = \frac{5}{2} \div \frac{1}{4}$$

Think
$\frac{1}{4} \times \frac{?}{?} = 1$

$$= \frac{5}{2} \times \frac{4}{1}$$

$$= \frac{5 \times \overset{2}{\cancel{4}}}{\underset{1}{\cancel{2}} \times 1} = \frac{5 \times 2}{1 \times 1}$$

$$= \frac{10}{1} = 10 \longleftarrow \boxed{\text{whole number}}$$

Carol can fill ten $\frac{1}{4}$-pound bags.

Study this example.

$$5\frac{1}{3} \div \frac{3}{5} = \frac{16}{3} \div \frac{3}{5}$$

Think
How many three fifths are in $5\frac{1}{3}$?

$$= \frac{16}{3} \times \frac{5}{3} = \frac{16 \times 5}{3 \times 3}$$

$$= \frac{80}{9} = 8\frac{8}{9} \longleftarrow \boxed{\text{mixed number}}$$

Complete each division.

1. $2\frac{1}{3} \div \frac{1}{6} = \frac{?}{3} \div \frac{1}{6}$

$= \frac{?}{3} \times \frac{?}{?}$

$= \underline{?}$

2. $1\frac{1}{2} \div \frac{9}{10} = \frac{?}{2} \div \frac{9}{10}$

$= \frac{?}{2} \times \frac{?}{?}$

$= \underline{?}$

3. $1\frac{1}{4} \div \frac{3}{8} = \frac{?}{?} \div \frac{3}{8}$

$= \frac{?}{?} \times \frac{?}{?}$

$= \underline{?}$

Practice

Divide.

4. $2\frac{1}{2} \div \frac{5}{6}$ **5.** $2\frac{1}{5} \div \frac{3}{4}$ **6.** $2\frac{11}{12} \div \frac{5}{12}$ **7.** $6\frac{7}{8} \div \frac{5}{8}$

8. $3\frac{1}{5} \div \frac{4}{15}$ **9.** $5\frac{1}{16} \div \frac{3}{8}$ **10.** $3\frac{1}{7} \div \frac{2}{7}$ **11.** $7\frac{1}{2} \div \frac{5}{6}$

12. $4\frac{4}{5} \div \frac{4}{15}$ **13.** $3\frac{6}{7} \div \frac{9}{14}$ **14.** $2\frac{1}{4} \div \frac{9}{10}$ **15.** $2\frac{8}{9} \div \frac{2}{3}$

16. $6\frac{3}{4} \div \frac{3}{5}$ **17.** $2\frac{3}{4} \div \frac{5}{12}$ **18.** $4\frac{1}{32} \div \frac{5}{16}$ **19.** $4\frac{1}{5} \div \frac{3}{7}$

20. $4\frac{5}{8} \div \frac{3}{4}$ **21.** $3\frac{7}{8} \div \frac{3}{8}$ **22.** $6\frac{5}{9} \div \frac{5}{9}$ **23.** $2\frac{4}{9} \div \frac{5}{6}$

Compare. Write $<$, $=$, or $>$.

24. $1\frac{1}{2} \div \frac{3}{4}$ ___?___ $1\frac{1}{3} \div \frac{1}{3}$ **25.** $2\frac{1}{2} \div \frac{1}{8}$ ___?___ $3\frac{1}{3} \div \frac{1}{6}$

26. $3\frac{3}{4} \div \frac{3}{4}$ ___?___ $3\frac{1}{5} \div \frac{4}{5}$ **27.** $3\frac{1}{5} \div \frac{4}{15}$ ___?___ $8\frac{1}{3} \div \frac{5}{6}$

28. $3\frac{1}{2} \div \frac{3}{4}$ ___?___ $1\frac{1}{4} \div \frac{3}{8}$ **29.** $4\frac{1}{2} \div \frac{1}{4}$ ___?___ $2\frac{1}{4} \div \frac{1}{2}$

Problem Solving

30. Pang has $8\frac{2}{3}$ pounds of coffee beans. How many $\frac{2}{3}$-pound bags can he fill?

31. Eli jogs $\frac{3}{4}$ mile a day. How many days will it take him to jog $6\frac{1}{4}$ miles?

32. Kim had $2\frac{3}{10}$ meters of copper tubing that he cut into $\frac{1}{5}$-meter pieces. How many $\frac{1}{5}$-meter pieces of tubing did he cut?

33. A carpenter cuts a $4\frac{1}{6}$-yard length of board into $\frac{5}{6}$-yard pieces. How many $\frac{5}{6}$-yard pieces of board does he cut?

MENTAL MATH

Divide.

34. $\frac{1}{2} \div \frac{1}{4}$ **35.** $\frac{1}{3} \div \frac{1}{9}$ **36.** $\frac{1}{4} \div \frac{1}{16}$ **37.** $\frac{1}{5} \div \frac{1}{25}$ **38.** $\frac{1}{6} \div \frac{1}{36}$

39. $2 \div \frac{1}{4}$ **40.** $3 \div \frac{1}{5}$ **41.** $4 \div \frac{1}{6}$ **42.** $5 \div \frac{1}{7}$ **43.** $6 \div \frac{1}{8}$

Divide Mixed Numbers

How many boxes are needed to pack $7\frac{1}{2}$ dozen apples if a box holds $2\frac{1}{2}$ dozen?

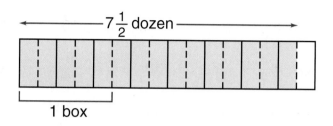

$7\frac{1}{2}$ dozen

1 box

To find how many boxes are needed, divide: $7\frac{1}{2} \div 2\frac{1}{2} = n$.

.Think.........
How many $2\frac{1}{2}$s are in $7\frac{1}{2}$?

▶ To **divide** a *mixed* or *whole number* by another *mixed* or *whole number*:

- Rename both numbers as fractions greater than one.

- Multiply by the reciprocal of the divisor.

- Simplify using the GCF where possible. Then multiply the numerators and multiply the denominators.

- Write the answer in simplest form.

$$7\frac{1}{2} \div 2\frac{1}{2} = \frac{15}{2} \div \frac{5}{2}$$

.Think.........
$$\frac{5}{2} \times \frac{?}{?} = 1$$

$$= \frac{15}{2} \times \frac{2}{5}$$

$$= \frac{\overset{3}{\cancel{15}} \times \overset{1}{\cancel{2}}}{\underset{1}{\cancel{2}} \times \underset{1}{\cancel{5}}} = \frac{3 \times 1}{1 \times 1}$$

$$= \frac{3}{1} = 3$$

Three boxes are needed to pack $7\frac{1}{2}$ dozen apples.

Study these examples.

$$7\frac{1}{5} \div 9 = \frac{36}{5} \div \frac{9}{1}$$

.Think.........
Divide $7\frac{1}{5}$ into 9 equal parts.

$$= \frac{36}{5} \times \frac{1}{9} = \frac{\overset{4}{\cancel{36}} \times 1}{5 \times \underset{1}{\cancel{9}}}$$

$$= \frac{4 \times 1}{5 \times 1} = \frac{4}{5}$$

$$16 \div 1\frac{1}{3} = \frac{16}{1} \div \frac{4}{3}$$

.Think.........
How many $1\frac{1}{3}$s are in 16?

$$= \frac{16}{1} \times \frac{3}{4} = \frac{\overset{4}{\cancel{16}} \times 3}{1 \times \underset{1}{\cancel{4}}}$$

$$= \frac{4 \times 3}{1 \times 1} = 12$$

Complete each division.

1. $3\frac{1}{3} \div 1\frac{2}{3} = \frac{10}{3} \div \frac{?}{3}$

$$= \frac{?}{?} \times \frac{?}{?}$$

$$= \underline{\ ?\ }$$

2. $7 \div 3\frac{1}{2} = \frac{7}{?} \div \frac{?}{?}$

$$= \frac{?}{?} \times \frac{?}{?}$$

$$= \underline{\ ?\ }$$

3. $2\frac{2}{3} \div 6 = \frac{?}{?} \div \frac{6}{?}$

$$= \frac{?}{?} \times \frac{?}{?}$$

$$= \underline{\ ?\ }$$

Divide.

4. $3\frac{1}{2} \div 1\frac{3}{4}$ **5.** $5\frac{1}{3} \div 1\frac{1}{3}$ **6.** $10\frac{1}{2} \div 3\frac{1}{2}$ **7.** $3\frac{6}{7} \div 1\frac{2}{7}$

8. $3\frac{1}{5} \div 8$ **9.** $3\frac{1}{3} \div 10$ **10.** $7\frac{1}{3} \div 11$ **11.** $3\frac{2}{5} \div 17$

12. $6 \div 1\frac{1}{2}$ **13.** $14 \div 4\frac{2}{3}$ **14.** $5 \div 6\frac{3}{5}$ **15.** $23 \div 3\frac{5}{6}$

16. $7\frac{1}{2} \div 1\frac{2}{3}$ **17.** $4\frac{1}{5} \div 1\frac{3}{4}$ **18.** $5\frac{1}{4} \div 2\frac{1}{3}$ **19.** $6\frac{2}{3} \div 1\frac{1}{4}$

20. $4\frac{1}{8} \div 2\frac{3}{4}$ **21.** $6\frac{3}{4} \div 1\frac{1}{2}$ **22.** $6\frac{1}{4} \div 5$ **23.** $6\frac{3}{7} \div 9$

24. $6\frac{2}{3} \div 10$ **25.** $9\frac{3}{5} \div 8$ **26.** $15 \div 1\frac{2}{3}$ **27.** $56 \div 3\frac{1}{2}$

28. $3\frac{3}{4} \div 1\frac{1}{4}$ **29.** $4\frac{4}{5} \div 1\frac{1}{5}$ **30.** $2\frac{2}{7} \div 1\frac{4}{7}$ **31.** $3\frac{3}{5} \div 2\frac{3}{10}$

32. $12 \div 2\frac{2}{5}$ **33.** $18 \div 1\frac{2}{7}$ **34.** $32 \div 1\frac{3}{5}$ **35.** $21 \div 2\frac{1}{3}$

Problem Solving

36. How many pieces of $1\frac{1}{4}$-ft board can be cut from a board that is $8\frac{3}{4}$ ft long?

37. Jorge cut a $5\frac{1}{5}$-m board into 5 equal pieces. How long was each piece?

38. Delia is making name tags that are each $3\frac{3}{4}$ in. long. How many can she make from a 30-in. roll of label paper?

39. Subas packed 5 dozen oranges in boxes. If he put $1\frac{3}{4}$ dozen in each box, how many boxes did he pack?

CHALLENGE Algebra

Compute using the order of operations.

40. $6\frac{1}{2} \times a \div b$ when $a = \frac{1}{5}$ and $b = 1\frac{1}{3}$ **41.** $a + b \times \frac{1}{2}$ when $a = 1\frac{1}{2}$ and $b = 2\frac{1}{3}$

42. $a \times (b \div c)$ when $a = 2\frac{5}{9}$, $b = \frac{2}{3}$, and $c = \frac{2}{9}$ **43.** $(a - b) \div c$ when $a = 3\frac{5}{6}$, $b = 2\frac{1}{4}$, and $c = \frac{3}{8}$

Estimate Products and Quotients with Mixed Numbers

▶ There are two strategies you can use to estimate products and quotients with mixed numbers: **Rounding** and **Compatible Numbers.**

Rounding

Estimate: $2\frac{2}{3} \times 6\frac{1}{9}$.

- Round each mixed number to the nearest whole number.

- Multiply the rounded numbers.

$$2\frac{2}{3} \times 6\frac{1}{9}$$
$$\downarrow \qquad \downarrow$$
$$3 \ \times \ 6$$
$$= 18 \leftarrow$$

$\boxed{\frac{2}{3} > \frac{1}{2} \text{ and } \frac{1}{9} < \frac{1}{2}.}$

$\boxed{\text{estimated product}}$

Estimate: $14\frac{1}{6} \div 1\frac{5}{8}$.

- Round each mixed number to the nearest whole number.

- Divide the rounded numbers.

$$14\frac{1}{6} \div 1\frac{5}{8}$$
$$\downarrow \qquad \downarrow$$
$$14 \ \div \ 2$$
$$= 7 \leftarrow$$

$\boxed{\frac{1}{6} < \frac{1}{2} \text{ and } \frac{5}{8} > \frac{1}{2}.}$

$\boxed{\text{estimated quotient}}$

$\boxed{\textbf{Compatible Numbers} \text{ are numbers that are easy to compute mentally.}}$

Compatible Numbers

Estimate: $\frac{2}{5} \times 11\frac{1}{8}$.

- Think of nearby numbers that are compatible.

- Multiply, using the compatible numbers.

$$\frac{2}{5} \times 11\frac{1}{8}$$
$$\downarrow \qquad \downarrow$$
$$\frac{2}{5} \times \ 10$$

$\boxed{\text{5 and 10 are compatible numbers.}}$

$$= \frac{2}{5} \times \frac{10}{1}$$
$$= \frac{2 \times \overset{2}{\cancel{10}}}{\underset{1}{\cancel{5}} \times 1}$$
$$= \frac{2 \times 2}{1} = \frac{4}{1}$$
$$= 4 \leftarrow$$

$\boxed{\text{Since } 11\frac{1}{8} > 10, \text{ the actual product is } \textit{greater than } 4.}$

$\boxed{\text{estimated product}}$

Estimate: $13 \div 3\frac{3}{7}$.

- Think of nearby numbers that are compatible.

- Divide, using the compatible numbers.

$$13 \div 3\frac{3}{7}$$
$$\downarrow \qquad \downarrow$$
$$12 \ \div \ 3$$

$\boxed{\text{12 and 3 are compatible numbers.}}$

$$= 4$$

$\boxed{\text{estimated quotient}}$

$\boxed{\text{Since } 3\frac{3}{7} > 3, \text{ the actual quotient is } \textit{less than } 4.}$

Estimate the product or quotient by rounding. Then compute to compare.

1. $4\frac{1}{4} \times 3\frac{1}{8}$ 2. $10\frac{3}{4} \times 1\frac{6}{7}$ 3. $4\frac{1}{2} \times 5\frac{1}{4}$ 4. $8\frac{1}{5} \times 3\frac{2}{3}$

5. $26\frac{1}{9} \div 13\frac{1}{3}$ 6. $35\frac{1}{8} \div 4\frac{3}{4}$ 7. $17\frac{2}{3} \div 1\frac{1}{7}$ 8. $55\frac{1}{2} \div 7\frac{1}{3}$

Estimate by using compatible numbers. Then write whether the actual product or quotient is *less than* or *greater than* the estimated product or quotient.

9. $\frac{2}{3} \times 8\frac{1}{5}$ 10. $25\frac{3}{5} \times \frac{3}{8}$ 11. $\frac{9}{10} \times 28\frac{1}{2}$ 12. $82\frac{3}{5} \times \frac{7}{8}$

13. $25 \div 3\frac{1}{3}$ 14. $43 \div 9\frac{1}{5}$ 15. $18\frac{7}{12} \div 5\frac{2}{7}$ 16. $73\frac{1}{8} \div 16\frac{11}{16}$

Use estimation strategies to predict the product or quotient. Choose the correct answer.

17. $4\frac{3}{7} \times 6\frac{1}{10}$ **a.** less than 24   **b.** between 24 and 25   **c.** greater than 25

18. $17\frac{1}{2} \div 2\frac{3}{4}$ **a.** less than 6   **b.** between 6 and 7   **c.** greater than 7

Estimate to compare. Write $<$, $=$, or $>$.

19. $\frac{3}{7} \times 20\frac{1}{5}$ __?__ $\frac{5}{8} \times 25\frac{1}{3}$ 20. $16\frac{4}{5} \times \frac{5}{9}$ __?__ $11\frac{3}{7} \times \frac{3}{5}$

21. $23\frac{4}{7} \div 5\frac{1}{4}$ __?__ $10\frac{5}{6} \div 4\frac{1}{3}$ 22. $33 \div 6\frac{7}{10}$ __?__ $66 \div 13\frac{1}{9}$

Problem Solving

23. Gina uses $3\frac{2}{3}$ cups of flour to make bread. Kate uses $2\frac{1}{2}$ times as much for her recipe. About how much flour does Kate use for her recipe?

24. A surveying team surveys 23 city blocks in $2\frac{3}{4}$ hours. About how many city blocks does the team survey per hour?

CRITICAL THINKING

Choose the best estimate for each quotient. Explain your choice.

25. $\frac{3}{8} \div 6\frac{1}{3}$ **a.** greater than 1   **b.** less than $\frac{1}{12}$ **c.** less than $\frac{1}{3}$

26. $2\frac{1}{6} \div \frac{2}{5}$ **a.** less than 1   **b.** greater than 2   **c.** greater than 4

Problem-Solving Strategy:
Use Simpler Numbers

How many days will it take Paula to walk $6\frac{2}{3}$ mi if she walks $\frac{5}{6}$ mi each day?

How many $\frac{5}{6}$s in $6\frac{2}{3}$?

Read

Visualize yourself in the problem above as you reread it. Focus on the facts and the question.

List what you know.

Facts: total distance —$6\frac{2}{3}$ mi

each day's walk — $\frac{5}{6}$ mi

Question: How many days will it take Paula to walk $6\frac{2}{3}$ mi?

Plan

Use any two simpler numbers to help you choose the operation to use.

..**Think**..............

Use 12 and 2 in place of $6\frac{2}{3}$ and $\frac{5}{6}$ to plan what to do.

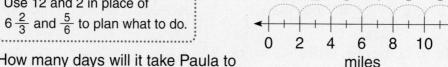

How many days will it take Paula to walk 12 mi if she walks 2 mi each day?
To find how many 2s in 12, divide: $12 \div 2 = 6$

So divide: $6\frac{2}{3}$ mi $\div$ $\frac{5}{6}$ mi = ___?___

Solve

$6\frac{2}{3}$ mi $\div$ $\frac{5}{6}$ mi $= \frac{20}{3} \div \frac{5}{6}$ ◄— The reciprocal of $\frac{5}{6}$ is $\frac{6}{5}$.

$= \frac{20}{3} \times \frac{6}{5}$

$= \frac{\overset{4}{\cancel{20}}}{\underset{1}{\cancel{3}}} \times \frac{\overset{2}{\cancel{6}}}{\underset{1}{\cancel{5}}} = \frac{8}{1}$

$= 8$

So Paula will walk $6\frac{2}{3}$ mi in 8 days if she walks $\frac{5}{6}$ mi each day.

Check

Use the inverse operation to check your answer.

$6\frac{2}{3} \div \frac{5}{6} = 8 \longrightarrow 8 \times \frac{5}{6} \overset{?}{=} 6\frac{2}{3}$

$\frac{\overset{4}{\cancel{8}}}{1} \times \frac{5}{\underset{3}{\cancel{6}}} = \frac{20}{3} = 6\frac{2}{3}$ The answer checks.

Use simpler numbers to solve each problem.

1. Raul reads at a constant rate of 38 pages an hour. If he reads for $3\frac{1}{4}$ h, how many pages will he read?

Read Visualize yourself in the problem above as you reread it. Focus on the facts and question.

List what you know.

Facts: 38 pages an hour read

$3\frac{1}{4}$ h total time

Question: How many pages will Raul read?

Plan Use simpler numbers. Suppose Raul reads 30 pages an hour. How many pages will he read in 3 h? To find how many pages in 3 h, multiply:

3×30 pages or 90 pages.

Now multiply: $3\frac{1}{4} \times 38 = n$

Solve .... **Check**

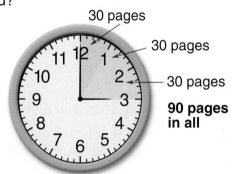

30 pages

30 pages

30 pages

90 pages in all

2. Each box holds $2\frac{1}{2}$ dozen apples. How many boxes are needed to pack $32\frac{1}{2}$ dozen apples?

3. What is the speed in miles per minute of an airplane that flies $18\frac{3}{4}$ mi in $2\frac{1}{2}$ min?

4. If fourteen children share $9\frac{1}{3}$ lb of a fruit mix, what part of a pound will each receive?

5. Rosa needs $14\frac{1}{2}$ lb of potatoes to make potato salad for the picnic. She has peeled $5\frac{1}{3}$ lb. How many more pounds does she need to peel?

6. Eduardo studies $1\frac{5}{6}$ h each night. How many hours will he study in 5 nights?

7. Write a problem that can be solved using simpler numbers. Have a classmate solve it.

Problem-Solving Applications: Mixed Review

Solve each problem and explain the method you used.

1. Martin has $\frac{5}{6}$ of a loaf of banana bread left. He gives half of it to a friend. What part of the loaf does he give to his friend?

2. A recipe calls for $\frac{3}{4}$ c of walnuts. Anna decides to use only $\frac{1}{4}$ of that amount. How much does Anna use?

3. Helen slices 8 carrots into tenths for stew. How many slices are there?

4. Van and Doug make bread. Van uses $\frac{1}{6}$ c of rye flour and Doug uses 4 times as much rye flour. How much rye flour does Doug use?

5. Van's recipe calls for $3\frac{1}{2}$ c of wheat flour. He decides to cut the recipe in half. How much wheat flour should Van use?

6. Holly has $3\frac{1}{4}$ pt of raspberries. She wants to make raspberry muffins. Each muffin uses $\frac{1}{8}$ pt of berries. How many muffins can Holly make?

7. Dorothy buys $10\frac{1}{2}$ lb of apples. She uses $\frac{1}{4}$ of the apples in a pie. How many pounds of apples does she use in the pie?

8. Tom is making burritos. Each burrito uses $\frac{3}{8}$ c of beans and $\frac{1}{4}$ c of rice. How many cups of beans and cups of rice does he need to make 2 dozen burritos?

9. It takes $1\frac{1}{4}$ h to bake a loaf of rye bread. How long will it take to bake a half-dozen loaves if they are baked one at a time?

Choose a strategy from the list or use another strategy you know to solve each problem.

10. Jeanine is making her own breakfast cereal. For every cup of oats, she uses $\frac{1}{4}$ c of dates, $\frac{1}{3}$ c of raisins, and $\frac{1}{8}$ c of puffed rice. How many cups of each ingredient will she use for 8 c of oats?

Strategy File

Use These Strategies
Work Backward
Use Simpler Numbers
Make an Organized List
Use More Than One Step
Make a Table/Find a Pattern

11. Robert is making party mix from raisins, nuts, cereal, and butter. How many different ways can he combine the ingredients if he decides to put the butter in last?

12. Adam decided to divide a carrot cake recipe in half, so he used $\frac{4}{5}$ lb of carrots. How many pounds of carrots did the original recipe require?

13. A recipe calls for $\frac{1}{8}$ lb of pistachio nuts. Heather has 3 oz of pistachios. Does she have enough to make the recipe?

14. Ashlee bakes a loaf of rye bread that weighs $18\frac{1}{3}$ oz. How many $\frac{5}{6}$-oz slices can she cut?

Use the table for problems 15–18.

15. Rosemary makes a double batch of garden salad and a triple batch of cucumber salad. How many pounds of cucumbers does she use? Explain.

16. Which uses more tomatoes: three garden salads or six cucumber salads? Explain.

17. Which use less oil and vinegar combined: four garden salads or three cucumber salads? Explain.

Salads		
Item	**Garden**	**Cucumber**
Tomatoes	$\frac{3}{4}$ lb	$\frac{1}{5}$ lb
Lettuce	$1\frac{1}{2}$ lb	none
Onions	$\frac{1}{6}$ lb	$\frac{1}{3}$ lb
Cucumbers	$\frac{1}{6}$ lb	$1\frac{1}{4}$ lb
Oil	$\frac{1}{4}$ c	$\frac{1}{3}$ c
Vinegar	$\frac{1}{8}$ c	$\frac{1}{3}$ c

18. Write a problem that uses the data in the table. Have someone solve it.

Check Your Progress
Lessons 1–17

Use the diagram to complete each statement. *(See pp. 198–199, 212–213.)*

1.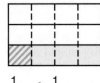

$\frac{1}{4}$ of $\frac{1}{3} = n$

2.

$\frac{2}{3} \times \frac{5}{6} = n$

3.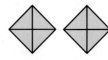

$2 \div \frac{1}{4} = n$

4.

$\frac{2}{3} \div \frac{1}{6} = n$

Multiply. *(See pp. 200–205.)*

5. $\frac{3}{5} \times \frac{1}{2}$

6. $\frac{7}{10} \times \frac{2}{21}$

7. $6 \times \frac{2}{11}$

8. $\frac{4}{9} \times 18$

9. $\frac{2}{3} \times \frac{7}{10}$

10. $\frac{9}{20} \times \frac{24}{45}$

11. $\frac{9}{11} \times 6$

12. $60 \times \frac{3}{5}$

Rename each as a fraction greater than one. *(See pp. 206–207.)*

13. $2\frac{1}{2}$

14. $3\frac{1}{7}$

15. $2\frac{1}{4}$

16. $4\frac{2}{3}$

17. $3\frac{1}{5}$

18. $6\frac{1}{8}$

Find the product. *(See pp. 208–211.)*

19. $5\frac{1}{3} \times 3\frac{3}{4}$

20. $2\frac{1}{2} \times \frac{4}{7}$

21. $9\frac{1}{5} \times \frac{1}{7}$

22. $1\frac{7}{9} \times \frac{4}{5}$

Are the numbers reciprocals? Write *Yes* or *No*. *(See pp. 214–215.)*

23. $5, \frac{1}{5}$

24. $\frac{2}{3}, 1\frac{1}{2}$

25. $3\frac{1}{4}, \frac{4}{13}$

26. $\frac{4}{5}, \frac{8}{10}$

Use manipulatives or drawings to divide. *(See pp. 216–225.)*

27. $9 \div \frac{3}{5}$

28. $\frac{3}{8} \div 6$

29. $\frac{3}{10} \div \frac{3}{5}$

30. $\frac{5}{8} \div \frac{3}{10}$

31. $3\frac{1}{5} \div \frac{1}{3}$

32. $3\frac{1}{2} \div 1\frac{3}{4}$

33. $5 \div 2\frac{2}{7}$

34. $6\frac{1}{8} \div 1\frac{3}{4}$

Estimate. *(See pp. 226–227.)*

35. $14\frac{2}{7} \times 4\frac{1}{5}$

36. $4\frac{2}{3} \times 2\frac{1}{2}$

37. $6\frac{1}{4} \div 1\frac{3}{4}$

38. $19\frac{1}{3} \times 5\frac{4}{5}$

Problem Solving
(See pp. 208–209, 224–225, 228–230.)

39. Tony ran $3\frac{5}{9}$ times farther than Dot. If Dot ran $\frac{3}{4}$ of a mile, how far did Tony run?

40. Ann uses a $2\frac{1}{2}$-gal container to fill a 20-gal tank with water. How many times must she fill the container?

(See Still More Practice, p. 482.)

Logic

In logic, two statements can be combined to form a compound statement using *and* or a compound statement using *or*.

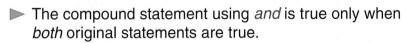
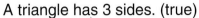

▶ The compound statement using *and* is true only when *both* original statements are true.

A triangle has 3 sides. (true)
A square has 4 angles. (true)
A triangle has 3 sides *and* a square has 4 angles. (true)

A triangle has 4 sides. (false)
A triangle has 4 sides *and* a square has 4 angles. (false)

▶ The compound statement using *or* is true when *both* original statements are true, or *one* of the original statements is true.

A triangle has 3 sides *or* a square has 4 angles. (true)

A square has 5 angles. (false)
A triangle has 3 sides *or* a square has 5 angles. (true)

A triangle has 4 sides *or* a square has 5 angles. (false)

Write compound statements using *and* and *or*. Then tell whether each compound statement is *true* or *false*.

1. A cat is an animal.
   A nickel is a coin.

2. Fall follows spring.
   December falls in winter.

3. Ten is divisible by 2.
   Twelve is divisible by 3.

4. Four is a prime number.
   Five is a composite number.

5. $45 \div 9 = 5$
   $8 - 3 = 6$

6. $4 \times 6 = 20$
   $9 + 5 = 14$

7. $8 + 2 = 10$
   $8 < 9$

8. $8 + 20 \div 2 = 18$
   $2 + 3 + 5 > 10$

9. $\frac{1}{2} + \frac{2}{3} = \frac{3}{5}$
   $\frac{6}{7} - \frac{2}{7} = \frac{4}{7}$

10. $\frac{1}{2} \times \frac{2}{3} = \frac{1}{3}$
    $\frac{6}{7} \div \frac{2}{7} = 3$

Use the diagram to complete each statement.

1.

   $\frac{3}{4} \times \frac{3}{5} = n$

2.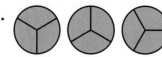

   $3 \div \frac{1}{3} = n$

3.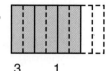

   $\frac{3}{4} \div \frac{1}{8} = n$

Rename each as a fraction greater than one.

4. $3\frac{3}{7}$
5. $9\frac{2}{5}$
6. $6\frac{4}{9}$
7. $2\frac{5}{11}$
8. $7\frac{1}{3}$

Multiply.

9. $\frac{4}{5} \times \frac{1}{2}$
10. $\frac{6}{7} \times 2\frac{1}{3}$
11. $4\frac{2}{5} \times 2$
12. $3\frac{1}{3} \times 2\frac{1}{5}$

Write the reciprocal of each number.

13. 13
14. $\frac{3}{17}$
15. $\frac{11}{9}$
16. $1\frac{4}{15}$

Divide.

17. $\frac{9}{20} \div 6$
18. $\frac{4}{15} \div \frac{4}{7}$
19. $8 \div \frac{2}{3}$
20. $\frac{1}{5} \div \frac{2}{5}$

21. $4\frac{1}{8} \div 11$
22. $2\frac{1}{2} \div \frac{5}{13}$
23. $2\frac{2}{5} \div 1\frac{1}{2}$
24. $4 \div 3\frac{1}{2}$

Problem Solving

Use a strategy you have learned.

25. Barbara lives 12 miles from work. Linda lives $1\frac{3}{4}$ times farther from work than Barbara. About how far does Linda live from work?

26. Joe cut off $\frac{5}{9}$ of a $4\frac{1}{2}$-foot-long rope. How many feet were cut off?

Tell About It

27. Explain how you can use:
    - manipulatives or drawings to divide: $12 \div 1\frac{1}{2}$.
    - the division steps to solve the same problem.

Performance Assessment

Use these rule cards.
Predict the rule for each pattern. Then tell the next number and rule.

28. $6, 2, \frac{2}{3}, \underline{\ ?\ }$

29. $6, 9, 13\frac{1}{2}, \underline{\ ?\ }$

30. $6, 8, 10\frac{2}{3}, \underline{\ ?\ }$

Test Preparation

Choose the best answer.

1. $3 \times \frac{5}{6}$

    a. $\frac{15}{18}$ **b.** $2\frac{1}{2}$

    c. $3\frac{5}{6}$ **d.** $\frac{5}{18}$

2. $7\frac{3}{4} + \frac{3}{8} + 6\frac{9}{32}$

    a. $14\frac{13}{32}$ **b.** $13\frac{13}{32}$

    c. $32\frac{13}{14}$ **d.** $31\frac{13}{14}$

3. $20 + 15 \div 5 - 6$

    a. 17
    b. 1
    c. 16
    d. 0

4. Choose two equivalent
    fractions for $\frac{7}{15}$.

    a. $\frac{7}{30}, \frac{40}{45}$ **b.** $\frac{14}{30}, \frac{21}{60}$

    c. $\frac{21}{45}, \frac{28}{60}$ **d.** $\frac{14}{30}, \frac{40}{45}$

5. Which is the least common multiple
    of 6, 9, and 12?

    a. 3
    b. 18
    c. 36
    d. 72

6. Which numbers are
    not reciprocals?

    a. 7 and $\frac{1}{7}$ **b.** $\frac{1}{15}$ and 15

    c. $1\frac{1}{3}$ and $\frac{4}{3}$ **d.** $\frac{3}{5}$ and $1\frac{2}{3}$

7. $3 \div \frac{1}{4}$

    a. $\frac{1}{12}$ **b.** $\frac{3}{4}$

    c. $1\frac{1}{3}$ **d.** 12

8. $41\frac{3}{5} - 17\frac{5}{6}$

    a. $24\frac{23}{30}$ **b.** $23\frac{23}{30}$

    c. $58\frac{23}{30}$ **d.** $36\frac{23}{30}$

9. Find the GCF of 36, 90,
    and 120.

    a. 12
    b. 9
    c. 6
    d. 3

10. Order from least to
    greatest $\frac{2}{7}, \frac{1}{5}, \frac{3}{10}$

    a. $\frac{1}{5}, \frac{2}{7}, \frac{3}{10}$ **b.** $\frac{2}{7}, \frac{1}{5}, \frac{3}{10}$

    c. $\frac{2}{7}, \frac{3}{10}, \frac{1}{5}$ **d.** $\frac{1}{5}, \frac{3}{10}, \frac{2}{7}$

11. Which number is divisible
    by both 2 and 4?

    a. 36,106
    b. 30,182
    c. 803,612
    d. 842,214

12. Which statement is true?

    a. $\frac{3}{5} < \frac{2}{9}$ **b.** $\frac{3}{8} = \frac{9}{15}$

    c. $\frac{4}{7} > \frac{5}{8}$ **d.** $\frac{10}{24} = \frac{15}{36}$

13. Choose the standard form.

eighteen million, seven thousand, four

    a. 18,700,004   **b.** 18,007,400
    c. 18,070,040   **d.** 18,007,004

14. Find the sum.

$6\frac{3}{4} + 8\frac{2}{5}$

    a. $14\frac{3}{20}$ **b.** $15\frac{3}{20}$

    c. $5\frac{1}{10}$ **d.** $4\frac{1}{10}$

15. Compute. Use the order of operations.

$132 - n \div 4 \times 2$ when $n = 8$

    a. 62   **b.** 64
    c. 128   **d.** 130

16. Choose the missing addend and the property of addition that is used.

$10 + 6 = n + 10$

    a. 6; identity
    b. 6; commutative
    c. 10; identity 0
    d. 10; commutative

17. Mr. Diaz needs $8\frac{5}{16}$ ft of molding to finish a closet. He has $7\frac{1}{8}$ ft of molding. How many more feet of molding does Mr. Diaz need?

    a. $1\frac{5}{16}$ ft   **b.** $1\frac{3}{16}$ ft

    c. $15\frac{7}{16}$ ft   **d.** $15\frac{3}{16}$ ft

18. Find the product.

81×745

    a. 60,435   **b.** 60,345
    c. 50,435   **d.** 50,345

19. Find the quotient.

$14\frac{2}{3} \div 4\frac{1}{8}$

    a. $3\frac{1}{3}$ **b.** $4\frac{1}{3}$

    c. $3\frac{5}{9}$ **d.** $4\frac{5}{9}$

20. Round to the place of the underlined digit.

4,5̲85,802

    a. 4,500,000   **b.** 5,000,000
    c. 4,000,000   **d.** 4,600,000

21. Find the quotient and choose the basic fact you use.

$300\overline{)27,000}$

    a. 9; $27 \div 3 = 9$
    b. 90; $27 \div 3 = 9$
    c. 900; $27 \div 3 = 9$
    d. 9000; $27 \div 3 = 9$

22. Bill needs canvas for three projects. One project requires $\frac{1}{4}$ yd, another requires $\frac{1}{2}$ yd, and the third requires $\frac{1}{8}$ yd. How much canvas does he need for all three projects?

    a. $\frac{7}{8}$ yd   **b.** $1\frac{1}{8}$ yd

    c. $\frac{15}{16}$ yd   **d.** $1\frac{1}{16}$ yd

Explain how you solved the problem. Show all your work.

23. Each letter in the statements below represents one number in the box. Find out which fraction, whole number, or mixed number to use for each letter.

$\frac{9}{16}$	1	$1\frac{1}{2}$	$\frac{3}{4}$	$2\frac{1}{4}$

$C - A = D$ $D \times D = E$ $B - D < E$

Probability and Statistics

Leaves
The winds that blow—
ask them, which leaf of the tree
will be next to go!

Soseki

In this chapter you will:
Learn about tree diagrams
  and independent and
  dependent events
Collect, organize, report,
  and interpret data
Interpret and make line plots,
  histograms, and line graphs
Use a model or diagram to
  solve problems

Critical Thinking/Finding Together
On Sunday, leaves start falling into the
swimming pool. The number of leaves
doubles each day, until the whole pool
is covered on the seventh day. On
which day is the pool half-covered?

Update your skills. See page 20.

Probability

Probability is the chance that a given *event* or situation will occur in an *experiment*.

Random experiments, like tossing a coin, rolling a number cube, spinning a spinner, and selecting an item from a set of items without looking, mean you do not know beforehand what the *outcome*, or result, will be.

Experiment: tossing a coin
Possible Outcomes: heads (*H*), tails (*T*)
Event: tossing heads

The experiment of spinning the given spinner involves finding the probability of a spinner landing on different colors. What is the probability of the spinner landing on red? *not* landing on blue?

► For *equally likely* outcomes, **the probability of an event, *P*(E),** to occur is given by the formula:

$$P(E) = \frac{\text{number of favorable outcomes}}{\text{number of possible outcomes}}$$

$P(\text{red}) = \frac{1}{3}$ — one red
— three possible outcomes

$P(\textit{not}\text{ blue}) = \frac{2}{3}$

Think
not blue: 1 red, 1 green

► You can use probability to make predictions. In 300 spins, predict about how many times the spinner above will land on red.

$$\frac{1}{\cancel{3}} \times \overset{100}{\cancel{300}} = 100$$
$$\uparrow$$
$$P(\text{red}) = \frac{1}{3}$$

The spinner will land on red about 100 out of 300 spins.

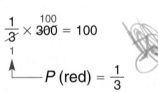

Practice

Use a coin to find the probability of each event. H = Heads   T = Tails

1. *P*(H)   **2.** *P*(T)   **3.** *P*(*not* H)   **4.** *P*(*not* T)

Use the spinner at the right to find the probability of each event.

5. *P*(1)   **6.** *P*(2)   **7.** *P*(3)   **8.** *P*(4)

9. In 700 spins, predict how many times the spinner at the right will land on: **a.** 1   **b.** 2   **c.** 3   **d.** 4

10. Explain how you made your predictions in exercise 9.

Use the number cube at the right to predict the probability of each event in 12 tosses.

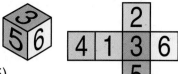

11. $P(3)$ **12.** $P(6)$ **13.** $P(not\,2)$ **14.** $P(not\,5)$

15. Use a real number cube to test your predictions in 11–14. Roll the cube 12 times. How do your predictions compare with your outcomes?

Combined and Special Events

A box contains 1 red cube, 3 green cubes, and 4 blue cubes. Pick one cube from the box at random. What is the probability you will pick red or green? yellow? *not* pink?

Number of possible outcomes: 8 since there are 8 cubes.

P (red or green) $= P$ (red) $+ P$ (green)

> **Think**
> 1 red cube
> 3 green cubes

$$= \frac{1}{8} + \frac{3}{8} = \frac{4}{8} = \frac{1}{2}$$

P (yellow) $= \frac{0}{8} = 0$

> **Think**
> *no* yellow cube

P (*not* pink) $= \frac{8}{8} = 1$

> **Think**
> 8 cubes are *not* pink.

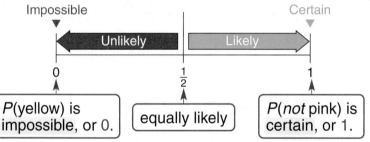

Impossible ▼   Certain ▼

◄ Unlikely | Likely ►

0          $\frac{1}{2}$ 1

P(yellow) is impossible, or 0.

equally likely

P(*not* pink) is certain, or 1.

Find the probability of each event. Use the box of cubes above.

16. P (red or blue) **17.** P (*not* purple) **18.** P (gray)

Problem Solving

19. A bank contains a nickel, a dime, and a quarter. James selects one coin at random. What is the probability that the coin is worth:

a. exactly 5¢? **b.** exactly 4¢? **c.** more than 4¢?

TEST PREPARATION

20. An envelope contains 4 blue cards, 5 yellow cards, and 3 red cards. One card is chosen at random. What is the probability that the card chosen is *not* blue?

A $\frac{1}{4}$ **B** $\frac{2}{3}$ **C** $\frac{3}{4}$ **D** $\frac{1}{12}$

Tree Diagrams

In an experiment, Taylor flips two counters. One side of each counter is green and the other side is red. Find all possible outcomes. What is the probability of both counters landing green side up?

▶ The set of all possible outcomes of a probability experiment is called the sample space. You can use a tree diagram to find the sample space and to determine the *probability of more than one event.*

Event 1 First Counter	Event 2 Second Counter	Outcomes	Write
Green (G)	Green (G) ⟶	Green-Green	(G, G)
	Red (R) ⟶	Green-Red	(G, R)
Red (R)	Green (G) ⟶	Red-Green	(R, G)
	Red (R) ⟶	Red-Red	(R, R)

Probability of both green ⟶ $P(G, G) = \dfrac{1}{4}$ ⟵ favorable outcomes / possible outcomes

Possible outcomes: $(G, G), (G, R), (R, G), (R, R)$
The probability of both counters landing green side up is $\dfrac{1}{4}$.

Complete the tree diagram to show all the possible outcomes of tossing two coins. Then use the completed tree diagram for exercises 3–4.

Heads (H)   Tails (T)

Event 1 First Coin	Event 2 Second Coin	Outcomes	Write
1. Heads (H)	Tails (T) ⟶	?	(?, ?)
	? ⟶	?	(?, ?)
2. Tails (T)	? ⟶	?	(?, ?)
	? ⟶	?	(?, ?)

3. How many possible outcomes are there altogether?

4. What is the probability of each outcome occurring?

Use the spinners for exercises 5–7.

A   **B**

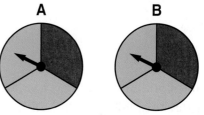

5. Draw a tree diagram to list all the possible outcomes of spinning both spinners.

6. How many possible outcomes are there altogether?

7. What is the probability of spinning:

    a. red-green?   **b.** green-blue?   **c.** the same color?

    d. red with spinner *A*?   **e.** blue with spinner *B*?

Draw a tree diagram and list all possible outcomes.

8. Toss a coin and roll a number cube.

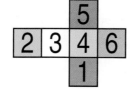

Heads (*H*)

9. Spin the spinner and pick a marble without looking.

Find each probability. Use the experiments in exercises 8–9.

10. *P* (*H*, 2)   **11.** *P* (*T*, 5)   **12.** *P* (*H*, even) **13.** *P* (*T*, odd)   **14.** *P* (*H*, 1 or 6)

15. *P* (red, red)   **16.** *P* (blue, orange) **17.** *P* (green, blue)   **18.** *P* (red, not blue)

Problem Solving

19. Lia spins a spinner with three equal sections twice. The sections of the spinner are marked 1, 4, and 7. The two numbers she spins are the first and the second digits of a number that tells her how much contest money she wins. List all possible outcomes.

Write About It

20. How is a tree diagram like an organized list of possible outcomes?

21. Describe how you can use a tree diagram to find the probability of more than one event.

Independent and Dependent Events

A bag contains 3 cubes: 1 yellow, 1 red, and 1 blue. Pick 2 cubes, one at a time, from the bag without looking. What is the probability of picking a blue and then a red?

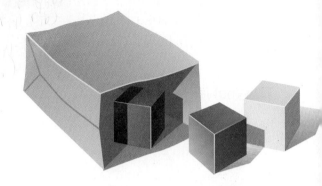

You can use tree diagrams to list all possible outcomes for experiments involving more than one event.

▶ **Independent events:** The first event does *not* affect the second event.

Pick the first cube. <u>Return</u> it to the bag. Then pick the second cube.

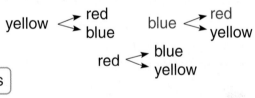

yellow ⟨ red, blue, yellow   blue ⟨ red, blue, yellow

red ⟨ red, blue, yellow

$P \text{ (blue, red)} = \frac{1}{9}$ ← favorable outcomes
                              ← possible outcomes

▶ **Dependent events:** The first event *does* affect the second event.

Pick the first cube. <u>Do *not*</u> return it to the bag. Then pick the second cube.

yellow ⟨ red, blue   blue ⟨ red, yellow

red ⟨ blue, yellow

$P \text{ (blue, red)} = \frac{1}{6}$ ← favorable outcomes
                              ← possible outcomes

Draw a tree diagram and list all possible outcomes.

1. A bag contains 4 cubes: 2 orange and 2 blue.

   a. Pick a cube from the bag at random and put it back. Then pick another cube.

   b. Pick a cube from the bag at random and do *not* put it back. Then pick another cube.

2. A purse contains 5 coins: 2 dimes and 3 nickels. Pick one coin from the purse at random and, without replacing it, pick another coin.

Draw a tree diagram for the random experiment. Then find the probability: (a) if the first choice is replaced; and (b) if the first choice is *not* replaced.

Experiment: Choose a card from an envelope containing 4 cards marked *A, B, C, D.*

Pick a card and put it back. Then choose another card.

3. $P(A, B)$ **4.** $P(C, not D)$ **5.** $P(not B, D)$

Problem Solving

Ben has 3 bananas and 2 apples in a bag. He will eat 2 of the fruits while waiting for the school bus.

6. Draw a tree diagram and list all possible outcomes showing which fruit could be eaten.

7. Find the probability that:

    a. both fruits will be bananas.

    b. neither of the fruits will be a banana.

    c. the fruits will be the same kind.

    d. at least one of the fruits will be a banana.

CHALLENGE

You can also find probabilities of independent and dependent events by multiplying the probabilities of each single event.

Find the probability: (a) if the first choice is replaced; and (b) if the first choice is *not* replaced.

Experiment: Choose a counter from a bag containing 10 red, 6 white, and 4 blue counters. Then choose another counter.

		With Replacement	Without Replacement
8.	$P(red, red)$	$P(red) \times P(red) =$ $\dfrac{10}{20} \times \dfrac{10}{20} = \dfrac{1}{4}$	$P(red) \times P(red) =$ $\dfrac{10}{20} \times \dfrac{9}{19} = \dfrac{9}{38}$
9.	$P(red, white)$	?	?
10.	$P(blue, red)$	?	?

Collect and Organize Data

Pilar wants to know which type of fish in the class aquarium is the favorite among her classmates.

▶ To *collect* the data, Pilar conducts a survey.

First, she makes a list of all the types of fish in the aquarium:

goldfish, angelfish, mollie, guppy

Then she asks each student this survey question: *Which type of fish, goldfish, angelfish, mollie, or guppy, is your favorite?*

▶ To *record* and *organize* the data, Pilar makes a frequency table. She uses tally marks to record each response. Then she counts the tallies to find the frequency. The frequency tells how many students choose each fish.

Favorite Fish		
Type of Fish	**Tally**	**Frequency**
goldfish	////	4
angelfish	~~HHt~~ ~~HHt~~ //	12
mollie	///	3
guppy	~~HHt~~ /	6

/ = 1 and ~~HHt~~ = 5

The angelfish is the most favorite and the mollie is the least favorite among the students.

▶ To show a running total of data and find the total number of students surveyed, Pilar makes a cumulative frequency table.

Favorite Fish		
Type of Fish	**Frequency**	**Cumulative Frequency**
goldfish	4	4
angelfish	12	16	← 4 + 12 = 16
mollie	3	19	← 16 + 3 = 19
guppy	6	25	← 19 + 6 = 25

The last entry in the cumulative frequency column gives the total frequency.

Pilar surveyed 25 students.

Copy and complete the table. Use the completed table for problems 5–8.

Fifth-Grade Students' Favorite Place to Visit Some Day		
Place	**Tally**	**Frequency**
1. Europe	~~HHT~~ ~~HHT~~ ///	?
2. Africa	~~HHT~~ //	?
3. Caribbean	?	10
4. Asia	?	5

5. Write a survey question that could have been used to obtain the data.

what is your favorite country

6. Which place was favored by the least number of students?

Asia

7. How many fewer students chose Asia than the Caribbean? *5*

8. How many students were surveyed?

35

Write a survey question that could have been used to obtain the data. Then complete the table.

Method of Travel to School		
Travel Method	**Frequency**	**Cumulative Frequency**
9. Bus	15	?
10. Walk	13	15 + ? = 28
11. Car	10	? + 10 = 38
12. Bike	?	38 + ? = 50

Survey your fifth grade class to find the favorite month of the year for each of your classmates.

13. Make up a question for your survey.

14. Record your data in a frequency table.

15. Make a cumulative frequency table from your frequency table.

16. Which month was favored by the most number of students?

17. Which month did the least number of students favor?

18. If you surveyed another class do you think that the most number of students will favor the same month?

19. Survey another class to test your prediction. Record your data in a frequency table.

20. Make a cumulative frequency table from your frequency table.

21. Compare the data from both surveys. Was your prediction correct?

22. Write a paragraph comparing the two sets of data.

Range, Median, Mean, and Mode

Raul has kept a record of the number of points his basketball team scored in six games. Now he is going to *interpret* the scores.

Game	1	2	3	4	5	6
Score	63	48	56	64	65	64

You can analyze a set of data by using *range, median, mean,* and *mode.* Median, mean, and mode are measures of central tendency.

▶ The range of a set of data is the difference between the greatest number and the least number.

$$65 - 48 = 17 \longleftarrow \boxed{\text{range}}$$

greatest number / least number

The team's scores vary by 17 points.

▶ The median is the middle number when the data are listed in order from least to greatest.

When there are an even number of data, the median is the average of the two middle numbers.

When there are an odd number of data, the median is the middle number.

6, 7, 8, 8, 10, 11, 14

$\boxed{\text{median}}$

• Order from least to greatest:

48, 56, 63, 64, 64, 65

middle numbers

• Divide the sum of the two middle numbers by 2 to find the median.

$$\frac{63 + 64}{2} = \frac{127}{2} = 63\frac{1}{2} \longleftarrow \boxed{\text{median}}$$

Half of the scores are below $63\frac{1}{2}$; half are above $63\frac{1}{2}$.

▶ The mean is the average of the data. To find the mean, add the numbers and then divide the sum by the number of addends.

$$63 + 48 + 56 + 64 + 65 + 64 = 360$$
$$360 \div 6 = 60 \longleftarrow \boxed{\text{mean}}$$

The team's mean, or average score, is 60.

▶ The mode is the number that occurs most frequently:

63, 48, 56, 64, 65, 64 → $\boxed{\text{mode: 64}}$

occurs most

Sometimes a set of data has *no* mode or has *more than one* mode.

The team scored 64 more frequently than any other score in its games.

55, 63, 58, 62, 65, 64 has no mode.
48, 53, 48, 58, 60, 58 has two modes: 48 and 58.

Find the range, median, mean, and mode, for each set of data.

1. 39, 31, 39, 27
2. 96, 88, 81, 80, 85
3. 90, 60, 85, 75, 100, 85
4. 31, 59, 73, 96, 30, 96, 118

5.

Five-Day Temperature				
Day 1	Day 2	Day 3	Day 4	Day 5
33°F	38°F	27°F	37°F	45°F

Tell which best describes each situation. Write *range, median, mean,* and *mode.* Explain why.

6. The most popular type of movie rented last week was a mystery.
7. The ages of game contestants varied by 5 years.
8. The average test grade of students in section A is 92.
9. Half of the runners finished a race in 12 minutes or less.

10. Write in your Math Journal how the median and mode of a set of data differ from the mean; then write how they differ from the range.

Problem Solving

Use the chart for problems 11–12.

Kim's Math and Science Test Scores	
Math:	98, 75, 90, 62, 82, 95, 98
Science:	96, 90, 74, 70, 80, 86

11. How much greater or less was Kim's median score for math tests than her median score for science tests?

12. A mean score of 90 or more for Kim's science tests would earn her an A in science. Did Kim get an A in science? Explain.

13. Kevin's average score after bowling 12 games was 140. He scored 179 in his next game. What was his new average score?

14. Change one number in the set of data: 6, 4, 8, 9, 6, 5, 8, 7, and 10, so that the range will be 5.

15. Add one number to the set of data: 88, 96, 88, 80, and 76, so that the median will be 86.

MENTAL MATH

16. Which set of data has the same number for the mean, median, and mode?
   a. 2, 2, 5
   b. 2, 3, 3, 4
   c. 2, 5, 5
   d. 2, 2, 5, 5

17. Which set of data has more than one mode?
   a. 2, 2, 4, 6, 7, 9
   b. 2, 2, 2, 6, 7, 9
   c. 2, 2, 4, 6, 9, 9
   d. 2, 3, 4, 6, 9, 9

Graphing Sense

Graphs are pictorial representations of data. They are used to illustrate data in an organized and easily understood way. Each type of graph is used for a particular purpose.

▶ A bar graph presents data so that comparisons of *different* items can be made. It uses vertical bars or horizontal bars of different lengths. The length of each bar is proportional to the number the bar represents. The *scale* on the bar graph is divided into equal intervals.

▶ A line graph presents data on one item so that changes and trends over time can be identified and comparisons can be made. It uses points and line segments on a grid. The *scale* on the line graph is divided into equal intervals.

▶ A pictograph presents data using pictures or symbols. Each picture or symbol represents an assigned amount of data. The *key* for a pictograph tells the number that each picture or symbol represents.

Bar Graph

Library Books

(Bar graph: Number vs. Kinds — Biography 40, Fiction 55, Science 25)

Line Graph

Magazine Sales

(Line graph: Number vs. Days — Mon. 20, Tues. 25, Wed. 45, Thurs. 55, Fri. 15)

Pictograph

Newspaper Drive				
Grade 5	📖	📖	📖	📖 ◗
Grade 6	📖 ◗			
Grade 7	📖	📖	📖 ◗	

Key: Each 📖 = 20 newspapers.
     Each ◗ = 10 newspapers.

▶ A circle graph presents the division of a total amount of data. It shows how parts of the data are related to the whole and to each other. The circle, as a whole, represents the whole data.

Circle Graph

Vanya's Magazine Collection

(Circle graph: News 6, Fashion 8, Home 3, Sports 5, Hobby 2)

Use the graphs on page 248.

1. Which graphs use scales divided into equal intervals?

2. Which graphs use vertical and horizontal axes?

3. How many library books does each unit on the vertical scale represent?

4. Of which kind of book is there the greatest number? What is the number?

5. Between which two days was the increase in magazine sales the greatest?

6. What is the number of newspapers collected by each grade?

7. How many magazines are in Vanya's collection?

8. How many home magazines are in Vanya's collection?

9. Explain in your Math Journal:

   • What advantages a graph has over a table of numerical data.

   • When a bar graph or pictograph is more suitable to use than another type of graph.

Name the most appropriate type of graph to use to show each set of data. Explain why.

A class has a bake sale for 1 week to raise money for a field trip. At the end of the week, the class wants to show:

10. increases or decreases in sales from one day to the next.

11. the sales for each day as part of the total sales for the week.

CHALLENGE

A magazine published the given bar graph to show how its number of subscriptions had increased for the past three years.

12. Find the approximate increase in the number of subscriptions from 2003 until 2005.

13. How is the graph misleading?

14. How could you change the graph to give a clearer representation of the situation?

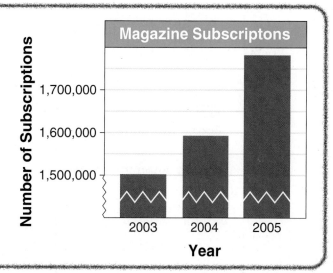

7-7

Line Plots

Nick's test scores in math are: 100, 90, 70, 85, 95, 85, 95, 90, 90, and 100. He records his scores in a frequency table and then organizes the data in a line plot.

Nick's Math Test Scores							
Score	100	95	90	85	80	75	70
Tally	//	//	///	//			/
Frequency	2	2	3	2	0	0	1

Materials: ruler, paper, colored pencils

Step 1 Use the data from the table to choose an appropriate scale and title for the graph.

What is the least score in the data? the greatest score?
What scale would be appropriate for the graph?
What intervals on the scale would you use?

Step 2 Draw a number line. Use the scale to label the intervals. Start with the least score.

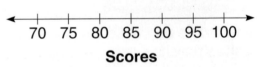

Step 3 Use an X to represent each score in the data. Vertically stack the correct number of Xs above each score on the scale.

How many Xs did you mark on the line plot?

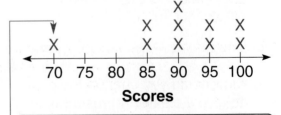

70 is an outlier since it is well separated from the rest of the data.

Use the line plot on page 250.

1. What is the range of Nick's test scores? the mode?

2. Around which score do Nick's test scores seem to cluster (or group)?

Use the line plot at the right for problems 3–5.

3. How many heights are in the data?

4. What is the mode of the data? Is there an outlier?

5. Around which height do the data seem to cluster?

Heights of Students in Ms. Lim's Class

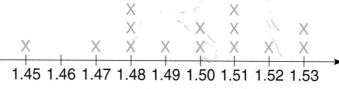

Heights in meters

**Make a line plot for each set of data.
Then find the range, the mode, and an outlier.**

6. Elsa's science test scores:
   100, 93, 93, 96, 89, 89, 89, 96,
   94, 95, 78, 92, 91, 89, 88

7. Matt's monthly deposits: $25, $28.50,
   $27.50, $26.50, $29, $28.50,
   $29, $26.50, $29, $32, $27.50, $29

Communicate

8. Why is it easy to find the mode and range of a set of data in a line plot?

9. Can you find the median of a set of data in a line plot? Explain your answer.

CRITICAL THINKING

Another way to organize data is to use a stem-and-leaf plot. The stem-and-leaf plot at the right shows the Grade 5 test scores at Sunlight School.

10. The stems are the tens digits of the data. What do the leaves represent?

11. How many test scores are shown in the stem-and-leaf plot?

12. What is the least and the greatest values of the data? How are the values represented in the plot?

13. What is the median of the test scores?

Grade 5 Test Scores

Stem	Leaves
5	2 3 5 8
6	0 0 3 5 6 7 8 8
7	0 1 1 2 4 5 7 8 9
8	0 0 1 2 3 3 3 3 6 8
9	1 2 5 5 6 7 9

5 | 8 represents 58.

7-8

Histograms

Helen organized the data in the survey shown at the right. First she made a frequency table and then she made a histogram.

A histogram is a bar graph that shows the *frequency* of equal intervals of data. In a histogram, the intervals must not overlap and the bars are not separated by spaces.

Ages of Marathon Runners
70 55 32 18 21 42 60 56
68 51 29 19 28 33 45 22
59 64 72 24 19 54 66 65
25 45 66 23 22 36 37 65

▶ To make a frequency table:

- Choose a reasonable interval to group the data.

  Since the data span from 18 to 72, use 7 intervals of 10 years.

- Tally the data for each interval and record the frequencies.

Ages	Tally	Frequency
10–19	///	3
20–29	⁄⁄⁄⁄ ///	8
30–39	////	4
40–49	///	3
50–59	⁄⁄⁄⁄	5
60–69	⁄⁄⁄⁄ //	7
70–79	//	2

▶ To make a histogram:

- Use the frequency table to choose and label a scale on the vertical axis for the frequencies.

- Label the horizontal axis, listing the intervals in order.

- Draw bars (with no space between them) to show the frequency of each interval.

- Write the title of the histogram.

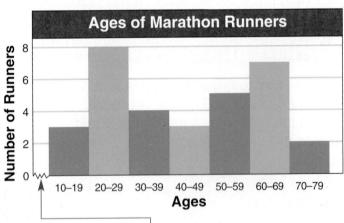

From which age group does the greatest number of marathon runners come?

A **broken scale** is used since the data start at 10.

▶ To find which age group, look for the tallest bar and read the interval it represents.

Most marathon runners are from 20–29 years old.

**Make a frequency table for the given data.
Then copy and complete the histogram.**

1.

Height (cm) of Fir Saplings
18 33 24
9 29 13 31
9 21 16 17
31 22 26

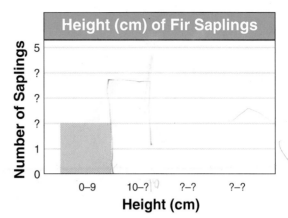

**Make a frequency table and a
histogram for each set of data.**

2.

Minutes Students Spent Doing Tuesday's Homework
53 72 45 60 50 42 60
37 63 40 77 44 56 35
65 55 75 41 31 30 58

3.

Heights of Fifth Graders (in cm)
160 153 148 171 147 148
151 155 159 170 148 146
162 156 162 156 151 153
155 149 162 152 158 155

Use the histogram at the right.

4. Which interval has the least frequency?

5. What does the histogram tell you about the kinds of dresses Dressmart probably sells?

6. Predict what the graph would look like if it included customers over 35.

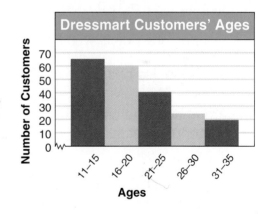

CHALLENGE

Use the histogram.

7. Make a frequency table for the histogram. Explain your method.

8. Use intervals of 50 acres to make a new histogram of your data. How do the bars differ from the bars of the given histogram?

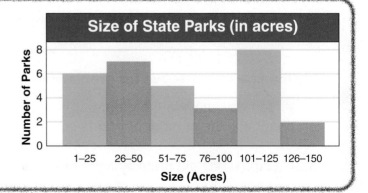

Algebra

7-9

Update your skills. See pages 18 and 19.

Make Line Graphs

Mr. Moreno organized the ticket sales data for the school play in a line graph.

Monroe School Play Ticket Sales						
Day	1	2	3	4	5	6
Tickets Sold	352	453	554	396	503	548

▶ To make a line graph:

- Use the data from the table to choose an appropriate scale.

  > If necessary, round the data to nearby numbers.
  > 352 → 350   453 → 450

- Draw and label the scale on the vertical axis. Start at 0.

- Draw and label the horizontal axis. List the name of each item.

- Locate the points on the grid.

- Connect the points with line segments.

- Write the title of the line graph.

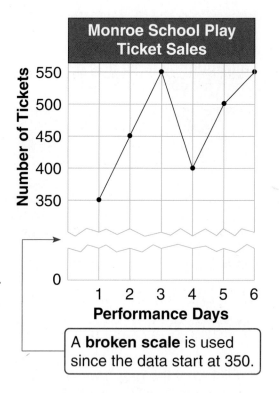

A **broken scale** is used since the data start at 350.

What trend does the graph show about the number of ticket sales?

▶ To determine a trend, look for a rise (shows the data is increasing) or a fall (shows the data is decreasing) in the line between two points.

The number of ticket sales increased from day 1 to day 3 and from day 4 to day 6; the number of ticket sales decreased from day 3 to day 4.

Use the line graph above for problems 1–3.

1. Which day showed the greatest change in the number of tickets sold?

2. About what was the average number of tickets sold each day?

3. On which day did the play have the least number of tickets sold? the greatest number?

Practice

Copy and complete the graph. Use the table.

4.

Jimenez's Math Test Grades						
Test	1	2	3	4	5	6
Grade	75	80	100	95	90	95

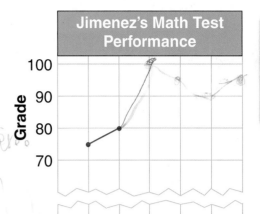

Jimenez's Math Test Performance

Use the completed graph.

5. What trend does the graph show?

6. What is the mean of Jimenez's math test grades? the range?

Make a line graph for each set of data.

7.

Booster Club Membership									
Year	1997	1998	1999	2000	2001	2002	2003	2004	2005
Number	30	25	40	55	60	70	65	75	80

8.

Juice Machine Profits							
Month	Sept.	Oct.	Nov.	Dec.	Jan.	Feb.	Mar.
Amount	$16.25	$17.50	$15.00	$10.25	$12.00	$14.50	$15.75

Use the completed line graphs for problems 9–12.

9. What trend does each graph show?

10. Find the median in each set of data.

11. Predict how much the juice machine profit will be in each of the months of April to August. Explain how you obtain your data.

12. What predictions can you make about the Booster Club membership in the year 2008? Explain your answer.

DO YOU REMEMBER?

Complete the sentences. Use the words in the box.

13. A _?_ shows the *frequency* of equal intervals of data.

14. A _?_ shows data by using pictures or symbols.

15. A _?_ shows how parts of the data are related to the whole and to each other.

> histogram
> circle graph
> line plot
> pictograph

Interpret Circle Graphs

Mr. Sweeney asked the students in his class to name their favorite kind of DVD.

The **circle graph** at the right shows the data.

Remember: A circle graph shows how parts of the data are related to the whole and to each other.

What fractional part of the class chose comedy as its favorite?

The Favorite DVDs of Mr. Sweeney's Class

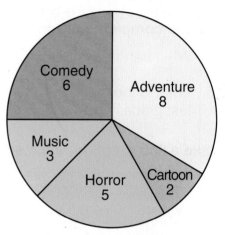

▶ To find what fractional part:

- Add the numbers in the sections of the graph.

  6 + 3 + 5 + 2 + 8 = 24

- Write the fraction with the number of students who like comedy as the numerator and total the number of students in class as the denominator.

  $\frac{6}{24}$ ← students who like comedy

  $\frac{6}{24}$ ← students in class

- Write the fraction in simplest form.

  $\frac{6}{24} = \frac{1}{4}$ ← simplest form

One fourth of the class chose comedy as its favorite.

Practice

Use the circle graph above.

1. What fractional part of Mr. Sweeney's class prefers each kind of DVD?

   a. music   **b.** horror   **c.** cartoon   **d.** adventure

2. How many students chose music or horror DVDs as their favorite? What fractional part of the class do they represent?

3. How many students did *not* choose adventure DVDs as their favorite? What fractional part of the class do they represent?

Budgets in Circle Graphs

A school team's annual budget is $900. How much does the team spend for snacks each year?

To find the amount spent for snacks, multiply: $\frac{3}{20} \times \$900 = n$

$$\frac{3}{20} \times \$900 = \frac{3}{20} \times \frac{\overset{45}{\cancel{900}}}{1}$$

part budgeted for snacks

annual budget $= \frac{3 \times 45}{1 \times 1} = \frac{135}{1}$

$= \$135 \leftarrow$ amount spent for snacks

A School Team's Annual Budget

Transportation $\frac{1}{5}$ | Uniforms $\frac{1}{4}$

Snacks $\frac{3}{20}$

Equipment $\frac{2}{5}$

The school team spends $135 for snacks each year.

Use the circle graph above.

4. How much does the school team spend each year for transportation? for equipment? for uniforms?

5. On which item does the school team spend the most? the least?

6. How much more money is spent for uniforms than transportation?

Use the circle graph at the right.

7. The circle graph shows how many of each kind of bird Diana saw on her class field trip to the zoo: 4 parakeets, 2 macaws, 15 pelicans, 2 snowy white owls, and 1 blue heron. Copy the graph and label it with the corresponding fractional parts. Explain how you did your labeling.

8. Do parakeets and macaws account for one quarter of the birds Diana saw? How do you know?

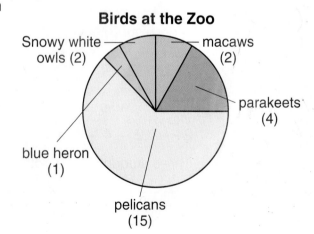

Birds at the Zoo

Snowy white owls (2) — macaws (2) — parakeets (4) — blue heron (1) — pelicans (15)

9. Explain how a circle graph can be useful.

Problem-Solving Strategy:
Use a Model/Diagram

Half of a class of 24 students have no pets. Four students have only dogs as pets, and five have only cats. The rest of the class have both a cat and a dog. How many students have both a cat and a dog?

Read

Visualize yourself in the problem above as you reread it. List the facts and the question.

Facts: class of 24 students
Half of the class have no pets.
4 students—dogs
5 students—cats

Question: How many students have both?

Plan

Use a Venn diagram.
Draw circles to represent the groups: no pets, dogs, cats. Make 2 of the circles overlap because some students have both a cat and a dog. Then write the numbers in each section.

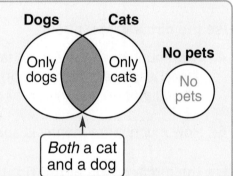

- To find how many students have no pets, multiply: $\frac{1}{2} \times 24 = n$

- To find how many students have both a cat and a dog, subtract the number in each group from 24.

Solve

$$\frac{1}{\cancel{2}} \times \overset{12}{\cancel{24}} = 12 \quad \text{no pets}$$

$$24 - 12 - 4 - 5 = 3$$

Three students have both a cat and a dog.

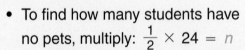

Check

You can act out the problem or add.

$12 + 4 + 5 + 3 = 24$ The answer checks.

Use a model/diagram to solve each problem.

1. Dee can join 1 art class from each area: painting and crafts. There are 3 painting classes and 3 crafts classes. What are all the possible combinations of classes she can join?

Art Classes
Available

Painting	**Crafts**
Oils	Pottery
Watercolors	Stitchery
Acrylics	Macramé

Read ▶ Visualize yourself in the problem above as you reread it. Focus on the facts and question.

List what you know.

Facts: 3 painting classes
3 crafts classes
Dee joins 1 class from each area.

Question: What are the possible combinations of classes she can join?

Plan ▶ To show all the possible combinations, make a tree diagram.

▶ **Solve** ·······▶ **Check** ▶

Think

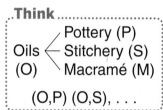

Oils (O) → Pottery (P)
Stitchery (S)
Macramé (M)

(O,P) (O,S), . . .

2. How many students are in 5th grade if 5 students do not take music lessons, 10 take piano lessons, 8 take guitar lessons, and 2 take both piano and guitar lessons?

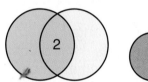

8 Guitar   10 Piano   No music

Valerie and Joel play a game. Each spins this spinner and chooses a card.

3. What are the possible outcomes?

4. What is the probability of spinning an odd number and choosing a vowel?

Truck Driver's Log

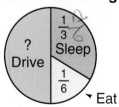

5. The circle graph shows how a truck driver spent his time. If he was on the road for five days, how many hours did he drive? sleep? eat?

6. Erica takes 3 types of lessons: piano, swimming, and ballet. Each of her three friends takes two of these lessons, but none of them takes the same two lessons. Jenny takes piano and ballet. Oxana takes piano and swimming. What does Danielle take?

Piano

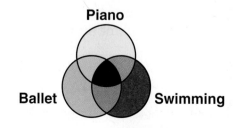

Ballet   **Swimming**

Solve each problem and explain the method you used.

Visitors to North Park Nature Center wear name tags shaped like an owl, a deer, a trout, and a woodpecker. What is the probability of choosing a name tag that is:

1. a deer?

2. a bird?

3. not an owl?

4. a raccoon?

In March, 812 people came to the Nature Center; in April, 1105; in May, 1229; in June, 1070; and in July, 910. In August, 126 fewer people came to the center than came in July.

5. How many people came in August?

6. Make a graph to show these data. Explain why you chose this type of graph.

7. Find the range, mean, and median of these data. How much greater is the median than the mean?

8. What fractional part of the birds rescued were sea birds?

9. What fractional part of the birds rescued were not birds of prey?

10. Suppose the center budgeted $2400 to rescue birds. How much was spent to rescue hummingbirds?

11. Which kind of tree planted was twice the number of cherry trees?

12. What kind of tree was about half the total number of trees planted?

13. What part of the planted trees produces fruit?

Birds Rescued

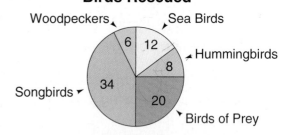

Woodpeckers 6, Sea Birds 12, Hummingbirds 8, Birds of Prey 20, Songbirds 34

Trees Planted

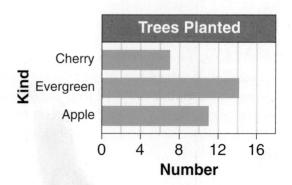

Kind: Cherry, Evergreen, Apple — Number 0 4 8 12 16

Use a strategy from the list or use another strategy you know to solve each problem.

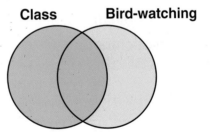

14. At the Center there are more squirrels than raccoons and more rabbits than squirrels. Are there more rabbits or raccoons?

15. North Park Center covers $289\frac{1}{4}$ acres. Central Park Center covers $193\frac{1}{8}$ acres. How much smaller is this than North Park Center?

Strategy File

Use These Strategies
Use a Model/Diagram
Make an Organized List
Work Backward
Use Simpler Numbers
Logical Reasoning

16. The North Park Center sells white, blue, or green shirts in 5 sizes: S, M, L, XL, and XXL. Pictured on each shirt is either an eagle or an owl. How many different kinds of shirts are sold?

17. In a 5-day period, a worker spends $4\frac{1}{2}$ h, $3\frac{1}{4}$ h, $5\frac{1}{8}$ h, $3\frac{3}{8}$ h, and $3\frac{1}{4}$ h pruning trees. What is the average amount of time the worker spends pruning each day?

18. In May, 18 birds' eggs hatched in the Center's incubator. This is $1\frac{1}{2}$ times the number that hatched in April. How many eggs hatched in April?

19. Yesterday 56 people came to the Center. How many people came to the Center to hike if 30 people took classes, 22 went bird-watching, and 12 people did both?

20. Two thirds of the visitors on Monday were children. Three fourths of the children came on a school trip. The rest, 21 children, came with their families. How many people visited the Center on Monday?

Write Your Own

21. Invent data about the Nature Center. Then create a graph to show your data. Write a problem that a classmate can solve using your invented data.

Use the number cube to find the probability of each event. *(See pp. 238–239.)*

1. $P(1)$ **2.** $P(2 \text{ or } 3)$ **3.** $P(< 4)$ **4.** $P(5)$

Draw a tree diagram. List all possible outcomes. *(See pp. 240–243.)*

5. Toss a coin and spin the spinner.

6. A bag contains 4 cubes: 3 orange and 1 purple. Pick a cube at random, put it back, and then pick another cube.

Find each probability. Use the experiments in exercises 5 and 6.

7. $P(T, not \text{ green})$ **8.** $P(H, \text{ red or yellow})$ **9.** $P(\text{orange}, not \text{ purple})$

Make a frequency table and a cumulative frequency table. *(See pp. 244–245.)*

10. Each student in Elsa's class was asked to choose his/her after-school activity from a list of after-school activities. The responses are listed below.

club	sports	club	club	sports	club	club
tutoring	club	sports	sports	club	tutoring	sports
sports	club	club	club	sports	club	tutoring

Find the range, median, mean, and mode for each set of data. *(See pp. 246–247.)*

11.

Center's Noontime Temperatures
65°F, 69°F, 82°F, 78°F, 66°F, 68°F, 72°F, 68°F, 70°F, 72°F, 73°F, 81°F, 67°F, 65°F, 72°F, 81°F, 67°F, 80°F

12.

Walter's Winning Matches in the Chess Tournament						
Month	Oct.	Nov.	Dec.	Jan.	Feb.	Mar.
Matches Won	9	8	4	6	8	7

Problem Solving

(See pp. 250–257, 258–261.)

13. Make a line plot and a histogram for the data in exercise 11.

14. Make a line graph for the data in exercise 12.

Use the circle graph.

15. What fractional part of the class has fish or cats as pets?

16. If there are 60 children in Grade 5, how many in all have pets?

Kinds of Pets in Grade 5

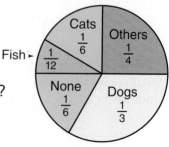

(See Still More Practice, p. 483.)

Double Line and Double Bar Graphs

A double line graph and a double bar graph are used to compare two sets of data. Each set of data is graphed separately, but on the same grid. The *key* identifies the sets of data.

Double Line Graph

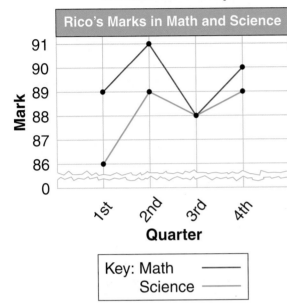

Double Bar Graph

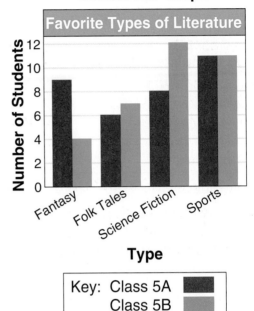

Problem Solving Use the graphs above.

1. In which quarter did Rico get the same mark in math and science?

2. What trend do you notice about Rico's marks in math and science?

3. Between which two quarters did Rico have the largest difference in his math marks?

4. In which quarters did Rico's science marks fall below that of his math marks?

5. Which type of literature is the least preferred by class 5A? the most preferred?

6. Which type of literature is the most preferred by class 5B? the least preferred?

7. Which type of literature is more preferred by students in 5A than in 5B? How many more students?

8. Which type of literature is preferred by an equal number of students in 5A and 5B?

Chapter 7 Test

Draw a tree diagram. Find each probability.

1. Pick a marble from the bag at random and toss a coin.

2. Pick a marble from the bag at random and do not put it back. Then pick another marble.

3. P(yellow, H) 4. P(*not* red, T) 5. P(red, yellow) 6. P(red, *not* red)

Copy and complete the table.

Number of Members of School Clubs			
Club	Tally	Frequency	Cumulative Frequency
7. Drama Club	ЖЖ ЖЖ ЖЖ ‖	?	?
8. Glee Club	ЖЖ ЖЖ ЖЖ ЖЖ ЖЖ ЖЖ ЖЖ	?	?
9. Math and Science Club	?	25	?
10. Debating Club	?	15	?

Use the data box for exercises 11–12.

11. Find the range, median, and mode of the data.

12. Make a line plot and a histogram for data.

First School District Grade 5 Classes' Enrollment

37, 21, 24, 28, 16, 29, 33, 35, 41, 28, 34, 29, 22, 19, 28, 20, 25, 31, 22, 21

Problem Solving

Use a strategy you have learned.

13. The mean score of Jerry's first three tests is 85. What score must he get on his fourth test if he wants to raise the mean score by 2 points?

Tell About It

14. Suppose you want to compare the quantities of different items that make up the stock in your clothing store. What kind of graph should you use? Why?

Performance Assessment

Make a spinner.
Use the data from exercises 15–18 to fill in the spinner.

15. P(1 or 2) $= \frac{3}{8}$ 16. P(not 3) $= \frac{5}{8}$

17. P($<$6) $= 1$ 18. P($>$5) $= 0$

Test Preparation

Choose the best answer.

1. Which shows the standard form of seven billion, ninety-six million?

    a. 7,096,000   **b.** 796,000,000
    c. 7,096,000,000   **d.** 7,960,000,000

2. Estimate.

    $86 \times \$2.98$

    a. $93.00
    b. $100.00
    c. $270.00
    d. $320.00

3. Which group shows numbers that are each divisible by 5?

    a. 725,840; 1051; 12,750
    b. 360,730; 986; 1422
    c. 231,620; 814; 2351
    d. 2510; 313,155; 21,100

4. Which shows the prime factorization of 24?

    a. 3×8
    b. $2^2 \times 6$
    c. $2^3 \times 3$
    d. $2^2 \times 3^2$

5. $\frac{3}{11} + \frac{5}{11} + \frac{8}{11}$

    a. $\frac{16}{33}$ **b.** $1\frac{5}{16}$

    c. $1\frac{5}{11}$ **d.** $1\frac{6}{11}$

6. Choose the fraction for $4\frac{3}{5}$.

    a. $\frac{12}{5}$ **b.** $\frac{23}{5}$

    c. $\frac{20}{3}$ **d.** $\frac{23}{3}$

7. Round to the nearest ten cents.

    $4.19

    a. $4.00   **b.** $4.09
    c. $4.10   **d.** $4.20

8. $\begin{array}{r} 2386 \\ \times\ 453 \\ \hline \end{array}$

    a. 1,080,858
    b. 2,612,118
    c. 8,216,014
    d. not given

9. Compute. Use the order of operations.

    $47 - 6 + 2 \times 3$

    a. 31
    b. 47
    c. 74
    d. 129

10. Which is ordered from greatest to least?

    a. $\frac{3}{10}, \frac{4}{5}, \frac{7}{10}, \frac{1}{5}$

    b. $\frac{1}{24}, \frac{1}{12}, \frac{1}{6}, \frac{1}{2}$

    c. $1, \frac{5}{6}, \frac{1}{3}, \frac{1}{2}$

    d. none of these

11. Estimate.

    $14\frac{9}{16} - 9\frac{1}{3}$

    a. 4   **b.** 6
    c. 15   **d.** 24

12. Choose the reciprocal of $2\frac{1}{4}$.

    a. $\frac{9}{4}$ **b.** $\frac{8}{9}$

    c. $\frac{7}{4}$ **d.** $\frac{4}{9}$

13. Which must always be a member of the set of data?

    a. range   **b.** mode
    c. median   **d.** mean

14. Use the circle graph to find what fractional part of a day Peter spends altogether at school or at play.

Peter's Day

    a. $\frac{1}{4}$

    b. $\frac{3}{8}$

    c. $\frac{1}{8}$

    d. $\frac{1}{3}$

15. Which of the following illustrates the Identity Property of Multiplication?

    a. $5 \times \frac{1}{5} = 1$

    b. $5 \times 1 = 5$

    c. $5 \times 6 = 6 \times 5$

    d. $5 \times (3 \times 6) = (5 \times 3) \times 6$

16. Feng tosses a coin and rolls a 1–6 number cube. What is the probability that he tosses a head and rolls a 7?

    a. 0   **b.** 1

    c. $\frac{1}{12}$ **d.** $\frac{7}{12}$

17. Shiela walks at the rate of $\frac{1}{16}$ mile per minute. How many hours would it take her to walk 3 miles?

    a. $\frac{4}{5}$ h   **b.** $\frac{2}{3}$ h

    c. 48 h   **d.** $5\frac{1}{3}$ h

18. To show a trend, comparison, or a growth pattern, which graph would be most useful?

    a. circle   **b.** histogram
    c. pictograph   **d.** line

19. Use the table to find the mode of the earnings.

Hourly Wage	Number of People
$4.00	3
$4.50	3
$4.75	5
$5.00	8
$5.25	11

    a. $4.50
    b. $4.75
    c. $5.13
    d. $5.25

20. Which fraction is closest to 0?

    a. $\frac{3}{54}$ **b.** $\frac{29}{30}$

    c. $\frac{40}{43}$ **d.** $\frac{26}{51}$

21. Eve worked 8 hours one holiday and was paid time and a half. If her hourly wage was $6.88, how much did she earn?

    a. $82.56   **b.** $55.04
    c. $110.08   **d.** not given

22. Mr. Tan sold $\frac{1}{2}$ of a 16-acre plot. He then sold $\frac{2}{3}$ of the remaining piece. How much of the 16 acres remained unsold?

    a. $5\frac{1}{3}$ acres   **b.** $2\frac{2}{3}$ acres

    c. 8 acres   **d.** 12 acres

Explain how you solved the problem. Show all your work.

23. In Mr. Clay's math class, 16 students are in band, 7 students play sports, 3 students participate in both activities, and 9 students are not in band and do not play sports. How many students are in Mr. Clay's math class?

Decimals: Addition and Subtraction

Speed!

no hands
down the hill
no hands
just the wheel

brisk breeze
in my hair
such ease
not a care

my feet
steer the bike
my seat
sitting tight

wheels spin
this is speed!
wheels spin
all I need

Monica Kulling

In this chapter you will:

Estimate, add, and subtract decimals
Solve problems with extra information by
   using more than one step

Critical Thinking/Finding Together

A cyclist biked one tenth of a mile less on
Tuesday than on Monday. He biked five
miles farther on Wednesday than on
Tuesday. He biked 13.8 miles on Monday.
Which day did he bike the farthest?

Decimal Sense

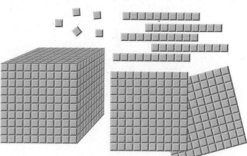

Decimals may be represented on a number line. As with whole numbers, a greater decimal is located to the right of a lesser decimal.

Study these number lines:

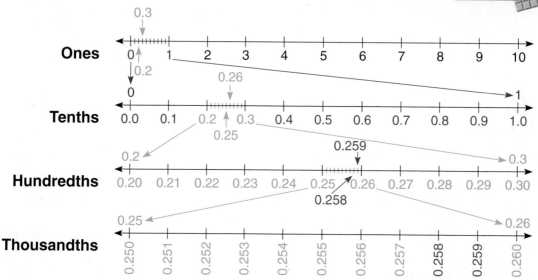

Point *A* represents 6.6.
Point *B* represents 7.3.
Point *C* represents 8.0.

Practice

Name the decimal represented by *A*, *B*, and *C* on each number line.

1.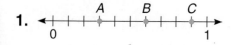
0 ... 1

2.
0.4 ... 0.5

3.
0.7 ... 0.8

4.
0.9 ... 1.0

5.
0.34 ... 0.35

6.
0.28 ... 0.29

7.
1 ... 2

8.
5.1 ... 5.2

Name the decimal for each point on the number line.

9. A   **10.** B   **11.** C   **12.** D   **13.** E   **14.** F

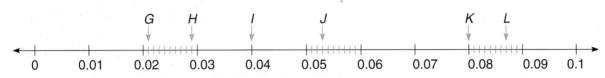

15. G   **16.** H   **17.** I   **18.** J   **19.** K   **20.** L

Name the point represented by each decimal.

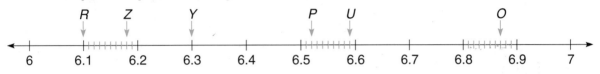

21. 6.87   **22.** 6.18   **23.** 6.52   **24.** 6.1   **25.** 6.3   **26.** 6.59

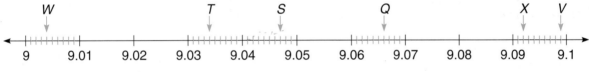

27. 9.066   **28.** 9.004   **29.** 9.092   **30.** 9.034   **31.** 9.099   **32.** 9.047

Use a number line to locate the points.

33. 0.42   **34.** 0.47   **35.** 0.85   **36.** 0.034   **37.** 0.036

38. a. Is 0.42 closer to 0.4 or 0.5?   **b.** Is 0.47 closer to 0.4 or 0.5?

39. a. Is 0.034 closer to 0.03 or 0.04?   **b.** Is 0.036 closer to 0.03 or 0.04?

CRITICAL THINKING   *Algebra*

Use a number line to compare. Write <, =, or >.

40. $0.5 \underline{\ ?\ } \frac{3}{4}$ **41.** $\frac{1}{4} \underline{\ ?\ } 0.21$ **42.** $0.4 \underline{\ ?\ } \frac{2}{5}$

43. $1\frac{1}{2} \underline{\ ?\ } 1.35$ **44.** $2.25 \underline{\ ?\ } 2\frac{1}{8}?$ **45.** $3\frac{1}{3} \underline{\ ?\ } 3.5$

46. Is 2 closer to 2.25 or $2\frac{1}{8}$?   **47.** Is 3 closer to $3\frac{1}{3}$ or 3.1?

Decimals and Place Value

You can show decimals in a **place-value chart**.

The value of each digit in a decimal depends on its **place** in the decimal. Each place is 10 times greater than the place to its right.

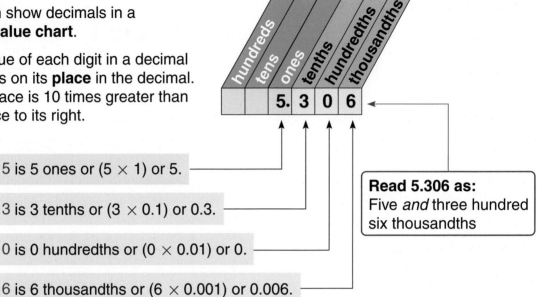

5 is 5 ones or (5 × 1) or 5.

3 is 3 tenths or (3 × 0.1) or 0.3.

0 is 0 hundredths or (0 × 0.01) or 0.

6 is 6 thousandths or (6 × 0.001) or 0.006.

Read 5.306 as:
Five *and* three hundred six thousandths

▶ You can write a decimal in standard form or in expanded form.

Standard Form	**Expanded Form**
5.306	5 + 0.3 + 0 + 0.006
	or
	(5 × 1) + (3 × 0.1) + (6 × 0.001)

A place that holds a zero may be omitted in expanded form.

▶ You can use decimals to write the *short word names* of large numbers.

Write the short word name of 1,200,000.

$1{,}200{,}000 = 1\frac{200{,}000}{1{,}000{,}000}$ million

$= 1\frac{200{,}000}{1{,}000{,}000}$ million

$= 1\frac{2}{10}$ million = 1.2 million

Standard Form: 1,200,000
Short Word Name: 1.2 million

Write the short word name of 3,580,000,000.

$3{,}580{,}000{,}000 = 3\frac{580{,}000{,}000}{1{,}000{,}000{,}000}$ billion

$= 3\frac{580{,}000{,}000}{1{,}000{,}000{,}000}$ billion

$= 3\frac{58}{100}$ billion = 3.58 billion

Standard Form: 3,580,000,000
Short Word Name: 3.58 billion

Write the place of the underlined digit. Then write its value.

1. 2.4<u>1</u>2
2. 1.5<u>3</u>0
3. 4.71<u>6</u>
4. 27.20<u>5</u>
5. 76.4<u>1</u>3

Write each in expanded form.

6. 4.512
7. 3.014
8. 5.025
9. 2.107
10. 6.51

11. 13.15
12. 131.5
13. 1.315
14. 0.315
15. 13.152

Write the short word name.

16. 7,800,000
17. 6,500,000
18. 8,300,000,000
19. 5,600,000,000

20. 5,760,000
21. 3,540,000
22. 9,214,000,000
23. 3,469,000,000

Write each in standard form.

24. two and nine thousandths
25. fifty-four and eight tenths

26. six and five hundredths
27. eleven and one thousandth

28. 8 + 0.1 + 0.05 + 0.003
29. 200 + 0.7 + 0.001

30. 4.14 million
31. 5.05 billion
32. 7.062 million
33. 9.008 billion

Write as a fraction in simplest form.

34. $0.5 \ \frac{5}{10} = \frac{5 \div 5}{10 \div 5} = \frac{1}{2}$
35. 0.2
36. 0.6
37. 0.08
38. 0.15

39. 0.25
40. 0.12
41. 0.735
42. 0.225
43. 0.018
44. 0.125

Problem Solving

45. A car travels at a speed of 0.915 miles per minute. Write the speed in expanded form.

46. An athlete won the gold medal for combined exercises in the Olympics. Her score was 79.275. What is the value of the digit 5 in her score?

DO YOU REMEMBER?

Align and add.

47. 478 + 96
48. 5509 + 693
49. 857 + 9278

50. 507 + 38 + 4
51. 45 + 317 + 6
52. 312 + 9 + 63

Update your skills. See page 11.

8-3

Add Decimals

David has 3 strips of wood measuring 0.28 m, 0.6 m, and 0.09 m, respectively. How many meters of wood does he have?

To find how many meters of wood, add: $0.28 + 0.6 + 0.09 = n$.

▶ You can use base ten blocks to model $0.28 + 0.6 + 0.09$.

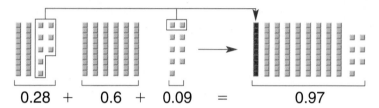

| Regroup 10 hundredths as 1 tenth. |

0.28 +   0.6 +   0.09   =   0.97

▶ To add decimals, add the same way as you add whole numbers.

Line up the decimal points.	Add the hundredths. Regroup.	Add the tenths.	Write the decimal point in the sum.
0.28 0.60 ← 0.6 = 0.60 + 0.09	¹ 0.28 0.60 + 0.09 ——— 7	¹ 0.28 0.60 + 0.09 ——— 97	0.28 0.60 + 0.09 ——— 0.97

David has 0.97 m of wood.

Study these examples.

```
        1 1
        0.34
0.53    0.72
+ 0.40  + 0.54
————    ————
0.93    1.60 = 1.6
```

Find the sum of $n + 0.42$
when $n = 0.3$.
$n + 0.42 = \underline{\ ?\ }$.
$0.3 + 0.42 = 0.72$

Use base ten blocks to model each sum. Then write the sum.

1.   0.2
  + 0.5

2.   0.63
  + 0.03

3.   0.42
  + 0.54

4.   0.3
   0.4
  + 0.2

5.   0.05
   0.82
  + 0.12

Practice

Add.

6.	0.39 +0.05	**7.**	0.49 +0.38	**8.**	0.8 +0.39	**9.**	0.98 +0.32	**10.**	0.87 +0.48

11.	0.6 0.5 +0.8	**12.**	0.09 0.75 +0.24	**13.**	0.7 0.29 +0.43	**14.**	0.4 0.75 +0.6	**15.**	0.07 0.3 +0.9

Align and add.

16. $0.2 + 0.79$　　　　**17.** $0.03 + 0.9$　　　　**18.** $0.54 + 0.05$

19. $0.38 + 0.06$　　　　**20.** $0.72 + 0.3$　　　　**21.** $0.7 + 0.97$

22. $0.6 + 0.54 + 0.05$　　　　**23.** $0.82 + 0.6 + 0.05$

24. $0.2 + 0.08 + 0.32$　　　　**25.** $0.9 + 0.01 + 0.65$

Find the sum.

26. $n + 0.05$ when $n = 0.75$　　　　**27.** $n + 0.67$ when $n = 0.6$

28. $0.41 + n$ when $n = 0.09$　　　　**29.** $0.98 + n$ when $n = 0.2$

30. $0.51 + 0.3 + n$ when $n = 0.08$　　　　**31.** $0.73 + n + 0.2$ when $n = 0.13$

True or false? Explain your answer.

32. The sum of two decimals less than 1 is always less than 1.

33. The sum of two decimals greater than 0.5 is always greater than 1.

Problem Solving

34. Rainfall for two days was measured as 0.24 in. and 0.39 in. at the city airport. What was the total rainfall measured over the two days?

35. Chana has 3 packages of cheese weighing 0.24 lb, 0.69 lb, and 0.8 lb, respectively. How many pounds of cheese does she have?

TEST PREPARATION

36. Art has three wood planks measuring 0.9 m, 0.75 m, and 0.68 m. What is the total length of the three wood planks?

A 1.52 m　　　　**B** 3.33 m　　　　**C** 2.52 m　　　　**D** 2.33 m

Estimate Decimal Sums

A bicycle trail has three sections measuring 5.5 mi, 6.45 mi, and 7.62 mi. About how long is the bicycle trail?

To find about how long, estimate the sum: 5.5 + 6.45 + 7.62.

You can use front-end estimation or rounding to estimate a decimal sum.

▶ To **estimate** a *decimal sum* by *front-end estimation*:

- Add the *nonzero* front digits.
- Write zeros for the other digits.

$$
\begin{array}{r}
5.5 \\
6.45 \\
+\,7.62 \\
\hline
\text{about } 18.00
\end{array}
$$

▶ To **estimate** a *decimal sum* by *rounding*:

- Round the decimals to the greatest *nonzero* place of the least number.
- Add the rounded numbers.

$$
\begin{array}{rcl}
5.5 & \longrightarrow & 6 \\
6.45 & \longrightarrow & 6 \\
+\,7.62 & \longrightarrow & +\,8 \\
\hline
& \text{about} & 20
\end{array}
$$

So the exact sum is between 18 and 20.

The bicycle trail is about 18 to 20 mi long.

Study these examples.

$$
\begin{array}{rcll}
0.591 & \longrightarrow & 0.591 & 0.6 \\
+\,0.305 & \longrightarrow & +\,0.305 & +\,0.3 \\
\hline
& & \text{about } 0.800 & \text{about } 0.9
\end{array}
\qquad
\begin{array}{rcll}
223.31 & \longrightarrow & 223.31 & 200 \\
+\,466.672 & \longrightarrow & +\,466.672 & +\,500 \\
\hline
& & \text{about } 600.000 & \text{about } 700
\end{array}
$$

So the exact sum is between 0.8 and 0.9.

So the exact sum is between 600 and 700.

Choose the best estimated sum.

1. 10.93 + 6.1   **a.** 17   **b.** 15   **c.** 11   **d.** 18

2. 0.872 + 0.141 + 0.56   **a.** 1.3   **b.** 1.2   **c.** 1.4   **d.** 1.1

3. 0.9 + 0.78 + 0.551   **a.** 2   **b.** 2.3   **c.** 2.4   **d.** 2.5

Practice

Estimate the sum by front-end estimation.

4. 0.19
0.74
+0.8

5. 7.8
5.2
+4.4

6. 2.65
6.2
+5.93

7. 0.228
0.376
+0.59

8. 3.791
4.38
+7.332

9. 3.2 + 6.43

10. 0.257 + 0.65

11. 1.708 + 6.391 + 3.94

Estimate the sum by rounding.

12. 0.57
0.91
+0.3

13. 6.6
1.8
+4.2

14. 8.57
0.73
+0.59

15. 0.771
0.567
+0.48

16. 5.412
2.793
+0.137

17. 7.39 + 5.3

18. 0.554 + 0.94

19. 3.07 + 7.5 + 4.273

Estimate by both front-end estimation and rounding. Between what two numbers will the exact sum be?

20. 0.93
+0.564

21. 3.283
+8.59

22. 50.78
+18.9

23. 35.472
+25.29

24. 683.24
+405.168

25. 5.23
4.7
+6.5

26. 8.61
2.315
+7.83

27. 45.31
88.2
+92.7

28. 2.653
3.91
+4.32

29. 192.134
235.14
+374.421

30. 17.08 + 25.9

31. 3.07 + 2.54 + 4.654

32. 374.91 + 592.6 + 271.732

Problem Solving

33. Elaine rode her bike 3.45 mi on Friday, 5.38 mi on Saturday, and 6.35 mi on Sunday. About how many miles did she ride her bike in these three days?

Complete the statement to make it true. Write *less than* or *greater than*. Explain your answer.

34. When rounding down the addends, the estimated sum is __?__ the actual sum.

35. When rounding up the addends, the estimated sum is __?__ the actual sum.

36. The estimated sum by front-end estimation is __?__ the actual sum.

Add More Decimals

In three trial runs of a luge competition, one team was timed at 86.082 seconds, 79.216 seconds, and 88.52 seconds. What is the total of all three runs?

First use rounding to estimate the sum: $90 + 80 + 90 = 260$

The exact sum must be less than 260.

To find the total of all three runs, add: $86.082 + 79.216 + 88.52 = n$.

| Line up the decimal points. | Add the thousandths. Then add the hundredths and the tenths. Regroup. | Add the whole numbers. |

```
  86.082                        86.082      86.082              2
  79.216                        79.216      79.216            86.082
+ 88.520 ← 0.52 = 0.520       + 88.520    + 88.520           79.216
                                      8          18        + 88.520
                                                            253.818
```

The total of all three runs is 253.818 seconds.

Think
253.818 is close to the estimate of 255.

Write the decimal point in the sum.

Study these examples.

```
    5.173        1 1             0.600           2             1
  + 3.215      0.365          + 2.035         18.41       213.000
    8.388    + 0.680            2.635         37.05       451.400
             1.045                          + 24.90      +382.071
                                             80.36       1046.471
```

Use rounding to estimate. Then add.

1. 3.6
   + 2.8

2. 3.02
   + 4.06

3. 4.12
   + 5.63

4. 0.597
   + 0.802

5. 3.125
   + 7.431

6. 36.3
   + 43.5

7. 15.4
   + 22.7

8. 56.03
   + 23.05

9. 13.48
   + 36.17

10. 17.004
    + 12.059

11. 37.01
    + 2.69

12. 29.6
    + 3.49

13. 42.75
    + 50.8

14. 4.071
    + 15.32

15. 56.021
    + 3.123

Practice

Use rounding to estimate. Then find the sum.

16.	5.4	17.	7.36	18.	0.825	19.	16.3	20.	911.435
	3.2		9.43		0.914		25.7		79.362
	+7.6		+5.72		+0.203		+32.4		+812.417

21.	3.45	22.	0.458	23.	4.4	24.	179.65	25.	919.435
	4.2		0.42		8.056		67.142		2.812
	+7.34		+0.31		+9.14		+324.23		+73.764

Align and add.

26. 7.05 + 9.5   **27.** 17 + 4.5 + 1.15   **28.** 2.114 + 4 + 1.07

29. 28.72 + 6.8   **30.** 7.424 + 3.005 + 10.1   **31.** 6.9 + 3.08 + 1.247

32. 97.602 + 5.98   **33.** 635 + 27.314 + 9.5   **34.** 0.63 + 237.819 + 24

Compare. Write $<$, $=$, or $>$.

35. 5.6 + 7.82 _?_ 13.52

36. 35.5 + 19.8 + 0.63 _?_ 55.73

37. 7.15 _?_ 2.079 + 5.08

38. 35.195 _?_ 24.08 + 5 + 6.115

39. 0.668 + 6.584 _?_ 3.154 + 6.661

40. 0.583 + 2.745 _?_ 0.1 + 0.02 + 3.003

41. 0.15 + 0.46 _?_ $\frac{1}{2} + \frac{3}{4}$

42. 0.23 + 0.54 _?_ $\frac{2}{5} + \frac{3}{10}$

Problem Solving

43. Tara biked 13.8 laps in the morning and 14.75 laps in the afternoon. How many laps did she bike in all?

44. Aldo ran 9.8 mi, Greg ran 13.7 mi, and Victor ran 12.5 mi. What was the total distance for the three?

45. The leading team's score in the Decimal Olympics was 40.816 points. The final team's three players scored 14.21, 12.924, and 13.689 points. Did they have enough points to take the lead? How do you know?

CRITICAL THINKING — Algebra

Find the missing digits. Use Guess and Test.

46.	☐8.67	47.	2☐.56	48.	39.☐☐2	49.	5☐.5☐4
	+35.☐9		+ 3.☐5		+☐6.34☐		+ 6.☐7☐
	74.46		32.2☐		9☐.729		☐2.301

Subtract Decimals

Aileen jumped 0.9 m on her first jump and 0.78 m on her second jump. How much farther did she jump on her first jump than on her second jump?

To find how much farther she jumped on her first jump, subtract: $0.9 - 0.78 = n$.

▶ You can use base ten blocks to model $0.9 - 0.78$.

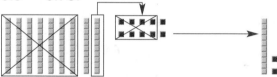

Regroup 1 tenth as 10 hundredths.

$0.9 - 0.78 = 0.12$

▶ To subtract decimals, subtract the same way as you subtract whole numbers.

Line up the decimal points.	Regroup. Subtract the hundredths.	Subtract the tenths.	Write the decimal point in the difference.
$\begin{array}{r} 0.90 \leftarrow \boxed{0.9 = 0.90} \\ -\,0.78 \\ \hline \end{array}$	$\begin{array}{r} {}^{8\ 10} \\ 0.\cancel{9}\cancel{0} \\ -\,0.7\ 8 \\ \hline 2 \end{array}$	$\begin{array}{r} {}^{8\ 10} \\ 0.\cancel{9}\cancel{0} \\ -\,0.7\ 8 \\ \hline 1\ 2 \end{array}$	$\begin{array}{r} {}^{8\ 10} \\ 0.\cancel{9}\cancel{0} \\ -\,0.7\ 8 \\ \hline 0.1\ 2 \end{array}$

Aileen jumped 0.12 m farther on her first jump.

Study these examples.

| $\begin{array}{r} 0.8 \\ -\,0.3 \\ \hline 0.5 \end{array}$ | $\begin{array}{r} 0.69 \\ -\,0.52 \\ \hline 0.17 \end{array}$ | $\begin{array}{r} 0.73 \\ -\,0.40 \\ \hline 0.33 \end{array}$ | $\begin{array}{r} {}^{4\ 18} \\ 0.\cancel{5}\cancel{8} \\ -\,0.3\ 9 \\ \hline 0.1\ 9 \end{array}$ | Find the difference of $0.69 - n$ when $n = 0.52$. $0.69 - 0.52 = 0.17$ |

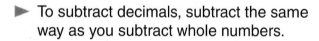

Use base ten blocks to model each difference. Then write the difference.

1. $\begin{array}{r} 0.7 \\ -\,0.2 \\ \hline \end{array}$
2. $\begin{array}{r} 0.75 \\ -\,0.2 \\ \hline \end{array}$
3. $\begin{array}{r} 0.95 \\ -\,0.54 \\ \hline \end{array}$
4. $\begin{array}{r} 0.7 \\ -\,0.25 \\ \hline \end{array}$
5. $\begin{array}{r} 0.76 \\ -\,0.08 \\ \hline \end{array}$

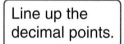

Find the difference.

6. 0.08
   − 0.04

7. 0.67
   − 0.36

8. 0.63
   − 0.38

9. 0.84
   − 0.46

10. 0.51
    − 0.29

11. 0.9
    − 0.2

12. 0.78
    − 0.3

13. 0.4
    − 0.06

14. 0.9
    − 0.37

15. 0.7
    − 0.54

16. $0.97 - n$ when $n = 0.6$

17. $0.8 - n$ when $n = 0.17$

18. $n - 0.2$ when $n = 0.39$

19. $n - 0.73$ when $n = 0.9$

Align and subtract.

20. $0.49 - 0.24$

21. $0.97 - 0.5$

22. $0.5 - 0.09$

23. $0.89 - 0.7$

24. $0.6 - 0.16$

25. $0.61 - 0.3$

26. $0.92 - 0.3$

27. $0.8 - 0.51$

28. $0.47 - 0.06$

Write the pattern rule and the next 2 terms in each set.

29. 0.1, 0.5, 0.9, 1.3, _?_ , _?_

30. 0.28, 0.31, 0.34, 0.37, _?_ , _?_

31. 0.9, 0.85, 0.8, 0.75, _?_ , _?_

32. 0.85, 0.7, 0.55, 0.4, _?_ , _?_

Write a subtraction sentence.

33. What is the difference between 0.9 and 0.09?

34. How much less than 0.91 is 0.4?

Problem Solving

35. Max had 0.85 m of ribbon. He used 0.5 m for a gift. How much of the ribbon was *not* used for the gift?

36. Elma walked 0.9 mi on Thursday. She walked 0.25 mi less on Friday. How far did she walk on Friday?

37. The length of a paramecium is about 0.24 mm and an amoeba is about 0.47 mm long. Find the difference in their lengths.

38. A miniature coal car is 0.39 m tall and a miniature refrigerator car is about 0.5 m tall. Which car is taller? by how much?

CHALLENGE

39. The combined height of Marvin and Ray is 3.4 m. This is 1.58 m more than Jim's height. Jim is 0.08 m taller than Marvin. How tall is Ray?

Estimate Decimal Differences

The horseback riding trail is 34.35 km. Jesse has ridden 17.78 km. About how much farther must he ride to finish the trail?

To find how much farther, estimate the difference: 34.35 − 17.78.

You can use front-end estimation or rounding to estimate a decimal difference.

▶ To estimate a *decimal difference* by **front-end estimation:**

- Subtract the *nonzero* front digits.
- Write zeros for the other digits.

$$\begin{array}{r} 34.35 \\ -\ 17.78 \\ \hline \text{about}\ \ 20.00 \end{array}$$

▶ To estimate a *decimal difference* by **rounding:**

- Round the decimals to the greatest *nonzero* place of the lesser number.
- Subtract the rounded numbers.

$$\begin{array}{r} 34.35 \longrightarrow \quad 30 \\ -\ 17.78 \longrightarrow -\ 20 \\ \hline \text{about}\ 10 \end{array}$$

So the exact difference is between 10 and 20.

Jesse needs to ride about 10 to 20 km farther.

Study these examples.

$$\begin{array}{r} 0.86 \longrightarrow \quad 0.86 \qquad\quad 0.9 \\ -\ 0.3 \longrightarrow -\ 0.3 \qquad -\ 0.3 \\ \hline \text{about}\ \ 0.50 \quad \text{about}\ \ 0.6 \end{array}$$

$$\begin{array}{r} 0.93 \longrightarrow \quad 0.93 \qquad\quad 0.9 \\ -\ 0.451 \longrightarrow -\ 0.451 \qquad -\ 0.5 \\ \hline \text{about}\ \ 0.500 \quad \text{about}\ \ 0.4 \end{array}$$

So the exact difference is between 0.5 and 0.6.

So the exact difference is between 0.4 and 0.5.

Choose the best estimated difference.

1. 0.89 − 0.22   **a.** 0.7   **b.** 0.8   **c.** 0.5   **d.** 0.9

2. 18.19 − 7.23   **a.** 12   **b.** 9   **c.** 11   **d.** 8

3. 0.506 − 0.38   **a.** 0.1   **b.** 0.3   **c.** 0.4   **d.** 0.5

Estimate the difference by rounding.

4.	0.73 − 0.4	**5.**	7.3 − 2.16	**6.**	0.582 − 0.43	**7.**	5.879 − 3.71	**8.**	26.259 − 13.4

9. 0.476 − 0.32   **10.** 14.8 − 9.223   **11.** 50.78 − 9.6

Estimate the difference. Use front-end estimation.

12.	0.87 − 0.4	**13.**	0.695 − 0.26	**14.**	9.347 − 8.12	**15.**	23.754 − 12.412	**16.**	35.471 − 11.53

17. 0.735 − 0.54   **18.** 26.73 − 14.52   **19.** 95.143 − 23.21

**Estimate by both rounding and front-end estimation.
Between what two numbers will the exact difference be?**

20.	0.986 − 0.21	**21.**	52.49 − 19.6	**22.**	63.231 − 49.16	**23.**	35.47 − 12.529	**24.**	69.3 − 12.135
25.	3.89 − 1.158	**26.**	78.5 − 14.371	**27.**	84.53 − 28.165	**28.**	69.451 − 12.3	**29.**	92.473 − 27.51

30. 30.64 − 19.3   **31.** 49.72 − 21.514   **32.** 94.713 − 78.4

Problem Solving

**Choose a computation method. Solve and explain the method you used.
Write whether you estimated or found an exact answer.**

33. Lani needs 9.5 m of ribbon. She has 2.8 m. About how many more meters of ribbon does she need?

34. From a 5.3 ft piece of rope, Omar cut off a piece and had 2.95 ft left. How much rope did he cut off?

35. Jason is 136.5 cm tall. He marked this length on the ground, then did a running jump. He jumped a distance of 152.3 cm. How much longer was his jump than his height?

36. Ruth tries to run on the treadmill at least 8 mi a week. Last week, she ran 1.45 mi on Tuesday, 1.7 mi on Thursday, and 2.25 mi on Saturday. Did she meet her goal of 8 mi last week? Explain.

Subtract More Decimals

Saturn takes 29.456 Earth years to revolve around the Sun. Jupiter takes 11.862 Earth years to revolve around the Sun. How much longer does Saturn take than Jupiter?

First use rounding to estimate the difference: 30 − 10 = 20

The exact difference must be close to 20.

To find the exact difference, subtract: 29.456 − 11.862 = *n*.

| Line up the decimal points. | Subtract the thousandths. Then subtract the hundredths and the tenths. Regroup. | Subtract the whole numbers. |

$$\begin{array}{r} 29.456 \\ -\ 11.862 \\ \hline \end{array}$$

$$\begin{array}{r} 29.456 \\ -\ 11.862 \\ \hline 4 \end{array}$$

$$\begin{array}{r} {\scriptstyle 13\ 15} \\ 29.4\cancel{5}\cancel{6} \\ -\ 11.862 \\ \hline 594 \end{array}$$

$$\begin{array}{r} 29.456 \\ -\ 11.862 \\ \hline 18.594 \end{array}$$

.Think....
: 18.594 is close to the estimate of 20. :

Write the decimal point in the difference.

Saturn takes 18.594 Earth years longer than Jupiter.

Study these examples.

$$\begin{array}{r} 8.6 \\ -\ 2.4 \\ \hline 6.2 \end{array}$$

$$\begin{array}{r} {\scriptstyle 8\ 17} \\ 19.\cancel{7}5 \\ -\ 3.80 \\ \hline 15.95 \end{array}$$

$$\begin{array}{r} 6.457 \\ -\ 3.215 \\ \hline 3.242 \end{array}$$

$$\begin{array}{r} {\scriptstyle\ \ 14} \\ {\scriptstyle 4\ \cancel{4}\ 10} \\ \cancel{5}.\cancel{5}\cancel{0} \\ -\ 1.9\ 6 \\ \hline 3.5\ 4 \end{array}$$

$$\begin{array}{r} {\scriptstyle 7\ 9\ 10} \\ 287.8\cancel{0}\cancel{0} \\ -\ 140.6\ 5\ 3 \\ \hline 147.1\ 4\ 7 \end{array}$$

Practice

Use rounding to estimate. Then subtract.

1. $\begin{array}{r}5.6\\-\ 2.4\end{array}$	**2.** $\begin{array}{r}7.03\\-\ 2.01\end{array}$	**3.** $\begin{array}{r}9.37\\-\ 4.26\end{array}$	**4.** $\begin{array}{r}0.646\\-\ 0.523\end{array}$	**5.** $\begin{array}{r}4.549\\-\ 1.317\end{array}$

6. $\begin{array}{r}27.8\\-\ 13.6\end{array}$	**7.** $\begin{array}{r}25.6\\-\ 19.1\end{array}$	**8.** $\begin{array}{r}15.32\\-\ 11.39\end{array}$	**9.** $\begin{array}{r}23.49\\-\ 11.93\end{array}$	**10.** $\begin{array}{r}19.009\\-\ 13.528\end{array}$

11. $\begin{array}{r}9\\-\ 6.3\end{array}$	**12.** $\begin{array}{r}3.9\\-\ 0.27\end{array}$	**13.** $\begin{array}{r}5.25\\-\ 4.5\end{array}$	**14.** $\begin{array}{r}4.45\\-\ 2.236\end{array}$	**15.** $\begin{array}{r}72.2\\-\ 36.597\end{array}$

Use rounding to estimate. Then find the difference.

16.　　8.6
　　　− 0.314

17.　　19.3
　　　− 17.47

18.　　23.47
　　　− 14.9

19.　　27.23
　　　− 3.518

20.　　36.458
　　　− 15.3

21.　　8.515
　　　− 7.6

22.　　17.51
　　　− 8.4

23.　　17.34
　　　− 3.545

24.　　9.763
　　　− 7.52

25.　　13.719
　　　− 1.9

Practice

Align and subtract.

26. 7.22 − 3.405

27. 9.459 − 6.48

28. 19.42 − 2.579

29. 40.16 − 25.714

30. 29.7 − 14.634

31. 38.1 − 9.134

Compare. Write < , = , or > .

32. 4.549 _?_ 12.6 − 7.051

33. 5.72 _?_ 7.73 − 2.104

34. 40.16 − 25.714 _?_ 14.5 − 0.006

35. 24.714 − 9.3 _?_ 25.414 − 10

36. 4.95 − 3.15 _?_ $2\frac{7}{8} - 1\frac{3}{4}$

37. 0.98 − 0.73 _?_ $\frac{1}{2} - \frac{1}{4}$

38. 6.034 − 2.95 _?_ $4\frac{2}{5} - 1\frac{1}{10}$

39. 7.5 − 5.062 _?_ $2\frac{3}{5} - 1\frac{1}{2}$

Find the missing minuend.

40.　　?
　　　− 3.6
　　　‾‾‾‾
　　　4.5

41.　　?
　　　− 4.59
　　　‾‾‾‾
　　　3.36

42.　　?
　　　− 0.532
　　　‾‾‾‾
　　　0.284

43.　　?
　　　− 2.109
　　　‾‾‾‾
　　　5.145

44.　　?
　　　− 4.062
　　　‾‾‾‾
　　　3.149

Problem Solving

45. Cesar is 1.52 m tall. Cheryl is 1.176 m tall. How much taller is Cesar than Cheryl?

46. Dean had 2.75 qt of paint. He used some and had 0.6 qt left. How much paint did he use?

47. A rapid rise on a barometer is 0.05 in. or more in 3 h or less. Toni's barometer rose from 29.98 in. to 30.02 in. between 8:00 A.M. and 11:00 A.M. Was this a rapid rise? Explain.

MENTAL MATH

Compute.

48.　　6.145
　　　− 2

49.　　5
　　　+ 2.143

50.　　9.53
　　　+ 7

51.　　8.57
　　　− 4

52.　　17.539
　　　− 9

Problem-Solving Strategy:
Use More Than One Step

The Blackstones drove 145.2 mi the first day and twice as many miles the next day of their vacation. They spent $15 for gas each day. How many miles did they travel?

Read Visualize yourself in the problem above as you reread it. List the facts and the question.

Facts: drove 145.2 mi one day
drove twice as many miles the next day
spent $15 each day for gas

Question: How many miles did they travel?

Plan Is all the information you need listed in the problem? Yes
Is there *extra information* in the problem? Yes

You do not need to know how much money the Blackstones spent for gas—$15 for gas each day.

You need to find the total mileage.

First find the mileage for the second day.
Multiply: $2 \times 145.2 = n$.

Then add the miles for both days. $145.2 + n = \underline{\ ?\ }$.

Solve To solve, first multiply: $2 \times 145.2 = 290.4$.

Then, add: $145.2 + 290.4 = 435.6$.

The total mileage is 435.6 mi.

Check Use the commutative property to check.

$$
\begin{array}{r}
\overset{1}{} \\
290.4 \\
+\ 145.2 \\
\hline
435.6
\end{array}
$$
The answer checks.

Identify the extra information. Then solve each problem.

1. Tony is saving to buy a CD player that costs $68.95. He won 3 CDs at the carnival. He earned $12.00 for mowing the lawn. He had already saved $43.50. How much more money does he need?

Read **Visualize yourself in the problem above as you reread it. Focus on the facts and the question.**

List what you know.

Facts: CD player costs $68.95
Tony has 3 CDs.
He earned $12.00.
He had saved $43.50.

Question: How much more money does he need?

Plan This problem has extra information.
You only need to know the cost of the CD player and how much Tony has already.

First, add: $43.50 + $12.00 = n.

Then, subtract to find how much more Tony needs.
$68.95 − \underline{\ ?\ } = \underline{\ ?\ }$.

Solve Check

2. Paul has three wood planks, measuring 0.5 m, 0.8 m, and 1.6 m. Carl has a circular piece of wood measuring 0.4 m in diameter and three wood planks measuring 0.7 m, 1.9 m, and 0.2 m. Whose three wood planks total the greater length?

3. Chen usually rides his bicycle for 30 minutes four days a week. One week he clocked mileage at 14.2 km, 12.6 km, 10.9 km, and 13.3 km. The next week he clocked mileage at 12.7 km, 11.8 km, 9.9 km, and 14.6 km. In which week did he clock the greater total mileage?

4. Cathy bought 5 lb of tomatoes at $1.08 a pound and 2 heads of lettuce at $0.89 each. She has $10. How much did she spend in all?

5. Ken's math scores for the month were 92, 93, 90, and 81. His creative writing score was 91. If the score of Ken's next math test is 99, by how many points will his math average increase?

Problem-Solving Applications: Mixed Review

Solve each problem and explain the method you used.

1. An organic string bean is 4.6 cm long. A nonorganic bean is 6.42 cm long. How much longer is the nonorganic bean?

2. Andy buys 1.05 kg of organic oranges and 0.96 kg of organic grapefruit. What is the total mass of the fruit Andy bought?

3. Missy measured an organic carrot's length in tenths of centimeters. Then she rounded its length to 11 cm. What is the longest length she could have measured?

4. Juan has 1.243 kg of organic flour. His recipe calls for 2 kg of flour. How much more flour does he need?

5. Organic strawberries cost $1.45 for a pint and $2.78 for a quart. Jen buys 1 pint and 2 quarts of strawberries. About how much does she spend?

6. Alma buys four organic apples. They have masses of 154.5 g, 120 g, 127.72 g, and 151.19 g. What is the total mass of the apples?

7. An organic peach weighed 142.3 g. Its pit weighed 18.48 g. How much did its skin and flesh weigh?

8. An apricot weighed 4.5 oz before drying. After drying, it weighed 1.375 oz. How many ounces of water did it lose while drying?

9. The line graph shows the amount of produce sold each month. In which months did Pélé's Produce sell about 2.5 metric tons of produce?

10. How much more did Pélé's Produce sell in June than in April?

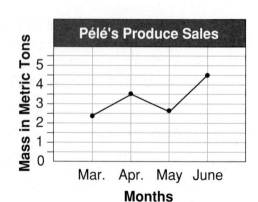

Pélé's Produce Sales

Mass in Metric Tons

Months — Mar. Apr. May June

Choose a strategy from the list or use another strategy you know to solve each problem.

11. A bag of 12 organic onions costs $3.49. A bag of organic carrots costs $1.69. How much would 2 bags of each cost?

12. Mary Ann bought some fruit. She gave 1.4 kg of pears to Jill, who gave her 1.15 kg of melon. Then she had 3 kg of fruit altogether. How much fruit had she bought?

13. Thea's organic tomato weighs 0.145 kg more than Fran's. Together their tomatoes weigh 3.945 kg. How much does Thea's tomato weigh?

14. Of 120 children surveyed, 80 like Red Delicious apples, 74 like McIntosh apples, and 34 like both kinds of apples. How many children like Red Delicious apples only? McIntosh apples only?

Strategy File

Use These Strategies
Use More Than One Step
Make an Organized List
Guess and Test
Work Backward
Use a Model/Diagram

Use this table for problems 15–17.

15. Belinda bought 2 pears and 1 of each of the other fruits. How much change did she receive from $10?

16. Rich spent exactly $3.83. What fruits did he purchase?

17. Ms. Fermat buys 3 different fruits. What combinations of fruits can she purchase? What is the most expensive combination?

Organic Fruit Prices	
Apples	$0.49 each
Pears	$0.39 each
Kiwis	$0.75 each
Melons	$1.89 each
Mangos	$2.95 each

Use this table for problems 18–19.

18. How much more expensive is it to buy 2 lb of each organic vegetable than 2 lb of each nonorganic vegetable?

19. Bill buys 5 pounds of spinach, some organic and some nonorganic. He spends $8.02. How many pounds of organic spinach does he buy?

Vegetable Prices (per lb)		
Food	Organic	Nonorganic
Beets	$1.19	$0.89
Carrots	$0.98	$0.45
Onions	$1.25	$0.99
Spinach	$2.09	$1.28

Write Your Own

20. Write a problem using the data in a graph or table in this lesson. Then solve it. Share your work with a classmate.

Check Your Progress
Lessons 1–10

Name the decimal for each point on the number line. *(See pp. 268–269.)*

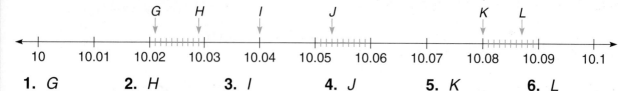

1. G **2.** H **3.** I **4.** J **5.** K **6.** L

Write the place of the underlined digit. Then write its value. *(See pp. 270–271.)*

7. 136.025 **8.** 2.754 **9.** 250.963 **10.** 647.912

Write each in expanded form.

11. 470.47 **12.** 39.062 **13.** 50.247 **14.** 349.308

Estimate by both rounding and front-end estimation. Between what two numbers will the exact sum or exact difference be? *(See pp. 274–275, 280–281.)*

15.	**16.**	**17.**	**18.**	**19.**
0.97	5.575	0.753	4.76	277.52
+ 0.465	+ 6.81	− 0.52	− 2.135	453.153
				+ 118.64

Add. *(See pp. 272–273, 276–277.)*

20.	**21.**	**22.**	**23.**	**24.**
0.58	3.142	0.4	3.25	17.154
+ 0.69	+ 13.236	+ 0.63	+ 1.7	+ 5.24

25. 5.2 + 8.13 + 9.152 **26.** 413.21 + 25.358 + 114.259

Subtract. *(See pp. 278–279, 282–283.)*

27.	**28.**	**29.**	**30.**	**31.**
6.85	20.84	0.9	72.35	17.9
− 0.72	− 9.18	− 0.254	− 8.513	− 6.129

32. 5.2 − 3.75 **33.** 15.67 − 3.4 **34.** 419.1 − 24.853

Problem Solving
(See pp. 276–277, 282–283, 284–287.)

35. Find the perimeter of a rectangle that has an area of 735 sq cm and sides of 17.5 cm and 42 cm.

36. Ana had 3.75 pt of milk. She used some for a recipe and had 1.5 pt left. How much did she use?

(See *Still More Practice*, p. 484.)

Scientific Notation

Scientists use scientific notation as a more compact and useful way to write very large numbers.

The distance from Earth to the Sun is about 93,000,000 miles. Write this number in scientific notation.

▶ To write a number in scientific notation, write it as a product of two factors.

- One factor is a number greater than or equal to 1, but less than 10.

- The other factor is a power of 10 in exponent form.

Some Powers of 10 in Exponent Form	
$10 = 10^1$	$100,000 = 10^5$
$100 = 10^2$	$1,000,000 = 10^6$
$1000 = 10^3$	$10,000,000 = 10^7$
$10,000 = 10^4$	$100,000,000 = 10^8$

$$93,000,000 = 9.3000000 \times 10,000,000 = 9.3 \times 10^7$$

7 places — 7 zeros

In scientific notation, $93,000.000 = 9.3 \times 10^7$.

Study these examples.

$300,000,000 = 3 \times 100,000,000$
$= 3 \times 10^8$

$127,000 = 1.27 \times 100,000$
$= 1.27 \times 10^5$

$5051 = 5.051 \times 1000$
$= 5.051 \times 10^3$

Write each number in scientific notation.

1. 400,000

2. 7,000,000

3. 50,000

4. 900,000,000

5. 9600

6. 57,000

7. 420,000,000

8. 78,000,000

9. 6760

10. 91,700

11. 48,900,000

12. 375,000,000

13. 57,510

14. 161,200,000

15. 723,400

16. 84,570,000,000

Problem Solving

17. The speed of light in a vacuum is about 186,000 miles per second. Use scientific notation to express how far light travels in one hour.

18. In 2000 there were about 248.7 million citizens in Country A. In 2005 the population grew to 269.8 million. What was the amount of increase in population? Express your answer in scientific notation.

Chapter 8 Test

Write the place of the underlined digit. Then write its value.

1. 84.2<u>6</u>8
2. 5.23<u>9</u>
3. 873.<u>1</u>59

Write each in expanded form.

4. 347.046
5. 5.902
6. 0.593

Estimate by both rounding and front-end estimation. Between what two numbers will the exact sum or exact difference be?

7.   0.86
      + 0.683

8.   785.53
         243.752
      + 451.385

9.   0.853
       − 0.52

10.   578.457
        − 123.3

Add or subtract.

11.   0.516
       + 0.47

12.   6.8
       + 0.72

13.   0.595
       − 0.41

14.   12.79
        − 3.581

15. 1.23 + 3.517 + 12.3

16. 153.236 + 98.2 + 5.34

17. 6.85 − 2.4

18. 354.9 − 98.183

Problem Solving

Use a strategy you have learned.

19. Pam needs 2 yd of blue ribbon. She has 0.497 yd. She buys 0.91 yd more. Then she buys 0.4 yd of red ribbon. How much more blue ribbon does Pam need?

Tell About It

20. Betty has 3 pieces of fabric measuring 0.45 m, 0.24 m, and 0.3 m. Is the total length more or less than one meter? Explain.

Performance Assessment

Use the number line.

21. Name the decimal for points *X* and *V*.

Draw a number line and locate each point.

22. *S* = 19.047
23. *T* = 19.034
24. *D* = 19.04

25. Name the thousandths between 19.0 and 19.010.

Test Preparation

Choose the best answer.

1. Which is equivalent to $\frac{19}{5}$?

   a. $3\frac{4}{5}$

   b. $4\frac{4}{5}$

   c. 3

   d. 5

2. What is the greatest common factor of 12, 18, and 36?

   a. 3
   b. 4
   c. 6
   d. 12

3. Choose the product of $3\frac{1}{3} \times 5\frac{2}{5}$.

   a. $1\frac{7}{18}$ b. $\frac{1}{18}$

   c. 15   d. 18

4. Which decimal represents fifty-four and nine thousandths?

   a. 54.9000
   b. 54.900
   c. 54.009
   d. 54.09

5. Choose the short word name for 5,750,000,000.

   a. 5.75 million
   b. 5.75 billion
   c. 57.5 million
   d. 575 billion

6. Choose the simplest form for $\frac{88}{104}$.

   a. $\frac{44}{52}$ b. $\frac{11}{13}$

   c. $\frac{22}{26}$ d. not given

7. There are 10 cards numbered 1 through 10. If one card is picked at random, what is $P\,(> 6)$?

   a. $\frac{1}{2}$ b. $\frac{3}{5}$

   c. $\frac{1}{5}$ d. not given

8. Subtract $2\frac{4}{7}$ from $8\frac{4}{7}$.

   a. $10\frac{4}{7}$

   b. $6\frac{8}{7}$

   c. 10

   d. 6

9. Which is a prime number?

   a. 14
   b. 12
   c. 10
   d. 7

10. Choose the quotient of $2\frac{5}{8} \div \frac{1}{2}$.

    a. $5\frac{1}{4}$ b. $5\frac{1}{2}$

    c. 5   d. 84

11. To the nearest hundredth, 68.876 would equal:

    a. 68.87
    b. 68.88
    c. 68.8
    d. 68.00

12. Round 382,576,121 to the nearest ten thousand.

    a. 382,576,000
    b. 382,600,000
    c. 382,580,000
    d. 382,577,000

13. Choose the sum of $6\frac{3}{4} + 8\frac{2}{5}$.

    a. $15\frac{3}{20}$ b. $14\frac{5}{9}$

    c. $15\frac{13}{20}$ d. not given

14. Which fractions are ordered from least to greatest?

    a. $\frac{9}{19}, \frac{1}{2}, \frac{8}{15}$ b. $\frac{1}{2}, \frac{8}{15}, \frac{9}{19}$

    c. $\frac{9}{19}, \frac{8}{15}, \frac{1}{2}$ d. $\frac{1}{2}, \frac{9}{19}, \frac{8}{15}$

15. Estimate by rounding.

9,879,632
+ 763,986

  a. 9,700,000
  b. 10,700,000
  c. 11,700,000
  d. 9,000,000,000

20. Which shows the standard form of 2 billion, 14 million, 800 thousand?

  a. 2,014,800
  b. 2,014,800,000
  c. 2,000,014,800
  d. not given

---

16. Choose the sum.

38.72 + 11.3 + 45.09

  a. 95.11   **b.** 95.01
  c. 84.94   **d.** not given

21. Choose the difference.

68.2 − 8.419

  a. 59.871   **b.** 59.781
  c. 58. 871   **d.** not given

---

17. Choose the product.

905
× 78

  a. 70,590   **b.** 75,090
  c. 75,900   **d.** not given

22. Choose the quotient.

6)4848

  a. 88   **b.** 800
  c. 808   **d.** not given

---

18. For which months do the first days have the same amount of daylight?

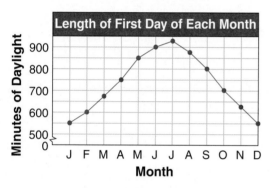

a. Jan. and Dec.   **b.** May and Aug.
c. Jan. and Nov.   **d.** not given

23. How many students received a score of 81 or greater?

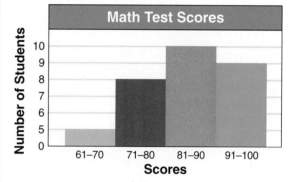

a. 9 students   **b.** 10 students
c. 19 students   **d.** not given

---

19. Susan received grades of 78, 93, 82, and 76 on four math exams. What is the lowest grade she can receive on her next math exam and have an average of at least 85 on the five exams?

  a. 96   **b.** 94
  c. 92   **d.** 90

24. In store A a scarf costs $12, and in store B the same scarf is on sale for $8. How many scarves can be bought in store B with the same amount of money, excluding tax, needed to buy 10 scarves in store A?

  a. 4 scarves   **b.** 12 scarves
  c. 15 scarves   **d.** 18 scarves

Explain how you solved the problem. Show all your work.

25. A manufacturer makes a certain machine part that measures 26.4 cm in length. A part will pass inspection if it is no more than 0.03 cm shorter than 26.4 cm or no more than 0.03 cm longer than 26.4 cm. What is the shortest and longest measures that can pass inspection? How do you know?

Decimals: Multiplication and Division

Sand Dollar

What can we buy
with this loose
money?

It spilled
from the green silk
pocket
of the sea
a white coin tossed up
a careless gift wet
shining
at the water's edge

Who can break a dollar?

What a bargain! Five
white doves
ready to fly to your hand

Sea change!

Barbara Juster Esbensen

In this chapter you will:

Multiply and divide by powers of ten
Estimate decimal products and
 quotients
Multiply and divide decimals and
 money
Write a number sentence to solve
 problems

Critical Thinking/Finding Together

You bought some supplies that cost
$2.59 and paid with $10. What is the
least possible combination of bills and
coins you could receive as change?

Multiply by 10, 100, and 1000

Materials: paper, pencil

Copy and complete the given table.
Look for patterns for multiplying decimals
by 10, 100, or 1000 mentally.

	n	$10 \times n$	$100 \times n$	$1000 \times n$
1.	0.352	3.52	35.2	352
2.	0.74	?	?	740
3.	0.6	?	?	600
4.	1.2	?	?	?

Compare the position of the decimal point in n with the position
of the decimal point in $10 \times n$, $100 \times n$, and $1000 \times n$.

5. What patterns do you notice in your complete table?
What happens to the decimal point when you multiply
a decimal by 10? by 100? by 1000?

6. Examine the products in exercises 2–4. What happens when
there are not enough places to move the decimal point
as far to the right as needed?

Use the patterns to find the products mentally.

7. 10×3.628
 100×3.628
 1000×3.628

8. 10×9.65
 100×9.65
 1000×9.65

9. 10×0.5
 100×0.5
 1000×0.5

10. 10×4.8
 100×4.8
 1000×4.8

11. Write a rule that you can use to multiply a decimal
by 10, 100, and 1000.

Use your rule to find the product mentally.

12. 10×0.02

13. 10×0.691

14. 10×0.03

15. 10×0.007

16. 100×37.9

17. 100×1.7

18. 100×2.63

19. 100×0.296

20. 1000×0.4

21. 1000×3.642

22. 1000×0.82

23. 1000×4.693

24. 10×0.006

25. 1000×0.69

26. 100×0.13

27. 10×5.047

Use the properties of multiplication to complete each sentence.

28. $20 \times 0.4 = n$
$2 \times (10 \times 0.4) = n$
$2 \times 4 = 8$
$200 \times 0.4 = n$
$2 \times (100 \times 0.4) = n$
$2 \times 40 = 80$

29. $70 \times 0.9 = n$
$700 \times 0.9 = n$

31. $60 \times 0.3 = n$
$600 \times 0.3 = n$

30. $40 \times 0.6 = n$
$400 \times 0.6 = n$

32. $90 \times 0.8 = n$
$900 \times 0.8 = n$

33. Write a rule that you can use to multiply a decimal by a multiple of 10 or 100. Use the rule for multiplying a decimal by 10, 100, and 1000 to help.

Use your rule to find the product. Check by using the properties of multiplication.

34. 500×0.9

35. 900×0.7

36. 40×0.8

37. 30×0.2

38. 80×0.8

39. 90×0.5

40. 300×0.9

41. 600×0.7

Communicate

42. Describe in your Math Journal the pattern formed when you multiply by 10, 100, or 1000 and the number of places the decimal point "moves."

43. When you multiply a decimal by a multiple of 10 or 100, why does the decimal point move to the right rather than to the left?

44. Find the missing factors. Explain your answers.

a. $n \times 0.309 = 309$
b. $n \times 0.028 = 0.28$
c. $n \times 0.054 = 5.4$

d. $10 \times n = 32.13$
e. $1000 \times n = 1580$
f. $100 \times n = 350$

45. Multiply each of the factors in box B by one of the factors in box A. Write each multiplication sentence.

50	800
60	300
40	700

A

0.1	0.4	0.7
0.2	0.5	0.8
0.3	0.6	0.9

B

DO YOU REMEMBER?

Use rounding to estimate. Then find the product.

46. 17×69
47. 540×7
48. 65×158
49. 150×700

50. 309×157
51. 104×503
52. 407×873
53. 1809×480

Estimate Decimal Products

Mr. Millar drove for 3.8 hours at a speed of 48.95 miles an hour. About how far did he drive?

To find about how far, estimate: 3.8 × 48.95.

▶ To **estimate** a *decimal product*:

- Round each factor to its greatest place.

- Multiply the rounded factors.

Mr. Millar drove about 200 miles.

$$
\begin{array}{r}
48.95 \longrightarrow 50 \\
\times\ \ 3.8 \longrightarrow \times\ 4 \\
\hline
\text{about}\ \ 200
\end{array}
$$

Both factors rounded *up*.
So the actual product *is less than* 200.

Study these examples.

$$
\begin{array}{r}
0.734 \longrightarrow 0.7 \\
\times 22.86 \longrightarrow \times 20 \\
\hline
\text{about}\ \ 14
\end{array}
$$

.Think.........
Both factors rounded *down*.

The actual product *is greater than* 14.

$$
\begin{array}{r}
0.56 \longrightarrow 0.6 \\
\times\ 9.7 \longrightarrow \times 10 \\
\hline
\text{about}\ \ 6
\end{array}
$$

.Think.........
Both factors rounded *up*.

The actual product *is less than* 6.

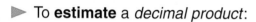

Practice

Estimate each product. Then tell whether the actual product *is greater than* or *is less than* the estimated product.

1. 4.81 × 2.6	**2.** 3.45 × 4.3	**3.** 5.56 × 9.7	**4.** 0.75 × 9.5	**5.** 0.88 × 9.8
6. 4.376 × 8.2	**7.** 9.135 × 4.2	**8.** 4.836 × 6.7	**9.** 7.036 × 2.31	**10.** 5.645 × 3.84
11. 13.96 × 0.84	**12.** 24.69 × 0.23	**13.** 17.68 × 0.55	**14.** 0.146 × 29.34	**15.** 0.341 × 32.49
16. 15.435 × 0.48	**17.** 28.776 × 0.76	**18.** 45.186 × 0.35	**19.** 83.607 × 0.64	**20.** 92.487 × 0.92

Estimation by Clustering

When a number of addends "cluster" around a certain number, an estimate for the sum may be obtained by multiplying that number by the number of addends.

Estimate: $8.91 + 9.05 + 8.92 + 9.07$

$9 + 9 + 9 + 9$

$4 \times 9 = 36$ ← estimated sum

Think Addends "cluster" around 9.

Estimate: $\$0.63 + \$0.59 + \$0.56 + \$0.61 + \$0.55$

$\$0.60 + \$0.60 + \$0.60 + \$0.60 + \$0.60$

$5 \times \$0.60 = \$3.00$

Think Addends "cluster" around $0.60.

Estimate the sum. Use clustering.

21. $0.93 + 1.1 + 1.08 + 0.9$

22. $2.05 + 1.986 + 2.014 + 1.895 + 2.1$

23. $\$0.84 + \$0.77 + \$0.81 + \$0.79$

24. $\$.35 + \$.41 + \$.39 + \$.44 + \$.36$

25. $\$.53 + \$.48 + \$.54 + \$.46 + \$.51$

26. $\$.99 + \$1.01 + \$.96 + \$1.10 + \$.95$

Problem Solving

27. Jon runs 5.3 miles in one hour. At this rate, about how far could he run in 1.7 hours?

28. Mila can swim 18.55 meters in one minute. About how far can she swim in 4.75 minutes?

29. If one sample of ore weighs 23.8 g, about how many grams will 87 equal samples weigh?

30. A set of 6 art books costs $41.25. A copy of one of the books, bought separately, costs $8.25. About how much less is the cost of the 6 books if you buy the set?

TEST PREPARATION

31. A 1-ft length of steel cable weighs 0.428 lb. About how much does a 22.6-ft length of steel cable weigh?

A about 80 lb   **B** about 40 lb   **C** about 8 lb   **D** about 4 lb

Multiply Decimals by Whole Numbers

If one cup of skim milk contains 0.31 grams of calcium, how much calcium is in 11 cups of skim milk?

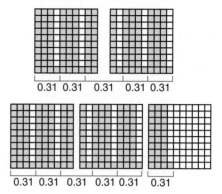

0.31 0.31   0.31   0.31 0.31

0.31 0.31   0.31   0.31 0.31   0.31

First estimate the product by rounding:
$10 \times 0.3 = 3$.

The actual product is greater than 3.

To find how much calcium,
multiply: $11 \times 0.31 = n$.

▶ To **multiply** a *decimal* by a *whole number*:

- Multiply as you would with whole numbers.
- Count the number of decimal places in each factor.
- Mark off the *same number* of decimal places in the product.

Multiply as with whole numbers.

$$
\begin{array}{r}
0.3\ 1 \\
\times\ \ \ 1\ 1 \\
\hline
3\ 1 \\
+3\ 1\ 0 \\
\hline
3\ 4\ 1
\end{array}
$$

Write the decimal point in the product.

$$
\begin{array}{r}
0.3\ 1 \\
\times\ \ \ 1\ 1 \\
\hline
3\ 1 \\
+3\ 1\ 0 \\
\hline
3.4\ 1
\end{array}
$$

2 decimal places

.Think
3.41 is close to
the estimate of 3.

Eleven cups of skim milk contain 3.41 grams of calcium.

Study these examples.

$$
\begin{array}{r}
0.121 \\
\times\ \ \ \ \ 4 \\
\hline
0.484
\end{array}
$$

3 decimal places

$$
\begin{array}{r}
9.3 \\
\times\ \ \ 5 \\
\hline
46.5
\end{array}
$$

1 decimal place

$$
\begin{array}{r}
\$4.55 \\
\times\ \ \ \ \ 9 \\
\hline
\$40.95
\end{array}
$$

Write the dollar sign.

Write the decimal point in each product. Explain your answer.

1.
$$
\begin{array}{r}
2.8 \\
\times\ \ \ 3 \\
\hline
8\ 4
\end{array}
$$

2.
$$
\begin{array}{r}
6.3\ 1 \\
\times\ \ \ 1\ 6 \\
\hline
1\ 0\ 0\ 9\ 6
\end{array}
$$

3.
$$
\begin{array}{r}
0.7\ 9 \\
\times\ \ \ \ \ 3 \\
\hline
2\ 3\ 7
\end{array}
$$

4.
$$
\begin{array}{r}
0.5\ 3\ 4 \\
\times\ \ \ \ \ \ \ 5 \\
\hline
2\ 6\ 7\ 0
\end{array}
$$

5.
$$
\begin{array}{r}
4.1\ 7\ 3 \\
\times\ \ \ \ \ 7\ 2 \\
\hline
3\ 0\ 0\ 4\ 5\ 6
\end{array}
$$

Use rounding to estimate. Then find the product.

6.   0.6
    × 13

7.   0.49
    × 29

8.   0.479
    ×   35

9.   9.2
    × 39

10.   3.05
    ×   26

11.   5.052
    ×   19

12.   7.891
    ×   56

13. $0.74
    ×   12

14. $8.39
    ×   62

15. $14.55
    ×   89

Find the product.

16. 3 × 0.4

17. 5 × 0.49

18. 9 × 0.019

19. 8 × 0.153

20. 2 × 8.519

21. 35 × 35.02

22. 15 × $0.67

23. 49 × $15.19

24. six times nineteen thousandths

25. two times five and two tenths

26. $n \times 3.29$ when $n = 3$

27. $n \times 18.34$ when $n = 27$

28. $43 \times n$ when $n = 26.514$

29. $36 \times n$ when $n = 1.03$

Problem Solving

30. One large banana contains 2.4 g of protein. How many grams of protein will a dozen large bananas contain?

31. Ms. Blake bought 3 lb of onions at $1.69 a pound, 2 lb of yams at $0.59 a pound, and 3 bunches of broccoli at $1.19 a bunch. Did she spend more than $10.00? Explain.

CRITICAL THINKING — Algebra

32. An arithmetic sequence is a pattern of numbers in which each succeeding number is obtained by **adding** the same number to the previous number.

    What number is added?   0.2   0.5   0.8   1.1   1.4

33. A geometric sequence is a pattern of numbers in which each succeeding number is obtained by **multiplying** the same number by the previous number.

    What number is multiplied?   0.2   0.4   0.8   1.6   3.2

34. **a.** Write other examples of arithmetic and geometric sequences.

    b. Find a sequence that is both arithmetic and geometric.
        (*Hint:* Try adding 0 and multiplying by 1.)

9-4 Multiply Decimals by Decimals

Carla cut 0.8 of a roll of fabric and used 0.6 of it for a project. How much of the fabric did she use on the project?

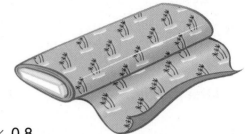

To find how much of the fabric she used, multiply: $0.6 \times 0.8 = n$.

▶ You can use a model to help you multiply 0.6×0.8.

- Shade *8 columns* of a 10×10 grid to show 0.8.

- Mark off *6 rows* of the 8 shaded columns to show 0.6 of 0.8.

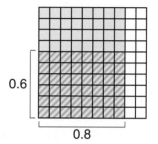

48 out of 100 squares are marked off.
$0.6 \times 0.8 = 0.48$

▶ To **multiply** a *decimal* by a *decimal:*

- Multiply as you would with whole numbers.

- Count the total number of decimal places in both factors.

- Mark off the *same number* of decimal places in the product.

Multiply as with whole numbers.

$$\begin{array}{r} 0.8 \\ \times 0.6 \\ \hline 4\ 8 \end{array}$$

Write the decimal point in the product.

$$\begin{array}{r} 0.8 \leftarrow \\ \times 0.6 \leftarrow \\ \hline 0.4\ 8 \leftarrow \end{array}$$

- 1 decimal place
- 1 decimal place
- 2 decimal places

Carla used 0.48 of the fabric on the project.

Study these examples.

$$\begin{array}{r} 6.5 \leftarrow \\ \times 0.7\ 3 \leftarrow \\ \hline 1\ 9\ 5 \\ 4\ 5\ 5\ \circ \\ \hline 4.7\ 4\ 5 \leftarrow \end{array}$$

- 1 decimal place
- 2 decimal places
- 3 decimal places

$$\begin{array}{r} 4.2 \leftarrow \\ \times\ \ 1.7 \leftarrow \\ \hline 2\ 9\ 4 \\ 4\ 2\ \circ \\ \hline 7.1\ 4 \leftarrow \end{array}$$

- 1 decimal place
- 1 decimal place
- 2 decimal places

Use the diagram to complete each statement.

1.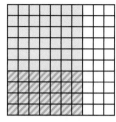

    $0.4 \times 0.7 = \underline{}$

2.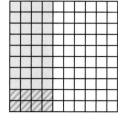

    $0.2 \times \underline{} = \underline{}$

3.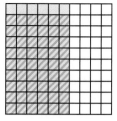

    $\underline{} \times \underline{} = 0.54$

Use a 10 × 10 grid to find each product.

4. 0.3×0.9
5. 0.8×0.7
6. 0.5×0.6
7. 0.9×0.4

Find the product.

8. $\begin{array}{r} 3.4 \\ \times\, 0.8 \\ \hline \end{array}$
9. $\begin{array}{r} 5.9 \\ \times\, 0.03 \\ \hline \end{array}$
10. $\begin{array}{r} 2.2 \\ \times\, 0.16 \\ \hline \end{array}$
11. $\begin{array}{r} 6.24 \\ \times\, 0.9 \\ \hline \end{array}$
12. $\begin{array}{r} 24.6 \\ \times\, 2.3 \\ \hline \end{array}$

13. 6.6×4.83
14. 4.8×5.94
15. 0.97×65.8
16. 3.17×19.5

17. $n \times 5.2$ when $n = 0.6$
18. $n \times 4.7$ when $n = 2.6$

19. $n \times 1.45$ when $n = 0.5$
20. $21.3 \times n$ when $n = 1.5$

21. $0.9 \times n$ when $n = 0.4$
22. $0.32 \times n$ when $n = 4.1$

Compare. Write <, =, or >.

23. $0.7 \times 6.2 \underline{} 0.45 \times 9.6$
24. $0.98 \times 0.7 \underline{} 0.4 \times 1.89$

25. $1.25 \times 0.2 \underline{} \frac{2}{3} \times \frac{3}{8}$
26. $0.3 \times 0.75 \underline{} \frac{1}{2} \times \frac{2}{5}$

Problem Solving

27. Krissie is 1.43 m tall. Her mother is 1.2 times Krissie's height. How tall is Krissie's mother?

28. If Jack can run 8.53 km in one hour, how far can he run in 3.5 hours?

CRITICAL THINKING — Algebra

Write the pattern rule. Then complete the pattern.

29. 50, 5, 0.5, $\underline{}$, $\underline{}$
30. 2.5, 7.5, 22.5, $\underline{}$, $\underline{}$

31. 1.2, 2.4, 4.8, $\underline{}$, $\underline{}$
32. 20, 6, 1.8, $\underline{}$, $\underline{}$

Zeros in the Product

Sometimes you need to write zeros to the left of nonzero digits in the product in order to place the decimal point correctly.

Multiply: $0.3 \times 0.03 = n$.

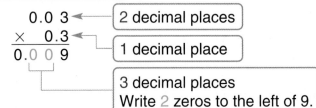

Multiply as with whole numbers.	Write the decimal point in the product.

$$\begin{array}{r} 0.0\ 3 \\ \times\ \ \ 0.3 \\ \hline 9 \end{array}$$

$$\begin{array}{r} 0.0\ 3 \quad \leftarrow \text{2 decimal places} \\ \times\ \ \ 0.3 \quad \leftarrow \text{1 decimal place} \\ \hline 0.0\ 0\ 9 \end{array}$$

3 decimal places
Write 2 zeros to the left of 9.

Study these examples.

$$\begin{array}{r} 0.4 \quad \leftarrow \text{1 decimal place} \\ \times 0.2 \quad \leftarrow \text{1 decimal place} \\ \hline 0.0\ 8 \end{array}$$

2 decimal places
Write 1 zero to the left of 8.

$$\begin{array}{r} 0.0\ 0\ 3 \quad \leftarrow \text{3 decimal places} \\ \times\ \ \ \ \ \ \ 2 \\ \hline 0.0\ 0\ 6 \end{array}$$

3 decimal places
Write 2 zeros to the left of 6.

Practice

**Write the decimal point in the product.
Write in zeros where necessary.**

1.
$$\begin{array}{r} 0.3 \\ \times 0.2 \\ \hline 0.06 \end{array}$$

2.
$$\begin{array}{r} 0.0\ 4 \\ \times\ \ \ 0.3 \\ \hline 1\ 2 \end{array}$$

3.
$$\begin{array}{r} 0.3\ 4 \\ \times\ \ \ 0.2 \\ \hline 6\ 8 \end{array}$$

4.
$$\begin{array}{r} 7.4 \\ \times 0.0\ 1 \\ \hline 7\ 4 \end{array}$$

5.
$$\begin{array}{r} 0.0\ 0\ 8 \\ \times\ \ \ \ \ \ \ 7 \\ \hline 5\ 6 \end{array}$$

Multiply.

6.
$$\begin{array}{r} 0.2 \\ \times 0.1 \end{array}$$

7.
$$\begin{array}{r} 0.04 \\ \times\ 0.2 \end{array}$$

8.
$$\begin{array}{r} 0.03 \\ \times\ \ \ \ 9 \end{array}$$

9.
$$\begin{array}{r} 0.003 \\ \times\ \ \ \ \ 3 \end{array}$$

10.
$$\begin{array}{r} 0.002 \\ \times\ \ \ \ \ 4 \end{array}$$

11.
$$\begin{array}{r} 0.16 \\ \times\ 0.3 \end{array}$$

12.
$$\begin{array}{r} 0.46 \\ \times\ 0.2 \end{array}$$

13.
$$\begin{array}{r} 0.19 \\ \times\ 0.4 \end{array}$$

14.
$$\begin{array}{r} 0.012 \\ \times\ \ \ \ \ 3 \end{array}$$

15.
$$\begin{array}{r} 0.021 \\ \times\ \ \ \ \ 4 \end{array}$$

16.
$$\begin{array}{r} 1.3 \\ \times 0.03 \end{array}$$

17.
$$\begin{array}{r} 1.1 \\ \times 0.05 \end{array}$$

18.
$$\begin{array}{r} 2.3 \\ \times 0.04 \end{array}$$

19.
$$\begin{array}{r} 6.7 \\ \times 0.01 \end{array}$$

20.
$$\begin{array}{r} 1.7 \\ \times 0.04 \end{array}$$

Find the product.

21. 3.2×0.02 **22.** 0.7×0.02 **23.** 5.2×0.01 **24.** 0.13×0.3

25. 2×0.021 **26.** 0.3×0.11 **27.** 0.5×0.05 **28.** 1.2×0.04

29. $n \times 0.006$ when $n = 8$ **30.** $n \times 0.4$ when $n = 0.05$

31. $0.3 \times n$ when $n = 0.07$ **32.** $0.04 \times n$ when $n = 1.9$

Compute. Use the order of operations.

33. $0.35 \times (3 - 0.5)$ **34.** $(0.09 \times 0.8) + (0.3 \times 0.6)$

35. $1.8 - 0.3 \times 0.02 + 0.9$ **36.** $(0.28 + 3.2) \times 0.4$

Problem Solving

37. A clock uses 0.02 kilowatt hours of electricity a day. How much electricity does it use in 4 days?

38. A postcard weighs 0.004 kg. How many kilograms would six of these weigh?

39. Cocoa hulls make up 0.08 of Jamal's organic fertilizer mix. Teresa uses nine tenths of that amount in her mix. What portion of Teresa's mix is cocoa hulls?

40. A radio uses three 1.5-volt batteries. It stops playing if the batteries lose two hundredths of their total power. What is the minimum voltage the radio needs?

CHALLENGE — Algebra

Find the products to discover a pattern.

41. 0.25×3200 **42.** $\frac{1}{4} \times 3200$ **43.** 0.25×320 **44.** $\frac{1}{4} \times 320$

45. 0.25×32 **46.** $\frac{1}{4} \times 32$ **47.** 0.25×3.2 **48.** $\frac{1}{4} \times 3.2$

49. Multiplying a number by 0.25 is the same as multiplying the number by the fraction __?__ .

50. 0.2×1500 **51.** 0.2×150 **52.** 0.2×15 **53.** 0.2×1.5

54. 0.2×2000 **55.** 0.2×200 **56.** 0.2×20 **57.** 0.2×2

58. Multiplying a number by 0.2 is the same as multiplying the number by the fraction __?__ .

Divide by 10, 100, and 1000

Materials: paper, pencil

Copy and complete the given table. Look for patterns for dividing decimals by 10, 100, or 1000 mentally.

	n	$n \div 10$	$n \div 100$	$n \div 1000$
1.	198	19.8	1.98	0.198
2.	64	?	?	0.064
3.	7	?	?	0.007

Compare the position of the decimal point in n with the position of the decimal point in $n \div 10$, $n \div 100$, and $n \div 1000$.

4. What patterns do you notice in your complete table? What happens to the decimal point when you divide a decimal by 10? by 100? by 1000?

5. Examine the quotients in exercises 2–3. What happens when there are not enough places to move the decimal point as far to the left as needed?

Use the patterns to find the quotients mentally.

6. $4321 \div 10$
   $4321 \div 100$
   $4321 \div 1000$

7. $765 \div 10$
   $765 \div 100$
   $765 \div 1000$

8. $81 \div 10$
   $81 \div 100$
   $81 \div 1000$

9. $6 \div 10$
   $6 \div 100$
   $6 \div 1000$

   Multiply to check your quotients.

10. Write a rule that you can use to divide a decimal by 10, 100, and 1000.

Use your rule to find the quotient mentally. Check by multiplying.

11. $0.06 \div 10$

12. $9 \div 10$

13. $0.7 \div 10$

14. $32 \div 10$

15. $32 \div 100$

16. $1.7 \div 100$

17. $9 \div 100$

18. $2719.5 \div 100$

19. $4 \div 1000$

20. $5384 \div 1000$

21. $39 \div 1000$

22. $16,483 \div 1000$

23. $68.3 \div 10$

24. $86.3 \div 100$

25. $456 \div 1000$

26. $57.35 \div 10$

Now use your rule to find if the divisor is 10, 100, or 1000.
Check by multiplying.

27. $2.08 \div n = 0.208$

28. $1.8 \div n = 0.018$

29. $59 \div n = 0.059$

30. $27.9 \div n = 0.279$

31. $865 \div n = 0.865$

32. $41.02 \div n = 4.102$

Communicate

33. Describe in your Math Journal the pattern formed by the number of zeros in 10, 100, and 1000 and the number of places the decimal point "moves" when you divide by these numbers.

34. When you divide a decimal by 10, 100, and 1000, why does the decimal point move to the left rather than to the right?

35. How is dividing a decimal by 10, 100, and 1000 the same as multiplying a decimal by 10, 100, and 1000? How is it different?

36. When and why do you need to write zeros in the quotient when dividing a decimal by 10, 100, and 1000?

37. Find the missing numbers. Explain your answers.

a. $n \div 100 = 0.021$

b. $n \div 10 = 0.35$

c. $n \div 1000 = 0.024$

d. $n \div 10 = 0.09$

e. $n \div 1000 = 2.006$

f. $n \div 100 = 0.012$

MENTAL MATH

Write the output number. Follow the steps for each machine.

Input ⟩— ÷10 —÷100 — Output ⟩

38. 8591   **39.** 578   **40.** 69

Input ⟩— ÷100 —×1000— Output ⟩

41. 53.6   **42.** 6.2   **43.** 0.032

Input ⟩— ×100 —÷1000— Output ⟩

44. 354.9   **45.** 63.7   **46.** 9.5

Input ⟩— ×100 — ×10 — Output ⟩

47. 23.595   **48.** 4.13   **49.** 1.8

Divide Decimals by Whole Numbers

Liam has 1.62 m of copper tubing that he cuts into 3 equal pieces. How long is each piece?

To find how long, divide: $1.62 \div 3 = n$.

▶ You can use a model to help you divide $1.62 \div 3$.

• Shade 1.62 on 10 × 10 grids.

• Cut the shaded grids apart as necessary to show 3 equal groups.

$1.62 \div 3 = 0.54$

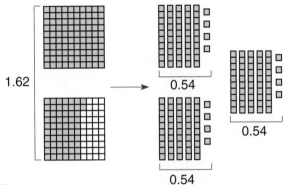

1.62   0.54

0.54

0.54

▶ To **divide** a *decimal* by a *whole number*:

Write the decimal point of the quotient above the decimal point of the dividend.	Divide as you would with whole numbers.

Check.

$$3\overline{)1.6\ 2}$$

$$\begin{array}{r} 0.5\ 4 \\ 3\overline{)1.6\ 2} \\ -1\ 5 \\ \hline 1\ 2 \\ -1\ 2 \\ \hline 0 \end{array}$$

3 > 1 **Not enough** ones
3 < 16 **Enough** tenths
The quotient begins in the tenths place.

2 decimal places

$$\begin{array}{r} 0.5\ 4 \\ \times\ 3 \\ \hline 1.6\ 2 \end{array}$$

2 decimal places

Each piece of copper tubing is 0.54 m long.

Study these examples.

$$\begin{array}{r} 1.1 \\ 8\overline{)8.8} \\ -8 \\ \hline 0\ 8 \\ -8 \\ \hline 0 \end{array}$$

$$\begin{array}{r} 0.5\ 5\ 5 \\ 5\overline{)2.7\ 7\ 5} \\ -2\ 5 \\ \hline 2\ 7 \\ -2\ 5 \\ \hline 2\ 5 \\ -2\ 5 \\ \hline 0 \end{array}$$

$$\begin{array}{r} \$0.2\ 4 \\ 4\overline{)\$0.9\ 6} \\ -8 \\ \hline 1\ 6 \\ -1\ 6 \\ \hline 0 \end{array}$$

Write the dollar sign and decimal point in the quotient.

Use the diagram to complete each statement.

1.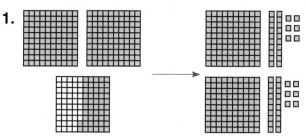

2.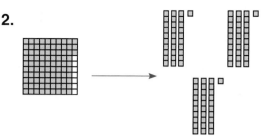

$\underline{\quad?\quad} \div 2 = \underline{\quad?\quad}$

$0.93 \div \underline{\quad?\quad} = \underline{\quad?\quad}$

Divide and check.

3. $8\overline{)5.6}$ 4. $9\overline{)5.4}$ 5. $6\overline{)0.96}$ 6. $5\overline{)0.75}$ 7. $4\overline{)0.76}$

8. $4\overline{)0.924}$ 9. $9\overline{)2.214}$ 10. $4\overline{)25.72}$ 11. $3\overline{)\$0.84}$ 12. $6\overline{)\$55.56}$

13. $76.8 \div 8$ 14. $9.513 \div 7$ 15. $\$364.50 \div 5$ 16. $\$346.32 \div 9$

Find the quotient.

17. $n \div 5$ when $n = 2.5$

18. $n \div 3$ when $n = 0.63$

19. $0.861 \div n$ when $n = 7$

20. $41.36 \div n$ when $n = 8$

Compare. Write <, =, or >.

21. $1.2 \div 3 \underline{\quad?\quad} 0.84 \div 2$

22. $31.92 \div 4 \underline{\quad?\quad} 23.55 \div 5$

23. $0.8 \div 2 \underline{\quad?\quad} \frac{4}{5} \div 2$

24. $2.4 \div 6 \underline{\quad?\quad} \frac{3}{4} \div 3$

Problem Solving

25. A large bag holds 24.9 lb. This is 3 times the weight a small bag holds. How much does a small bag hold?

26. Mr. Lee drove 232.5 km in 5 days. If he drove the same distance each day, what distance did he drive in one day?

CHALLENGE — Algebra

Use a number line to complete each division sentence.

27. $2 \div 0.4 = n$

28. $6 \div 0.5 = n$ 29. $4 \div 0.8 = n$ 30. $7 \div 0.2 = n$

31. $4.5 \div 0.3 = n$ 32. $3.6 \div 0.9 = n$ 33. $4.2 \div 0.7 = n$

Zeros in Division

▶ Sometimes you must write zeros in the *quotient* to show correct place value.

Divide: $0.637 \div 7 = n$.

Write the decimal point in the quotient.

$$7\overline{)0.6\ 3\ 7}$$

Divide.

$$7\overline{)0.0\ 9\ 1}$$

7 > 6 **Not enough** tenths
Write 0 in the tenths place.
7 < 63 **Enough** hundredths
The quotient begins in the
hundredths place.

Check.	$7 \times 0.091 = 0.637$

▶ Sometimes you must write zeros in the *dividend* to complete the division.

Divide: $3.6 \div 8 = n$.

Write the decimal point in the quotient. Divide until you have a remainder.

$$8\overline{)3.6\ ^4}$$
    0.4

8 > 3 **Not enough** ones
8 < 36 **Enough** tenths
The quotient begins
in the tenths place.

Write zeros as needed in the dividend to complete the division.

$$8\overline{)3.6\ ^40}$$
    0.4 5

$3.6 = 3.60$

Check.	$8 \times 0.45 = 3.60$

Study these examples.

$$6\overline{)6.3\ ^36}$$
  1.0 6

Not enough tenths
Write 0 in the
tenths place.

$$4\overline{)\$5.^10\ ^20}$$
  \$ 1. 2 5

Write zeros as needed
in the dividend to
complete the division.

Divide and check.

1. $2\overline{)0.014}$ 2. $9\overline{)27.81}$ 3. $6\overline{)0.63}$ 4. $6\overline{)6.15}$ 5. $5\overline{)7.51}$

6. $4\overline{)0.424}$ 7. $9\overline{)2.745}$ 8. $7\overline{)21.364}$ 9. $8\overline{)\$16.72}$ 10. $5\overline{)\$28}$

11. $16.2 \div 4$ 12. $18.87 \div 6$ 13. $33.32 \div 8$ 14. $25.848 \div 6$

Find the quotient.

15. $n \div 6$ when $n = 18.156$

16. $n \div 9$ when $n = 81.54$

17. $0.44 \div n$ when $n = 8$

18. $13 \div n$ when $n = 4$

More Zeros in the Dividend

For some divisions, writing zeros in the dividend does *not* complete the division. The quotient is a repeating decimal and is rounded to a given place.

Divide: $4.4 \div 6 = n$.

$$\begin{array}{r} 0.7\ 3\ 3\ 3\ \ldots = 0.733 \\ 6\overline{)4.4\ ^2 0\ ^2 0\ ^2 0\ ^2} \end{array}$$

rounded to the nearest thousandth

Divide: $3.56 \div 7 = n$.

$$\begin{array}{r} 0.5\ 0\ 8\ 5\ \ldots = 0.509 \\ 7\overline{)3.5\ 6\ ^6 0\ ^4 0\ ^5} \end{array}$$

rounded to the nearest thousandth

Divide. Round the quotient to the nearest thousandth.

19. $3\overline{)2.9}$ 20. $7\overline{)1.5}$ 21. $6\overline{)3.8}$ 22. $9\overline{)1.83}$ 23. $3\overline{)9.34}$

24. $6\overline{)0.64}$ 25. $9\overline{)0.83}$ 26. $3\overline{)0.95}$ 27. $7\overline{)0.85}$ 28. $6\overline{)0.59}$

Problem Solving

29. Ed rode 4 laps on his bike in 9.46 min. What was his average time for each lap?

30. Liz bought 9 identical key chains for $27.72. How much did each key chain cost?

DO YOU REMEMBER?

A set of data is ordered from least to greatest. Use the words in the box to complete each sentence.

| median | mode |
| mean | range |

31. The _?_ is the number that occurs most often.

32. The _?_ is the difference between the greatest and the least number.

Estimate Decimal Quotients

On a bicycle trip, Marc plans to travel 226.85 km in 7 days. About how many kilometers a day will he travel if he travels the same distance each day?

To find about how many kilometers, estimate: 226.85 ÷ 7

▶ To **estimate** a *decimal quotient*:

- Write the decimal point in the quotient.

- Decide in which place the first nonzero digit of the quotient begins.

- Find the *first* nonzero digit of the quotient.

- Write zeros for the remaining digits.

$$\begin{array}{r} 3\ 0.0\ 0 \\ 7)\overline{2\ 2\ 6.8\ 5} \end{array}$$

> 7 > 2 **Not enough** hundreds
> 7 < 22 **Enough** tens
> The quotient begins in the tens place.
> About how many 7s in 22? 3

Marc will travel about 30 km a day.

Study these examples.

$$\begin{array}{r} 0.4\ 0\ 0 \\ 8)\overline{3.2\ 4\ 8} \end{array}$$

> 8 > 3 **Not enough** ones
> 8 < 32 **Enough** tenths
> About how many 8s in 32? 4

The quotient is close to 0.4.

$$\begin{array}{r} 0.0\ 5\ 0 \\ 6)\overline{0.3\ 1\ 4} \end{array}$$

> 6 > 3 **Not enough** tenths
> 6 < 31 **Enough** hundredths
> About how many 6s in 31? 5

The quotient is greater than 0.05.

Practice

Estimate the quotient.

1. 6)0.234
2. 7)0.244
3. 8)0.746
4. 3)0.997
5. 4)0.872

6. 7)6.566
7. 6)2.472
8. 3)2.976
9. 8)3.295
10. 5)3.315

11. 3)29.506
12. 9)36.279
13. 4)12.688
14. 5)39.719
15. 9)47.821

16. 7)36.494
17. 6)23.523
18. 8)38.344
19. 4)312.123
20. 9)286.391

Estimate the quotient.

21. $0.874 \div 5$　　**22.** $0.855 \div 3$　　**23.** $5.364 \div 4$　　**24.** $9.088 \div 9$

25. $47.372 \div 9$　　**26.** $23.018 \div 4$　　**27.** $58.761 \div 8$　　**28.** $38.554 \div 6$

Using Compatible Numbers

To **estimate decimal quotients** using *compatible numbers*:

• Think of nearby numbers that are compatible.

• Divide.

Estimate: $8.316 \div 9$.　

Think
9 and 81 are compatible numbers.

Estimate: $1.684 \div 42$.　

Think
40 and 160 are compatible numbers.

$$9\overline{)8.3\ 1\ 6} \rightarrow 9\overline{)8.1\ 0}^{\,0.9}$$

$$42\overline{)1.6\ 8\ 4} \rightarrow 40\overline{)1\ 6\ 0}^{\,4\ \text{hundredths}}\ \text{hundredths}$$

The quotient is about 0.9.　　　The quotient is about 0.04.

Estimate the quotient. Use compatible numbers.

29. $4\overline{)2.302}$　　**30.** $9\overline{)1.935}$　　**31.** $7\overline{)4.351}$　　**32.** $8\overline{)4.253}$　　**33.** $6\overline{)3.756}$

34. $5\overline{)34.057}$　　**35.** $7\overline{)29.361}$　　**36.** $3\overline{)28.536}$　　**37.** $8\overline{)63.016}$　　**38.** $9\overline{)71.789}$

39. $1.339 \div 31$　　**40.** $2.654 \div 53$　　**41.** $3.128 \div 62$　　**42.** $2.095 \div 38$

43. $62.158 \div 28$　　**44.** $36.751 \div 61$　　**45.** $461.651 \div 53$　　**46.** $105.995 \div 19$

Problem Solving

47. Alan rode his bicycle 34.325 km in 5 hours. If he rode an equal distance each hour, about how many kilometers did he ride in one hour?

48. Beth can run 5.985 km in 21 minutes. About how many kilometers can she run in one minute?

Write Your Own

49. Write in your Math Journal at least three situations in which making an estimate is more useful or efficient than finding an exact answer.

Estimate with Money

MELONS

Four melons cost $3.39. About how much is the melon's unit price?

To find about how much the unit price (cost of one item) is, estimate: $3.39 ÷ 4.

▶ You can **estimate quotients** involving *money* by using *compatible numbers*.

$$4\overline{)\$3.39} \longrightarrow \begin{array}{r} \$\,0.8\;0 \\ 4\overline{)\$\,3.2\;0} \end{array}$$

.Think.........
4 and 32 are compatible numbers.

Since $3.20 < $3.39 the exact quotient must be greater than $0.80.

The unit price is about $0.80.

▶ Sometimes you use different sets of compatible numbers to estimate a quotient involving money.

Estimate: $2.87 ÷ 5

$$5\overline{)\$2.87}\begin{cases} \begin{array}{r} \$\,0.5\;0 \\ 5\overline{)\$\,2.5\;0} \end{array} \\ \begin{array}{r} \$\,0.6\;0 \\ 5\overline{)\$\,3.0\;0} \end{array} \end{cases}$$

The exact quotient is between $0.50 and $0.60.

Estimate: $29.85 ÷ 32

$$32\overline{)\$29.85}\begin{cases} \begin{array}{r} \$\;\;0.9\;0 \\ 3\,0\overline{)\$\,2\,7.0\;0} \end{array} \\ \begin{array}{r} \$\;\;1.0\;0 \\ 3\,0\overline{)\$\,3\,0.0\;0} \end{array} \end{cases}$$

The exact quotient is between $0.90 and $1.00.

Practice

Estimate the unit price.

	Item	Total Cost	Estimated Unit Price
1.	6 bottles of apple juice	$ 2.49	?
2.	9 tomatoes	$ 3.45	?
3.	4 quarts of milk	$ 3.38	?
4.	12 mugs	$59.76	?
5.	23 oranges	$12.96	?

Write what compatible numbers you would use.
Then estimate the quotient.

6. 3)$1.06   **7.** 5)$9.32   **8.** 9)$8.25   **9.** 7)$34.95   **10.** 6)$13.79

11. 62)$29.14   **12.** 54)$37.84   **13.** 92)$82.88   **14.** 31)$59.96   **15.** 28)$56.65

16. $149.50 ÷ 15   **17.** $231.25 ÷ 42   **18.** $412.18 ÷ 83   **19.** $186.62 ÷ 31

Rounding to the Nearest Cent

Four mugs cost $9.89. How much does one mug cost?
Round the amount to the nearest cent.

To find how much, divide: $9.89 ÷ 4 = *n*.

> Write the decimal point
> in the quotient. Divide.

$$\begin{array}{r} \$\,2.\,4\;7\;2 \\ 4\overline{)\,\$\,9.^18\;^29\;^10} \end{array}$$

> Add a zero in
> the dividend.
> $9.89 = $9.890

> Round the quotient
> to the nearest cent.

$$\begin{array}{r} \$\,2.\,4\;7\;2 \\ 4\overline{)\,\$\,9.^18\;^29\;^10} \end{array} = \$2.47$$

> 2 < 5
> Round **down**
> to $2.47.

One mug costs about $2.47.

Divide. Round the quotient to the nearest cent.

20. 8)$1.24   **21.** 5)$3.78   **22.** 2)$1.11   **23.** 3)$5.29   **24.** 6)$8.20

25. 6)$33.32   **26.** 4)$22.61   **27.** 5)$26.12   **28.** 9)$51.09   **29.** 7)$28.46

Problem Solving

30. Ruby earns $52.50 in 6 hours. About how much does she earn in one hour?

31. A set of 35 identical books costs $236.25. About how much does one book cost?

CHALLENGE

32. A monthly pass for a commuter train costs $84. A single ticket costs $2.75. Rose rides the train an average of 44 times a month. About how much does she save per ride if she buys a monthly pass instead of single tickets?

Problem-Solving Strategy:
Write a Number Sentence

On their field trip to the circus, the 30 students in Ms. Dalton's class plan to buy 15 bags of peanuts to share.

Each bag of peanuts at the circus holds 0.9 kg. How much is needed to fill 15 bags?

Read ▶ **Visualize yourself in the problem above as you reread it. List the facts and the question.**

Facts: Each bag holds 0.9 kg of peanuts.
There are 15 bags.

Question: How much is needed to fill 15 bags?

Plan ▶ Write and label a number sentence using the given information. Use a diagram to help.

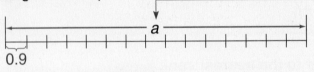

a

0.9

Number of bags	times	Amount in each	equals	Amount of peanuts needed for 15 bags
15	×	0.9 kg	=	a ◀

Let a represent the unknown amount of peanuts.

Solve ▶ $15 \times 0.9 \text{ kg} = a$
$15 \times 0.9 \text{ kg} = 13.5 \text{ kg}$

The amount 13.5 kg is needed to fill 15 bags.

Check ▶ Change the order of the factors and then multiply to check your computations.

Write a number sentence to solve each problem.

1. A bicyclist travels 36.3 miles in 2 hours.
   What is her rate of speed in miles per hour?

> Rate of speed is distance traveled per unit of time.

Read ▶ Visualize yourself in the problem above as you reread it. Focus on the facts and the question.

List what you know.

Facts: distance—36.3 miles
time—2 hours

Question: How many miles per hour did the bicyclist travel?

$$\overset{\longleftarrow\ 36.3\ \longrightarrow}{\underset{r}{\rule{0pt}{0pt}}}$$

Plan ▶ Write a word sentence for the problem, then write a number sentence. Let r represent rate. Divide to find the missing factor.

> **Think**
> Write the related division sentence.

Distance equals rate of speed times time.
36.3 mi   = r mph   ×   2 h

Solve ▶ ········▶ **Check** ▶

2. Devon lives 8.25 km from the river. In the morning he walks 5.7 km toward the river. How much farther does he need to walk to reach the river?

3. The length of a river is 27.6 mi. Joan kayaked half the length of the river. How many miles did Joan kayak?

4. A swimmer took 2.75 h to swim upstream and 1.8 h to swim downstream. How long did it take the swimmer to cover the entire distance?

5. A set of 32 new fifth-grade math books costs $468.96. About how much does each math book cost?

6. Ninety books weigh 720.9 lb. What is the weight of one book if they all weigh the same amount?

7. Mr. Brophy traveled 232.5 km in 5 days. If he traveled the same distance each day, what was the distance he traveled in one day?

Solve and explain the method you used.

1. In a science experiment one lens is positioned 0.25 m from a light source, and a second lens is positioned ten times farther away. How far is the second lens from the light source?

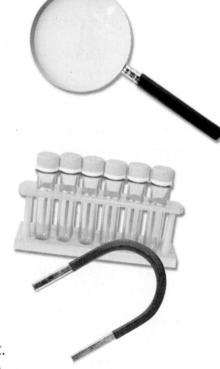

2. Adam discovers that the first lens has a focal length of 1.4 m. The second lens has a focal length 3 times greater. What is the focal length of the second lens?

3. The radius of Sara's lens is 0.235 dm. What is the diameter of her lens?

4. Carlotta divides 0.09 L of bleach equally among 3 beakers. How much bleach is in each beaker?

5. A set of 8 magnets costs $19.84. How much does each magnet cost?

6. The largest magnet is 4 times the size of the smallest. The largest magnet is 31.48 cm long. How long is the smallest magnet?

7. In each of four experiments Marta uses 23.2 mL, 20.8 mL, 17.3 mL, and 19.7 mL of distilled water. About how many milliliters does she use in all?

8. It took Adam 100.3 s to light a candle using a small lens. It took one half as long using a large lens. How long did it take to light a candle using a large lens?

9. The tone of a large tuning fork lasts for 125.75 s. The tone of a small tuning fork lasts two tenths of this time. How long does the tone of the small fork last?

10. A solution's temperature increased 11.3°C in 5 minutes. What was the average temperature increase per minute?

Choose a strategy from the list or use another strategy you know to solve each problem.

11. For their experiments, Ty, Ann, and Bob each paid a different amount for a battery: $1.49, $0.99, and $2.59. Ty did not pay the least and Ann spent over $1.75. Who bought which battery?

Strategy File

Use These Strategies
Write a Number Sentence
Use More Than One Step
Logical Reasoning
Use a Model/Diagram

12. Jill worked on her physics project 0.5 h each day for one week and 1 h each day the next week. How many hours did Jill work on her project?

13. Each magnet can lift 0.542 kg. Can fourteen magnets together lift a 6.5-kg metal box? How do you know?

14. Each magnet has a mass of 95.5 g. Kim uses 9 magnets to lift a 4.5-kg box. What is the total mass of the magnets and the box?

15. A tank holds 0.38 cubic meters. Vicki fills 0.1 of the tank with gravel. How many cubic meters of water does she need to fill the tank?

16. A heat lamp shines on Joni's plants four days a week for 3 h a day. Three days a week, it shines for 3.5 h each day. An incandescent bulb shines on the plants for twice as long as the heat lamp every day. How long is the incandescent bulb on in one full week?

17. Each of these test tubes can hold 0.015 L. Mr. Henry pours out half of the water in test tube *B*. How much water is left in test tube *B*?

18. Ms. Cooper fills the rest of test tube *A* with an acid. How much acid does she use?

19. Mr. Henry uses 0.3 of the water from test tube *C*. Now can he add 0.006 L of bleach to test tube *C*?

0.009 L 0.004 L 0.01 L

A **B** **C**

Write Your Own

20. Write a problem that involves multiplication or division of decimals using one or more strategies from the list above. Then have a classmate solve it.

Find the value of *n*. Use the rules for multiplying or dividing (See pp. 294–295, 304–305.)
by 10, 100, or 1000.

1. $n \times 6.1 = 61$

2. $n \times 42.3 = 4230$

3. $n \times 6.23 = 6230$

4. $43.7 \div n = 4.37$

5. $2.7 \div n = 0.027$

6. $25 \div n = 0.025$

7. $10 \times n = 14.3$

8. $1000 \times n = 593$

9. $100 \times n = 74.6$

10. $n \div 10 = 7.914$

11. $n \div 100 = 4.567$

12. $n \div 1000 = 0.009$

Estimate each product by rounding. Then tell whether the actual (See pp. 296–297.)
product *is greater than* or *is less than* the estimated product.

13.
$$\begin{array}{r} 3.396 \\ \times\ \ \ 7.4 \\ \hline \end{array}$$

14.
$$\begin{array}{r} 14.87 \\ \times\ \ 0.73 \\ \hline \end{array}$$

15.
$$\begin{array}{r} 8.147 \\ \times\ \ \ 6.3 \\ \hline \end{array}$$

16.
$$\begin{array}{r} 25.423 \\ \times\ \ \ \ 0.58 \\ \hline \end{array}$$

Use a 10 × 10 grid to find the product or quotient. (See pp. 300–301, 306–307.)

17. 0.4×0.6

18. 0.9×0.5

19. $1.98 \div 2$

20. $0.87 \div 3$

Multiply. (See pp. 298–303.)

21. 6×0.43

22. 3.8×0.6

23. 0.64×0.4

24. 7×1.4

25. 0.18×0.4

26. 4.3×0.2

Divide and check. (See pp. 306–309.)

27. $0.546 \div 2$

28. $0.4 \div 8$

29. $6.4 \div 4$

30. $7.56 \div 3$

31. $9.5 \div 5$

32. $0.49 \div 7$

Estimate the quotient. Use compatible numbers. (See pp. 310–313.)

33. $8\overline{)1.754}$

34. $6\overline{)4.159}$

35. $7\overline{)29.543}$

36. $21\overline{)43.359}$

37. $9\overline{)\$28.53}$

38. $4\overline{)\$37.34}$

39. $3\overline{)\$19.97}$

40. $43\overline{)\$89.15}$

Problem Solving
(See pp. 300–301, 312–317.)

41. A community newspaper reports the average monthly rainfall for each season. Recorded rainfall for the summer months was 8.81 in., 7 in., and 9.2 in. To the nearest hundredth, what was the average monthly rainfall for the season?

42. Nine part-time workers earned $463.15. About how much was each worker paid if the money was divided equally?

(See *Still More Practice*, p. 485.)

Fractions to Decimals

Every fraction is *equivalent to* or can be *renamed as* a decimal.

$\dfrac{a}{b}$ ◄——The **fraction bar** means *division*.

To rename a fraction as a decimal:

► Find an equivalent fraction whose denominator is a power of 10, since a decimal is a fraction with a denominator that is a power of 10.

Powers of 10 are: 1, 10, 100, 1000, . . .

$$\dfrac{1}{2} = \dfrac{1 \times 5}{2 \times 5} = \dfrac{5}{10} = 0.5 \qquad \dfrac{3}{4} = \dfrac{3 \times 25}{4 \times 25} = \dfrac{75}{100} = 0.75$$

power of 10

or

► Divide the numerator by the denominator since a fraction $\dfrac{a}{b} = a \div b$.

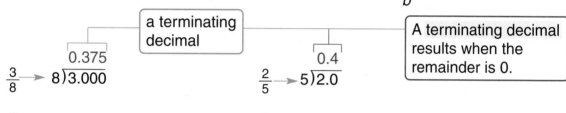

a terminating decimal

A terminating decimal results when the remainder is 0.

$$\dfrac{3}{8} \to 8\overline{)3.000} \quad 0.375 \qquad \dfrac{2}{5} \to 5\overline{)2.0} \quad 0.4$$

$$\dfrac{3}{8} = 0.375 \qquad\qquad \dfrac{2}{5} = 0.4$$

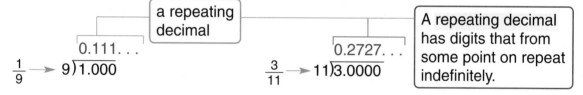

a repeating decimal

A repeating decimal has digits that from some point on repeat indefinitely.

$$\dfrac{1}{9} \to 9\overline{)1.000} \quad 0.111\ldots \qquad \dfrac{3}{11} \to 11\overline{)3.0000} \quad 0.2727\ldots$$

$$\dfrac{1}{9} = 0.111\ldots = 0.\overline{1} \qquad\qquad \dfrac{3}{11} = 0.2727\ldots = 0.\overline{27}$$

Write a bar over the digit or digits that repeat.

Rename each fraction as a decimal. Use a power of 10.

1. $\dfrac{1}{4}$ **2.** $\dfrac{1}{5}$ **3.** $\dfrac{1}{8}$ **4.** $\dfrac{7}{20}$ **5.** $\dfrac{6}{25}$ **6.** $\dfrac{49}{50}$

Rename each fraction as a repeating or terminating decimal.

7. $\dfrac{5}{8}$ **8.** $\dfrac{4}{5}$ **9.** $\dfrac{2}{3}$ **10.** $\dfrac{5}{6}$ **11.** $\dfrac{2}{15}$ **12.** $\dfrac{7}{40}$

Chapter 9 Test

Estimate each product by rounding. Then tell whether the actual product *is greater than* or *is less than* the estimated product.

1.	5.65	2.	8.436	3.	18.76	4.	26.877
	× 3.4		× 7.6		× 0.44		× 0.47

Use a 10 × 10 grid to find the product or quotient.

5. 0.8 × 0.7   **6.** 0.2 × 0.9   **7.** 2.42 ÷ 2   **8.** 3.16 ÷ 4

Find the product or quotient.

9. $n × 0.3$ when $n = 0.72$ **10.** $n × 0.85$ when $n = 9.6$

11. $8 × n$ when $n = 0.43$ **12.** $0.07 × n$ when $n = 0.6$

13. $n ÷ 6$ when $n = 0.24$ **14.** $n ÷ 5$ when $n = 4.12$

15. $0.63 ÷ n$ when $n = 7$ **16.** $1.908 ÷ n$ when $n = 3$

Estimate the quotient. Use compatible numbers.

17. $6\overline{)29.457}$ **18.** $8\overline{)41.053}$ **19.** $72\overline{)139.125}$ **20.** $54\overline{)\$295.72}$

Problem Solving

Use a strategy you have learned.

21. Sarah has 10 m of cloth. An elephant pillow requires 2 m of cloth and a bear pillow requires 0.95 m. If Sarah makes 4 bear pillows, how many elephant pillows can she make with the remaining cloth?

Tell About It

Explain how you solved the problem. Show all your work.

22. A team's finishing time in a 100-km marathon was 639.3 min. The team finished the last kilometer in 5.73 min. How much longer is the team's average time than the team's time in the last kilometer?

Performance Assessment

Write the missing output and write a rule for each table.

23.

Input	7.8	0.13	0.6
Output	0.78	0.013	?

24.

Input	0.065	1.03	0.008
Output	6.5	103	?

Make up an input-output table for each rule.

25. rule: × 1000   **26.** rule: ÷ 100

Test Preparation

Choose the best answer.

1. In the number 12,345,678,000, which digit is in the billions place?

   a. 1   **b.** 2
   c. 3   **d.** 5

2. Which number is divisible by 3 and by 6 but not divisible by 9?

   a. 20,007   **b.** 72,000
   c. 72,111   **d.** 73,110

3. How much greater than

   $8\frac{1}{3} - 6\frac{1}{4}$ is

   $8\frac{1}{3} + 6\frac{1}{4}$?

   a. 12   **b.** $12\frac{1}{12}$

   c. $12\frac{5}{24}$ **d.** $12\frac{1}{2}$

4. Use the data. Which is greatest: range, mean, median, mode?

School Enrollment				
Grade	3	4	5	6
Number of Students	83	79	87	79

   a. range   **b.** mean
   c. median   **d.** mode

5. Estimate by rounding.

   $31.09 + 7.86$

   a. 11.5
   b. 23.9
   c. 39
   d. 45

6. 8.1×7.56

   a. 61.236
   b. 68.04
   c. 612.36
   d. not given

7. $406 \times \$17.98$

   a. $827.08   **b.** $7299.88
   c. $7479.68   **d.** not given

8. Which is the least common denominator of

   $\frac{3}{5}, \frac{1}{2}, \frac{5}{6}$?

   a. 18   **b.** 30
   c. 60   **d.** 16

9. $2\frac{2}{5} \div 1\frac{1}{7}$

   a. $1\frac{2}{35}$ **b.** $2\frac{1}{10}$

   c. $2\frac{26}{35}$ **d.** $1\frac{1}{10}$

10. The circle graph shows the distribution of an investment of $4800 among four different stocks. In which stock is the investment closest in value to $1200?

    a. stock A
    b. stock B
    c. stock C
    d. stock D

11. $45.8 - 4.294$

    a. 0.286
    b. 41.606
    c. 41.694
    d. 41.506

12. $3.612 \div 4$

    a. 0.903
    b. 0.93
    c. 9.03
    d. 9.3

13. What is the prime factorization of 88?

    a. $2^4 \times 11$
    b. $2^3 \times 11$
    c. $2^2 \times 11$
    d. $2 \times 4 \times 11$

14. $2834 \div 1000 = n$

    a. 2.834
    b. 28.34
    c. 283.4
    d. 283,400

15. What number is twenty-eight and one hundred two thousandths?

    a. 28.012
    b. 28.102
    c. 28,120
    d. not given

16. $4\frac{2}{5} \times 7\frac{1}{8}$

    a. $\frac{176}{285}$ **b.** $28\frac{1}{20}$

    c. $31\frac{7}{20}$ **d.** not given

17. Clara bought 7 sweaters at $15.50 each and sold them for $5 more each. Find the amount she charged for all the sweaters.

    a. $73.50   **b.** $108.50
    c. $143.50   **d.** not given

18. A scale model train is 14.2 cm long. Each centimeter represents 87 m on the actual train. How long is the actual train?

    a. 6674 m   **b.** 667.4 m
    c. 66.74 m   **d.** not given

19. Estimate by rounding.

54×287

    a. 18,000
    b. 15,000
    c. 10,000
    d. 1,000

20. Estimate. Use compatible numbers.

$324\overline{)9573}$

    a. 3
    b. 30
    c. 300
    d. 3000

21. What is the value of the 3 in 731,078,650?

    a. 300,000,000
    b. 30,000,000
    c. 3,000,000
    d. 300,000

22. Order $\frac{2}{3}, \frac{3}{7}, \frac{7}{19}$ from least to greatest.

    a. $\frac{7}{19}, \frac{3}{7}, \frac{2}{3}$ **b.** $\frac{3}{7}, \frac{2}{3}, \frac{7}{19}$

    c. $\frac{3}{7}, \frac{7}{19}, \frac{2}{3}$ **d.** not given

23. Mr. Ramos rented a store for 2 years for $13,380 per year. How much was his monthly rent?

    a. $1115   **b.** $13,380
    c. $26,760   **d.** not given

24. Bill caught three catfish and one trout. Two of the catfish were 19 in. long. The other was 16.9 in. long and the trout was 17.2 in. long. What was the average length of the catfish?

    a. 16.2 in.   **b.** 17.6 in.
    c. 18.3 in.   **d.** not given

Explain how you solved the problem. Show all your work.

25. Luz multiplied a number by 3 and then divided the result by 5. The answer was 0.36. Find Luz's original number.

Geometry

One day, the triangle began to feel dissatisfied. "I'm tired of doing the same old things," it grumbled. "There must be more to life." So the triangle went to see the local shapeshifter.

"How may I help you?" the shapeshifter asked the triangle.

"I think if I had just one more side and one more angle," said the triangle, "my life would be more interesting."

"That's easy to do," said the shapeshifter.

From *The Greedy Triangle* by *Marilyn Burns*

In this chapter you will:

Classify angles and polygons
Explore congruence, similarity, symmetry, transformations, and tessellations
Use perimeter and circumference formulas
Solve problems using formulas

Critical Thinking/Finding Together

Six equilateral triangles are placed together to form a hexagon. If the perimeter of each equilateral triangle is 20 cm, what is the perimeter of the hexagon?

10-1

Measure and Draw Angles

An angle is formed by two rays with a common endpoint. The rays are the **sides** of the angle. The common endpoint is the **vertex** (plural: vertices) of the angle. The **interior** and **exterior** of the angle are also shown.

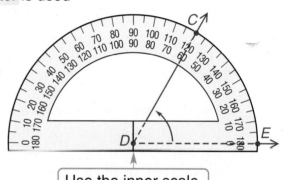

sides: $\overrightarrow{DC}$, $\overrightarrow{DE}$ **name:** $\angle D$ or $\angle CDE$ or $\angle EDC$
vertex: D

Point X is in the **interior** of $\angle CDE$.
Point Y is in the **exterior** of $\angle CDE$.

Angles are measured in **degrees** (°). A protractor is used to measure or draw an angle.

▶ **To measure ∠CDE:**

- Place the protractor so that its *base* rests along $\overrightarrow{DE}$ and its *center mark* is at D.

- Find the "0" on the scale where $\overrightarrow{DE}$ crosses the protractor.

- Follow along the scale to the point where $\overrightarrow{DC}$ crosses the protractor. The number of degrees at that point is the measure of $\angle CDE$. $\angle CDE$ measures 60°.

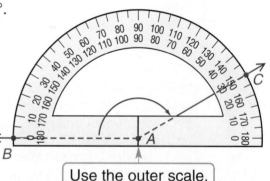

Use the inner scale.

▶ **To draw an ∠ABC that measures 150°:**

- Draw a ray, $\overrightarrow{AB}$.

- Place the center mark of the protractor on A so that the 0° mark is along $\overrightarrow{AB}$.

- Follow along the scale to the 150° mark and mark point C.

- Draw $\overrightarrow{AC}$. $\angle CAB = 150°$.

Use the outer scale.

Name the sides and the vertex of each angle and tell whether point X is in the *interior* or *exterior* of the angle.

1.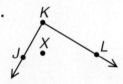

2.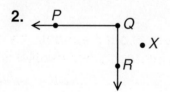

3.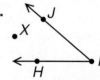

Name the angle. Then use a protractor to find the measure.

4.
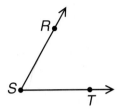

5.
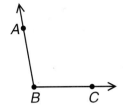

6.
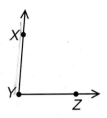

7.

8.
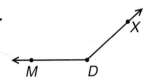

9.

Use a protractor to draw each angle.

10. 30° **11.** 45° **12.** 90° **13.** 110° **14.** 135° **15.** 170°

Estimate the measure of each angle. Then use a protractor to find the exact measure.

16.
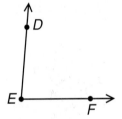

17.
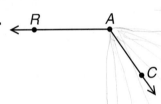

18.
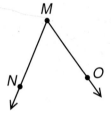

CRITICAL THINKING

Use a protractor to find the measure of each angle.

In the figure, $\overleftrightarrow{DC}$ and $\overleftrightarrow{FG}$ are parallel. $\overleftrightarrow{DC}$ intersects $\overleftrightarrow{AE}$ at point B. $\overleftrightarrow{FG}$ intersects $\overleftrightarrow{AE}$ at point E.

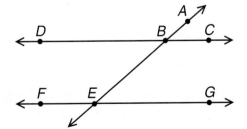

19. ∠DBA **20.** ∠ABC **21.** ∠DBE

22. ∠FEB **23.** ∠BEG **24.** ∠EBC

25. What do your results suggest about the measures of angles formed when a line intersects two parallel lines?

Identify Angles

▶ Angles are classified by their measures.

A right angle is an angle that has a measure of *exactly* 90°.

An acute angle is an angle that has a measure *less than* 90°.

An obtuse angle is an angle that has a measure *greater than* 90° but *less than* 180°.

A straight angle is an angle that has a measure of *exactly* 180°.

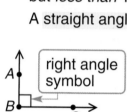

right angle symbol

right angle
∠ABC = 90°

acute angle
∠DEF < 90°

obtuse angle
90° < ∠GHM < 180°

straight angle
∠JKL = 180°

▶ Perpendicular lines are intersecting lines that form four right angles.

$\overleftrightarrow{RS}$ and $\overleftrightarrow{PQ}$ are perpendicular lines.
∠RTP, ∠PTS, ∠RTQ, and ∠QTS are right angles.

The symbol ⊥ means "is perpendicular to."
$\overleftrightarrow{RS} \perp \overleftrightarrow{PQ}$

Write whether each angle is *acute, right, obtuse*, or *straight*.

1. 34°   **2.** 110°   **3.** 12°   **4.** 90°   **5.** 180°   **6.** 6°

7. 163°   **8.** 91°   **9.** 25°   **10.** 137°   **11.** 75°   **12.** 179°

13.   **14.** 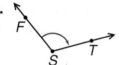   **15.**   **16.**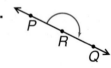

Name the following angles. Use the figure.

17. 4 acute angles

18. 2 right angles

19. a straight angle

20. 3 obtuse angles

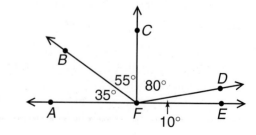

Find the measure of each angle.
Use the figure.

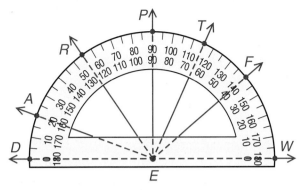

21. ∠WED

22. ∠DET

23. ∠WER

24. ∠PEW

25. ∠AER

26. ∠FEA

**Choose the best estimate for its measure. Then measure with
a protractor to check your estimate.**

27.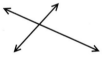

28.

29.

a. 85° **b.** 90° **c.** 135°   **a.** 45° **b.** 85° **c.** 105°   **a.** 75° **b.** 90° **c.** 95°

Find the measure of each angle. Then classify the angle.

30.    **31.**   **32.**    **33.**

Are the lines perpendicular? Write _Yes_ or _No_.
Use a protractor to check your answers.

34.    **35.**   **36.**   **37.**

Problem Solving

38. The measure of ∠X is twice the
measure of ∠Y. The sum of the
measures of ∠X and ∠Y is 90°. What
are the measures of ∠X and ∠Y?

39. Draw $\overleftrightarrow{AB}$. Then draw a point X between
points A and B. Use a protractor to
draw $\overrightarrow{XY} \perp \overleftrightarrow{AB}$. What is the sum of the
measures of ∠YXA and ∠YXB?

TEST PREPARATION

40. In the figure at the right,
$\overrightarrow{MA} \perp \overrightarrow{MD}$, ∠BMC = 25°, and ∠AMC = 75°.
What is the measure of ∠BMD?

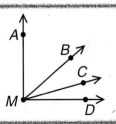

A 15°   **B** 40°   **C** 50°   **D** 65°

10-3

HANDS-ON UNDERSTANDING   *Update your skills. See page 13.*

Polygons

Materials: dot paper or geoboard, ruler, protractor, dictionary

Plane figures are made up of points that are all in the same plane. They lie on a flat surface.

A plane figure is either an open or a closed figure. Look at the figures below.

Open

Closed

1. How are the open figures similar to the closed figures? How are they different?

2. Use a geoboard or dot paper to make several closed figures.

3. Describe each figure you made. How many line segments does each figure have? How many angles?

4. What is the relationship between the number of line segments and the number of angles of each figure?

Some closed plane figures are called polygons. Polygons are closed plane figures made up of line segments, called sides. Pairs of sides meet at a point called a vertex (plural: vertices) and do not cross.

The figures on the geoboards shown at the right are polygons. Polygons are classified by the number of sides.

heptagon

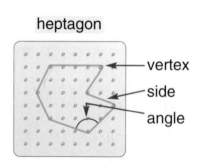

— vertex

— side

— angle

octagon

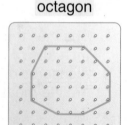

5. How many sides does a heptagon have? How many angles?

6. How many sides does an octagon have? How many angles?

7. Use a geoboard or dot paper to model 5 different polygons.

8. What relationship can you find between the number of sides and the number of angles of each of your models?

9. Copy and complete the table of polygons. You may use your polygon models.

Name of Polygon	Number of Sides	Number of Angles	Drawing of Polygon
Heptagon	?	7	
Octagon	8	?	?
Nonagon	?	9	?
Decagon	10	?	?

Polygons that have all sides of the same length and all angles of the same measure are called regular polygons. Look at the figures below.

10. Trace the figures and make a table or a concept map to classify each as a regular or *not* regular polygon.

Communicate

11. Is a closed plane figure always a polygon? Explain your answer.

12. Can a polygon have sides that are of the same length and angles that are *not* the same measure? Explain your answer.

13. Name some examples of real objects that have polygon shapes.

Write About It

14. Find the meaning of the prefixes *tri*, *quad*, *penta*, *hexa*, *octa*, and *deca*. Write a story about life in a land where all objects are only shapes beginning with these prefixes.

Congruent and Similar Figures

Two figures are **congruent** if one can be moved to fit exactly over the other.

These pairs of figures are congruent:

► Congruent polygons have exactly the same size and shape. Matching or **corresponding parts** (sides and angles) of congruent polygons are congruent.

is congruent to

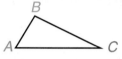

Write: △ABC ≅ △DEF

Read: Triangle ABC is congruent to triangle DEF.

corresponding sides: corresponding angles:

$\overline{AB} \cong \overline{DE}$ ∠A ≅ ∠D

$\overline{BC} \cong \overline{EF}$ ∠B ≅ ∠E

$\overline{AC} \cong \overline{DF}$ ∠C ≅ ∠F

► Congruent polygons are also similar polygons.
Similar polygons have the same shape.
They may or may *not* have the same size.
Corresponding angles of similar polygons are congruent.

is similar to

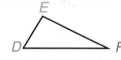

Write: △GHI ~ △JKL

Read: Triangle GHI is similar to triangle JKL.

corresponding angles: ∠G ≅ ∠J
∠H ≅ ∠K
∠I ≅ ∠L

Find the corresponding sides and the corresponding angles of the given congruent triangles.

 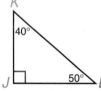   △RPQ ≅ △MNO

1. $\overline{RP} \cong$?   2. ∠M ≅ ?

3. $\overline{RQ} \cong$?   4. ∠N ≅ ?

5. $\overline{PQ} \cong$?   6. ∠O ≅ ?

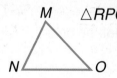

Are the figures similar? Write *Yes* or *No*. Explain your answer.

7.   8.  9.   10.

Use the symbol ≅ to identify corresponding angles.

11.

$\triangle XYZ \sim \triangle RST$

12.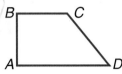

Quadrilateral *ABCD* ~ Quadrilateral *EFGH*

Constructing a Congruent Line Segment

A **compass** can be used to construct a line segment congruent to a given line segment.

To construct a line segment congruent to $\overline{AB}$:

- Use a straightedge to draw a line segment of any length.

- Open a compass to match the length of $\overline{AB}$.

- Keeping the compass opening the same, place the compass point at any point *P* on the line segment.

- From point *P*, swing the compass across the line segment to intersect it at point *Q*.

$\overline{PQ} \cong \overline{AB}$

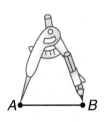

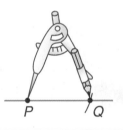

For each segment, construct a congruent line segment. Explain the steps used.

13.
    A   *B*

14.

15.

16.

Problem Solving

17. Jim enlarges $\triangle DEF$, labeling it $\triangle MNO$. In $\triangle DEF$, $\angle D = 60°$, $\angle E = 55°$, and $\angle F = 65°$. What are the measures of the angles in $\triangle MNO$? How do you know?

18. Pia draws an exact copy of rectangle *ABCD*, labeling it *RSTV*. In rectangle *ABCD*, $\overline{AB} = 5$ in. and $\overline{BC} = 8$ in. What are the lengths of $\overline{RS}$ and $\overline{ST}$? How do you know?

10-5 Triangles

> Identical marks indicate congruent sides of the figure.

▶ Triangles may be classified by the length of their sides.

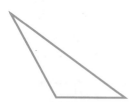 

scalene triangle
no sides congruent

isosceles triangle
2 sides congruent

equilateral triangle
all sides congruent

▶ Triangles may also be classified by the measures of their angles.

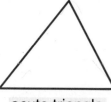 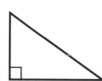 

acute triangle
3 acute angles

right triangle
1 right angle
2 acute angles

obtuse triangle
1 obtuse angle
2 acute angles

Practice

Classify each triangle as *scalene*, *isosceles*, or *equilateral*.

1.
2.
3.
4.

5.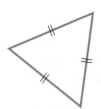
6.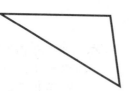
7.
8.

Classify each triangle as *acute*, *right*, or *obtuse*.

9.
10.
11.
12.

13.
14.
15.
16.

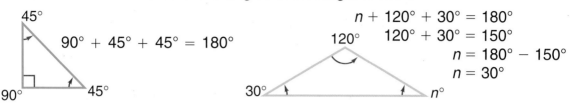

Angles of a Triangle

The sum of the measures of the angles of a triangle is 180°.

$90° + 45° + 45° = 180°$

$n + 120° + 30° = 180°$
$120° + 30° = 150°$
$n = 180° - 150°$
$n = 30°$

Is it possible for each triangle to have the given angle measures? Write *Yes* or *No*. Explain your answer.

17. 70° 90° 30°

18. 15° 100° 20°

19. 60° 60° 60°

20. 20° 80° 80°

Find the degree measure of the third angle of each triangle.

21. 85° 80° $n°$

22. 35° $n°$ 40°
105

23. $n°$ 65° 65°

24. 60° 60° $n°$
620

Problem Solving

25. One angle of a triangle is 98° and another is half that. What is the measure of the third angle?

26. One angle of a triangle is 105°. If the other two angles have equal measures, what is the measure of each?

CRITICAL THINKING

Draw each triangle. You may use dot paper.

27. an acute isosceles triangle

28. a right scalene triangle

29. a right isosceles triangle

30. an obtuse scalene triangle

Quadrilaterals

Some quadrilaterals have special names.

A **trapezoid** is a quadrilateral with exactly 1 pair of parallel sides.

A **parallelogram** is a quadrilateral with 2 pairs of parallel congruent sides.

A **rectangle** is a parallelogram with 4 right angles.

A **square** is a parallelogram with 4 congruent sides and 4 right angles.

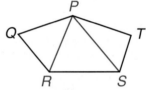

A **rhombus** is a parallelogram with 4 congruent sides.

▶ A **diagonal** of a polygon is a line segment that joins two vertices of the polygon but is *not* a side of the polygon.

$\overline{AC}$ is a diagonal.

$\overline{PR}$ and $\overline{PS}$ are diagonals.

Classify each quadrilateral in as many ways as possible: parallelogram, rectangle, square, rhombus, or trapezoid.

1. 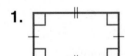 2. 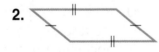 3. 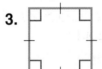 4.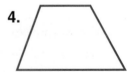

5. 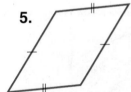 6.  7. 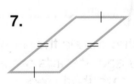 8.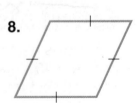

Use the polygons *ABCD* and *PQRST* above.

9. Name another diagonal that can be drawn in quadrilateral *ABCD*.

10. Name another 3 diagonals that can be drawn in pentagon *PQRST*.

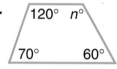

Use the quadrilaterals in exercises 1–8. Write the exercise number.

11. Which have 4 right angles?
no right angles?

12. Which have 4 congruent sides?
2 pairs of parallel sides?

Trace each figure. Then draw all its diagonals and count how many you have drawn.

13.

14.

15.

Angles of a Quadrilateral

The sum of the measures of the angles of a quadrilateral is 360°.

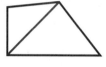

.**Think**....................
Draw a diagonal to
form 2 triangles.

$2 \times 180° = 360°$

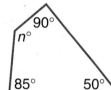

$n + 90° + 50° + 85° = 360°$
$90° + 50° + 85° = 225°$
$n = 360° - 225°$
$n = 135°$

Find the measure of the missing angle.

16.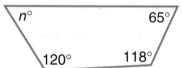
$n°$ ⟋ 65°
120° 118°

17.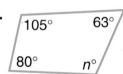
105° 63°
80° $n°$

18.
120° $n°$
70° 60°

Problem Solving

19. What is the sum of the measures of the angles of a trapezoid? of a rhombus? How do you know?

20. What is the sum of the measures of the angles of a *pentagon*? Explain how you found your answer.

CHALLENGE

A tangram is a geometric puzzle that originated in China over 4000 years ago. It starts out as a square, and is then cut into 7 prescribed pieces.

21. Trace the 7 pieces of the tangram shown at the right. Cut out the pieces. Then rearrange them to form different quadrilaterals. How many quadrilaterals can you make? Name them.

Perimeter

The perimeter of a polygon (P) is the distance around the polygon.

► Formulas can be used to find the perimeter of regular polygons and rectangles.

square

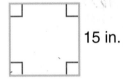

15 in.

$P = 4 \times s$ ◄— Let s represent one side of the square.
$P = 4 \times 15$ in.
$P = 60$ in.

regular hexagon

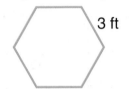

3 ft

$P = 6 \times s$ ◄— Let s represent one side of the regular hexagon.
$P = 6 \times 3$ ft
$P = 18$ ft

rectangle

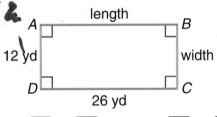

length

A — B
12 yd — width
D — C
26 yd

$\overline{AB} \cong \overline{DC}$ $\overline{AD} \cong \overline{BC}$

length   width

$P = (2 \times \ell) + (2 \times w)$
$P = (2 \times 26 \text{ yd}) + (2 \times 12 \text{ yd})$
$P = 52 \text{ yd} + 24 \text{ yd}$
$P = 76 \text{ yd}$

► To find the perimeter of a more complex figure, break it down into components and then add the lengths of its actual sides.

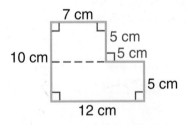

7 cm
5 cm
10 cm — 5 cm
5 cm
12 cm

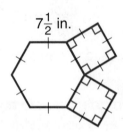

$7\frac{1}{2}$ in.

$P = 7 \text{ cm} + (3 \times 5 \text{ cm}) + 12 \text{ cm} + 10 \text{ cm}$

$= 7 \text{ cm} + 15 \text{ cm} + 12 \text{ cm} + 10 \text{ cm}$

$= 44 \text{ cm}$

$P = 10 \times 7\frac{1}{2}$ in.

$= 75$ in.

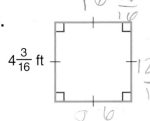

Find the perimeter of each polygon.

1.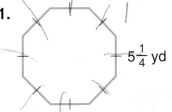

$5\frac{1}{4}$ yd

2.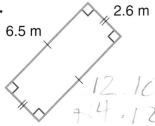

6.5 m   2.6 m

3.

$4\frac{3}{16}$ ft

4.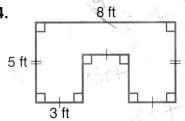

8 ft
5 ft
3 ft

5. 20 in.

30 in.

10 in.

6.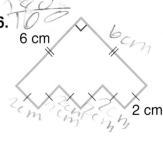

6 cm   2 cm

Problem Solving

7. Egypt's Great Pyramid has a square base. One side of the base is 230 meters long. What is its perimeter?

8. A park is shaped like a regular hexagon. Each of its sides is 26 yd long. Find the perimeter of the park.

9. How many feet of trim border a rug that is $5\frac{2}{3}$ ft wide and $8\frac{1}{6}$ ft long?

10. How many feet of satin trim the edges of a $6\frac{1}{4}$-ft wide and $12\frac{1}{8}$-ft-long blanket?

11. A roll of weather stripping is 24 m long. How many rolls are needed to go around 12 square windows that are 0.9 m on each side?

12. The length of one side of a rectangle is 30 m. The perimeter of the rectangle is 80 m. What is the width of the rectangle?

13. A field in the shape of a rectangle is 550 yd wide and 880 yd long. If Karen jogs around the field twice, how many yards does she jog?

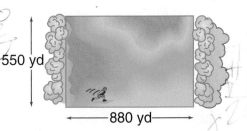

550 yd

880 yd

DO YOU REMEMBER?

Compute.

14. $3 \times 2 \times 7.5$

15. $3 \times 2 \times 16.5$

16. $3 \times 2 \times 3\frac{1}{2}$

17. $\frac{22}{7} \times 2 \times 7$

18. $3.14 \times 2 \times 2.5$

19. 3.14×9.2

Circles

▶ A circle is a plane figure. All points on the circle are the same distance from a given point, called the center.

Point *C* is the center of circle *C*.

circle C

A circle is named by its center.

▶ The parts of a circle have special names.

A chord is a line segment with its endpoints on the circle. $\overline{LK}$ and $\overline{MN}$ are chords of circle *C*.

A diameter is a chord that passes through the center. $\overline{LK}$ is a diameter of circle *C*.

A radius is a line segment with one endpoint at the center of the circle and the other endpoint on the circle. $\overline{CL}$, $\overline{CK}$, $\overline{CN}$ are radii (plural of radius) of circle *C*.

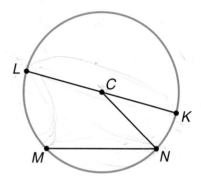

A central angle in a circle is an angle with its vertex at the center of the circle. $\angle LCN$ and $\angle KCN$ are central angles of circle *C*.

The length of the diameter (*d*) is twice the length of the radius (*r*).
$$d = 2 \times r \qquad r = d \div 2$$

An arc (⌒) is a part of a circle, with all of its points on the circle. $\overset{\frown}{KN}$, $\overset{\frown}{NM}$, $\overset{\frown}{ML}$, and $\overset{\frown}{LK}$ are arcs of circle *C*.

Practice

Match each term with the correct definition.

1. chord

2. radius

3. diameter

4. center

5. arc

6. central angle

a. a chord that passes through the center of the circle

b. a point that names the circle

c. a line segment joining any two points on the circle

d. a line segment drawn from the center of the circle to any point on the circle

e. an angle whose vertex is at the center of a circle

f. a part of a circle, with all of its points on the circle

Use the circle at the right.

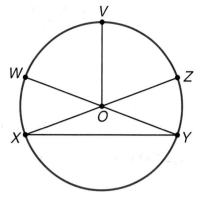

7. Name the circle and its center.

8. Name 5 points of the circle.

9. How many chords of the circle are shown? Name them.

10. Is $\overline{XY}$ a diameter of the circle? Explain why or why not.

11. How many diameters of the circle are shown? Name them.

12. How many radii of the circle are shown? Name them.

13. How many central angles of the circle are shown? Name them.

14. Name five arcs of the circle.

15. What kind of triangle is $\triangle XOY$?

Constructing a Circle

A **compass** can be used to construct a circle. The compass tip marks the **center** of the circle. The distance the compass is open is the **radius** of the circle.

A ruler or straightedge is used to draw the parts of the circle.

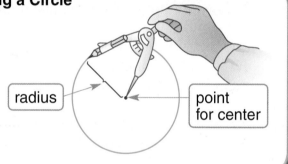

radius

point for center

Use a compass to construct a circle. Then do the following:

16. Label the center point, X.

17. Draw chord $\overline{MN}$.

18. Draw diameter $\overline{VT}$.

19. Draw radius $\overline{XR}$.

Use a compass and a ruler to construct a circle with a:

20. radius of $1\frac{1}{2}$ in.

21. diameter of 6 cm.

Problem Solving

22. The diameter of a circular track is 140 yd. What is the radius?

23. The radius of a circular flower bed is $8\frac{5}{6}$ ft. What is the diameter?

Circumference

The distance around a circle is called
the circumference (C) of the circle.

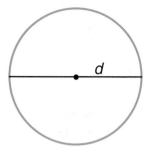

▶ Mark a point A on a circle and on grid paper, as shown below.
Roll the circle along the paper until A returns
to its original position. Mark this point B on the paper.
The line segment $\overline{AB}$ is the same length as the circumference.

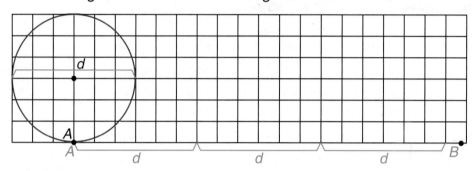

The length of the circumference (C) is about equal to
three times the length of the diameter (d).

$C \approx 3 \times d$

| is approximately equal to |

Mathematicians have shown that for every circle,
the circumference (C) divided by the diameter (d)
is always the same value. This value is represented
by the Greek letter π (read: "pi").

$\dfrac{\text{Circumference}}{\text{diameter}} = \dfrac{C}{d} = \pi$

Approximate values of π that are commonly used are 3.14 and $\dfrac{22}{7}$.

▶ To find the circumference (C) of a circle:

| $d = 2 \times r$ or |
| $r = d \div 2$ |

• Multiply π by the length of
the diameter (d).

$C = \pi \times d$

$C \approx 3.14 \times 5.5$ m

$C \approx 17.27$ m

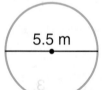

5.5 m

• Multiply π by twice the
length of the radius (r).

$C = \pi \times 2 \times r$

$C \approx \dfrac{22}{7} \times 2 \times 28$ in.

$C \approx \dfrac{22}{\overset{}{\underset{1}{7}}} \times \dfrac{2}{1} \times \dfrac{\overset{4}{28}}{1}$ in.

$C \approx \dfrac{176}{1}$ in. ≈ 176 in.

28 in.

Find the circumference of each circle. Use π ≈ 3.14.

1.
2 m

2.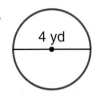
4 yd

3.
3 m

4.
7 yd

5. a circle with a diameter of 150 cm

6. a circle with a radius of 65 mm

7. a circle with a diameter = 1.2 yd

Find the circumference of each circle. Use π ≈ $\frac{22}{7}$. 3.17

8.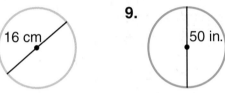
16 cm

9.
50 in.

10.
$1\frac{1}{3}$ in.

11.
$3\frac{1}{6}$ ft

12. a circle with a diameter of $12\frac{1}{3}$ in.

13. a circle with a radius of $3\frac{1}{9}$ yd

14. a circle with a diameter of $10\frac{1}{2}$ ft

Problem Solving

15. Earth's equator is a circle with a radius of 6378 km. Find Earth's circumference.

16. How much fencing is needed to enclose a circular garden whose radius is 4.5 yd?

17. A Ferris wheel has a diameter of 80 ft. Find its circumference.

18. A circular table has a radius of $2\frac{1}{2}$ ft. Find its circumference.

19. The diameter of Rod's bicycle wheel is 68 cm. How many centimeters will the wheel travel in 8 complete turns?

20. If the diameter of a circle is doubled, what happens to its circumference? Explain how you found your answer.

21. By how much does the circumference of a circle whose radius is 31 in. exceed that of a circle whose radius is 22 in.?

MENTAL MATH

Estimate the circumference of each circle. Use π = 3.

22. diameter = 20 cm

23. radius = 6 ft

24. diameter = 13 yd

25. radius = 3.5 m

26. diameter = 2.5 in.

27. radius = 5.5 cm

Lines of Symmetry

If a figure can be folded along a line so that the two halves are congruent, the figure has line symmetry. The fold line is called the line of symmetry.

Some figures have *more than one* line of symmetry.

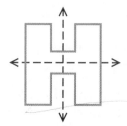

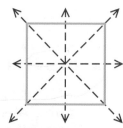

This capital letter has *two* lines of symmetry.

This square has *four* lines of symmetry.

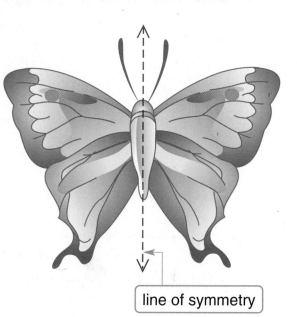

line of symmetry

▶ If a figure can be turned halfway around a point so that it looks exactly the same, the figure has half-turn symmetry.

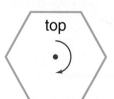

after half turn

top

dot

This regular hexagon has half-turn symmetry.

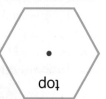

after half turn

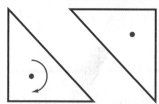

This triangle does *not* have half-turn symmetry.

How many lines of symmetry does each figure have?

1.

2.

3.

4.

5.

6.

7.

8.

Find how many lines of symmetry each figure has.

9.

10.

11.

12.

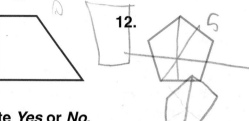

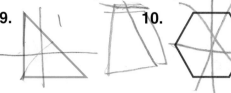

Does the figure have half-turn symmetry? Write *Yes* or *No*.

13. ◇ *yes*

14. I *yes*

15. ▱ *yes*

16. ◯ *no*

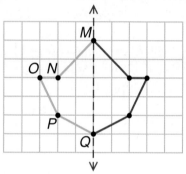

Drawing a Figure Using a Line of Symmetry

Draw the rest of this figure so that the dashed line is the line of symmetry.

Fold along the dashed line. Mark the points where *M*, *N*, *O*, *P*, and *Q* touch. Join these points to complete the figure.

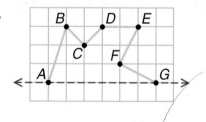

Trace and complete each figure so that the dashed line is a line of symmetry.

17.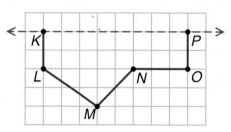

18.

Write About It

19. Can a figure have line symmetry but no half-turn symmetry? line symmetry and half-turn symmetry? half-turn symmetry but no line symmetry? Explain your answers.

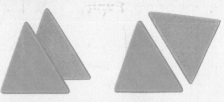

Transformations

There are three basic types of transformations of geometric figures in a plane:

- **translation (or slide)** — Every point of a figure moves the same distance and in the same direction.

- **reflection (or flip)** — A figure is flipped over a line so that its mirror image is formed.

- **rotation (or turn)** — A figure is turned around a center point.

Materials: pattern blocks, grid paper, ruler

Step 1 Fold a sheet of grid paper in thirds. Open it up and label each section *A*, *B*, and *C*.

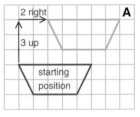

Step 2 Place a trapezoid in section *A* and trace around it to record a starting position. **Translate**, or slide, the trapezoid up 3 units and right 2 units.

What changed when you translated the trapezoid? Did the size and shape change?

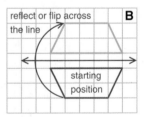

Step 3 Now trace the trapezoid in section *B*. **Reflect**, or flip, the trapezoid across a reflection line.

Are the two trapezoids in section *B* congruent? How did the position of the trapezoid change?

Step 4 Trace the trapezoid in section C. **Rotate**, or turn, the trapezoid 90° clockwise around a vertex to a new position. Label it *1*. Next, rotate the trapezoid another 90° clockwise (180° rotation from original position). Label it *2*. Then, rotate the trapezoid another 90° clockwise (270° rotation from original position). Label it *3*.

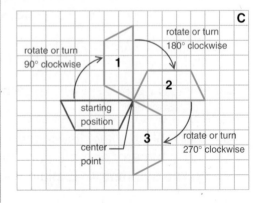

What changed when you rotated the trapezoid? What did *not* change?

**Decide whether figure B is a result of a transformation of figure A.
Write Yes or No. Explain your answers.**

1.

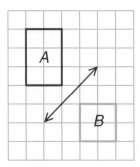

2.

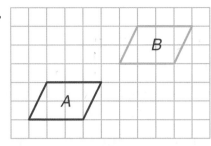

3.

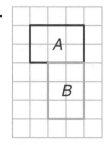

**Copy each figure on grid paper. Then draw a second figure
to show the result of a translation, reflection, or rotation.
Use pattern blocks to model.**

4. Translate parallelogram *RSTP* down 4 units and left 5 units.

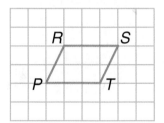

5. Reflect square *NOLM* across the line.

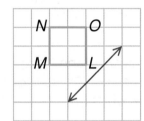

6. Rotate triangle *ABC* 90° clockwise around vertex *C*; then rotate 180° counterclockwise.

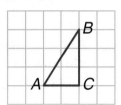

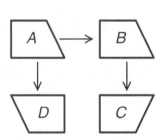

Communicate

7. How can you tell if figure B is a result of a transformation of figure A?

8. In the figures at the right, name the transformation(s) when *A* is moved to *B*; *A* is moved to *C*; *A* is moved to *D*. Explain your answers.

9. What clockwise rotation of a figure is equivalent to a 270°-rotation counterclockwise?

DO YOU REMEMBER?

Match each definition with a term in the box.

10. a part of a line that has one endpoint

11. a set of one or more outcomes of a probability experiment

12. a figure formed by two rays that have a common end-

13. a pictorial representation of data

angle
event
graph
interval
ray

Update your skills. See page 12.

Tessellations

Interesting patterns, often made of polygons, are used in designs on fabrics, wallpaper, floors, and sidewalks. These patterns, like the one at the right, are called tessellations.

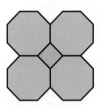

A tessellation is a pattern formed by covering a plane surface with a set of polygons so that no polygons overlap and no gaps exist between the polygons.

▶ You can make a tessellation by tracing a figure or figures and then using a translation, a reflection, or a rotation.

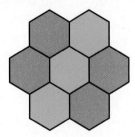

Hexagons are used in the tessellation.

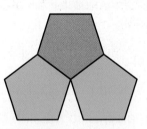

Octagons and a rhombus are used in the tessellation.

Study these examples.

Each of these hexagons has been tessellated with various shapes.

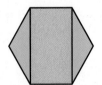

Regular pentagons cannot tessellate.

Name the polygons used in each tessellation.

1.

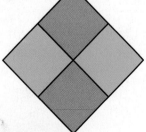

2.

3.

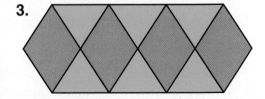

Practice

Trace each polygon. Then try to make a tessellation using each polygon. Use dot paper to help you.

4.

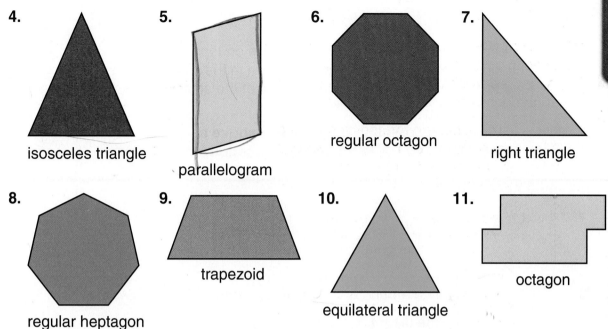

isosceles triangle

5.

parallelogram

6.

regular octagon

7.

right triangle

8.

regular heptagon

9.

trapezoid

10.

equilateral triangle

11.

octagon

12. Which of the polygons above could not be used for tessellation?

Problem Solving

Use dot paper to help you.

13. If all triangles tessellate, do all parallelograms tessellate? Explain.

14. Do all regular polygons tessellate? Give examples to support your answer.

15. What room in your house has a tessellating pattern on its floor, ceiling, or walls? What polygons appear in the pattern?

16. Create your own tessellation by using a combination of polygons.

17. Ryan has diamond and half-diamond tiles to tile his hallway. Show how he can use the tiles together to tile the hallway.

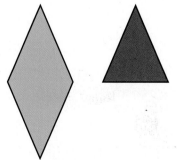

Write About It

18. Write a report about the Dutch artist M. C. Escher, focusing on how he used tessellations in his artwork.

Problem-Solving Strategy:
Use a Diagram/Model

A steeple shaped like a square pyramid is on top of a building.
The dimensions of the pyramid are shown in the diagram.
Find the perimeter of *one* triangular face of the steeple.

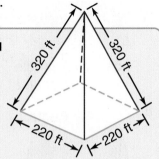

Read **Visualize yourself in the problem above as you reread it. List the facts and the question.**

Facts: Face of the steeple is an isosceles triangle (two congruent sides)

Question: What is the perimeter of *one* triangular face of the steeple?

Plan The distance around an object is its perimeter.

First use the diagram to find the perimeter of an isosceles triangle.
Let *a* represent the length of each congruent side.
Let *b* represent the length of the third side.

$$P = a + a + b$$

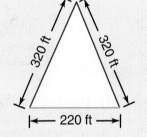

two congruent sides

$$P = (2 \times a) + b$$

Then substitute the values of the variables in the formula,
$P = (2 \times a) + b$.

Solve $P = (2 \times 320 \text{ ft}) + 220 \text{ ft}$

$= 640 \text{ ft} + 220 \text{ ft} = 860 \text{ ft}$

The perimeter of one triangular face of the steeple is 860 ft.

Check Use the formula $P = a + a + b$ to check your computation.

$$P = a + a + b$$

$860 \text{ ft} \stackrel{?}{=} 320 \text{ ft} + 320 \text{ ft} + 220 \text{ ft}$

$860 \text{ ft} = 860 \text{ ft}$ The answer checks.

Use formulas to solve each problem.

1. A quilt design consists of a regular pentagon with a square attached to each side. If the perimeter of the pentagon is $7\frac{1}{2}$ in., what is the perimeter of the design?

Read ▸ Visualize yourself in the problem above as you reread it. Focus on the facts and the question.

List what you know.

Facts: shape—regular pentagon with a square attached to each side

perimeter of pentagon is $7\frac{1}{2}$ in.

Question: What is the perimeter of the design?

Plan ▸ First, use the diagram and the formula $P = 5 \times s$ to find the length of a side of the pentagon. Then, use the formula $P = 15 \times s$ to find the perimeter of the design.

Solve ┈┈┈➤ **Check**

2. The perimeter of a gazebo floor shaped like a regular octagon is 96 ft. What is the length of one side of the floor?

3. A merry-go-round at the children's playground has a radius of 5 ft. Find the circumference of the merry-go-round.

4. A parallelogram has two pairs of congruent sides. Find the perimeter of a parallelogram whose parallel sides have lengths of 21 ft and 29 ft.

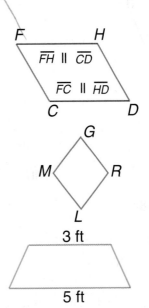

$\overline{FH} \parallel \overline{CD}$

$\overline{FC} \parallel \overline{HD}$

5. Figure *MGRL* is a rhombus. If $\angle M \cong \angle R$ and $\angle G \cong \angle L$, and $\angle G$ equals 50°, what is the measure of $\angle R$?

6. The parallel sides of this window measure 3 ft and 5 ft. The other sides of the window are congruent. If the perimeter is 16 ft, what is the length of each congruent side?

Problem-Solving Applications: Mixed Review

Read Plan Solve Check

Solve each problem and explain the method you used.

1. Darlene drew right angle *DAR*. Name the two rays she drew.

2. Arnie's polygon has 2 pairs of parallel sides but no right angles. What might his polygon be?

3. Josh drew a square and a rhombus. Then he drew the diagonals of each. Name the types of triangles he formed.

4. In a quilt 2 congruent isosceles right triangles were joined at one side. What possible figures were formed?

5. Cleo put new trim around the edge of a circular rug that had a radius of 2 ft. About how much trim did she use?

6. Helen drew figure *FHMSVR*.

    a. Name the two rays.

    b. Name an acute angle and an obtuse angle.

    c. Name the polygon.

    d. $\overline{HF}$ is 2 cm long. Find the perimeter.

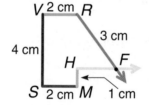

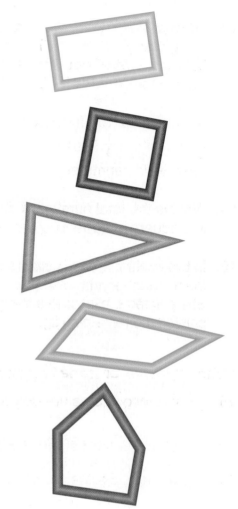

Use the drawing for problems 7–10.

7. A rectangular rug has this pattern. What polygon is congruent to △*AGC*?

8. Classify quadrilateral *FBCG*.

9. How many trapezoids are in this pattern?

10. How many lines of symmetry does this figure have? Does it have half-turn symmetry?

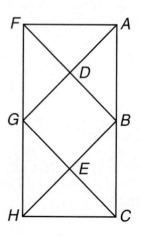

Choose a strategy from the list or use another strategy you know to solve each problem.

11. Judy makes a quilt square that has a perimeter of 18 in. How long is each side?

12. Ed drew 2 rays from the vertex of straight angle *FHM*. ∠*FHC* equals 35°, and ∠*MHD* equals twice that. How many degrees is ∠*CHD*?

Strategy File

Use These Strategies
Use a Diagram/Model
Logical Reasoning
Work Backward
Guess and Test
Use More Than One Step

13. A rectangular rug has a length of $7\frac{1}{2}$ ft. Its width is $2\frac{1}{4}$ ft less than its length. What is its perimeter?

14. What is the total number of diagonals that can be drawn in a square? in a regular pentagon? in a regular hexagon?

15. In this design, Rita painted the equilateral triangle blue, the rectangles yellow, and the obtuse triangles green. She painted the isosceles triangle orange. Finally she painted the remaining figures red. Name them.

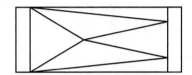

Write *all*, *some*, or *none* to make true statements.

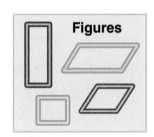

Figures

16. ? of these figures are polygons.

17. ? of these figures have acute angles.

18. ? of these figures are parallelograms.

19. Each of four friends made 1 of these quilt squares. Tina's has 4 triangles and 2 trapezoids. Frank's has the most rectangles. Julio's has 7 right triangles. Hope's has triangles, squares, and trapezoids. Which friend drew each square?

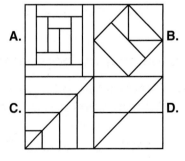

A.   B.

C.   D.

Write Your Own

20. Use the drawing of the rug on page 350 and these data to write two problems. Then solve them. Share your work with a classmate.

$\overline{FA} = 4$ ft

$\overline{FH} = 8$ ft

Use your protractor. Write the measure of each angle. Then classify the angle. *(See pp. 324–337, 340–343, 346–347.)*

1.
2.
3.
4.

Name each polygon.

5.
6.

Are the figures congruent? similar?

7.
8.
9. *(squares figure)*

Classify each triangle.

10.
11.

Classify each quadrilateral.

12.
13.

Find the perimeter of each polygon.

14. $2\frac{1}{2}$ cm
15. 30 mm 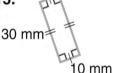 10 mm

Find the circumference of each circle.

16. 14 ft
17. 13 m

Is the dashed line in each figure a line of symmetry? Write *Yes* or *No.*

18.
19. *(triangle figure)*

Tell what polygons are used in the tessellation.

20. *(tessellation figure)*

Trace each figure on grid paper. Then draw a second figure to show each transformation. Use pattern blocks to model. *(See pp. 344–345.)*

21. Translate triangle *ABC* up 4 units and left 3 units.
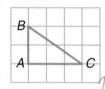

22. Rotate rhombus *DGFE* 180° clockwise around vertex *G*.
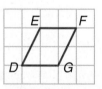

Problem Solving

(See pp. 340–341, 348–351.)

23. A tennis court is 78 ft long and 36 ft wide. Find its perimeter.

24. The diameter of a bicycle wheel is 28 in. Find its radius.

(See Still More Practice, p. 486.)

Triangular and Square Numbers

A number sequence is a pattern of numbers arranged in a particular order. Triangular and square numbers are sequences of whole numbers.

▶ Triangular numbers are numbers that can be arranged in a compact triangular pattern. The triangular arrays of dots below show the first five triangular numbers.

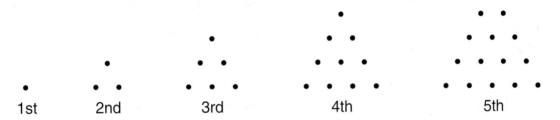

1st   2nd   3rd   4th   5th

▶ Square numbers are numbers that can be arranged in a compact square pattern. The square arrays of dots below show the first four square numbers.

1st   2nd   3rd   4th

Use the figures above to complete each table. Look for a pattern.

1.

Triangular Numbers	
Number	Number of Dots
1st	?
2nd	?
3rd	?
4th	?
5th	?

2.

Square Numbers	
Number	Number of Dots
1st	?
2nd	?
3rd	?
4th	?

Problem Solving

3. How many dots will be in the 6th triangular number? in the 7th triangular number?

4. How many dots will be in the 5th square number? in the 6th square number?

5. What patterns do you see in the triangular numbers?

6. What pattern do you see in the square numbers?

Name each polygon.

1.

2.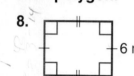

Are the figures congruent? similar?

3.

4.

Classify each quadrilateral.

5.

6.

Find the perimeter of each polygon.

7. $2\frac{1}{3}$ ft

8.  6 m

10 m

Find the circumference of each circle.

9. 5 ft

10. 27 cm

Tell whether the dotted line shows a line of symmetry.

11.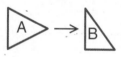

12.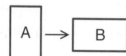

Tell what polygons are used in the tessellation.

13.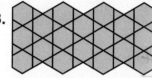

Decide whether figure B is a result of transformation of figure A. Write *Yes* or *No*. Explain your answer.

14. A → B

15. A → B

16. A → B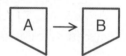

Problem Solving

Use a strategy you have learned.

17. If $\frac{3}{8}$ of the perimeter of an equilateral triangle is 6 ft, what is the length of one side?

Tell About It

Explain how you solved the problem. Show all your work.

18. Draw a parallelogram with one angle of 45° and another angle of 135°. Measure the other angles. What do you discover?

Performance Assessment

This is one possible triangle you can draw whose vertices are on a 3-dot-by-3-dot square. Draw 3 triangles that are not congruent.

19. Use your protractor to measure and classify each angle.

20. Classify each triangle by its angles and by the length of its sides.

Test Preparation

Choose the best answer.

1. Sally's test grades in English are 75 and 80. What grade must she get on her next test so that her average is an 85?

   a. 80   b. 90
   c. 95   d. 100

2. The diameter of a circle is 6 in. What is the circumference of the circle? Use 3.14 for π.

   a. 9.42 in.   b. 15.84 in.
   c. 18.84 in.   d. 37.68 in.

3. Which number has a quotient of 2.3 when divided by 8?

   a. 162.4
   b. 16.24
   c. 18.4
   d. 184

4. Which is not equivalent to the product of $1\frac{2}{3}$ and $3\frac{3}{5}$?

   a. $\frac{18}{3}$ b. $4\frac{19}{15}$

   c. $\frac{90}{15}$ d. 6

5. What type of graph best compares intervals of data?

   a. pictograph
   b. line graph
   c. histogram
   d. circle graph

6. A bag holds 5.8 lb of corn. How many pounds do 2.5 bags hold?

   a. 14. 5 lb   b. 8.3 lb
   c. 3.3 lb   d. 1.45 lb

7. Which is not a true statement?

   a. $2.7 \times 100 > 270 \div 100$
   b. $340 \div 1000 = 3.4 \div 10$
   c. $16.5 \div 2 < 18 \div 3$
   d. $9.8 \times 10 < 9800 \div 10$

8. Which of the following best describes a triangle with a 90° angle and two sides of equal length?

   a. scalene right   b. isosceles right
   c. equilateral obtuse d. equilateral acute

9. What must be added to 16.8 to equal 48?

   a. 64.8
   b. 32
   c. 31.8
   d. 31.2

10. A box contains 24 pair of socks that are blue, black, or white. If $\frac{1}{3}$ are blue and $\frac{1}{6}$ are black, then how many pairs are white?

    a. 12 pairs   b. 8 pairs
    c. 6 pairs   d. 4 pairs

11. What is the value of 5 in the number 47,536,098

    a. 5 hundred thousand
    b. 5 hundred million
    c. 5 hundred
    d. 5 tens

12. Choose the standard form of 70,000,000 + 400,000 + 3000 + 60 + 9.

    a. 70,403,069   b. 70,400,369
    c. 70,403,690   d. 743,690

13. Find the sum of

0.092 + 2.314 + 3.185

    a. 5.591
    b. 6.419
    c. 14.699
    d. 5591

18. What is the LCM of 3, 16, and 24?

    a. 24
    b. 48
    c. 64
    d. not given

---

14. What is the probability of tossing an odd number with a 6-sided number cube?

    a. $\frac{1}{6}$ **b.** $\frac{1}{3}$

    c. $\frac{1}{2}$ **d.** not given

19. What kind of line segment is $\overline{CD}$?

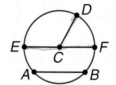

    a. diameter
    b. radius
    c. chord
    d. not given

---

15. Compute: $8\frac{1}{3} + 4\frac{3}{4}$

    a. $3\frac{7}{12}$ **b.** $13\frac{1}{12}$

    c. 11   **d.** not given

20. Compute: $5\frac{1}{8} - 3\frac{5}{6}$

    a. $1\frac{7}{24}$ **b.** $1\frac{1}{2}$

    c. $2\frac{1}{14}$ **d.** not given

---

16. Polygon $ABCD \cong$ polygon $KLMN$. Which are congruent parts?

    a. $\overline{AB}$ and $\overline{LN}$
    b. $\angle A$ and $\angle N$
    c. $\overline{BC}$ and $\overline{LM}$
    d. not given

21. Find the measure of the missing angle.

    a. 42°
    b. 52°
    c. 62°
    d. not given

---

17. A wagon train traveled an average of 4.9 mi a day for two weeks and an average of 5.4 mi a day the next three weeks. How many miles did the wagon trail travel in those five weeks?

    a. 26 mi   **b.** 182 mi
    c. 260 mi   **d.** not given

22. A bicycle costs $189.98. Gordon has $5 less than half that amount. How much more does Gordon need to buy the bicycle?

    a. $94.99   **b.** $99.99
    c. $109.99   **d.** not given

Explain how you solved the problem. Show all your work.

23. Feng's grandfather gave him $120 for his birthday. The circle graph shows how he spent the money.

    a. How much money did Feng spend on each item?

    b. How would the circle graph look different if Feng spent the same amount on clothes and snacks? What amount of money is that?

Feng's Expenses

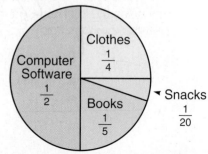

Measurement Topics

CHAPTER 11

In this chapter you will:

Investigate customary units of length, capacity,
and weight
Read Fahrenheit and Celsius temperature scales
Learn about time zones
Compute customary units with regrouping
Solve problems by using more than one step

Critical Thinking/Finding Together

A ship's watch began at midnight on the mid-Atlantic
with one bell rung to signal the time. If one additional
bell is rung as each half hour passes and 9 bells were
just rung, what time is it?

Midnight on the mid-Atlantic

Nothing blacker than the water,
nothing wider than the sky.
Pitch and toss, pitch and toss.
The Big Dipper might just ladle
a drink out of the sea.
Midnight on the mid-Atlantic is...

From Nine O'Clock Lullaby by Marilyn Singer

HANDS-ON UNDERSTANDING *Update your skills. See page 14.*

Relate Customary Units of Length

Materials: inch ruler or measuring tape, paper, pencil

The inch (in.), foot (ft), yard (yd), and
mile (mi) are customary units of length.

> 12 inches (in.) = 1 foot (ft)
> 3 feet = 1 yard (yd)
> 5280 ft or 1760 yd = 1 mile (mi)

1. Choose the following objects to measure:
   - two objects that are longer than 1 inch
     but less than 1 foot,
   - two objects that are between 1 foot and 1 yard long,
   - two objects that are longer than 1 yard.

2. Estimate the length of each object. Then use
   a ruler or a measuring tape to measure each
   of them. Record your answers in a table
   like the one shown at the right.

Object	Estimate	Actual Measure

3. What unit of measure did you use for lengths
   between 1 inch and 1 foot? between 1 foot
   and 1 yard? longer than 1 yard?

4. How does each estimate in your table compare
   with the actual measurement?

5. What unit would you use to measure the width
   of your math book? Why?

6. What unit would you use to measure the height
   of a table? Why?

7. What unit would you use to measure the distance
   of a race? Why?

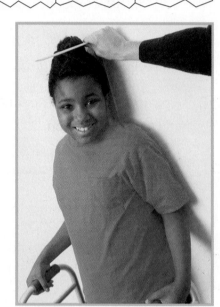

8. What unit would you use to measure the distance
   between New York City and Washington, DC? Why?

Sometimes we use two units instead of one to give a measurement.
It is usually easier to think about a person's height as 5 ft 4 in. rather
than 64 in. To rename larger units as smaller units, *multiply;* to
rename smaller units as larger units, *divide.*

9. Describe how you would rename:

   a. 5 ft 4 in. as inches

   b. 3 yd 2 ft as feet

   c. 58 in. as feet and inches

   d. 1105 feet as yards and feet

You can also use a ruler to measure the length of an object to the nearest inch, nearest $\frac{1}{2}$ inch, nearest $\frac{1}{4}$ inch, and nearest $\frac{1}{8}$ inch.

10. Lay your ruler along the crayon at the right. Is the length closer to 3 inches or to 4 inches?

11. What is the length of the crayon to the nearest inch?

12. Is the length of the crayon closer to 3 inches or to $3\frac{1}{2}$ inches? What is the length to the nearest $\frac{1}{2}$ inch?

13. Is the length of the crayon closer to 3 inches or to $3\frac{1}{4}$ inches? What is the length to the nearest $\frac{1}{4}$ inch?

14. Is the length of the crayon closer to 3 inches or to $3\frac{1}{8}$ inches? What is the length to the nearest $\frac{1}{8}$ inch?

15. Why is measuring to the nearest $\frac{1}{8}$ inch more precise than measuring to the nearest $\frac{1}{4}$ or $\frac{1}{2}$ inch?

16. Measure each to the nearest inch, nearest $\frac{1}{2}$ inch, nearest $\frac{1}{4}$ inch, and nearest $\frac{1}{8}$ inch.

a.

b.

c. A |————————————————| B   d. R |————————————| P

Communicate

17. Why are there different units of measurement?

18. How do you decide which customary unit of length to use in a particular situation?

19. Give examples of when an estimate of length is needed and when a precise measurement is essential.

20. You needed 85 in. of ribbon. You bought 8 ft of ribbon. Did you have enough ribbon? If so, will you have any left over? How much? Explain your answer.

Update your skills. See page 15.

Relate Customary Units of Capacity

Raul needs to put 6 gallons of water in his aquarium. He is using a quart jar to fill it. How many times will he need to fill the jar to get 6 gallons of water into the aquarium?

To find how many times Raul will need to fill the jar, find how many quarts are in 6 gallons or rename 6 gallons as quarts.

Customary Units of Capacity
8 fluid ounces (fl oz) = 1 cup (c)
2 cups = 1 pint (pt)
2 pints = 1 quart (qt)
2 quarts = 1 half gallon
4 quarts = 1 gallon (gal)

▶ To rename customary units of capacity:
  • *Multiply* to rename larger units as smaller units.
  • *Divide* to rename smaller units as larger units.

6 gal = __?__ qt
6 gal = (6 × 4) qt
6 gal = 24 qt

.Think..........
1 gal = 4 qt
Multiply by 4.

Raul will need to fill the quart jar 24 times to get 6 gallons of water.

Study these examples.

13 pt = __?__ qt

13 pt = (13 ÷ 2) qt

13 pt = $6\frac{1}{2}$ qt

.Think.........
2 pt = 1qt
Divide by 2.

23 qt = __?__ gal __?__ qt

23 qt = 5 gal 3 qt

$$\begin{array}{r} 5 \text{ R3} \\ 4\overline{)23} \\ -20 \\ \hline 3 \end{array}$$ ⌐remaining
⌐quarts

Practice

Rename each unit of measure.

1. 6 pt = __?__ qt

2. 22 qt = __?__ gal

3. 4 qt = __?__ pt

4. 4 c = __?__ fl oz

5. 16 pt = __?__ gal

6. 28 fl oz = __?__ c

7. 22 fl oz = __?__ c __?__ fl oz

8. 23 c = __?__ pt __?__ c

Compare. Use <, =, or >.

9. 42 fl oz __?__ 5 c 2 fl oz

10. 22 qt __?__ 5 gal 3 qt

11. 2 qt __?__ 5 pt

12. 25 c __?__ 6 qt

Find the picture that matches each measure. Then complete.

13. ? cups of apple juice

14. ? pints of frozen yogurt

15. ? fluid ounces of lemonade

16. ? quarts of milk

Do the pictures show the correct amount for exercises 17–20? Explain why or why not.

17. 8 fl oz honey

18. 1 c ketchup

19. 8 qt paint

20. 1 pt maple syrup

Problem Solving

21. Dale bought 4 gal of milk. The milk came in half gallons. How many half gallons of milk did she buy?

22. If Sally mixes $\frac{1}{2}$ c of poster paint with $\frac{1}{4}$ c of water, how many fluid ounces will she have?

23. Harvey wanted to buy 3 gal of honey. The beekeeper had 10 qt of honey on hand. Was Harvey able to purchase the amount of honey he wanted? Why or why not?

24. Philip needs to buy 1 gal of paint. The store sells 1 gal of paint for $18.49 or 1 qt of paint for $4.85. Which is the less expensive way for him to buy 1 gal of paint? Why?

CRITICAL THINKING

25. A leaky faucet drips 2 fl oz of water each hour. About how many gallons of water are lost from the faucet in a week? in a month? in a year? Share your results with a classmate.

11-3

HANDS-ON UNDERSTANDING   *Update your skills. See page 15.*

Relate Customary Units of Weight

Estimate the weights of some
classroom objects.

Materials: balance scale, pencils, almanac

The ounce (oz), pound (lb), and ton (T)
are customary units of weight.

A pencil weighs about one ounce (oz).

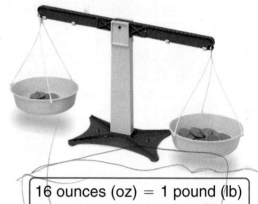

1. Hold a pencil in your hand and feel its weight.
   Find 3 classroom objects that would each
   weigh about 1 oz.

   | 16 ounces (oz) = 1 pound (lb) |
   | 2000 pounds = 1 ton (T) |

2. Place the pencil on one side of a balance scale.
   Then place each object that you found, one at
   a time, on the other side of the scale.

3. Is the weight of the object less than (<),
   equal to (=), or greater than (>) 1 oz? Record
   your findings in a table like the one shown at the right.

Object	<, =, or > 1 oz

4. Compare your findings with those of other
   groups' findings. Make a class list of objects
   that weigh about 1 oz.

Sixteen ounces equal one pound (lb). Combine your
pencils so you have enough to weigh about 1 lb.

5. About how many pencils are in 1 lb?

6. Find 3 classroom objects that each seem
   to weigh about 1 lb. Weigh each object on the
   balance scale using the pencils on the other
   side of the scale.

7. Is the weight of each object less than, equal to,
   or greater than 1 lb? Record your findings
   in a table like the one shown at the right.

Object	<, =, or > 1 lb

8. Compare your findings with those of other groups'
   findings. Make a class list of objects that weigh
   about 1 lb.

Two thousand pounds equal one ton (T).

9. About how many pencils are in 1 T?

10. Name some objects that would weigh about 1 T or more than 1 T.

11. Why are you less likely to use the ton than the pound or the ounce as a unit of weight in your everyday life?

Customary units of weight can also be renamed by multiplying or dividing.

12. Describe how you would rename 3 tons as 6000 pounds.

13. Rename 4 T 105 lb as pounds. Explain the method you used.

14. Why do you multiply to rename tons as pounds? divide to rename ounces as pounds?

Communicate

15. What unit would you use to measure the weight of an elephant? a bag of flour? a slice of cheese? Explain your answers.

16 When might you need to know the weight of an object?

17. A sign on a bridge lists a load limit of 4 tons. Can a truck with a loaded weight of 12,000 lb safely cross the bridge? Why or why not?

18. Estimate the weight of the items, then write the name of the objects in order from heaviest to lightest.
    a. a book, a pen, a letter, a ruler
    b. a bicycle, a motorcycle, a shopping cart, a truck
    c. a bowling ball, a golf ball, a basketball, a Ping-Pong ball

Write About It

19. Research and write a report on the history of units of weight in the customary (English) system. Include an explanation of Troy units and avoirdupois units.

Temperature

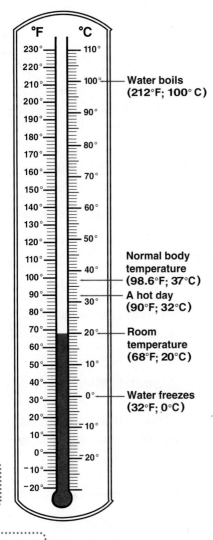

▶ A **thermometer** is used to measure temperature. Temperature can be measured in degrees Fahrenheit (°F), or in degrees Celsius (°C).

The thermometer at the right shows some common temperatures.

Water freezes at 32°F or 0°C, and boils at 212°F or 100°C.

▶ Use (⁻) sign to write temperatures below zero.

Write: ⁻10°F
Read: 10 degrees Fahrenheit below zero or negative ten degrees Fahrenheit

Write: ⁻5°C
Read: 5 degrees Celsius below zero or negative five degrees Celsius

▶ If you know the starting temperature and how many degrees the temperature rises or falls, you can find the final temperature.

Starting Temperature: 37°F
Change: rises 8°
Final Temperature: 45°F

.Think.................................
Rises means increases.
  Add: 37° + 8° = 45°
....

Starting Temperature: 12°C
Change: falls 16°
Final Temperature: ⁻4°C

.Think.................................
Falls means decreases:
  From 12° to 0° → 12°
  Subtract: 16° − 12° = 4°
  4° below zero = ⁻4°
....

Practice

Choose the most reasonable temperature for each.

1. ice skating outdoors   **a.** ⁻40°F   **b.** 10°F   **c.** 60°F

2. oven temperature to bake a cake   **a.** 60°F   **b.** 120°F   **c.** 350°F

3. a summer day in Miami   **a.** 20°C   **b.** 75°C   **c.** 35°C

4. snow skiing   **a.** ⁻10°C   **b.** 20°C   **c.** 40°C

Write each temperature.

5. °F

6. °F

7. °C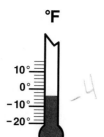

8. °C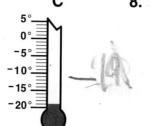

Find the final temperature.

	Starting Temperature	Change	Final Temperature
9.	26°F	rises 6°	?
10.	3°F	falls 10°	?
11.	19°C	rises 4°	?
12.	11°C	falls 20°	?

Problem Solving

13. The temperature yesterday was −4°F in the morning and 13°F in the evening. How many degrees did the temperature rise?

14. A snowstorm drove the temperature down 3°C each hour. The thermometer read 8°C before the storm began. What did it read 4 hours later?

15. During the week the temperature each day at noon was 25°C, 23°C, 20°C, 22°C, 22°C, 18°C, and 17°C. What was the average daily noon temperature?

16. The morning temperatures during the school week were 37°F, 45°F, 41°F, 21°F, and 26°F. What was the average daily morning temperature?

DO YOU REMEMBER?

Compute.

17. 5 × 60

18. 13 × 7

19. 6 × 12

20. 8 × 100

21. 3 × 60 + 8

22. 5 × 7 + 4

23. 2 × 12 + 5

24. 3 × 100 + 2

25. 480 ÷ 60

26. 242 ÷ 7

27. 138 ÷ 12

28. 4000 ÷ 100

Skip count to make each pattern.

29. by 5 from 0 to 60

30. by 10 from 0 to 360

Units of Time

The second (s), minute (min), hour (h), day (d), week (wk), month (mo), year (y), and century (cent.) are units of time.

> To rename units of time:
> • *Multiply* to rename larger units as smaller units.
> • *Divide* to rename smaller units as larger units.

60 seconds (s) = 1 minute (min)
60 minutes = 1 hour (h)
24 hours = 1 day (d)
7 days = 1 week (wk)
12 months (mo) = 1 year (y)
365 days = 1 year
100 years = 1 century (cent.)

5 h = __?__ min
5 h = (5 × 60) min
5 h = 300 min

Think
1 h = 60 min
Multiply by 60.

28 d = __?__ wk
28 d = (28 ÷ 7) wk
28 d = 4 wk

Think
7 d = 1 wk
Divide by 7.

Study these examples.

$6\frac{1}{2}$ y = __?__ mo
$6\frac{1}{2}$ y = 78 mo

Think
$6\frac{1}{2} \times 12$
= 78

4 y 9 mo = __?__ mo
4 y 9 mo = 57 mo

Think
(4 × 12) + 9
= 57 mo

160 min = __?__ h
160 min = $2\frac{2}{3}$ h

Think
160 ÷ 60
= 2 R40
= $2\frac{40}{60} = 2\frac{2}{3}$

380 d = __?__ y __?__ d
380 d = 1 y 15 d

Think
380 ÷ 365
= 1 R15

Write *s, min, h, d, wk,* or *mo* to complete.

1. Baseball season lasts about 7 __?__ .

2. Jane exercised for 15 __?__ .

3. The lightning flashed for about 3 __?__ .

4. Leo's cold lasted 1 __?__ .

5. The circus performed 263 __?__ last year.

6. The movie was about 2 __?__ long.

Rename each unit of time. Explain the method you used.

7. 9 min = __?__ s

8. 4 d = __?__ h

9. $2\frac{1}{2}$ y = __?__ mo

10. 400 y = __?__ cent.

11. 42 d = __?__ wk

12. 260 min = __?__ h

13. 192 min = __?__ h __?__ min

14. 300 wk = __?__ y __?__ wk

15. 7 y 5 mo = __?__ mo

16. 220 s = __?__ min __?__ s

Computing Elapsed Time

School begins at 8:30 A.M. and ends at 2:45 P.M. How much time does Anna spend in school?

To find how much time, find the elapsed time from 8:30 A.M. to 2:45 P.M. Count the number of hours and then the number of minutes.

From 8:30 A.M. to 2:30 P.M. is 6 h.
From 2:30 P.M. to 2:45 P.M. is 15 min.

Anna spends 6 h 15 min in school.

Find the elapsed time.

17. from 2:15 P.M. to 5:30 P.M.

18. from 6:55 A.M. to 8:30 A.M.

19. from 9:30 A.M. to 4:15 P.M.

20. from 8:20 A.M. to 5:30 P.M.

21. from 10:25 P.M. to 6:38 A.M.

22. from 3:10 P.M. to 7:23 A.M.

23. Explain in your Math Journal why we need A.M. and P.M. when referring to time.

Problem Solving

24. Tim ran the marathon in 4 h 13 min. Neil ran the marathon in 310 min. Who ran the marathon in less time?

25. Elsa practiced the piano for 2 h 20 min. If she began at 2:50 P.M., at what time did she finish?

26. Melissa has to be at school at 8:10 A.M. She takes 25 minutes to shower and get dressed, 20 minutes to eat breakfast, and 18 minutes to walk to school. What is the latest time she should get up?

27. The Earth takes $365\frac{1}{4}$ days or 1 year to complete its orbit of the Sun. To account for the $\frac{1}{4}$ day, a leap year of 366 days occurs every 4 years. How many days are there in 4 consecutive years?

MENTAL MATH

Use the table to solve.

28. How long does Tom's delivery time take on Monday? on Wednesday?

29. Tom started work 1 h 20 min earlier on Monday. What time did he start work?

Tom's Delivery Times		
Day	**Start**	**Finish**
Mon.	8:15 A.M.	11:15 A.M.
Wed.	7:30 A.M.	1:00 P.M.

Time Zones

The United States is divided into six time zones.
This map shows four time zones of the United States:
Pacific, Mountain, Central, and Eastern.

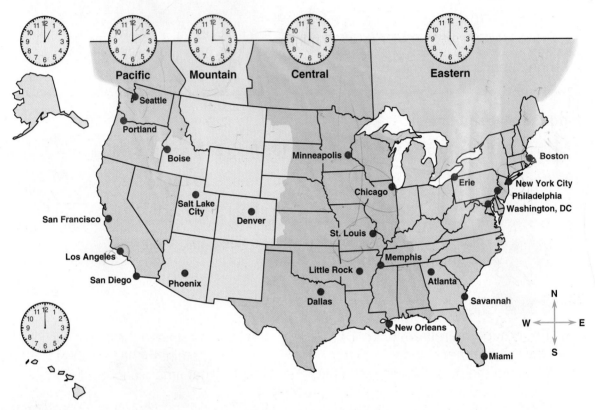

► From time zone to time zone, it is one hour earlier as you
travel west, and one hour later as you travel east.

When it is 3:00 A.M. in Phoenix, Arizona,
it is 2:00 A.M. in San Francisco, California.

When it is 4:00 P.M. in Chicago, Illinois,
it is 5:00 P.M. in New York City, New York.

Write the time zone where each is located. Use the map above.

1. Boise

2. Portland

3. Dallas

4. St. Louis

5. San Diego

6. Washington, DC

7. Denver

8. Miami

9. Why do you think that time gets earlier as you move from east to west?

Practice

Use the given time to complete each column. Use the map on page 368.

	Time Zone	Time			
10.	Pacific	7:00 A.M.	?	?	?
11.	Mountain	?	?	11:30 A.M.	?
12.	Central	?	1:15 P.M.	?	?
13.	Eastern	?	?	?	10:45 P.M.

	Cities	Time			
14.	Philadelphia	9:30 P.M.	?	?	?
15.	Memphis	?	3:15 P.M.	?	?
16.	Salt Lake City	?	?	7:20 A.M.	?
17.	Los Angeles	?	?	?	8:45 A.M.

Problem Solving Use the map on page 368.

18. Sandra wants to call a friend in St. Louis at 4:00 P.M. At what time should she call from Seattle?

19. Darin called his aunt in Boise from Savannah at 8:00 P.M. What time was it in Boise when he called?

20. A plane bound for Minneapolis leaves Philadelphia at 9:00 A.M. If the flight takes 2 hours, what time does the plane arrive in Minneapolis?

21. Mr. Kenney took a nonstop flight from New York to San Francisco. His plane left New York at 11:00 A.M. Eastern time and arrived in San Francisco at 1:30 P.M. Pacific time. How long was his flight?

22. An overnight train to Chicago left Erie at 8:15 P.M. Eastern time. It was supposed to arrive in Chicago after $15\frac{1}{2}$ h, but it was 45 min behind schedule. When did the train arrive in Chicago, Central time?

TEST PREPARATION

23. A flight to New York left Los Angeles at 1:00 A.M. Pacific Time. The flying time was 6 h 25 min. When did the plane arrive in New York, Eastern time?

   A 7:25 A.M.   **B** 7:25 P.M.   **C** 10:25 A.M.   **D** 10:25 P.M.

Compute with Customary Units

▶ To add customary units:

- Add like units. Start with smaller units.

- Rename units as needed. Regroup.

5 ft 10 in.
+ 8 ft 6 in.
13 ft 16 in. = 13 ft + 1 ft + 4 in. = 14 ft 4 in.

16 in. = 12 in. + 4 in.
    = 1 ft + 4 in.

▶ To subtract customary units:

- Rename units as needed. Regroup.

- Subtract like units. Start with smaller units.

$\overset{3}{\cancel{4}}$ gal $\overset{6}{\cancel{2}}$ qt
− 2 gal 3 qt
1 gal 3 qt

2 qt < 3 qt. Rename 4 gal 2 qt.

4 gal 2 qt = 3 gal + 1 gal + 2 qt

= 3 gal + 4 qt + 2 qt

= 3 gal + 6 qt

Study these examples.

6 yd 1 ft
+ 5 yd 1 ft
11 yd 2 ft

8 lb 17 oz
+   15 oz
8 lb 32 oz = 8 lb + 2 lb
           = 10 lb

$\overset{8}{\cancel{9}}$ h $\overset{60\ min}{}$
−   50 min
8 h 10 min

Add.

1.   8 yd 5 in.
+ 3 yd 4 in.

2.   17 ft 2 in.
+ 8 ft 9 in.

3.   2 mi 450 yd
+ 1 mi 330 yd

4.   6 c 5 fl oz
+ 3 c 2 fl oz

5.   2 qt 1 pt
+ 3 qt 1 pt

6.   2 gal 2 qt
+ 5 gal 3 qt

7.   2 lb 12 oz
+ 4 lb 12 oz

8.   2 h 51 min
+ 4 h 29 min

9.   4 wk 5 d
+ 7 wk 6 d

10.   13 ft 10 in.
+ 5 ft 9 in.

11.   4 mi 870 yd
+ 3 mi 1085 yd

12.   7 pt 3 c
+ 2 pt 1 c

Subtract.

13. 10 yd 2 ft
　　 $-$ 4 yd 1 ft

14. 3 ft 10 in.
　　 $-$ 1 ft 10 in.

15. 10 gal 1 qt
　　 $-$ 7 gal 2 qt

16. 9 lb 3 oz
　　 $-$ 3 lb 5 oz

17. 8 pt 1 c
　　 $-$ 2 pt

18. 6 T 100 lb
　　 $-$ 2 T 800 lb

19. 5 h 10 min
　　 $-$ 3 h 40 min

20. 6 y 8 mo
　　 $-$ 2 y 10 mo

21. 6 qt
　　 $-$ 2 qt 1 pt

Find the sum or difference.

22. 7 pt + 2 pt 1 c

23. 6 ft 10 in. $-$ 11 in.

24. 12 yd 1 ft + 2 ft

25. 5 d 10 h $-$ 16 h

26. 10 lb 5 oz + 16 lb 12 oz

27. 18 c 5 fl oz $-$ 13 c 7 fl oz

Problem Solving

28. Alfonso needs 1 ft 3 in. of ribbon to wrap one present and 1 ft 11 in. of ribbon to wrap another one. How much ribbon does he need in all?

29. Three packages weigh a total of 19 lb 4 oz. Two of these packages weigh 12 lb 7 oz. What is the weight of the third package?

30. Nestor worked for 6 h 45 min. Carla worked 4 h 20 min more than Nestor. How much time did Carla work?

31. A barrel holds 14 gal 1 qt of liquid. After removing 10 gal 3 qt, how much liquid is in the barrel?

32. Max weighs 82 lb 6 oz. He stands on a scale with his cat and the scale reads 95 lb 2 oz. How much does his cat weigh?

CHALLENGE

33. Jean bought 3 gal 2 qt of paint. She used 1 gal 3 qt to paint the walls of her room and some more to paint the kitchen. She had 2 qt of paint left over. How much paint did she use to paint the kitchen?

Problem-Solving Strategy:
Use More Than One Step

TIME CARD

5:30

Marina Petro worked from 8:15 A.M. to 5:30 P.M. on Monday. She spent 45 min for lunch. She was told she had worked only 7 hours. Marina disagreed and asked her employer to check her time card. Who was correct?

Read Visualize yourself in the problem above as you reread it. List the facts and the question.

Facts: worked from 8:15 A.M. to 5:30 P.M.
had lunch for 45 min

Question: How long did Marina work on Monday?

Plan **Step 1** To find the time difference between 8:15 A.M. and 5:30 P.M.:

Find the difference.
8:15 A.M. − 5:15 P.M. = _?_ h
5:30 P.M. − 5:15 P.M. = _?_ min
Add the two differences.

8:15

5:30

Step 2 Subtract 45 min from the time difference between 8:15 A.M. and 5:30 P.M.

Solve
8:15 A.M. − 5:15 P.M. = 9 h ⎤ 9 h + 15 min
5:30 P.M. − 5:15 P.M. = 15 min ⎦
(9 h + 15 min) − 45 min = n

$$\begin{array}{r} 8 \quad 75 \\ \cancel{9}\text{ h } \cancel{15}\text{ min} = 8\text{ h }75\text{ min} \\ -\qquad 45\text{ min} = \qquad 45\text{ min} \\ \hline 8\text{ h }30\text{ min} \end{array}$$

Rename 1 h as 60 min.

Marina was correct. 8 h 30 min > 7 h

Check Count on using the clock above to check that Marina worked 8 h 30 min.

Solve each problem by using more than one step.

1. Last week the average temperature was 18°C. The daily temperatures this week were: 21°C, 17°C, 25°C, 22°C, 23°C, 18°C, 21°C. How many degrees did the average temperature increase?

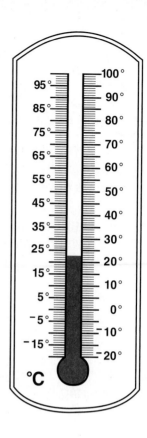

Read Visualize yourself in the problem above as you reread it. Focus on the facts and the question.

List what you know.

Facts: Last week's average—18°C
This week's temperatures—21°C, 17°C, 25°C, 22°C, 23°C, 18°C, 21°C

Question: How many degrees did the average temperature increase?

Plan First find the average temperature for this week. Then subtract to find the increase.

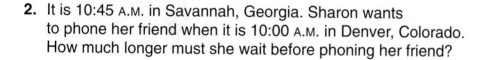

2. It is 10:45 A.M. in Savannah, Georgia. Sharon wants to phone her friend when it is 10:00 A.M. in Denver, Colorado. How much longer must she wait before phoning her friend?

3. The Morse family attended the school concert at 7:30 P.M. The concert lasted 1 hour 50 min. If it took them 15 minutes to drive home, what time did they arrive home?

4. A barrel holds 14 gal 1 qt of water. A gardener used 8 gal 2 qt to water the flowers and 2 gal 1 qt to fill the birdbath. How much water was left?

5. Jan bought 4 bags of oatmeal cookies and 3 bags of raisin cookies. Each bag of oatmeal cookies weighed 2 lb 7 oz, and each bag of raisin cookies weighed 1 lb 12 oz. What was the total weight of the cookies Jan bought?

6. Margaret leaves Newark, New Jersey, at 2:30 P.M. on Monday. She arrives in Honolulu, Hawaii, 13 hours later. Time in Hawaii is 2 hours earlier than in the Pacific time zone. What day and time will it be when she arrives?

Problem-Solving Applications: Mixed Review

Read **Plan** **Solve** **Check**

Solve each problem and explain the method you used.

1. A frozen yogurt cart at the Midwood Mall weighs about half a ton. About how many pounds does the cart weigh?

2. The yogurt cart's awning is 50 in. high. The awning on a nearby jewelry cart is 4 ft 9 in. high. Which awning is higher?

3. The jewelry cart owner opens it at 11:25 A.M. and closes it at 10:00 P.M. How long is the cart open each day?

4. Each side of a square sign is 2 ft 3 in. How long is the trim that goes around it?

5. How many pints of yogurt are there in a 2-gallon container?

6. The temperature outdoors was 48°F. Inside the mall the temperature was 70°F. How much colder was it outdoors?

Use the data box for problems 7 and 8.

7. What is the cost per ounce of each special?

8. Which special is the best buy?

9. The jewelry cart has a rectangular sign 3 ft long and 2 ft 5 in. wide. What is its perimeter?

10. This pictograph shows the number of yogurt cones sold last Friday. How many more peach than melon cones were sold?

11. What symbol would be used to represent 3 cones? 9 cones?

Today's Specials	
5	6-oz cups for $3.00
4	8-oz cups for $3.00
2	pints for $2.50

Yogurt Sales	
melon	🍦🍦🍦
peach	🍦🍦🍦🍦🍦
lime	🍦🍦🍦🍦🍦🍦
orange	🍦🍦🍦🍦
Key: Each 🍦 = 12 cones.	

Choose a strategy from the list or use another strategy you know to solve each problem.

12. Amelia opened the jewelry cart at 9:15 A.M. and worked for $5\frac{1}{4}$ h. Then Marie took over until 9:45 P.M. How long did Marie work?

13. There are 4 carts at the mall. Each cart is 4 in. taller than the previous one. The tallest cart is 6 ft 2 in. What are the heights of the two shortest carts?

14. Five flavors of yogurt are sold. How many possible combinations of 3 different flavors can Jules order?

15. The diagonal of the square in the mall sign is 3 ft 9 in. Find the circumference of the sign.

16. Three people each brought 3 gal of juice to a party. If $5\frac{1}{4}$ gal of juice was used and they shared equally what was left over, how many gallons did each person take home?

17. David won a charm at the jewelry cart by naming the tenth number in the sequence 1, 3, 7, 15, ... What number did he name?

18. Cheryl gives this business card to each new customer. Measure each side to the nearest $\frac{1}{8}$ inch. Then find the perimeter.

19. The yogurt cart features a special on peach and lime. Fifteen people bought a pint of each. If 2 dozen pints of peach and 20 pints of lime were sold, how many people bought a pint of yogurt on sale?

Strategy File

Use These Strategies
Use More Than One Step
Use a Model/Diagram
Make an Organized List
Find a Pattern

Gems 'n' Jewels
With every $25 purchase, receive a $2 discount.

Midwood Mall

Write Your Own

20. Write a problem that can be solved by using more than one step. Then have a classmate solve it.

Write the letter of the best estimate. *(See pp. 358–365.)*

1. width of a camera   **a.** 8 yd   **b.** 8 ft   **c.** 8 in.

2. capacity of a blender   **a.** 2 gal   **b.** 2 c   **c.** 2 qt

3. weight of a whale   **a.** $1\frac{2}{3}$ oz   **b.** $1\frac{2}{3}$ T   **c.** $1\frac{2}{3}$ lb

4. temperature on a beach day   **a.** 40°F   **b.** 50°F   **c.** 90°F

5. temperature for water to freeze   **a.** 0°C   **b.** 32°C   **c.** 10°C

Rename each unit of measure. *(See pp. 358–363, 366–367.)*

6. 72 in. = ? yd   7. 490 min = ? h   8. 112 oz = ? lb

9. 5 qt = ? pt   10. 4 yd = ? ft   11. 12 min = ? s

12. 3 c = ? fl oz   13. 6 gal = ? pt   14. 2 T = ? lb

Use the given time to complete each column.
You may use the map on page 368.   *(See pp. 368–369.)*

	City	Time			
15.	Washington, DC	6:00 A.M.	?	?	?
16.	Chicago, Illinois	?	7:30 A.M.	?	?
17.	Denver, Colorado	?	?	8:15 P.M.	?
18.	Los Angeles, California	?	?	?	9:45 P.M.

Add or subtract. *(See pp. 370–371.)*

19. 4 gal 2 qt
    − 1 gal 3 qt

20. 5 ft 2 in.
    + 11 ft 11 in.

21. 4 wk 1 d
    − 2 wk 5 d

22. 2 lb 10 oz
    + 5 lb 9 oz

23. 4 yd 18 in.
    − 2 yd 26 in.

24. 9 pt 1 c
    + 2 pt 1 c

Problem Solving
(See pp. 364–365, 372–375.)

25. The temperature last Monday was 12°F in the morning and −8°F in the evening. How many degrees did the temperature drop?

26. If David jogs once around the $2\frac{1}{2}$-mile perimeter of the lake 6 days a week and twice on Sundays, how many miles does David jog in one week?

(See Still More Practice, p. 486.)

Pascal's Triangle

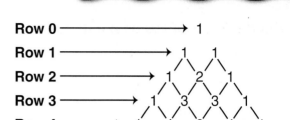

The arrangement of numbers at the right is known as Pascal's Triangle. It is named for the seventeenth-century French mathematician Blaise Pascal.

There are certain useful patterns in this triangle. For example:

- 1 is the first and last number in each row.

- Every number other than 1 is the sum of the two numbers directly above it.

▶ The sum of the first two numbers in each row form a pattern. Putting the data in a table makes it easier to identify and to extend the pattern.

Pascal's Triangle					
Row Number	0	1	2	3	4
Sum of First Two Numbers	1	2	3	4	5

> The sum of the first two numbers in each row is one greater than the row number.

1. Copy Pascal's Triangle above and complete row 5. Then extend the triangle two more rows.

2. Use the pattern above to find the sum of the first two numbers in row 10 of Pascal's Triangle; in row 25.

3. Copy and complete each table. Look for a pattern.

a.

Pascal's Triangle						
Row Number	0	1	2	3	4	5
Number of Numbers in the Row	1	2	?	?	?	?

b.

Pascal's Triangle						
Row Number	0	1	2	3	4	5
Sum of the Numbers in the Row	1	2	?	?	?	?

4. Use the pattern in exercise 3a to find how many numbers are in row 8 of Pascal's triangle; in row 20.

5. Use the pattern in exercise 3b to find the sum of the numbers in row 6 of Pascal's triangle; in row 8.

6. Except for the 1s, which of the rows 1 through 7 of Pascal's Triangle contain all even numbers? of the rows 8 through 10?

7. Which of the rows 1 through 7 of Pascal's Triangle contain all odd numbers? of the rows 8 through 10?

8. List the numbers in row 9 of Pascal's Triangle. What pattern do you see, excluding the ones?

9. Which numbers in row 7 of Pascal's Triangle are divisible by 7?

Write the letter of the best estimate.

1. length of a bed
   a. 6 in.   **b.** 6 yd   **c.** 6 ft

2. weight of a bag of flour
   a. 6 lb   **b.** 6 oz   **c.** 6 T

3. capacity of a large bowl
   a. 4 gal   **b.** 4 pt   **c.** 4 qt

4. temperature on a cold, snowy day
   a. 0°C   **b.** −10°C   **c.** 10°C

5. temperature on a good day to swim
   a. 5°F   **b.** 45°F   **c.** 90°F

Compare. Write <, =, or >.

6. 42 ft ? 14 yd

7. 3 qt ? 7 pt

8. 1 gal 5 qt ? 2 gal 2 pt

9. 15 c ? 4 qt

10. 120 in. ? 10 ft

11. 350 min ? 3 h

Use the given time to complete each column.

	Time Zone	Time			
12.	Pacific	11:30 P.M.	?	?	?
13.	Mountain	?	9:15 P.M.	?	?
14.	Central	?	?	8:45 A.M.	?
15.	Eastern	?	?	?	6:00 A.M.

Problem Solving

Use a strategy you have learned.

16. Lisa works at the library 3 h 15 min each morning and 2 h 45 min each afternoon, 5 days a week. How many hours does she work in 2 weeks?

Tell About It

Explain how you solved the problem. Show all your work.

17. The temperature at midnight was −6°C. It rose to 3°C by 8:00 A.M. How many degrees did it rise?

Performance Assessment

Mia recorded data about her pets in this table.

18. How much older is Goldie than Tiny?

19. What is the combined weight of her pets?

20. Write and solve a problem using the data.

Pet	Age	Weight
Rex	4 y 2 mo	42 lb 10 oz
Tiny	1 y 10 mo	1 lb 13 oz
Goldie	2 y 6 mo	9 lb 8 oz

Choose the best answer.

1. Which is ordered from greatest to least?

    a. 2.3, 2.4, 2.0, 2.9
    b. 0.14, 0.16, 0.18, 0.2
    c. 7.43, 7.42, 7.41, 7.4
    d. none of these

2. $16 \overline{) \$138.88}$

    a. $8.68
    b. $9.38
    c. $18.68
    d. $19.38

3. $\begin{aligned} 23\frac{3}{8} \\ -17\frac{3}{4} \\ \hline \end{aligned}$

    a. $5\frac{5}{8}$ **b.** $6\frac{5}{8}$

    c. $6\frac{3}{4}$ **d.** $5\frac{3}{4}$

4. Which is a true statement about the data?

Average Weekly Temperature (in °F)							
Week	1	2	3	4	5	6	7
Temperature	28	20	33	34	28	30	21

    a. median = 33   **b.** median = mode
    c. mean > median   **d.** range = 13

5. Which type of angle is shown?

    a. acute   **b.** obtuse
    c. scalene   **d.** right

6. How much more than

$$658 - 309 \text{ is } 658 \times 309?$$

    a. 22,208
    b. 202,971
    c. 202,973
    d. 203,671

7. Choose the simplest form of the mixed number.

$$27\frac{20}{15}$$

    a. $27\frac{1}{3}$ **b.** $27\frac{3}{4}$

    c. $28\frac{1}{3}$ **d.** $28\frac{1}{2}$

8. $5\frac{1}{5} \div 5$

    a. $\frac{1}{5}$ **b.** $1\frac{1}{26}$

    c. 26   **d.** not given

9. Use the spinner. Which is a true probability statement?

    a. $P(3) = \frac{1}{8}$

    b. $P(not\ 3) = \frac{1}{3}$

    c. $P(3) = \frac{3}{8}$

    d. $P(not\ 3) = \frac{1}{5}$

10. Which is true about the polygons?

    a. congruent, *not* similar
    b. congruent and similar
    c. similar, *not* congruent
    d. none of these

11. Which statement about quadrilaterals is true?

    a. All quadrilaterals have four sides.
    b. All quadrilaterals have equal sides.
    c. All quadrilaterals have four right angles.
    d. All quadrilaterals are parallelograms.

12. Round to the nearest cent.

    8)$17.33

    a. $2.16
    b. $2.17
    c. $21.70
    d. not given

13. Choose the appropriate unit to measure orange juice.

    a. feet
    b. quarts
    c. pounds
    d. not given

14. What number is 389 million, 235 thousand?

    a. 389,235
    b. 389,200,035
    c. 389,235,000
    d. not given

15. A 3-pound bag of whole-wheat flour is on sale for $2.88. The regular price is $3.75 for a 3-pound bag. What is the regular price per pound of whole-wheat flour?

    a. $3.75   **b.** $1.25
    c. $.96   **d.** $2.21

16. One of the angles of a right triangle measures 53°. What are the degree measures of the other two angles?

    a. 90°; 37°   **b.** 90°; 47°
    c. 90°; 53°   **d.** not given

17. Which statement is *false*?

    a. A square is a regular polygon.
    b. A triangle has no diagonals.
    c. A rhombus is a square.
    d. A square is a rectangle.

18. Choose the elapsed time between 10:45 A.M. and 1:15 P.M.

    a. 3 h
    b. 3 h 30 min
    c. 2 h 30 min
    d. 2 h 20 min

19. 18 ft 9 in. − 11 ft 11 in. = ___?

    a. 6 ft 10 in.
    b. 7 ft 11 in.
    c. 7 ft 2 in.
    d. not given

20. Compare: 6 c ___?___ $1\frac{1}{2}$ qt

    a. <
    b. >
    c. =
    d. not given

21. Every morning Alan jogs once around his property, which is a rectangular block 230 m long and 160 m wide. How far does Alan jog in five mornings?

    a. 390 m   **b.** 780 m
    c. 3900 m   **d.** not given

22. Your dog weighs 16 lb 4 oz. You put your cat on the scale with your dog. The scale reads 20 lb 1 oz. How much does the cat weigh?

    a. 4 lb 3 oz   **b.** 3 lb 13 oz
    c. 3 lb 3 oz   **d.** not given

Explain how you solved the problem. Show all your work.

23. A forward on the Lansing varsity basketball team is 6 ft 4 in. tall. A guard is 5 ft 11 in. The center is 6 ft 9 in. What is the average (mean) height of the three players?

Metric Measurement, Area, and Volume

METRICAL MEASUREMENT

When measuring a distance
like the length of any river,
or calculating volume
such as water it delivers,
or figuring how much it weighs,
determining its mass,
it helps to know some simple things
that you can learn in class.
It's useful knowing that you measure
volume with the *liter*,
that mass you measure with the *gram*
and distance with the *meter*.
With just a few more simple rules
you'll find it is a pleasure
to use the metric system
as an easy way to measure.

Kenn Nesbitt

In this chapter you will:

Investigate metric units of length,
  capacity, and mass
Use area formulas
Classify solid figures
Learn about cubic measure
  and volume
Solve problems by drawing
  a picture

**Critical Thinking/
Finding Together**

You have one piece of pipe 1.3 m
long and another piece 30 cm
long. How can you use these two
pieces of pipe to measure 2 m on
a third piece of pipe?

12-1

Metric Measurement

The metric system is a *decimal* system of measurement. The standard metric units are the meter (m), which is used to measure length; the liter (L), which is used to measure capacity; and the gram (g), which is used to measure mass.

▶ The table below shows how the metric units of length, capacity, or mass are related to the standard metric units and to each other.

Metric Units of Length	(1 × 1000) m = 1000 m	—	(1 ÷ 10) m = 0.1 m	(1 ÷ 100) m = 0.01 m	(1 ÷ 1000) m = 0.001 m
	1 kilometer (km)	1 meter (m)	1 decimeter (dm)	1 centimeter (cm)	1 millimeter (mm)
Metric Units of Capacity	(1 × 1000) L = 1000 L	—	(1 ÷ 10) L = 0.1 L	(1 ÷ 100) L = 0.01 L	(1 ÷ 1000) L = 0.001 L
	1 kiloliter (kL)	1 liter (L)	1 deciliter (dL)	1 centiliter (cL)	1 milliliter (mL)
Metric Units of Mass	(1 × 1000) g = 1000 g	—	(1 ÷ 10) g = 0.1 g	(1 ÷ 100) g = 0.01 g	(1 ÷ 1000) g = 0.001 g
	1 kilogram (kg)	1 gram (g)	1 decigram (dg)	1 centigram (cg)	1 milligram (mg)

▶ To rename metric units, use the relations between the units as shown in the table below.

1 km = 1000 m	1 kL = 1000 L	1 kg = 1000 g
1 m = 10 dm	1 L = 10 dL	1 g = 10 dg
1 m = 100 cm	1 L = 100 cL	1 g = 100 cg
1 m = 1000 mm	1 L = 1000 mL	1 g = 1000 mg
1 dm = 10 cm	1 dL = 10 cL	1 dg = 10 cg
1 dm = 100 mm	1 dL = 100 mL	1 dg = 100 mg
1 cm = 10 mm	1 cL = 10 mL	1 cg = 10 mg

▶ *Multiply* to rename larger units as smaller units.

85 dm = _?_ cm

.....Think.............
: 1 dm = 10 cm :
....

85 dm = (85 × 10) cm

85 dm = 850 cm

▶ *Divide* to rename smaller units as larger units.

638 L = _?_ kL

.....Think.............
: 1000 L = 1 kL :
....

638 L = (638 ÷ 1000) kL

638 L = 0.638 kL

Which is the smaller unit of measure? Write the letter of the correct answer.

1. **a.** milliter
   b. liter

2. **a.** meter
   b. decimeter

3. **a.** gram
   b. kilogram

4. **a.** centimeter
   b. millimeter

Rename each unit of measure.

5. 84 g = ? cg

6. 4000 cL = ? L

7. 16 000 g = ? kg

8. 11.5 dm = ? m

9. 25 300 m = ? km

10. 50 dL = ? L

11. 3.78 cm = ? mm

12. 40.3 kL = ? L

13. 734 g = ? kg

14. 585 m = ? km

15. 836 mm = ? m

16. 479 cg = ? g

17. Explain in your Math Journal how the metric system of measurement differs from the customary system of measurement.

Problem Solving

18. Sergey Bubka's Olympic gold-medal-winning pole vault in 1988 was 5.90 m. Would a vault of 595 cm be higher or lower than Bubka's jump?

19. Isabel needs 350 mL of milk to make a loaf of bread. How many liters of milk does she need to make 8 loaves of bread?

20. An orange contains about 0.07 g of vitamin C. About how many milligrams of vitamin C does it contain?

21. Marco was running in the 600-m race. He had run 45 000 cm. How many meters farther did he have to run to complete the race?

CHALLENGE — Algebra

Find the missing number to discover a pattern in each row.

22. 18.5 m = ? dm

23. 185 dm = ? cm

24. 1850 cm = ? mm

25. 173 L = ? dL

26. 1730 dL = ? cL

27. 17 300 cL = ? mL

28. 2500 mm = ? cm

29. 250 cm = ? dm

30. 25 dm = ? m

31. 68 000 mg = ? cg

32. 6800 cg = ? dg

33. 680 dg = ? g

34. To which direction, right or left, is the decimal point moved when renaming a larger metric unit as a smaller metric unit? a smaller metric unit as a larger metric unit?

Relate Metric Units of Length

Materials: metric ruler or meterstick, paper, pencil

The millimeter (mm), centimeter (cm), decimeter (dm), meter (m), and kilometer (km) are metric units of length.

1 m	=	1000 mm
1 m	=	100 cm
1 m	=	10 dm
1 km	=	1000 m

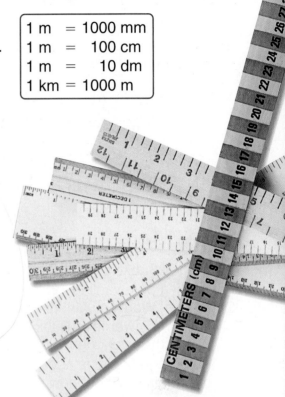

1. Which units are smaller than a meter? larger than a meter?

2. Which unit would you use to measure the height of your desk? Explain why you think your choice is reasonable.

3. What objects in your classroom would you measure in meters? Explain why your choices are reasonable.

4. What unit would you use to measure the distance between two cities? Explain why you think your choice is reasonable.

5. What unit would you use to measure the length of an ant? Explain why you think your choice is reasonable.

You can use a metric ruler or a meterstick to measure the length of an object. A meterstick usually shows decimeters, millimeters, and centimeters.

6. Find the marks that represent each unit on your metric ruler.

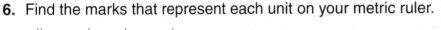

1 mm   1 cm   1 dm

7. How many millimeters long is your metric ruler? How many centimeters? How many decimeters?

8. How many millimeters long is a meterstick? How many centimeters? How many decimeters?

9. Use your metric ruler to measure each of the following objects in millimeters; in centimeters; in decimeters.

    a. width of your desktop   **b.** height of your chair

    c. length of your thumb   **d.** thickness of your math book

10. Name 3 objects you would measure in millimeters; in centimeters; in decimeters; in meters; in kilometers.

Sometimes it is necessary to take precise measurements. The smaller the unit of measure you use, the more precise your measurement will be. When you measure an object, you measure to the nearest unit of that measure.

11. Use your metric ruler as shown to measure the length of the given ribbon.

What is the length of the ribbon to the nearest mm? the nearest cm? the nearest dm?

12. Estimate. Then measure each to the nearest mm, nearest cm, and nearest dm.

    a. length of your pen   **b.** diameter of a coin   **c.** height of the board

Communicate

13. What is the smallest metric unit of length? the largest metric unit of length?

14. Which is the most precise unit of measure to use: meter, decimeter, centimeter, or millimeter? Why?

15. At the hardware store Alex asked for an extension cord that was 4 km long. Was this an appropriate length to ask for? If not, what length do you think he should have asked for?

CRITICAL THINKING

Find the missing unit. Explain how you found your answer.

16. 9.5 dm = 950 ___?___   **17.** 4 cm = 0.04 ___?___   **18.** 2.5 mm = 0.25 ___?___

19. 1200 m = 1.2 ___?___   **20.** 2.5 m = 2500 ___?___   **21.** 0.34 km = 34 000 ___?___

12-3

Relate Metric Units of Capacity

The milliliter (mL), centiliter (cL), deciliter (dL),
liter (L), and kiloliter (kL), are metric units of capacity.

1 L	=	1000 mL
1 L	=	100 cL
1 L	=	10 dL
1 kL	=	1000 L

▶ The liter, milliliter, and kiloliter are the most
commonly used metric units of capacity.

A tall thermos
holds about 1 L.

A medicine dropper
holds about 0.5 mL.

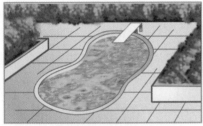

The water in a swimming
pool is measured in kL.

▶ You can use graduated cylinders of various sizes
to measure liquid capacity.

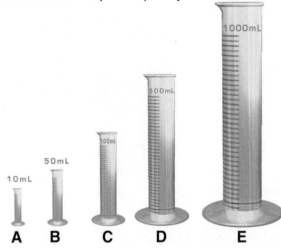

A   B   C   D   E

- Cylinder *A* holds 10 mL or 1 cL.
- Cylinder *B* holds 50 mL.
- Cylinder *C* holds 100 mL or 1 dL.
- Cylinder *D* holds 500 mL.
- Cylinder *E* holds 1000 mL or 1 L.

Study these examples.

15 L __?__ 1500 mL

Think
1 L = 1000 mL

15 L = (15 × 1000) mL
15 L = 15 000 mL
15 000 mL > 1500 mL

So 15 L > 1500 mL.

360 L __?__ 3.6 kL

Think
1000 L = 1 kL

360 L = (360 ÷ 1000) kL
360 L = 0.36 kL
0.36 kL < 3.6 kL

So 360 L < 3.6 kL.

Which metric unit would best measure the capacity of each?
Write _mL_, _L_, or _kL_.

1. a fish tank   **2.** an oil tanker   **3.** an ice tray

4. a milk truck   **5.** a baby bottle   **6.** a washing machine

Compare. Write <, =, or >.

7. 2 L __?__ 250 cL   **8.** 13 L __?__ 130 mL   **9.** 36 kL __?__ 36 000 L

10. 52 L __?__ 515 dL   **11.** 2600 L __?__ 26 kL   **12.** 35 dL __?__ 4 L

13. 760 cL __?__ 75 L   **14.** 12 L __?__ 12 000 mL   **15.** 173 L __?__ 1730 cL

16. 860 mL __?__ 8.6 L   **17.** 17.3 kL __?__ 1730 L   **18.** 2.5 L __?__ 25 dL

Problem Solving

19. Rhoda wants to add a small amount of food coloring to the pie she is making. What metric unit of capacity should she use to measure the food coloring?

20. Mr. Navarro has 28 students in his science class. Each student in his class needs 250 mL of salt solution to do one experiment. How many liters of salt solution does the class need for the experiment?

21. Ms. Haraguchi made fruit punch for her party. To make the punch, she used 1.5 L of orange juice, 300 cL of ginger ale, 5 dL of lemon juice, and 1 L of club soda. How many deciliters of punch did Ms. Haraguchi make?

CHALLENGE

Choose 4 empty containers of different sizes and shapes.

22. Use a small paper cup as your unit of measure.
  • Estimate how many times you would have to fill the paper cup with water to fill each of the 4 empty containers.
  • Use the paper cup and water to measure the actual capacity of each container.

23. Use a graduated cylinder to measure the capacity of each container in milliliters. Then tell whether each container holds less than, equal to, or greater than one liter.

24. Report to your class on the results of your experiment.

Update your skills. See page 17.

12-4

Relate Metric Units of Mass

The milligram (mg), centigram (cg), decigram (dg), gram (g), kilogram (kg), and metric ton (t) are metric units of mass.

The most commonly used metric units of mass are the milligram, gram, kilogram, and metric ton.

1 g	=	1000 mg
1 g	=	100 cg
1 g	=	10 dg
1 kg	=	1000 g
1 t	=	1000 kg

Materials: metric balance, gram masses, nickel, paper, pencil

1. Which units are smaller than a gram? larger than a gram?

2. A grain of salt has a mass of about one milligram.
   Name other objects that have a mass of about 1 mg.

3. What objects would you use to measure mass in milligrams?

4. A standard paper clip has a mass of about one gram.
   Name other objects that have a mass of about 1 g.

5. Estimate the mass of a nickel by comparing it with the mass of a standard paper clip. How many standard paper clips do you think are equal to the mass of a nickel?

6. About how many grams do you think a nickel would weigh?

7. Use a metric balance to find the actual mass of a nickel. Then compare the mass with your estimate. How does your estimate compare with the mass?

8. **a.** Estimate the mass of a pencil by comparing it with the mass of a standard paper clip. About how many grams do you think a pencil would weigh?

   b. Use a metric balance to find the actual mass of the pencil. Then compare the mass with your estimate. How does your estimate compare with the mass?

Now choose 5 classroom objects, each of different size and mass.

9. Estimate the mass of each object. Then use a metric balance to find the mass in grams. Record your answers in a table like the one shown.

10. How does each estimate in your table compare with the actual measurement?

Object	Estimate	Mass in Grams

11. Estimate the mass of a hardcover dictionary by comparing it with the mass of a bag of 1000 standard paper clips. About how many grams do you think a hardcover dictionary would weigh?

12. If 1000 g = 1 kg, about how many kilograms do you think a hardcover dictionary would weigh?

13. Name some objects you know that have their mass measured in kilograms.

The mass of extremely heavy objects is expressed in metric tons. A bus has a mass of about 3 t.

14. Name some objects you know that have their mass measured in metric tons.

15. How many grams are in one metric ton?

16. Why are you less likely to use the metric ton than the gram, the milligram, or the kilogram as a unit of mass in your everyday life?

> 1 metric ton (t) = 1000 kilograms (kg)

17. Which is a greater mass: 3 g or 300 mg? 400 g or 4.5 kg? 2.75 t or 2000 kg? Explain your answers.

Communicate

18. What is the smallest metric unit of mass? the largest metric unit of mass?

19. What unit would you use to measure the mass of a small leaf? a loaf of bread? an automobile? a table? Explain your answers.

20. You are cooking chicken for dinner. The recipe calls for a large chicken. Will you buy a chicken that is about 4 g or 4 kg? Why?

MENTAL MATH

21. Express in cm: 5 dm, 10 dm, 15 dm, 100 mm, 150 mm, 200 mm

22. Express in m: 8 km, 6 km, 7 km, 50 dm, 70 dm, 400 dm

23. Express in g: 2 kg, 4 kg, 9 kg, 70 dg, 80 dg, 600 dg

24. Express in L: 3 kL, 5 kL, 8 kL, 40 dL, 90 dL, 700 dL

Square Measure

The area of a figure is the number of square units that cover its surface.

▶ Square measures can be expressed in both metric and customary units.

1 cm

1 cm

This square measures 1 cm on each side. Its area is one square centimeter (cm^2).

| Read: "square centimeter" |

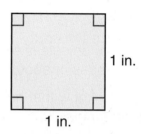

1 in.

1 in.

This square measures 1 in. on each side. Its area is one square inch ($in.^2$).

| Read: "square inch" |

Other metric square measures are: square millimeter (mm^2), square decimeter (dm^2), square meter (m^2), and square kilometer (km^2).

Other customary square measures are: square foot (ft^2), square yard (yd^2), and square mile (mi^2).

Find the area of each figure.

1. ◂1 mm^2

<u>14</u> mm^2

2. ◂1 dm^2

<u>?</u> dm^2

3. ◂ 1 m^2

<u>?</u> m^2

4. ◂1 ft^2

<u>?</u> ft^2

5. ◂1 yd^2

<u>?</u> yd^2

6. ◂1 mi^2

<u>?</u> mi^2

7. ◂1 km^2

<u>?</u> km^2

8. ◂1 ft^2

<u>?</u> ft^2

9. ◂1 m^2

<u>?</u> m^2

Practice

Estimating Area

Mr. Ramirez uses a grid to find about how many square feet of glass he will need to cover the top of a counter. About how many square feet of glass will he need?

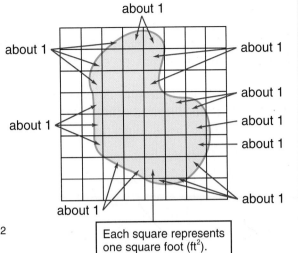

To find about how many square feet of glass is needed, estimate the area of the top of the counter.

Area of whole squares: 17 ft^2

Area of partial squares: about 9 ft^2

Estimated area: 17 ft^2 + 9 ft^2 = 26 ft^2

Mr. Ramirez will need about 26 square feet of glass.

Estimate the area of each figure.

10.

1 in.^{2} ▸

11.
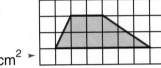
1 cm^2 ▸

12.

1 dm^2 ▸

13.
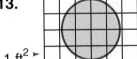
1 ft^2 ▸

14.

1 m^2 ▸

15.
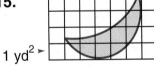
1 yd^2 ▸

Problem Solving

16. Karina is making a design by using a grid as shown. About how many square feet is her design if each square in the grid represents one square foot?

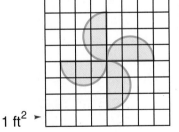
1 ft^2 ▸

Write About It

17. Use grid paper to make a design like Karina's in exercise 16. Then estimate its area. In your Math Journal, explain how you planned your design and how you estimated the number of square feet used in your design.

Areas of Rectangles and Squares

▶ The rectangle on the right contains 45 squares, or 9 rows of 5 squares each.

The area of the rectangle is found by *multiplying* the *length by* the *width.* So, the *formula* for finding the area of a rectangle is:

$$\begin{array}{ccc} \textbf{Area} & \textbf{length} & \textbf{width} \\ \downarrow & \downarrow & \downarrow \end{array}$$

$$A = \ell \times w$$
$$A = 9 \text{ yd} \times 5 \text{ yd}$$
$$A = 45 \text{ yd}^2$$

The area of the rectangle is 45 square yards.

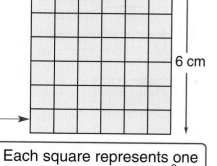

Each square represents one square yard (1 yd²).

▶ The square on the right contains 36 squares, or 6 rows of 6 squares each.

The area of the square is found by *multiplying* the *side by* the *side.* So, the *formula* for finding the area of a square is:

$$\begin{array}{ccc} \textbf{Area} & \textbf{side} & \textbf{side} \\ \downarrow & \downarrow & \downarrow \end{array}$$

$$A = s \times s = \boxed{s^2}$$
$$A = 6 \text{ cm} \times 6 \text{ cm} \qquad \text{Read: "} s \text{ squared"}$$
$$A = 36 \text{ cm}^2$$

Each square represents one square centimeter (1 cm²).

The area of the square is 36 square centimeters.

Study these examples.

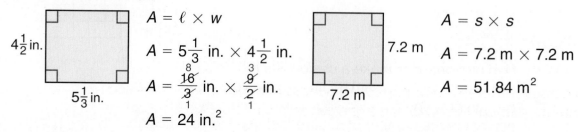

$4\frac{1}{2}$ in.

$5\frac{1}{3}$ in.

$$A = \ell \times w$$
$$A = 5\frac{1}{3} \text{ in.} \times 4\frac{1}{2} \text{ in.}$$
$$A = \frac{\overset{8}{\cancel{16}}}{\underset{1}{\cancel{3}}} \text{ in.} \times \frac{\overset{3}{\cancel{9}}}{\underset{1}{\cancel{2}}} \text{ in.}$$
$$A = 24 \text{ in.}^2$$

7.2 m

7.2 m

$$A = s \times s$$
$$A = 7.2 \text{ m} \times 7.2 \text{ m}$$
$$A = 51.84 \text{ m}^2$$

Find the area of each figure.

1.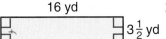
16 yd
$3\frac{1}{2}$ yd

2.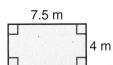
7.5 m
4 m

3.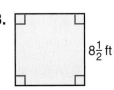
$8\frac{1}{2}$ ft

4.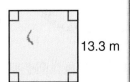
13.3 m

Find the area of each figure to complete each table.

Rectangle		
ℓ	w	$A = \ell \times w$
5. 7.3 cm	3.1 cm	?
6. $13\frac{1}{3}$ ft	$3\frac{3}{4}$ ft	?

Square	
s	$A = s \times s$
7. 4.5 cm	?
8. $4\frac{1}{3}$ in.	?

Use your centimeter ruler to measure the sides to the nearest millimeter. Then find the area.

9.

10.

11.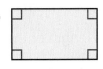

12.

Find the area of each figure by forming rectangles. Explain your answer.

13.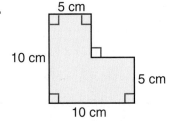
5 cm
10 cm
5 cm
10 cm

14.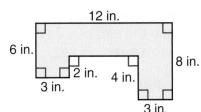
12 in.
6 in.
2 in.
3 in.
4 in.
8 in.
3 in.

15.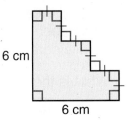
6 cm
6 cm

Problem Solving

16. Which has a greater area, a rectangle that has a length of 80 cm and a width of 20 cm, or a square that measures 40 cm on each side?

17. How many cans of paint are needed to paint 2 walls that are each 8 ft high and 18 ft long if one can of paint covers an area of 100 square feet?

CRITICAL THINKING — *Algebra*

How many different rectangles with whole number dimensions can you make for each given area? Use grid paper to construct each figure.

18. 7 square units

19. 10 square units

20. 8 square units

Areas of Parallelograms and Triangles

Materials: grid paper, pencil, ruler, scissors

You can use what you know about finding the area of a rectangle to help you find the area of other polygons.

Look at the parallelograms below.

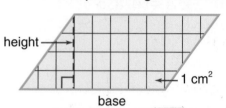
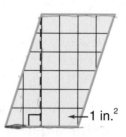
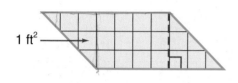

Any side of a parallelogram can serve as the *base*. The *height* is the length of the perpendicular segment from the base to the opposite vertex.

1. Find and record the length of the base (*b*) and the height (*h*) of each parallelogram.

2. How would you find the height of each parallelogram if it was not marked with a dotted line?

3. On grid paper copy and then cut out each parallelogram along each dotted line. Place the two pieces of each parallelogram together to form a rectangle.

4. What is the area of each rectangle formed?

5. How do the base and height of each parallelogram relate to the length and width of its related rectangle?

6. What is the area of each parallelogram? How does the area of each parallelogram compare with the area of its related rectangle?

7. What formula would you use to find the area of a parallelogram with base *b* and height *h*?

8. Use the formula to find the area of each parallelogram below.

a.
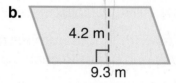
6 cm
8 cm

b.
4.2 m
9.3 m

c.
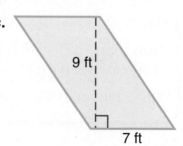
9 ft
7 ft

Now look at the parallelograms below.

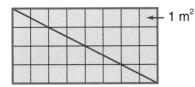

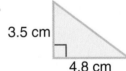

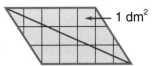

9. Record the length of the base (*b*) and the height (*h*) of each parallelogram. Then find its area.

10. On grid paper copy and cut out each parallelogram. Then cut along each diagonal to make two triangles. Are the two triangles of each parallelogram congruent?

11. How do the base and height of each triangle relate to the base and height of its related parallelogram?

12. How does the area of each triangle compare with the area of its related parallelogram? What is the area of each of the triangles?

13. What formula would you use to find the area of a triangle with base *b* and height *h*?

14. Use the formula to find the area of each triangle below.

a.
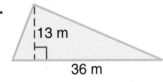
13 m
36 m

b.
3.5 cm
4.8 cm

c.
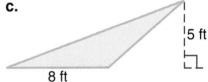
5 ft
8 ft

Communicate

15. What two measurements are needed for finding the area of parallelograms and of triangles?

16. Write in your Math Journal the formulas for finding the area of parallelograms and of triangles. Give an example using each formula.

CHALLENGE

17. In the given figure, *ABCD* is a parallelogram. If $\overline{DM}$ and $\overline{CM}$ are the same length, how does the area of triangle *ABM* relate to the area of parallelogram *ABCD*? Use grid paper to model and explain your answer.

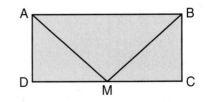

12-8 Solid Figures

Solid figures are three-dimensional. They are also called space figures. Some of their parts are not in the same plane.

Polyhedrons are solid figures whose faces are polygons.

▶ A prism is a polyhedron with two parallel and congruent bases. The shape of the base names the prism. The other faces are rectangles.

A cube is a special kind of prism with 6 square faces.

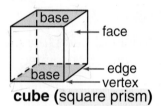

base — face
base — edge — vertex
cube (square prism)

A face is a flat surface of a solid figure bounded by line segments.
An edge is a line segment where 2 faces meet.
A vertex is a point where 2 or more edges meet.

triangular prism

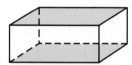
rectangular prism

pentagonal prism

hexagonal prism

▶ A pyramid is a polyhedron with one base. The shape of the base names the pyramid. The other faces are triangles that meet at a common vertex.

square pyramid

rectangular pyramid

triangular pyramid

pentagonal pyramid

hexagonal pyramid

Some solid figures have curved surfaces.

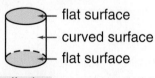
— flat surface
— curved surface
— flat surface
cylinder

cone

sphere

Cones and cylinders have circular bases.

Write the name of the solid figure each is most like.

1.
2.
3.
4.

Write the number of faces, vertices, and edges for each solid figure.

	Solid Figure	Faces	Vertices	Edges
5.	triangular prism	?	?	?
6.	pentagonal prism	?	?	?
7.	hexagonal prism	?	?	?
8.	triangular pyramid	?	?	?
9.	pentagonal pyramid	?	?	?
10.	hexagonal pyramid	?	?	?

Write *True* or *False* for each statement. If false, tell why.

11. Cylinders have no edges or vertices.

12. A sphere has no flat surfaces.

13. Cylinders and cones have flat surfaces.

14. A cone has more than one base.

Net of a Solid Figure

A solid figure can be unfolded to make a two-dimensional pattern, called a net.

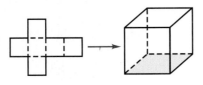

Cube Net

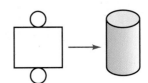

Cylinder Net

Write the solid figure that can be made from each net.

15.
16.
17.
18.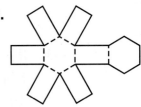

Problem Solving

19. Which solid figure has 1 less vertex than a cube and no rectangular faces?

20. Which solid figure has 3 rectangular faces and 2 congruent triangular bases?

Surface Area

The surface area (S) of a solid figure is the sum of the areas of all its faces. To find the surface area of a polyhedron, look at its net.

Find the surface area of a cube that measures 3 cm on an edge.

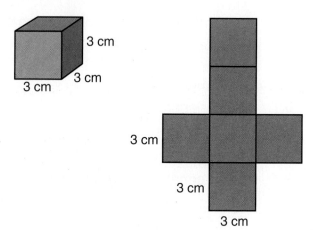

▶ **To find the surface area of a cube:**

- Find the area of one face.

- Multiply the area by 6 since all six faces of a cube are congruent.

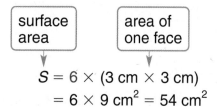

surface area	area of one face

$$S = 6 \times (3 \text{ cm} \times 3 \text{ cm})$$
$$= 6 \times 9 \text{ cm}^2 = 54 \text{ cm}^2$$

The surface area of the cube is 54 cm².

Find the surface area of a rectangular prism that measures 6 in. long, 5 in. wide, and 12 in. high.

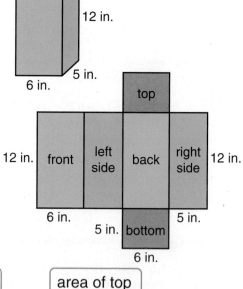

▶ **To find the surface area of a rectangular prism:**

- Find the area of one of each of the parallel faces and then double the area.

- Find the sum of the areas.

A rectangular prism has 3 pairs of congruent *parallel rectangular* faces.

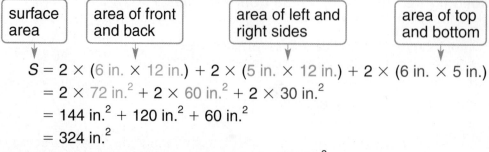

surface area	area of front and back	area of left and right sides	area of top and bottom

$$S = 2 \times (6 \text{ in.} \times 12 \text{ in.}) + 2 \times (5 \text{ in.} \times 12 \text{ in.}) + 2 \times (6 \text{ in.} \times 5 \text{ in.})$$
$$= 2 \times 72 \text{ in.}^2 + 2 \times 60 \text{ in.}^2 + 2 \times 30 \text{ in.}^2$$
$$= 144 \text{ in.}^2 + 120 \text{ in.}^2 + 60 \text{ in.}^2$$
$$= 324 \text{ in.}^2$$

The surface area of the rectangular prism is 324 in.².

Find the surface area of each figure.

1.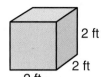
2 ft, 2 ft, 2 ft

2.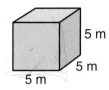
5 m, 5 m, 5 m

3.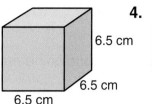
6.5 cm, 6.5 cm, 6.5 cm

4.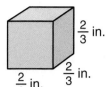
$\frac{2}{3}$ in., $\frac{2}{3}$ in., $\frac{2}{3}$ in.

5. $s = 1.2$ dm

6. $s = 15$ in.

7. $s = 8$ m

8. $s = 1\frac{1}{2}$ yd

Find the surface area of each rectangular prism.

9.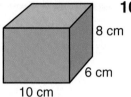
8 cm, 6 cm, 10 cm

10.
3 in., 1.5 in., 2 in.

11.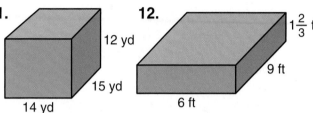
12 yd, 15 yd, 14 yd

12.
$1\frac{2}{3}$ ft, 9 ft, 6 ft

13. $\ell = 10$ ft,
    $w = 5$ ft,
    $h = 4$ ft

14. $\ell = 100$ mm,
    $w = 40$ mm,
    $h = 5$ mm

15. $\ell = 15$ m,
    $w = 1.4$ m,
    $h = 3$ m

16. $\ell = 6$ yd,
    $w = 2\frac{1}{3}$ yd,
    $h = 1\frac{1}{2}$ yd

Problem Solving

17. How many square centimeters of cardboard were used to make a cubical carton that is 3.5 cm on each edge?

18. What is the surface area of a utility cabinet that is 60 cm long, 46 cm wide, and 32 cm high?

19. What is the difference between the surface area of a cube that is 20 cm on an edge and a rectangular prism that is 20 cm long, 20 cm wide, and 18 cm high?

DO YOU REMEMBER?

Match each description with a word in the box.

hexagonal prism
cylinder
triangular prism
sphere
triangular pyramid

20. a curved solid figure in which all the points are the same distance from a point called the *center*

21. a solid figure with two bases, each with six edges

22. a solid figure with a base having three edges and with triangular faces

23. a solid figure with two congruent circular bases and a curved surface

Cubic Measure

The volume of a solid figure is the number of cubic units it contains.

▶ Cubic measures can be expressed in both metric and customary units.

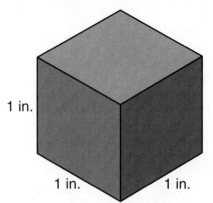

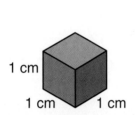

1 cm

1 cm   1 cm

This cube measures 1 cm on each edge. Its volume is 1 cubic centimeter (cm³).

Read: "cubic centimeter"

This cube measures 1 in. on each edge. Its volume is 1 cubic inch (in.³).

Read: "cubic inch"

Other metric cubic measures are: cubic millimeter (mm³), cubic decimeter (dm³), and cubic meter (m³).

Other customary cubic measures are: cubic feet (ft³) and cubic yard (yd³).

Practice

Find the cubic measure of each.

1. 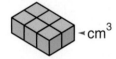 ◄cm³

   _?_ cm³

2. 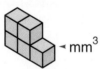 ◄mm³

   _?_ mm³

3. ◄in.³

   _?_ in.³

4. 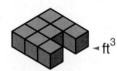 ◄ft³

   _?_ ft³

5. 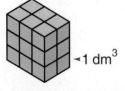 ◄1 dm³

   _?_ dm³

6. 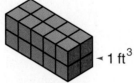 ◄1 ft³

   _?_ ft³

7. 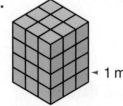 ◄ 1 m³

   _?_ m³

8. 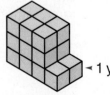 ◄1 yd³

   _?_ yd³

Relating Metric Measures

In the metric system under standard conditions,

▶ **One cubic centimeter (cm³)** holds **1 milliliter (mL)** of water, which has a mass of **1 gram (g)**.

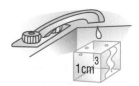
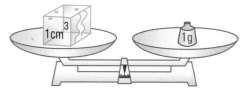

▶ **One cubic decimeter (dm³)** holds **1 liter (L)** of water, which has a mass of **1 kilogram (kg)**.

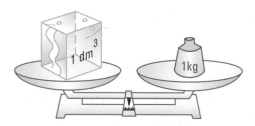

Find the equivalent measure to complete the table.

	Cubic Measure	Capacity of Water	Mass of Water
9.	3 cm³	3 mL	?
10.	5 dm³	?	5 kg
11.	?	2 mL	2 g
12.	?	5 mL	?
13.	?	?	8.4 kg
14.	4000 cm³	?	?

Problem Solving

15. What cubic measure can hold 25 mL of water?

16. What cubic measure can hold 8 kg of water?

17. A water truck holds 24 000 kg of water. What is the capacity of the water?

18. A fish tank holds 21 000 cm³ of water. What is the mass of the water?

Volume

Find the volume of a rectangular prism that measures 4 cm long, 2 cm wide, and 3 cm high.

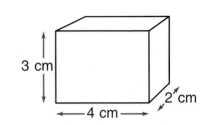

▶ The volume of a solid figure is its cubic measure, or the number of cubic units it contains.

You can find the volume of the prism by *counting the cubes* it contains:

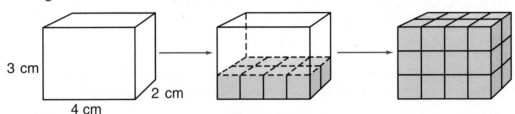

There are 4 × 2, or 8, cubes in each layer and there are 3 layers of cubes. So 8 × 3, or 24, cubes fill the prism.

or

You can use the *formula* to find the volume of a rectangular prism:

Volume	**length**		**width**		**height**
↓	↓		↓		↓

$$V = \ell \times w \times h$$
$$V = 4 \text{ cm} \times 2 \text{ cm} \times 3 \text{ cm}$$
$$V = 24 \text{ cm}^3$$

Read: "24 cubic centimeters"

The volume of the rectangular prism is 24 cm^3.

Find the length, width, and height of each rectangular prism. Then use the formula to find the volume.

1.

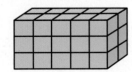

$\ell =$ _?_ units; $w =$ _?_ units

$h =$ _?_ units; $V =$ _?_ cubic units

2.

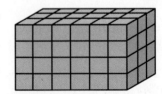

$\ell =$ _?_ units; $w =$ _?_ units

$h =$ _?_ units; $V =$ _?_ cubic units

Find the volume of each rectangular prism.

3. 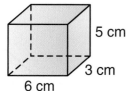 5 cm
3 cm
6 cm

4. 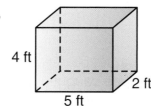 4 ft
5 ft
2 ft

5. 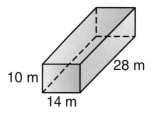 28 m
10 m
14 m

6. 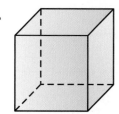 5 dm
1.4 dm
8 dm

7. 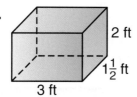 2 ft
$1\frac{1}{2}$ ft
3 ft

8. 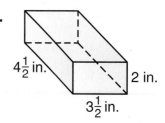 $4\frac{1}{2}$ in.
2 in.
$3\frac{1}{2}$ in.

Use your centimeter ruler to measure the length, width, and height of each rectangular prism to the nearest millimeter. Then find the volume.

9.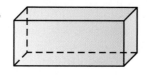

10.

11.

Problem Solving

12. A sandbox measures 6 feet long, 5 feet wide, and 3 feet deep. How many cubic feet of sand are needed to fill it?

13. Find the volume of a gift box that measures 8 inches long, $5\frac{1}{2}$ inches wide, and 2 inches high.

14. Bob has an aquarium that is 80 cm long, 45.2 cm wide, and 40.5 cm deep. How many cubic centimeters of water are needed to fill the aquarium?

15. A jewelry case is in the shape of a cube and has an edge of 75 cm. What is the volume of the jewelry case?

TEST PREPARATION

16. Find the volume of a rectangular basket 20 cm long, 15.6 cm wide, and 30.4 cm high.

A 9464.75 cm^3 **B** 9464.8 cm^3 **C** 9484.75 cm^3 **D** 9484.8 cm^3

HANDS-ON UNDERSTANDING

Estimate Volume

Marco wants to build a cube-shaped box large enough to hold a baseball he caught at the stadium. He is deciding whether to build a box with a volume of 1 cubic centimeter or a box with a volume of 1 cubic decimeter. Which size is more reasonable for the baseball?

To find which size box is more reasonable, make the boxes and test in which box the baseball fits.

Materials: centimeter grid paper, tape, scissors, pencil, ruler, base ten blocks, baseball

Step 1 Draw the net at the right on centimeter grid paper.

Step 2 Draw a second net so that each square of the net is 1 decimeter on each side.

Step 3 Cut out the outline of each net. Then fold and tape each net to form a box.

What is the volume of each box? Which of these boxes is a more reasonable size to hold a baseball?

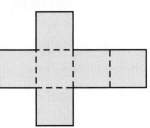

Each square of the net is 1 cm on each side.

Remember:
1 dm = 10 cm

Practice

1. What objects do you know that would fit into a cube-shaped box with a volume of 1 cm^3? with a volume of 1 dm^3?

2. How many centimeter cubes would you need to fill a decimeter cube? What is the volume of a cubic decimeter box in cubic centimeters?

3. How many decimeter cubes would you need to fill a meter cube? What is the volume of a cubic meter box in cubic decimeters? in cubic centimeters?

Which size, *cm*³ or *dm*³, is a reasonable size to hold each object?

4. a sunflower seed

5. a tennis ball

6. a miniature car

7. a ring

8. a cat's-eye marble

9. a Ping-Pong ball

10. Find or make a cube-shaped box that has a volume of about 1 in.³ Then use this as a model to find larger objects, such as boxes, that are about 12 times the length, width, and height of a cubic inch.

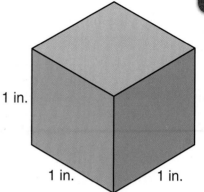

1 in.

1 in.   1 in.

11. What are the length, width, and height of each of the objects found in exercise 10?

12. What other unit of length can you use for the dimensions of these objects besides inches? Why?

13. What is the approximate volume of each object?

14. What is the volume of a cubic foot box in cubic inches?

Estimate the volume of each object. Write the letter of the best estimate.

15. crayon box

a. 500 m³ **b.** 500 dm³ **c.** 500 cm³

16. tissue box

a. 90 in.³ **b.** 90 ft³ **c.** 90 yd³

17. CD

a. 140 mm³ **b.** 140 cm³ **c.** 140 m³

Communicate

18. Which is larger: 10 cm³ or 1 dm³? 100 dm³ or 1 m³? 12 in.³ or 1 ft³? Explain your answers.

19. Can rectangular prisms look different but have the same volume? Explain your answer.

CHALLENGE

20. Choose 3 classroom objects that are shaped like rectangular prisms. Find a way to estimate the volume of each object. Explain the method you used.

Problem-Solving Strategy:
Draw a Picture

Marlene cut a frame for a picture from a sheet of paper 24 inches by 15 inches. If the frame is 2 inches wide, what is the area of the frame she used?

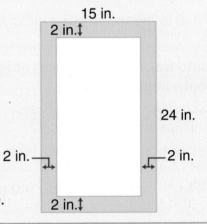

15 in.

24 in.

Read ▶ **Visualize yourself in the problem above as you reread it. List the facts and the question.**

Facts: paper—24 in. by 15 in.
width of frame—2 in.

Question: What is the area of the frame?

Plan ▶ Draw a picture of the frame.

Find the length and width of the inside rectangle by subtracting 2 × 2 in., or 4 inches, from each side.

Then use the area formula to find the area of the sheet of paper and the inside rectangle.

Next subtract the smaller area from the larger to find the area of the frame.

15 in.
2 in.↕

24 in.

2 in.— ⟷   ⟷ —2 in.

2 in.↕

Solve ▶ **Smaller Rectangle**

ℓ = 24 in. − 4 in. = 20 in.
w = 15 in. − 4 in. = 11 in.
$A = \ell \times w$
  = 20 in. × 11 in. = 220 in.^{2}

Larger Rectangle

$A = \ell \times w$
  = 24 in. × 15 in.
  = 360 in.^{2}

Difference⟶ 360 in.^{2} − 220 in.^{2} = 140 in.^{2}

The area of the frame is 140 in.^{2}

Check ▶ You can draw the picture on grid paper and count the number of square units of mat.

Use inverse operations to check your computations.

Draw a picture to solve each problem.

1. Daryl drew a right triangle on grid paper. The length of its base was double the length of its height. Its area was 16 square units. If both dimensions were whole numbers, find its height and base.

Read ▶ Visualize yourself in the problem above as you reread it. Focus on the facts and the question.

List what you know.

Facts: base of right triangle—double its height
Area—16 square units

Question: What were the base and height?

Plan ▶ Draw the picture of the right triangle. Find the combination of dimensions that satisfies both conditions:
$A = 16$ sq units; $b = 2 \times h$

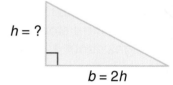

Solve ▶ ⋯ ▶ **Check**

2. Kate made a cube that has a volume of 27 cubic units. She painted each of the 3 sets of parallel faces the same color: red, blue, or yellow. What part of the cubic units has all 3 colors?

3. What is the least perimeter Jason can make by joining 5 regular hexagons side to side if each side is 2.5 cm? What is the greatest perimeter?

4. A right triangle has an area of 9 cm². The base and height are whole numbers. What are two possible lengths?

5. Kelly made a design by pasting an isosceles right triangle in the center of a square 10 cm on each side. If the length of each perpendicular side of the triangle is 5.2 cm, what is the area of the square that is still showing?

6. Draw 3 different polygons that have an area of 9 cm². Which polygon has the greatest perimeter? the least? Share your work with a classmate.

Solve each problem and explain the method you used.

1. A giant fold-out greeting card is 48.5 cm long. How much shorter than a meter is the card?

2. A musical card is 1.65 dm long and 1.1 dm wide. Its envelope is 0.2 cm longer on each side. What are the length and width of the envelope?

3 A special pop-up birthday card has a mass of 12.5 g. The card store sells these cards in a pack that weighs about 1 kg. About how many pop-up cards are in each pack?

4. Each holder on the postcard rack can take up to 10 centimeters of cards. Postcards are printed on 2-mm thick paper. How many postcards can fit in one holder?

5. Each perfumed card uses 0.5 mL of perfume. How many cards can be made with a liter of perfume?

6. Each colored square of this greeting card represents 1 cm². What is the area of the front of the card? of the word?

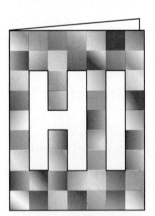

7. Whimsical Greeting Cards come in odd shapes. One greeting card is a 12-cm square. What is the area of this card in square centimeters?

8. A box contains cards with a hologram on the front. Each hologram is 53.2 mm wide and 81.5 mm tall. What is the area of each hologram?

9. A right-triangular birthday pennant has a base of 7.2 dm and a height of 2.6 dm. What is its area?

Choose a strategy from the list or use another strategy you know to solve each problem.

Strategy File

Use These Strategies
Guess and Test
Use a Model/Diagram
Draw a Picture
Use More Than One Step
Logical Reasoning

10. A card shaped like a regular pentagon has a perimeter of 35 decimeters. How many centimeters long is each side?

11. A rectangular greeting card has an area of 176 cm². One side is 16 cm. How long is the other side?

12. One birthday card comes with 2 g of confetti inside. Can 195 cards be made with 385 g of confetti?

13. Ron, Yvonne, and Fran tried to guess the age of their grandmother. Their guesses were 68, 70, and 75. One guess was incorrect by 4 years, one by 3 years, and one by 2 years. How old is their grandmother?

14. A giant right-triangular card has an area of 210 cm². The height of the triangle is 28 cm. How long is the base of this card?

15. A clerk is arranging 192 cubic units that are 1 decimeter on each edge in a display. If the display's height cannot exceed 8 dm, what might the clerk use as the length and width of the display?

16. What is the circumference of the largest circle you can cut from a piece of paper 2.15 dm by 2.8 dm?

Use the diagram for problems 17–20.
Tell whether each statement is *True* or *False*.

17. No birthday cards are pop-up cards.

18. All postcards are rectangular.

19. All triangular cards are birthday cards.

20. Some pop-up cards are rectangular birthday cards.

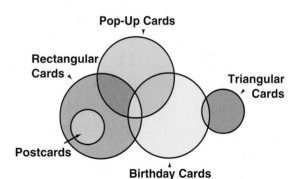

Write Your Own

21. Write a problem that uses the information in the diagram. Have someone solve it.

Rename each unit of measure.   *(See pp. 382–391; 398–399.)*

1. 5 L = __?__ mL

2. 70 mm = __?__ cm

3. 3000 mg = __?__ g

4. 2.8 cm = __?__ mm

5. 20.5 mg = __?__ cg

6. 2.96 km = __?__ m

7. 1.2 m = __?__ dm

8. 2.65 kg = __?__ g

9. 3.9 L = __?__ mL

Estimate the area of each figure.

10.
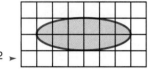
1 yd²

11.
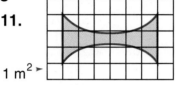
1 m²

Find the surface area.

12.
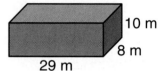
10 m
8 m
29 m

Find the area of each figure.   *(See pp. 392–397; 402–403.)*

13.
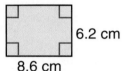
6.2 cm
8.6 cm

14.
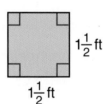
1½ ft
1½ ft

15.
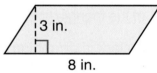
3 in.
8 in.

16.
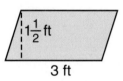
1½ ft
3 ft

17.
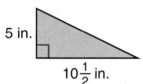
5 in.
10½ in.

18.
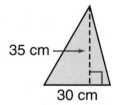
35 cm
30 cm

Write the name of the solid figure each is most like.   **Find the volume.**

19.

20.

21.

22.
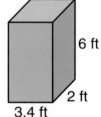
6 ft
2 ft
3.4 ft

Problem Solving   *(See pp. 400–405, 406–409.)*

23. How many cubic centimeters will 65 mL of water fill?

24. A doghouse is 3 ft by 4 ft by 4 ft. Is the volume of the doghouse more or less than a doghouse with a volume of 1 yd³?

(See Still More Practice, p. 487.)

Views of Solid Figures

When you view a polyhedron from the top, the front, or the side, you will see a polygon since all the faces are polygons.

The box at the right is a rectangular prism, a polyhedron. Its top view, front view, and side view are shown below.

| top view | front view | side view |

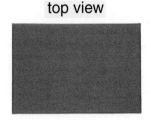

Compare the views above with the views of a cylinder as shown below.

| cylinder | top view | front view | side view |

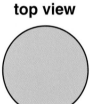

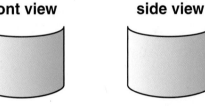

► When a plane intersects a solid figure, the intersection is a cross section of the solid figure. The cross section is a plane figure.

The cross section of a cylinder is a rectangle. The width of the rectangle is the diameter of the base of the cylinder; the length of the rectangle is the height of the cylinder.

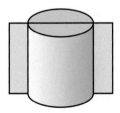

Tell what solid figure(s) could have each polygon as a front, side, or top view.

1.   **2.**   **3.**   **4.**

Name the cross section in each diagram.

5.   **6.**   **7.**  **8.**

Chapter 12 Test

Write the letter of the best estimate.

1. mass of an envelope   **a.** 2 mg   **b.** 2 g   **c.** 1 kg

2. capacity of a thimble   **a.** 3 mL   **b.** 30 mL   **c.** 3 L

Compare. Write <, =, or >.

3. 7.3 km __?__ 7000 m   **4.** 940 mL __?__ 9.4 L   **5.** 8.4 kg __?__ 8400 g

Estimate the area of each figure.

6. 1 in.²

7. 1 m²

Find the surface area.

8. 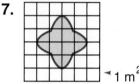 8 ft, 10 ft, 33 ft

Find the area of each figure.

9. 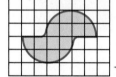 10 dm, 12.5 dm

10. 8 ft, 7½ ft

11. 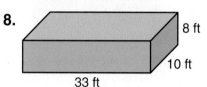 3 cm, 3 cm, 7 cm, 4 cm, 6 cm

What solid figure is each object most like?

12.    **13.**    **14.**

Find the volume.

15. 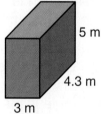 5 m, 4.3 m, 3 m

Problem Solving

Use a strategy you have learned.

16. Adam planted a 30-ft-by-18-ft garden. If he planted a 2-ft border of flowers, how much area was left to plant vegetables?

Tell About It

17. A birdfeeder is 16 cm by 20 cm by 12 cm. A sack of birdseed has a volume of 4 dm³. Is this enough birdseed to fill the feeder? How do you know?

Performance Assessment

18. Measure the length and width of the rectangular stamp, then find its area.

Test Preparation

Choose the best answer.

1. If the opposite sides of a quadrilateral are parallel, then the quadrilateral must *not* be a:

   a. rectangle   **b.** parallelogram
   c. square   **d.** trapezoid

2. Which expression is *not* equivalent to $\frac{1}{2}(3 + 2)$?

   a. $(3 + 2) \times (0.5)$ **b.** $\frac{1}{2} \times (3 \times 2)$

   c. $\frac{3 + 2}{2}$ **d.** $\frac{5}{2}$

3. Which of the given fractions is less than $\frac{1}{5}$?

   a. $\frac{4}{15}$ **b.** $\frac{9}{35}$

   c. $\frac{21}{100}$ **d.** $\frac{26}{135}$

4. For the set of scores, 68, 72, 94, 84, 62, the mean is:

   a. 32
   b. 72
   c. 76
   d. 84

5. Find the sum.

   4 ft 7 in. + 3 ft 8 in.

   a. 7 ft 5 in.
   b. 7 ft 3 in.
   c. 8 ft 3 in.
   d. 8 ft 5 in.

6. Subtract: $4\frac{7}{8} - 2\frac{1}{6}$

   a. $2\frac{6}{2}$ **b.** $2\frac{17}{24}$

   c. $2\frac{15}{24}$ **d.** $2\frac{5}{24}$

7. The measure of a straight angle is:

   a. less than 90°   **b.** exactly 90°
   c. less than 180°   **d.** exactly 180°

8. A garden is in the shape of a regular pentagon with sides 13 ft long. Which is the perimeter of the garden?

   a. 5 × 13 ft   **b.** 3 × 13 ft
   c. 13 × 13 ft   **d.** 5 × 13 × 13 ft

9. Find the surface area.

   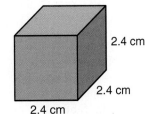

   2.4 cm

   2.4 cm

   2.4 cm

   a. 5.76 cm^2
   b. 13.824 cm^2
   c. 23.04 cm^2
   d. 34.56 cm^2

10. A polygon with 8 sides is called:

    a. a pentagon
    b. a hexagon
    c. an octagon
    d. a triangle

11. Which is equivalent to 4650 m?

    a. 4.65 km
    b. 46.5 km
    c. 46 500 km
    d. 4 650 000 m

12. Find the sum.

    5 + 2.079 + 41.41

    a. 48.489   **b.** 111.21
    c. 11.219   **d.** not given

13. Which solid figure has no curved surface?

    a. cylinder
    b. cone
    c. prism
    d. sphere

14. What is the volume of the rectangular prism?

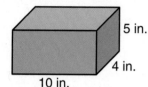

    a. 100 in.^{3}
    b. 110 in.^{3}
    c. 200 in.^{3}
    d. 220 in.^{3}

15. Which numbers are divisible by 3?

    A. 1275   **B.** 7103   **C.** 3546

    a. A and B only   **b.** A and C only
    c. B and C only   **d.** A, B, and C

16. Find the mass of 4.65 m of copper tubing if the mass of one meter is 1.2 kg.

    a. 4.58 kg   **b.** 5.58 kg
    c. 5.85 kg   **d.** not given

17. What part of an hour elapses from 4:56 P.M. to 5:32 P.M.?

    a. $\frac{1}{4}$ **b.** $\frac{1}{2}$
    c. $\frac{3}{5}$ **d.** $\frac{2}{3}$

18. By how much does the product of 8 and 25 exceed the product of 15 and 10.

    a. 25   **b.** 50
    c. 75   **d.** 100

19. 91 lb 1 oz is how much heavier than 82 lb 4 oz?

    a. 8 lb 4 oz
    b. 8 lb 13 oz
    c. 9 lb 4 oz
    d. 9 lb 13 oz

20. How many lines of symmetry does the given figure have?

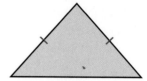

    a. none
    b. one
    c. two
    d. three

21. Which decimal has 3 in the thousandths place and 5 in the tenths place?

    a. 3009.5   **b.** 8.543
    c. 3.359   **d.** 3.157

22. Choose the standard form.

    3 billion, 5 hundred million, 4

    a. 3,500,400   **b.** 3,500,004
    c. 3,500,000,004   **d.** 3,500,000,400

23. Jose buys 2 dozen belts for $334.80. He sells the belts for $19.50 each. How much profit does he make?

    a. $5.55   **b.** $55.20
    c. $133.20   **d.** $468

24. The circumference of a circle that has a radius of 3.5 cm is:

    a. 38.5 cm   **b.** 22 cm
    c. 11 cm   **d.** not given

Explain how you solved the problem. Show all your work.

25. If an 8-oz carton of juice costs $0.69 and a 12-oz carton of juice costs $0.95, how much money can be saved by purchasing 48 oz of juice in 12-oz rather than 8-oz cartons?

26. Ann cut a 9-yard piece of ribbon into three pieces. The first two pieces were each $2\frac{2}{3}$ yd long. What was the length of the other piece?

Ratio, Proportion, and Percent

In this chapter you will:

Relate ratios to fractions
Use proportion in scale drawings and maps
Relate fractions and decimals to percents
Find the percent of a number
Solve problems by combining strategies

Critical Thinking/Finding Together

The cashier gave you 9 coins in change, totaling one dollar. The coin with the greatest value was a quarter and the coin with the least value was a nickel. How many of each kind of coin did you receive?

Smart

My dad gave me one dollar bill
'Cause I'm his smartest son,
And I swapped it for two shiny quarters
'Cause two is more than one!

And then I took the quarters
And traded them to Lou
For three dimes—I guess he don't know
That three is more than two!

Just then, along came old blind Bates
And just 'cause he can't see
He gave me four nickels for my three dimes,
And four is more than three!

And I took the nickels to Hiram Coombs
Down at the seed-feed store,
And the fool gave me five pennies for them,
And five is more than four!

And then I went and showed my dad,
And he got red in the cheeks
And closed his eyes and shook his head—
Too proud of me to speak!

Shel Silverstein

Ratios as Fractions

A number of balls are on display in the sports store window. What is the ratio of the number of baseballs to the number of soccer balls?

A ratio is a way of comparing two numbers or quantities by division.

The ratio of the number of baseballs to the number of soccer balls is 5 to 3.

There are three ways to write a ratio:

$$5 \text{ to } 3 \quad \text{or} \quad 5 : 3 \quad \text{or} \quad \frac{5}{3}$$

▶ Some ratios can be written in simplest form.

The ratio of the number of soccer balls to the number of tennis balls is:

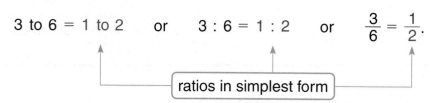

$$3 \text{ to } 6 = 1 \text{ to } 2 \quad \text{or} \quad 3 : 6 = 1 : 2 \quad \text{or} \quad \frac{3}{6} = \frac{1}{2}.$$

ratios in simplest form

▶ 3 to 2 and 2 to 3 are two different ratios.

The ratio of the number of soccer balls to basketballs is:

$$3 \text{ to } 2 \quad \text{or} \quad 3 : 2 \quad \text{or} \quad \frac{3}{2}.$$

The ratio of the number of basketballs to soccer balls is:

$$2 \text{ to } 3 \quad \text{or} \quad 2 : 3 \quad \text{or} \quad \frac{2}{3}.$$

$$3 \text{ to } 2 \neq 2 \text{ to } 3 \quad \text{or} \quad 3 : 2 \neq 2 : 3 \quad \text{or} \quad \frac{3}{2} \neq \frac{2}{3}$$

means "is not equal to"

Write each ratio in 3 ways.

1. gloves to bats
2. gloves to caps
3. bats to caps
4. balls to bats

Write each ratio in simplest form.

5. 4 to 6
6. 9 : 27
7. $\dfrac{14}{21}$
8. 12 to 24
9. 13 : 25

10. 16 to 4
11. $\dfrac{26}{39}$
12. 24 : 36
13. 100 : 125
14. $\dfrac{5}{33}$

Equivalent Ratios

Equivalent ratios have the same value. Equivalent ratios can be written as *equivalent fractions*.

To write an equivalent ratio:

6 : 10

- Write the given ratio as a fraction.

$\dfrac{6}{10}$

- Multiply or divide both the numerator and the denominator by the same number.

$\dfrac{6 \times 3}{10 \times 3} = \dfrac{18}{30}$ or $\dfrac{6 \div 2}{10 \div 2} = \dfrac{3}{5}$

- Express the result as a fraction.

$\dfrac{6}{10} = \dfrac{18}{30} = \dfrac{3}{5}$ ← equivalent ratios

---

Find the value of *n* to show equivalent ratios.

15. $\dfrac{1}{5} = \dfrac{n}{10}$
16. $\dfrac{3}{4} = \dfrac{n}{12}$
17. $\dfrac{2}{3} = \dfrac{n}{15}$
18. $\dfrac{2}{5} = \dfrac{n}{10}$

19. $\dfrac{6}{16} = \dfrac{n}{8}$
20. $\dfrac{9}{30} = \dfrac{n}{10}$
21. $\dfrac{8}{12} = \dfrac{n}{3}$
22. $\dfrac{25}{35} = \dfrac{n}{7}$

23. During one baseball season, Glenn was at bat 25 times and had 13 hits. What is the ratio of hits to times at bat?

24. Sally took a 30-question grammar test. She had 23 answers correct. What is the ratio of the number of correct answers to the number of incorrect answers?

Write About It

25. Explain why the order of the numbers is important when you read and write a ratio. Give an example to justify your answer.

Proportions

A **proportion** is a number sentence stating that two ratios are equal.

Some examples of proportions are:

$$\frac{1 \text{ liter}}{4 \text{ glasses}} = \frac{2 \text{ liters}}{8 \text{ glasses}}$$

2 is to 5 as 6 is to 15 $2 : 5 = 6 : 15$ $\frac{2}{5} = \frac{6}{15}$

There are two ways to determine if two ratios form a proportion.

- Write the ratios as fractions in simplest form. Two ratios form a proportion if they can be simplified to give the same fraction.

$$\frac{8}{12} \overset{?}{=} \frac{6}{9} \longrightarrow \frac{8 \div 4}{12 \div 4} = \frac{2}{3} \quad \text{and} \quad \frac{6 \div 3}{9 \div 3} = \frac{2}{3}$$

$\frac{8}{12} = \frac{6}{9}$ is a proportion.

Fractions are the same.

- Use the **cross-products rule**. Two ratios form a proportion if their cross products are equal.

first $\frac{1}{3}$ ⤫ $\frac{3}{9}$ third
second   fourth

$1 \times 9 = 3 \times 3$

9   9

$\frac{1}{3} = \frac{3}{9}$ is a proportion.

Think
The product of the first and fourth numbers and the product of the second and third numbers are equal.

Explain the way you used to determine if each pair of fractions forms a proportion.

1. $\frac{1}{6}, \frac{3}{18}$ 2. $\frac{2}{3}, \frac{4}{9}$ 3. $\frac{4}{5}, \frac{8}{15}$ 4. $\frac{12}{10}, \frac{5}{6}$ 5. $\frac{2}{7}, \frac{6}{21}$

Use the cross-products rule to determine which of these are proportions. Write Yes or No.

6. $\frac{5}{7} \overset{?}{=} \frac{10}{14}$ 7. $\frac{8}{5} \overset{?}{=} \frac{40}{25}$ 8. $\frac{2}{11} \overset{?}{=} \frac{14}{22}$ 9. $\frac{5}{3} \overset{?}{=} \frac{39}{16}$

Practice

Missing Number in a Proportion

To find the missing number in a proportion:

- Use equivalent ratios.

Two cups of rice serve 6 people.
How many people do 3 cups of rice serve?

$$\frac{2 \text{ cups rice}}{3 \text{ cups rice}} = \frac{6 \text{ people}}{n \text{ people}} \longrightarrow \frac{2}{3} = \frac{6}{n} \longrightarrow \frac{2 \times 3}{3 \times 3} = \frac{6}{9}, \; n = 9$$

Three cups of rice serve 9 people.

- Use the cross-products rule.

$$\frac{1}{4} \diagdown \frac{3\frac{3}{4}}{n} \longrightarrow 1 \times n = 4 \times 3\frac{3}{4} \longrightarrow n = 4 \times 3\frac{3}{4} = \frac{\cancel{4}}{1} \times \frac{15}{\cancel{4}} = 15$$

Find the missing number in the proportion.

10. $\dfrac{3}{4} = \dfrac{12}{n}$

11. $\dfrac{12}{14} = \dfrac{n}{28}$

12. $\dfrac{16}{n} = \dfrac{4}{5}$

13. $\dfrac{n}{15} = \dfrac{6}{10}$

14. $\dfrac{1}{2} = \dfrac{2\frac{1}{2}}{n}$

15. $\dfrac{1}{8} = \dfrac{1\frac{1}{8}}{n}$

16. $\dfrac{2\frac{1}{4}}{n} = \dfrac{1}{4}$

17. $\dfrac{n}{2} = \dfrac{10}{1}$

18. $\dfrac{n}{0.72} = \dfrac{5}{8}$

19. $\dfrac{3}{7} = \dfrac{n}{0.91}$

20. $\dfrac{0.6}{n} = \dfrac{54}{99}$

21. $\dfrac{0.2}{0.9} = \dfrac{n}{72}$

22. $\dfrac{2 \text{ oz cheese}}{6 \text{ oz cheese}} = \dfrac{4 \text{ sandwiches}}{n \text{ sandwiches}}$

23. $\dfrac{1 \text{ box}}{3 \text{ boxes}} = \dfrac{16 \text{ crayons}}{n \text{ crayons}}$

Problem Solving

24. If 2 apples cost 40¢, how much will 4 apples cost?

25. If 3 oranges cost 75¢, how many oranges could you buy for 25¢?

TEST PREPARATION

26. A can of tomatoes holds $2\frac{1}{2}$ cups and is used in a recipe to serve 6 people. If Ellen wants to serve 2 people, how many cups of tomatoes must she use?

A $\dfrac{5}{12}$ c   **B** $\dfrac{1}{15}$ c   **C** $\dfrac{5}{6}$ c   **D** $\dfrac{1}{2}$ c

Scale and Maps

A scale drawing of something is accurate, but *different* in size.

A scale is the ratio of the pictured measure to the actual measure.

The scale distance between San Antonio and Houston is $1\frac{5}{8}$ in.

To find the actual distance between San Antonio and Houston:

• Use the scale to set up a proportion.

$$\frac{\text{Scale measure}}{\text{Actual measure}} = \frac{\text{Scale distance}}{\text{Actual distance}}$$

$$\frac{1 \text{ in.}}{120 \text{ miles}} = \frac{1\frac{5}{8} \text{ in.}}{n \text{ miles}}$$

Scale: 1 in. = 120 miles

0   60   120 miles

$\frac{1}{8}$ in.   1 in.

• Use the cross-products rule to solve.

$$\frac{1}{120} \times \frac{1\frac{5}{8}}{n} \rightarrow 1 \times n = 120 \times 1\frac{5}{8} \rightarrow n = \frac{\overset{15}{\cancel{120}}}{1} \times \frac{13}{\underset{1}{\cancel{8}}} = \frac{15 \times 13}{1 \times 1} = 195$$

The actual distance between San Antonio and Houston is about 195 miles.

Measure the scale distance on the map above to the nearest $\frac{1}{8}$ in. Then find the actual distance between cities.

	Between Cities	Scale Distance (in.)	Actual Distance (mi)
1.	Houston—Beaumont	$\frac{5}{8}$ in.	?
2.	Dallas—Shreveport	?	?
3.	Austin—San Antonio	?	?
4.	Waco—Dallas	?	?
5.	Corpus Christi—Galveston	?	?

Use the scale 1 in. = 8 mi to find the actual distance.

	To go from:	Scale Distance	Actual Distance
6.	Dunes to Park	2 in.	?
7.	Hotel to Beach	$2\frac{3}{4}$ in.	?
8.	Lake to Park	$3\frac{1}{2}$ in.	?

	To go from:	Scale Distance	Actual Distance
9.	City to Hotel	$1\frac{1}{2}$ in.	?
10.	Beach to City	$2\frac{1}{2}$ in.	?
11.	Dunes to City	$4\frac{3}{4}$ in.	?

Measure the scale distance to the nearest centimeter. Then estimate the distance from the treasure to each place.

12. Rockaway Cove

13. Town

14. West Mount

15. Old Oak Tree

16. The scale distance between Watch Tower and East Mount is about 5 centimeters. Estimate the distance.

17. The distance between Sandy Beach and Sleepy Lagoon is about 40 kilometers. About how many centimeters is the scale distance?

18. Estimate the distance between Watch Tower and Sandy Beach.

19. Create a small map of your school yard. Explain in your Math Journal why a scale is needed when making a map.

TREASURE ISLAND

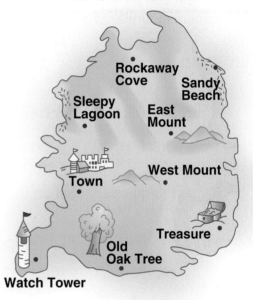

Scale: 1 cm = 10 km

0   30 km
0 cm   1 cm   2 cm   3 cm

DO YOU REMEMBER?

Write in simplest form.

20. $\frac{2}{10}$ **21.** $\frac{6}{10}$ **22.** $\frac{5}{10}$ **23.** $\frac{25}{100}$ **24.** $\frac{80}{100}$ **25.** $\frac{16}{100}$

Relate Fractions to Percents

In the 100-square grid, 32 squares are green and 6 squares are red.

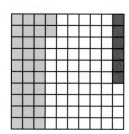

$\dfrac{32}{100}$ of the grid is green.

$\dfrac{6}{100}$ of the grid is red.

▶ A fraction can be written as percent. Percent means "per hundred."
A percent is a ratio of a number to 100. The symbol for percent is %.

	Fraction		**Percent**	
32 out of 100 ⟶	$\dfrac{32}{100}$	⟶	32%	32% of the grid is green.
6 out of 100 ⟶	$\dfrac{6}{100}$	⟶	6%	6% of the grid is red.

▶ To write a fraction, with a denominator that is a factor of 100, as a percent:

- Write an equivalent fraction with a denominator of 100.

- Write the fraction as a percent.

$$\frac{3}{25} = ?$$

$$\frac{3}{25} = \frac{3 \times 4}{25 \times 4} = \frac{12}{100} = 12\%$$

$$\frac{3}{25} = 12\%$$

▶ To write a percent as a fraction:

- Drop the percent symbol (%). Then write the number as the numerator and 100 as the denominator.

- Write the fraction in simplest form.

$$80\% = ?$$

$$80\% = \frac{80}{100}$$

$$80\% = \frac{80 \div 20}{100 \div 20} = \frac{4}{5}$$

**Tell what fractional part of the grid is shaded.
Then write the fraction as a percent.**

1.

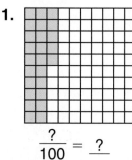

$$\frac{?}{100} = \frac{?}{\rule{1cm}{0.4pt}}$$

2.

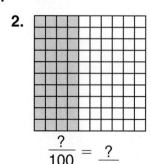

$$\frac{?}{100} = \frac{?}{\rule{1cm}{0.4pt}}$$

3.

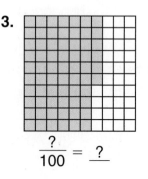

$$\frac{?}{100} = \frac{?}{\rule{1cm}{0.4pt}}$$

Write as a percent.

4. $\frac{3}{4}$ 5. $\frac{4}{5}$ 6. $\frac{7}{20}$ 7. $\frac{13}{50}$ 8. $\frac{9}{10}$ 9. $\frac{6}{25}$

10. 2 out of 5   11. 3 out of 20   12. 21 out of 25   13. 7 out of 10

Shade a 10 × 10 grid to model each percent.
Then write as a fraction in simplest form.

14. 28%   15. 5%   16. 30%   17. 64%   18. 44%   19. 29%

20. 52%   21. 4%   22. 85%   23. 13%   24. 18%   25. 30%

Problem Solving

Use the table for problems 26–27.

26. What percent of Paul's day is spent playing and eating? Write this percent as a fraction.

27. What percent of Paul's day is *not* spent in school? Write this as a fraction.

Paul's Day	
Activity	**Part of Day**
school	25%
sleep	35%
play	18%
eating	10%
other	12%

28. What percent of the grid is modeled on a 10 × 10 grid if all squares of the grid are shaded? if none are shaded?

29. Leesan received a score of 84% on a math quiz. What fraction of the questions did she answer incorrectly?

30. Is it possible to shade a 10 × 10 grid so that it is 15% blue, 75% red, and 20% green? Explain your answer.

31. Al has a collection of 100 stamps. Forty are international stamps. What percent of his collection are international stamps?

MENTAL MATH

Write as a percent.

32. $\frac{16}{100}$ 33. $\frac{9}{100}$ 34. $\frac{95}{100}$ 35. $\frac{44}{100}$ 36. $\frac{30}{100}$ 37. $\frac{89}{100}$

38. $\frac{15}{100}$ 39. $\frac{57}{100}$ 40. $\frac{88}{100}$ 41. $\frac{1}{100}$ 42. $\frac{65}{100}$ 43. $\frac{100}{100}$

Write as a fraction with a denominator of 100.

44. 77%   45. 8%   46. 82%   47. 10%   48. 55%   49. 79%

50. 23%   51. 98%   52. 37%   53. 19%   54. 46%   55. 5%

Relate Percents to Decimals

You can use the meaning of percent to rename a percent as a decimal or a decimal as a percent.

% means *per hundred.*

45% red
5% blue

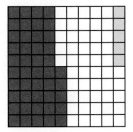

▶ To rename a percent as a decimal:
  • Rename the percent as a fraction with a denominator of 100.
  • Write the fraction as a decimal.

Percent	Fraction	Decimal
45%	$\frac{45}{100}$	0.45
5%	$\frac{5}{100}$	0.05

▶ To rename a decimal as a percent:
  • Rename the decimal as a fraction with a denominator of 100.
  • Write the fraction as a percent.

% means *hundredths.*

59% green
40% purple

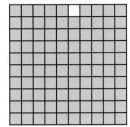

Decimal	Fraction	Percent
0.59	$\frac{59}{100}$	59%
0.4	$\frac{40}{100}$	40%

You can use a shortcut to write a percent as a decimal or a decimal as a percent.

• Drop the percent (%) symbol. Then move the decimal point *two* places to the left.

Percent		Decimal
45% ⟶	.45. ⟶	0.45
5% ⟶	.05. ⟶	0.05

• Move the decimal point *two* places to the right. Then write the percent (%) symbol.

Decimal		Percent
0.59 ⟶	0.59. ⟶	59%
0.4 ⟶	0.40. ⟶	40%

Practice

Write as a decimal.

1. 65% **2.** 83% **3.** 7% **4.** 23.6% **5.** 10% **6.** 12.7%

Write as a percent.

7. 0.15 **8.** 0.73 **9.** 0.08 **10.** 0.4 **11.** 0.123 **12.** 1.85

Find the percent, fraction, and decimal equivalents to complete each table.

	Percent	Fraction	Decimal
13.	10%	?	?
14.	?	$\frac{1}{5}$	?
15.	?	?	0.25

	Percent	Fraction	Decimal
16.	?	?	0.4
17.	50%	?	?
18.	?	$\frac{3}{4}$	?

Money as Percent of a Dollar

Coins can be expressed as a **percent** of a dollar.

1 penny   = \$0.01 or $\frac{1}{100}$ of a dollar ⟶ 1%

1 nickel   = \$0.05 or $\frac{5}{100}$ of a dollar ⟶ 5%

1 dime   = \$0.10 or $\frac{10}{100}$ of a dollar ⟶ 10%

1 quarter = \$0.25 or $\frac{25}{100}$ of a dollar ⟶ 25%

1 half-dollar = \$0.50 or $\frac{50}{100}$ of a dollar ⟶ 50%

Study these examples.

5 nickels ⟶ 5 × \$0.05 = \$0.25 ⟶ 25% of a dollar

2 quarters, 4 pennies ⟶ (2 × \$0.25) + (4 × \$0.01)

                      = \$0.50 + \$0.04 = \$0.54 ⟶ 54% of a dollar

Write as a percent of a dollar.

19. 9 nickels   **20.** 7 pennies   **21.** 3 dimes   **22.** 2 quarters

23. 2 nickels, 3 pennies   **24.** 2 quarters, 1 dime   **25.** 1 half-dollar, 2 pennies

Problem Solving

26. Al needs 0.02 liter of acid for a project. What percent of a liter does he need?

27. Ed had \$1.00. He spent 65¢. What percent of his money did he spend?

CRITICAL THINKING — Algebra

Compare. Write <, =, or >. Explain how you got your answer.

28. 0.13 _?_ 1.3%   **29.** 0.06 _?_ 60%   **30.** 0.032 _?_ 3.2%

Find the Percent of a Number

There are 60 questions on a social studies exam. Twenty-five percent of the questions are about map skills. How many of the questions are about map skills?

To find how many of the questions are about map skills, find the percent of a number:

25% of 60 = n

To find the percent of a number:	25% of 60 = n
• Write the percent as a decimal.	25% = 0.25
• Multiply.	0.25 × 60 = 15.00

or

• Write the percent as a fraction.	25% = $\frac{25}{100}$ = $\frac{1}{4}$
• Multiply.	$\frac{1}{\cancel{4}_1} \times \cancel{60}^{15} = 15$

There are 15 questions about map skills.

▶ You can also estimate the percent of a number by using the equivalent fraction and compatible numbers.

Estimate: 48% of 209

$$50\% \text{ of } 200 = 50\% \times 200$$
$$= \frac{1}{\cancel{2}} \times \cancel{200}^{100}$$
$$= 100$$

> **Think**..............................
> 48% of 209 is about 50% of 200.

So 48% of 209 is about 100.

Find the percent of the number.

1. 10% of 120
2. 50% of 46
3. 25% of 224

4. 75% of 48
5. 20% of 325
6. 30% of 80

7. 80% of 240
8. 15% of 180
9. 60% of 315

10. 40% of 300
11. 90% of 200
12. 35% of 120

Estimate the percent of the number.

13. 55% of 800   **14.** 19% of 516   **15.** 45% of 120

16. 73% of 316   **17.** 11% of 630   **18.** 23% of 482

19. 22% of 103   **20.** 18% of 500   **21.** 24% of 394

Compare. Use $<$, $=$, or $>$.

22. 10% of 20 _?_ 20% of 40   **23.** 30% of 60 _?_ 40% of 20

24. 15% of 60 _?_ 25% of 60   **25.** 20% of 150 _?_ 20% of 180

26. 30% of 40 _?_ 60% of 20   **27.** 45% of 300 _?_ 65% of 200

Problem Solving Use the percent table for problems 28–30.

28. Five percent of 80 fifth graders have red hair. How many fifth graders have red hair?

29. Ten percent of the 150 new cars that are on display at the Auto-Rama are minivans. How many minivans are on display?

30. At Irwin School, 75% of the 348 students ride the bus to school. How many students ride the bus to school?

Percent Table		
Percent	**Decimal**	**Fraction**
1%	0.01	$\frac{1}{100}$
5%	0.05	$\frac{5}{100} = \frac{1}{20}$
10%	0.10	$\frac{10}{100} = \frac{1}{10}$
25%	0.25	$\frac{25}{100} = \frac{1}{4}$
50%	0.50	$\frac{50}{100} = \frac{1}{2}$
75%	0.75	$\frac{75}{100} = \frac{3}{4}$

31. **Draw and color on one circle to show about:**

 a. 50% green   **b.** 25% yellow   **c.** 10% blue   **d.** 15% red

CHALLENGE **Algebra**

Find the value of *n*.

32. 50% of *n* is 16.   **33.** 25% of *n* is 4.   **34.** 10% of *n* is 5.

35. 20% of *n* is 5.   **36.** 35% of *n* is 7.   **37.** 40% of *n* is 8.

38. 15% of *n* is 6.   **39.** 6% of *n* is 12.   **40.** 4% of *n* is 10.

Use Percent

At Kennedy School, 180 students take Allied Arts courses. How many students take Fine Arts?

The **circle graph** at the right shows the percent of students taking each Allied Arts course.

To find how many students take Fine Arts, find the percent of a number: 25% of 180 = *n*

Allied Arts Courses

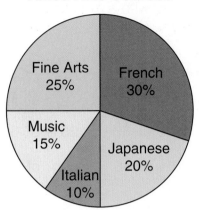

	Percent	×	Total	Number of Students	

$$25\% \quad \text{of} \quad 180 = n$$

$$\frac{1}{\cancel{4}} \times \overset{45}{\cancel{180}} = 45 \quad \text{or}$$

$$\begin{array}{r} 1\,8\,0 \\ \times\ 0.2\,5 \\ \hline 9\,0\,0 \\ +\ 3\,6\,0 \\ \hline 4\,5.0\,0 \end{array}$$

There are 45 students taking Fine Arts.

Use the circle graph above to complete the table.

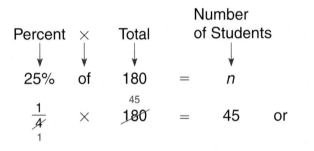

	Subject	Percent	Number of Students
1.	Music	?	?
2.	Italian	?	?
3.	Japanese	?	?
4.	French	?	?

Use the circle graph at right.

Mr. Smith's monthly income is $3500. How much is his budget for:

5. education? **6.** food?

7. shelter? **8.** clothing?

9. recreation? **10.** savings?

Mr. Smith's Monthly Budget

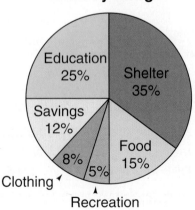

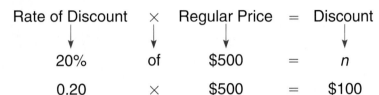

Finding Discount

During a sale, LP Electronics offers a discount of 20% on an entertainment system with a regular price of $500. How much is the discount?

A discount is a savings on the regular price of an item. The rate of discount is given as a percent.

To find the discount, find: 20% of $500 = n

Rate of Discount	×	Regular Price	=	Discount
↓		↓		↓
20%	of	$500	=	n
0.20	×	$500	=	$100

The discount is $100.

Find the discount for each item.

	Item	Regular Price	Rate of Discount	Discount
11.	towel	$14	25%	?
12.	tablecloth	$30	15%	?
13.	bed sheets	$200	30%	?
14.	shower curtain	$25	5%	?

Problem Solving

15. Bikes with a regular price of $120 are offered at a 35% discount. What is the discount?

16. Beach chairs with a regular price of $30 are on sale at a 15% discount. What is the discount?

17. Explain in your Math Journal why stores advertise percent off rather than dollars off.

CHALLENGE — Algebra

18. A store offers a 4% discount if a consumer pays cash rather than paying by credit card. If the cash price of an item is $84, what is the credit-card purchase price of the same item?

Problem-Solving Strategy:
Combine Strategies

Tasha decides to save some money. The first day she puts a nickel in a bank. Each day she plans to double the amount she put in the day before. How much money will she have saved in a week?

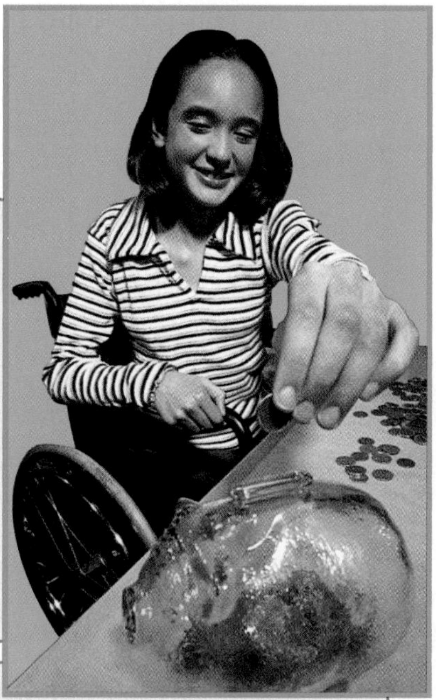

Read

Visualize yourself in the problem above as you reread it. List the facts and the question.

Facts: First day—Tasha saves a nickel.

Each day following, she doubles the amount she puts in the bank.

Question: How much money will Tasha have saved in a week?

Plan

Some problems are easier to solve by combining strategies.

Is there hidden information? Yes.

1 nickel = $0.05   and   1 week = 7 days

Make a table to record the amount saved each day.

Find a pattern.

Solve

	1st	2nd	3rd	4th	5th	6th	7th
Saved	$0.05	$0.10	$0.20	$0.40	$0.80	$1.60	$3.20
Total	$0.05	$0.15	$0.35	$0.75	$1.55	$3.15	$6.35

Check

In 1 week Tasha saved $6.35.

You can act out the problem or add.

$0.05 + $0.10 + $0.20 + $0.40 + $0.80 + $1.60 + $3.20 = $6.35

The answer checks.

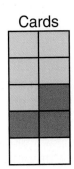

Combine strategies to solve each problem.

1. Caren bought some greeting cards. She gave 5 cards to her sister. After sending 3 of the remaining cards, Caren had 2 left. What percent of the cards Caren bought does she have left?

> **Read**

Visualize yourself in the problem above as you reread it. Focus on the facts and the question.

List what you know.

> **Plan**

Facts:
    bought some cards
    gave 5 cards away
    sent 3 cards
    had 2 cards left

Question: What percent of the bought cards are left?

First find the number of cards Caren bought by *working backward*. $2 + 3 + 5 = \underline{\ ?\ }$

Then find the percent by *writing a number sentence* or *using drawings*.

Cards

> **Solve** **Check**

2. In a box of 40 assorted cards, 12 were birthday cards, 10 were anniversary cards, 6 were get-well cards, and the rest were all-occasion cards. What percent of the box of cards were all-occasion cards?

3. Two out of every seven pieces of mail the Zimmer family receives are bills. If they received a half-dozen bills last week and 4 bills this week, how many pieces of mail did they receive in those two weeks?

4. Three out of every 5 thank-you cards Diane wrote were to her family. The rest were to her friends. If Diane wrote 8 cards to her friends, how many thank-you cards did she write altogether?

5. Mary has 162 cards to put into 15 boxes. Some boxes hold 10 cards; others hold a dozen. Fifty cards are yellow. How many of each size box will Mary use?

Solve each problem and explain the method you used.

1. The stationery store is having a spring sale. For every 5 pencils you buy, you get 2 free. If Arnie pays for 15 pencils, how many does he get free?

2. The store clerk notices that he sold pens and pencils in a ratio of 4 : 9. He sold 24 pens. How many pencils did he sell?

3. Two out of every 5 customers bought markers. What percent did *not* buy markers?

4. The store earns $.12 on every $.49 eraser it sells. How much money will the store earn on the sale of 2 dozen erasers?

5. This week eight tenths of the stationery items are on sale. What percent of the stationery items are *not* on sale?

6. A book bag usually costs $15, but during the sale its price is reduced by 30%. How much will be saved?

7. The list price of a dictionary is $24.00. Helen saved $6.00 when she bought it at the sale. What percent of the list price did she save?

8. Which is less expensive during the sale: a $12 sweatshirt reduced by 25% or a $15 sweatshirt reduced by 45%?

9. In a brochure the scale for a picture of a computer is 1 cm = 4 cm. The computer screen has a scale length of 7 cm and a scale width of 5 cm. What are its actual dimensions?

10. The scale length of the keyboard is 12 cm. Its actual width is 37.5% of its length. What are its length and width?

11. For every $20 spent, a customer pays a $1.20 sales tax. Lori bought 3 pen-and-pencil sets and paid $2.16 in sales tax. How much did she spend?

Choose a strategy from the list or use another strategy you know to solve each problem.
You may combine strategies.

12. Angela bought a ream of paper listed at $20 for 10% less. How much money did she save? She was charged an additional $1.08 in sales tax. How much did she pay for the paper?

13. A $7 T–shirt at the bookstore is reduced by 50%. What is the final cost, including $0.21 sales tax?

14. Each day the price of a school umbrella will be reduced by another 10% until all the umbrellas have been sold. The original price of each umbrella is $10. What is the price on the 5th day of the sale?

15. This table shows the original prices of calculators on sale for 30% off. Kirk spent less than $11. Which 2 calculators did he buy? Explain how you found your answer.

16. Li bought 2 calculators from the table at the 30% discount. He spent $11.76. Which 2 calculators did he buy? Explain how you found your answer.

17. Greg buys a sheet of paper 24 in. by 18 in. First he folds it in half vertically, then horizontally. What is the perimeter of the final rectangle?

Use the circle graph for problems 18–21.

18. Which 3 items represent about 50% of the profits? How do you know?

19. The bookstore's profits were $1470 last week. What was the profit from sales of writing tools?

20. How much more profit was there on paper supplies than on clothing?

Strategy File

Use These Strategies
Use a Model/Diagram
More Than One Solution
Use More Than One Step
Guess and Test
Make a Table
Use a Graph

Calculator Model	Original
Mini-Max	$7.30
Midi-Max	$9.10
Super Sum	$8.10
Turbo Plus	$9.50

Last Week's Profits

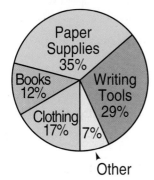

Paper Supplies 35%
Books 12%
Writing Tools 29%
Clothing 17%
7%
Other

Write Your Own

21. Write a problem that uses the data from the circle graph and can be solved by using more than one step. Have a classmate solve it.

Write in 3 ways the ratio of the number of: *(See pp. 416–417.)*

1. kites to balls

2. cars to kites

3. balls to cars

a)  b) c)

Find the missing number in the proportion. *(See pp. 418–419.)*

4. $\dfrac{3}{4} = \dfrac{n}{12}$

5. $\dfrac{6}{7} = \dfrac{18}{n}$

6. $\dfrac{n}{16} = \dfrac{7}{8}$

7. $\dfrac{5}{n} = \dfrac{7}{35}$

Find the actual measurements. *(See pp. 420–421.)*

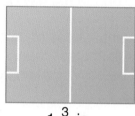

8. What is the length of the soccer field?

1 in.

9. What is the width of the soccer field?

$1\dfrac{3}{8}$ in. Scale: 1 in. = 80 yd

Write as a percent. *(See pp. 422–425.)*

10. $\dfrac{27}{100}$

11. $\dfrac{65}{100}$

12. 0.83

13. 0.52

14. 0.3

Shade a 10 × 10 grid to model each percent. Then write as a fraction. *(See pp. 422–423.)*

15. 20%

16. 45%

17. 16%

18. 70%

19. 81%

Write as a decimal. *(See pp. 424–425.)*

20. 46%

21. 68%

22. 5%

23. 9%

24. 76%

Find the percent of the number. *(See pp. 426–427.)*

25. 20% of 200

26. 50% of 136

27. 25% of 120

Problem Solving

(See pp. 418–419, 426–427, 430–433.)

28. William paid $1.20 for 2 hot dogs. He also paid $.75 for a soda and $1.09 for french fries. How much would he pay for 6 hot dogs?

29. Ten percent of a $25 gas bill is tax. How much is the tax?

(See Still More Practice, p. 488.)

Percent Patterns

Study the pattern for these percents and their
equivalent fractions.

$2\% = \dfrac{2}{100} = \dfrac{1}{50}$

$4\% = 2 \times 2\% = 2 \times \dfrac{1}{50} = \dfrac{2}{50}$

$6\% = 3 \times 2\% = 3 \times \dfrac{1}{50} = \dfrac{3}{50}$

$8\% = 4 \times 2\% = 4 \times \dfrac{1}{50} = \dfrac{4}{50}$

$4\% = \dfrac{4}{100} = \dfrac{1}{25}$

$12\% = 3 \times 4\% = 3 \times \dfrac{1}{25} = \dfrac{3}{25}$

$20\% = 5 \times 4\% = 5 \times \dfrac{1}{25} = \dfrac{5}{25}$

$28\% = 7 \times 4\% = 7 \times \dfrac{1}{25} = \dfrac{7}{25}$

$5\% = \dfrac{5}{100} = \dfrac{1}{20}$

$25\% = 5 \times 5\% = 5 \times \dfrac{1}{20} = \dfrac{5}{20}$

$45\% = 9 \times 5\% = 9 \times \dfrac{1}{20} = \dfrac{9}{20}$

$65\% = 13 \times 5\% = 13 \times \dfrac{1}{20} = \dfrac{13}{20}$

$10\% = \dfrac{10}{100} = \dfrac{1}{10}$

$30\% = 3 \times 10\% = 3 \times \dfrac{1}{10} = \dfrac{3}{10}$

$50\% = 5 \times 10\% = 5 \times \dfrac{1}{10} = \dfrac{5}{10}$

$70\% = 7 \times 10\% = 7 \times \dfrac{1}{10} = \dfrac{7}{10}$

Find the equivalent fractions. Look for a pattern.

1. 10%, 20%, 30%, 40%

2. 20%, 40%, 60%, 80%

3. 25%, 50%, 75%, 100%

4. 15%, 30%, 45%, 60%

5. 12%, 24%, 36%, 48%

6. 8%, 16%, 32%, 64%

7. 5%, 20%, 35%, 50%

8. 4%, 32%, 60%, 88%

Problem Solving

9. If $\dfrac{1}{8} = 12.5\%$, then what percent is equivalent to $\dfrac{3}{8}$?

10. If $\dfrac{1}{3} = 33\frac{1}{3}\%$, then what percent is equivalent to $\dfrac{2}{3}$?

11. If $\dfrac{1}{9} = 11\frac{1}{9}\%$, then what percent is equivalent to $\dfrac{7}{9}$?

12. If $\dfrac{1}{7} = 14\frac{2}{7}\%$, then what percent is equivalent to $\dfrac{3}{7}$?

13. If $\dfrac{1}{6} = 16\frac{2}{3}\%$, then what percent is equivalent to $\dfrac{5}{6}$?

Chapter 13 Test

Solve for *n*.

1. $\dfrac{5}{n} = \dfrac{25}{3}$

2. $\dfrac{7}{9} = \dfrac{n}{81}$

3. $\dfrac{n}{12} = \dfrac{7}{4}$

Write as a percent.

4. $\dfrac{42}{100}$

5. $\dfrac{57}{100}$

6. $\dfrac{3}{5}$

7. $\dfrac{13}{20}$

8. 0.26

9. 0.31

10. 0.7

11. 0.03

**Shade a 10 × 10 grid to model each percent.
Then write as a fraction in simplest form.**

12. 40%

13. 51%

14. 75%

15. 14%

Write as a decimal.

16. 19%

17. 90%

18. 7%

19. 4%

Find the percent of the number.

20. 4% of 120

21. 30% of 250

22. 90% of 300

23. 75% of 150

Problem Solving

Use a strategy you have learned.

24. Kim bought a beach towel and a cooler. The beach towel, regularly $15, was discounted 20%. The cooler, regularly $30, was discounted 10%. How much did Kim save?

Tell About It

Explain how you solved the problem. Show all your work.

25. On a map 1 cm represents 6 m. What does 7 cm represent?

Performance Assessment

Show all the ratios in exercises 26–28 on one fraction strip.

26. Color the fraction strip so that the ratio of:
    a. red to blue is 2 to 5
    b. yellow to blue is 3 to 5
    c. not yellow to red is 9 to 2

27. Write each ratio in exercise 26 in 2 other ways.

28. Describe what the ratio of 2 to 2 represents.

Test Preparation

Choose the best answer.

1. Which shows 5 billion in expanded form?
   - **a.** $5 \times 1,000,000$
   - **b.** $5 \times 1,000,000,000$
   - **c.** $5 \times 10,000,000,000$
   - **d.** $5 \times 100,000,000$

2. Which number is divisible by 2, 3, 5, 6, 9, and 10?
   - **a.** 135
   - **b.** 600
   - **c.** 1620
   - **d.** 2025

3. $18 - 1\frac{1}{8}$
   - **a.** $17\frac{1}{8}$
   - **b.** $17\frac{7}{8}$
   - **c.** $19\frac{1}{8}$
   - **d.** not given

4. Which graph shows how a whole is divided into fractional parts?
   - **a.** bar graph
   - **b.** circle graph
   - **c.** pictograph
   - **d.** line graph

5. Rename.

   10 qt = ___?___
   - **a.** 5 c
   - **b.** 5 pt
   - **c.** 16 pt
   - **d.** $2\frac{1}{2}$ gal

6. Find the area.

    2.5 m

   2.5 m
   - **a.** 2.5 m²
   - **b.** 5 m²
   - **c.** 6.25 m²
   - **d.** 10 m²

7. Rename 48% as a fraction in lowest terms.
   - **a.** $\frac{12}{25}$
   - **b.** $\frac{24}{50}$
   - **c.** $\frac{48}{100}$
   - **d.** $\frac{4}{15}$

8. Estimate.

   221×4632
   - **a.** 800,000
   - **b.** 1,400,000
   - **c.** 8,000,000
   - **d.** 1,000,000

9. Which shows the prime factorization of 84?
   - **a.** 2×42
   - **b.** $2 \times 3 \times 7$
   - **c.** $2 \times 2 \times 3 \times 7$
   - **d.** $3 \times 4 \times 7$

10. $18 \div 1\frac{1}{8}$
    - **a.** 4
    - **b.** 16
    - **c.** $20\frac{1}{4}$
    - **d.** not given

11. Which of the following is *not* a quadrilateral?
    - **a.** trapezoid
    - **b.** rhombus
    - **c.** parallelogram
    - **d.** hexagon

12. Round 7.248 to the nearest hundredth.
    - **a.** 0.725
    - **b.** 7.24
    - **c.** 7.25
    - **d.** 7.3

13. Which solid figure is shown?

    - **a.** triangular pyramid
    - **b.** rectangular prism
    - **c.** rectangular pyramid
    - **d.** square prism

14. Find the missing number.

    $\frac{4}{9} = \frac{12}{n}$
    - **a.** 8
    - **b.** 18
    - **c.** 27
    - **d.** 36

15. Which fraction names the ratio 144 to 16?

    a. $\frac{12}{1}$ **b.** $\frac{9}{1}$

    c. $\frac{1}{9}$ **d.** $\frac{11}{100}$

16. Choose the quotient.

$7\overline{)284,914}$

    a. 472
    b. 4702
    c. 40,702
    d. 400,702

17. What is the area of a parallelogram with a base of 4.5 m and a height of 4 m?

    a. 8.5 m^2
    b. 9 m^2
    c. 18 m^2
    d. not given

18. What is the surface area of a cube with one edge 2.5 m long?

    a. 6.25 m^2
    b. 15.625 m^2
    c. 37.5 m^2
    d. not given

19. Find the mode of this set of data.

83, 91, 83, 95, 85, 93, 79

    a. 83   **b.** 85
    c. 93   **d.** not given

20. If the scale is $\frac{1}{2}$ in. = 4 ft, what is the actual length of a room that is $3\frac{3}{4}$ in. long on the scale drawing?

    a. 60 ft   **b.** 30 ft
    c. 15 ft   **d.** $7\frac{1}{2}$ ft

21. Which is a true proportion?

    a. $\frac{7}{10} = \frac{14}{22}$ **b.** $\frac{2}{3} = \frac{1}{6}$

    c. $\frac{3}{8} = \frac{6}{16}$ **d.** $\frac{4}{5} = \frac{32}{42}$

22. In quadrilateral *ABCD*, $\angle A = 75°$, $\angle B = 115°$, and $\angle C = 70°$. What is the measure of $\angle D$?

    a. 30°
    b. 45°
    c. 90°
    d. 100°

23. Find the volume of a rectangular prism with a length of 4 m, width of 0.5 m, and height of 6 m.

    a. 12 m^3
    b. 10.5 m^3
    c. 6 m^3
    d. not given

24. Find the missing length.
850 mm = __?__ m

    a. 0.085
    b. 0.85
    c. 8.5
    d. 85

25. A container of milk holds 1.9 L. Nancy used 280 mL to make bread. How many milliliters of milk are left?

    a. 0.9 mL   **b.** 90 mL
    c. 162 mL   **d.** 1 620 mL

26. Which number is *not* equivalent to the other numbers?

$\frac{2}{5}$, 0.4, $\frac{2}{5}$%, 40%

    a. $\frac{2}{5}$ **b.** 0.4
    c. $\frac{2}{5}$%   **d.** 40%

Explain how you solved each problem. Show all your work.

27. A bag contains 1 red, 1 green, 1 blue, and 1 yellow marble. Pick a marble from the bag without looking and put it back. Then pick another marble. What are all the possible outcomes?

28. Lois has 3 packages. Each weighs 2 lb 10 oz. Find the total weight of the 3 packages.

More Concepts in Algebra

CHAPTER 14

Exit X

Let *x* be this
and *y* be that,
my teacher says. And I
expecting *x* to be complex
enough, put wily *y*
to work. If *vex*
is x^2, *rex*
will equal one-no-three.
But that's not why
x over my
right shoulder laughs at me.

David McCord

In this chapter you will:

Write and evaluate expressions
Write and solve equations
Learn about integers, function tables,
  coordinate graphs, and linear functions
Solve problems by writing an equation

Critical Thinking/Finding Together

If *x* and *y* in the equations below stand for
different numbers, but are the same in
every equation, what are their values?

$$x + y = 12 \qquad y \times y = x$$

$$x - y = 6 \qquad 27 \div x = y$$

Algebraic Expressions and Equations

▶ An **algebraic expression** is a mathematical expression that contains variables, numbers, and symbols of operations.

$$10mn \qquad 7x^2y + \frac{1}{2}xy + x - 5 \qquad 5a - 7a + c \qquad \frac{3xy - 1}{y}$$

Word Phrase	Algebraic Expression
c more than n	$c + n$
x less than y	$y - x$
the product of a and b	ab or $a \cdot b$ or $a(b)$
the quotient when p is divided by q	$p \div q$ or $\frac{p}{q}$

▶ An **equation** is a statement that two expressions are equal.

$$n + 16 = 29 \qquad 35 = x - 11 \qquad 3m = 30.75 \qquad \frac{p}{9} = 2.73$$

Word Sentence	Equation
Two added to a number equals 9.	$a + 2 = 9$
The difference between a number and 4 is 6.	$y - 4 = 6$
The product of a number and 5 is 15.	$5c = 15$
The quotient of a number divided by 6 is 5.	$\frac{n}{6} = 5$

Write whether each is an *expression* or an *equation*.

1. $n + 8$ **2.** $n + 4 = 12$ **3.** $n - 9 = 9$ **4.** $5 + 2y$

5. $y + w$ **6.** $3n + 8$ **7.** $n + x = 7$ **8.** $9t$

Write each word phrase as an algebraic expression.

9. the sum of a number m and 8

10. five less than a number p

11. three times a number z, increased by 4

12. 25 less than the product of 4 times a number n

13. the sum of the square of a number a and 5

14. the quotient of a number b and 3

Practice

Write each word sentence as an equation.

15. A number subtracted from 29 is equal to 11.

16. 4 more than the quotient of a number and 6 is 40.

17. A number added to 4.87 is equal to 14.84.

18. 65 less than the product of 3 times a number is 50.

Evaluate Algebraic Expressions or Equations

To evaluate algebraic expressions or equations:

- Substitute a number(s) for the variable(s).
- Simplify. Apply the rules for the order of operations.

> **Evaluate** means to find the value of.

Evaluate $5a - (b + c)$ when $a = 4$, $b = 3$, and $c = 1.5$.

$$5a - (b + c) = 5 \cdot 4 - (3 + 1.5)$$
$$= 20 - 4.5$$
$$= 15.5$$

Find a value of n that will make $2(a + b) - c = n$ a true equation. Let $a = 10$, $b = 6$, and $c = 2$.

$$2(a + b) - c = n$$
$$2(10 + 6) - 2 = 2 \cdot 16 - 2 = 30$$
$$n = 30$$

Evaluate the algebraic expression when $x = 20$, $y = 3$, and $w = 1.25$.

19. $(x - w)y$

20. $x - 3w + 2$

21. $2^2 + 2(y + w)$

22. $\dfrac{xy}{2} + w$

23. $\dfrac{9(x - w)}{y}$

24. $\dfrac{3y + 8}{x}$

Find a value of n that will make each a true equation. Let $a = 36$, $b = 12$, and $c = 3$.

25. $\dfrac{a}{b} + c = n$

26. $\dfrac{4(a + b)}{6} = n$

27. $\dfrac{6a}{c} + b = n$

Problem Solving

28. The lengths, in inches, of the sides of a triangle are represented by x, $x + 3$, and $x - 2$. Find the perimeter of the triangle when $x = 10$.

CHALLENGE — Algebra

Simplify each expression by combining like terms.

29. $4y + 5y$ $(4 + 5)y = 9y$

⎿ like terms

30. $4w + w + 5$

31. $7n + n + 3$

32. $5y + 3xy + 2y$

33. $y + y + x$

Properties of Equality

An equation is like a balanced scale. Both sides of an equation remain equal if you *add, subtract, multiply,* or *divide* by the same number on each side.

► The properties of equality tell what you can do to both sides of an equation so that the sides remain equal.

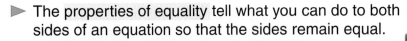

Property of Equality	Example
Addition Property of Equality If the same number is added to both sides of an equation, the sides remain equal.	$8 + 4 = 10 + 2$ $8 + 4 + 6 = 10 + 2 + 6$ $18 = 18$
Subtraction Property of Equality If the same number is subtracted from both sides of an equation, the sides remain equal.	$8 + 4 = 10 + 2$ $8 + 4 - 5 = 10 + 2 - 5$ $7 = 7$
Multiplication Property of Equality If both sides of an equation are multiplied by the same nonzero number, the sides remain equal.	$8 + 4 = 10 + 2$ $(8 + 4) \cdot 4 = (10 + 2) \cdot 4$ $48 = 48$
Division Property of Equality If both sides of an equation are divided by the same nonzero number, the sides remain equal.	$8 + 4 = 10 + 2$ $(8 + 4) \div 3 = (10 + 2) \div 3$ $4 = 4$

When solving equations, you use the properties of equality and inverse operations. Inverse operations undo each other. Addition and subtraction, as well as multiplication and division, are inverse operations.

► Before solving equations, you need to *isolate* the variable.

$n + 4 = 7$	$n - 3 = 7$	$2n = 8$	$\frac{n}{5} = 4$
Subtraction undoes addition.	Addition undoes subtraction.	Division undoes multiplication.	Multiplication undoes division.
Subtract 4.	Add 3.	Divide by 2.	Multiply by 5.
$n + 4 - 4 = 7 - 4$	$n - 3 + 3 = 7 + 3$	$\frac{2n}{2} = \frac{8}{2}$	$\frac{n}{5} \cdot 5 = 4 \cdot 5$
$n = 3$	$n = 10$	$n = 4$	$n = 20$

Name the property of equality used.

1. $15 + 4 = 19$
   $(15 + 4) - 9 = 19 - 9$

2. $7 \cdot 6 = 2 \cdot 21$
   $(7 \cdot 6) \div 2 = (2 \cdot 21) \div 2$

3. $20 - 5 = 19 - 4$
   $(20 - 5) + 5 = (19 - 4) + 5$

4. $16 = 48 \div 3$
   $16 \cdot 8 = (48 \div 3) \cdot 8$

5. $\frac{8}{16} = \frac{3}{6}$
   $\frac{8}{16} - \frac{1}{4} = \frac{3}{6} - \frac{1}{4}$

6. $\frac{9}{12 + 3} = \frac{2 + 1}{5}$
   $\frac{9}{12 + 3} \cdot 15 = \frac{2 + 1}{5} \cdot 15$

Write the inverse operation that would isolate the variable.

7. $w - 9 = 0$

8. $x + 25 = 30$

9. $6h = 12$

10. $a + 5.4 = 7$

11. $k \div 17 = 2$

12. $c - 201 = 2$

13. $27p = 27$

14. $g - 53 = 2$

15. $\frac{m}{8.1} = 1$

16. $17.8x = 35.6$

17. $9.2s = 18.4$

18. $\frac{b}{0.003} = 1$

19. $5.53f$

20. $t - 0.43 = 0.2$

21. $u + 4.21 = 5$

22. $39.5q = 39.5$

Write the number, variable, or operation that makes each equation true.

23. $(5 + 7) - \underline{\ ?\ } = 5$

24. $(8 - 6) + \underline{\ ?\ } = 8$

25. $(n + 3) - \underline{\ ?\ } = n$

26. $(4 \times 7) \div \underline{\ ?\ } = 4$

27. $\left(\frac{n}{4}\right) \cdot \underline{\ ?\ } = n$

28. $(5 + 9) \underline{\ ?\ } 9 = 5$

29. $3r \div \underline{\ ?\ } = 3$

30. $(y - 6) \underline{\ ?\ } 6 = y$

31. $(n + w) - \underline{\ ?\ } = n$

Problem Solving

32. Kevin was given his allowance on Sunday. On Monday, he bought a book for $8.95. On Tuesday, Tim paid Kevin the $5.55 he owed him. Kevin now has $16.60. How much was his allowance?

DO YOU REMEMBER?

Use a vocabulary word in the box to complete each sentence.

33. A $\underline{\ ?\ }$ is a parallelogram with all sides congruent.

34. A $\underline{\ ?\ }$ is a flat pattern that folds into a solid figure.

35. A $\underline{\ ?\ }$ is when a figure is moved without changing its size or shape.

square
transformation
rhombus
net

Addition and Subtraction Equations

Mr. Adams is 26 years older than his daughter, Kelly. If Mr. Adams is 38 years old, how old is Kelly?

To find how old Kelly is, write and solve an equation.

Let y = Kelly's age.

Mr. Adams's age is Kelly's age plus 26.

$$38 \quad = \quad y + 26$$

addition equation

▶ To solve an **addition equation**, use the Subtraction Property of Equality to isolate the variable.

> Remember: Addition and subtraction are inverse operations.

$$38 = y + 26$$
$$38 - 26 = y + 26 - 26 \quad \longleftarrow \text{Subtract 26 from } both \text{ sides.}$$
$$12 = y$$

Check your answer by replacing y with 12 in the original equation.

$$38 = y + 26$$
$$38 \overset{?}{=} 12 + 26$$
$$38 = 38 \quad \text{The answer checks.}$$

Kelly is 12 years old.

Study this example.

Solve: $x - 2.56 = 14.503$ ◀— subtraction equation

To solve, use the Addition Property of Equality.

$$x - 2.56 = 14.503$$
$$x - 2.56 + 2.56 = 14.503 + 2.56 \quad \longleftarrow \text{Add 2.56 to } both \text{ sides.}$$
$$x = 17.063$$

Check: $x - 2.56 = 14.503$

$$17.063 - 2.56 \overset{?}{=} 14.503$$
$$14.503 = 14.503 \quad \text{The answer checks.}$$

Solve and check each addition equation.

1. $n + 39 = 14$
2. $y + 327 = 522$
3. $c + 14.81 = 14.81$
4. $616 = m + 125$
5. $327 + x = 794$
6. $f + 1.018 = 3.19$

Solve and check each subtraction equation.

7. $n - 25 = 72$
8. $y - 319 = 105$
9. $c - 20.5 = 20.5$
10. $219 = m - 516$
11. $3.79 = x - 9.59$
12. $f - 4.08 = 19.005$

Solve for x. Check your answers.

13. $x - 225 = 723$
14. $x + 749 = 4605$
15. $x - 47.9 = 1.34$
16. $58.7 = x - 9.03$
17. $8.34 = x + 0.53$
18. $4.8 + x = 6.001$

Write and solve an equation for the variable used.

19. A number y added to 7 is equal to 12.
20. A number w decreased by 12 is equal to 22.
21. The sum of a number x and 9 is equal to 49.
22. When 24 is subtracted from y, the result is 6.

Problem Solving

23. A book has 328 pages. Niko has 203 pages left to read. How many pages has he read?
24. In 11 years, Carla will be 23 years old. How old is she now?
25. Jake has earned $200, which is $120 less than Iris has earned. How much money has Iris earned?
26. If the Sears Tower in Chicago were 200 ft shorter, it would be the same height as the Empire State Building in New York. The Empire State Building is 1250 ft tall. How high is the Sears Tower?

MENTAL MATH — Algebra

Solve and check each equation.

27. $n + 9 = 14$
28. $n + 7 = 22$
29. $n + 4 = 4$
30. $n + 12 = 16$
31. $6 + n = 16$
32. $n + 11 = 31$
33. $n - 3 = 17$
34. $n - 2 = 15$
35. $n - 5 = 12$
36. $n - 9 = 10$
37. $n - 20 = 24$
38. $n - 3 = 6$

Multiplication and Division Equations

A rectangular parking lot has an area of 8000 square meters. If the width of the lot is 32 m, what is the length?

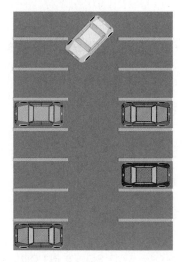

To find the length, write and solve an equation.

Let y = length of the parking lot.

The area of the parking lot is the length times the width.

$$8000 \qquad = \qquad 32y$$

multiplication equation

▶ To solve a **multiplication equation**, use the Division Property of Equality to isolate the variable.

Remember: Multiplication and division are inverse operations.	

$$8000 = 32y$$
$$\frac{8000}{32} = \frac{32y}{32} \quad \longleftarrow \text{Divide } both \text{ sides by 32.}$$
$$250 = y$$

Check your answer by replacing y with 250 in the original equation.

$$8000 = 32y$$
$$8000 \overset{?}{=} 32 \cdot 250$$
$$8000 = 8000 \quad \text{The answer checks.}$$

The length of the parking lot is 250 m.

Study this example.

Solve: $\frac{x}{12} = 18.75$ ◀— division equation

To solve, use the Multiplication Property of Equality.

$$\frac{x}{12} \cdot 12 = 18.75 \cdot 12 \quad \longleftarrow \text{Multiply } both \text{ sides by 12.}$$
$$x = 225$$

Check: $\frac{x}{12} = 18.75 \rightarrow \frac{225}{12} \overset{?}{=} 18.75$
$$18.75 = 18.75 \quad \text{The answer checks.}$$

Solve and check each multiplication equation.

1. $29n = 1392$
2. $17y = 2057$
3. $513c = 513$

4. $362.5 = 29m$
5. $14x = 508.2$
6. $35f = 817.25$

Solve and check each division equation.

7. $\frac{n}{50} = 125$
8. $\frac{y}{319} = 11$
9. $\frac{c}{23.5} = 0.8$

10. $2.26 = \frac{m}{14}$
11. $5.07 = \frac{x}{0.4}$
12. $\frac{f}{526} = 1.201$

Solve for x. Check your answers.

13. $456x = 0$
14. $18x = 4644$
15. $55x = 67.65$

16. $1.25 = \frac{x}{25}$
17. $8.34 = \frac{x}{0.9}$
18. $\frac{x}{65} = 65$

Write and solve an equation.

19. The product of a number y and 6 is equal to 72.

20. When a number x is multiplied by 9, the product is 108.

21. A number w divided by 4 is equal to 32.

22. When a number y is divided by 16, the quotient is 6.

Problem Solving

23. A parallelogram has an area of 126 cm^2. The base is 12 cm. What is the height of the parallelogram?

24. Carl's age is one third his father's age. Carl is 17 years old. How old is Carl's father?

25. Monica saved $37.95. This is one fifth of the cost of the bicycle she wants to buy. How much more money does she need?

26. Ted's room is a rectangle. Its length is twice its width. If the length is 22 ft, what is the perimeter of the room?

CHALLENGE   Algebra

Solve and check each equation.

27. $2x + 6 = 16$
$2x + 6 - 6 = 16 - 6$
$2x = 10$
$\frac{2x}{2} = \frac{10}{2}$
$x = 5$

28. $3k - 7 = 14$

30. $\frac{w}{10} - 3 = 9$

32. $\frac{n}{5} + 4 = 7.8$

29. $6n + 1.2 = 4.2$

31. $\frac{m}{12} + 45 = 47.2$

33. $8.1 + 4.2y = 17.76$

Equations with Fractions

Some equations, such as equations with fractions, can be solved by using the properties of addition or multiplication.

Equation	Solution	Property Applied
$n + \frac{1}{2} = \frac{1}{2}$	$n = 0$	Identity Property of Addition
$\frac{5}{7} + \frac{1}{7} = \frac{1}{7} + n$	$n = \frac{5}{7}$	Commutative Property of Addition
$\frac{1}{3} \cdot n = \frac{1}{3}$	$n = 1$	Identity Property of Multiplication
$\left(3 \cdot \frac{1}{2}\right) \cdot n = 3 \cdot \left(\frac{1}{2} \cdot \frac{3}{5}\right)$	$n = \frac{3}{5}$	Associative Property of Multiplication
$n \cdot \frac{1}{4} = 0$	$n = 0$	Zero Property of Multiplication

Solve for _a_. Use the properties to help you.

1. $\frac{2}{3} \cdot a = 4 \cdot \frac{2}{3}$ $a = 4$
Commutative Property of Multiplication

2. $\frac{3}{4} + a = \frac{3}{4}$

3. $a + 0 = \frac{3}{5}$

4. $\frac{7}{8} \cdot a = \frac{1}{3} \cdot \frac{7}{8}$

5. $a + \frac{1}{2} = \frac{1}{2} + \frac{2}{3}$

6. $\frac{2}{5} + a = \frac{1}{5} + \frac{2}{5}$

7. $\frac{6}{7} \cdot a = \frac{6}{7}$

8. $a \cdot \frac{1}{9} = 0$

9. $\frac{2}{5} \cdot a = 0$

10. $\frac{3}{8} + a = \frac{3}{8}$

11. $1 \cdot a = \frac{2}{3}$

12. $a \cdot \frac{1}{6} = \frac{1}{6}$

13. $\frac{6}{11} + \frac{3}{10} = a + \frac{6}{11}$

14. $\frac{3}{4} + \left(\frac{1}{2} + \frac{3}{5}\right) = \left(\frac{3}{4} + \frac{1}{2}\right) + a$

15. $\frac{5}{9} + \left(a + \frac{2}{3}\right) = \left(\frac{5}{9} + \frac{1}{6}\right) + \frac{2}{3}$

16. $\frac{1}{4} \times \left(a + \frac{1}{5}\right) = \left(\frac{1}{4} \times \frac{1}{3}\right) + \left(\frac{1}{4} \times \frac{1}{5}\right)$

Solve Equations with Fractions

You can also solve equations with fractions by using inverse operations and the properties of equality.

Solve the equations.

$$n + \frac{2}{7} = \frac{6}{7}$$

$$n + \frac{2}{7} - \frac{2}{7} = \frac{6}{7} - \frac{2}{7}$$ ← Subtract $\frac{2}{7}$ from both sides.

$$n = \frac{4}{7}$$

.Think.....

$$\frac{1}{3}x = \frac{x}{3}$$

$$\frac{1}{3}x = \frac{1}{12}$$

$$\frac{x}{3} \cdot 3 = \frac{1}{12} \cdot 3$$ ← Multiply both sides by 3.

$$x = \frac{1}{4}$$

Solve the equation. Use inverse operations and properties of equality.

17. $y + \frac{1}{3} = \frac{2}{3}$

18. $a - \frac{1}{5} = \frac{4}{5}$

19. $\frac{1}{2} \cdot b = \frac{1}{4}$

20. $\frac{1}{4} \cdot m = \frac{1}{8}$

21. $\frac{5}{6} = c + \frac{1}{6}$

22. $\frac{1}{8} = \frac{1}{2} \cdot d$

23. $\frac{2}{7} + n = \frac{9}{14}$

24. $\frac{2}{5} \cdot n = \frac{1}{3}$

25. $7\frac{4}{9} = x - \frac{1}{3}$

Solve the equation. Use properties of addition and multiplication or inverse operations.

26. $\frac{2}{3} \cdot y = \frac{2}{3}$

27. $\frac{4}{9} + z = \frac{4}{9}$

28. $\frac{3}{4} = t + \frac{1}{4}$

29. $\frac{1}{5} \cdot \frac{1}{2} = \frac{1}{2} \cdot n$

30. $\frac{1}{14} = \frac{1}{7} \cdot m$

31. $\frac{5}{9} + \frac{1}{3} = \frac{1}{3} + a$

32. $\left(\frac{1}{2} + \frac{1}{3}\right) + \frac{1}{4} = \frac{1}{2} + \left(\frac{1}{3} + r\right)$

33. $\frac{3}{5} \cdot \left(\frac{1}{2} \cdot s\right) = \left(\frac{3}{5} \cdot \frac{1}{2}\right) \cdot \frac{1}{10}$

DO YOU REMEMBER?

Write the number or letter for each point.

34. A

35. B

36. M

37. E

38. H

39. 4

40. 6

41. 12

42. 16

43. 10

Introduction to Integers

Integers are all of the whole numbers and their opposites.
They are either positive, negative, or zero.

Kyle earned $8 running errands for neighbors.
He spent $3.

You can write these numbers as integers.

earned $8 $^+$8 dollars   ◀── Read: "positive eight dollars"

spent $3 $^-$3 dollars   ◀── Read: "negative three dollars"

▶ Integers can be shown on a number line.

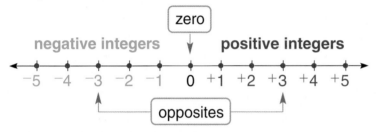

Positive ($^+$) integers are to the *right* of 0. They are *greater than* 0.
Negative ($^-$) integers are to the *left* of 0. They are *less than* 0.
Zero is *neither* a positive integer *nor* a negative integer.

▶ Every integer has an opposite. $^+$3 and $^-$3 are opposites.
The opposite of 0 is 0.

Practice

Write each as an integer.

1. a loss of $2   **2.** 4 floors up   **3.** 5 degrees cooler

4. a gain of 2 pounds   **5.** $6 profit   **6.** 3 meters forward

Name the integer that matches each point on the number line.

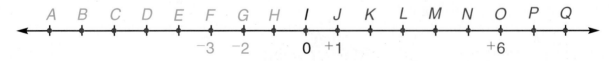

7. P   **8.** B   **9.** N   **10.** L   **11.** Q   **12.** A

13. E   **14.** M   **15.** C   **16.** K   **17.** D   **18.** H

For each integer, name the integer that is just *before* and just *after* it on a number line.

19. ⁺9 **20.** ⁻17 **21.** ⁻6 **22.** 0 **23.** ⁻10 **24.** ⁺1

25. ⁻1 **26.** ⁺13 **27.** ⁻26 **28.** ⁻8 **29.** ⁺4 **30.** ⁻2

Write the opposite of each integer.

31. ⁺5 **32.** ⁺8 **33.** ⁻6 **34.** ⁺9 **35.** ⁻17 **36.** ⁻3

37. ⁻11 **38.** ⁺88 **39.** ⁻1 **40.** 0 **41.** ⁻67 **42.** ⁺49

43. ⁺14 **44.** ⁻63 **45.** ⁺70 **46.** ⁺105 **47.** ⁻213 **48.** ⁺300

Problem Solving

49. If you record a deposit of eighteen dollars as ⁺$18, how would you record a withdrawal of eighteen dollars?

50. In a game the card for ⁺7 says "Go Ahead 7 Steps." What would the card for ⁻7 say?

51. Begin at 0. What happens if you go up 6 steps (⁺6) and then down 6 steps (⁻6)?

52. On a vertical number line, are the numbers above zero positive or negative?

53. If 0 is sea level, how would twenty-five feet below sea level be written?

54. If 0 is sea level, how would forty-seven feet above sea level be written?

55. In your Math Journal, list real-life situations in which positive and negative integers are used.

0 ft sea level

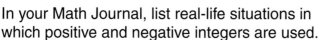

Name each integer on a horizontal number line.

56. six to the right of negative three **57.** four to the left of one

Compare and Order Integers

You can use a number line to compare and order integers.

-8 -7 -6 -5 -4 -3 -2 -1 0 +1 +2 +3 +4 +5 +6 +7 +8

▶ To **compare integers** using a horizontal number line, any integer is greater than an integer to its left.

$+4 > +2$ since $+4$ is right of $+2$.

$-3 < +1$ since -3 is left of $+1$.

$-3 > -5$ since -3 is right of -5.

> A positive integer is greater than any negative integer.

Order $+5$, -4, 0.

▶ To **order integers** using a horizontal number line:

• Least to greatest — Begin with the integer farthest to the *left*.

• Greatest to least — Begin with the integer farthest to the *right*.

.Think...
-4 is farthest to the left and $+5$ is farthest to the
right on the number line; 0 is between $+5$ and -4.

The order from least to greatest is: -4, 0, $+5$

The order from greatest to least is: $+5$, 0, -4

Choose the greater integer.

1. $+3$, $+5$ **2.** 0, -6 **3.** $+4$, $+1$ **4.** 0, $+3$

5. $+2$, -2 **6.** $+1$, 0 **7.** -2, $+4$ **8.** $+5$, $+6$

9. $+2$, $+4$ **10.** -3, -7 **11.** -1, $+1$ **12.** -6, -2

Compare. Write < or >.

13. $-1 \underline{\;?\;} +1$ **14.** $+6 \underline{\;?\;} -5$ **15.** $+4 \underline{\;?\;} +1$ **16.** $-11 \underline{\;?\;} -14$

$-2 \underline{\;?\;} +6$ **18.** $+12 \underline{\;?\;} -10$ **19.** $-6 \underline{\;?\;} 0$ **20.** $+9 \underline{\;?\;} 0$

Arrange in order from least to greatest.

21. ⁻5, 0, ⁻4

22. ⁺5, ⁺3, ⁻7

23. ⁻1, ⁻9, ⁺2

24. ⁺14, ⁻6, ⁻1

25. ⁻8, ⁺5, 0

26. ⁺9, ⁺8, ⁻1

27. ⁻6, ⁻9, ⁻3

28. ⁻2, ⁺7, ⁻1

29. ⁻4, ⁺14, 0

Arrange in order from greatest to least.

30. ⁻3, ⁺6, ⁺5

31. ⁻6, ⁻3, ⁺4

32. ⁻4, ⁺5, ⁺3

33. ⁺8, ⁻8, 0

34. ⁻12, ⁻8, ⁻10

35. ⁻15, ⁺6, ⁺8

Write *always*, *sometimes*, or *never* to make true statements.

36. A negative integer is __?__ less than a positive integer.

37. A negative integer is __?__ greater than 0.

38. A negative integer is __?__ less than another negative integer.

39. A positive integer is __?__ greater than 0.

Problem Solving

The table shows the daily average temperature for five days.

40. Which day had the coldest average temperature?

41. Which day had the warmest average temperature?

42. What was the median (middle) temperature?

43. Which day was the average temperature between ⁻3°C and ⁺1°C?

Day	Average Temperature
Monday	⁻2°C
Tuesday	⁺5°C
Wednesday	⁻3°C
Thursday	⁺1°C
Friday	⁺2°C

TEST PREPARATION

44. Which statement is true?

   A ⁺5 > ⁻5   **B** ⁻6 < ⁻9

   C ⁻12 > ⁺2   **D** ⁺1 = ⁻1

45. Which is ordered from least to greatest?

   F ⁺4, ⁻3, ⁻5   **G** ⁻3, ⁻5, ⁺4

   H ⁺4, ⁻5, ⁻3   **J** ⁻5, ⁻3, ⁺4

Add Integers with Like Signs

An anchor is 2 ft below sea level. It goes down 4 more feet. What is its new depth written as an integer?

2 ft below sea level	⁻2
4 ft down	⁻4

To find the anchor's new depth, add: ⁻2 + ⁻4 = n.

▶ You can use a number line to model the addition of integers.

- Start at 0.
- Move *left* for negative integers.
- Move *right* for positive integers.

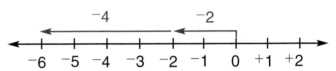

▶ To add integers with *like* signs:

- Add the integers.   2 + 4 = 6
- Use the sign of the addends.   ⁻2 + ⁻4 = ⁻6

Think.........
2 + 4 = 6
Use a negative sign.

The anchor's depth written as an integer is ⁻6 ft.

Study these examples.

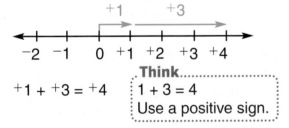

⁺1 + ⁺3 = ⁺4

Think.........
1 + 3 = 4
Use a positive sign.

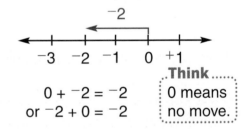

0 + ⁻2 = ⁻2
or ⁻2 + 0 = ⁻2

Think.........
0 means
no move.

Practice

Write an addition sentence for each number line.

1.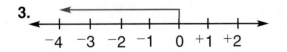

2.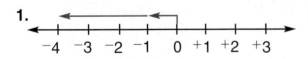

3.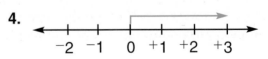

4.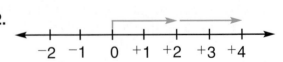

Add. Use a number line to help you.

5. $^+5 + {}^+2$ 6. $^+6 + {}^+4$ 7. $^+9 + {}^+3$ 8. $^+7 + {}^+12$

9. $^-12 + {}^-3$ 10. $^-8 + {}^-9$ 11. $^-4 + {}^-11$ 12. $^-8 + {}^-13$

13. $0 + {}^+8$ 14. $^+7 + 0$ 15. $^-10 + 0$ 16. $0 + {}^-5$

17. Describe a rule for each row of exercises above and give another example.

Evaluate the expression to complete each table. Let n represent an integer.

18.

n	$n + 5$
$^+3$	$3 + 5 = 8$
$^+6$	?
$^+9$	?
0	?
$^+5$	?

19.

n	$n + {}^-4$
$^-4$	$^-4 + {}^-4 = {}^-8$
$^-8$	?
0	?
$^-3$	?
$^-7$	?

Find the sum.

20. $^-5 + ({}^-3 + {}^-2)$

   $^-5 + \underline{\ ?\ } = \underline{\ ?\ }$

21. $({}^+8 + {}^+2) + {}^+9$

   $\underline{\ ?\ } + {}^+9 = \underline{\ ?\ }$

22. $^+3 + ({}^+7 + {}^+5)$ 23. $({}^-2 + {}^-9) + {}^-6$ 24. $({}^+4 + {}^+1) + {}^+13$

25. $({}^-1 + {}^-10) + {}^-12$ 26. $^-6 + ({}^-3 + {}^-3)$ 27. $({}^-5 + 0) + {}^-10$

Problem Solving Write each answer in words and as an integer.

28. A geologist worked at a site 3 m above sea level. Later he moved to a site 5 m higher. How far above or below sea level is the new site?

29. Team A's score in one card game is $^-9$. If the team makes another score of $^-20$, what is its total score?

30. The selling price of stock X fell 8 points one day and 12 points the next day. What was the total change over the two-day period?

31. The football team had a gain of 6 yd on one play and a gain of 5 yd on the next play. How many yards were gained on the two plays?

Add Integers with Unlike Signs

Jan lost 8 points in the first round of a game.
He earned 3 points in the second round.
What was his score after the second round?

lost 8 points	$^-8$
earned 3 points	$^+3$

To find Jan's score after the second round,
add: $^-8 + {}^+3 = n$.

▶ You can use a number line to
model $^-8 + {}^+3$.
- Start at 0.
- Move *left* for negative integers.
- Move *right* for positive integers.

$^-8 + {}^+3 = {}^-5$

▶ To add integers with *unlike* signs:
- Find the difference. (Drop the signs $8 - 3 = 5$
  and subtract the numbers.)
- Use the sign of the addend farther $^-8 + {}^+3 = {}^-5$
  from zero.

.Think.........
$^-8$ is farther from
zero than $^+3$. Use
a negative sign.
....

Jan's score after the second round was $^-5$.

Study these examples.

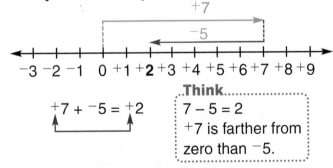

$^+7 + {}^-5 = {}^+2$

.Think..............
$7 - 5 = 2$
$^+7$ is farther from
zero than $^-5$.
....

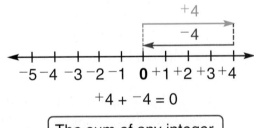

$^+4 + {}^-4 = 0$

The sum of any integer
and its opposite is zero.

Complete the addition sentence for each number line.

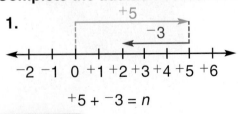

1.

$^+5 + {}^-3 = n$

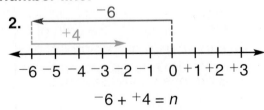

2.

$^-6 + {}^+4 = n$

Practice

Write an addition sentence for each number line.

3.

4.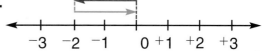

5.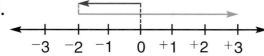

6.

Find the sum. Use a number line to help you.

7. $^+10 + {}^-4$ 8. $^+9 + {}^-11$ 9. $^+7 + {}^-1$ 10. $^+13 + {}^-17$

11. $^-9 + {}^+2$ 12. $^-13 + {}^+15$ 13. $^-8 + {}^+2$ 14. $^-7 + {}^+5$

15. $^+8 + {}^-8$ 16. $^-9 + {}^+9$ 17. $^+11 + {}^-11$ 18. $^+25 + {}^-25$

19. $^-15 + {}^+7$ 20. $^+21 + {}^-13$ 21. $^-36 + {}^+25$ 22. $^+11 + {}^-9$

Problem Solving Write each answer in words and as an integer.

23. Sally's checking account has a balance of $^-\$12$. If she deposits $30, what will be her new balance?

24. A quarterback gained 16 yd on one play. Then he lost 13 yd on the next play. What was the total gain?

25. An anchor hung against the side of a boat 4 ft below sea level. A sailor lowered the anchor 20 ft. What is the total depth of the anchor?

26. At noon on a Monday in May, the temperature was 53°F. At sunset, the temperature was 12° lower. What was the temperature at sunset?

27. In March, Ben gained 2 lb. In April, he lost 4 lb. What was Ben's total gain or loss in March and April?

28. Electrons have a charge of $^-1$ and protons have a charge of $^+1$. The total charge of an ion is the sum of its electrons and protons. Find the total charge of an ion of:

   a. 13 protons and 17 electrons

   b. 9 protons and 4 electrons.

   c. 8 protons and 8 electrons.

Subtract Integers

You can use two-color counters to subtract integers.

Subtract: $^-3 - {}^-5 = n$; $^+3 - {}^-5 = n$
$^+3 - {}^+5 = n$; $^-3 - {}^+5 = n$

Key

| 1 🔴 = $^+1$ |
| 1 ⚫ = $^-1$ |

$^+1 + {}^-1 = 0$

zero pair: 🔴⚫

Materials: two-color counters, workmat

Step 1   Place 3 red counters on your integer mat. What integer do the counters represent?

Can you subtract $^-5$ from the integer on your mat?

Integer Mat

⚫   ⚫   ⚫

Step 2   Add 2 zero pairs to your mat.

Can you subtract $^-5$ now?

What is $^-3 - {}^-5$?

Integer Mat

⊗   ⊗   ⊗
🔴⊗   🔴⊗

Step 3   Remove all counters from your mat.

Place 3 green counters on your mat. What integer do the counters represent?

Can you subtract $^-5$ from the integer on your mat?

Step 4   Add 5 zero pairs to your mat.

Can you subtract $^-5$ now?

What is $^+3 - {}^-5$?

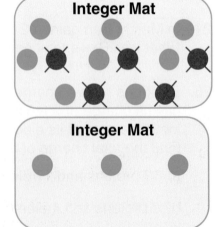

Integer Mat

Step 5   Remove all counters from your mat.

Place 3 green counters on your mat. What integer do the counters represent?

Can you subtract $^+5$ from the integer on your mat?

Integer Mat

🟢   🟢   🟢

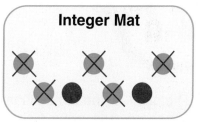

Integer Mat

Step 6 | Add 2 zero pairs to your mat.

Can you subtract $^+5$ now?

What is $^+3 - {}^+5$?

Step 7 | Remove all counters from your mat.

Place 3 red counters on your mat.
What integer do the counters represent?

Can you subtract $^+5$ from the integer
on your mat?

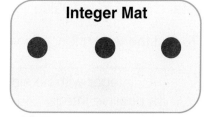

Integer Mat

Step 8 | Add 5 zero pairs to your mat.

Can you subtract $^+5$ now?

What is $^-3 - {}^+5$?

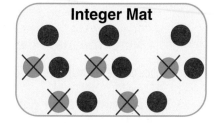

Integer Mat

Use counters to subtract.

1. $^-6 - {}^-2$ **2.** $^+6 - {}^-2$ **3.** $^+6 - {}^+2$ **4.** $^-6 - {}^+2$

5. $^-9 - {}^-4$ **6.** $^+9 - {}^-4$ **7.** $^+9 - {}^+4$ **8.** $^-9 - {}^+4$

9. $^-5 - {}^-8$ **10.** $^+5 - {}^-8$ **11.** $^+5 - {}^+8$ **12.** $^-5 - {}^+8$

Find the value of *n*.

13.

Subtraction Sentences	Addition Sentences
$^-3 - {}^-5 = n$	$^-3 + {}^+5 = n$
$^+3 - {}^-5 = n$	$^+3 + {}^+5 = n$
$^+3 - {}^+5 = n$	$^+3 + {}^-5 = n$
$^-3 - {}^+5 = n$	$^-3 + {}^-5 = n$

Communicate

14. How does adding zero pairs help to model
subtraction of integers?

15. How can you use addition to subtract integers?
Give examples to explain your answer.

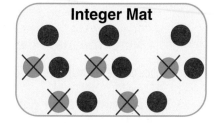

Practice

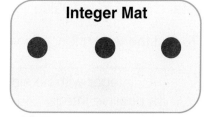

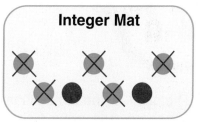

Multiply Integers

The stock of the Jones Company dropped $3 per share. Ana owns 4 shares. What is the total change in the value of Ana's shares?

To find the total change in value, multiply: $4 \times {}^-3 = n$.

> An integer with no sign is a positive integer: $4 = {}^+4$, $12 = {}^+12$, and so on.

$4 \times {}^-3$ means ${}^+4 \times {}^-3$

| positive four | | negative three |

The pattern at the right shows that ${}^+4 \times {}^-3 = {}^-12$.

$4 \times 3 =$		12
$4 \times 2 =$		8
$4 \times 1 =$		4
$4 \times 0 =$		0
$4 \times {}^-1 =$		${}^-4$
$4 \times {}^-2 =$		${}^-8$
$4 \times {}^-3 =$	${}^-12$	

The total change in the value of Ana's shares is ${}^-\$12$.

▶ To find the product ${}^-4 \times {}^-3$, study the pattern below.

$${}^-4 \times {}^-3$$

| negative four | | negative three |

So ${}^-4 \times {}^-3 = 12$ or ${}^+12$.

$4 \times {}^-3 =$	${}^-12$
$3 \times {}^-3 =$	${}^-9$
$2 \times {}^-3 =$	${}^-6$
$1 \times {}^-3 =$	${}^-3$
$0 \times {}^-3 =$	0
${}^-1 \times {}^-3 =$	3
${}^-2 \times {}^-3 =$	6
${}^-3 \times {}^-3 =$	9
${}^-4 \times {}^-3 =$	12

▶ > The product of two integers:
> - is *positive* if they have the *same* sign.
> - is *negative* if they have *different* signs.
> - is *zero* if one or both is *zero*.

Study these examples.

$${}^+5 \times {}^+6 = {}^+30 \qquad ({}^-7)\,({}^+8) = {}^-56 \qquad 0\,({}^+9) = 0 \qquad 0 \cdot 0 = 0$$

Use the rules on page 460 to find each product.

1. $^{-}7 \times {^{+}5}$
2. $^{+}3 \times {^{-}4}$
3. $^{-}2 \times {^{-}5}$
4. $^{+}8 \times {^{+}5}$

5. $^{+}9 \times {^{-}6}$
6. $^{-}5 \times {^{+}5}$
7. $^{-}8 \times {^{+}10}$
8. $0 \times {^{+}8}$

9. $^{-}4 \cdot 0$
10. $^{-}1 \cdot {^{+}11}$
11. $^{+}1 \cdot {^{-}20}$
12. $^{-}7 \cdot {^{-}7}$

13. $(^{-}8)(^{-}8)$
14. $^{+}1\,(^{-}1)$
15. $5\,(^{-}10)$
16. $(^{-}12)(^{-}11)$

Choose the correct answer to complete each statement. Give an example to support each answer. Let p = positive integer and n = negative integer.

17. $p \times p =$ ___?___
     a. positive   **b.** negative   **c.** cannot tell

18. $n \times n =$ ___?___
     a. positive   **b.** negative   **c.** cannot tell

19. $p \times n =$ ___?___
     a. positive   **b.** negative   **c.** cannot tell

20. $(p \times p) \times p =$ ___?___
     a. positive   **b.** negative   **c.** cannot tell

21. $(n \times n) \times n =$ ___?___
     a. positive   **b.** negative   **c.** cannot tell

Compute. Use the order of operations.

22. $^{+}5\,(^{+}3 + {^{+}9})$
23. $^{+}3\,(^{-}1 + {^{+}2})$
24. $^{-}9\,(^{-}7 + {^{+}4})$

25. $^{-}8\,(^{-}2 + {^{-}2})$
26. $^{-}5\,(^{+}6 + {^{-}8})$
27. $^{-}6\,(^{-}3 + {^{-}4})$

Problem Solving

28. At noon the temperature was 8°C. The temperature dropped 2°C per hour. What was the total change in 6 hours?

29. The Acme Tigers football team loses 8 yards on each of the first 3 plays of the game. Write an integer to express the results.

Write About It

30. Write in your Math Journal how to add two negative integers and how to multiply two negative integers. Write a number pattern for each operation that could be used to "discover" the rules.

Divide Integers

Pia wants to lose 8 lb in 4 weeks. If she loses the same number of pounds each week, how many pounds will she lose per week?

lose 8 lb $^-8$

To find how many pounds Pia will lose per week, find the missing factor:

Remember: $4 = {}^+4$	$n \times {}^+4 = {}^-8$ $n = {}^-2$ or

> **Think**
> What integer times $^+4$
> equals $^-8$? $^-2 \times {}^+4 = {}^-8$

divide, since you are *sharing* a set (8 lb) among equal groups (4 wk).

$$^-8 \div {}^+4 = {}^-2$$

Pia will lose 2 lb per week.

Multiplication Sentence	Related Division Sentences
$^-2 \times {}^+4 = {}^-8$	$^-8 \div {}^+4 = {}^-2$ $^-8 \div {}^-2 = {}^+4$
$^+3 \times {}^-5 = {}^-15$	$^-15 \div {}^-5 = {}^+3$ $^-15 \div {}^+3 = {}^-5$
$^-6 \times {}^-9 = {}^+54$	$^+54 \div {}^-9 = {}^-6$ $^+54 \div {}^-6 = {}^-9$

> **Think**
> Division is the inverse of multiplication.

Complete each related division sentence.

1. $^-6 \times {}^-7 = {}^+42$

    $^+42 \div {}^-7 = n$

    $^+42 \div {}^-6 = n$

2. $^-9 \cdot {}^+5 = {}^-45$

    $^-45 \div {}^+5 = n$

    $^-45 \div {}^-9 = n$

3. $^+8\,({}^+3) = {}^+24$

    $^+24 \div {}^+3 = n$

    $^+24 \div {}^+8 = n$

Write two related division sentences.

4. $^-5 \times {}^+6 = {}^-30$

5. $^+6 \cdot {}^-4 = {}^-24$

6. $^-7 \cdot ({}^-4) = {}^+28$

7. $^+9 \times {}^+8 = {}^+72$

8. $^-2 \cdot {}^-8 = {}^+16$

9. $^+6\,({}^-9) = {}^-54$

Rules of Division

Here are rules of division that can help you divide integers quickly and correctly.

- The quotient of integers with *like* signs is positive.

$$^+18 \div {}^+3 = {}^+6 \qquad\qquad ^-20 \div {}^-5 = {}^+4$$

$$^+15 \div {}^+5 = {}^+3 \qquad\qquad ^-54 \div {}^-9 = {}^+6$$

- The quotient of integers with *unlike* signs is negative.

$$^-10 \div {}^+5 = {}^-2 \qquad\qquad ^-30 \div {}^+6 = {}^-5$$

$$^+36 \div {}^-9 = {}^-4 \qquad\qquad ^+42 \div {}^-7 = {}^-6$$

Find each quotient.

10. $^+60 \div {}^+5$ **11.** $^+32 \div {}^-8$ **12.** $^-63 \div {}^+9$ **13.** $^-55 \div {}^-11$

14. $^+48 \div {}^+12$ **15.** $^+52 \div {}^-4$ **16.** $^-10 \div {}^-10$ **17.** $^-30 \div {}^-6$

18. $^+45 \div {}^+9$ **19.** $^+44 \div {}^-11$ **20.** $^-100 \div {}^+5$ **21.** $^-45 \div {}^-45$

Compute. Use the order of operations.

22. $\dfrac{(^-7 + {}^-8)}{^+3}$ **23.** $\dfrac{(^+9 + {}^-5)}{^-4}$ **24.** $\dfrac{(^-5 + {}^+3)\,(^-4 + {}^+3)}{^+2}$

Write a division sentence. Then solve it.

25. The dividend is $^-48$. The quotient is $^+8$. What is the divisor?

26. The divisor is $^+12$. The quotient is 0. What is the dividend?

Problem Solving

27. The temperature drops 25°F in 5 hours. What is the average change per hour, written as an integer?

28. Tony withdraws $180 from his account in 3 weeks. What was the average withdrawal per week, written as an integer?

CHALLENGE — Algebra

Find the pattern rule. Then complete the pattern.

29. $^-80, {}^+40, {}^-20,$ __?__ , __?__

30. $^-243, {}^-81, {}^-27,$ __?__ , __?__

31. $^+3, {}^-12, {}^+48,$ __?__ , __?__

32. $^+1, {}^+5, {}^+25,$ __?__ , __?__

The Coordinate Plane

A coordinate plane, or grid, is formed by two perpendicular number lines, called axes. The horizontal line is called the *x*-axis and the vertical line is called the *y*-axis. The point where the two axes intersect is (0, 0). It is called the origin.

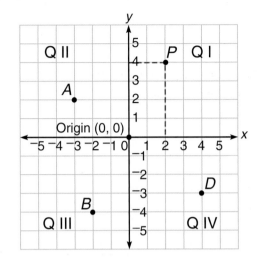

▶ Ordered pairs (*x*, *y*) are numbers used to locate points on a grid. The numbers that are used to represent a point are called coordinates.

(2, 4) are the coordinates of point *P*.

x-coordinate

y-coordinate

A grid can be divided into four sections, called quadrants. Point *P* is in quadrant I.

▶ To locate, or graph, a point on a grid:

- Start at (0, 0). Move the number of units on the *x*-axis indicated by the *x*-coordinate. The ⁻ sign tells you to move left.

- Move the number of units on the *y*-axis indicated by the *y*-coordinate. The ⁻ sign tells you to move down.

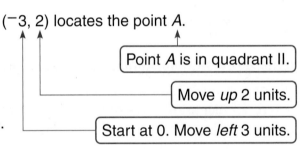

(⁻3, 2) locates the point *A*.

Point *A* is in quadrant II.

Move *up* 2 units.

Start at 0. Move *left* 3 units.

Study these examples.

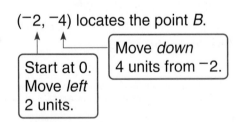

(⁻2, ⁻4) locates the point *B*.

Start at 0. Move *left* 2 units.

Move *down* 4 units from ⁻2.

Point *B* is in quadrant III.

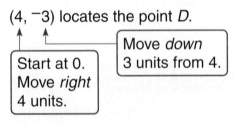

(4, ⁻3) locates the point *D*.

Start at 0. Move *right* 4 units.

Move *down* 3 units from 4.

Point *D* is in quadrant IV.

Use the grid at the right. Write the coordinates of each point.

1. *E*   2. *O*   3. *F*

4. *R*   5. *N*   6. *L*

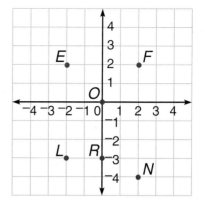

Use the grid at the right. Name the point to complete the table.

	Coordinates	Point
7.	(⁻5, 1)	?
8.	(⁻1, 1)	?
9.	(⁻1, ⁻2)	?
10.	(⁻5, ⁻2)	?
11.	(3, 2)	?
12.	(5, 0)	?
13.	(5, ⁻2)	?
14.	(3, ⁻4)	?
15.	(1, ⁻2)	?
16.	(1, 0)	?

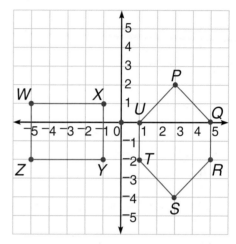

17. Classify the polygons *WXYZ* and *PQRSTU*.

Use a grid to locate the points. Then connect them.

18. *A* (1, 4); *M* (4, 4); *H* (1, 8)
19. *P* (⁻2, 8); *S* (⁻8, 8); *T* (⁻2, 16)

20. *B* (3, ⁻1); *C* (5, ⁻1); *D* (5, ⁻3); *E* (3, ⁻3)

21. *W* (⁻7, ⁻2); *X* (⁻11, ⁻2); *Y* (⁻11, ⁻6); *Z* (⁻7, ⁻6)

22. What figures have you made? Find the area of each figure.

CHALLENGE ····Algebra····

23. Given the points (0, 4) and (6, 4), find two sets of points that can be used to complete a square.

24. Given the points (0, 3), (1, 0), and (5, 3), find the point that can be used to complete a parallelogram.

Function Tables

A **function** is a relationship between two quantities in which one quantity depends on the other.

The **function table** below shows the charges for an overdue library book for different numbers of days that the book is late. The table matches each input value, *d* (days late), with an output value, *c* (charges).

Days Late, *d*	1	2	3	4	5	*d*
Charges (in cents), *c*	5	10	15	20	25	?

Think: The charges are 5 cents *times* the number of days the book is late.

Charges for 1 day: 5¢ · 1 or 5 cents
2 days: 5¢ · 2 or 10 cents
d days: 5¢ · *d* or 5*d* cents

A **rule** for the function table above is defined by the equation, $c = 5d$.

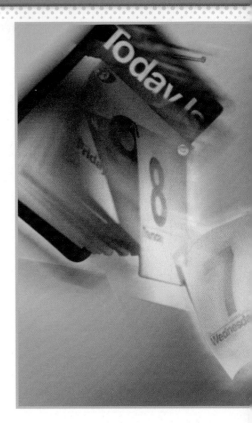

Use the table above to find the charge for each overdue book.

1. 6 days late

2. 10 days late

3. 0 days late

Use the table above to find the number of days each book is late.

4. $0.25

5. $0.50

6. $0.30

7. $0.45

Use the rule to complete each function table.

8. $a = f + 6$

f	16	33	50	67	74
a	?	?	?	?	?

9. $w = \dfrac{a}{7}$

a	7	14	35	77	$3\frac{1}{2}$
w	?	?	?	?	?

Use the rule to complete each function table.

10. $y = x\%$ of 300

x	y
10	?
20	?
30	?
40	?

11. $y = 20\%$ of x

x	y
5	?
15	?
25	?
30	?

12. $y = 10\%$ of x

x	y
?	2
?	4
?	8
?	10

13. $y = x\%$ of 100

x	y
?	5
?	10
?	15
?	20

Write a rule for each function table.

14.

x	y
2	6
3	9
4	12
5	15

Think:

$3 \cdot 2 = 6$

$3 \cdot 3 = 9$

$\vdots$

Rule: $y = 3x$

15.

m	n
20	4
21	5
22	6
23	7

16.

x	y
$\frac{1}{2}$	$\frac{1}{4}$
$\frac{1}{3}$	$\frac{1}{6}$
$\frac{1}{4}$	$\frac{1}{8}$
$\frac{1}{5}$	$\frac{1}{10}$

17.

m	n
$\frac{1}{2}$	$\frac{1}{3}$
$\frac{1}{4}$	$\frac{1}{6}$
$\frac{1}{6}$	$\frac{1}{9}$
$\frac{1}{8}$	$\frac{1}{12}$

CRITICAL THINKING — Algebra

Match the rule with the correct table.

Remember: Use the order of operations.

18. $y = 2x + 1$ **19.** $y = 3x - 1$ **20.** $y = 2x + 2$

a.

x	2	3	4	5
y	5	7	9	11

b.

x	2	3	4	5
y	6	8	10	12

c.

x	2	3	4	5
y	5	8	11	14

Functions and Coordinate Graphs

You can use a rule or equation to make a function table and use ordered pairs to locate points on a coordinate plane.

Graph the function $y = x + 1$ on a coordinate plane using integer values from $^-2$ to $^+2$. Then use the graph to find the value of y when $x = {}^+4$.

▶ **To graph a function on a coordinate plane:**

- Make a function table.
    - Substitute values for x in the rule or equation.
    - Find the corresponding y-values.
    - Write an ordered pair for each x- and y-value.

- Graph each ordered pair.

- Connect the points.

x	x + 1	y	(x, y)
$^-2$	$^-2 + 1 = {}^-1$	$^-1$	$(^-2, {}^-1)$
$^-1$	$^-1 + 1 = 0$	0	$(^-1, 0)$
0	$0 + 1 = {}^+1$	$^+1$	$(0, {}^+1)$
$^+1$	$^+1 + 1 = {}^+2$	$^+2$	$(^+1, {}^+2)$
$^+2$	$^+2 + 1 = {}^+3$	$^+3$	$(^+2, {}^+3)$

Remember: Start at the origin and move x units to the *right* or *left*. Then move y units *up* or *down*.

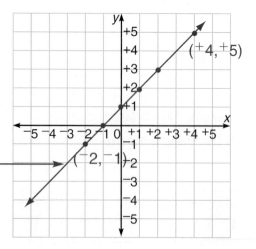

The graph of the function $y = x + 1$.

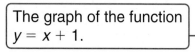

When $x = {}^+4$, $y = {}^+5$.

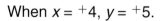

Find the values of y and write the ordered pairs in each function table. Then graph on a coordinate plane.

1.

x	$y = x$	y	(x, y)
$^-1$	$y = {}^-1$	$^-1$	$(^-1, ^-1)$
0	?	?	?
$^+1$	?	?	?
$^+2$	?	?	?

2.

x	$y = x + 2$	y	(x, y)
0	?	?	?
$^+1$	?	?	?
$^+2$	?	?	?
$^+3$	?	?	?

Use the given graph of $y = x + {}^-1$.

3. When $x = 0$, what is the value of y?

4. When $x = {}^-1$, what is the value of y?

5. When $x = {}^-3$, what is the value of y?

6. For what value of x is $y = {}^+1$?

7. For what value of x is $y = {}^-3$?

8. For what value of x is $y = 0$?

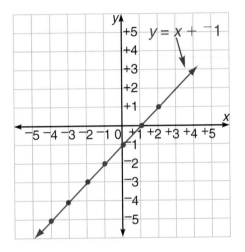

Make a function table using integer values from $^-2$ to $^+2$ for x and graph each function on a coordinate plane. Then use the graph to find the value of y when $x = {}^+3$.

9. $y = x + 3$

10. $y = x + {}^-2$

11. $y = x + {}^-3$

12. $y = {}^-x$

Problem Solving

Function tables and coordinate graphs are used in problem solving.

Given a constant wind speed of 7 miles per hour, a windchill table shows that the windchill temperature (y) in °F is equal to the actual temperature (x) in °F reduced by 5°F: $y = x + {}^-5$.

13. Use the rule to complete the function table. Then graph on a coordinate plane. Find x when $y = {}^-15$ from the graph.

Actual Temperature x	Windchill Temperature $y = x + {}^-5$	(x, y)
$^-5$	$y = {}^-5 + {}^-5 = {}^-10$	$(^-5, ^-10)$
0	?	?
$^+5$	?	?
$^+10$	?	?

Problem-Solving Strategy:
Write an Equation

There are 19 boys in Mr. Robinson's music class. This is 5 less than twice the number of girls. How many girls are in Mr. Robinson's music class?

Read ▶ **Visualize yourself in the problem above as you reread it. List the facts and the question.**

Facts: number of boys—19
number of boys—5 less than twice
the number of girls

Question: How many girls are in Mr. Robinson's music class?

Plan ▶ First write a word sentence to show the relationship between the number of boys and the number of girls. Then *write an equation* equivalent to it. Choose a letter to represent the variable.

Let *n* represent the number of girls.

number of boys	is	5 less than twice the number of girls
19	=	$2n - 5$

Then solve the equation by using inverse operations and properties of equality.

Solve ▶ Solve for *n*: $19 = 2n - 5$

$2n - 5 = 19$
$2n - 5 + 5 = 19 + 5$ ◀— Add 5 to both sides.
$2n = 24$
$\dfrac{2n}{2} = \dfrac{24}{2}$ ◀— Divide both sides by 2.
$n = 12$

There are 12 girls in Mr. Robinson's music class.

Check ▶ Substitute 12 for *n*.

$2 \times 12 - 5 = 24 - 5 = 19$

The answer checks.

Write an equation to solve each problem.

1. Tresse practiced 30 min longer than Lyle. Together they practiced 1 h 50 min. How long did each one practice?

Read Visualize yourself in the problem above as you reread it. List the facts and the question.

   Facts: Tresse practiced 30 min longer than Lyle.
   Total practice time—1 h 50 min

   Question: How long did each one practice?

Plan First *write an equation*. Choose a letter to represent the variable.
   Let *t* represent the time Lyle practiced and *t* + 30 represent the time
   Tresse practiced. $t + t + 30 = 110$ ← | 1 h 50 min |

Solve ········· **Check**

2. There are 35 students in chorus. Nine students sing alto, 8 sing tenor, 4 sing bass, and the rest sing soprano. How many sing soprano?

3. Ms. Murphy teaches 18 students music. Three more than half of them take piano lessons. How many piano students does Ms. Murphy teach?

4. There are 18 fifth graders in the band. This is 8 more than one fourth of the students in the band. How many students are in the band?

5. Helene has taken flute lessons $1\frac{1}{2}$ years longer than Doug. Lynn has taken flute lessons 1 year less than Doug. If Lynn has taken flute lessons for 2 years, for how long has Helene taken flute lessons?

6. Write an equation. Then write a problem that you can solve using it. Share your work with a classmate.

Problem-Solving Applications: Mixed Review

Solve each problem and explain the method you used.

1. Math-o-Matic is a mathematics video game. Players try to solve equations and puzzles. The Math-o-Matic screen shows two expressions: $n(4 + 4)$, when $n = 5$, and $150 ÷ (n + 1)$, when $n = 2$. Which expression has the greater value? Explain your answer.

2. The Math-o-Matic screen shows this sentence: $5 + n × 3$ __?__ $5 × n + 3$, when $n = 4$. Should the player input $<$, $=$, or $>$ to make a true sentence? Explain.

3. Math-o-Matic asks players to find the missing operation symbol to make the expression $80 ÷ (10$ __?__ $n)$, when $n = 2$, equal 10. Which key should the player hit?

4. The Math-o-Matic function machine printed this input and output material. Find its rule.

m	12	10	6	3
n	6	5	3	1.5

5. What is the value of b in this Math-o-Matic equation: $17 × b = 50 + 1$?

6. The variables c and d have the same value in all these equations. Find the values of c and d.
   $c + d = 21$ $c - d = 1$ $c × d = 110$

7. Rolland's final Math-o-Matic score is twice Ben's final score, which is 2750. What is Rolland's score?

8. Melanie's score is one third of Loni's score, which is 3327. What is Melanie's score?

9. Tina computed these expressions to equal $\frac{1}{2}$. Which ones are correct?

   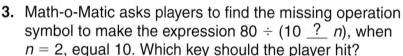

   25% of 8 $3\frac{1}{8} - n$, when $n = \frac{5}{8}$

   $n ÷ 3$, when $n = 1.50$ $\frac{5}{n} × \frac{n}{10}$, when $n = 7$

10. Math-o-Matic shows this series of equations.
    $5e = 7.5 \longrightarrow e + f = 2 \longrightarrow f - g = 0.2$
    Solve the equation to find the value of g.

Choose a strategy from the list or use another strategy you know to solve each problem. You may combine strategies.

11. The value of x in this magic square is $\frac{3}{4}$ of 12. What is its value?

18	s	t
q	p	r
24	x	12

12. The sum of each horizontal, vertical, and diagonal row in the magic square is the same. What is the sum of each row?

13. Write and solve equations to find the value of p, q, r, s, and t in the magic square.

14. The game machine prints a 2-digit number. The sum of the digits is 15 and the difference between them is 1. What are the possible numbers?

15. Ashlee figures out that 35% of the 60 questions in the Math-o-Matic game involve solving equations. How many of them do not involve solving equations?

16. Adam plays 2 rounds of Math-o-Matic. His first score is 24 less than his second score. His total for both rounds is 264. What is his mean score?

17. The length, width, and height of a rectangular prism are whole numbers and each is 1 in. longer than the other. If the volume is 120 in.^{3} and the length is the longest edge, what is the length?

18. Glen plays 5 rounds of Math-o-Matic. He answers $\frac{3}{4}$ of the questions correctly in each round. He gets 8 points for each correct answer and finishes with a total of 600 points. How many questions does he miss?

19. Pattie moved the entire figure formed by joining the coordinates (5, 3), (9, 3), (9, 6) left 3 and down 2. Name its new coordinates and find its area.

20. The perimeter of an isosceles triangle is 18 in. The congruent sides are odd numbers between 4 and 10. What are the lengths of the three sides?

Evaluate each expression. *(See pp. 440–441.)*

1. $a - 6\frac{1}{4}$, when $a = 10$

2. $13\frac{1}{8} + c$, when $c = 15\frac{1}{2}$

3. $12m$, when $m = \frac{1}{6}$

4. $y \div 12$, when $y = 3\frac{1}{2}$

Solve each equation. *(See pp. 442–453.)*

5. $x + 256 = 715$

6. $75b = 262.5$

7. $\frac{1}{3}s = 18.6$

8. $\frac{2}{3} + p = \frac{2}{3}$

9. $\frac{2}{3}d = \frac{2}{3}$

10. $\frac{2}{3} \cdot \frac{3}{4} = \frac{3}{4} \cdot c$

Write the opposite.

11. $^-7$ 12. $^+5$ 13. 0

Compare. Write $<$ or $>$.

14. $^-2 \underline{\ ?\ } ^+2$ 15. $0 \underline{\ ?\ } ^-2$

Complete each function table. *(See pp. 454–463, 466–467.)*

$n = m + 4$

16.

m	2	3	4	5	6
n	?	?	?	?	?

$c = \dfrac{b}{3}$

17.

b	9	12	15	18	21
c	?	?	?	?	?

Compute.

18. $^+5 + {}^+11$

19. $^-12 + {}^+4$

20. $^-3 + {}^-5$

21. $^-6 - {}^+4$

22. $^-2 - {}^-7$

23. $^+9 - {}^+10$

24. $^-1 \times {}^-18$

25. $^+6(0)$

26. $^+4 \cdot {}^-12$

27. $^-63 \div {}^+7$

28. $^-81 \div {}^+9$

29. $^+48 \div {}^+3$

Use the graph on the right. *(See pp. 464–465, 468–469.)*

30. Name the point for:

    a. $(^-4, {}^-4)$ b. $(0, 0)$ c. $(^+3, {}^+3)$

31. When $x = {}^-1$, what is the value of y?

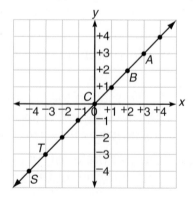

Problem Solving

32. There are 46 people on the bus. Five more than half of them will transfer to other buses. How many will transfer?

(See Still More Practice, p. 488.)

Rational Numbers

Stock A-B-C fell $8\frac{1}{2}$ points one day and gained $12\frac{1}{4}$ points the next day.

You can write these numbers as positive and negative numbers.

fell $8\frac{1}{2}$ points $\longrightarrow$ $^-8\frac{1}{2}$

gained $12\frac{1}{4}$ points $\longrightarrow$ $^+12\frac{1}{4}$

$^-8\frac{1}{2}$ and $^+12\frac{1}{4}$ are rational numbers.

The diagram above shows that whole numbers, integers, and fractions are rational numbers. Some decimals are also rational numbers.

Rational Numbers

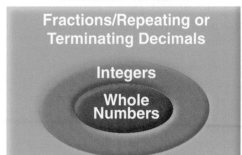

Like integers, every rational number has an opposite and all rational numbers can be shown on a number line.

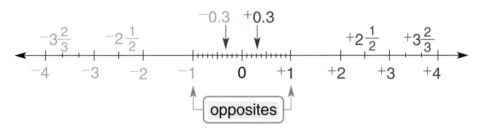

Write a rational number for each expression.

1. a deposit of $20.50

2. 2.5 km underwater

3. 3 floors up

4. a loss of $5\frac{1}{2}$ pounds

5. 6.2 m above sea level

6. $8.50 profit

Write the opposite of each rational number.

7. $^+1.1$

8. $^-\frac{5}{3}$

9. $^-\frac{1}{9}$

10. 0

11. $^+1\frac{1}{7}$

12. $^-5\frac{2}{5}$

Draw a number line and locate each rational number.

13. $^-0.5$

14. $^+\frac{1}{3}$

15. $^+1\frac{1}{8}$

16. $^-2$

17. $^-2\frac{1}{4}$

18. $^-4\frac{2}{5}$

Evaluate each expression.

1. $19 + x$, when $x = 32$ **2.** $5c$, when $c = 6$ **3.** $50 \div q$, when $q = \frac{1}{2}$

Solve each equation.

4. $5 + x = 18$ **5.** $\frac{1}{4}m = 6$ **6.** $\frac{4}{7} + \frac{2}{3} = \frac{2}{3} + b$

Write the rule for the function table.

7.

a	b
20	2
30	3
40	4
50	5

Find the values of y and write the ordered pairs.

8.

x	y = x + 3	y	(x, y)
+1	?	?	?
0	?	?	?
−1	?	?	?
−2	?	?	?

Write as an integer.

9. a gain of $3   **10.** 5 floors down

Order from greatest to least.

11. $^+7, ^-7, 0$ **12.** $^+2, ^-6, ^-5$

Compute.

13. $^-5 + {}^-13$ **14.** $^+17 + {}^-4$ **15.** $^+6 - {}^-8$ **16.** $^+21 - {}^+13$

17. $^+7 \times {}^-9$ **18.** $^-8 \times {}^-3$ **19.** $^+84 \div {}^+4$ **20.** $^-54 \div {}^+6$

Problem Solving

Use a strategy you have learned.

21. Li won 14 games. Ed won 9 less than twice the number of games that Li won. How many games did Ed win?

Tell About It

Explain how you solved the problem. Show all your work.

22. What is the value of q in the equation $2 \times 5 + 6 \times p = q$ if $p = \frac{2}{3}$?

Performance Assessment

23. Draw a rectangle that has one vertex in each quadrant of a coordinate plane. Name each vertex and give its coordinates.

24. Name the coordinates of each point where the rectangle crosses the x-axis; the y-axis. Find the perimeter and area of your rectangle.

Still More Practice

CHAPTER 1

Practice 1-1

In the number 9,513,607,482, write the digit in each place. Then give its value.

1a. thousands   **b.** tens   **c.** millions

   d. ten millions   **e.** billions

Write the number in standard form.

2. six billion, twelve million, ninety-eight

3. $9,000,000 + 70,000 + 6000 + 70 + 3$

4. seventy-six and fourteen thousandths

Compare. Write $<$, $=$, or $>$.

5a. 326.49 $\underline{\ ?\ }$ 326.94   **b.** 0.2 $\underline{\ ?\ }$ 0.20

6a. 247,913 $\underline{\ ?\ }$ 247,193   **b.** 7.05 $\underline{\ ?\ }$ 7.5

Round each number to the place of the underlined digit.

7a. 7,2̲80,961   **b.** $967.3̲5   **c.** 6.14̲3

Round each number to the greatest place.

8a. 3,498,276   **b.** 459.604   **c.** 0.89

Write in order from least to greatest.

9. 721,056; 702,156; 720,156; 72,156

Problem Solving

10. Give the value of each 6 in 6326.061.

11. Write a number that can be rounded to 0.76 using the digits 5, 7, 9.

12. A pecan weighs 31.06 g. A walnut weighs 27.631 g. An almond weighs 30.9 g. Which nut weighs the most? the least?

13. Order the following numbers from greatest to least: 739.7, 793.7, 730.9.

14. Give the word name for 36.147.

15. How are the numbers 96.37 and 963.7 alike? different? Which is the greater number?

Practice 1-2

Find the missing number.

1a. $7 + 6 = \square + 7$ **b.** $9 = \square + 9$

2a. $(4 + 5) + 8 = 4 + (\square + 8)$ **b.** $\square - 5 = 0$

Add or subtract.

3a. 34,729   **b.** 48,924   **c.** $180.77
   $+ 29,886$ $+ 9,789$ $+ 99.65$

4a. 6000   **b.** 9103   **c.** $447.03
   $- 2534$ $- 894$ $- 195.80$

5a. 125,704   **b.** 756,183   **c.** $375.89
   306,199   19,975   46.50
   $+ 511,111$ $+ 103,078$ $+ 97.28$

Estimate. Use front-end estimation.

6a. $74.20   **b.** 2841   **c.** $946.21
   $+ 63.81$ $- 1607$ $- 370.88$

7a. $3627 + 9720 + 2156 + 829$
  b. $947.27 + $635.12 + 47.38

Estimate. Use rounding.

8a. $4732 + 649 + 7893$ **b.** $3749 - 2314$

Align. Then add or subtract.

9a. $4307 + 75,857 + 212$ **b.** $8006 - 3179$

Problem Solving

10. Kyle bought a fishing rod for $18.75, a reel for $27.50, lures for $9.25, and bait for $3.88. How much did he spend?

11. A toll machine counted 37,894 cars and 9198 trucks crossing a bridge. How many more cars crossed the bridge?

12. Find the difference of $703.07 and $116.98.

13. The sum is 97,000. One addend is 42,809. What is the other addend?

14. Claire saw this Roman numeral on the court house: MDCCCLXXIX. Write the number in standard form.

REINFORCEMENT

(477)

CHAPTER 2

Practice 2-1

Find the missing factor.

1a. $7 \times \underline{?} = 28$ **b.** $\underline{?} \times 4 = 36$

2a. $8 \times \underline{?} = 56$ **b.** $\underline{?} \times 6 = 48$

Name the property of multiplication used.

3a. $8 \times 1 = 8$ **b.** $2 \times 6 = 6 \times 2$

4a. $5 \times 0 = 0$ **b.** $(3 \times 2) \times 5 = 3 \times (2 \times 5)$

5a. $1 \times 6 = 6$ **b.** $3 \times 9 = 9 \times 3$

Find the products.

6a. 8×4 **b.** 3×9 **c.** 6×5
8×40 3×90 6×50
8×400 3×900 6×500

Use rounding to estimate. Then multiply.

7a. $\begin{array}{r} 10{,}074 \\ \times \quad 6 \\ \hline \end{array}$ **b.** $\begin{array}{r} 9827 \\ \times \quad 31 \\ \hline \end{array}$ **c.** $\begin{array}{r} \$14.07 \\ \times \quad 88 \\ \hline \end{array}$

Multiply.

8a. $\begin{array}{r} 204 \\ \times \quad 93 \\ \hline \end{array}$ **b.** $\begin{array}{r} 375 \\ \times \quad 46 \\ \hline \end{array}$ **c.** $\begin{array}{r} \$50.36 \\ \times \quad 70 \\ \hline \end{array}$

Problem Solving

9. Find the product if the factors are 3807 and 49.

10. Each of the 6 parking levels holds 109 cars. What is the total capacity of the parking garage?

11. Sharon bought 7 paperback books. Each cost $3.95. How much did she spend?

12. About 480 people visit the science museum each day. Estimate how many people visit in a month.

13. A jet travels 525 mi an hour. How far can the jet travel in 13 hours?

14. A factory produces 1360 boxes in an hour. How many boxes does it make in 12 hours?

Practice 2-2

Multiply.

1a. $6 \times 42{,}003$ **b.** 37×7018

2a. 473×3219 **b.** $78 \times \$40.98$

3a. $945 \times \$30.88$ **b.** 500×7873

Use rounding to estimate. Then multiply.

4a. $\begin{array}{r} \$11.82 \\ \times \quad 647 \\ \hline \end{array}$ **b.** $\begin{array}{r} \$34.03 \\ \times \quad 608 \\ \hline \end{array}$ **c.** $\begin{array}{r} \$90.91 \\ \times \quad 356 \\ \hline \end{array}$

5a. $\begin{array}{r} 7583 \\ \times \quad 209 \\ \hline \end{array}$ **b.** $\begin{array}{r} 6108 \\ \times \quad 978 \\ \hline \end{array}$ **c.** $\begin{array}{r} 3315 \\ \times \quad 462 \\ \hline \end{array}$

6a. $\begin{array}{r} 8848 \\ \times \quad 729 \\ \hline \end{array}$ **b.** $\begin{array}{r} 2056 \\ \times \quad 943 \\ \hline \end{array}$ **c.** $\begin{array}{r} 7902 \\ \times \quad 574 \\ \hline \end{array}$

Find the product.

7a. $\begin{array}{r} 349 \\ \times \quad 800 \\ \hline \end{array}$ **b.** $\begin{array}{r} 3946 \\ \times \quad 700 \\ \hline \end{array}$ **c.** $\begin{array}{r} \$34.77 \\ \times \quad 300 \\ \hline \end{array}$

Find the product.

8a. $n \times 376$ when $n = 129$

b. $917 \times n$ when $n = 705$

Problem Solving

9. At a sale, Leslie sold 2000 stickers for $0.25 each. How much money did she collect?

10. A ticket agent sold 458 tickets at $16.75 each. How much money did she collect?

11. The factors are 3905 and 748. Find the product.

12. Marty's heart beats 72 times in one minute. At this rate, how many times will Marty's heart beat in an hour?

13. What is the total cost of 394 hats that cost $7.49 each?

14. Write a two-digit number and a four-digit number that have a product of 810,000.

CHAPTER 3

Practice 3-1

Write four related facts using the given numbers.

1a. 7, 9, 63　　**b.** 4, 9, 36　　**c.** 3, 8, 24

Find the quotients.

2a.　56 ÷ 7　　　**b.**　72 ÷ 8
　　560 ÷ 7　　　　　720 ÷ 80
　　5600 ÷ 7　　　　7200 ÷ 800
　56,000 ÷ 7　　　72,000 ÷ 8000

Estimate the quotient by using compatible numbers.

3a. 2435 ÷ 6　　**b.** 8251 ÷ 9　　**c.** 5516 ÷ 7

4a. 8230 ÷ 19　　**b.** 4986 ÷ 23　　**c.** 8937 ÷ 34

5a. 57,178 ÷ 29　　　　**b.** 78,359 ÷ 42

Divide and check.

6a. $7\overline{)4963}$　　**b.** $6\overline{)7958}$　　**c.** $8\overline{)95,104}$

7a. $3\overline{)217,916}$　**b.** $5\overline{)372,135}$　**c.** $4\overline{)257,689}$

8a. $6\overline{)\$10.20}$　**b.** $9\overline{)\$79.38}$　**c.** $3\overline{)\$156.09}$

Problem Solving

9. Ron has saved 1425 pennies. If he divides them equally into 5 piles, how many pennies will go into each pile?

10. A store made $9876 in 3 weeks. Find the average amount of money the store made each week.

11. One hundred nineteen books are packed in 7 boxes. If the same number of books are packed in each box, how many books are in each box?

12. A gift costs $38.00. If 5 friends share the cost equally, how much will each person pay?

13. How many nickels are in $17.25?

Practice 3-2

Divide and check.

1a. $40\overline{)160}$　　**b.** $50\overline{)2500}$　　**c.** $30\overline{)90,000}$

2a. $17\overline{)399}$　　**b.** $36\overline{)780}$　　**c.** $25\overline{)906}$

3a. $51\overline{)3488}$　　**b.** $82\overline{)9486}$　　**c.** $46\overline{)7700}$

4a. $62\overline{)\$45.88}$　　　　**b.** $13\overline{)\$44.33}$

5a. $78\overline{)69,408}$　　　　**b.** $46\overline{)\$175.72}$

6a. $31\overline{)624,516}$　　　　**b.** $16\overline{)963,008}$

Write whether each number is divisible by 2, 3, 4, 5, 6, 9, and/or 10.

7a. 1800　　　**b.** 32,508　　　**c.** 602,535

Compute. Use the order of operations.

8a. 52 + 6 × 7 ÷ 3　**b.** 12 − 8 ÷ 4 + (7 − 3) × 5

9a. 8 × 3 − 21 ÷ 7　**b.** (3 × 9) − 8 + (48 ÷ 6)

Problem Solving

10. Ms. Cooper has 182 markers. If she has 14 students in her art club, what is the greatest number of markers each student can have?

11. Fifty-two ticket agents sold 16,640 tickets. If each agent sold the same number of tickets, how many tickets did each sell?

12. Elena has 1372 stamps. She has 96 pages in her stamp album. How many stamps can go on each page? How many stamps will be left over?

13. Jed consumed 2680 calories yesterday. If he ate an equal number of calories in 3 meals, estimate the number of calories per meal.

14. Estimate to compare the quotient of 9158 divided by 38 with the quotient of 10,148 divided by 43.

15. How many quarters are in $70.75?

Practice 4-1

Write whether each is a prime or composite number.

1a. 59 **b.** 121 **c.** 309

Find the missing term.

2a. $\dfrac{2}{5} = \dfrac{n}{10}$ **b.** $\dfrac{6}{7} = \dfrac{30}{n}$

3a. $\dfrac{10}{13} = \dfrac{30}{?} = \dfrac{?}{78}$ **b.** $\dfrac{3}{4} = \dfrac{?}{24} = \dfrac{54}{?}$

Find the greatest common factor (GCF) for each set of numbers.

4a. 6 and 12 **b.** 8, 12, and 32

Write each fraction in lowest terms.

5a. $\dfrac{15}{27}$ **b.** $\dfrac{24}{36}$ **c.** $\dfrac{35}{49}$

6a. $\dfrac{18}{48}$ **b.** $\dfrac{20}{28}$ **c.** $\dfrac{49}{63}$

Find all the factors of:

7a. 40 **b.** 308 **c.** 246

Find the least common denominator (LCD) of each set of fractions.

8a. $\dfrac{3}{5}, \dfrac{2}{3}$ **b.** $\dfrac{1}{6}, \dfrac{3}{4}$, and $\dfrac{5}{8}$

Problem Solving

9. Use a factor tree to find the prime factorization of 28.

10. Mario has seen 5 of the 8 films at the multiplex. What fractional part of the films has he not yet seen?

11. Liz painted $\dfrac{3}{12}$ of her design blue and $\dfrac{2}{8}$ of it red. Did she paint the same amount in each color? Explain your answer.

12. Write $\dfrac{4}{5}$ as an equivalent fraction with a denominator of 20.

13. Seven tenths is equivalent to how many fortieths?

14. Which fraction is closer to $\dfrac{1}{2}$: $\dfrac{5}{6}$, $\dfrac{6}{13}$, or $\dfrac{3}{9}$?

15. What number is a common factor of every set of numbers? Why?

Practice 4-2

Round to the nearest whole number.

1a. $3\dfrac{7}{8}$ **b.** $4\dfrac{1}{5}$ **c.** $9\dfrac{3}{7}$

Write each as a whole number or mixed number in simplest form.

2a. $\dfrac{13}{3}$ **b.** $\dfrac{35}{8}$ **c.** $\dfrac{49}{7}$

3a. $\dfrac{80}{11}$ **b.** $\dfrac{29}{2}$ **c.** $\dfrac{63}{8}$

Compare. Write $<$, $=$, or $>$.

4a. $\dfrac{5}{8} \ \underline{?} \ \dfrac{1}{8}$ **b.** $3\dfrac{2}{5} \ \underline{?} \ 3\dfrac{4}{5}$

5a. $\dfrac{3}{5} \ \underline{?} \ \dfrac{3}{7}$ **b.** $2\dfrac{1}{2} \ \underline{?} \ 2\dfrac{3}{6}$

Order from least to greatest.

6a. $\dfrac{1}{2}, \dfrac{3}{12}, \dfrac{1}{3}$ **b.** $\dfrac{2}{3}, \dfrac{7}{8}, \dfrac{1}{6}$

Problem Solving

7. Peter cut a loaf of bread into 6 equal parts. He ate 2 of these parts. Write a fraction for the parts he did not eat.

8. Thad has read $\dfrac{5}{8}$ of the book. Mia has read $\dfrac{3}{4}$ of the same book. Who has read less?

9. Jenna has sanded $3\dfrac{1}{3}$ boards. Hal has sanded $3\dfrac{1}{2}$ boards. Who has done more sanding?

10. Rico picked 16 lb of peaches and shared them equally with 6 friends. Write a mixed number to show how many pounds of peaches each person received.

11. A film lasted $1\dfrac{7}{8}$ hours. About how many hours long was the film?

12. How many half-dollar coins are in three and a half dollars?

CHAPTER 5

Practice 5-1

Use number lines to model each sum or difference. Then write an addition or subtraction sentence.

1a. $\frac{7}{15} + \frac{8}{15}$ **b.** $\frac{7}{8} + \frac{5}{8}$ **c.** $\frac{8}{9} + \frac{5}{9}$

2a. $\frac{5}{8} - \frac{3}{8}$ **b.** $\frac{11}{6} - \frac{5}{6}$ **c.** $\frac{19}{10} - \frac{7}{10}$

Add or subtract. Write each answer in simplest form.

3a. $\frac{1}{4} + \frac{1}{3}$ **b.** $\frac{3}{5} + \frac{3}{10}$ **c.** $\frac{1}{6} + \frac{1}{2}$

4a. $5\frac{1}{2} + 3\frac{1}{4}$ **b.** $2\frac{1}{6} + 3\frac{1}{2}$

5a. $\frac{1}{2} + \frac{1}{4} + \frac{1}{3}$ **b.** $3 + \frac{1}{5} + 1\frac{7}{10}$

6a. $\frac{7}{8} - \frac{3}{4}$ **b.** $\frac{7}{10} - \frac{2}{5}$ **c.** $\frac{11}{12} - \frac{3}{4}$

7a. $3\frac{3}{4} - 1\frac{1}{2}$ **b.** $4\frac{6}{7} - 2$

8a. $5\frac{1}{2} - 1\frac{1}{5}$ **b.** $8\frac{7}{9} - 5\frac{1}{3}$

9a. $\frac{7}{8} + \frac{1}{2} + \frac{3}{4}$ **b.** $10\frac{3}{4} - 4\frac{1}{3}$

Problem Solving

10. Steve weighs $67\frac{1}{4}$ lb. Mark weighs $\frac{3}{4}$ lb more. Find Mark's weight.

11. Rachel sang for $1\frac{1}{3}$ h and danced for $\frac{3}{4}$ h. How much longer did she sing?

12. On three hikes, Andrew walked $6\frac{1}{8}$ mi, $7\frac{1}{4}$ mi, and $12\frac{1}{2}$ mi. How far did Andrew hike altogether?

13. The sum of two fractions is $\frac{11}{16}$. One fraction is $\frac{3}{8}$. What is the other?

14. Liza has $\frac{4}{5}$ yd of ribbon. If she cuts off $\frac{3}{10}$ yd, how much ribbon does she have left?

15. Jacob needs 8 pounds of apples. If he has already picked $3\frac{5}{8}$ lb, how many more pounds of apples must he pick?

Practice 5-2

Add. Write each sum in simplest form.

1a. $\frac{9}{12} + \frac{1}{5}$ **b.** $\frac{7}{20} + \frac{3}{8}$ **c.** $\frac{1}{7} + \frac{3}{4}$

2a. $\frac{3}{4} + \frac{5}{6}$ **b.** $\frac{2}{3} + \frac{6}{7}$ **c.** $\frac{4}{9} + \frac{3}{7}$

3a. $1\frac{5}{9} + 1\frac{3}{4}$ **b.** $10\frac{1}{3} + 4\frac{7}{8}$

4a. $6\frac{1}{8} + 8\frac{5}{6}$ **b.** $9\frac{1}{4} + 3\frac{2}{3} + 2\frac{2}{5}$

Subtract. Write each difference in simplest form.

5a. $\frac{4}{5} - \frac{2}{3}$ **b.** $\frac{8}{9} - \frac{3}{5}$ **c.** $\frac{5}{6} - \frac{2}{7}$

6a. $\frac{11}{12} - \frac{5}{8}$ **b.** $\frac{13}{15} - \frac{1}{6}$ **c.** $\frac{4}{7} - \frac{1}{5}$

7a. $3\frac{3}{5} - 1\frac{1}{4}$ **b.** $5\frac{7}{8} - 1\frac{2}{3}$

8a. $10 - 3\frac{2}{3}$ **b.** $9\frac{1}{4} - 5\frac{4}{5}$

9a. $3 - 1\frac{9}{10}$ **b.** $8\frac{2}{3} - 7\frac{9}{10}$

Estimate. Use front-end estimation.

10a. $6\frac{5}{6} + 4\frac{1}{2}$ **b.** $8\frac{1}{6} - 3\frac{7}{8}$

11. $13\frac{4}{5} + 9\frac{1}{6} + 7\frac{9}{10}$

Problem Solving

12. Jeanne is $10\frac{1}{2}$ years old. Her brother Jake is $6\frac{3}{4}$ years old. How much older is Jeanne?

13. Maria rode her bike $2\frac{1}{3}$ mi to the store and then another $1\frac{4}{5}$ mi to the library. How far did she ride in all?

14. Ellen ordered 6 pizzas for a party. Guests ate $4\frac{7}{8}$ pizzas. How much pizza was left over?

15. The theater is showing a double feature. One movie lasts $1\frac{7}{8}$ h. The second movie lasts $2\frac{1}{4}$ h. Estimate the total length of the double feature.

Practice 6-1

Rename each as a fraction.

1a. $3\frac{1}{4}$ **b.** $7\frac{2}{5}$ **c.** $6\frac{9}{10}$

Write the reciprocal of each number.

2a. 5 **b.** $3\frac{1}{2}$ **c.** $2\frac{1}{4}$

Draw a diagram to show each product. Then write a multiplication sentence.

3a. $\frac{1}{2} \times \frac{3}{4}$ **b.** $\frac{1}{3} \times \frac{3}{5}$ **c.** $\frac{2}{5} \times \frac{5}{6}$

Multiply.

4a. $\frac{3}{4} \times \frac{7}{10}$ **b.** $\frac{5}{8} \times \frac{3}{4}$ **c.** $\frac{1}{8} \times \frac{5}{9}$

5a. $4 \times \frac{5}{6}$ **b.** $3 \times \frac{2}{3}$ **c.** $\frac{4}{5} \times 9$

6a. $\frac{1}{3} \times 3$ **b.** $\frac{6}{7} \times \frac{9}{8}$ **c.** $8 \times \frac{3}{5}$

Use fraction strips or circles to model each quotient. Then write a division sentence.

7. $4 \div \frac{1}{5}$ **b.** $3 \div \frac{3}{4}$ **c.** $\frac{3}{4} \div \frac{1}{8}$

Divide.

8a. $\frac{3}{4} \div 4$ **b.** $\frac{5}{8} \div 10$ **c.** $\frac{3}{4} \div \frac{1}{2}$

9a. $\frac{4}{9} \div \frac{3}{5}$ **b.** $\frac{7}{15} \div \frac{3}{5}$ **c.** $\frac{3}{4} \div \frac{5}{8}$

10a. $6 \div \frac{2}{3}$ **b.** $5 \div \frac{10}{13}$ **c.** $9 \div \frac{3}{7}$

Problem Solving

11. In a class of 28 students, $\frac{1}{7}$ wear glasses. How many students wear glasses?

12. Evan swam $\frac{7}{8}$ mi. He broke up the swim into $\frac{1}{12}$ -mi laps. How many laps did he swim?

13. James grew $\frac{2}{3}$ in. each month for the last five months. How much has he grown?

14. Six friends share $\frac{3}{4}$ lb of chocolates. How much chocolate does each get?

Practice 6-2

Rename each as a fraction.

1a. $1\frac{7}{10}$ **b.** $8\frac{11}{12}$ **c.** $9\frac{3}{7}$

Write the reciprocal of each number.

2a. 2 **b.** $\frac{14}{9}$ **c.** $3\frac{8}{11}$

Multiply.

3a. $\frac{3}{5} \times 5\frac{1}{3}$ **b.** $\frac{8}{9} \times 4\frac{1}{2}$

4a. $7 \times 3\frac{1}{4}$ **b.** $8\frac{2}{3} \times 5$

5a. $5\frac{2}{3} \times 4\frac{1}{9}$ **b.** $2\frac{1}{2} \times 6\frac{5}{6}$

6a. $9 \times 3\frac{4}{5}$ **b.** $6\frac{1}{3} \times 3\frac{1}{6}$

Divide.

7a. $3\frac{1}{3} \div 10$ **b.** $5\frac{2}{5} \div 9$

8a. $2\frac{1}{4} \div 3$ **b.** $5 \div 3\frac{3}{4}$

9a. $4\frac{1}{5} \div 2\frac{1}{3}$ **b.** $5\frac{5}{6} \div 1\frac{2}{3}$

Estimate by rounding. Then compute to compare.

10a. $12\frac{2}{9} \times 3\frac{1}{5}$ **b.** $5\frac{3}{4} \div 2\frac{1}{3}$

Estimate by using compatible numbers.

11a. $23\frac{1}{4} \times \frac{7}{8}$ **b.** $28\frac{1}{5} \div 6\frac{2}{3}$

Problem Solving

12. Eli has $16\frac{1}{2}$ lb of nuts. How many $\frac{11}{12}$ -lb bags can he fill?

13. Katy packed $10\frac{1}{2}$ gal of ice cream into $1\frac{3}{4}$ -gal cartons. How many cartons did she fill?

14. Lisa ran $2\frac{1}{2}$ times farther than Dana. If Dana ran $\frac{7}{8}$ mi, how far did Lisa run?

15. Karen lives 3 miles from school. Her teacher lives $3\frac{3}{4}$ times that distance. About how far from school does the teacher live?

CHAPTER 7.

Practice 7-1

Problem Solving

Use the spinner to find the probability of each event.

1a. *P* (even) **b.** *P* (<10)

2a. *P* (5 or 10) **b.** *P* (8)

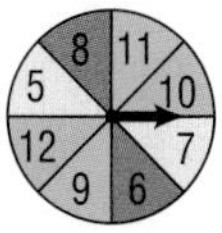
8
11
5
10
12
7
9
6

Use the circle graph to solve problems 3–4.

3. How many art projects are on display?

4. What fraction of the projects is:
a. drawings?
b. clay?
c. paintings

Art Projects

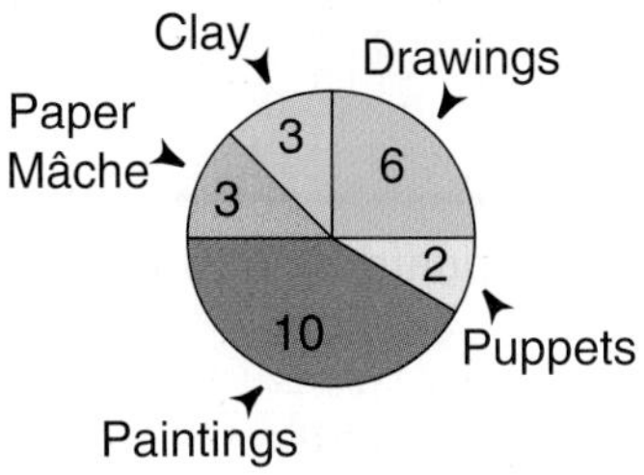
Clay
Drawings
Paper Mâche
3
6
3
2
10
Puppets
Paintings

Draw a tree diagram and list all possible outcomes.

5. Spin a spinner with 3 equal sections marked *A*, *B*, *C*, and pick a marble without looking from a bag containing 2 red marbles and 2 green marbles.

6. Make a tree diagram to find the probability of rolling a 5 on a cube numbered 1–6 *and* tossing a penny to land on tails.

The table gives class sizes at Nora's school. Use it to solve problems 7–8.

Class Size					
Class	5A	5B	5C	5D	5E
Number of Students	32	29	34	32	33

7. Find the range, mean, median, and mode of the class sizes.

8. Suppose each class gets one new student. Which would *not* change: range, mean, median, mode? Explain your answer.

9. Tom scored 90, 95, 92, and 94 on four tests. After the fifth test the mode of his scores was 92. What did he score on the fifth test?

Practice 7-2

Problem Solving

Write a survey question that could have been used to obtain the data. Then complete the cumulative frequency table.

	Trees Seen on Hike			
	Tree	Tally	Frequency	Cumulative Frequency
1.	Elm	𝍸 𝍸 𝍸	?	?
2.	Oak	𝍸 𝍸 //	?	?
3.	Pine	?	13	?
4.	Birch	?	10	?

5. The table shows Andre's pulse rate during a long bike ride. Make a line graph to show Andre's pulse rate.

Andre's Pulse Rate					
Time	2:00	2:15	2:30	2:45	3:00
Pulse	72	108	120	96	88

6. Make a histogram to show the following data:

Height of Seedlings in cm				
45	52	57	70	35
20	60	46	62	40
55	52	65	32	42

7. Diane's test scores for the first grading period are; 81, 82, 76, 95, 88, 83, 85, 84, 83, and 93. Draw a line plot for Diane's test scores. Then find the range and mode.

8. A bag contains 4 red marbles, 2 green marbles, 6 blue marbles, 3 black marbles, and 1 yellow marble. What is the probability of picking a green *or* a black marble? *not* a blue marble?

9. What is the probability of picking 1 blue marble from a bag of 15 green marbles?

Which type of graph would you use to show:

10a. increases or decreases in sales from 1 week to the next?

b. how the sales for each week compare with sales for other weeks?

c. what part of the sales for the month was made during each of the weeks.

CHAPTER 8

Practice 8-1

Write the place of the underlined digit. Then write its value.

1a. 4<u>9</u>.6   **b.** 0.34<u>8</u>   **c.** 12.6<u>7</u>2

Write each decimal in expanded form.

2a. 367.04   **b.** 70.163   **c.** 6.45

Estimate by both rounding and front-end estimation. Between what two numbers will the exact sum or difference be?

3a.   0.77   **b.**   3.54   **c.**   0.923
     $+\ 0.586$ 9.078 $-\ 0.68$
                  $+\ 5.166$

Estimate by rounding. Then add or subtract.

4a.   0.473   **b.**   36.3   **c.**   17.004
     $+\ 0.96$ $+\ 43.5$ $+\ 12.059$

5a.   0.75   **b.**   1.6   **c.**   17.439
     $-\ 0.2$ $-\ 0.74$ $-\ 8.8$

6a. 94.637 + 17.08 + 24.3   **b.** 12 − 7.84

Problem Solving

7. Write the decimal that has seven thousandths, nine tenths, and six ones.

8. Marc rode his bike 4.35 km from home to the park. Then he rode along the park and back home again, a distance of 16.9 km. About how far did he ride?

9. What is 74.16 increased by 9.056?

10. Snow accumulation in March was 1.26 in., 3.75 in., and 2.049 in. Find the total snowfall in March.

11. A board is 36.37 cm long. If Richard cuts off 9.5 cm from it, how much of the board is left?

12. Janis spent $7.99 on invitations, $3.79 on balloons, and $4.75 on streamers for a party. How much change did she get back from a $20 bill?

13. Eleni measured two books. One was 22 mm thick. The other was 18.25 mm thick. How much thicker was the first book?

CHAPTER 9

Practice 9-1

Find the missing number.

1a. $n \times 3.7 = 370$ **b.** $1000 \times n = 324$

2a. $42.6 \div n = 4.26$ **b.** $n \div 1000 = 0.007$

Multiply.

3a. 7×0.65 **b.** 2.7×0.8 **c.** 0.16×0.9

4a. 3.2×0.7 **b.** 0.63×0.3 **c.** 7×0.32

5a. 0.6×3.74 **b.** 4.3×6.92 **c.** 0.08×11.5

Divide and check.

6a. $0.374 \div 2$ **b.** $0.3 \div 6$ **c.** $1.6 \div 8$

7a. $0.64 \div 8$ **b.** $5.39 \div 5$ **c.** $1.308 \div 6$

8a. $2.4 \div 2$ **b.** $0.92 \div 4$ **c.** $0.744 \div 6$

Problem Solving

9. Estimate the product of 2.287 and 6.9. Is the actual product greater or less than the estimated product?

10. Is the estimated product of 13.608 and 0.62 greater or less than the exact product?

11. Estimate the quotient of 47.32 and 6 using compatible numbers.

12. The school year has 180 days. If 0.05 of them are missed due to bad weather, how many days are missed?

13. Burritos are $2.79 each. How much do 100 burritos cost?

14. Evan spent $74.33 for 3 video games. Estimate the cost of each game.

15. Liam picked 64.3 pounds of fruit. Three tenths of the fruit were pears. How many pounds of pears did Liam pick?

CHAPTER 10

Practice 10-1

Classify each angle. Name its vertex and sides.

1a.

b.

2a.

b.

Are the lines perpendicular? Write *Yes* or *No*. Use a protractor to check your answers.

3a.

b.

c.

Name each polygon.

4a.

b.

Classify each quadrilateral.

5a.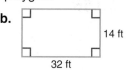

b.

6a.

b.

Problem Solving

7. Draw an isosceles triangle that has a right angle.

8. How would you classify a triangle whose sides measures 8 m, 8 m, and 8 m?

9. A quadrilateral has three angles that measure 30°, 112°, and 148°. Find the measure of the fourth angle.

10. A triangle has an obtuse angle and two sides that are congruent. Is each of the congruent sides longer or shorter than the third side?

11. Explain why triangle *MNO* and triangle *RLP* are *not* similar.

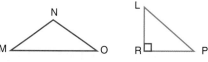

12. Draw two congruent rectangles. How do you know they are congruent?

13. Use a compass to construct a circle *Y*. Draw diameter $\overline{AB}$ and central angle *CYX*.

Practice 10-2

Find the perimeter of each polygon.

1a.

b.

Find the circumference of each circle.

2a.

b.

Is the dotted line a line of symmetry?

3a.

b.

4a.

b.

Write *reflection, rotation,* or *translation* to identify the transformation.

5a.

b.

6a.

b.

Problem Solving

7. Name a regular polygon that cannot be used alone in a tessellation.

8. Find the perimeter of a regular hexagon with a side of 9 m.

9. Sue is knitting a baby blanket that is a rectangle 100 cm by 140 cm. How much ribbon will she need to trim the edge?

10. Find the circumference of a circular clock whose radius is 8 inches.

CHAPTER 11

Practice 11-1

Write the letter of the best estimate.

1. A bed might be 76 _?_ long.
   a. ft   **b.** yd   **c.** in.

2. A brick might weigh 3 _?_ .
   a. lb   **b.** oz   **c.** T

3. A coffee pot might hold 2 _?_ .
   a. gal   **b.** pt   **c.** qt

4. The temperature during a snow
   storm might be _?_ .
   a. 20°F   **b.** 40°F   **c.** 60°F

Compare. Write <, =, or >.

5a. 6 lb _?_ 86 oz   **b.** 250 min _?_ 4 h

6a. 4 gal _?_ 20 qt   **b.** 5 yd _?_ 180 in.

Problem Solving

7. Lois bought a bag of ice cubes to keep the punch cold. Would the bag of ice weigh 10 oz or 10 lb?

9. Rob estimated the distance he had to walk from the school to his house as 1.2 yd. Would this be a reasonable estimate? Why or why not?

8. Moira needs 2 pt of honey for a recipe. She has 3 c of honey. Does she have enough? Explain.

9. Ben knitted a scarf that was 70 in. long. Was it more or less than 6 ft long? How much more or less?

10. The thermometer says 32°C. Should Sally wear a parka or shorts?

11. One moving van holds 1800 lb. Another van holds 1 T. Which holds more?

Practice 11-2

Use the given time to complete each column.

Time Zone		Time		
1.	Pacific	4:10 A.M.	?	?	?
2.	Mountain	?	11:00 P.M.	?	?
3.	Central	?	?	1:15 A.M.	?
4.	Eastern	?	?	?	2:00 P.M.

Add or subtract.

5a. 3 d 17 h
     + 2 d 15 h

b. 4 ft 9 in.
     + 3 ft 7 in.

6a. 5 qt 1 c
     − 3 qt 3 c

b. 7 T 380 lb
     − 3 T 900 lb

7a. 2 wk 6 d
     + 7 wk 5 d

b. 3 y
     − 1 y 7 mo

8a. 9 yd 27 in.
     + 3 yd 30 in.

b. 10 lb 5 oz
     − 5 lb 6 oz

9a. 3 gal 3 qt
     + 2 gal 1 qt

b. 6 y
     − 3 y 280 d

Problem Solving

10. Amy has two scarves. One is 5 ft long and the other is 7 ft long. How many yards are there in the combined length of both scarves?

11. Amos cut 2 yd 2 ft from a board that was 4 yd long. How long is the remaining piece of board?

12. How much more than a gallon is 7 quarts?

13. A punch recipe calls for 1 pt grape juice, 1 qt pineapple juice, 1 gal lemonade, and 3 c orange juice. Find the total quantity of punch this recipe makes.

14. Three railroad cars measure 19 ft 8 in., 21 ft 3 in., and 20 ft 10 in. Find their total length.

15. The carnival began at 11:15 A.M. and ended at 10:45 P.M. How long did it last?

16. Karla bought 1lb of cheese. If the cheese cost $1.75 for 8 oz, how much did Karla pay?

Practice 12-1

Write the letter of the best estimate.

1. A tree might be ? tall.
   a. 4m   **b.** 4 cm   **c.** 4 km

2. A thumbtack might have a mass of ? .
   a. 3 g   **b.** 3 mg   **c.** 3 kg

3. A medicine dropper might hold ? .
   a. 5 mL   **b.** 50 L   **c.** 50 mL

4. A refrigerator might be ? wide.
   a. 1 m   **b.** 1 cm   **c.** 1 dm

5. A bear might have a mass of ? .
   a. 4 kg   **b.** 400 g   **c.** 400 kg

Compare. Write <, =, or >.

6a. 5 dm ? 0.5 m   **b.** 2 kg ? 2100 g

7a. 870 mL ? 8.7 L   **b.** 3.1 km ? 310 cm

8. A snake measures 89.4 cm. Is this more or less than 1 meter?

9. Which holds more: a pitcher whose capacity is 1.5 L or 150 mL?

10. Alena bought two bags of nuts. Each weighs 600 g. Will the nuts fit into a box that holds 1 kg of nuts? Explain.

11. Sean runs a 1500-m race. Does he finish the race if he runs 1km 500 m? Why or why not?

12. A recipe suggests serving 250 g of meat for each person. How many kilograms of meat should Lena buy if she is serving 6 people at dinner?

13. David is using a glass that holds 250 mL to fill a 4.5 L fishbowl. How many full glassses will he need to fill the fishbowl?

Practice 12-2

Estimate the area of each figure.

1a. 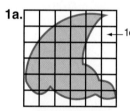   **b.**

1cm²   1yd²

Find the area of each figure.

2a.    **b.**
3.4 m
3.4 m

3a. 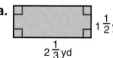 $1\frac{1}{2}$ yd   **b.** 3 m 7.2 m
$2\frac{1}{3}$ yd

4a. 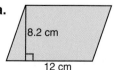 8.2 cm 12 cm   **b.** $3\frac{1}{2}$ in. 9 in.

Find the volume of each figure.

5a.   **b.**

Name each solid figure.

6a.   **b.**   **c.**

7a.   **b.**

8. What is the surface area of a rectangular box 5 in. long, 3 in. wide, and 4 in. high?

9. Find the volume of a box that is 3 dm wide, 5 dm deep, and 6 dm high.

10. How many cubic centimeters will 7.9 grams of water fill?

11. An aquarium measures 3 ft long, 2.5 ft wide, and 3.5 ft high. Is the volume of the aquarium more or less than an aquarium with a volume of 1 yd³? Explain your answer.

CHAPTER 13

Practice 13-1

Write the ratio of the number of:

☆ ☆ ☆ ☆
○ ○ ○
▽ ▽

1a. circles to stars   **b.** triangles to stars

2a. circles to triangles   **b.** triangles to circles

Which are proportions? Write $=$ or $\neq$.

3a. $\dfrac{5}{6}$? $\dfrac{11}{12}$ **b.** $\dfrac{13}{4}$? $\dfrac{39}{12}$

Find the missing term in each proportion.

4a. $\dfrac{4}{5} = \dfrac{n}{20}$ **b.** $\dfrac{7}{8} = \dfrac{49}{n}$ **c.** $\dfrac{5}{n} = \dfrac{25}{40}$

Write as a percent.

5a. $\dfrac{39}{100}$ **b.** $\dfrac{78}{100}$ **c.** $\dfrac{9}{100}$

6a. 0.46   **b.** 0.7   **c.** 0.05

Write as a fraction in simplest form.

7a. 60%   **b.** 85%   **c.** 5%

Write as a decimal.

8a. 35%   **b.** 6%   **c.** 10%

Problem Solving

9. On a map, 1 cm represents 12 km. What does 5 cm represent?

10. A basement playroom is 10.5 m long. Using the scale of 2 cm = 3 m, what is the length of the playroom in a scale drawing?

11. Seventy-five percent of registered voters cast ballots in the election. If there were 4000 registered voters, how many voted?

12. Tapes that usually cost $8 each are on sale for 30% off. What is the price for a tape on sale?

13. Hank paid $3.50 for 2 hamburgers. How much will he pay for 8 hamburgers?

14. What percent of the letters in *CALIFORNIA* are vowels?

CHAPTER 14

Practice 14-1

Label each expression as *expression* or *equation*.

1a. $13 - 7$ **b.** $15d = 75$ **c.** $3a + 7 = 9$

Evaluate each expression.

2a. $1\frac{1}{2} + b$, when $b = 3\frac{3}{5}$

b. $30.5 - n$, when $n = 1.6$

3a. $y \div 4$, when $y = 88$

b. $\frac{1}{2}\, x$, when $x = 24$

Solve each equation.

4a. $h + 3.6 = 10$ **b.** $150 = 50d$

5a. $\frac{3}{5}\, k = \frac{3}{5}$ **b.** $18 = a + 8\frac{1}{2}$

6a. $\frac{1}{7} \cdot \frac{1}{3} = \frac{1}{3} \cdot m$ **b.** $\frac{5}{6} + c = \frac{5}{6}$

Write as an integer.

7a. a deposit of $20   **b.** 3 miles underwater

8a. a loss of 16 pounds   **b.** 4°C above zero

Complete the function table.

9.

y	0	1	3	5	7
$7y$	?	?	?	?	?

Use the graph.

10. Name the point for:

a. $(^+2, ^-3)$

b. $(^+1, ^-2)$

c. $(^-1, 0)$

d. $(^-3, ^+2)$

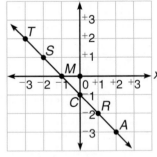

11. When $x = 0$, what is the value of y?

Compute.

12a. $^+3 + ^-12$ **b.** $^-6 + ^-7$

13a. $^-13 - ^+3$ **b.** $^+9 - ^+11$

14a. $^-2 \times ^-13$ **b.** $^+3 \times ^-7$

15a. $^+36 \div ^+4$ **b.** $^+27 \div ^-3$

Brain Builders

SET 1

1. $31 + 73 + 69$
2. $75 - 27 + 40 - 75$
3. $\frac{1}{4}$ of 1 gal = __?__ qt
4. $48.95 - $22.70
5. $3002 - 1369$
6. From $3 take $.08.
7. How much less than $20 is $17.95?

Compare. Use $<$, $=$, or $>$.

8. 3 million 6 __?__ 1 billion 2
9. $60,000 + 7000$ __?__ $60,000 + 900$
10. 3 and 4 hundredths __?__ 3 and 40 thousandths

11. John spent $.79 and had $.15 left. How much did he have to begin with?
12. A town's population increased by 275. This brought the population to 12,240. What was the population before the increase?
13. How many times greater is the digit in the tens place than the same digit in the tenths place?
14. What is the total number of days in September, October, and November?
15. A four-digit number is odd. It is divisible by 5. The first digit is 4 less than the last digit. The second digit is 4 times the first digit. The third digit is zero. What is the number?

SET 2

1a. $1428 \div 7$ b. 8×292
2a. XCVII + LIII   b. 90 is __?__ more than 26.
3. From $9 take $0.15.
4. 78 increased by 46 is __?__ .

Complete the pattern.

5. 3.01, 3.0, 2.99, __?__ , __?__
6. $4 \times (6 \times 2) =$ __?__
7. $9 \times (3 \times 4) =$ __?__
8. $\frac{1}{10}$ is to 0.1 as $\frac{1}{1000}$ is to __?__ .
9. CXL is to 140 as MDI is to __?__ .

10. How much greater than 6 hundredths is 6 tenths?
11. At $0.39 a pt, what is the cost of 24 qt of milk?
12. Express in increasing order: 1.5, 0.3, $\frac{4}{10}$, 5 tenths.
13. What numbers have a product of 54 and a difference of 3?
14. About how much is the cost of 185 headbands at $2.79 each?
15. Tom spent $.75 for a ball and $1.75 for a card. What was his change from $3?

SET 3

1a. 306×24 b. 7.08×35
2. How much greater is 30×8000 than 3×800?
3. $9.03 + $0.85 + $0.04
4. $5 + $2.35 + $0.08
5. $83.16 \div 27$
6. $8\overline{)2416}$
7. $6000 \times 12 - 100$
8. $2 + 6 \times 3 - 10 \div 5$
9. $12 \div 3 + 4 \times 2$
10. $2000 \times 9 - 100$

11. What numbers have a quotient of 9 and a sum of 70?
12. A school musical was attended by 250 adults and 120 children. If adults paid $1.50 and children paid $.75 for each admission, how much money was taken in?
13. Find the cost of 7 gal of milk at $.74 a quart.
14. A car was driven 575 mi last week. This was 275 mi more than it had been driven the previous week. How many miles was the car driven the previous week?
15. If the multiplicand is 724 and the multiplier is 608, what is the product?

SET 4

Compare. Use <, =, or >.

1a. $\frac{5}{8}$ _?_ $\frac{1}{2}$ **b.** $\frac{9}{10}$ _?_ 1   **c.** 0 _?_ $\frac{2}{11}$

2a. $\frac{3}{8}$ _?_ $\frac{4}{16}$ **b.** $2\frac{1}{5}$ _?_ $2\frac{2}{10}$ **c.** $\frac{31}{8}$ _?_ 4

Complete.

3. 12 is to 2 × 2 × 3 as 30 is to _?_ .

4. $1\frac{1}{8}, 1\frac{3}{8}, 1\frac{5}{8}, 1\frac{7}{8},$ _?_

5. Find: **a.** GCF of 12 and 18   **b.** LCD of $\frac{2}{9}$ and $\frac{2}{3}$

6. Name the composite numbers between 1 and 20.

7. Find the sum of three eighths and one eighth.

8. Rename eight sevenths as a mixed number.

9. Rename seven eighths as sixteenths.

10. $7.08 × 35 − $100

11. If a dozen pens cost $5.76, find the cost of a single pen.

12. Mr. DeMasi's sales for 3 months amounted to $2448. Find his average amount of sales for one month.

13. Jason worked $\frac{4}{5}$ of an hour on his homework. Juan worked $\frac{7}{10}$ of an hour on his. Who worked longer?

14. Six out of 24 fifth graders are on the football team. What part of the students are not football players?

15. How much does Mrs. Lawlor save in buying one 32-oz container of yogurt at $2.29 instead of four 8-oz containers at $.69 each?

SET 5

1. Find the fourth term: 16,000, 4000, 1000, _?_

2. $\frac{3}{10} + \frac{9}{10}$ **3.** 6000 − 38

4. $0.62 × 86   **5.** 2350 ÷ 47

6. Find the tenth fraction. $\frac{2}{3}, \frac{4}{6}, \frac{6}{9}, \ldots$

Find the missing digits.

7.
```
  5 6 □ 7
+   7 9 □
  6 □ 9 8
```

8.
```
  $5 □ . 7 □
 −    4 . 2 6
  $□ 2 . □ 7
```

9. $2\frac{5}{6} + 4\frac{4}{6}$ **10.** $6\frac{1}{3} + 4\frac{3}{4}$

11. Larry had $0.95. He had more quarters than dimes. How many dimes did he have?

12. How many even three-digit numbers can Bea make using the digits 3, 4, and 5 without repeating any digit?

13. The temperature at 6:00 a.m. was 28°F. It rose 2° every hour until 3:00 P.M. What was the temperature at 3:00 P.M.?

14. Alan, Bill, and Chad have papers of three different weights: 1.2 g, 0.9 g, 1.05 g. Alan's weighs less than Bill's and Chad's weighs the most. Find the weight of each boy's paper.

15. How many different ways can 2 red, 2 blue, and 2 green beads be arranged on a string so no two beads of the same color are side by side?

SET 6

Compare. Use <, =, or >.

1. $\frac{2}{3} × \frac{1}{4}$ _?_ $\frac{3}{4} × \frac{1}{2}$

2. $\frac{1}{6} × \frac{1}{2}$ _?_ $\frac{3}{12} × \frac{1}{6}$

Solve for n.

3. $\frac{3}{4}$ of 48 = n **4.** $9\frac{3}{7} = \frac{n}{7}$

5. $3\frac{3}{5} × 1\frac{1}{9} = n$ **6.** $\frac{1}{5} ÷ \frac{1}{3} = n$

7. $3\frac{1}{2} ÷ \frac{1}{6} = n$

8. From $\frac{2}{5} + \frac{1}{4}$ take $\frac{3}{20}$.

9. 1000 cents = _?_ dollars

10. Rename the number 8 as twelfths.

11. Nine students have a brother; seven have a sister; twelve have neither a brother nor a sister. If there are 25 in the class, how many students have both a brother and a sister?

12. A car travels at 55 mph. About how far will it go in $3\frac{3}{4}$ hours?

13. Kim used $\frac{1}{2}$ c of flour. She gave 2 c of flour to Fay and then had $3\frac{3}{4}$ c left. How many cups of flour did Kim start with?

14. Joan had $60. Each day, starting Monday, she spent $\frac{1}{2}$ of what she had the day before. How much money did she have left on the fourth day?

15. One third of what number equals eight?

SET 7

1a. 1003 − 999 **b.** Divide 27,234 by 9.

2a. 479 + 963 **b.** $5.80 × 80

3a. $\frac{1}{5} + \frac{1}{20} + \frac{1}{10}$ **b.** $5\frac{5}{6} - 2\frac{3}{4}$

4a. $8\frac{5}{6} + 10\frac{1}{2}$ **b.** $\frac{8}{12} = \frac{n}{3}$

5a. 643 + 872 + 948 **b.** 204 × 700

6. How much less than $6\frac{3}{4}$ is $4\frac{2}{3}$?

7. How many eighths are there in $\frac{3}{4}$?

8. Divide 1296 by 18.

9. From $9 take $6.35.

10. MCMLXV is to 1965 as MMI is to ___?___ .

11. Justin missed $\frac{1}{8}$ of his spelling words. If 24 was the perfect score, how many did he spell correctly?

12. Sue tosses a coin and spins a dial marked 1, 2, 3, and 4. What is the probability of getting heads and an even number? (*Hint:* Use a tree diagram.)

13. In each of 5 rounds Shalika scored 16, 20, 13, 24, and 28 points. Find the range, median, and mode of Shalika's scores.

14. Find the cost of 5 meters of wire at $0.42 a meter.

15. At $1.40 a dozen, how many oranges can be bought for $0.70?

SET 8

1a. $8 ÷ 2\frac{2}{5}$ **b.** $6\frac{1}{4} × 240$

2. 288 eggs = ___?___ dozen

Compare. Use <, =, or >.

3. 9.5 − 4.062 ___?___ 7.85 − 2.104

4. 6.004 + 2.003 + 0.864 ___?___ 7.062 + 1.809

5. 4.398 + 6.07 ___?___ 16.09 − 3.42

6. 0.6 + 0.132 + 0.25

7. 14.4 + 21.89 **8.** 0.731 − 0.209

9. 3.6 × 0.45 **10.** 2.864 ÷ 4

11. Dennis bought 7.5 m of felt to make a banner. If he had 4.6 m left, how much did he use?

12. What decimal is one hundredth more than 0.4?

13. Ray rode his bicycle 9.6 mi Monday, 4.8 mi Tuesday, and 6.6 mi Wednesday. What is the average distance he traveled each day?

14. A bakery's sales for a six-day week are: $525, $720, $625, $475, $588, and $640. It bakes about 35 doz donuts each day. Find its average sales for that week.

15. Miguel jogs 6.3 km each day. He swims 12 laps daily. How many kilometers does he jog in four days?

SET 9

1a. 136 in. = ___?___ ft ___?___ in.

 b. 2 yd 2 ft = ___?___ in.

2a. 7 pt 1 c = ___?___ c

 b. 77 fl oz = ___?___ c ___?___ fl oz

Compare. Use <, =, or >.

3a. 20 lb 6 oz ___?___ 236 oz

 b. 2 T 650 lb ___?___ 5000 lb

4a. 56 d = ___?___ wk

 b. 10 min = ___?___ s

5. 3 lb 12 oz + 1 lb 7 oz

6. 5 yd 2 ft + 3 yd 2 ft

7. 6 h 20 min − 2 h 35 min

8. 12 + 3 × 5 ÷ 5

9. (7 × 8) − 14

10a. 4.9 + 6.5 **b.** 9.2 − 6.4

11. A stained glass ornament in the shape of a regular pentagon has a perimeter of 40 in. What is the length of one side?

12. At $.40 a quart, what is the cost of 3 gallons of syrup?

13. At $2.28 a yard, find the cost of 2 feet of terry cloth fabric.

14. The original temperature was 26°F. The first two hours the temperature dropped 4°F. The next two hours it increased $1\frac{1}{2}$°F. What was the final temperature?

15. A waitress earned $265.80 last week in salary and tips. If her tips amounted to $102.20, what was her salary?

CHALLENGE

SET 10

1. Draw 2 lines that are perpendicular. How many angles did you form?
2. Find the missing angle of $\triangle ABC$:
   a. 45°, 45°, _?_   **b.** 65°, 70°, _?_
3. Given the radius, find the diameter.
   a. 12 cm   **b.** $4\frac{3}{8}$ in.   **c.** 1.07 m
4. How many diagonal lines of symmetry are in:
   a. a regular pentagon? **b.** a regular hexagon?
5. $840 + 30 + 78$
6. $\frac{14}{15} \div \frac{14}{15}$
7. $2\frac{7}{10} \div \frac{18}{25}$
8. From 6 take $\frac{3}{8}$.
9. How much less than $6\frac{3}{4}$ is $4\frac{2}{3}$?

10. Write 2028 in Roman numerals.
11. Find the perimeter of a rectangular rug 2 yd long and 4 ft wide.
12. Tony has 3 pairs of slacks: brown, blue, and black. He also has 4 shirts: white, yellow, pink, and green. How many different outfits can he wear?
13. About how many times greater than the diameter of a circle is the circumference?
14. A jet averages 675 mph. In how many hours will it fly 22,950 miles?
15. Find the circumference of a table with a diameter of 5 ft.

SET 11

Divide by 10, then multiply by 100.
1a. 0.06   **b.** 2.5   **c.** 0.9

Complete.
2a. 3 km = _?_ m   **b.** 180 cm = _?_ dm
3a. 62 m = _?_ cm   **b.** 500 mL = _?_ dL
4a. 2 dg = _?_ mg   **b.** 2000 L = _?_ kL
5a. 4000 g = _?_ kg   **b.** 3 g = _?_ dg
6a. 15 cg = _?_ mg   **b.** 12 cm = _?_ mm
7. A square pyramid is to 5 vertices as a triangular prism is to _?_ .
8. 60% is to $\frac{3}{5}$ as 75% is to _?_ .

Solve for n.
9. $\frac{8}{36} = \frac{n}{9}$ 10. $\frac{9}{10} = \frac{81}{n}$
11. Find the volume of a cereal box that measures 14 in. by 9 in. by 3 in.
12. Seventy-two cakes were sold at a school fair. Each cake costs $3.75. How much was raised?
13. If Jan saves $24.60 a month, how much money will she save in one year?
14. If Ramón walks 1 km in 12.5 min, how many meters does he walk in 1 minute?
15. If the diameter of a circular picture frame is 40 cm, what is the circumference in meters?

SET 12

1. Which is greater: 7.3×2.04 or 7.03×2.4?

Evaluate $a + 3\frac{1}{2}$ when a is:
2a. $6\frac{1}{4}$ **b.** $12\frac{1}{2}$ **c.** $26\frac{1}{3}$

Evaluate $b - 0.06$ when b is:
3a. 3.7   **b.** 11.03   **c.** 20.192

Evaluate $24x$ when x is:
4a. 32   **b.** 16   **c.** 103

Evaluate $\frac{y}{6}$ when y is:
5a. $4\frac{1}{3}$ **b.** $12\frac{1}{2}$ **c.** $16\frac{1}{4}$
6. Solve for z: $3 + 6 + 2 - 7 + z = 12$
7. Solve for a: $(4 \times 4) + (a \times 5) = 26$
8. Solve for g: $\frac{1}{g} \times 0.012 = 0.004$

9. What percent of a dollar is 2 quarters, 3 dimes, 1 nickel, and 4 pennies?
10. Which is greater: 3×10^2 or 3×20?
11. The sum of a number and twice the number is 21. Find the number.
12. On a map, the library is $1\frac{1}{4}$ cm west and $2\frac{1}{2}$ cm north of Ron's house. The scale is 1 cm = 2 km. What is the actual distance from the library to Ron's house? (*Hint:* Use a grid.)
13. Find the area of a triangle whose height is $1\frac{1}{2}$ ft and base is 8 in.
14. On a grid, connect points (1, 1), (5, 1), (1, 4) to form a polygon. Find its area.
15. The base of a triangle is 3 more than its height. Its area is 54 sq units. Find its base and height.

Mental Math

SET 1

1. 9 + 2   6 + 6   7 + 8   4 + 7
   16 − 8   13 − 5   14 − 6   12 − 3

2. 7 + 0   0 + 12   8 + 5   6 + 9
   0 + 7   12 + 0   5 + 8   9 + 6

3. 11 − 11   8 − 0   28 − 28   10 − 0
   17 − 0   18 − 9   16 − 5   13 − 13

4. Estimate by rounding: 18 + 21 + 11   38 + 42
   807 + 48   281 + 398   97 + 9

5. Round to the nearest dollar.
   $7.26 $19.84 $148.80 $4.79

6. What is seven increased by two?

7. Eleven is two greater than what number?

8. If Ellen weighs 82 lb, how much must she gain to weigh 91 lb?

9. What is 14 increased by 7?

10. Estimate by rounding: $9.95 + $7.45.

11. Dan weighs 40 kg and Terry weighs 12 kg less. What is Terry's weight?

12. How many more inches than 2 ft is 30 in.?

13. Nine equals 12 minus what number?

14. Zero added to 9 equals how much?

15. Jon has $0.31, and Ben has $0.49 more than Jon. How much does Ben have?

SET 2

1. 3 + 4 + 7 + 6   9 + 1 + 2 + 6
   8 + 4 + 2 + 4   5 + 5 + 4 + 6

2. Estimate by rounding: 53 − 38   67 − 16   41 − 27
   39 − 11   22 − 9

3. Add 2 to: 99, 79, 12, 22, 42, 82, 102, 39, 59, 62, 92, 109

4. Take 2 from: 91, 71, 61, 21, 11, 111, 51, 41, 101, 31, 81

5. Estimate by rounding: $16.20 + $23.85
   $8.07 + $24.49 $39.75 + $11.66
   $42.18 + $28.06

6. What is five less than twenty-one?

7. How many ten thousands are in 1,352,896?

8. 469,210 = 400,000 + _?_ + 9000 + _?_ + _?_

9. What is the value of 8 in 862,004?

10. If 245 students are enrolled and 15 are absent, how many are present?

11. 16 + 14 + 25 = n. Find n.

12. Write the numeral: twenty thousand, five hundred two

13. What is 31 decreased by 8?

14. What is 33 increased by 8?

15. If Jeff has $0.87, how much does he need to make $1.00?

SET 3

1. Give the value of the underlined digit.
   8<u>2</u>35   <u>6</u>719   35<u>4</u>2   1<u>1</u>31

2. Add 1000 to: 40, 140, 240, 340, 440, 540, 640

3. Compare. Use < or >: 3781 _?_ 3187
   13,482 _?_ 13,284   7532 _?_ 7352

4. Order least to greatest: 87, 81, 89;
   136, 361, 316; 2460, 2640, 2046

5. Read: 0.7   0.68   0.003   0.1   0.259
   0.99   0.06

6. Write the numeral: six thousand, two

7. In the number 60,543, what is the value of 5?

8. What decimal is one tenth more than 7.1?

9. A fish weighs 16.07 lb. Another weighs 16.7 lb. Which weighs more?

10. Complete the pattern.
    0.01, 0.03, 0.05, _?_, _?_, _?_

11. Jen has $12.75 in quarters and $6.15 in nickels. About how much money does she have?

12. Which is less: 456,017 or 465,007?

13. In the number 26,908, the 2 means
    2 × _?_ .

14. Write 3,628,405,012 in expanded form.

15. Write the Roman numeral for 1946.

SET 4

1. Give the value of the underlined digit.
   1.<u>6</u>6, <u>7</u>.394, 35.9<u>8</u>, <u>4</u>0.136, 1<u>2</u>.41

2. Compare. Use <, =, or >: 8.89 <u>?</u> 8.8
   2.3 <u>?</u> 0.3   6.60 <u>?</u> 6.6   2 <u>?</u> 1.8

3. Round to the nearest ten thousand.
   12,365   38,114   75,489   31,777
   57,261   44,119   67,123   25,986

4. Give the standard numeral: XXXV
   CXLIII   DCCVII   MCMXCIII   MDL

5. Add 8 to: 3, 33, 93, 43, 13, 83, 53,
   63, 73, 23

6. What is the value of 4 in 3456?

7. Write the numeral: seven million,
   six hundred thousand, forty-three

8. Write LXXV as a standard numeral.

9. Write the numeral: six and four tenths

10. Which is greater: 3 tenths or 3 hundredths?

11. Write each as a decimal:
    $1\frac{7}{10}, 3\frac{1}{10}, 2\frac{3}{10}$

12. Eighteen is how many less than 2 dozen?

13. What is 49 increased by 3?

14. What is 22 decreased by 3?

15. If 18 cards were left in the box after Cindy
    used 4, how many were there at first?

SET 5

1. Multiply by 6, then add 3: 2, 0, 4, 1,
   3, 6, 5, 7, 8

2. 8 × <u>?</u> = 72   9 × <u>?</u> = 36
   <u>?</u> × 7 = 28   <u>?</u> × 6 = 66
   7 × <u>?</u> = 49   9 × <u>?</u> = 81

3. 3 × 2 × 4   6 × 2 × 2   3 × 0 × 8
   4 × 1 × 7   5 × 2 × 7   2 × 3 × 10

4. Multiply by 40: 3, 5, 9, 6, 4, 8, 0, 7, 1, 2

5. Multiply by 1000: 6, 12, 24, 32, 8, 16, 44,
   58, 63, 15

6. Estimate the product by rounding:
   38 × 24

7. At $0.20 each, find the cost of 6 rulers.

8. One of the factors of 18 is 9. What is
   the other factor?

9. One tape costs $9.95. Estimate the
   cost of 5.

10. Estimate the product by rounding: 425 × 29

11. How many days are in 9 weeks?

12. Estimate the cost of 6 games, if one game
    costs $8.98.

13. There are 60 books on each of 4 shelves.
    How many books are there in all?

14. The Tran family traveled 105 mi each day of
    vacation. If they traveled for 3 days, how
    many miles did they travel?

15. How much greater is 4 × 6 than 3 × 7?

SET 6

1. Round to the nearest hundred: 623, 755,
   288, 143, 892, 324, 509

2. Give the first 10 multiples of: 3, 2, 6, 4, 5,
   7, 9, 8, 1

3. Multiply by 5, then add 4: 80, 90, 40, 70,
   60, 30, 20, 50

4. Take 8 from: 11, 41, 91, 61, 21, 81, 71,
   51, 31, 101

5. Add 4 to: 57, 97, 67, 14, 84, 24, 74, 44,
   37, 77, 54, 17

6. The sum of Tanya's and Paul's ages is 18
   years. If Tanya is six, how old is Paul?

7. Estimate the cost of 6 boxes of cards,
   if one box costs $4.99.

8. At $8 an hour, how much will a worker earn
   in 4 hours?

9. If one factor of 32 is 4, what is the other factor?

10. What is the standard numeral for CXX?

11. What is 27 increased by 6?

12. Write the numeral: three million, four hundred
    fifty thousand, ninety

13. Ann has 7 dimes, 5 nickels, and 13 pennies.
    How much money does Ann have?

14. At 50 mph, how far can a train travel in
    8 hours?

15. Glenn bought 9 pencils at $0.30 each.
    What was his change from $3.00?

MAINTENANCE

SET 7

1. Give 4 related facts.
   2, 7, 14   7, 5, 35   6, 8, 48   4, 9, 36
2. Divide by 2: 4, 40, 400, 4000, 40,000, 400,000
3. $7 \div 1$ $0 \div 84$ $34 \div 34$
   $62 \div 1$ $0 \div 17$ $20 \div 20$
4. $72 \div \underline{?} = 9$ $64 \div 8 = \underline{?}$
   $27 \div \underline{?} = 9$ $42 \div 6 = \underline{?}$
   $25 \div \underline{?} = 5$ $20 \div 2 = \underline{?}$
5. Divide by 4: 8, 4, 24, 40, 36, 12, 32, 28
6. The quotient is 7. The dividend is 56. What is the divisor?
7. If the quotient is 6 and the dividend is 6, what is the divisor?
8. If the cost of 9 folding chairs is $54, what is the cost per chair?
9. If two balls cost $2.80, what is the cost of one ball?
10. When 27 is divided by 8, what is the remainder?
11. If 3 workers each earned $15.20 in one hour, what was their total earnings?
12. At $9 each, how many blankets can be purchased for $108?
13. Use compatible numbers to estimate the quotient: $39,798 \div 8$
14. Which is cheaper: $0.30 each or $3.50 a dozen?
15. At $45 per day, how many days must Adam work to earn $450?

SET 8

1. Divide by 8: 71, 68, 72, 73, 75, 76
2. Which are divisible by 3?
   15, 22, 39, 45, 32, 61, 53, 57, 72, 87, 92
3. Divide by 5: 6, 7, 11, 12, 16, 34, 42, 27
4. $45 \div 15$ $24 \div 12$ $42 \div 14$
   $39 \div 13$ $64 \div 16$ $33 \div 11$
5. Take 6 from: 15, 35, 95, 85, 45, 25, 55, 75, 65
6. How many dozen in 120 eggs?
7. A 2-lb box of nuts costs $18.60. What is the cost per pound?
8. Divide 639 by 3.
9. Compute: $6 \times 2 \div 4 + 7 = \underline{?}$
10. At $1.20 each, how many pairs of socks can be bought for $8.40?
11. There are 24,000 seats in the stadium with 24 seats in each row. How many rows are there?
12. Ted picked 7 baskets of 20 apples each and 5 baskets of 20 peaches each. How much fruit did Ted pick?
13. Frank paid $5.40 for 9 bottles of spring water. What is the cost per bottle?
14. An airplane traveled 30,600 mi in 30 days. How many miles did it travel each day?
15. Jan paid $1.80 for 9 bran muffins. How much does one muffin cost?

SET 9

1. Add 3 to: 99, 29, 33, 53, 69, 83, 103
2. Take 5 from: 12, 32, 72, 92, 82, 62, 22
3. Is the fraction closer to 0 or 1?
   $\frac{1}{3}, \frac{5}{6}, \frac{2}{8}, \frac{4}{10}, \frac{6}{7}, \frac{2}{5}, \frac{1}{4}, \frac{2}{3}$
4. Which fractions are in lowest terms?
   $\frac{1}{2}, \frac{2}{3}, \frac{3}{6}, \frac{5}{10}, \frac{4}{7}, \frac{6}{15}, \frac{3}{5}, \frac{7}{8}$
5. Which have a GCF of 2?
   8 and 10   21 and 24   16 and 30
6. How much is 48 decreased by 6?
7. Which fraction has a different denominator:
   $\frac{3}{7}, \frac{2}{7},$ or $\frac{3}{5}$?
8. What is the numerator in $\frac{5}{8}$?
9. How many fifths are in one whole?
10. What fractional part of an hour is 10 minutes?
11. Express $\frac{30}{54}$ in simplest form.
12. $\frac{3}{4} = \frac{?}{8} = \frac{?}{16} = \frac{24}{?} = \frac{?}{64} = \frac{96}{?}$
13. Sean read for $\frac{2}{3}$h and Sara for $\frac{3}{4}$h. Who read longer?
14. Rename $\frac{31}{6}$ as a mixed number.
15. Which is the greatest: $\frac{1}{4}, \frac{1}{6}, \frac{1}{8}, \frac{1}{10},$ or $\frac{1}{2}$?

SET 10

1. Name prime or composite number.
   2, 5, 8, 15, 17, 36, 41, 29, 16, 10, 9, 11

2. Add 9¢ to: $1.21, $2.61, $0.91, $4.41, $7.00

3. Order from least to greatest.
   $\frac{2}{5}, \frac{4}{5}, \frac{1}{5}, \frac{3}{5}$ $\frac{1}{10}, \frac{1}{4}, \frac{1}{5}, \frac{1}{7}$

4. Name the fractions greater than or equal to 1.
   $\frac{4}{4}, \frac{5}{2}, \frac{1}{2}, \frac{2}{8}, \frac{9}{7}, \frac{5}{5}, \frac{10}{11}, \frac{12}{9}, \frac{2}{3}$

5. Express as a mixed number.
   $\frac{11}{7}, \frac{13}{8}, \frac{21}{2}, \frac{15}{6}, \frac{8}{3}, \frac{25}{4}, \frac{31}{5}, \frac{19}{9}$

6. Which is the smallest: $\frac{1}{4}$, $\frac{1}{2}$, or $\frac{1}{8}$?

7. How much more than $\frac{1}{14}$ is $\frac{2}{7}$?

8. Rename $4\frac{5}{6}$ as a fraction.

9. Express $\frac{30}{48}$ in simplest form.

10. Name the prime numbers between 1 and 20.

11. What fractional part of 1 year is 4 months?

12. Which of these fractions is not in simplest form: $\frac{5}{8}$, $\frac{5}{9}$, $\frac{6}{9}$, or $\frac{8}{11}$?

13. Express $\frac{74}{9}$ as a mixed number.

14. $\frac{4}{5} = \frac{?}{10} = \frac{?}{20} = \frac{32}{?} = \frac{64}{?} = \frac{?}{160}$

15. Find the LCD of $\frac{1}{9}$ and $\frac{1}{12}$.

SET 11

1. Express as a fraction.
   $3\frac{1}{6}, 2\frac{1}{6}, 4\frac{5}{6}, 8\frac{4}{6}, 9\frac{1}{6}, 5\frac{1}{6}, 7\frac{5}{6}, 10\frac{1}{6}$

2. Express as a mixed number.
   $\frac{31}{6}, \frac{19}{6}, \frac{11}{6}, \frac{25}{6}, \frac{13}{6}, \frac{27}{6}, \frac{61}{6}, \frac{17}{6}, \frac{29}{6}$

3. $\frac{2}{6} + \frac{1}{6}$ $\frac{3}{7} + \frac{2}{7}$ $\frac{8}{18} + \frac{5}{18}$ $\frac{3}{8} + \frac{4}{8}$

4. Add $\frac{1}{2}$ to: $\frac{1}{2}, 2, 3\frac{1}{4}, 1\frac{1}{2}, 4, 5\frac{1}{4}$

5. $1\frac{3}{8} + 2\frac{4}{8}$ $3\frac{7}{12} + 4\frac{2}{12}$ $5\frac{6}{11} + 1\frac{3}{11}$

6. What is the sum of $1\frac{3}{8}$ and $\frac{5}{8}$?

7. Joe worked for $3\frac{1}{2}$ h. Sam worked for $4\frac{1}{4}$ h. How much time did they work altogether?

8. Add: $\frac{1}{6} + \frac{1}{3} + \frac{1}{2}$ 9. $9\frac{5}{4} = \frac{?}{4}$

10. Len weighed $78\frac{1}{2}$ lb and then gained $1\frac{1}{2}$ lb. How much does he weigh now?

11. How much larger than $\frac{1}{4}$ of a circle is $\frac{3}{4}$ of the same circle?

12. How much less than 3 is $2\frac{1}{3}$?

13. From $1\frac{1}{5}$ subtract $\frac{1}{10}$.

14. Hikers are $7\frac{1}{2}$ m from camp. After walking $3\frac{1}{4}$ m back, how far do they have to go?

15. From 2 take $\frac{4}{9}$.

SET 12

1. $\frac{5}{9} - \frac{3}{9}$ $\frac{17}{21} - \frac{9}{21}$ $\frac{18}{19} - \frac{10}{19}$ $\frac{13}{15} - \frac{6}{15}$

2. Take $\frac{1}{10}$ from: $\frac{9}{10}, \frac{2}{10}, \frac{6}{10}, \frac{3}{10}, \frac{4}{10}, \frac{7}{10}$

3. $6\frac{4}{10} - 2\frac{2}{10}$ $5\frac{3}{4} - 3\frac{2}{4}$ $4\frac{4}{5} - 1\frac{1}{5}$

4. Express in lowest terms.
   $\frac{7}{14}, \frac{7}{21}, \frac{7}{28}, \frac{7}{63}, \frac{7}{35}, \frac{7}{56}, \frac{7}{49}, \frac{7}{42}$

5. Express as a fraction.
   $2\frac{1}{9}, 3\frac{4}{9}, 5\frac{2}{9}, 8\frac{1}{9}, 9\frac{4}{9}, 7\frac{1}{9}, 4\frac{4}{9}, 6\frac{5}{9}$

6. $7\frac{3}{5} = 6\frac{?}{5}$

7. What is $\frac{1}{10}$ less than $\frac{1}{5}$?

8. How much greater than $\frac{3}{4}$ is 2?

9. If Lee weighed $90\frac{1}{2}$ lb and lost $2\frac{1}{2}$ lb, how much does he weigh?

10. How many yards of cloth are there in two remnants, one of which contains $\frac{5}{8}$ yd and the other $\frac{3}{8}$ yd?

11. Estimate the cost of 8 mugs at $2.89 each.

12. Take $\frac{8}{9}$ from 6.

13. Fay had 4 yd of tape. She used $3\frac{7}{8}$ yd. How many yards does she have left?

14. Ralph studied $1\frac{1}{2}$ h on Monday and $2\frac{1}{2}$ h on Tuesday. How many hours did Ralph study?

15. Add: $\frac{2}{5} + \frac{1}{10} + \frac{3}{5}$

SET 13

1. $\frac{1}{2} \times \frac{3}{4}$ $\frac{2}{3} \times \frac{1}{3}$ $\frac{3}{4} \times \frac{1}{8}$ $\frac{2}{3} \times \frac{4}{5}$

2. $6 \times \frac{1}{2}$ $12 \times \frac{1}{3}$ $\frac{2}{3} \times 30$ $\frac{2}{5} \times 20$

3. Find the GCF: 3 and 9   2 and 6
   7 and 21   8 and 16   3 and 16

4. Express as a fraction.
   $6\frac{1}{8}, 5\frac{3}{8}, 3\frac{5}{8}, 4\frac{3}{8}, 8 = \frac{?}{10}$ $5 = \frac{?}{8}$

5. Round to the nearest whole number.
   $4\frac{1}{3}, 10\frac{6}{11}, 8\frac{6}{7}, 11\frac{1}{5}$

6. How much greater than $\frac{1}{6}$ of 24 is $\frac{1}{6}$ of 36?

7. Express $9\frac{3}{7}$ as a fraction.

8. Jim lives $\frac{3}{4}$ km from the zoo. Tom lives 4 times that distance from the zoo. How far from the zoo does Tom live?

9. How many minutes are in $\frac{1}{3}$ of an hour?

10. Find $\frac{5}{8}$ of 40.

11. At the rate of 40 mph, how far will a car travel in $\frac{3}{4}$ of an hour?

12. Tim needs to study 3 h. He has studied $\frac{2}{3}$ of that time. How much more of that time does he have to study?

13. How many $\frac{3}{4}$- c portions can be made from $3\frac{3}{4}$ c of pudding?

14. Jill worked $\frac{1}{2}$ h. Sue worked $\frac{2}{3}$ h. How long did they both work?

15. Divide 6 lb into $\frac{1}{2}$-lb packages.

SET 14

1. $9 \div \frac{1}{4}$ $3 \div \frac{1}{4}$ $4 \div \frac{1}{2}$ $6 \div \frac{1}{3}$ $2 \div \frac{1}{8}$

2. Give the reciprocal: $6, \frac{1}{7}, \frac{2}{3}, 8, 3\frac{1}{4}$

3. $\frac{2}{5} \div \frac{1}{5}$ $\frac{7}{9} \div \frac{1}{9}$ $\frac{5}{6} \div \frac{1}{6}$ $\frac{3}{8} \div \frac{1}{8}$

4. $\frac{1}{6} \div 6$ $\frac{7}{10} \div 7$ $\frac{1}{3} \div 6$ $\frac{2}{3} \div 2$ $\frac{6}{7} \div 6$

5. $\frac{3}{4} = \frac{?}{8} = \frac{?}{16} = \frac{?}{32} = \frac{?}{64} = \frac{?}{128} = \frac{?}{256}$

6. Is the reciprocal of 8: $\frac{1}{8}$ or 8?

7. Which is greater: $\frac{4}{5} \div \frac{1}{2}$ or $\frac{4}{5} \times \frac{1}{2}$?

8. Dividing a number by $1\frac{1}{4}$ is the same as multiplying it by $\underline{\ ?\ }$.

9. Is $\frac{33}{4}$ greater or less than 8?

10. Divide 8 yd into $\frac{1}{4}$- yd pieces.

11. Three people divided $\frac{1}{2}$ of a pizza. How much did each person receive?

12. How many sixths are there in $\frac{1}{3}$?

13. Express $\frac{46}{9}$ as a mixed numeral.

14. Write XCVIII as a standard numeral.

15. How many minutes are there in $\frac{3}{4}$ hour?

SET 15

1. Add 7 to: 9, 19, 39, 79, 89, 49, 59, 29

2. Multiply by 9 and add 2: 8, 3, 10, 2, 0, 9, 5

3. Express as a mixed number.
   $\frac{37}{6}, \frac{35}{6}, \frac{43}{6}, \frac{49}{6}, \frac{19}{6}, \frac{29}{6}, \frac{25}{6}, \frac{55}{6}, \frac{61}{6}$

4. $2 = 1\frac{?}{8}$ $2 = 1\frac{?}{6}$ $2 = 1\frac{?}{4}$ $3 = 2\frac{?}{9}$

5. $2 - \frac{3}{8}$ $2 - \frac{5}{6}$ $2 - \frac{3}{4}$ $2 - \frac{1}{5}$

6. On three days, Meg worked 8 h, 6 h, and 10 h. What was the average number of hours worked?

7. How many books are there?

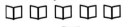

Key: Each [] = 25 books.

A bank contains 5 quarters, 3 dimes, and 2 nickels. Pick a coin at random. Find the probability.

8. P(quarters)   P(nickels)

9. P(dimes)   P(quarters or dimes)

10. P(pennies)   P(coins)
   Danielle's math test scores were:
   82, 86, 86, 90, 93, 95.

11. Find the median of the scores.

12. Find the range of the scores.

13. Find the mode of the scores.

14. Ned is 63 in. tall. Nell is $\frac{2}{3}$ as tall. How tall is Nell?

15. What is 32 decreased by 5?

SET 16

1. Give the range.
   6, 11, 8, 15   17, 5, 9, 20   10, 12, 18, 9

2. Give the median: 86, 74, 81, 87
   92, 87, 96   72, 80, 76, 84

3. $\dfrac{1}{8} = \dfrac{?}{16} = \dfrac{?}{32} = \dfrac{?}{64} = \dfrac{?}{128} = \dfrac{?}{256} = \dfrac{?}{512}$

4. Express in simplest form.
   $\dfrac{8}{16}, \dfrac{8}{32}, \dfrac{8}{64}, \dfrac{8}{72}, \dfrac{8}{56}, \dfrac{8}{24}$

5. Divide by 8, then subtract 2: 48, 56, 64, 32,
   72, 80, 16, 40, 24

6. In a 6-h school day there are 8 equal time
   periods, including 6 subjects, a study period,
   and lunch. What part of an hour is
   there for lunch?

7. Write XCIII as a standard numeral.

8. What is 85 decreased by 6?

9. How many days are in 9 weeks?

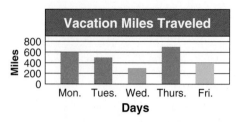

Vacation Miles Traveled

10. When were more than 500 mi traveled?

11. How many more miles were traveled on
    Thursday than on Tuesday?

12. How many miles were traveled on the last
    three days?

13. A square playpen measures 4 ft on each
    side. Find the perimeter.

14. If a bird flies 10 mph, how far can it fly in
    30 minutes?

15. At $0.30 each, what will 7 rolls cost?

SET 17

1. Give the value of the underlined digit.
   0.1<u>3</u>5, 0.<u>4</u>8, 0.<u>7</u>, 0.25<u>9</u>, 0.<u>6</u>10, 0.<u>1</u>, 0.7<u>3</u>,

2. Add 6 to: 9, 19, 39, 79, 99, 69, 29, 49

3. Express in simplest form: $\dfrac{32}{40}, \dfrac{24}{72}, \dfrac{16}{32}, \dfrac{40}{48}$

4. Compare. Use <, =, or >.
   0.62 _?_ 0.26   0.9 _?_ 0.90
   1.345 _?_ 1.435   0.519 _?_ 0.159

5. Order from least to greatest.
   0.2, 0.02, 0.21   0.36, 0.63, 0.33
   5.111, 5.101, 5.110   0.429, 0.492, 0.9

6. What decimal is one thousandth more
   than 0.05?

7. Which is greater: 36.08 or 36.80?

8. Complete the pattern.
   1.3, 1.6, 1.9, _?_, _?_, 2.8, _?_

9. Round 45.629 to the nearest hundredth.

10. Round $50.51 to the nearest dollar.

11. Kay bought 0.25 lb of ham, 0.5 lb of cheese,
    and 0.3 lb of bologna. Is the total more or
    less than a pound and by how much?

12. Compare. Use <, =, or >.
    0.203 + 0.650 _?_ 0.808

13. Place the decimal point in the answer.
    1.734 + 2.15 = 3884

14. Ned bought stickers for $1.80 and a stamper
    for $2.05. Find the total cost.

15. Find the difference between 0.01 and 0.001.

SET 18

1. 0.3 + 0.4   0.24 + 0.6   0.54 + 0.05
   0.8 + 0.08   0.2 + 0.13

2. 0.9 − 0.2   0.38 − 0.07   0.07 − 0.03
   0.66 − 0.3   0.74 − 0.03

3. Express as a whole or mixed number.
   $\dfrac{56}{8}, \dfrac{57}{8}, \dfrac{59}{8}, \dfrac{61}{8}, \dfrac{63}{8}, \dfrac{64}{8}, \dfrac{65}{8}, \dfrac{67}{8}$

4. Express as a fraction.
   $8\dfrac{1}{9}, 4\dfrac{5}{9}, 6\dfrac{2}{9}, 3\dfrac{7}{9}, 9\dfrac{4}{9}, 7\dfrac{5}{9}, 5\dfrac{4}{9}, 2\dfrac{2}{9}$

5. Divide by 9: 64, 57, 29, 22, 83, 73, 69, 50, 14,
   19, 30, 85, 47

6. Chad saved $42.75. He bought a computer
   game for $38.75. How much money does
   he have left?

7. What fractional part of a foot is 6 inches?

8. One day Pat earned $42. The day before
   she earned $13 less. How much did she
   earn the day before?

9. At a speed of 7 mph, how long will it take
   a boat to travel 154 miles?

10. If the length of a rug is 21 ft, what is its
    length in yards?

11. At $2.03 each, find the cost of 7 pens.

12. Take 2.4 from 6.7. Then add 1.2 to the difference.

13. Donna's times on her runs were 0.25 h,
    1.4 h, and 0.75 h. What was her total time?

14. At $1.20 each pair, how many pairs of socks
    can be bought for $8.40?

15. The class collected 22.75 lb of newspapers on
    Mon. and 14.15 lb on Tues. About how many
    pounds did they collect?

SET 19

1. Multiply by 10: 0.6, 0.05, 1.02, 36.3, 0.009, 2.103, 0.013

2. Multiply by 100: 0.2, 0.43, 0.6, 4.01, 6.005, 24.3, 71.8, 0.09

3. Multiply by 1000: 0.1, 0.04, 2.3, 0.003, 49.7, 52.34, 0.016

4. Estimate by rounding: 0.62×0.29 3.1×4.6
0.08×1.4 50.3×2.2 19.7×0.94

5. Estimate by using compatible numbers:
$2.431 \div 6$ $561.9 \div 7$ $36.22 \div 9$
$4.49 \div 15$ $605.14 \div 8$

6. Don makes $4.85 an hour. How much will he make in 10 hours? in 100 hours?

7. A spool of ribbon has 9.2 yd. How many yards are there on 1000 spools?

8. If 9 identical items cost $724.62 about how much does one item cost?

9. If 12.5 kg of popping corn is put equally into 100 bags, how much corn will there be in each bag?

10. Estimate the cost of 4 shirts at $49.75 each.

11. Each glass holds 8.3 oz of milk. How much milk is in 5 glasses?

12. Which is less: 0.06×0.4 or 0.60×0.4?

13. Jill had 1.5 lb of cheese. She used 0.75 lb in lasagna. How much did she have left?

14. At $2.80 a pound, what will 0.5 lb of tea cost?

15. How much less than 2×8 is 7×2?

SET 20

1. Name each symbol: $\overrightarrow{AB}$, $\overrightarrow{DE}$, $\angle XYZ$, $\overleftrightarrow{KL}$, $\angle T$, $\overrightarrow{RS}$, $\overrightarrow{TU}$, $\overleftrightarrow{JC}$

2. Name parallel, perpendicular, or neither.

3. Acute, right, or obtuse angle? 27°, 174°, 90°, 45°, 12°, 115°, 5°, 162°

4. Identify:

5. Congruent? Yes or No.

6. A ? is used to measure angles.

7. An ? triangle has at least 2 congruent sides.

8. What is the perimeter of a room 20 ft long and 12 ft wide?

9. A triangular field measures 30 yd by 42 yd by 60 yd. What is the perimeter?

10. Find the perimeter of a picture frame 12 in. long and 10 in. wide.

11. A ? is a rectangle with 4 congruent sides.

12. The diameter of a circular clock is 15 in. What is the radius?

13. Estimate the circumference of a merry-go-round whose diameter is 50 ft.

14. Draw two congruent figures.

15. A circular table has a radius of 3 ft. Estimate the circumference.

SET 21

1. Which are divisible by both 2 and 5? 25, 10, 8, 20, 12, 35, 40, 30, 18, 24

2. Choose fractions close to 1.
$\frac{1}{9}$, $\frac{7}{8}$, $\frac{3}{16}$, $\frac{23}{24}$, $\frac{18}{20}$, $\frac{2}{9}$, $\frac{3}{11}$, $\frac{16}{17}$

3. Express in feet: 60 in., 36 in., 84 in., 48 in., 96 in., 72 in., 108 in.

4. Compare. Use $<$, $=$, or $>$.
20 c ? 5 qt   6 c ? 50 oz
3 qt ? 8 pt   16 oz ? 1 lb

5. 2 T = ? lb   80 oz = ? lb
2000 lb = ? T   2 lb 3 oz = ? oz

6. What speed must a boat maintain in order to go 54 miles in 6 hours?

7. How many yards equal 21 ft?

8. What is the best estimate of weight for an elephant: 200 lb, 6000 oz, or 2 T?

9. How many feet are in 1 yd 2 ft?

10. At the rate of 500 mph, how far does a jet travel in 30 minutes?

11. $\frac{1}{4}$ lb = ? oz

12. Which is more and by how much: 2 ft or 26 in.?

13. $6\frac{2}{7} = \frac{?}{7}$

14. Al weighed 7 lb 9 oz at birth. At 1 year he weighed 21 lb 13 oz. How much weight did he gain?

15. Express $\frac{36}{72}$ in simplest form.

SET 22

1. Is the temperature hot or cold?
   5°C, 80°C, 25°F, 250°F, 32°C, 100°C

2. Give the number of minutes in: 4 h, 2 h,
   120 s, 300 s, 5 h, 420 s, 1 h

3. Add 15 minutes to: 9:45, 12:15, 7:30, 2:00,
   10:05, 3:25, 11:30

4. Give the number of days in: 3 wk, 8 wk,
   2 wk, 10 wk, 5 wk, 7 wk, 4 wk

5. Express in quarts: 16 pt, 36 pt, 20 pt,
   8 pt, 28 pt, 12 pt, 32 pt

6. What fractional part of a day is one hour?

7. How many minutes are there in 9 hours?

8. 1 century = __?__ years

9. It is 3 hours earlier in California. When it is 1 P.M.
   in New York, what time is it in California?

10. The temperature at 12 noon was 24°F.
    By 8 P.M. it had dropped 30°. What was
    the temperature at 8 P.M.?

11. Water freezes at __?__ °C and __?__ °F.

12. Could you swim in water heated to
    100°C?

13. If the game began at 8:00 P.M. and
    ended $2\frac{1}{4}$ h later, what time did
    the game end?

14. If a jet leaves Oregon at 9 A.M. and
    travels 5 hours to Florida, what time will
    the plane land in Florida?

15. How many pints are contained in a
    9-quart jug?

SET 23

1. Multiply each by 2: 0.3, 0.02, 0.4, 0.08,
   0.5, 0.07, 0.6, 0.2

2. Divide by 10: 2.6, 0.8, 3.5, 7.34, 0.03,
   15.9, 24.7

3. Divide by 100: 13.7, 51.1, 0.9, 0.6,
   422.9, 27.5, 43.8, 0.7

4. Divide by 1000: 5000, 4500, 300, 380, 60,
   65, 5

5. $0.18 \div 9$ $0.08 \div 2$ $0.32 \div 4$
   $3.12 \div 3$ $4.016 \div 8$

6. Estimate the cost of 5 blank tapes
   at $2.99 a tape.

7. How many kilometers are in 1000 m?

8. Eight notebooks all the same price cost
   $7.20. How much does 1 notebook cost?

9. How many centimeters are in 3 m?

10. If there are 100 cm in 1 meter, how many
    meters are there in 500 cm?

11. Which is more and by how much: 2 kg or
    1800 g?

12. Which is more and by how much: 220 cm
    or 2 m?

13. How many grams are there in 1 kg?

14. What decimal part of a meter is 1 cm?

15. Find the area of a rectangular rug
    8 ft by 4 ft.

SET 24

1. Complete: 2 L = __?__ dL   60 dL = __?__ L
   12 dL = __?__ mL   3000 L = __?__ kL

2. Complete: 1 m = __?__ cm   1 L = __?__ cL
   1000 g = __?__ kg   1 dm = __?__ cm

3. Take 7 from: 16, 56, 86, 26, 96, 76

4. $\frac{2}{3} = \frac{?}{9} = \frac{?}{27} = \frac{?}{81} = \frac{?}{243} = \frac{?}{729}$

5. Divide by 7, then subtract 3: 21, 42, 63,
   28, 56, 70, 35, 49

6. How many square feet of plastic are needed
   to cover the bottom of a square playpen
   that measures 5 ft on each side?

7. What solid figure has 6 faces, 12 edges,
   and 8 vertices?

8. A triangle has a base of 9 ft and an altitude
   of 6 ft. What is its area?

9. A stack of newspapers measures
   20 in. long, 10 in. wide, and 30 in. high.
   Find the volume.

10. Write MCCXL in standard form.

11. Estimate the area of a tile floor that
    measures 9.7 ft by 13.2 ft.

12. Which is more and by how much:
    3 L or 2800 mL?

13. If 25 raisins weigh about 25 g, how many
    milligrams is that?

14. If a ship sails 270 km in 9 h, what is its
    average speed per hour?

15. What is the cost of 2 basketballs at
    $18 each?

SET 25

1. Find n: $\dfrac{1}{3} = \dfrac{n}{9}$ $\dfrac{1}{2} = \dfrac{n}{20}$
   $\dfrac{2}{3} = \dfrac{n}{18}$ $\dfrac{3}{5} = \dfrac{n}{25}$ $\dfrac{3}{4} = \dfrac{n}{24}$

2. Read the ratio: 17:24, 8:12, 36:5, 1:18, 2:27

3. Express as $=$ or $\neq$: $\dfrac{6}{8} \; ? \; \dfrac{3}{4}$
   $\dfrac{10}{20} \; ? \; \dfrac{2}{3}$ $\dfrac{45}{30} \; ? \; \dfrac{3}{2}$ $\dfrac{2}{1} \; ? \; \dfrac{6}{10}$

4. Express as a percent.
   $\dfrac{45}{100}, \dfrac{16}{100}, \dfrac{7}{100}, \dfrac{92}{100}, \dfrac{71}{100}, \dfrac{10}{100}, \dfrac{14}{100}$

5. Express as a fraction.
   63%, 85%, 5%, 28%, 1%, 98%, 11%

6. What percent of a dollar is $.25?

7. On a map, City A is $3\dfrac{1}{2}$ in. from City B.
   The scale is 1 in. = 20 mi. What is the actual distance from City A to City B?

8. 16 is $\dfrac{4}{5} \times 20$ as 4 is __?__ of 20.

9. What percent of a dollar is 1 penny?

10. Of 60 animals in the pet shop, 20 percent are dogs. How many are dogs?

11. Sneakers are on sale at 60% off the original price of $80. How much is the discount?

12. Of 100 children, 32% wear sneakers. How many children is that?

13. If a map scale reads 1 cm = 5 km, how many centimeters would represent a distance of 60 km?

14. 7 is to 1 as 35 is to __?__.

15. 39 in. = 3 ft __?__ in.

SET 26

1. Express as a percent.
   0.4, 0.73, 0.05, 0.91, 0.1, 0.88, 0.56

2. Express as a decimal.
   38%, 4%, 10%, 52%, 44%, 30%, 60%

3. Express as a whole or a mixed number.
   $\dfrac{63}{9}, \dfrac{64}{9}, \dfrac{67}{9}, \dfrac{70}{9}, \dfrac{72}{9}, \dfrac{73}{9}, \dfrac{76}{9}$

4. Express in lowest terms: $\dfrac{36}{45}, \dfrac{27}{36}, \dfrac{45}{54}, \dfrac{54}{63}, \dfrac{63}{72}, \dfrac{72}{81}$

5. Double, then add 0.1 to: 0.9, 0.04, 0.13, 0.20, 0.25, 0.7, 0.31

6. If 6 h are spent sleeping, what percent of the day is that?

7. $\dfrac{5}{8} = \dfrac{?}{16} = \dfrac{?}{32} = \dfrac{?}{40} = \dfrac{?}{56} = \dfrac{?}{48} = \dfrac{?}{64}$

8. Of 100 people surveyed, 42 voted yes, 34 voted no, and the rest were undecided. What percentage was undecided?

9. If 1 in. represents 60 ft, how many feet will 7 in. represent?

10. Jean and Joe used 4 yard of ribbon to make 5 bows. If the bows were all the same size, what part of a yard was used for each?

11. At a speed of 48 mph, how far will a car travel in 15 minutes?

12. Which of the following fractions is not in simplest form: $\dfrac{7}{17}, \dfrac{9}{35}, \dfrac{14}{35}$, or $\dfrac{15}{34}$?

13. How much less than 3 dozen is 28?

14. How many pints are in 10 quarts?

15. If one notepad costs $0.90, find the cost of 4 notepads.

SET 27

1. Evaluate $a + 7$ when a is: 9, 15, 3, 7, 11, 21, 32, 40, 54

2. Evaluate $b - 10$ when b is: 56, 72, 84, 96, 25, 11, 38, 47

3. Evaluate $6x$ when x is: 9, 7, 10, 12, 13, 15, 11, 8, 6

4. Evaluate $\dfrac{y}{5}$ when y is: 35, 45, 50, 60, 75, 90, 25, 15

5. $3 + 4 + 5$ $2 \times 3 \div 3 \times 4$
   $4 \times 1 + 6 - 7$ $5 \times 2 - 8 + 4$

6. Express Joan's age 4 years from now.
   Let z = Joan's age now.

7. $\dfrac{4}{7} = \dfrac{?}{14} = \dfrac{?}{28} = \dfrac{?}{56} = \dfrac{?}{112} = \dfrac{?}{224} = \dfrac{?}{448}$

8. Solve for n: $n + 3 + 5 = 18$

9. Solve for c: $5c = 40$

10. Express as an equation: The cost of 1 lb of peaches is 3 times the cost of 1 lb of apples. Let g = cost of apples.

11. Solve for m: $\dfrac{1}{m} \times 72 = 9$

12. Solve for p: $\dfrac{4}{5} = p + \dfrac{1}{5}$

13. Express as an equation:
    Ted's height is 3 in. less than Bob's. Let d = Bob's height.

14. Write XCII in standard form.

15. Ben's total of 4 scores was 30. He remembers three scores: 9, 7, 8. What score did he forget?

Glossary
also on-line

A

acute angle   An angle that measures less than 90°. (p. 326)

acute triangle   A triangle with three acute angles. (p. 332)

Addition Property of Equality   If the same number is added to both sides of an equation, the sides remain equal. (p. 442)

algebraic expression   A mathematical expression that contains variables, numbers, and symbols of operations. (p. 129)

arc   A part of a circle, with all of its points on the circle. (p. 338)

area   The number of square units needed to cover a flat surface. (p. 390)

arithmetic sequence   A sequence generated by repeatedly adding or subtracting the same number. (p. 322)

array   An arrangement of objects in rows and columns. (p. 134)

Associative (grouping) Property   Changing the grouping of the addends (or factors) does not change the sum (or product). (pp. 44, 68)

axis   The horizontal or vertical number line of a graph or coordinate plane. (pp. 252, 254, 464)

B

base   One of the equal factors in a product; a selected side or face of a geometric figure. (pp. 91, 394)

benchmark   An object of known measure used to estimate the measure of other objects.

C

capacity   The amount, usually of liquid, a container can hold.

Celsius (°C) scale   The temperature scale in which 0°C is the freezing point of water and 100°C is the boiling point of water. (p. 364)

central angle   An angle whose vertex is the center of a circle. (p. 338)

chord   A line segment with both endpoints on a circle. (p. 338)

circle   A set of points in a plane, all of which are the same distance from a given point called the *center*. (p. 284)

circle graph   A graph that uses the area of a circle to show the division of a total amount of data. (p. 248)

circumference   The distance around a circle.

clustering   To find addends that are nearly alike in order to estimate their sum. (p. 75)

Commutative (order) Property   Changing the order of the addends (or factors) does not change the sum (or product). (pp. 44, 68)

compatible numbers   Numbers that are easy to compute with mentally. (p. 112)

composite number   A whole number greater than 1 that has more than two factors. (p. 136)

compound event   In probability, when one event follows another. (p. 242)

cone   A solid, or space, figure with one circular base, one vertex, and a curved surface. (p. 396)

congruent figures   Figures that have the same size and shape. (p. 330)

conjunction   A compound statement formed by joining two statements with the connective *and*. (p. 233)

coordinate plane   The plane formed by two perpendicular number lines. (p. 464)

corresponding parts   Matching sides or angles of two figures. (p. 330)

cross products   The products obtained by multiplying the numerator of one fraction by the denominator of a second fraction and the denominator of the first fraction by the numerator of the second fraction. (p. 418)

cross section   A plane figure formed when a plane cuts through a solid figure. (p. 411)

cumulative frequency   A running total of data. (p. 244)

customary system   The measurement system that uses inch, foot, yard, and mile; fluid ounce, cup, pint, quart, and gallon; ounce, pound, and ton. (See *Table of Measures*, p. 515.)

D

data   Facts or information.

decagon   A polygon with ten sides. (p. 328)

decimal   A number with a decimal point separating the ones from the tenths place.

degree (°)   A unit used to measure angles; a unit used to measure temperature on the Celsius (°C) or the Fahrenheit (F°) scale. (pp. 324, 364)

dependent events   In probability, when the second event is affected by the first. (p. 242)

diagonal   A line segment, other than a side, that joins two vertices of a polygon. (p. 334)

diameter   A line segment that passes through the center of a circle and has both endpoints on the circle. (p. 338)

discount   A reduction in the regular, or list, price of an item. (p. 428)

disjunction   A compound statement formed by joining two statements with the connective *or*. (p. 233)

Distributive Property   Multiplying a number by a sum is the same as multiplying the number by each addend of the sum and then adding the products. (p. 69)

divisible   A number is divisible by another number if the remainder is 0 when the number is divided by the other number. (p. 108)

Division Property of Equality   If both sides of an equation are divided by the same nonzero number, the sides remain equal. (p. 442)

double bar (line) graph   A graph that uses pairs of bars (line segments) to compare two sets of data. (p. 263)

E

edge   The line segment where two faces of a space figure meet.

elapsed time   The amount of time that passes between the start and end of a given period. (p. 367)

equally likely outcomes   In probability, when the chance is the same of getting any one of the described outcomes. (p. 20)

equation   A number sentence that shows equality of two mathematical expressions. (p. 440)

equilateral triangle   A triangle with three congruent sides and three congruent angles. (p. 332)

equivalent fractions   Different fractions that name the same amount. (p. 9)

estimate   An approximate answer; to find an answer that is close to the exact answer.

evaluate   To find the value. (p. 441)

event   A set of one or more outcomes of a probability experiment.

expanded form   The written form of a number that shows the place value of each of its digits. (p. 34)

exponent   A number that tells how many times another number is to be used as a factor. (p. 93)

F

face   A flat surface of a solid figure.

factor   One of two or more numbers that are multiplied to form a product.

factor tree   A diagram used to find the prime factors of a number. (p. 137)

Fahrenheit (°F) scale   The temperature scale in which 32°F is the freezing point of water and 212°F is the boiling point of water.

formula   A rule that is expressed by using symbols. (p. 336)

fraction   A number that names a part of a whole, a region, or a set.

frequency table   A chart that shows how often each item appears in a set of data. (p. 244)

front-end estimation   A way of estimating by using the front, or greatest, digits to find an approximate answer.

G

geometric construction   A drawing that is made using only an unmarked *straightedge* and a *compass*. (p. 331)

geometric sequence   A sequence generated by repeatedly multiplying or dividing by the same number. (p. 322)

graph   A pictorial representation of data.

greatest common factor (GCF)   The greatest number that is a factor of two or more numbers. (p. 138)

H

half-turn symmetry   The symmetry that occurs when a figure is turned halfway (180°) around its center point and the figure that results looks exactly the same. (p. 342)

height   The perpendicular distance between the bases of a geometric figure. In a triangle, the perpendicular distance from the opposite vertex to the line containing the base. (p. 394)

heptagon   A polygon with seven sides. (p. 328)

hexagon   A polygon with six sides. (p. 13)

hexagonal prism   A prism with two parallel hexagonal bases. (p. 396)

hexagonal pyramid   A pyramid with a hexagonal base. (p. 396)

histogram   A graph in which bars, with no space between them, are used to display how frequently data occurs within equal intervals. (p. 254)

I

Identity Property   Adding 0 to a number or multiplying a number by 1 does not change the number's value. (pp. 44, 68)

improper fraction   A fraction with its numerator equal to or greater than its denominator. (p. 150)

inequality   A number sentence that uses an inequality symbol: $<$, $>$, or $\neq$.

integers   The whole numbers and their opposites. (p. 450)

intersecting lines   Lines that meet or cross. (p. 12)

interval   The number of units between spaces on a graph.

inverse operations   Mathematical operations that *undo* each other, such as addition and subtraction or multiplication and division.

isosceles triangle   A triangle with two congruent sides. (p. 332)

L

line graph   A graph that uses points on a grid connected by line segments to show data. (p. 254)

line of symmetry   A line that divides a figure into two congruent parts. (p. 342)

line plot   A graph that uses Xs to show information and to compare quantities. (p. 250)

line segment   A part of a line that has two endpoints. (p. 12)

linear measure   A measure of length.

M

mass   The measure of the amount of matter an object contains.

mathematical expression   A symbol or a combination of symbols that represents a number.

mean   The average of a set of numbers. (p. 246)

measures of central tendency   The *mean, median,* and *mode* of a set of data (p. 246)

median   The middle number of a set of numbers arranged in order. If there is an even number of numbers, the median is the average of the two middle numbers. (p. 246)

metric system   The measurement system based on the meter, gram, and liter. (See *Table of Measures,* p. 515.)

mixed number   A number that is made up of a whole number and a fraction. (p. 148)

mode   The number that appears most frequently in a set of numbers. (p. 246)

multiple   A number that is the product of a given number and any whole number. (p. 146)

Multiplication Property of Equality   If both sides of an equation are multiplied by the same nonzero number, the sides remain equal. (p. 442)

N

negation   The denial of a given statement. (p. 61)

net   A flat pattern that folds into a solid figure. (p. 397)

numerator   The number above the bar in a fraction.

O

obtuse angle   An angle with a measure greater than 90° and less than 180°. (p. 326)

obtuse triangle   A triangle with one obtuse angle. (p. 332)

octagon   A polygon with eight sides. (p. 329)

order of operations   The order in which operations must be performed when more than one operation is involved. (p. 122)

ordered pair   A pair of numbers that is used to locate a point on a coordinate plane. (p. 464)

origin   The point (0,0) in the coordinate plane where the *x*-axis and the *y*-axis intersect. (p. 464)

outcome   The result of a probability experiment.

outlier   A value separated from the rest of the data. (p. 250)

P

parallel lines   Lines in a plane that never intersect. (p. 12)

parallelogram   A quadrilateral with two pairs of parallel sides. (p. 334)

pentagon   A polygon with five sides. (p. 13)

pentagonal prism   A prism with two parallel pentagonal bases. (p. 396)

pentagonal pyramid   A pyramid with a pentagonal base. (p. 396)

percent   The ratio or comparison of a number to 100. (p. 422)

perimeter   The distance around a figure.

period   A set of three digits set off by a comma in a whole number.

perpendicular lines   Lines that intersect to form right angles. (p. 326)

pi (π)   The ratio of the circumference of a circle to its diameter. An approximate value of π is 3.14, or $\frac{22}{7}$. (p. 340)

place value   The value of a digit depending on its position, or place, in a number.

plane figure   A two-dimensional figure that has straight or curved sides.

polygon   A closed plane figure made up of line segments that meet at vertices but do not cross. (pp. 13, 328)

polyhedron   A solid, or space, figure whose faces are polygons. (p. 396)

power of a number   The result of using a number as a factor a given number of times. An exponent is used to express the power. $10^3 = 10 \times 10 \times 10$, or 1000. (p. 289)

prime factorization   Expressing a composite number as the product of prime numbers. (p. 137)

prime number   A whole number greater than 1 that has only two factors, itself and 1. (p. 136)

prism   A solid figure with two faces called *bases* bounded by polygons that are parallel and congruent. (p. 396)

probability   A branch of mathematics that analyzes the chance that a given outcome will occur. The probability of an event is expressed as the ratio of the number of desired outcomes to the total number of possible outcomes.

proportion   A number sentence that shows that two ratios are equal. (p. 418)

protractor   An instrument used to measure angles. (p. 324)

pyramid   A solid figure whose base is a polygon and whose faces are triangles with a common vertex. (p. 396)

Q

quadrilateral   A polygon with four sides. (p. 13)

R

radius (plural *radii*)   A line segment from the center of a circle to a point on the circle. (p. 338)

random sample   A subgroup or part of a total group, each of which or whom has an equally likely chance of being chosen. (p. 238)

range   The difference between the greatest and least numbers in a set of numbers. (p. 246)

ratio   A comparison of two numbers or quantities by division. (p. 416)

rational number   Any number that can be expressed as the quotient of two *integers* in which the divisor is not zero. (p. 475)

reciprocals   Two numbers whose product is 1. (p. 214)

rectangle   A parallelogram with four right angles. (p. 334)

rectangular prism   A prism with six rectangular faces. (p. 396)

rectangular pyramid   A pyramid with a rectangular base. (p. 396)

reflection   A transformation that moves a figure by flipping it along a line. (p. 334)

regular polygon   A polygon with all sides and all angles congruent. (p. 329)

regular price   The original, marked, or list price of an item before a discount has been given.

repeating decimal   A decimal with digits that from some point on repeat indefinitely. (p. 319)

rhombus   A parallelogram with all sides congruent. (p. 334)

right angle   An angle that measures 90°. (p. 326)

right triangle   A triangle with one right angle. (p. 332)

Roman numerals   Symbols for numbers used by the Romans. (p. 54)

rotation   A transformation that moves a figure by turning it about a fixed point. (p. 344)

S

sale price   The sale price is the difference between the list price and the discount.

sales tax   The amount added to the marked price of an item and collected as tax. (p. 428)

sample   A segment of a population selected for study to predict characteristics of the whole. (p. 244)

sample space   A set of all possible *outcomes* of an experiment. (p. 240)

scale   The ratio of a pictured measure to the actual measure; the tool used to measure weight.

scale drawing   A drawing of something accurate but different in size. (p. 420)

scalene triangle A triangle with no congruent sides. (p. 326)

scientific notation The expression of a number as the product of a power of 10 and a number greater than or equal to 1 but less than 10. (p. 289)

sequence A set of numbers given in a certain order. Each number is called a *term*. (p. 320)

similar figures Figures that have the same shape. They may or may not be the same size. (p. 330)

simplest form The form of a fraction when the numerator and denominator have no common factor other than 1. (p. 142)

solution A value of a variable that makes an equation true. (p. 440)

sphere A curved solid figure in which all the points are the same distance from a point called the *center*. (p. 396)

square measure A measure of area.

square pyramid A pyramid with a square base. (p. 398)

statistics The study of the collection, interpretation, and display of data.

stem-and-leaf plot A graph that arranges numerical data in order of place value. The last digits of the numbers are the *leaves*. The digits to the left of the leaves are the *stems*. (p. 251)

straight angle An angle that measures 180°. (p. 326)

Subtraction Property of Equality If the same number is subtracted from both sides of an equation, the sides remain equal. (p. 442)

surface area The sum of the areas of all the faces of a solid figure.

survey A way to collect data to answer a question. (p. 244)

symmetrical figure A plane figure that can be folded on a line so that the two halves are congruent. (p. 342)

T

terminating decimal A decimal in which digits do not show a repeating pattern. A terminating decimal results when the division of the numerator of a fraction by the denominator leaves a 0 remainder. (p. 319)

tessellation The pattern formed by fitting plane figures together without overlapping or leaving gaps. (p. 346)

transformation A flip, slide, or turn that changes the location of a figure on a plane without changing its size or shape. (p. 344)

translation A transformation that moves a figure by sliding along a line without flipping or turning it. (p. 344)

trapezoid A quadrilateral with only one pair of parallel sides. (p. 334)

tree diagram A diagram that shows all possible outcomes of an event or events. (p. 240)

triangular prism A prism with two parallel triangular bases. (p. 396)

triangular pyramid A pyramid with a triangular base. (p. 396)

U

unit fraction A fraction with a numerator of 1. (p. 193)

unit price The cost of one item. (p. 312)

V

variable A symbol, usually a letter, used to represent a number. (p. 80)

Venn diagram A drawing that shows relationships among sets of numbers or objects. (p. 61)

vertex (plural *vertices*) The common endpoint of two rays in an angle, of two line segments in a polygon, or of three or more edges in a space figure.

volume The number of cubic units needed to fill a solid figure.

W

weight The heaviness of an object.

whole number Any of the numbers 0, 1, 2, 3, ...

X

x-axis The horizontal number line in a coordinate plane. (p. 464)

Y

y-axis The vertical number line in a coordinate plane. (p. 464)

Z

zero pair A pair of algebra tiles, or counters, consisting of one positive and one negative. (p. 458)

zero property Multiplying a number by 0 always results in a product of 0. (p. 68)

GLOSSARY

Key: Italics = Enrichment/Challenge

Mathematical Symbols

$=$	is equal to	$\cdot$	decimal point	$\overleftrightarrow{AB}$	line AB
$\neq$	is not equal to	$\circ$	degree	$\overline{AB}$	line segment AB
$<$	is less than	$+$	plus	$\overrightarrow{AB}$	ray AB
$>$	is greater than	$-$	minus	$\angle ABC$	angle ABC
$\approx$	is approximately equal to	$\times$	times	ABC	plane ABC
		$\div$	divided by	$\sim$	is similar to
$\ldots$	continues without end	$P(E)$	probability of an event	$\cong$	is congruent to
$\%$	percent	cm^2	square centimeter	$\parallel$	is parallel to
$2:3$	two to three (ratio)	$in.^3$	cubic inch	$\perp$	is perpendicular to
$\$$	dollars			$(3, 4)$	ordered pair
$\cent$	cents				

Table of Measures

Time

60 seconds (s) = 1 minute (min)
60 minutes = 1 hour (h)
24 hours = 1 day (d)
7 days = 1 week (wk)

12 months (mo) = 1 year (y)
52 weeks = 1 year
365 days = 1 year
100 years = 1 century (cent.)

Metric Units

Length

10 millimeters (mm) = 1 centimeter (cm)
100 centimeters = 1 meter (m)
10 centimeters = 1 decimeter (dm)
10 decimeters = 1 meter
1000 meters = 1 kilometer (km)

Capacity

10 milliliters (mL) = 1 centiliter (cL)
100 centiliters = 1 liter (L)
10 centiliters = 1 deciliter (dL)
10 deciliters = 1 liter
1000 liters = 1 kiloliter (kL)

Mass

10 milligrams (mg) = 1 centigram (cg)
100 centigrams = 1 gram (g)
10 centigrams = 1 decigram (dg)

10 decigrams = 1 gram
1000 grams = 1 kilogram (kg)
1000 kilograms = 1 metric ton (t)

Customary Units

Length

12 inches (in.) = 1 foot (ft)
3 feet = 1 yard (yd)
36 inches = 1 yard
5280 feet = 1 mile (mi)
1760 yards = 1 mile

Capacity

8 fluid ounces (fl oz) = 1 cup (c)
2 cups = 1 pint (pt)
2 pints = 1 quart (qt)
4 quarts = 1 gallon (gal)

Weight

16 ounces (oz) = 1 pound (lb)
2000 pounds = 1 ton (T)

Geometric Formulas

Perimeter

Rectangle: $P = (2 \times \ell) + (2 \times w)$

Square: $P = 4 \times s$

Area

Rectangle: $A = \ell \times w$

Square: $A = s \times s = s^2$

Parallelogram: $A = b \times h$

Triangle: $A = \frac{1}{2} \times b \times h$

Circumference of Circle

$C = \pi \times d = \pi \times 2 \times r$

Surface Area

Rectangular Prism:

$S = 2 \times (\ell \times w) + 2 \times (\ell \times h) + 2 \times (w \times h)$

Cube: $S = 6 \times e \times e = 6 \times e^2$

Volume

Rectangular Prism: $V = \ell \times w \times h$

Cube: $V = e \times e \times e = e^3$

Other Formulas

Distance $=$ Rate $\times$ Time: $d = r \times t$

Discount $=$ List Price $\times$ Rate of Discount: $D = LP \times R$ of D

Sale Price $=$ Regular Price $-$ Discount: $SP = RP - D$

Sales Tax $=$ Marked Price $\times$ Rate of Sales Tax: $T = MP \times R$ of T

Percent Table

$10\% = \frac{1}{10} = 0.1$

$20\% = \frac{1}{5} = 0.2$

$30\% = \frac{3}{10} = 0.3$

$40\% = \frac{2}{5} = 0.4$

$60\% = \frac{3}{5} = 0.6$

$70\% = \frac{7}{10} = 0.7$

$80\% = \frac{4}{5} = 0.8$

$90\% = \frac{9}{10} = 0.9$

$1\% = \frac{1}{100} = 0.01$

$2\% = \frac{1}{50} = 0.02$

$4\% = \frac{1}{25} = 0.04$

$5\% = \frac{1}{20} = 0.05$

$25\% = \frac{1}{4} = 0.25$

$50\% = \frac{1}{2} = 0.5$

$75\% = \frac{3}{4} = 0.75$

FORMULAS / PERCENTS